THE FEDERAL INCOME TAX

BY

ROY G. BLAKEY

and

GLADYS C. BLAKEY

UNIVERSITY OF MINNESOTA

THE LAWBOOK EXCHANGE, LTD.

Clark, New Jersey

ISBN 9781584776468 (hardcover)
ISBN 9781616191092 (paperback)

Lawbook Exchange edition 2010

The quality of this reprint is equivalent to the quality of the original work.

THE LAWBOOK EXCHANGE, LTD.
33 Terminal Avenue
Clark, New Jersey 07066-1321

Please see our website for a selection of our other publications and fine facsimile reprints of classic works of legal history:
www.lawbookexchange.com

Library of Congress Cataloging-in-Publication Data

Blakey, Roy G. (Roy Gillispie), b. 1880.
The federal income tax / Roy G. Blakey, Gladys C. Blakey.
p. cm.
Includes bibliographical references and index.
ISBN-13: 978-1-58477-646-8 (alk. paper)
ISBN-10: 1-58477-646-3 (alk. paper)
1. Income tax--Law and legislation--United States--History. I. Blakey, Gladys C. II. Title.

KF6369.3.B565 2005
343.7305'2--dc22 2006002847

Printed in the United States of America on acid-free paper

THE FEDERAL INCOME TAX

BY

ROY G. BLAKEY

and

GLADYS C. BLAKEY

UNIVERSITY OF MINNESOTA

LONGMANS, GREEN AND CO.

LONDON · NEW YORK · TORONTO

1940

LONGMANS, GREEN AND CO.
55 FIFTH AVENUE, NEW YORK
221 EAST 20TH STREET, CHICAGO
88 TREMONT STREET, BOSTON

LONGMANS, GREEN AND CO. LTD.
39 PATERNOSTER ROW, LONDON, E.C. 4
17 CHITTARANJAN AVENUE, CALCUTTA
NICOL ROAD, BOMBAY
36A MOUNT ROAD, MADRAS

LONGMANS, GREEN AND CO.
215 VICTORIA STREET, TORONTO

BLAKEY

THE FEDERAL INCOME TAX

FIRST EDITION

PRINTED IN THE UNITED STATES OF AMERICA

FOREWORD

Few things are more revelatory of all phases of a democratic polity than the history of fiscal measure, especially a proposal for new or increased taxes. Such a measure galvanizes into life all the groups, interests, classes and sections, and in the persons of their proponents they parade before the observant eye, revealing much more than they say in words. The purposes for which new moneys are sought, whether deduced from the bill or urged by its supporters, tell their story of the strength of selfish interests or of broadening social purposes. The comparisons that may be drawn from dates alone of similar measures in other lands, tell a story not of imitation so much as of the irresistible forces which make nations and their problems all too similar in a shrinking world. All this and more can be distilled from the history of the public consideration of the inception and growth of income taxes in the United States better perhaps than from the history of any other fiscal measures, even tariff bills to which Hamilton gave the color of statesmanship and Fordney-McCumber reduced to the smell of pork.

All students would agree that a scholarly history of federal income taxation was something that needed writing. Most of those at all familiar with the field would agree that Professor Blakey was the living American scholar best equipped by long study to undertake the task. From the days of his first published paper on the sixteenth amendment to the present, he has made the income tax a major concern of his research and publishing activities. The files of the *American Economic Review,* as well as stout volumes such as *Taxation in Minnesota* and other surveys by him as the leader of a group of experts, bear witness to his continuing absorption with the subject of taxation and especially of the income tax in the field of both federal and state legislation.

In the preparation of this long maturing volume he has had other signal advantages. One is the collaboration of Mrs. Blakey who has done independent published work but has collaborated with him in this and other studies. The second significant advantage is that through his residence in Washington and service in the Treasury Department he has had opened to him the papers and memories of men who were active in making the history here recorded. It is a great service to have preserved for scholars this personal material that might never have been gleaned by anyone less in possession of the confidence of the leaders in the early battles over the income tax. When this volume was first projected there was a lively possibility that the Honorable Cordell Hull would be an active collaborator. No one who knows Mr. Hull's devotion to the discharge of his present great office needs to be told why his name is in footnotes and not on the title page.

Undoubtedly there will, in years to come, be other volumes by other authors dealing with the income tax. I venture to say that however good they may be, this volume will remain basic and indispensable. It is a history of the federal income tax as near first-hand in its sources as can be written and it is a contribution to the social, economic and political history of the American people.

GUY STANTON FORD

PREFACE

The income tax brought a revolution in national taxation in the United States in the decade 1909-1919. This revolution had its roots in the preceding decades; it has continued its course during the last two decades; in fact, it is still in progress. Its most violent phase quantitatively was in 1917 and 1918, but it has developed what may prove to be some of its most significant phases in the last few years. The end is not yet; indeed, it does not appear to be near at hand. No one can really understand the present income tax, the present fiscal situation and probable future developments, without some appreciation of the genesis and development of this tax and of the federal system of which it forms the most important part.

This volume presents the tax as it is today and, in addition, it shows how it has been changed from what was earlier, and why. It discusses the numerous important problems that have arisen throughout the years and the earlier as well as the later methods proposed for meeting them. Some of these proposals have succeeded and some have failed. From time to time some of the old discarded remedies have been brought forward again by new legislators and administrators as if they were newly discovered cures; certain improvements and certain perversions have developed; sometimes the tax and its administration have been strengthened; at other times they have been weakened and even misused.

In other words, this study indicates how economic, political, legal and administrative considerations have worked to create the income tax that we have and it also indicates how they are working to change it in the future. Laymen and even many specialists, including practitioners who know the terms of the current statutes and decisions, frequently exhibit only a superficial knowledge of the tax and of the law. It is only through an understanding of the changes and of the forces that bring them about that they or other students can have a real grasp of the income tax. The purpose of this volume is to fill the gap thus indicated, to meet a need not met by any other work published since the adoption of the Sixteenth Amendment.

The obligations of the authors for assistance in the preparation of this study are unusually numerous and great. Secretary of State Cordell Hull, long a member of the Committee on Ways and Means and chairman of the Subcommittee on Income Taxation when the new measure was introduced, who has probably done more than any living man to establish and develop a good income tax in the United States, has been especially helpful in furnishing data from his rich experience, besides reading and making many suggestions concerning several chapters. Judge William R. Green, Chairman of the Committee on Ways and Means from 1922 to 1928, has assisted extensively in similar ways. In fact, Secretary Hull, Judge Green, and others not mentioned, but intimately connected with the making of various federal income tax laws, have furnished a great deal of valuable information concerning issues, men, and tactics not found in published sources. Professor Carl Shoup of Columbia University, for several years a special consultant of the United States Treasury, has read practically all of the manuscript and offered many valuable suggestions. Very extensive and invaluable also has been the assistance of Mr. W. T. Sherwood, Assistant Deputy Commissioner of Internal Revenue, and various members of his staff.

Among others now or formerly of the Treasury and/or the Bureau of Internal Revenue to whom we are indebted are Messrs. William G. McAdoo, Daniel C. Roper, Guy T. Helvering, Roswell Magill, John W. Hanes, Robert H. Jackson, Arthur H. Kent, Charles T. Russell, E. C. Alvord, Edward White, T. C. Atkeson, George C. Haas, Roy Blough, and Ralph Dwan. Assistance has been given also by Messrs. L. H. Parker, Colin F. Stam and others of the staff of the Joint Committee on Internal Revenue Taxation. Professor Henry Rottschaefer, of the Law School of the University of Minnesota, has given indispensable aid and various chapters have been read by Professors F. B. Garver (Economics) and William Anderson (Political Science) of the same university. Both general and specific assistance has been given for many years by the late Professor E. R. A. Seligman of Columbia University. The extensive obligations to authors of published works are obvious, but some of the most valuable assistance has come from sources that must be anonymous.

We are peculiarly indebted to the Brookings Institution for a year in Washington, devoted to the study of this tax, to the Social Science Research Committee of the University of Minnesota for special assistance, and to the School of Business Administration and the University of Minnesota for leaves of absence to spend several years in Washington at various periods.

We are very grateful to all who have assisted and absolve them, of course, from responsibility for any errors that we may have made or may have permitted to creep into this volume.

Roy G. Blakey
Gladys C. Blakey

February 1, 1940

CONTENTS

LIST OF TABLES

LIST OF CHARTS

THE FEDERAL INCOME TAX

THE FEDERAL INCOME TAX

CHAPTER I

THE BEGINNINGS OF THE REVOLUTION IN NATIONAL TAXATION

A new era of national taxation was ushered into the United States with the adoption of the Sixteenth (Income Tax) Amendment to the Constitution, February 3, 1913. The first federal income taxes were supplementary emergency measures of the Civil War period,[1] but it was not possible for the United States to have a broad general income tax as a main source of revenue, for peace times as well as for war and other emergencies, until the adoption of the Sixteenth Amendment.

ANTECEDENTS OF THE SIXTEENTH AMENDMENT

The two great battles which made that amendment possible were fought in 1894-1895 and 1909-1913. The abortive income tax of 1894 (declared unconstitutional in 1895) had only a loose causal connection with the Civil War income taxes; it was really the result of a great equalitarian movement generated by two prolonged post-war depressions of great severity. Although frustrated for nearly two more decades, the leaders of this democratic movement won in 1909 what later proved to be a decisive victory by forcing a conservative President and even more conservative congressional leaders to submit a Constitutional amendment to the states and, also, by forcing them to authorize an entering-wedge income tax under the guise of an excise tax on corporations. These two 1909 income tax measures were not originated by immediate and urgent fiscal pressures, rather they were results of a no longer postponable conflict between holders of opposing economic interests and political philosophies. The ratification of the amendment by three fourths of the states — contrary to the expectations of the conservative leaders — showed on which side the victory lay, and was followed promptly by the adoption of a general income tax which included the previous tax on corporations and much more besides.

[1] An income tax was suggested during the War of 1812.

These short and simple laws were the forerunners of a series of measures that were soon to multiply many fold the revenues of the government, and to affect profoundly and permanently, not only the national government, but also state and local governments, all industry and finance in the United States and, consequently, the lives of its millions of citizens.

The really new era which got well under way in 1909 and 1913 is the one with which this treatise is chiefly concerned, though a brief account of what went before will assist in understanding why and how this era came into existence, and will aid also in evaluating the significance of later developments.

Prior to the Civil War the national government was financed chiefly by receipts from customs duties. Some revenue was received from the sale of public lands and from a few temporary excise and other internal taxes. (Table 1.) The tariff, although the main source of revenue, was not ideal for several reasons, one of them being that the yield fluctuated violently according to the condition of business and bore little relation to the needs of the government. At times the government faced a deficit. Then it borrowed, relying on a hoped-for surplus some time in the future. At times the surplus became embarrassing and tempted Congress to spend recklessly. Twice at least, in the 1830's and again in the decade preceding the panic of 1893, such surpluses were important factors contributing to economic depressions, though other factors were more important in the latter period.

THE CIVIL WAR TAXES

When the opening gun of the Civil War was fired on Fort Sumter, the national government was neither financially nor psychologically prepared for the long struggle. The panic of 1857 had left its mark on business and the decline in receipts from customs had left a Treasury deficit. Disagreement as to financial policy between northern and southern members of Congress and President Buchanan's apparent indifference or indecision forced the Treasury to borrow more and more.

Even before the war broke out the national credit was so poor that New York banks were reluctant to lend to the government. For example, in December 1860 the Administration experienced great difficulty in floating a $5,000,000 issue of treasury notes bearing 12% interest.[2]

In the first months after the outbreak of war neither Congress nor the Secretary of the Treasury had much courage when it came to imposing taxes, but perhaps it is difficult now to appreciate the

[2] 36th Congress, 2d Session, *House Miscellaneous Document* 20, p. 3.

psychology of a people totally unaccustomed to paying anything for support of the national government except indirectly through the tariff. There had not been even a federal excise tax on alcoholic liquors since 1817 when a temporary war measure was repealed. Furthermore, no one expected the war between the states to be difficult or of long duration.

Table 1

Receipts of the Federal Government 1789-1939 [a]
(In millions of dollars)

Year	*Customs* (including tonnage tax)[b]	*Internal Revenue*		*Miscellaneous* [c]	*Total*	*Surplus* or *deficit* of ordinary receipts covered into the Treasury compared with expenditures chargeable against ordinary receipts
		Income and Profits Taxes	*Miscellaneous*			
1789–91	$4.39	....	....	$.11	$4.50	+$.15
1800	9.08	....	$.81	1.16	11.05	+.06
1810	8.58	....	d	1.35	9.93	+1.23
1820	15.01	....	.11	3.87	18.99	−.38
1830	21.92	....	d	4.77	26.69	+9.70
1840	13.50	....	d	10.50	24.02	−4.84
1850	39.67	....	....	9.43	49.10	+4.06
1860	53.19	....	....	11.39	64.58	−7.07
1865	84.93	$60.98	148.48	53.88	348.27	−963.84
1870	194.54	37.78	147.12	50.69	430.13	+101.60
1880	186.52	....	124.01	56.31	366.84	+65.88
1890	229.67	....	142.61	91.68	463.96	+85.04
1900	233.16	....	295.33	141.09	669.59	+46.38
1910	333.68	20.95	268.98	276.02	899.64	−18.11
1919 [e]	184.46	3,018.78	1,296.50	927.45	5,427.19	−13,370.64
1920	322.90	3,945.95	1,460.08	1,398.57	7,126.50	+212.47
1930	587.00	2,410.99	628.31	1,257.12	4,883.43	+183.79
1932 [f]	327.75 [b]	1,057.34	503.67 [b]	705.13	2,593.89	−3,147.92
1937	486.36	2,157.53	2,439.61	936.98	6,020.04	−2,811.32
1938	359.19	2,634.62	3,039.70	936.79	6,970.29	−1,449.63
1939 [g]	318.84	2,182.30	2,978.92	187.76	5,667.82	−3,600.51

[a] Compiled from *Report of the Secretary of the Treasury* 1938, pp. 410-412. For annual receipts, 1908-1939, see Table 39, Appendix.

[b] Beginning in 1932, tonnage tax receipts are included in miscellaneous internal revenue.

[c] Includes sales of public lands, surplus postal receipts covered into the Treasury, and other postal revenues.

[d] Less than $100,000.

[e] Included because it was the year of greatest deficit.

[f] Included because it was the year of smallest receipts since 1918.

[g] From Daily Statement of the Treasury, June 30, 1939.

Aside from borrowing, three new expedients were devised to finance the war: (1) fiat money (greenbacks); (2) the internal revenue system, that is, excises on liquor, tobacco, and other consumption goods, licenses on business, and gross-receipts taxes on certain corporations; and (3) taxes on incomes of individuals. As the eloquent Morrill explained to his colleagues in the House:

Driven . . . like Milton's Adam, from our untaxed garden, to rely upon the sweat of our brow for support, like Adam, we have "all the world before us where to choose." [3]

The decision to impose an income tax was the result of a determination by the West and South that the eastern part of the United States should pay a fairer share of taxes. The amendment to include an income tax was forced upon the Committee on Ways and Means when Congress met in the special session of July 1861. Chairman Thaddeus Stevens (Rep., Pa.), who considered himself the ruler of the House, was doubtless much surprised at the refusal to accept the Committee measure when it was first introduced. He proposed to raise $30,000,000 annually by a direct tax on land apportioned among the states according to population [4] and an additional amount by a tariff on such articles of common consumption as tea, coffee, and sugar – hitherto on the free list. Western members resented the imposition of a direct tax on their part of the country where land was plentiful but the population sparse and poor. They were fully aware, too, that much of the burden of the tariff, though concealed, fell on them. So great was the objection to the bill that it was withdrawn and rewritten to reduce the amount of direct tax on land and to include an income tax that would fall more upon the industrial sections than upon the rural areas.

This first income tax law, that of 1861, was very simple and short; in fact, it did not specify whether the tax was on gross or net income nor did it enumerate any allowable deductions other than taxes. Before it went into effect Congress met again (in regular session) and drafted another measure. This law of 1862 is interesting not only because it provided for the first national income tax to be levied in this country but also because it established the office of Commissioner of Internal Revenue. The law was revised again in 1864 in order to bring in more revenue and also to make its provisions more definite. This basic law was amended somewhat in 1865 and 1866 and was drastically rewritten in 1867 and 1870 when revenue needs were not so pressing.

In the 1861 law the rates were graduated according to source of income and residence of taxpayer. They were 3% on income of residents of the United States, on amounts over a personal exemption of $800, and 5% on income of United States citizens living abroad, but 1½% on income from government securities. In the 1862

[3] *The Congressional Globe*, 37th Congress, 2d Session, p. 1194.

[4] It was originally planned to impose this tax on the "rebel states" as well as on the others but, of course, little was collected from them. In fact, the tax was a failure, never levied but once, and what was collected was returned to the states in the 1890's, partly on alleged grounds of justice, but mostly to reduce the Treasury surplus of that period and thus to lessen the agitation for reducing the rates of the protective tariff.

law the rates were graduated according to the amount of income — 3% on a person's income in excess of $600 and not in excess of $10,000, and 5% on income in excess of $10,000. In the 1864 law the rates were 5% on income over $600 and not over $5000, 7½% on income over $5000 and not over $10,000, and 10% on income over $10,000. The next law, that of 1865, taxed income in excess of $5000 at 10%. By 1867 the war was over and, although the debt remained, Congressmen were eager to reduce the tax burden; therefore, the personal exemption was increased to $1000 and the rate lowered to 5%. In 1870 the exemption was raised to $2000 and the rate was reduced to 2½%.[5]

Several features of these laws were important as precedents for later legislation. One was the direct dealing between the national government and large numbers of individuals in the collection of non-shiftable personal taxes; another and somewhat opposite was the partial adoption of the British "stoppage-at-the-source" method of collecting the tax; for example, on government salaries and certain corporation dividends and interest.

The concept of taxable net income was evolved gradually. In drafting the first two laws members of Congress were not sure whether gross or net income was what should be taxed. They were afraid to say "net" income for fear that taxpayers would take out too many personal expenses.[6] In the laws of 1861 and 1862 the only specified deductions were "national, state, and local taxes." The law of 1864 allowed deductions for business expenses, interest, taxes, rent — even rent paid for homes — but did not mention depletion of natural resources, although this matter was debated. The law of 1866 and succeeding measures permitted the allowance of "losses actually sustained during the year arising from fires, shipwreck, or incurred in trade, and debts ascertained to be worthless but excluding all estimated depreciation of values." Much of the phraseology of the Civil War laws was carried over into the laws written after the adoption of the Sixteenth Amendment.

Members of Congress in the Civil War period were as puzzled as those in recent times over the taxation of profits from sales of capital assets. The law of 1864 taxed net profits realized from sales of real estate purchased within the year for which income was estimated. In 1867 an amendment was made to tax net profits from sales of real estate purchased within two years previous to the year for which income was estimated. Efforts to extend this provision to personal property were unsuccessful.

Mention has been made of the establishment of the office of Com-

[5] For rates and personal exemptions of other laws, see Chap. XXII below.
[6] *Congressional Globe*, 37th Congress, 1st Session, p. 315.

missioner of Internal Revenue in 1862. Because of the vagueness of many of the provisions of the laws the interpretations of the Commissioner in the form of rulings and regulations were of great importance. This office was continued even after the repeal of the income tax (1872) in order to administer the liquor and tobacco excise

Table 2

Receipts of the Federal Government[a] 1860-1875
(In millions of dollars)

Year	*Customs*	*Internal Revenue*		*Miscellaneous*[b]	*Total*	*Surplus or deficit*
		Income and Profits Taxes	*Miscellaneous*			
1860	$53.19	....	....	$11.39	$64.58	$-7.07
1861	39.58	....	....	10.28	49.86	-25.04
1862	49.06	....	....	11.23	60.29	-422.77
1863	69.06	$2.74	$34.90	17.16	123.86	-602.04
1864	102.32	20.29	89.45	65.01	277.07	-600.70
1865	84.93	60.98	148.48	53.88	348.27	-963.84
1866	179.05	72.98	236.24	84.17	572.42	+37.22
1867	176.42	66.01	200.01	63.43	505.87	+133.09
1868	164.46	41.46	149.63	66.38	421.93	+28.29
1869	180.05	34.79	123.56	49.85	388.26	+48.08
1870	194.54	37.78	147.12	50.69	430.14	+101.60
1871	206.27	19.16	123.94	53.99	403.36	+91.15
1872	216.37	14.44	116.20	49.00	396.02	+96.59
1873	188.09	5.06	108.67	54.92	356.73	+43.39
1874	163.10	.14	102.27	65.93	331.45	+2.34
1875	157.17	....	110.01	47.61	314.79	+13.37

[a] *Report of the Secretary of the Treasury* 1938, p. 410.
[b] Includes sales of public lands and surplus postal receipts.

taxes; consequently when the later income tax laws were enacted there was in existence the nucleus of an administrative organization armed with many precedents and some valuable experience.[7]

From a fiscal point of view the Civil War income tax was a success. Although the yield was not large it was substantial at a time when every dollar counted. The greatest annual yield was over

[7] George S. Boutwell, the first commissioner, has left a description of the organization of the office in his memoirs, *Sixty Years in Public Office.* His regulations were published in 1863 in a volume entitled *Manual of the Direct and Excise Tax System of the United States.*

seventy-three million dollars in 1866.[8] During the ten years it was imposed the total collections were $376,000,000.

In all these years the income tax was considered a temporary wartime expedient. Each of the acts passed in 1864, 1865, 1866, and 1867 contained a provision that the law was to be in force until 1870 "and no longer." In 1870, therefore, the question had to be settled. It was then voted, by a close margin, that the tax should be collected for 1870 and 1871 "and no longer."

TABLE 3

EXPENDITURES OF THE FEDERAL GOVERNMENT[a] 1860-1875
(In millions of dollars)

Year	*Civil, Misc., and Indians*	*War Dept.*	*Navy Dept.*	*Pensions*	*Postal Deficiencies*	*Interest on the Public Debt*	*Postal Expenditures* exclusive of postal deficiencies	*Total*
1860	$21.13	$16.41	$11.51	$1.10	$9.89	$3.18	$9.28	$72.41
1861	21.93	22.98	12.42	1.04	5.17	4.00	8.43	74.98
1862	20.11	394.37	42.67	.85	3.56	13.19	7.56	482.33
1863	25.66	599.30	63.22	1.08	.75	24.73	10.56	725.30
1864	28.13	690.79	85.73	4.98	.99	53.69	11.84	877.17
1865	49.63	1031.32	122.61	16.34	.25	77.40	13.39	1310.94
1866	44.36	284.50	43.32	15.61	......	133.07	15.32	536.13
1867	58.35	95.22	31.03	20.94	3.52	143.78	15.69	373.24
1868	60.16	123.25	25.78	23.78	4.05	140.42	18.78	396.13
1869	59.79	78.50	20.00	28.48	5.40	130.69	18.28	341.15
1870	67.80	57.66	21.78	28.34	4.84	129.24	19.13	328.79
1871	71.79	35.80	19.43	34.44	5.13	125.58	19.26	311.44
1872	69.83	35.37	21.25	28.53	5.18	117.36	21.49	299.01
1873	80.89	46.32	23.53	29.36	5.49	104.75	23.64	313.98
1874	88.51	42.31	30.93	29.04	4.71	107.12	27.51	330.15
1875	72.24	41.12	21.50	29.46	7.21	103.09	26.40	301.03

[a] Compiled from *Report of the Secretary of the Treasury* 1938, p. 415.

What were the reasons for its unpopularity? Perhaps it was too successful; perhaps it reached too many influential people. Certainly it was not popular. Few had anything good to say for it. Naturally the critics were more vocal than most of those who favored it; but, despite its merits, it is difficult to find in the newspapers or memoirs or other writings of the period any enthusiasm for its continuation. Objections made to the Civil War income taxes may be grouped under four heads: (1) the revenue was not needed after the war, (2) the law was inequitable in many of its provisions,

[8] The Commissioner of Internal Revenue reported collections of $73,434,709 for 1866, including $452,550 from the special tax of 1865, not included in the *Report of the Secretary of the Treasury* as shown in Table 2.

(3) the administrative methods were inquisitorial, and (4) the administration was inefficient and subject to political influence.

TABLE 4

PRINCIPAL OF THE PUBLIC DEBT OUTSTANDING
CLOSE OF EACH FISCAL YEAR 1860–1875 [a]
(Columns 2 to 5 in millions of dollars)

June 30	*Interest-Bearing*	*Matured*	*Noninterest-Bearing*	*Total Gross Debt*	*Gross Debt per Capita*
1860	$64.68	$.16	....	$64.84	$2.06
1861	90.42	.16	....	90.58	2.83
1862	365.36	.23	$158.59	524.18	16.03
1863	707.83	.17	411.77	1,119.77	33.56
1864	1,360.03	.37	455.44	1,815.83	53.33
1865	2,217.71	2.13	458.09	2,677.93	77.07
1866	2,322.12	4.44	429.21	2,755.76	77.69
1867	2,238.95	1.74	409.47	2,650.17	73.19
1868	2,191.33	1.25	390.87	2,583.45	69.87
1869	2,151.50	5.11	388.50	2,545.11	67.41
1870	2,035.88	3.57	397.00	2,436.45	63.19
1871	1,920.70	1.95	399.41	2,322.05	58.70
1872	1,800.79	7.93	401.27	2,209.99	54.44
1873	1,696.48	51.93	402.80	2,151.21	51.62
1874	1,724.93	3.22	431.79	2,159.93	50.47
1875	1,708.68	11.43	436.17	2,156.28	49.06

[a] *Report of the Secretary of the Treasury* 1938, p. 489.

THE EQUALITARIAN MOVEMENT

Twenty-two years elapsed after the expiration of the Civil War income tax before the enactment of another by the national government. Meanwhile, advocacy of the tax was taken up by numerous protest groups and third parties, not merely as a fiscal measure but chiefly as a symbol and instrument of reform. In other words, most of the agitation for this tax during this period was by those active in the "share-the-wealth" and "soak-the-rich" campaigns that are characteristic of severe and prolonged depressions. The Civil War income tax had scarcely expired when the country was hit by the panic of 1873 and the devastating post-war depression which followed. Two income tax bills were presented to Congress the following year (1874) and, thereafter, scarcely a session passed without the introduction of from one to ten such proposals. All of the authors of these many bills were from the South and West, none was from the East.[9] The projected measures were duly referred to the Committee on Ways and Means, by whom they were securely and permanently interred.

But this did not mean the death of the movement for a federal income tax. In fact, the movement was carried on more vigorously outside of Congress than in that body, particularly by organizations and representatives of disillusioned farmers who had gone West in the hope of finding cheap land and a good living. The difficulties of these farmers and of the sections dependent upon them were numerous and complicated by countless factors; only a few of them can be mentioned here. Prices of farm products declined steadily from 1870 to 1897. Attempts to offset declines in farm income by increasing production brought still lower prices and thus aggravated the situation. On the other hand, prices of things which farmers purchased either increased or failed to decline in proportion to prices of products sold. The farmers saw themselves as unorganized, helpless individuals at the mercy of those who controlled their markets and their credit. They resented the power of the groups with which they had to deal: the bankers, the grain exchanges, the elevator operators, the commission men, the meat packers and the other powerful organizations and business units that set or appeared to set their buying and selling prices.

This was the era of early prominence of the "trusts," the beef trust, the sugar trust, the oil trust, and other "octopuses" that seemed to be fastening their tentacles permanently upon business and, indeed, upon the very life of the people. The railroads, also, were among the offenders. After being given generous aid in the form of land grants and cash bonuses they were found to be in

[9] Income Tax bills introduced into Congress, 1874-1893:

Congress			*Year*	*Number of Bills*	*Author's State of Residence*
43d	Congress, 1st	Session	1874	2	Ill., Iowa
43d	" 2d	"	1874–1875	2	Iowa, Ky.
45th	" 2d	"	1877–1878	3	Ill., Ky.
46th	" 1st	"	1879	6	La., Ohio, Ky., Tenn.
46th	" 2d	"	1879–1880	1	Tenn.
47th	" 1st	"	1881–1882	2	La., Tenn.
48th	" 1st	"	1883–1884	1	Ky.
49th	" 1st	"	1885–1886	4	Ark., Ga., Mich., Mo., Tenn.
49th	" 2d	"	1886–1887	1	N. C.
50th	" 1st	"	1887–1888	2	Ark., Mich.
50th	" 2d	"	1888–1889	1	Ga.
51st	" 1st	"	1889–1890	10	Ark., Ga., Ill., Ind., La., Mo., N. C., N. D., Minn.
51st	" 2d	"	1890–1891	4	Ark., Ill., La., Tenn.
52d	" 1st	"	1891–1892	19	Ala., Ark., Ga., Ill., Ind., La., Mich., Mo., N. C., S. C., Tenn., Texas
53d	" 1st	"	1893	10	Ala., Ark., Miss., Tenn., Va.

(Compiled from the *Congressional Record*.)

league with other oppressors, giving discriminatory favorable rates and rebates to large shippers, including the worst monopolists, while increasing farmers' costs of transportation and thus grinding them down still further.

Many farmers were heavily in debt and as farm prices declined they resented paying interest or principal in terms of fixed numbers of dollars with increasing numbers of bushels of grain or pounds of hogs and other produce. Another grievance was the tax burden, principally the local property tax burden, but some knew or suspected that the bulk of the hidden federal tariffs and excises fell with disproportionate weight upon the farmer and laborer. Thus the eastern manufacturers as well as the capitalists conspired with the other monopolists to exploit them. Southern farmers had all the troubles of their western brothers and others in addition, such as the negro problem, the dependence on cotton, and the crop lien system.

No wonder the hard pressed classes listened sympathetically to the panaceas promised by the advocates of co-operatives, railroad regulation, more greenbacks, free silver, trust busting, income and inheritance taxes on the rich, etc.

The platform of the Populist party in 1892 set forth some of the woes in the following preamble:

> We meet in the midst of a nation brought to the verge of moral, political and material ruin. Corruption dominates the ballot box, the legislatures, the Congress, and touches even the ermine of the Bench. The people are demoralized. . . The newspapers are largely subsidized or muzzled, public opinion silenced, business prostrated, our homes covered with mortgages, labor impoverished, and the land concentrating in the hands of capitalists. . . The fruits of the toil of millions are boldly stolen to build up colossal fortunes, unprecedented in the history of the world, while their possessors despise the Republic and endanger liberty. . .
>
> The national power to create money is appropriated to enrich bondholders . . . and the supply of currency is purposely abridged to fatten usurers, bankrupt enterprise, and enslave industry.[10]

Many organizations were formed to right these wrongs. In the 1870's and 1880's these organizations were chiefly of a social, propagandist nature; in the nineties they were primarily political. Patrons of Husbandry, the Grange, the Greenback party, the National Farmers' Alliance and Industrial Union, and the Knights of Labor were some of the more influential ones. It was estimated in 1889 that there were 4,500,000 farmers in the United States of whom 1,000,000 were members of some propagandist organization.[11]

It was perfectly logical that a demand for an income tax should be

[10] *The Annual Encyclopedia* 1892, p. 753.

[11] Peffer, W. A., "The Farmers' Defensive Movement," *The Forum* 8: 464 (Dec. 1889). The Greenbackers were most influential in the earlier part of this period; many had become "silverites" by the 1890's.

part of the program of this movement. It was a tax that would be paid by the rich, not the poor, and the yield would relieve the poor of some of the burdens of supporting the government. In 1877, 1879, and 1880 the Greenback party platform contained planks for an income tax. In 1884 the Anti-Monopoly party came out for a graduated income tax. The parties that represented labor also took up the proposal as part of their reform movement and in 1878 the platform of the Knights of Labor "demanded" a graduated income tax.

The elections of 1890 and 1892 saw the results of the Populist ferment, not only in the election of state officials from that ticket, but also in the adoption by the Democrats of many Populist doctrines and in the fusion of the two parties in some cases. Although the national Democratic platform of 1892 bore little indication of pressure from the Populists, many state platforms, particularly in the South, contained planks designed to appeal to those in sympathy with the reform movement and, in some states, the platforms of the two parties were so similar as to be almost indistinguishable.[12] Enough Populist members were elected to the legislatures of midwestern states to give definite color to legislation and to make the old parties decidedly anxious as to their future. Thus it came about that the income tax was associated in the minds of many with "wild-eyed" radicalism, with "socialism, communism, devilism." [13]

In the East, an impetus was given to the income tax movement by a great publisher, Joseph Pulitzer, who took up the cause of the downtrodden man. In New York, of all places, he started a campaign for this tax. The campaign was basically much broader than one for tax reform only. In May 1883, when this new proprietor took over the *World* he dedicated it "to the cause of the people rather than that of purse proud potentates." His ten-line platform was the following:

1. Tax luxuries
2. Tax inheritances
3. Tax large incomes

12 Hicks, John, *The Populist Revolt*, p. 248. Many Easterners thought the party had changed radically. The following excerpt from an editorial in the New York *Daily Tribune* for April 11, 1894 is cited as an example:

"The Democratic Party of today is a fad party, and curiously enough a party intense with the ancient spirit of opposition. Nobody can be sure what it is that the Democrats believe and aim to enforce, but insofar as they are agreed about anything, they agree in opposing the tariff doctrines of Jefferson and Jackson, and in supporting Mugwump Free Trade and the Populist fads of free silver, "free raw materials" and an income tax. Mr. Hill may succeed in effecting a change in the present Democratic programme. He certainly would succeed if he were dealing with men whose personal careers depended on loyalty to popular sentiment. But to the Democrats of the South — and they are the absolute rulers of their party — warnings and protests are a matter of no concern whatever."

13 Senator Sherman in the debate on the 1894 income tax. (*Cong. Rec.* 26: 6695.)

4. Tax monopolies
5. Tax the privileged corporation
6. A tariff for revenue
7. Reform the Civil Service
8. Punish corrupt officers
9. Punish vote buying
10. Punish employers who coerce their employees in elections.[14]

From that time until the enactment of the 1894 law the *World* kept before its readers the desirability of an income tax.[15]

Naturally the clamor of the farmers and other distressed classes of that period reverberated in the state and national legislative halls and resulted in an unusual number of bills and measures for cheap money and also for the regulation of offending organizations. Noteworthy, besides the greenback and silver bills of the seventies, were the many state "granger" laws, the federal Interstate Commerce Act (1887), the Sherman Anti-Trust Act (1890), the Sherman Silver Purchase Act (1890), and the income tax of 1894. Even "free silver" came near enough to carrying the presidential election of 1896 to scare many conservatives. It is with the income tax phase of this movement that this study is primarily concerned, and to that feature of the movement in the 1890's we now turn our attention because of its close relation to the present era.

INCOME TAX ACT OF 1894

The hopes of the downtrodden were pinned on Grover Cleveland who was ushered into the White House in 1893 for the second time, after a four-year interval, by the most decisive victory since that of Lincoln in 1864. Yet Cleveland was modest. "Sir, it is a solemn thing to be President of the United States," he said to one of his friends on election night.[16]

The cold, sleety, and depressing March day on which he took the oath of office was emblematic of the ominous clouds of economic and social depression which darkened other parts of the country and were prophetic of a stormy term of office. Farmers in the West were burning corn for fuel and dumping wheat because the prices offered were insufficient to pay the cost of seed, freight, and marketing. Interest on mortgages rose to 10%. In the South five-cent cotton meant hunger and rags. Country folk were not the only ones who suffered.

[14] The *World*, May 17, 1883. Reprinted in Seitz, Don C., *Joseph Pulitzer*, p. 141.

[15] "This year 1893 marks the general recognition that American society has been stratified anew, that out of the economic reconstruction, fruit of the Civil War, a new social system had emerged. . . And now the genius of the *World*, and of others in the new-fangled 'yellow press,' was aiming at a party of the proletariat." Stephenson, Nathaniel W., *Nelson W. Aldrich*, p. 101.

[16] Nevins, Allan, *Grover Cleveland*, p. 508.

Those living in the cities also were in the doldrums. The panic of 1893 left a trail of closed factories, defunct banks, lost fortunes, labor wars, and hungry people.

The federal Treasury quickly felt the impact of the business depression. Cleveland was forced to exert all his energy to maintain the public credit. In the summer of 1893 he summoned Congress to a special session for the purpose of repealing the Silver Purchase Act of 1890. This move was considered nothing less than traitorous by the Silver Democrats. In Congress and in the press the President was pictured as a "blackguard" who had sold out to Wall Street.

The differences of opinion aroused by the silver issue among members of the President's party were reflected in the failure of the President to secure co-operation for his legislative program in the regular session that convened early in December 1893.

The Committee on Ways and Means [17] began its work in the fall on the tariff bill that was to fulfill the President's election pledge of a measure for revenue only. Chairman William L. Wilson of West Virginia had supported the President on the silver repeal measure, in fact, had led the Administration forces. Those fighting the repeal measure were marshalled by William J. Bryan then serving his second term in Congress and almost by accident a member of the important Committee on Ways and Means.[18] In fact, Bryan first came into prominence as an orator on the occasion of the powerful three-hour speech he made against the President's silver repeal measure in the special session.

Bryan and Wilson agreed on tariff reduction, but they did not agree on the advisability of an income tax for making up the deficit that was sure to result if import duties were cut. Wilson did not object to the theory of the income tax; in fact, he was favorable to it, but he wanted to carry out the wishes of the President who was opposed to an income tax measure at that time largely because he

[17] The members of the Committee were:

Democrats	*Republicans*
William L. Wilson (W. Va.), Ch.	Thomas B. Reed (Maine)
Benton McMillin (Tenn.)	Julius C. Burrows (Mich.)
Henry G. Turner (Ga.)	Sereno E. Payne (N. Y.)
Alexander G. Montgomery (Ky.)	John Dalzell (Pa.)
Justin R. Whiting (Mich.)	Albert Hopkins (Ill.)
W. Bourke Cockran (N. Y.)	John H. Gear (Iowa)
Moses T. Stevens (Mass.)	
William J. Bryan (Neb.)	
Clifton R. Breckenridge (Ark.)	
William D. Bynum (Ind.)	
John C. Tarsney (Mo.)	

[18] In a contest over the speakership in 1891 Springer (Dem., Ill.), one of three candidates, agreed to throw his support to Crisp provided he would make Springer Chairman of the Committee on Ways and Means and make William J. Bryan a member of the Committee. (Clark, Champ, *My Quarter Century of American Politics,* I: 273.)

did not want to arouse any further party dissension that might prevent or even delay his tariff program.[19]

The Democratic members of the Committee were almost equally divided on the practical problem of the expediency of an income tax at that time, although a majority favored the income tax in principle. One of the greatest enthusiasts for the immediate enactment of the income tax was Benton McMillin (Tenn.), chairman of the subcommittee on internal revenue. He had been studying the tax for years and as early as 1882 had introduced a bill providing for such a tax.

Bryan also had studied extensively the operation of the tax in other countries. In the spring of 1893 he had had some correspondence with the editor of the St. Louis *Republic* who proposed to the young congressman that he make a name for himself as a leader in income tax legislation.[20] What influence this had on Bryan is not known with certainty, but there is abundant evidence that he studied what information he could secure from England and France. The idea was in harmony with his social philosophy, much of which he had absorbed from the Populists.[21] Three other members of the Committee approved the principle of the tax but wavered in their advocacy of it as a part of the revenue act then under consideration.

Two of the majority members were opposed to the income tax under any circumstances. They were Cockran (N. Y.) and Stevens (Mass.), representatives of the industrial East who fought the very principle of the tax because its burden would fall on their constituents. Needless to say, most of the Republican members on the Committee were opposed to the income tax but they were given no part in writing the bill.

THE DEMOCRATIC HEN HATCHES A POPULIST CHICKEN

Wilson engineered the drafting of the tariff section of the bill and succeeded in getting it done before other revenue measures were decided upon. Meanwhile the income tax advocates persuaded a

[19] Cleveland was a "mystery" president and limited his confidences to few. After the silver repeal session he was not a leader of Congress and hesitated to force his views on the legislative body, so he worked in indirect ways that were not always effective. At the time, almost no member of the House knew his attitude toward the income tax. At the close of the session a letter to Wilson was made public in which it was shown that he opposed the tax throughout the session. This letter is printed in the New York *World*, July 20, 1894; Nevins, *Letters of Cleveland*, p. 357; and the *Annual Encyclopedia* 1894, p. 186.

[20] Bryan Papers, Library of Congress. Colonel C. H. Jones, who thus urged Bryan, was later made editor of the New York *World* and conducted the campaign for the tax mentioned above.

[21] Ignatius Donnelly of Minnesota wrote, "We put him to school and he wound up by stealing the school books." (St. Paul *Representative*, Sept. 28, 1898; quoted also in Hicks, *The Populist Revolt*, p. 356.)

majority of the Committee that the income tax was necessary, not only for fiscal reasons, but also for political considerations;[22] that is, it would be effective bait for holding those western and southern Democrats who were in danger of being caught by the Populist propaganda. Chairman Wilson finally agreed that such a bill might be introduced, not as part of the tariff bill, but as a separate measure.

So live was the income tax issue in Congress that members of the House did not wait for a formal presentation of the amendment before they began to discuss it. During the fight over the sugar tariff schedules Louisiana members expressed their fears that if an income tax were imposed there would not be the fiscal need for a duty on sugar. "Vote for free sugar and an income tax" was the rallying cry of those opposed to the Louisiana point of view, and they were successful. When sugar was put on the free list, an important income tax hurdle was passed. The fiscal argument for it was then strong.

Nevertheless, opposing Democrats then planned various parliamentary schemes for preventing the introduction of the income tax amendment. Cockran and his eastern supporters were desperate. On the day set for the presentation of the revenue bill they moved for adjournment. At the critical moment, McMillin rose to get the Speaker's attention. Realizing his precarious situation, he rushed down the aisle frantically waving the bill, shouting that he had a committee report. Fortunately for him the Speaker was friendly to the measure and gave him recognition. The measure was referred to the Committee of the Whole on the State of the Union.

Not content with this success the income tax advocates immediately moved to join it to the tariff bill. This step was taken at a party caucus despite Wilson's fervent protest. He knew it was tantamount to acceptance of the income tax. When the news was out, one of the New York papers announced: "The Democratic hen has hatched a Populist chicken at last."[23]

It was not hard for the Democrats to justify their acceptance of the income tax as a party measure despite the fact that the platform in the campaign of the preceding fall had made no mention of it.[24]

22 Much of the pressure brought on the Committee was organized by Uriel S. Hall, a member from Missouri, who was called the father of the income tax. He had been active in the Farmers' Alliance until it became political. Although not on the Committee on Ways and Means, he talked and worked for the tax, especially impressing the Committee by petitions from state delegations in Congress. (Hall, U. S., "An Income Tax: Reasons in Its Favor," *Forum* 17: 14, March 1894.)

23 New York *Daily Tribune,* January 3, 1894.

24 When Hall was asked to justify this move, he said, "I maintain that when the Democratic platform adopted at Chicago declared that a protective tariff was robbery . . . it laid the ground for some form of direct taxation such as this. Let us wipe away the robber and unconstitutional tariff and that brings us to the income tax as a logical result of that platform." (*Cong. Rec.* 26: 1610.)

Eastern Democrats, however, remained adamant in their opposition, and very vocal. A leader of Tammany came down from New York City to see what could be done about it. The sessions became almost melodramatic. Bryan, swathed in an American flag, thrilled the House and the galleries with his exultant oratory. Even Wilson became a willing convert to the cause, and when the bill was passed Bryan and St. George Tucker (Va.) carried the lovable chairman out of the hall on their shoulders as the crowds yelled and cheered their approval.

Despite President Cleveland's disapproval of the income tax, the Wilson bill was acceptable to him because the tariff rates were moderated and many articles of common consumption were transferred to the free list.

BETRAYAL OF THE PRESIDENT BY PROTECTIONIST DEMOCRATIC SENATORS

In the Senate the leading income tax advocates were Voorhees, Chairman of the Senate Finance Committee,[25] Vest of Missouri, and Peffer, the Populist Senator from Kansas.

But Hill (Dem., N. Y.) fought the measure bitterly. He charged that the income tax was unnecessary, ill-timed, and mischievous; that it was unjust because the exemption was too large and the rate too high; that it was inquisitorial and undemocratic, a step towards socialism and a violation of state rights. He protested against the Democratic party "being made a tail to the Populist kite"!

Eastern Republicans also were opposed to it. Sherman (Rep., Ohio), who had urged the retention of the tax in 1870, objected to it in 1894 because of the high exemption, because it was not needed for fiscal reasons, and because it should be left to the states.

When the revenue measure was considered on the floor of the Senate, the conservative high protectionists led by Gorman (Dem., Md.), Aldrich, and McMillan (Rep., Mich.) succeeded in radically increasing the rates on many articles. The sugar scandal was especially malodorous. Despite hostility to the income tax, it was retained in the bill, not so much for fiscal reasons as to prevent the protective tariff schedules from being overturned by western members.

25 The members of the Senate Committee on Finance were:

Democrats	*Republicans*
Daniel Voorhees (Ind.), Chairman	Justin S. Morrill (Vt.)
John R. McPherson (N. J.)	John Sherman (Ohio)
Isham G. Harris (Tenn.)	John P. Jones (Nev.)
Zebulon B. Vance (N. C.)	William B. Allison (Iowa)
George G. Vest (Mo.)	Nelson W. Aldrich (R. I.)
James K. Jones (Ark.)	

The President was thoroughly disheartened at the emasculation of his tariff reform bill and at his own betrayal at the hands of Senators of his own party; indeed, he was so outraged that he refused to sign the measure. However, he kept Congress in session the required ten days so that the measure became law without his signature.[26]

The income tax section of the tariff bill provided for a small tax, 2%, on taxable income of individuals and corporations. Included in the tax base were the values of all "personal property [not real estate] acquired by gift or inheritance" during the year. Individuals were allowed a personal exemption of $4000. This exemption was criticized by Easterners and cited as proof that advocates of the tax were motivated by sectionalism thus deliberately to concentrate the tax burden on the wealth of New York, Massachusetts, and New Jersey.[27]

THE SUPREME COURT HOLDS THE TAX UNCONSTITUTIONAL

So the "radicals" of the South and West won a victory in the struggle for democracy of taxation, but their triumph was short lived. The validity of the tax was attacked almost immediately and, in 1895, the Supreme Court declared it unconstitutional in the famous case of *Pollock* v. *Farmers Loan and Trust Company*.[28]

The chief questions before the Court were as follows: (1) whether or not the tax on income from real estate was a direct tax; (2) whether or not the tax on income from personal property was a direct tax; (3) whether or not the tax violated the rule of uniformity; and (4) whether or not the law was constitutional in view of its imposition of a tax on incomes from stocks and bonds of the states of the United States and their counties and municipalities.

[26] The President explained his position in a letter to Congressman Catchings (Miss.): "I take my place with the rank and file of the Democratic party who believe in tariff reform and who know what it is, who refuse to accept the results embodied in this bill as the close of the war, who are not blinded to the fact that the livery of Democratic reform has been stolen and worn in the service of Republican protection, and who have watched the places where the deadly blight of treason has blasted the counsels of the brave in their hour of might." (Quoted in McElroy, Robert, *Grover Cleveland,* II: 116-117.)

[27] Chairman Wilson denied that the bill involved either sectional or class legislation. "Why, sir, when for a generation New England has been sending out from her colleges men imbued with the doctrine that an income tax is a wise and equal system of taxation, when through the textbooks of her great economists, her Sumner, and Walker, and Perry, she has taught that doctrine in the colleges of the South and West, she cannot justly complain that her own teachings are used as a sectional weapon against her. No, sir, I am in close touch with the men of the North — I am in close touch with the men of the West — I am bone of the bone of the men of the South. And today I can affirm . . . that in all my conferences with them, I have heard no man suggest as the motive for this scheme of taxation that he supported it in any sectional spirit or with any feeling of resentment or hostility to any part of the country." (*Cong. Rec.* 26: appendix, 204.)

[28] 157 U. S. 429; 158 U. S. 601.

The main argument of the case was on the first point, that the tax on income from real estate was a direct tax within the meaning of Article I, Section 2 of the Constitution, hence could not be levied unless it was apportioned among the states according to their respective populations. Counsel for the plaintiff maintained that, despite earlier court rulings to the contrary, an income tax was a direct tax; that the justices arrived at their conclusions from economic definitions and from their incorrect interpretation of the debates in the Constitutional Convention.

Much more significant, in view of the psychology of the times, was the argument of Joseph Choate, one of the attorneys for the plaintiff, who represented the eastern capitalistic point of view. To him the income tax was dangerous because it was an entering wedge by which the whole system of private property might be shaken. Had not the counsel for the government admitted that the exemption might have been made $20,000 as well as $4000 and the rate 20% instead of 2%? He asked if such a "communistic march" were allowed to begin, how could the Court then make a protest after it had validated the law under consideration? He warned his hearers that there must be protection "now or never." Choate was thoroughly alarmed over the Populist revolt and its effect on Congress. He called the income tax act "communistic in its purposes and tendencies" and "defended here upon principles as communistic, socialistic — what shall I call them — populistic as ever have been addressed to any political assembly in the world."

The United States Attorney General argued that it made no difference what the meaning of direct taxes might be from an economic, scientific, or practical point of view, the question before the Court was what the words meant in the Constitution. That document did not define the terms. Two of the justices who decided the Hylton case [29] had been members of the Constitutional Convention. In that case the Court interpreted the words "direct tax" as used in the Constitution to mean only land and poll taxes, and in four later cases the Court had decided that an income tax was not a direct tax.[30] The Attorney General also relied on the favorable decisions in these later cases relative to the validity of the Civil War taxes on dividends, real estate, inheritances, and personal income.

On the third point, that the tax was not uniform, the Attorney General showed that the Constitution prescribed territorial uniformity only; that Congress had a right to provide for an exemption

[29] 3 Dall. 171 (1796). In this case the Court held that a federal tax on carriages was not a direct tax.

[30] *Pacific Insurance Co.* v. *Soule*, 7 Wall. 433 (1868); *Veazie Bank* v. *Fenno*, 8 Wall. 533 (1869); *Scholey* v. *Rew*, 23 Wall. 331 (1874); *Springer* v. *U. S.*, 102 U. S. 586 (1880).

of $4000 because it was "seeking to adjust the load of taxation" in such a way as to make it most easily borne.

These arguments were evidently not convincing to the Court. A majority agreed that the tax on land was a direct tax; therefore, the tax on income from land was a direct tax. They agreed unanimously that the section imposing a tax on income from state bonds was unconstitutional, not on the ground that the tax was direct, but because the federal government had no power to tax instrumentalities or means of the state. In the absence of one member they split evenly on the following propositions and, therefore, expressed no opinion: (1) whether the void provisions as to rents and income from real estate invalidated the whole act; (2) whether, as to income from personal property, the act was unconstitutional as laying direct taxes; (3) whether any part of the tax, if not considered direct, was invalid for want of uniformity.

So confusing was the status of the law as a result of this decision that a re-hearing was ordered. Nine justices were present at this second hearing. A majority agreed to the following conclusions: (1) taxes on rents or income of real estate are direct taxes; (2) taxes on personal property or on the income of personal property are direct taxes; (3) "the tax imposed, . . . so far as it falls on the income of real estate and of personal property, being a direct tax within the meaning of the Constitution, and, therefore, unconstitutional and void because not apportioned according to representation, all those sections, constituting one entire scheme of taxation, are necessarily invalid." One of the judges who had voted for the constitutionality of the tax on income from real estate at the time of the first hearing switched his position at the re-hearing and voted the other way. So the entire income tax section of the act was declared void by a vote of 5 to 4.

Professor Seligman has carefully analyzed the decisions and the material upon which they were based from both historical and economic points of view.[31] He states that little of the economic discussion was sound. For example, in Senator Edmunds' argument were definitions of direct taxes which the senator thought would be "generally found to be universally true." "It is fortunate," says Professor Seligman, "that legal reputation is so entirely divorced from economic knowledge, for, with all respect to Senator Edmunds, it must be said that the merest tyro in present day economics could easily puncture almost every successive clause in his definition." He points out that many misstatements of historical fact were made.

[31] Seligman, E. R. A., *Income Tax*, 1st ed., pp. 538, 579-581.

But such errors and misstatements . . . pale into insignificance compared with the glaring misinterpretation put upon the origin and purpose of the direct-tax clause — a misinterpretation which, like most of the preceding mistakes, was adopted bodily by the majority of the Court, who evidently found no time for an independent investigation of the subject.

Sectionalism and class feeling aroused by the decision expressed itself in voluminous press comment. Eastern capitalists rejoiced at the "downfall of Populism and extreme Socialism." They rejoiced also that "the people escaped the most dangerous Populistic law ever enacted," and that the Communists had learned that "they could not override the Constitution of the United States." [32]

On the other side, the liberal press pointed out that the obvious result of the decision would be to strengthen the Populist movement and to provoke social antagonism. One paper asked if there was not a spoke loose in the Constitutional wheel when the Astors and other great landed proprietors could shift the burdens of federal taxation from their own shoulders to the backs of the poor laborers.[33] The New York *World* — for years a staunch supporter of the income tax and other "radical" measures — said, "The tax is dead, but the principle upon which it is based is alive and will yet in some form prevail." [34]

THE LOW EBB OF INTEREST IN AN INCOME TAX

The feelings of discontent and frustration resulting from the court decision were slow in disappearing, but they lessened gradually with the passing of the depression and the lapse of time. With the subsequent increase of prosperity the ardor for an income tax waned perceptibly. It never entirely disappeared, however. A few members of Congress persisted in introducing income tax measures into the House. Three of the more radical political parties — the Populist, the Socialist Labor, and the Bryan wing of the Democratic party — wrote income tax planks into their party platforms in 1896. In 1898 the tax was proposed as a means of financing the Spanish American War, but the idea was discarded.

Left-wing activities were shifted into other channels. First the silver movement, long an issue in the West, attained nation-wide importance with Bryan's campaigns for the presidency. Then antitrust legislation and similar agitation against the concentration of great wealth became of paramount interest.

[32] The New York *Times,* May 21, 1895, printed interviews with prominent citizens. For an example of this point of view see Edmunds, George F., "The Salutary Results of the Income-tax Decision," *Forum* 19: 513 (July 1895).

[33] Syracuse (New York) *News,* quoted in the New York *World,* May 23, 1895.

[34] May 21, 1895.

Upon the return of the Republicans to power in 1897 the radical groups found little sympathy at the White House. McKinley's interests were concentrated on the war with Spain, tariffs, and the currency. In his second term, however, he asked Congress to study and assert its power to control monopolies and trusts. One of the interesting moves was that for an amendment to the Constitution to give Congress adequate power to deal with trusts. The resolution presented to Congress, however, did not secure the necessary two-thirds vote in the House.

In 1904 even Bryan was unable to get support for an income tax plank in the Democratic platform. He said that he was persuaded to abandon the idea on the condition that the committee would agree to a stronger anti-trust plank.

As Bryan let his zeal for the income tax wane, another political leader sounded a call for grappling with the problems of massive fortunes, including those related to the creation and the use of those fortunes. On the occasion of the laying of the corner-stone of the House Office Building, April 14, 1906, President Theodore Roosevelt made a reference to the desirability of limiting fortunes by taxation. The effect of the speech has been thus described:

> The President made a flamboyant Fourth of July speech for ten minutes, an uplift speech for fifteen, skinned the muckrakers within an inch of their lives, and delivered a few light taps on Democratic ribs. The mouths of the eminent Republican magnates were spread in smiles reaching from ear to ear. They were having the time of their lives, when suddenly, without any connection whatever with anything he had said, apropos of nothing, he declared vehemently for both a graduated income tax and a graduated inheritance tax. The Democrats were jubilant and applauded hilariously, while the smiles froze on the faces of the Republicans. . . The President seemed to be delighted with the sensation he had created and the consternation he had wrought among Republican statesmen. Their curses on him for that speech were not only deep, but loud.[35]

In his message to Congress in December 1906, he discussed the graduated income tax in some detail. He emphasized the responsibility that men of wealth owed to the state because they derived "special advantages from the mere existence of government." The problem of enacting a law was rightly described as "intricate, delicate, and troublesome." The difficulty of amending the Constitution was considered so great that "only real necessity" could justify a resort to that method. These speeches were merely sporadic. Theodore Roosevelt made no further move toward the enactment of such a tax, and no other prominent Republican showed any interest in it at that time.

[35] Clark, Champ, *My Quarter Century of American Politics,* I: 440.

CHAPTER II

THE CORPORATION EXCISE TAX OF 1909 AND THE SIXTEENTH AMENDMENT

FAINT BUT NEW INTEREST IN THE INCOME TAX (1895-1909)

Many of the proponents of the income tax felt that they were "robbed" of their victory in 1895. Though they appeared quiescent for more than a decade thereafter, the forces working for such a tax were in reality far from dead; in fact, they were too deeply rooted to be easily destroyed and too vigorous to be suppressed for long. Moreover, by one of the strange ironies of fate, these forces were destined to compel the conservative leaders of a conservative party to make a complete right about face and to aid their political opponents in establishing the "radical," "socialistic," or "communistic" income tax which they had fought so stubbornly for a generation.

President Theodore Roosevelt's unheralded outburst in 1906, mentioned in the preceding chapter, was a slight indication of the sub-surface ferment at work in those seemingly quiescent years. Indicative of the same ferment were the activities of various other individuals and organizations. Outstanding among these were the efforts of Representative Cordell Hull (Tenn.), a protege of Benton McMillin, who introduced his first income tax measure in December 1907, and who started a real campaign to educate Congress in the following session by drafting such resolutions as the following:

Providing for printing in one volume all United States Statutes relating to duties on imports and taxes on incomes.[1]

Directing the Committee on the Judiciary to report certain information to the House relative to the collection of taxes under the income tax law of 1861.[2]

Directing the Secretary of State to instruct our representatives abroad to make certain investigations concerning the income tax.[3]

In 1908 the Democratic Convention adopted the following platform plank:

We favor an income tax as part of our revenue system, and we urge the submission of a constitutional amendment specifically authorizing Congress to levy and collect a tax upon individual and corporate incomes, to the end that wealth may bear its proportional share of the burdens of the federal government.

1 *Cong. Rec.* 43: 684.

2 *Cong. Rec.* 43: 1324. The "1861" in the *Record* is probably a misprint for "1867." See text and footnote 16 below and Chapter XXI, text and footnote 78.

3 *Cong. Rec.* 43: 2532.

Two of the minor parties "demanded" a graduated income tax. The Republican platform was silent on the subject. It was with some surprise, therefore, that the public heard the following statement of Judge Taft upon the occasion of his formal acceptance of the nomination for the presidency at Cincinnati, July 28, 1908:

The Democratic platform demands two constitutional amendments, one providing for an income tax and the other for the election of Senators by the people. In my judgment an amendment to the Constitution for an income tax is not necessary. I believe that an income tax, when the protective system of customs and the internal revenue tax shall not furnish income enough for governmental needs, can and should be devised which, under the decisions of the Supreme Court, will conform to the Constitution.[4]

Mr. Bryan, the Democratic nominee, replied at Des Moines August 21, saying:

The Democratic party has declared for an income tax as part of the revenue system, and for a Constitutional Amendment as a means of securing this tax. Secretary Taft announces in his notification speech that he is in favor of an income tax whenever the revenues are so low as to require it, and expresses his belief that it is possible to secure such a tax without a constitutional amendment. If it is possible to frame a law which will avoid the objections raised to the income tax law of 1894, well and good, but that is uncertain. If an income tax is desirable, surely Secretary Taft cannot consistently oppose the adoption of a Constitutional Amendment. If the principle is right and the tax wise, Congress ought to have authority to levy and collect such a tax, and no supporter of Secretary Taft can oppose our position without dissenting from the Republican candidate.[5]

Tariff reform, not the income tax, however, was the issue in the 1908 campaign, if there can be said to have been any real issue at all; indeed, it has been said that no campaign up to that time had been more devoid of great issues. After Taft's election he made no mention of the income tax either in his inaugural address or in his short message to the special session of Congress that he called in March 1909.

THE SPECIAL SESSION OF 1909

It was particularly ironic that the impending tax revolution should have been given such an impetus by the Sixty-first Congress. Conservatism seemed to be its dominant attribute. Both the House and the Senate had a large majority of Republican members. The President had been elected as the most conservative of the candidates. The House was controlled by the Speaker, Joseph Cannon (Ill.), a man of strong will who developed a tyrannical code of parliamentary

[4] New York *Daily Tribune*, July 29, 1908.
[5] *Annual Encyclopedia* 1908, p. 588.

procedure to suppress the minority. The leaders of the majority party in the House were such "stand patters" as Payne (N. Y.), Longworth (Ohio), Dalzell (Penn.), and Fordney (Mich.). In the Senate, the leaders were Lodge (Mass.), Aldrich (R. I.), Penrose (Penn.), and Cullom (Ill.), none of whom could be imagined as willing to allow anything so radical as an income tax bill to be introduced, much less to be considered. There were, however, a few western Republican members who were more liberal. They joined with the progressive Democrats in both houses to launch a surprise attack and to force the income tax issue upon the Administration.

An opportunity for the President to propose an income tax was offered at the beginning of his administration. The report of the Secretary of the Treasury for the preceding fiscal year, 1908, showed the effect of the depression on federal revenues. Receipts from customs had fallen off $46,000,000, those from the internal revenue, $18,000,000. On the other hand, expenditures had increased more than $136,000,000.

In view of Taft's campaign statement as to his belief in the constitutionality of an income tax, it might have been expected that he would propose such a tax to make up the deficit. Instead he proposed an inheritance tax. It is difficult to understand why he ever made such a reference to the income tax as that in his acceptance speech because he never afterward evinced any enthusiasm for it.[6]

THE PROGRAM OF THE COMMITTEE ON WAYS AND MEANS

Chairman Payne of the Committee on Ways and Means,[7] described as "an honest devotee of privilege," co-operated with Speaker Cannon and other conservatives to enforce the will of the eastern high protectionists.[8] He stunned even the President by immediately proposing a new bill which revised upwards the tariff rates, contrary to the

6 Even after the Sixteenth Amendment was submitted to the states he is reported to have said to a press correspondent that he would not resort to the ordinary income tax except in an emergency such as war, although he believed in the principle of the tax. (*The Outlook*, 99: 816, Dec. 2, 1911.)

7 The members of the Committee on Ways and Means were:

Republicans	*Democrats*
Sereno E. Payne (N. Y.), Ch.	Champ Clark (Mo.)
Nicholas Longworth (Ohio)	Oscar W. Underwood (Ala.)
John Dalzell (Pa.)	James M. Griggs (Ga.)
Joseph H. Gaines (W. Va.)	Edward W. Pou (N. C.)
Joseph W. Fordney (Mich.)	Choice B. Randell (Tenn.)
Sam McCall (Mass.)	Frances B. Harrison (N. Y.)
Henry S. Boutell (Ill.)	Robert F. Broussard (La.)
Ebenezer J. Hill (Conn.)	
James C. Needham (Calif.)	
William A. Calderhead (Kan.)	
Edgar A. Crumpacker (Ind.)	
Francis W. Cushman (Wash.)	

8 Bowers, Claude G., *Beveridge and the Progressive Era*, p. 334.

principles espoused by the Republican party in the preceding campaign and contrary to the general opinion as to the purpose for which Congress had been summoned. The tariff bill had been drafted, however, according to the usual method, that is, after interested manufacturers had been heard from. This was before Taft was inaugurated, but the Committee saw no reason to change its bill after he took office.

The President was unhappy about it. He strongly disapproved of the proposed taxes on "the breakfast table," on clothing, or on any of the necessities of life. When congressional leaders countered with the claim that if such taxes were eliminated the bill would not bring in the necessary amount of revenue, Taft's reply was that the revenue could be raised from other sources.[9] The newspapers carried frequent dispatches as to what these sources might be. One frequently mentioned was a tax of 2% on corporation dividends.[10] Chairman Payne stated that the Ways and Means Committee had considered such a proposal but did not favor it because the financial condition of many corporations was precarious and because taxes levied on them by states and local governmental units were already burdensome.[11] Furthermore, even if a fairly heavy tax were imposed, it would probably bring in less than $20,000,000. Payne questioned also the constitutionality of such a tax. It was learned later in the session that the suggestion for this tax came from the President. In fact, he had submitted to the Committee on Ways and Means several proposals which had been drawn up for him by Attorney General George W. Wickersham. These embodied the principle of an income tax and attempted to comply with the decisions of the Supreme Court.[12]

The Committee eventually made some concessions. An inheritance tax[13] was included before the measure was introduced and some tariff rates were lowered slightly before the bill was passed. It was estimated that the bill would bring in $30,000,000 additional revenue from the tariff and $20,000,000 from the inheritance tax.

The report of the minority members of the Committee on Ways and Means criticized the bill on the grounds that the tariff rate reductions were more apparent than real and that the consumers' cost of living would not be decreased. Their report made no mention of the inheritance tax, but when the bill was presented on the floor

[9] New York *World,* March 10, March 30, 1909; New York *Times,* March 30, 1909; Washington *Post,* March 23, 1909.

[10] New York *Times,* March 23, March 24, 1909. See below, pp. 35 and 36.

[11] *Cong. Rec.* 44: 194-195; Washington *Post,* March 24, 1909.

[12] *Cong. Rec.* 44: 4003, 4717.

[13] The rates were graduated from 1% to 5% according to the amount of the bequest and the relation of the heir to the decedent. This tax was eliminated from the Senate bill and not restored by the Conferees.

of the House there was much criticism of it chiefly because 33 states were already using this form of taxation and should not be interfered with by the federal government.

ATTEMPTS TO INTRODUCE AN INCOME TAX IN THE HOUSE

Several members commented on the failure of the Committee to provide for an income tax. In answer to questioning, especially by Champ Clark, minority leader, Chairman Payne replied that several proposals for such a measure were made to the Committee but that he did not favor them because (1) he had strong convictions about the constitutionality of an income tax and (2) he thought it would occasion "perjury and fraud unlimited." [14] The members of the minority were convinced that "any utterance of Mr. Payne giving the two reasons for not incorporating an income tax were purely reasons for opposing the tax, in common with eastern influences general at that time." [15]

Despite the apparent hopelessness of their cause, three Representatives had the courage to introduce into such a hostile atmosphere income tax bills and resolutions. They were Hull (Tenn.), James (Ky.), and Stevens (Minn.), the last a Republican. They knew that they could never get a bill through that House, yet were convinced that some education along this line might eventually be successful.

Hull's efforts, it will be recalled, had commenced in 1907. His bills were interesting. One was almost a duplicate of the 1894 law, slightly modified because of the ruling of the Supreme Court in the Pollock case. One was to "require the assessment and collection of taxes imposed by the income tax law of 1894." Hull's resolutions were "to investigate the validity of acts under which an income tax had been collected," and "to secure information as to the operation of the income tax in foreign countries." [16] His speeches showed careful thought and a thorough study of earlier United States laws and court decisions as well as of the laws in force in England, Prussia, Switzerland, Norway, and Sweden.

James' resolution was much like Hull's, that is, to request the President to advise Congress as to the need of an income tax.[17] Stevens wanted his measure not to be linked with the tariff bill but to be considered on its own merits. His plan was to use the revenue from an income tax to build up a large fund for internal improvements.

[14] *Cong. Rec.* 44: 194-195. Later in the session Longworth said that the members of the Committee rejected the income tax because they thought it would yield insufficient revenue.

[15] Memorandum of Secretary Cordell Hull to the authors, Feb. 11, 1936.

[16] *Cong. Rec.* 44: 36, 105.

[17] *Cong. Rec.* 44: 105.

He had acquainted President Roosevelt with his suggestion the preceding December [18] and was offered the assistance of the Secretary of the Treasury. In fact, with the help of the Treasury, a bill was drawn up, but it was too late in the session to do anything with it. Stevens secured a comment of approval from President Taft but no evidence of much interest, so the bill was not introduced.

As to the constitutional difficulties, Stevens and Hull agreed that it was necessary to secure a reversal of the previous decision of the Supreme Court before an equitable and comprehensive income tax law would have much chance of survival.[19]

All of these three men — Hull, James and Stevens — knew that their work for the income tax would probably not accomplish immediate results, nevertheless they kept it up for educational purposes. The one tangible result was the insertion of a demand for a graduated income tax in the motion of the minority leader to recommit the bill.[20]

In reply to the question as to why the Democrats in the House of Representatives were not so successful as those in the Senate in pushing the income tax idea, Hull gave this answer some years later :

> The democrats in the Senate had entire freedom of discussion and debate and the benefit of senatorial courtesy in other essential respects, whereas the democratic minority in the House was hopelessly curbed and restrained by every sort of muzzle method under the despotic Cannon rule. All we could do would be to get a chance to deliver a speech compressed into a brief time, on taxation or similar subject. We had no chance to offer an amendment in the form of an income tax proposal. The most I could do was to prevail upon the democratic minority leader, Mr. Champ Clark, to insert the income tax doctrine in his motion to recommit the Payne-Aldrich tariff bill.[21]

THE INCOME TAX INJECTED INTO THE SENATE TARIFF BILL

While the House was debating the Payne bill, the Senate Committee on Finance [22] worked out its own measure at the dictation of Chairman Aldrich. The members of the Committee had been "hand

[18] At that time the National River and Harbor Congress convened in Washington and passed a resolution favoring a bond issue of $500,000,000 for internal improvements.

[19] *Cong. Rec.* 44: 266-267.

[20] *Cong. Rec.* 44: 1300.

[21] Memorandum of Secretary Cordell Hull to the authors, Feb. 11, 1936.

[22] The members of the Senate Committee on Finance were :

Republicans	*Democrats*
Nelson W. Aldrich (R. I.) Ch.	John W. Daniel (Va.)
Julius C. Burrows (Mich.)	Hernando D. Money (Miss.)
Boies Penrose (Pa.)	Joseph W. Bailey (Texas)
Eugene Hale (Maine)	James P. Taliaferro (Fla.)
Shelby Cullom (Ill.)	F. M. Simmons (N. C.)
Henry Cabot Lodge (Mass.)	
Porter J. McCumber (N. D.)	
Reed Smoot (Utah)	
Frank P. Flint (Cal.)	

picked" so that there would be no difference of opinion on protection. Aldrich frankly boasted that there would be nothing in the bill when it finally passed the Senate except the straight schedules — no income tax, no inheritance tax, no stamp tax, no corporation tax.[23]

He anticipated no difficulty in pushing his measure through. The Senate, as has been said, was conservative, even to a greater degree than the House, and Aldrich controlled it. He has been described as a tall, handsome, aristocratic, self-possessed, and socially charming gentleman who "wore his crown of kingship as one who did not feel its weight upon his head." [24] His clients were railroads, bankers, industrialists — called by opponents the reactionary privileged groups. Towards the common man he felt nothing but indifference or contempt. Towards Senators, he felt himself their ruler and them the ruled.

It was said to have been characteristic of Aldrich's opponents that they painted him in black colors, the "exponent of heartless wealth, trying to prevent its just taxation." [25] Naturally he wanted to protect the interests of his class. His biographer implies that La Follette played up this trait for strategic reasons. La Follette, however, was not alone in holding this impression of Aldrich. It was widespread. For example, a special correspondent in an eastern paper wrote the following comment in his column :

> Aldrich's job is to prevent, emasculate, or postpone legislation which threatens to interfere with the profits of big business interests. . . For years Aldrich has prevented postal reforms . . . from being discussed, let alone coming to a vote. . . Employers' liability laws, eight hour legislation, conservation of public resources, improvements of waterways, reform of the injunction laws, better security for bank depositors, regulation of corporations and civil pensions are among numerous other economic reforms Aldrich has sidetracked or smothered.[26]

In the same party but with completely dissimilar views on economics and political theory was La Follette (Wis.). Four others supported this "Fighting Bob :" Bristow (Kan.), Dolliver (Iowa), Cummins (Iowa), and Clapp (Minn.). Their ranks were soon swelled by the "conversion" of Brown (Neb.), and Borah (Idaho), then a new member. Occasionally Beveridge (Ind.), one of Taft's most devoted campaigners, voted with them. All of these men were "of character and ability, and some among them had more than a spark of genius." [27] They were fighters, seasoned in local conflicts. They carried on the tradition of the social revolution, the fight against

23 New York *Times,* April 10, 12 and 13, 1909.
24 Bowers, *Beveridge and the Progressive Era,* p. 323.
25 Stephenson, *Nelson W. Aldrich,* p. 353.
26 Newark (N. J.) *Evening News,* July 1, 1909.
27 Bowers, *Beveridge and the Progressive Era,* p. 324.

monopoly, intrenched privilege, and the power of money — all that Aldrich stood for.

These insurgents entered the tariff fight under the illusion that they had the blessing of the Administration. They knew that the President did not approve of the House draft of the tariff bill. The Aldrich bill was worse but, instead of saying so frankly to the Senate, the President chose indirect methods. He consulted with La Follette, told him to go ahead and amend the bill, and promised to veto it unless it complied with the platform.[28]

Thus opened the tariff fight of 1909, one act of the historic drama — the splitting of the Republican party. Only as the income tax became part of the plot can the scenes be delineated here.

Forty-eight hours after the House bill was passed the Aldrich bill was substituted in the Senate. No explanation was made of the hundreds of increases in rates. The author planned to rush it through unchallenged. Objection to the high-handed procedure of the conservative Republicans could be seen only as shadows of coming events. Thirty young western Republicans courageously but futilely attacked Cannonism in the House. Several western Republican Senators made no attempt to hide their disappointment at being left off the important Finance Committee.[29] Others broadcast the information that the West would not stand for higher protective duties.

The Insurgents[30] divided the bill so that each of them could specialize on certain schedules. The Democrats held a caucus to formulate their plans for a fight on the measure and agreed unanimously to push an income tax amendment.

Bailey was ready for this campaign. When Hull realized the impossibility of getting any action on the income tax in the House, he persuaded Bailey to take up the cause in the Senate. He presented him with a valuable collection of material on the subject. It dealt with the operation of the tax in all parts of the world and was brought up to date for his benefit.[31] This idea was in line with Bailey's interests. For at least twelve years he had been a congressional proponent of the income tax.

Bailey was a striking figure, tall and well built, intellectually well informed and of keen judgment, but his temperament was often irritating because he was dictatorial and quick to take offense.[32] His

28 La Follette, Robert M., *Autobiography*, p. 440.

29 La Follette, *Autobiography*, p. 432.

30 At this period these "radicals" did not consider themselves a separate party. They were Republicans, but because of their later separation they have been designated in this chapter as "Insurgents."

31 Memorandum of Cordell Hull to the authors, Feb. 11, 1936.

32 Bowers, *Beveridge and the Progressive Era*, p. 185.

voice was melodious; his oratorical manner impressive. When he rose in the Senate to offer his amendment on April 15, everyone listened. The occasion was described some years later by Hull, as follows:

> In defense of his proposal Senator Bailey delivered a remarkable . . . speech of two hours and a half, with the floor and galleries completely filled every moment of the time. Both the great ability of Senator Bailey and the opportunity to speak at any length at almost any time in the Senate, compared to virtually no opportunity in the House except in a most limited way, made this performance possible. After his speech the income tax movement flared up noticeably throughout the Nation.[33]

This amendment proposed a tax of 3% on the net income of individuals and corporations above $5000 but income received from states, counties, and municipalities was exempt. This exception was made because of the decision of the Supreme Court in the case of *Pollock* v. *Farmers' Loan and Trust Co.* in 1895 but, in all other respects, the law was practically a copy of the 1894 law and challenged the decision. The author wrote the law in this way so that it might be submitted to the Court for reconsideration.

As one of the counter-reactionary moves on the part of western Republicans, Cummins also drew up an income tax amendment. Cummins came to the Senate well trained in constructive statesmanship through his fights to control the railroads when governor of Iowa. He was one of the oldest of the Insurgent group, but was one of the newer men in the Senate.[34] As a speaker he was characterized as convincing but not flowery nor even eloquent, a plain blunt man who looked seriously on life.[35]

In less than a week after Bailey's measure was proposed Cummins offered his income tax amendment, which differed from that of Bailey in two respects: (1) it taxed only individual income; (2) the rates were graduated from 2% on incomes of over $5000 and not over $10,000 to 6% on those over $100,000.[36] The author explained that he objected to a direct tax on corporations because it put too much burden on stockholders as opposed to bondholders, and because comparatively too much of the burden on stockholders fell on the small investor. By the plan that he proposed corporation earnings would be taxed after distribution to individuals whose total incomes were more than bare living wages.

Aldrich sensed the strength of the income tax movement and, even before Cummins' amendment was introduced, offered statistical material to show that the Senate tariff measure would produce revenue

[33] Memorandum of Cordell Hull to the authors, Feb. 11, 1936.
[34] He entered the Senate in November 1908.
[35] Bowers, *Beveridge and the Progressive Era*, p. 330.
[36] *Cong. Rec.* 44: 1420.

sufficient to meet the expenses of government "without the imposition of additional taxes." If, however, his estimates of yield proved too high, he considered it the duty of Congress to reduce expenditures, not to impose new tax burdens.[37]

He expressed surprise that Bailey would propose taxes that would take $60,000,000 from the incomes of the people, although he admitted that Bailey wished to reduce proportionately other taxes upon "necessaries of life." This was the rub so far as Aldrich was concerned. If this theory were carried out many articles would be put on the free list. He remarked caustically that perhaps the Senators would like to take steps to destroy the protective system. He cited the Wilson bill (of 1894) as a horrible example of an attempt to reduce the tariff. The rates had been lowered, to be sure, he said, it did reduce revenues. How? By ruining business, he replied. He painted a black picture of the effects — machinery was stopped, the fires of furnaces were put out, industries were prostrated. He did not state, however, that much of the depression had come before the 1894 tariff bill was enacted.

Daniel answered Aldrich at length.[38] An editorial in a New York paper the next day also answered him, as follows:

> Senator Aldrich is opposed to an income tax. . . Yet Senator Aldrich must see what everybody else sees, that tariff legislation such as he urges upon Congress, legislation that would increase the rates proposed in the Payne bill, increase the rates actually imposed by the Dingley Act, forces his opponents, from motives of the plainest political expediency, to urge income taxes and inheritance taxes, and directly and powerfully stimulates the popular demand for the imposition of such taxes.
>
> Mr. Aldrich knows very well that the South and the West favor income and inheritance taxes because they would be collected largely in the North and East. Tariff taxes are distributed in proportion to consumption, income taxes and inheritance taxes would be paid largely out of accumulations. That single consideration is enough to make an income tax popular. It is enough to create and enforce the demand that taxes upon incomes and inheritances be substituted, so far as possible, for tariff taxes. . .
>
> There is no occasion for surprise in the fact that Senator Daniel and Senator Bailey propose as a substitute for this impost taxes that would

[37] *Cong. Rec.* 44: 1378. The *Commercial and Financial Chronicle* (April 24, 1909) printed the following comment on Cummins' amendment: "The real reason, which is never or rarely honest enough and bold enough to announce itself in plain language, is the desire . . . of penalizing wealth. This country has always been the possible eldorado of every man. Its most prominent and most boasted idea is, or used to be, that every man shall be secure in holding the utmost he is able honestly to get. . . How a thing which everybody may seek becomes criminal as soon as anybody gets it is an economic puzzle which can be solved psychologically by jealousy. The wrong people have the property, that is all.

"The pestilent anger at the prosperity of others is at the bottom of all our 'regulative' disturbances. . ."

[38] Daniel had introduced an amendment to tax corporations on their gross income at the rate of 1/4 of 1%. (*Cong. Rec.* 44: 4236.)

not compel the people to pay $6.50 to the protected manufacturers for every dollar collected at the Custom Houses. The protectionist ship is a pretty staunch old craft. . . But, really, Senator Aldrich is steering her straight on the rocks. When the people come to a full understanding of the extravagant cost to them of the Republican policy of protection, the stand-patters will be confronted with a real and imperative demand for a tariff for revenue only, coupled in all probability with those taxes upon the business and industries of the United States which Mr. Daniel and Mr. Bailey propose, and of which the Rhode Island Senator stands in such dread.[39]

In the debate of April 21, Bacon (Ga.) secured a statement from Cummins that he would favor an income tax even if the tariff bill provided for sufficient revenue,[40] thus showing that the principle of the thing was at stake. The following day was the historic occasion on which the small but effective group of Insurgents astonished the Senate by proclaiming their great objection to the tariff bill because of its failure really to revise the rates as the party had promised. This move marked the opening of the Insurgent Republican revolt. It "made a marked impression on the [Finance] Committee." As one paper stated, they realized "that they must either present arguments to convince the Insurgents of the reality of the revision or at least give them an excuse for coming back into the fold of the organization." [41]

The strength of the Insurgents was shown when ten Republicans joined the Democrats in opposing an increase in one of the schedules.[42] A change of four votes would have defeated the Administration and everyone knew that on more important matters the radicals could muster more than ten votes. Aldrich was a shrewd enough politician to see what was happening. If three groups, namely, the progressive Republicans, the Democrats, and certain eastern Republicans who carried on the Theodore Roosevelt tradition, formed an alliance to pass an income tax measure they could win. The Republican party would be seriously split, party discipline would be utterly ruined, and something even more important than a tariff bill would be lost.[43]

Lodge and Aldrich attempted to defend the work of the Commit-

[39] New York *Times*, April 21, 1909.

[40] *Cong. Rec.* 44: 1429.

[41] New York *Times*, April 25, 1909. The *Times* of March 23, 1909 made this statement: "The fact is, Mr. Aldrich has seen as clearly as any man in the Senate and equally as early the growth of the 'progressive' or the insurgent element. . ."

[42] *Cong. Rec.* 44: 1759. The ten were: Joseph Bristow and Charles Curtis (Kan.), Norris Brown and Elmer Burkett (Neb.), Coe Crawford (S. D.), Albert Cummins and Jonathan Dolliver (Iowa), Martin Johnson (N. D.), Robert La Follette (Wis.), and Knute Nelson (Minn.). Beveridge and Bourne were among the fifteen who did not vote.

[43] Aldrich's biographer ascribes part of the Senator's opposition to the tax to the fear that the bad feeling thus engendered would jeopardize the banking and currency legislation in which he was so deeply interested. (Stephenson, *Aldrich*, p. 353.)

tee, but the Insurgents were not to be misled by oratory nor were they in a mood to yield because of minor concessions that Aldrich was about ready to make. There seemed to be a possibility of intervention by the President. Moreover, even Root came out against the tactics of the conservative Republicans so that Aldrich saw that it was a matter of good generalship to concede lower rates on several schedules, though he took care to prevent the Insurgents from making "political capital" out of them.[44]

About a month after Bailey introduced his amendment he asked Aldrich when the vote on it could be taken. Aldrich put him off and Bailey well knew how such tactics could kill his bill.[45] He said:

> I want to admonish all the friends of the income tax on both sides . . . that if we postpone it until the Senator from Rhode Island is ready to vote we will not carry it for he will stay here until the dog days before he will allow us to come to a vote on this question, if he can help it, until he feels reasonably sure of defeating it.[46]

Within a few days it was rumored that Aldrich had decided to kill the income tax by having Cummins' amendment voted on first. He heard objections to the graduated rates and thought there was enough opposition from Democratic ranks to kill it. Then he hoped that enough Insurgents would retaliate by voting against the Bailey amendment.[47]

Knowing this situation and the temper of the Senate majority leaders, it is understandable why the Insurgents and Democrats realized that it would be to their tactical advantage to unite on an income tax program. With this in mind, a meeting was held May 18 at which they agreed on a compromise between the measures of Cummins and Bailey but Bailey did not withdraw his amendment. Cummins was to write the joint measure, which would be a tax on both corporation and individual incomes over $5000 at a flat rate of either 2% or 3%. There was to be some arrangement for a rebate to prevent double taxation of individual income received from corporations.[48] It was estimated that about sixteen [49] Insurgent votes

44 New York *Times*, May 18, 1909. See also issues of May 12 and 13, and Newark *Evening News*, May 13, 1909. A special correspondent of the *Evening News* who had a clear picture of the Congressional scene said that Root showed signs of becoming an insurgent and that there was talk that the President was also "beginning to be a little nervous over the Aldrich program."

45 On May 13, Aldrich replied that he was not ready to give an answer then, but he might be ready the next day. On the 14th he replied that he saw no objection to taking a vote the first of June, but secured an agreement from Bailey that the vote would be on the tariff bill and all amendments.

46 *Cong. Rec.* 44: 2454.

47 Newark *Evening News*, May 19, 1909.

48 New York *Times*, May 19, 1909; New York *World*, May 19, 1909.

49 The sixteen were: Bourne, Borah, Bristow, Brown, Burkett, Clapp, Crawford, Cummins, Carter, Dixon, Dolliver, Johnson, Jones, La Follette, Piles, Stephenson. The Progressive vote fluctuated from 12 to 21.

could be counted on, and that about six more Republicans might be won over if they were urged sufficiently.[50]

The two champions of the income tax were willing to make some concessions on the details of the measure but they were unwilling to accept a compromise on the tactics of when to push it to a vote. Bailey was convinced that immediate action must be taken while the Insurgents were enthusiastic for the measure. Cummins, on the other hand, thought they would be in a stronger position if they waited until after the tariff schedules were completed and it was known what revenues could be expected. Bailey feared that this strategy would play into the hands of Aldrich and would mean certain defeat. Nevertheless Cummins proceeded to rewrite the amendment and agreed that if Bailey's amendment came up first he would support it.

To the annoyance of the Progressives, Bailey became impetuous and on May 25 made a speech in which he threatened to prevent action on the tariff bill unless some agreement were reached as to a date for the consideration of his amendment. In the midst of the discussion of the sugar tariff schedules on May 27, he introduced his amendment. "The income tax fight came up like an unexpected summer storm," wrote a Washington correspondent.[51] With his characteristically clever parliamentary strategy Aldrich immediately rose and moved that consideration of the amendment be postponed until June 10. He wanted an opportune time to get the amendment referred to his committee, "ostensibly for consideration, but really for refrigeration." [52] Bailey warned his supporters of the "dish the Senator sets before them, postponement after postponement." The motion was carried 50 to 33.[53] Only six Republicans voted against it. Both Cummins and Bailey admitted that much strength was lost by the peculiar character of the proposition on which the vote was taken. It also afforded an opportunity for the expression of petty disagreement and a show of temper between Bailey and Cummins. The scene was thus pictured by one writer :

A snapping point to the strained situation between the Progressives and Democrats appeared at hand when Mr. Cummins requested that the agreement be made for his own amendment, and that of Mr. Bailey be left to take care of itself. . . The two income tax leaders looked across at each other with flushed faces and lowering brows.[54]

[50] Du Pont, McCumber, Guggenheim, Gamble, Nelson, and Wm. Warner.

[51] New York *World*, May 28, 1909.

[52] *La Follette's Magazine*, June 26, 1909, p. 8.

[53] *Cong. Rec.* 44: 2457. At least one correspondent did not consider this vote a test of strength of the income tax advocates. Several radical Republicans favored the tax but "were unwilling to follow Bailey's lead because he refused to abide by the agreement with Cummins that the Democrats and radical Republicans would stick together." (Herman B. Walker in the Newark *Evening News*, May 25, 1909.)

[54] New York *World*, May 28, 1909.

Nevertheless, this disagreement was not of long duration nor over fundamental matters, so the drive for an income tax was not halted.

Although the President made it his policy not to interfere unnecessarily with Congress, it became clear early in June that he was disturbed over the situation. The torrid heat of Washington's summer made dispositions more touchy than normal. The humidity made the Senate Chamber almost unbearable. There were plenty of rumors of a lack of understanding between the Senate and the White House and of conferences to iron out difficulties. It was reported that the President was worried because Aldrich did not seem to be meeting the expectations of the western Republicans nor, what was more serious, to be showing "respect for the Republican platform declaration" but, on the other hand, was making the tariff measure distrusted and feared by the whole country. "It is being made perfectly plain to all that Aldrich is trying to prevent income, inheritance, and special taxes, and in so doing is trying to keep in force or raise the present schedules."[55] Republican Senate leaders protested, however, that they knew nothing of the dissatisfaction of the President.[56]

Aldrich also was worried. Apparently afraid that Taft would support the income tax amendments, he made it his mission to convince the President that he had been wrong when he said in his acceptance speech that an income tax was constitutional and that a constitutional amendment was unnecessary.[57]

All these suspicions and anxieties were directed, however, towards a much more critical situation. What was happening to the Republican party? If the insurgent movement became more solidified it would be a real threat to the party. Any victories won by the "progressive" bloc would strengthen their ranks. Apparently it was this fear of a rupture in party harmony more than of the income tax *per se* that worried Aldrich and the President most. In fact the rift was not over the income tax issue alone, but "found expression in the West in opposition to high cost of living, trusts, high tariffs, and other economic and social welfare conditions."[58]

As the date approached for the vote on the income tax amendment, set for June 10, Aldrich became more and more apprehensive that it would pass. In fact, according to his information the vote would be too close to risk a roll call.[59] He conferred with the President who was convinced that some substitute for the income tax must

55 New York *World,* June 7, 1909.
56 Washington *Post,* June 5, 1909.
57 *La Follette's Magazine,* June 26, 1909.
58 Memorandum of Cordell Hull to the authors, Feb. 11, 1936.
59 "It is an axiom in the Senate that when Nelson W. Aldrich permits a question to come to a vote he knows before the roll is called precisely what the outcome will be." (Washington *Post,* June 18, 1909.)

be offered. He persuaded Aldrich to sound out his colleagues as to the desirability of a tax on corporation dividends such as he had proposed to the House in March.[60] Aldrich consulted the regular Republicans, while Borah saw the Insurgents on this proposition. They were met with cool receptions. Bailey was somewhat more willing to listen, but only on two conditions: (1) that the rate would be high enough to yield $80,000,000, which was the estimated yield of the proposed income tax, and (2) that it would be kept in the bill by the Conferees. No assurance could be given that either of these demands would be met.[61]

Efforts to persuade the Insurgents of the folly of pushing a measure that was certainly unconstitutional were fruitless;[62] rather they stimulated the Insurgents to action. Fearing defeat, the latter again moved to come to an agreement with the Democrats.[63]

On June 10, the Senate was so deeply engrossed in the wool schedules that Bailey waited until the next day to ask for consideration of the measure as promised. Then Aldrich again used his parliamentary device of postponing the vote. Bailey assented, knowing that some of those who were co-operating with him wanted more time. Apparently he was assured that the supporters of the measure would "stick."[64] A few moments later Cummins presented the amendment that incorporated the compromises which the two men and their followers had finally agreed upon in order to consolidate their efforts for an income tax.

The bill as amended provided for a tax of 2% on all net income of individuals and corporations in excess of $5000. In addition to reducing the rate from 3% to 2%, Cummins rewrote one section dealing with corporations so as to provide that individuals whose incomes were less than $5000 and who owned taxable stock might be reimbursed by the government for the amount of tax that had been paid on income of their stock by the company.

Bailey and Cummins asked for an agreement that the income tax "be taken up at the end of the tariff schedules and disposed of by a direct vote." Aldrich refused this but he set June 18 as the date for consideration of the measure. By the time this date had been reached the situation had so changed that the issue was completely befogged by other considerations and the vote was not on the merits of the tax.

Before proceeding with the chronological account, it may be well to summarize the main debate on the tax.

60 New York *World*, Washington *Post*, June 10, 1909.
61 Washington *Post*, June 10, 1909.
62 New York *Times*, June 15, 1909.
63 New York *Herald*, June 11, 1909.
64 There were "enough votes pledged to insure its passing the Senate by five majority." (*La Follette's Magazine*, June 26, 1909.)

SUMMARY OF MAIN ARGUMENTS PRESENTED FOR AND AGAINST THE INCOME TAX

It will be readily understood from the preceding account that the Senate had little opportunity to debate the merits of the income tax. The arguments advanced *pro* and *contra* may be briefly stated. They are not new to present-day readers; in fact, it is not easy now to appreciate that the income tax proposal was a startling or radical one then.

Bailey made much of the need for more revenue to meet the extraordinary increase in public expenditures, so great, in fact, as to "almost confuse the human mind"! Fiscal results, however, he considered of secondary importance. Primarily his sponsorship of the income tax was due to his belief in the justice of the tax, the only one ever devised that "rose or fell with a man's ability to pay it." For twelve years he had worked to make the tax a part of the federal tax system so that the burden would fall according to a more equitable measure than according to the amount of goods consumed.[65]

Cummins made a similar argument. He said that the income tax placed burdens where they belonged, because it discarded unproductive property and unproductive labor as a basis and exacted but a small percentage of gains, profits, and earnings actually received.[66]

Borah was one of the strong supporters of the amendment. He wanted it understood that in advocating an income tax he was not advocating new or radical principles. He favored an income tax, "not for the purpose of putting all the burdens of government upon property or all the burdens of government upon wealth, but that it may bear its just and fair proportion of the burdens of this government." He believed that every tax system based upon consumption should be supplemented by a system which taxed property and the wealth of the country. Furthermore, he believed that the income tax might be a teacher of economy in public expenditures.[67]

He then presented a legal brief for the tax upon which he had been working for some months. Analyzing the Pollock case he showed that the decision was based on two propositions: (1) that the economic definition of a direct tax was the proper definition, and (2) that the framers of the Constitution included in the meaning of the phrase "direct tax" all property, personal and real, and the income therefrom.

Borah took issue in no uncertain terms with the reasoning in this case. He objected to the definition of a direct tax as one that could

[65] *Cong. Rec.* 44: 1351, 1538, 2447.
[66] *Cong. Rec.* 44: 3969. The Senator's reasons for an income tax are well presented in an article in the *Independent* 67: 178 (July 1909).
[67] *Cong. Rec.* 44: 1680-1683.

not be shifted, that is, one whose economic burden was borne by the person against whom it was laid. He stated that, although it was accepted by the Court in 1895, it was not a new argument then but had been discussed and rejected for a hundred years previously; after 1895 also that interpretation was rejected. Similarly there was no precedent for the interpretation of a direct tax as one that applied to all property, personal and real, and the income therefrom. He pointed out that the transfer of rent did not transfer the real estate or any interest in the real estate, that the transfer of real estate did not transfer either the earned and uncollected or the collected rents, and that collected rent is personal property and always has been so held by the courts. He stated that in fact there had been no other case in the history of English jurisprudence in which it had been held that a tax upon collected rent was a tax upon real estate. It seemed logical to Borah, therefore, that the matter could very well be re-submitted to the Supreme Court on two propositions: (1) upon the facts of history which were not presented to the Court in 1895, and (2) in the light of decisions which had been rendered by the Court since the Pollock case was decided.

The speaker's case for the tax was well summarized in these words:

> I place my advocacy of the income-tax proposition upon a higher plane than that of raising a little revenue for the Government for the next few years. I believe it involves a great Constitutional power, one of the great powers which in many instances might be absolutely necessary for the preservation of the Government itself. I believe that the Constitution as construed is the same as granting an exemption to the vast accumulated wealth of the country and saying that it shall be relieved from the great burden of taxation. I do not believe that the great framers of the Constitution, the men who were framing a government for the people, of the people, and by the people, intended that all the taxes of this Government should be placed upon the backs of those who toil, upon consumption, while the great accumulated wealth of the Nation should stand exempt, even in an exigency which might involve the very life of the Nation itself.
>
> This cannot be true; it was never so intended; it was a republic they were building, where all men were to be equal and bear equally the burdens of government, and not an oligarchy, for that must a government be, in the end, which exempts property and wealth from all taxes.[68]

There was surprisingly little disagreement with the main proposition of the income tax advocates. True, Root offered some data to show that the owners of real estate were the chief supporters of state and local government, that property in the United States bore a burden for the support of government in the United States equal to nearly eight times the income tax that was proposed, but Bailey

[68] *Cong. Rec.* 44: 1701.

answered that property did not contribute anything to the support of the federal government.[69]

Aldrich, however, was the leading spokesman for the opponents. The record of his stand in 1894 was read by Bailey, namely, that he understood that the tax "was supported by the Socialist party, by the Populist party, and by the Democratic party with a few honorable exceptions, simply as a means of redistribution of wealth." Aldrich was not pleased by this reference.[70] In 1909, with greater caution, he put his objections on other grounds, chiefly that such a tax would tend to destroy the protective system,[71] that it would raise unnecessary revenue, and that it would harm laboring men because it would reduce "the protection which the law affords them in competition with the cheap labor of other countries, when the proposition has, in the words of the Senator from Texas, that avowed and distinct purpose." [72]

An editorial in the New York *Times* of April 20, 1909, made this comment :

> Senator Aldrich has set his face like flint against additional schemes of taxation. That means the inheritance taxes, the income tax. Politically this is wise and on grounds of economy and equity much can be said for his position. Anyone can see that if an income tax is imposed and death duties collected, the tariff would have to come down. It is not the present intention of the Republican party to lower the tariff. So the standpatters have at least this merit that they will resolutely resist any venture into new fields of taxation.

Depew (N. Y.) supported Aldrich in this argument and added that the revenue from the income tax would produce a dangerous surplus. In his opinion the time had come to draw a line between the federal and state revenues.[73] Lodge commented on the difficulty of administration of state income taxes and from this fact drew the conclusion that a great deal of income would also escape a federal income tax.[74]

On the whole there were few speeches and no orations made against the tax. The opponents were primarily interested in keeping the Democrats and the Insurgents within bounds, and in pushing the tariff schedules to completion. Therefore they considered the income tax discussions as intrusions. Furthermore, mere talk was much less effective than strategic parliamentary maneuvers to postpone the vote on the tax.[75]

[69] *Cong. Rec.* 44: 1701-1702.
[70] *Cong. Rec.* 44: 1536.
[71] *Cong. Rec.* 44: 1379.
[72] *Cong. Rec.* 44: 1539.
[73] *Cong. Rec.* 44: 2102-2104.
[74] *Cong. Rec.* 44: 1683.
[75] Other arguments for and against the tax were brought out in the debates on the Conference Report and on the 16th Amendment. See below, pp. 47, 50, 60 ff.

THE CORPORATION EXCISE TAX

While the Senate was thus engaged in debating the income tax and the tariff schedules the President was frantically hunting for some tie to bind his splitting party. It will be recalled that early in June the President asked Aldrich to sound out his colleagues on their opinions of a tax on corporate dividends as a substitute for a general income tax.[76]

The President had had such a tax in mind for some time. Before his inauguration he requested Mr. Wickersham, who was to be his Attorney General, to draw up a bill for a tax on corporation income.[77] That the President did not consider it very seriously then may be inferred from the fact that in his inaugural address he suggested an inheritance tax — not the corporation or other forms of income tax — as a means of raising additional revenue. As stated above, he presented to the Ways and Means Committee the corporation tax bill of the Attorney General, but it was not accepted as part of the tariff bill.[78] The President, however, maintained enough interest in the proposition to ask for estimates of possible yield and seemed to have been disappointed at the smallness of the amount.[79]

When the critical situation of June developed in Congress, because of the apparent success of the Insurgents with the income tax and the consequent rift in the party, the President again brought out his plan for a tax on dividends. When the proposal was first made to Aldrich that this be substituted for the general income tax he did not react favorably.

He could not see that it was much better than the income tax he wanted to kill, but apparently he "experienced a rude awakening upon his visit to the White House where the President told him a plain mistake would be made in the attempt . . . to defeat the income tax without offering something in its stead." [80] He doubtless recalled Daniel's amendment, introduced April 12, for a tax on the gross income of corporations. The conservative Republicans did not want to push the corporation tax, not only because it was an income tax in another form, but also because it might appear as a Democratic idea. The President, however, kept advancing arguments and citing the need of more revenue than the tariff would produce and at the same time protesting against the issuance of bonds.[81]

76 See above, pp. 35 and 36.

77 *Cong. Rec.* 44: 670; New York *World*, March 30, 1909; New York *Times*, April 21, 1909.

78 See above, p. 25.

79 Washington *Post*, March 23, 1909; New York *Times*, March 24, March 30, 1909.

80 New York *World*, June 11, 1909.

81 The deficit for the year was reported to be $96,000,000. Such an amount seemed larger then than it does now.

Furthermore, he insisted that there must be some alternative for the income tax amendment. Therefore he suggested to Aldrich a tax of 2% on net income of corporations where the earnings were in excess of some specific figure, such as $100,000 or $200,000.[82] Aldrich was asked to sound out the other Senators on this proposal.

Undaunted by the lack of enthusiasm for his suggestion, the President requested Root to work out the legal aspects of the proposed tax. This activity stimulated the income tax advocates of both parties to unite on a program and to make it known that a majority of votes could be counted on for the bill. This in turn seemed to convert Aldrich to the need of some constructive proposal to head them off.

It was mentioned above that Aldrich succeeded in postponing the vote on the income tax amendment on May 27 and again on June 10, even though he drove the promoters of the two somewhat divergent plans to unite. This postponement gave the chairman time to plan his next move and to counsel the members of his party that it was a bad policy "to pass an ill-digested scheme as a revenue measure when there was no necessity for adding to the revenues such an enormous amount as an income tax would raise, and especially bad policy for a few republicans to give control of the Senate to the democratic minority." [83]

The newspaper comment of those days is interesting. An anti-Aldrich paper printed the following remarks:

> Aldrich and his associates are verging on the point of being panic stricken by the consolidation of the income tax forces and the possibility that such legislation will be annexed to the pending tariff measure. Their entire campaign has degenerated into that of seeking any subterfuge to defeat the income taxers and defer that subject for decisive determination until the next regular session of Congress.
>
> But four days remain in which they must map out a final programme, and this is causing more worriment than any other feature of the troublesome bill.[84]

It was also reported that Aldrich was disturbed by the fact that several of his Republican supporters from the West notified him that their constituents were exerting such great pressure upon them that they could no longer oppose the income tax.[85]

Then followed a series of conferences as to means of achieving harmony.[86] They were chiefly between the President and Aldrich,

82 New York *World*, Washington *Post*, June 10, 1909.
83 New York *Herald*, June 12, 1909.
84 New York *World*, June 14, 1909.
85 Washington *Post*, June 10, 1909.
86 "The President is doing everything in his power to bring about harmony so that the session will end with a united Republican party. His stand has perhaps prevented a serious split in the Senate which might have been followed by a similar parting of the ways in the House." (New York *Herald*, June 16, 1909.)

but other Senators including the Insurgents and leading Democrats were also called in.[87] Probably no one will ever know the details of these meetings which have been so well described by Aldrich's biographer:

> No tariff has had a more interesting concealed history than the tariff of 1909. Far more important than anything that took place on the floor of the Senate or in the House were long rides through Rock Creek Park 'in the cool of the evening,' on which Aldrich and the House leaders discussed possibilities; other night rides, the President and Mr. Payne 'roaming all over the countryside,' in the President's automobile, anxiously casting up chances; talks in the portico of the White House late into the darkness when Aldrich and the President shut themselves from the press; dinners with political managers on the White House Terrace; games of golf when Mr. Taft's geniality drew out – or instilled – the same quality in senators and representatives.[88]

Finally this compromise was proposed, that if the President would agree to limiting the corporation tax to only a two-year period, Aldrich would agree to go half-way and support a constitutional amendment legalizing an income tax.[89] The President was not willing to accept this limitation. Soon afterwards a group of western Senators[90] "told the President that if he would send in a message favoring the corporation tax they would be enabled to drop the income tax and support the corporation tax." Cummins conferred with the President at length, but failed to convince him that it would be a wise move to enact an income tax statute despite the 1895 Supreme Court decision.[91] Crane took to the White House the word that Aldrich would acquiesce in the corporation tax without time limit.[92] So the die was cast and the Presidential message was prepared.

On June 16 the Senate heard the message of President Taft in which he made two astonishing proposals; in fact, they were revolutionary. The President first called attention to the need for funds

[87] Senator Bailey was personally attracted to President Taft, and was a frequent visitor at the White House. (Acheson, Sam, *Joe Bailey, The Last Democrat*, p. 257.)

[88] Stephenson, *Nelson W. Aldrich*, p. 351.

[89] New York *Herald*, June 2, 1909. La Follette wrote some years later: "He [Aldrich] was obliged, however, in order to secure enough votes for his corporation tax, to agree to the submission of a resolution for a constitutional amendment providing for a tax upon incomes." (*La Follette's Weekly*, September 6, 1913.)

[90] Curtis, Bourne, and Brown. (New York *Times*, July 2, 1909.)

[91] New York *World*, June 17, 1909.

[92] Once Aldrich agreed to the plan he seemed to want it known that it was his idea and that he had urged it on the President. In fact, it may have been his idea. It seems more probable, however, that it was Taft's idea because he originally proposed it early in the session. Taft's letters express his delight at winning over Aldrich, of "chloroforming" him. The press generally credited the President with the plan. On the other hand, Aldrich's biographer makes out a thesis that Aldrich originated it. It would be natural that Aldrich would want his colleagues and posterity to think he had worked out such a clever bit of strategy; the President and his friends might reason similarly. (Later.–See Pringle, H., *Life of Taft*, I: 434.)

to care for the rapidly growing deficit, but so little was made of this point that it was obviously not the main reason for the message. He recalled the suggestion he had made in his inaugural address for the inheritance tax, a measure which the House of Representatives had adopted. Then he spoke of the income tax. He had thought it was possible to make some limited use of the principle without an amendment but the Court had deprived the government of full use of the tax. Such power the government ought to have. It might be indispensable in a great crisis. He therefore recommended that Congress propose an amendment to the Constitution conferring upon the federal government "the power to levy an income tax without apportionment among the states in proportion to population." [93]

The second suggestion was for a 2% excise tax either as a substitute for, or in addition to, the inheritance tax, to be measured by net income and to be levied on all corporations except national banks, savings banks, and building and loan associations. This was of somewhat broader scope than the tax on dividends originally proposed, because it covered income put into surplus as well as that paid out to stockholders. Furthermore, the President had evolved a social justification for the tax. He said:

> If now, by a perfectly legitimate and effective system of taxation, we are incidentally able to possess the government and the stockholders and the public of the knowledge of the real business transactions and the gains and the profits of every corporation in the country, we have made a long step toward that supervisory control of corporations which may prevent a further abuse of power.[94]

The President based his opinion of the constitutionality of this tax on the ruling in the Pollock case [95] which left the government the right of levying an excise tax without apportionment, and on

[93] For a discussion of the adoption of this amendment see below, pp. 60 ff.

[94] *Cong. Rec.* 44: 3344. This part of the speech made business very uneasy. The New York *Herald* (June 18, 1909) quoted the Hartford (Conn.) *Times*: "If the federal government is to put a hook in the nose of every big corporation in the country and compel it to make a full report of its business annually to the Department of Commerce and Labor or to the Treasury Department at Washington, a law levying a tax on net profits may accomplish the same result. But it remains to be seen whether the majority in the Senate, friendly as they are to corporate interests of the country, are ready to approve so radical a step which may result in giving the Federal Government the drastic power over corporations which Mr. Roosevelt and Mr. Bryan proposed to attain through their scheme of requiring all corporations doing interstate business to take out a license in Washington."

The *Commercial and Financial Chronicle* (June 19, 1909) made this comment: "President Taft's special message . . . is a blow from an unexpected direction. Propositions of that kind were common enough with the late Administration. Then everybody looked for them and was prepared in advance to antagonize them. . . Mr. Taft's proposal is not only highly objectionable but is doubly disturbing by reason of the arguments he advances in support of the same. . . This is the Roosevelt doctrine all over again. . . The inevitable result of such a law would be that everyone engaged in business would constantly have a pack of government officials at his heels."

[95] 158 U. S. 601.

the constitutionality of the excise tax based on gross receipts of sugar refiners imposed during the Spanish-American War.[96]

When the message was completed, Heyburn (Idaho), a standpat Republican, again secured the floor after the interruption and expressed the opinion of all the members that probably the Senate had never seen an occasion when the situation had changed so radically within five short minutes — a revolution had occurred. He expressed his reaction to the proposal thus:

> We were not called together here for the purpose of getting even with somebody or punishing somebody. We were called together for the purpose of revising the revenue law that provides the money for the expenses of the Government, and in doing that the man who would allow the spirit of resentment or the spirit of opposition to enter into it — well, in my judgment, he would have forgotten the duty that rested upon him.[97]

The Senator from Idaho was only one of a group of surprised and disgusted members. The Insurgents were at first indignant and full of resentment at the President. For three months, they said, they had begged him to say one word in favor of lower tariff duties but he refused to interfere. In fact these members believed that they were carrying out the President's tariff pledge in trying to reduce rates. Then, when Aldrich was confronted with defeat, the President rushed to help him. They had not been consulted nor even warned of the President's change of mind as to the constitutionality of the tax. As a matter of fact, the President's message "took nearly all the fight out of them." Only six attended a meeting called to decide what position they would take, namely, Borah, Brown, Bristow, Clapp, Cummins, and La Follette.[98]

The Democrats also had a conference and they, too, were annoyed at the clever tactics of the Administration. It was not the first time that the Republican party had stolen their thunder. They decided to stand firm for the more general income tax, supported by the six Republicans who agreed to stay with them, yet they realized they were beaten.[99]

The message of the President was one of the shrewdest bits of strategy that could have been arranged. In the first place he secured the unity of the party. The conservative Republicans would approve

96 *Spreckels Sugar Refining Company* v. *McClain,* 192 U. S. 397.

97 *Cong. Rec.* 44: 3347.

98 New York *World,* June 16, 1909. This is one of the few instances of La Follette's active and open interest in the income tax. He was completely engrossed in the tariff fight that demanded all his energies. In his *Magazine,* however, he reported the progress of the income tax amendments and published stirring editorials favoring such a tax.

99 "The Democrats, madder than hornets, fled to the cloak room to talk it over, with Bailey in the lead." "More lemonade in the Democratic cloak room" was the chorus. (New York *Herald,* June 17, 1909; New York *World,* June 17, 18, 1909.)

the corporation tax as one of their own measures, in order to defeat the more general income tax amendment.[100] Furthermore, it put Aldrich in the position of being the President's ally. It "took off his shoulders the onus under which he has rested of opposing the President's ideas." In the second place the President secured the approval of many Democrats, also, for he had "planted himself squarely on the Democratic platform of 1908." [101]

Within ten days the corporation excise measure was in shape for presentation to the Senate. Meanwhile, on June 18, Aldrich again secured the postponement of the vote on the Cummins-Bailey amendment, not wishing to have it come up before the Administration bill was ready.

In order to have the Administration measure "impervious to attacks in the courts" and "so phrased as to meet the least resistance in Congress" it was very carefully scrutinized by the Senate Finance Committee [102] and the Cabinet after it was drafted by Root [103] and Wickersham. The President, too, kept a surprisingly close watch

100 "Senators Borah, Bristow, Cummins, La Follette, and Clapp conferred last night and issued this statement:

'The friends of the income tax feel it a duty to continue to put forth every effort to secure the adoption of the measure. They, therefore, will urge the adoption of the amendment. They also stand ready to support a resolution providing for an amendment to the Constitution of the United States.

'While they believe that the Supreme Court will sustain the law, yet, to provide against any possible contingency that might result from an adverse decision, they gladly favor the proposition to amend the Constitution. They do not feel satisfied with simply a corporation tax.

'A tax upon the net income of corporations alone will very imperfectly reach the desired result. It will tax tens of thousands of stockholders whose total incomes are very small, and will exempt in large measure the immense personal incomes of the country.' " (Washington *Post*, June 17, 1909.)

The New York *World*, June 18, 1909 said: "The Progressive Republicans have cooled down materially. They were angry last night, but are now more reconciled to the situation and will all vote to amend the Constitution if it is found impossible to pass their own measure."

101 New York *World*, Washington *Post*, June 17, 1909; New York *World*, June 26, 1909. The President's change of position is recorded in a letter of Archie Butt describing a conversation between the President and his brothers: "I prefer an income tax, but the truth is I am afraid of the discussion which will follow and the criticism which will ensue if there is another serious division in the Supreme Court on the subject of the income tax. Nothing has ever injured the prestige of the Supreme Court more than that last decision, and I think that many of the most violent advocates of the income tax will be glad of the substitution in their hearts for the same reason. I am going to push the Constitutional Amendment, which will admit an income tax without question, but I am afraid of it without such an amendment." (*Taft and Roosevelt* I: 134.)

102 New York *World*, June 26, 1909.

103 The President's military aide wrote this interesting comment on Root: "Speaking of the astonishment that some of the papers seem to express that Senator Root was in favor of this tax, the President said yesterday: 'The fact is that while neither Root nor I even got the credit for being the progressive members of the last Cabinet, we were the most progressive and the two who usually aided and abetted President Roosevelt in what were called his radical policies. I don't know if that would be a popular thing to admit just at this juncture, but it is true and I felt that when the time came to push this program that I could rely on Root to stand by me.' " (Butt, *Taft and Roosevelt*, I: 128.)

on every detail. In order to win as much good will as possible from the Finance Committee members who were somewhat in the position of being forced by the executive, he gave several dinners preceding the conferences and used his sociable geniality for good political ends.[104]

As originally written, the measure was intended to fulfill the expectations of the President in: (1) raising revenue of approximately $50,000,000 a year, (2) imposing government supervision of corporations, and (3) discouraging the excessive borrowing of corporations.[105] By the time the Finance Committee had amended it, some of these hoped-for results appeared rather dim if not forgotten. First of all they were afraid the measure would raise too much revenue for the good of their tariff policy. Next they were fearful that the publicity and supervisory features were too drastic.[106] They insisted on some exemptions for small corporations,[107] savings banks, and, under certain limitations, holding companies that controlled the stock of subsidiary corporations.[108]

The Committee and Root were puzzled over the difficult question as to whether or not corporations should be permitted to deduct from net earnings interest paid on bonds. Most of the members were at first opposed to such deduction because they thought it would encourage the substitution of bonds for stocks so as to avoid the tax.

104 The President's satisfaction at the outcome may be judged by this description of a conversation with the Attorney General during a drive on June 25, the day the amendment was offered in the Senate:

" 'Well, George, for a man who has always eschewed politics of all kinds, you certainly have got knee deep in it. It remained for my non-political attorney general to draft a law for Congress. The strangest part is that the Congress was willing to have a member of the Cabinet draw up such an important amendment, for as a rule the Senate Committee on Finance is rather jealous of its prerogatives.'

"The Attorney General said that he was merely the instrument of the President himself, for while he had largely put the amendment into shape he only embodied the suggestions of the President.

" 'It has been a long time since Congress has come to the White House for its advice,' said the Attorney General, 'and I do not know any incident such as the framing of this amendment ever happening there before.'

" 'However,' said the President, 'I think that both Hale and Aldrich felt that unless they acceded to some of my views there would be no tariff bill. In fact, I said to them, when they first met with me on the subject, that it was either the corporation tax or the income tax or no bill at all, and Aldrich answered frankly, 'That is why we came to you.' Aldrich is frank if anything." (Butt, *Taft and Roosevelt,* I: 130-131.)

105 New York *World,* June 19, 1909.

106 New York *Herald,* June 25, 1909; June 26, 1909; New York *World,* June 23, 1909, June 24, 1909.

107 New York *Herald,* June 22, 1909. The Washington *Post* of June 22, 1909 reported Hale as saying that if amendments did not provide for exemption, representatives of hundreds of small corporations would swoop down on Washington and not only make things miserable for senators and representatives but get up such an agitation against the corporation tax that general tariff legislation itself would stand in danger of defeat.

108 New York *World,* June 24, 1909; Washington *Post,* June 28, 1909. There was some talk that the tax was only a blind and that an inheritance tax would be substituted by the Conferees. (Newark *Evening News,* June 30, 1909.)

Some questioned the legality of taxing earnings set aside for interest payment; others argued that a tax upon such funds was really a tax upon stockholders, inasmuch as their dividends would be reduced by the amount deducted from earnings for this purpose. Root insisted that at least part of the interest should be taxed. One member cited a Supreme Court decision in which it was held that net earnings included interest upon bonded indebtedness.[109] The final decision, a victory for Root, was to permit corporations to deduct interest on an amount of bonds not in excess of paid-up capital stock.

SENATE DEBATE ON THE CORPORATION EXCISE BILL

On June 29 the tariff schedules were completed so Aldrich was ready with a neat plan for introducing the corporation tax and pushing it through as drafted. Adroitly he called up the Bailey amendment, taking advantage of the fact that Bailey was absent.[110] Immediately Lodge moved that the inheritance tax amendment be substituted for Bailey's income tax amendment. Then Aldrich moved to amend Lodge's substitute by the substitution of the corporation excise tax as drawn up by the Committee.[111] Thus Bailey's income tax was quickly and "painlessly" shelved and amendment of Aldrich's measure was practically banned.[112]

Flint (Cal.) the newest member of the Finance Committee, explained that the measure was drafted in accordance with the recommendation of the President. Various excuses were offered for the decision not to accept the more general income tax as proposed in the Senate, and the inheritance tax as passed by the House, but the real reason for proposing the tax had been admitted by Aldrich earlier in the day when he said, "I shall vote for a corporation tax as a means to defeat the income tax." [113]

109 New York *Herald,* June 22, 1909. In 1916 Hull gave this explanation of the limitation on deduction of interest in the excise tax: "I think the original theory . . . was that corporations could issue quite a lot of watered stock, transfer that into bonds, mortgage their property and incur interest and make a great many shifts in many ways that would result in avoiding the real purpose of the law." (*Cong. Rec.* 53: 10656.)

110 New York *World,* June 30, 1909.

111 *Cong. Rec.* 44: 3935.

112 It was an amendment of the third degree, in parliamentary parlance. That he had so planned is shown in the following characteristic conversation:

The President told of Representative Payne's objection to the proposition to frame any corporation tax, when he said, "There will be lots of amendments offered in the Senate so why agree on anything now?"

"There will not be any amendments," answered Aldrich with a jerk of his head. (Butt, *Taft and Roosevelt,* I: 131.)

113 *Cong. Rec.* 44: 3929. Root said: "Gentlemen may assume I am for the corporation tax to beat the income tax. I care not. I am for the corporation tax because I think it is better policy, better patriotism, and higher wisdom than the general income tax, at this time, and under the circumstances."

Cummins spoke for almost five hours on the issue of a corporation tax versus a general income tax. He called attention to the fact that until a few days before the question had been, "Shall an income tax be added to the revenue bill under consideration?" In the twinkling of an eye the issue became, "What kind of income tax law shall be added to the bill?"

Cummins based his case for the more general income tax on its greater equity. The corporation tax in his estimation was unfair; it did not distribute the burdens of government as they ought to be distributed but concentrated them on those who had invested their capital in stock of corporations. He put a great deal of emphasis on the need for more revenue and linked that argument to the one used by his opponents who feared that the income tax would kill the protective tariff system. He pointed out that, contrary to the argument of the high protectionists, the tariff did not raise enough revenue and, indeed, if it served its purpose of preventing importation of goods it would yield very little revenue and would of necessity have to be supplemented.

He replied at great length to the charge that a general income tax was unconstitutional, pointing out that the Court had never before nor after the Pollock case called a tax on income a direct tax within the meaning of the Constitution. If the Court had made a great error in the Pollock case he considered it not only proper but the duty of Congress to ask for a new interpretation of that part of the Constitution. On the other hand, if the income tax was unconstitutional then he considered the excise tax equally unconstitutional, whether it was an income tax or a tax on the right to do business as a corporation.[114]

Borah opened his speech by saying that it was not his purpose to compare the income tax and the corporation tax. He realized that the chances for enactment of the former were gone so far as that session was concerned but he had faith to believe that they were only postponed. He spoke particularly of the incidence of the corporation tax. The burden, he was sure, would be shifted upon those who already "bore an unjust and undue proportion of the burdens of the government." Rather than vote for such a tax he preferred to accept the policy of Aldrich as expressed at the opening of the debate, that is, to reduce expenditures as much as possible if the tariff did not supply sufficient revenue.[115]

Root made the chief defense of the corporation excise measure. He argued that it was preferable to the more general income tax

[114] *Cong. Rec.* 44: 3975-3979. Cummins' position was also stated in an article in the *Independent*, 67: 178-182 (July 22, 1909.)

[115] *Cong. Rec.* 44: 3985.

measure for several reasons: (1) the income tax was unconstitutional, (2) the bills introduced by both Bailey and Cummins were defective in that they failed to distinguish between earned and unearned incomes and permitted very high personal exemptions. Root pointed out that one constructive feature of the corporation excise tax was that it would furnish Congress information on the profits of corporations for use when the time came to revise the tariff bill.[116]

The time for debate on the corporation excise tax was short and Aldrich's strategy in introducing his measure practically precluded any amendments. Because of the general objection to including such non-profit-making corporations as fraternal societies, building and loan associations, labor organizations, and educational institutions, the Committee drew up an amendment to exempt them.[117] Clapp (Minn.) succeeded in getting a favorable vote to eliminate the exemption of dividends allowed to holding companies.[118] Aldrich objected to this motion but let it go through without a vote in order to prevent a fight for it by Insurgents and Democrats.[119] He saw to it, however, that it was deleted in conference. Aldrich also accepted La Follette's amendment to exempt agricultural and horticultural societies and Bulkeley's addition of municipal taxes to the allowable deductions.[120]

The corporation tax amendment to the tariff bill was substituted for the income tax in Committee of the Whole, July 2, by a vote of 59 to 11.[121] Bailey's final effort to substitute the general income tax for the corporation tax amendment met with defeat in the Senate, July 7.[122] On the following day the tariff bill including the excise tax measure was passed by a vote of 45 to 34.[123]

A year later Borah wrote:

> This amendment and the corporation tax were the twin children of legislative necessity. Those of us who favored the amendment to the tariff bill providing for an income tax, believing the court would reverse

[116] *Cong. Rec.* 44: 4003.

[117] *Cong. Rec.* 44: 4148-4156.

[118] *Cong. Rec.* 44: 4228-4229.

[119] New York *World*, July 8, 1909.

[120] *Cong. Rec.* 44: 4236. The allowance of municipal taxes was deleted in conference.

[121] *Cong. Rec.* 44: 4066.

[122] *Cong. Rec.* 44: 4228. The vote was 28 yeas, 47 nays, 17 not voting. Those not voting were: Bourne, Clark (Ark.), Clay, Cullom, Curtis, Davis, Dillingham, Guggenheim, Lodge, McEnery, Owen, Paynter, Rayner, Richardson, Root, Smith (Md.), Tillman.

[123] Ten Republicans voted against it, namely, Borah, Beveridge, Brown, Burkett, Clapp, Crawford, Cummins, Dolliver, La Follette, and Nelson. "The Progressive Republicans realize that: They have nothing to expect hereafter from Mr. Aldrich and the Republican leaders. They must make their own fight. . . They cannot rely on the President for comfort and consolation, as he gave them never a whisper during their long struggle to secure a genuine downward revision." (New York *World*, July 10, 1909.)

the Pollock case if the question were resubmitted, had secured enough votes to pass the amendment. Something had to be done. So this amendment and the corporation tax were brought in as a substitute, with the understanding and notice served that both had been formulated in the region of the immaculate and both were clothed and accompanied by the sustaining benediction of those who could not err and that no changes in the amendments were to be contemplated for a moment. And thus with that solemn and serious but complacent consideration which always obtains when divine things are passing by they went through the senate.[124]

THE CONFERENCE REPORT

The Senate immediately sent the bill to the House with notice of the appointment of conferees to consider the 847 amendments that had been made. It was no secret that the House managers did not want the corporation excise tax and that they were determined to have the inheritance tax. They resented the many amendments in the tariff schedules made by the Senate as well as the infringement upon their prerogatives, so they said, when the Senate added the corporation tax. The President lost no time in trying to harmonize their differences. He let it be known that it was his personal desire to have the corporation tax written into the bill, but in doing so he used his usual indirect, diplomatic methods of conferences and dinner parties.[125] Though the Senate managers were personally very lukewarm about the tax, they were pledged to it and knew that if they dropped it they could not "avoid the inevitable rupture that would follow in the Senate."

The discussions between the various factions involved much bargaining as to the rates of tariff duties, most of which is not very germane to this study. Suffice it to say that the President won the immediate victory in keeping the corporation excise tax, but this only prolonged the war between the two branches of the party because of the Insurgents' objection to the tariff rates.

The corporation excise tax was one of the first parts of the revised bill to be discussed by the House. In fact it was the most talked of amendment when the House voted to agree to a conference on the divergent measures. A typical speech of the opposing Democrats was that of Townsend (Mich.):

I am not enamored of any of these new forms of taxation, but if we are to have an income tax, I would have it general. . . It is possible that a tax on net earnings of corporations is desirable, but the matter is too big to be settled on the last day of a special session called to deal with another question. To me it seems like Federal regulation and control

[124] Borah, William E., "The Income-Tax Amendment," *North American Review,* 191: 760. (June 1910.)

[125] Washington *Post,* July 15, 16, 20, and 21, 1909; New York *World,* July 20, 1909.

of all corporations. Are we prepared to enter upon this gigantic undertaking? [126]

Champ Clark came out flatly for a general income tax:

> You brought in a corporation tax over in the Senate. I say that you had no right to add to the bill a proposition that was never broached in the House. The House passed an inheritance tax. I would like to dump into this conference the proposition for an income tax.
>
> The people of the United States by an overwhelming majority are in favor of a graduated income tax – a large majority of the membership of the House favors it – and in my humble judgment this corporation tax was cooked up for the purpose of defeating the proposition for an income tax.[127]

The report of the Conference Committee was made July 30. It recommended few changes in the corporation excise bill. As a concession to the House the rate was reduced from 2% to 1%. The amendment to make the law apply to holding companies was struck out. The section applying to insurance companies was rewritten by the Attorney General so that it was acceptable to them.

Chairman Payne, who presented the report, said frankly that he had no use for an income tax and that what use he had for a corporation tax was due to the fact that by it one could get "rid of an unconstitutional income tax appended to a bill." [128] Longworth defended the Administration with the following remarkable bit of rationalization:

> It was apparent from the outset that whatever the final action of this Congress upon the tariff question might be . . . there would be, in one respect at least, a marked departure from the mode of raising revenue which has prevailed during the past twelve years . . .
>
> . . . I believe that it will be the settled policy of this Government hereafter to tax certain forms of wealth which today pay no tax to the Government.
>
> Far from being a legislative trick, designed to meet a particular condition in the Senate, or designed to beat any particular measure, this corporation tax is a well-considered plan, designed to go upon the statute books on account of the merit it has in it.[129]

When questioned on the inquisitorial nature of the corporation tax, the speaker drew a distinction between "inquisition into the affairs of an individual and inquisition into the affairs of a corporation.[130] He upheld the publicity sections because he thought that not only the public at large but the stockholders would benefit from

[126] *Cong. Rec.* 44: 4365.
[127] *Cong. Rec.* 44: 4383.
[128] *Cong. Rec.* 44: 4696.
[129] *Cong. Rec.* 44: 4717.
[130] *Cong. Rec.* 44: 4719.

knowing how corporation funds were spent, what amount went for salaries or was "diverted from its proper channels."

Underwood played up the Republican argument that the ultimate object of the excise tax was control of corporations. If such control was to be undertaken, he asked whether it should be exercised by the states or by the federal government. He objected to the theory of the excise tax because of its injustice; for example, merely because a merchant or small business man had incorporated he would be subject to the tax, but a millionaire could escape the tax if he had his funds invested in bonds or in real estate.[131]

The House accepted the report of the Conference Committee July 31, by a vote of 195 to 183; [132] the Senate, August 5, by a vote of 47 to 31.[133]

The passage of the corporation excise tax section of the Tariff Act of 1909 was unusual for several reasons. In the first place the measure did not originate in the House of Representatives but in the Senate, and was so extraneous to the tariff bill that House members charged that it was contrary to the spirit of Article I, Section 7, of the Constitution.[134] Furthermore, it was not presented to the House officially until it was reported by the Conferees and until then was discussed for only a short time and very informally. It was not even voted upon in the House as a separate measure but only as a part of the tariff bill. In the third place, there were no public hearings on it. In the fourth place, neither house had much to say about its contents. It was drawn up at the behest of the President by Senator Root and Attorney General Wickersham, and passed almost as introduced. Lastly, the leaders in both House and Senate disliked the measure and accepted it only because it was pushed by the President and because it was hoped that it would save the party organization.[135]

SUMMARY OF MAIN FEATURES OF THE CORPORATION EXCISE LAW

Although the tax was to be measured by corporate net income, it was called "a special excise tax with respect to the carrying on or doing business by such corporation, joint stock company, or associa-

[131] *Cong. Rec.* 44: 4725.
[132] *Cong. Rec.* 44: 4755.
[133] *Cong. Rec.* 44: 4949.
[134] *Cong. Rec.* 44: 4365. See also preceding discussion in this chapter.
[135] "Its coming into being is one of the most remarkable of recent legislative events. It was not discussed during the campaign; it was not mentioned in President Taft's inaugural; it was not proposed in the compact and deliberate program laid down by the President in his message at the opening of the special session, nor was it brought forward as any part of the pending revenue measure by any Member of Congress." (*Review of Reviews*, 40: 136, August 1, 1910, quoted in the *Cong. Rec.* 48:3510.)

tion,"[136] in order to avoid the constitutional pitfalls which might have endangered a direct tax.

The law provided that every corporation engaged in business in the United States should be subject to an excise tax of 1% of the entire net income in excess of $5000 received from all sources, exclusive of amounts received as dividends from corporations subject to tax.

Certain non-profit organizations were exempt from the Act; for example, agricultural societies, certain fraternal beneficiary orders, building and loan associations organized exclusively for the mutual benefit of their members, and labor, religious, charitable, or educational organizations "no part of the net income of which inures to the benefit of any private stockholder or individual."

Net income was to be ascertained by deducting from gross income: the amounts spent for all ordinary and necessary operating expenses; losses actually sustained within the year and not compensated by insurance or otherwise; interest paid on bonded or other indebtedness to an amount "not exceeding the paid-up capital stock . . . outstanding at the close of the year . . ."; taxes of the United States or any state or any foreign country; and dividends from stock of taxable corporations.

In the case of foreign corporations doing business in the United States, net income was to be ascertained by deducting from gross income received in the United States the same expenses incurred in the United States as were deductible for domestic corporations.

The law required each taxable company to file a return by the first of March of each year, giving the following information as of the preceding December 31: (1) the total amount of paid-up capital stock outstanding; (2) the amount of bonded debt; (3) the gross income; (4) the total amount of all ordinary and necessary expenses; (5) the total amount of all losses, the amount allowed for depreciation and, in the case of insurance companies, the sums other than dividends paid within the year on policy and annuity contracts; (6) interest paid on debt and, in the case of banks, interest paid on deposits; (7) taxes, showing separately the amounts paid to foreign governments; and (8) the net income, after making the deductions authorized. On or before the first of June corporations were to be notified of the amount of tax due.

The administrative provisions gave the Commissioner of Internal Revenue power to require a corporation to file a return if it had failed to do so and to examine any books and papers of a corporation "for the purpose of ascertaining the correctness of" the return or

[136] 36 *Statutes at Large* 112. For text of the measure as introduced into the Senate see *Cong. Rec.* 44: 3836.

"for the purpose of making a return where none has been made," to require the attendance of any officer or employee, and to invoke the aid of any court. "All proceedings taken by the Commissioner of Internal Revenue under the provisions of this section shall be subject to the approval of the Secretary of the Treasury."

The penalty for making a false return with fraudulent intent was put at 100% of the tax; for refusal or neglect to make a return, at 50% of the tax due; for failure to pay tax on time, at 5% of the amount of tax unpaid and interest at the rate of 1% a month from the time the tax was due. Furthermore, if a company refused or neglected to make a return or made a false return it was liable to a penalty of not less than $1000 and not more than $10,000.

When the assessments were made, the returns were to be filed in the office of the Commissioner of Internal Revenue and were to "constitute public records and be open to inspection as such." In 1910 this section was amended by the addition of the following words:

> That any and all such returns shall be open to inspection only upon the order of the President under rules and regulations to be prescribed by the Secretary of the Treasury and approved by the President.

Anyone who divulged any information obtained from corporation books or from their returns, "except upon the special direction of the President," was liable to a fine not exceeding $1000 or to imprisonment not exceeding one year, or both, at the discretion of the court.

THE CONSTITUTIONALITY OF THE CORPORATION EXCISE TAX

The Supreme Court heard the case of *Flint* v. *Stone Tracy Company* in March 1910, and again in January 1911.[137] It gave its decision upholding the law in March 1911. The main points brought out were that the tax was not a direct tax but an excise tax on the privilege of doing business in a corporate capacity. As an excise, the tax was properly measured by the entire income of the parties subject to it, notwithstanding the fact that a part of the income may have been derived from non-taxable property.

The Court held that the Act was part of the tariff bill, hence the fact that the corporation tax provision originated in the Senate instead of the House of Representatives did not make it unconstitutional. "The amendment was germane to the subject matter of the bill and not beyond the power of the Senate to propose."

[137] 220 U. S. 107. There were 15 similar cases decided at the same time, among them: *Van Derhoeff* v. *Coney Island and Brooklyn R. R. Co.*; *Hine* v. *Home Life Insurance Co.*; *Smith* v. *Northern Trust Co.*; *Miner* v. *Corn Exchange National Bank*; *Cedar Street Co.* v. *Park Realty Co.*; *Jared* v. *American Multigraph Co.*; *Gay* v. *Baltic Mining Co.*

In answer to the contention that "the measurement of the tax by the net income . . . is not only unequal but so arbitrary and baseless as to fall outside of the taxing power," the Court held that, "conceding the power of Congress to tax the business activities of private corporations . . . the tax must be measured by some standard, and none can be chosen which will operate with absolute justice and equality upon all corporations."

It was also objected that the exemption of certain non-profit organizations invalidated the tax, but the Court did not sustain this contention.

One of the arguments for the unconstitutionality of the Act was that the clause permitting returns to be open to the public was a violation of the Fourth Amendment to the Constitution. It was contended that the section, even after the amendment which modified its severity, "could have no legitimate connection with the collection of the tax, and in substance amounts to no more than an unlawful attempt to exhibit the private affairs of corporations to public or private inspection without any substantial connection with, or legitimate purpose to be served, in the collection of the tax now under consideration." In reply the Court held that "Congress may have deemed the public inspection of such returns a means of more properly securing the fullness and accuracy thereof." Therefore it concluded that this feature of the law did not "do violence to the constitutional protection of the Fourth Amendment, and this is equally true of the Fifth Amendment. . ."

At least two sections of the law were not interpreted by the Court as they were by the Treasury. One was the clause imposing the tax on "every corporation . . . organized for profit and having a capital stock represented by shares . . . and engaged in business." The other was that relating to the deduction by insurance companies of "sums other than dividends paid within the year on policy and annuity contracts."

The first clause was considered in connection with suits brought against the government by inactive corporations and holding companies. In the case of *McCoach, Collector* v. *Minehill and Schuylkill Haven Railroad Company*, the Supreme Court ruled that a company holding leases was not engaged in business as defined by the excise tax law. Part of the decision read:

A railroad corporation, which has leased its property for a term of years and parted with its control and management, but which maintains its corporate organization and collects rentals from the lessee company and distributes the same among its stockholders, is not "engaged in business" within the meaning of the corporation tax act of 1909, and is not liable for taxes thereunder, notwithstanding the lease provides for recovery of the property in case of default.[138]

This decision was a shock to the office of the Commissioner of Internal Revenue. It meant that a company could escape the excise tax by leasing its plant to an operating company. Attorney General McReynolds asked for a rehearing but it was not granted. Many questions were left undecided. Some of the cases resulting from this decision were settled by the courts in a way that was favorable to the government and some were unfavorable.[139]

"The true test of distinction," the Court held in one case, "must be, as applied to corporations of the class, whether they are continuing the body and substance of the business for which they were organized and in which they set out, or whether they have substantially retired from it and turned it over to another." [140] Again the Court held that "The question is rather what the corporation is doing than what it could do." [141] More favorable to the government was the ruling that:

> A lessor corporation which exercises its corporate powers and functions by adding to its properties, disposing of its investments, making others in co-operation with or at request of lessee with a view of enhancing the value of the leased estate, is outside of the rule in *McCoach* v. *Minehill Railway Company* (228 U. S. 295), and is doing business.[142]

The second clause which has been referred to as receiving an unexpected interpretation from the courts was that allowing insurance companies to deduct from income "sums other than dividends paid within the year on policy and annuity contracts." The question at issue was the interpretation of the word "dividend." Insurance companies used the term to apply to the portion of the premium charged in excess of insurance cost and returned annually to policy holders. Hearings were held for six months during which time the insurance companies sent representatives and filed briefs. The Treasury then announced that so-called dividends were not deductible from the gross income of such companies, that when such dividends were applied to payment of renewal premiums, to shorten

138 228 U. S. 295, quoted in *Report of the Secretary of the Treasury* 1913, p. 511.

139 In the case of *Zonne* v. *Minneapolis Syndicate,* 220 U. S. 187, the Court held that a corporation organized for the purpose of owning and renting an office building but which had wholly parted with the management and control of the property . . . its sole authority being to hold the title subject to lease for 130 years, and to receive and distribute the rentals . . . or the proceeds of any sale of the land, if it should be sold, was not subject to tax.

140 *Traction Companies* v. *Collectors,* 223 Fed. 984, quoted in *Report of the Commissioner of Internal Revenue* 1915, pp. 34, 35.

141 *U. S.* v. *Emery, Bird, Thayer Realty Company,* 237 U. S. 38.

142 *Public Service Ry. Co.* v. *Moffett.* Quoted in *Report of the Commissioner of Internal Revenue* 1915, pp. 34, 35.

endowment or premium-paying period, to purchase paid-up additions and annuities, they were sums retransferred to the company. They constituted income "in every sense identically as though the actual cash was paid therefor," hence must be included in and accounted for as income.[143]

As the companies were not satisfied with this ruling, several cases were taken to court. The decisions were in favor of the insurance companies, namely that:

> The excess loading of premiums collected by a mutual life insurance company on the level premium plan, applied at the end of the year in reduction of future premiums of the policy holders, etc., held not "dividends."[144]

ADMINISTRATION OF THE LAW

That the administration of the law was difficult at first is evidenced by a report from the Treasury in 1911. The Secretary of the Treasury was not wholly in sympathy with some of the provisions. Major Butt described a conversation between President Taft and Secretary of the Treasury MacVeagh in 1910 wherein the Secretary told the President that he was opposed to the publicity features, as far as small corporations were concerned. The President rather discouraged him by saying that it was the publicity feature which appealed to him more than any other part of the law. The Secretary replied that it was meeting with the greatest objection everywhere. He thought the collection of the tax would result in good, whereas the publication of the facts regarding the small corporations would only bring about great discontent and no special good. The President thought many small corporations had a good deal that should be made known and that the publicity could have only healthy results. "Even you," said the Secretary, "would not like all your business affairs to become public property; what income you had and from what sources it was derived." "I would not mind in the least," said the President, "would you?" "I certainly would," said the Secretary, "and I would do all I could to evade the law. . ." To this the President answered: "Mr. MacVeagh, I am in favor of letting the law work out as it was framed to do. To me the publicity feature of the law is the only thing which makes the law of any special value for it is not going to be a great revenue producer." [145]

The Commissioner of Internal Revenue made the following comment:

143 T. D., 1743, Dec. 16, 1911, quoted in *Cong. Rec.* 50: 515.

144 *Connecticut General Life Insurance Company* v. *Eaton,* 218 Fed. 188, affirmed in C. C. A.; quoted in *Report of the Commissioner of Internal Revenue* 1915, p. 33.

145 Butt, *Taft and Roosevelt,* I: 262-263.

> The amount of detail work involved in the preparation of the first year's collection was very great, and employees of this bureau and collectors and their forces throughout the country worked in a most cheerful and enthusiastic manner day and night, Sundays and holidays included, in order to complete the work within the limits prescribed by the statute. . . [146]

When it is remembered that no special appropriation was made to enforce this law the achievement of the Bureau appears remarkable. There were only fifteen field agents. In the following year a request was made to Congress for funds to double that number.[147] It must also be borne in mind that collecting this excise tax was work of an entirely different character from that previously carried on by the Bureau, hence involved a new technique as well as an expansion of activity.[148]

FISCAL RESULTS

The law went into effect August 5, 1909 and the first returns were due for the calendar year 1909. Inasmuch as the reports of the government are issued for fiscal years ending on June 30, the collection figures are not always clear. They are further confused by the fact that refunds and penalties were not allocated to the years for which the taxes were due originally.

The total amounts collected under the corporation excise law are shown in Table 5. In the first fiscal year that the law was in effect the Bureau collected almost $21,000,000. In the second year collections were over $33,500,000, of which approximately $6,400,000 was on assessments for the calendar year 1909. In the fiscal year 1911, assessments of the 50-per-cent additional taxes for failure to file in 1910 amounted to $159,862 and, for 1911, to $323,221. In spite of the inadequate staff, the Bureau reported that the examinations made by the field force in 1911 resulted in "increasing the tax collections reported by the companies themselves by approximately $550,000." [149] In 1912 the collections were about $5,000,000 less than in the preceding year. The Commissioner explained:

> This apparent decrease is accounted for by the fact that penalties, interest, and amounts paid in compromise of violations of the law are this year reported separately, while they were included in the amount reported for the fiscal year 1911. An actual decrease, however, did occur during the past fiscal year with respect to the 50 per cent additional

[146] *Report of the Secretary of the Treasury* 1910, p. 462.

[147] *Report of the Secretary of the Treasury* 1911, p. 451. The grant made was $150,000 for the collection of the tax and $30,000 for classifying and otherwise caring for the returns.

[148] For a more complete account of the income tax administration see below, Chap. XXIII.

[149] *Report of the Commissioner of Internal Revenue* 1911, p. 15.

tax – the amounts being $90,518.88 for 1912 as compared with $323,221.20 assessed in 1911, showing a decrease of $232,702.32 in the penalties assessed during the year.[150]

TABLE 5

NUMBER OF RETURNS AND AMOUNT OF REVENUE FROM THE CORPORATION EXCISE TAX [a]

Tax Year [b]	*Total number of returns*	*Returns showing taxable income* [c]	*Returns showing no taxable income*	*Net income*	*Revenue*
1909	262,490	52,498	209,992	$3,590,000,000	$20,959,783.74
1910	279,202	54,040	216,162	3,761,000,000	33,511,525.00
1911	288,352	55,129	233,223	3,503,000,000	28,583,259.81
1912	305,336	61,116	244,220	4,151,000,000	35,006,299.84
Total					$118,060,868.39
Additional assessments, fines, penalties, etc.[d]					10,671,077.22
Total					$128,731,945.61

[a] U. S. Treasury, *Statistics of Income* 1920, p. 29; *Report of the Commissioner of Internal Revenue* 1914, p. 19.

[b] Year income received by taxpayer. Most of the revenue based on income of year indicated was received in the fiscal year ending June 30 following.

[c] Net income in excess of $5000 exemption allowed each corporation.

[d] Including receipts for Jan. and Feb. 1913, before the federal income tax of 1913 applied.

The collections for the fiscal year 1913, over $35,000,000, were the highest of any of the four years in which the 1909 law was in effect. In 1914 there was collected as special excise tax, $10,671,077.22, of which $3,000,000 was from assessments made for 1912 and $7,000,000 for previous years and for the two months of January and February 1913, under the law of October 3, 1913. These amounts indicate very tangible results from the enlarged field staff and from additional experience. The Commissioner stated in his Annual Report that not all of the benefits could be so measured:

> These examinations are educational in character, in that the corporations gain from intelligent and competent examiners a clearer conception and understanding of the law and regulations, and are induced to install, if they have not already done so, a system of bookkeeping and accounting that will enable them to make their returns in conformity with the requirements of this office.[151]

150 *Report of the Commissioner of Internal Revenue* 1912, p. 15; *Report of the Secretary of the Treasury* 1912, p. 463.

151 *Report of the Commissioner of Internal Revenue* 1914, p. 19.

THE SIXTEENTH AMENDMENT TO THE CONSTITUTION

The message sent by President Taft to Congress June 16, 1909 requested, in addition to the corporation excise tax just discussed, a joint resolution for an amendment to the Constitution to be ratified by the states so that the federal government might levy an income tax without regard to apportionment among the states.

This action was a deliberate right-about-face from the position taken by the President before his inauguration,[152] in fact, it was an acceptance of one plank of the 1908 platform of the Democratic party. There is no doubt that the President had carefully reviewed the income tax decisions of the Supreme Court and had also asked his Attorney General for advice. "A mature consideration has satisfied me that an amendment is the only proper course," he said in his June message. Enough has been said in earlier sections of this chapter to show that the President's hand was forced by the political situation in Congress and in the country. Outside of Congress, the income tax was receiving much favorable comment.

The President's move was a strategically clever one. By it he won the approval of all groups. The conservative Republicans accepted the plan partly because they considered it a harmless gesture. What assurance did they have that enough states would ratify it? Even such liberals as Cummins thought it would not be ratified.[153] La Follette believed that it would be more probable to expect the Supreme Court to reverse itself. He wrote:

> The first twelve amendments were adopted by common consent as things which ought not to have been omitted in the first place. But since that time it has been found quite impossible to amend the Constitution by constitutional means. The Civil War amendments were put in the Constitution by guns. Whether amendments which are really proposed can be won in any other way remains to be seen. This is certainly true, that the success of any given amendment is very improbable.[154]

The Progressives accepted it as the best substitute for the general income tax that they were likely to get, realizing full well that the President had cut the ground from under their measure. The Democrats considered it as their own plan originally, filched for political purposes by the party in power. They, too, were not very sanguine of success in getting the amendment ratified.

152 See above, p. 23.
153 *Cong. Rec.* 44: 3974.
154 *La Follette's Magazine,* July 3, 1909, p. 12. When the amendment was discussed in the Senate, Money (Miss.) said he believed there would never be another amendment to the Constitution. (*Cong. Rec.* 44: 4115.)

DISCUSSION IN THE SENATE

Brown (Rep., Neb.), one of the Insurgents, had introduced a resolution for a constitutional amendment in April, and again on June 11. It was rather vague and as soon as he could get recognition on June 18, he offered another in better phrasing that read:

> The Congress shall have power to lay and collect direct taxes on incomes without apportionment among the several States according to population.

This resolution was referred to the Senate Finance Committee which was at work on the Administration resolution.[155] According to a letter published in 1920, it was there amended at the insistence of Nelson (Rep., Minn.) of the Judiciary Committee to include the phrase "from whatever source derived" and omit the word "direct" so that it read:

> The Congress shall have power to lay and collect taxes on incomes, from whatever source derived, without apportionment among the several States, and without regard to any census or enumeration.[156]

So zealous was Brown for connection with the amendment that he rose on Saturday, July 3, to ask for consideration of the Administration resolution which had been presented on June 28.[157] Chairman Aldrich was not through with the tariff bill and resented this interruption, but he could not ignore it entirely. He agreed that it be considered on condition that a vote be taken by one o'clock that same day, thereby eliminating all debate. When Senators objected to being so hurried he agreed to postpone the vote until the following Monday.

Senatorial debate on the Administration resolution was, therefore, limited to a part of the day of July 5. Few amendments were offered. Bailey proposed that the Sixteenth Amendment be submitted to state conventions chosen for that purpose, instead of to legislatures elected with reference to many issues,[158] so that the danger of rejection would be diminished. Borah spoke favorably of this change, but Beveridge thought it more complicated than necessary.

Bailey also presented an amendment to give Congress the power to graduate the rates of the tax, which he admitted was probably not

155 *Cong. Rec.* 44: 1568, 1570 (April 28); 3138 (June 11); 3377 (June 18). The New York *Herald* of June 18 commented: "If a constitutional amendment goes through by virtue of the understanding between President Taft and Senator Aldrich, it will probably bear the name of some Senator who has not been taking pot shots at the elder statesmen."

156 Hubbard, Harry, "From Whatever Source Derived," *American Law Journal* VI (b); 202-207 (Sept. 1920).

157 *Cong. Rec.* 44: 3900; 4067. According to Borah, the Amendment was written by Wickersham. *Cong. Rec.* 65: 8208.

158 *Cong. Rec.* 44: 4108.

necessary but proposed "only as a matter of abundant caution" because of the statement of Justice Brewer in the case of *Knowlton* v. *Moore* (178 U. S. 41, 1920) that he dissented from the opinion of the Court sustaining the validity of the inheritance tax law upon the ground that Congress had no power to grade it.[159] "Plainly," said Bailey, "if Congress is without power . . . to grade an inheritance tax, it would be without power under this amendment to grade an income tax."

McLaurin (Miss.) offered a substitute, that is, he wanted to rewrite the amendment so as to strike out the words "and direct taxes" in Section 2, Article 1, and the words "or other direct taxes" in Section 9, Article I of the Constitution. These sections would then read as follows:

> Representatives shall be apportioned among the several States which may be included within this Union. . .
> No capitation tax shall be laid unless in proportion to the census or enumeration hereinbefore directed to be taken.

He wanted to avoid the possible argument of contestants of the tax that the amendment provided for apportionment of some kind even if apportionment by population was excluded. He objected to the original wording of the amendment also on the ground that by it Congress recognized the income tax as a direct tax. Bristow attempted to add an amendment providing for direct election of Senators but Aldrich raised a point of order which the Vice-President upheld.[160]

All amendments were either voted down or withdrawn. The resolution was passed by a vote of 77 yeas, no nays.[161]

THE AMENDMENT IN THE HOUSE OF REPRESENTATIVES

The resolution was debated in the House of Representatives July 12 for four hours, at the end of which time the vote was taken — 318 yeas, 14 nays, 55 not voting.[162] All of the negative votes were cast by Republicans.

The debate centered on the desirability of an income tax. Chairman Payne frankly stated that he was opposed to such a tax because he believed that it would make "a nation of liars," that it was the "most difficult of enforcement," "the hardest to collect of any tax," that it was "a tax upon the income of the honest men and an exemption, to a greater or less extent, on the income of rascals." Never-

159 *Cong. Rec.* 44: 4108, 4120.
160 *Cong. Rec.* 44: 4105-4106.
161 *Cong. Rec.* 44: 4121. The fifteen members who did not vote were: Brandegee, Bulkeley, Clarke (Ark.), Clay, Dolliver, Elkins, Hale, Lodge, Lorimer, Paynter, Piles, Richardson, Smith (Md.), Smith (Mich.), and Tillman.
162 *Cong. Rec.* 44: 4440.

theless he did not wish the nation to be left in time of war without an opportunity to avail itself of every resource. So he favored the passage of an amendment to give Congress power to levy an income tax which he hoped would be used only in war time.[163]

McCall (Mass.) thought the amendment abrogated "one of the fundamental principles of the Constitution" by doing away with the rule of apportionment which safeguarded the big states. If this protection were given up there should be some compensation, such as a provision that the House should have sole power to introduce income tax bills and that the Senate should not be allowed to amend them. In contrast to Payne, McCall thought that the income tax was not primarily for war, as the chairman had argued, but for social purposes, that is, "to regulate the citizen and regenerate the moral nature of man." He warned his colleagues that if an income tax were enforced, each individual citizen would be called upon "to lay bare the innermost recesses of his soul in affidavits, and with the aid of the federal inspector, who will supervise his books and papers and business secrets, he may be made to be good, according to the notions of virtue at the moment prevailing in Washington." [164]

The eastern Republican view was also expressed by Hill (Conn.) who opposed the amendment because: (1) he did not believe that Congress had been called "to completely change and revolutionize the taxation system of the United States," and that a question of such magnitude should be submitted to the people and discussed in a campaign; (2) the income tax might be justified in war time but in time of peace expenses should be cut "so as to keep them within our national income." He considered it fair enough that everyone should be taxed for such a project as the Panama Canal but objected to taxing the East for local western projects such as inland waterways and irrigation developments.[165]

The Democratic position was first presented by Champ Clark (Mo.) who showed that the income tax was put into the tariff law of 1894 by his party, had been advocated by it ever since, and finally was accepted by the Republicans. He challenged the historical interpretation of his colleague, McCall (Mass.), as to the desirability of the rule of apportionment for the reason that the conditions of the country had changed since the Constitution was written, when population and wealth were approximately evenly divided among the states.[166] Congress would never levy a direct tax because it would be so palpably unjust.

[163] *Cong. Rec.* 44: 4390.
[164] *Cong. Rec.* 44: 4391.
[165] *Cong. Rec.* 44: 4393-4394.
[166] *Cong. Rec.* 44: 4392.

Hull began his speech by stating that:

during the past few weeks the unexpected spectacle of certain so-called "old-line conservative" Republican leaders in Congress suddenly reversing their attitude of a lifetime and seemingly espousing, though with ill-concealed reluctance, the proposed income-tax amendment to the Constitution has been the occasion of universal surprise and wonder.

He showed how the Republicans had been driven to their position by the crystallization of public sentiment throughout the country and the success of the income tax movement in the Senate. Hull therefore agreed to vote for the proposed constitutional amendment but would not agree to relax his efforts for a new income tax law to give the Supreme Court a chance to reconsider its former decision. He surveyed the history of constitutional amendments, emphasizing the difficulties that had arisen and showing that ratification of the Sixteenth would require the alertness and vigilance of all friends of an income tax.[167]

Only one amendment was offered in the House, and it did not come to a vote. It would have had the states ratify by conventions instead of by legislatures.[168]

THE MEANING OF THE AMENDMENT

The joint resolution proposing the Sixteenth Amendment to the Constitution of the United States was worded as follows:

The Congress shall have power to lay and collect taxes on incomes, from whatever source derived, without apportionment among the several States, and without regard to any census or enumeration.

Early in January 1910, Governor Hughes[169] sent a special message to the Assembly of the State of New York in which he affirmed that he was in favor of conferring upon the federal government the power to levy an income tax but he thought that the terms of the grant should not be so broad as to give the federal government the power to tax bonds issued by the state or municipal governments. He argued:

To place the borrowing capacity of the State and of its governmental agencies at the mercy of the Federal taxing power would be an impairment of the essential rights of the State, which, as its officers, we are bound to defend.

The governor objected especially to the inclusion of the phrase "from whatever source derived" because he considered that it would make impossible a claim that any property of the state, even its

[167] *Cong. Rec.* 44: 4400-4404.
[168] It was introduced by Henry (Tex.). (*Cong. Rec.* 44: 4438).
[169] Now Chief Justice of the United States Supreme Court.

bonds, would be out of reach of the taxing power of the federal government. He wrote:

> The immunity from Federal taxation that the State and its instrumentalities now enjoy is derived not from any express provision of the Federal Constitution but from what has been deemed to be necessary implication. Who can say that any such implication will survive the adoption of this explicit and comprehensive amendment?

Stuyvesant Fish[170] supported the recommendation of Governor Hughes that the Assembly should not ratify the amendment, but for the following very different reasons: (1) That the joint resolution was passed by Congress in great haste and without much thought; (2) that the amendment had been before the legislatures of the various states for eighteen months but had attracted no attention and excited no interest; (3) that if the amendment were adopted Congress might impose income taxes "without regard to either apportionment or uniformity and may vary them from time to time at pleasure" and that the removal of the restraint of apportionment would enable Congress "to wield a weapon which may in the hands of partisan leaders readily destroy the chief industry of any state"; (4) that Congress did not need any added power to levy direct taxes; and (5) that the states could not afford "to give the Federal Government this or any indefinite increased taxing power." He concluded his letter to the Assembly with these words:

> Does not the State of New York and every State in the Union need to husband its own resources and to keep down taxation rather than to vote for all future time, into the hands of a Congress sitting at a distance, additional and unlimited power in respect thereto, especially in these times when all classes are suffering from the "high cost of living."[171]

Another brief was presented to the Assembly by Joseph Choate and four others.[172] They opposed the ratification for much the same reasons that Governor Hughes had given.

The reply of the federal Administration to the governor is found in a letter written by Senator Root to Frederick Davenport, a state senator of New York.[173] Root took exception to the statement of Governor Hughes that the proposed amendment would grant authority to the federal government to tax income from state bonds or from those of local governmental units. He did not consider that the amendment would enlarge "in any degree whatever . . . the

170 A prominent New York banker and railroad executive.

171 This appeal was published in the form of an open letter (a pamphlet), Jan. 30, 1911.

172 William D. Guthrie, Victor Morawetz, Austen G. Fox, and John G. Milburn, all of whom were prominent attorneys. Guthrie and Choate had opposed the government in the Pollock case in 1895.

173 61st Congress, 2d Session, *Senate Document* 398.

taxing power of the National Government," or would "have any effect whatever except to relieve the exercise of that taxing power from the requirement that the tax shall be apportioned among the several states. . ." He gave a short summary of the court decisions regarding income tax legislation of the federal government and showed that the government could tax income from business or occupation but could not tax income from real estate or personal property, that "this history shows that the end sought by the amendment was simply a removal of the restrictions as to apportionment and not a change in the well-settled rule which restrains the national government from taxing State securities."

In the next session of Congress Borah introduced a resolution requesting the Judiciary Committee to report to the Senate whether or not the proposed amendment would authorize Congress to tax the income of state and municipal bonds or would authorize Congress "to tax the instrumentalities or means or property of the State or the salary of state officers." [174] In presenting this request the Senator expressed his disagreement with the interpretation given by Governor Hughes to the phrase "from whatever source derived" on the following grounds: (1) that the amendment, if adopted, would add nothing to the power of the National Government to lay and collect taxes; (2) that the words "from whatever source derived" added nothing to the force or strength of the amendment itself, and (3) that "the amendment did not deal, does not purport to deal with the question of power. It intended to deal, and does deal, alone with the manner of exercising that power which is already complete, that which is already without any limit." [175] Brown, who introduced the amendment, agreed with Borah's interpretation and emphasized the fact that the amendment did not impose the tax, it merely gave to Congress the power to levy such a tax.[176] He said:

> My own judgment is that the words against which complaint is lodged "from whatever source derived" neither add to nor take away from the power of the Government to reach the incomes of the country, provided the proposed amendment is adopted. But I further maintain . . . that, without regard to whether or not the proposed amendment will reach the incomes of state officers or the incomes arising from state securities, nevertheless the amendment should be adopted.[177]

Professor Seligman, in his work on the income tax, put the whole discussion on a much broader basis. After paying his respects to

174 *Cong. Rec.* 45: 1585, 1694. (Feb. 8, 10, 1910.) The resolution was laid on the table.
175 *Cong. Rec.* 45: 1694-1695.
176 *Cong. Rec.* 45: 1649, 2245-2247.
177 *Cong. Rec.* 45: 1699.

Governor Hughes' ability as a lawyer and a statesman, he pointed out three reasons for considering his opinion erroneous.[178]

The first reason was that the governor's interpretation of the legal force of the amendment was incorrect. Professor Seligman cited a series of decisions to show that by an established rule of constitutional construction, certain kinds of income taxes were direct, certain kinds were indirect, and a third kind were invalid, whether they were direct or indirect. State and local government bonds were not subject to federal taxation. The Sixteenth Amendment would simply remove the discrimination between these direct and indirect income taxes, that is, it would remove the necessity that the former be apportioned. In other words, the amendment made it possible to tax incomes without apportionment, whether the sources of income belonged to one category or another. The amendment made no change in the taxability of income beyond the taxing power of the federal government, the third group mentioned above. Therefore it did not extend the power of the government to tax income of state and municipal bonds.

The second reason was that, even were his (Governor Hughes') legal interpretation correct, he failed to take account of economic facts which would prevent the consequences which he feared. Professor Seligman explained that there was a difference in effect between a special tax and a general tax. The economic effect of tax exemption of bonds would be to increase their market value in accordance with the principle of the capitalization or amortization of the tax. The income tax, however, would be a general, not a special tax, hence would have no discriminating effect on state bonds if applied to them, for the amendment specified that the tax would apply to all income, hence there would be no tax-free investments. All income would be equally diminished by the tax.

The third point was that, if the governor were correct in believing that the constitutional amendment would operate to change the law in the direction indicated, that is, to tax state bonds, there were valid reasons why constitutional interpretation should keep pace with the changing political and social conditions. National development of economic forces had created the need for national regulation in many matters since the framing of the Constitution. Central authority should not be opposed in those cases where self-government meant retrogression rather than progress.

Many thoughtful citizens, he concluded, still had their doubts as to the practicability of an income tax but the question must be faced. "Shall the government of the United States be precluded from even

178 Seligman, E. R. A., *The Income Tax,* 1st ed., pp. 596-628. This book was written but not published before Senator Root made his statement. (*Ibid.,* 601, note.)

making the attempt to levy an income tax?" he asked. No one would deny that the government might be seriously handicapped in times of national emergency by lacking "so powerful a fiscal engine," a "power which is possessed by the smallest of its competitors." He concluded therefore that the pending constitutional amendment was not only "legally defensible and politically innocuous," but it was, above all, economically sound. Hence it was from every point of view eminently desirable.[179]

RATIFICATION BY THE STATES

Alabama was the first state to ratify the amendment, and the only one to do so in 1909. In the following year eight states ratified it, namely, Georgia, Illinois, Kentucky, Maryland, Mississippi, Oklahoma, South Carolina, and Texas. The rest of the states were slower in taking action and the thirty-sixth state did not ratify it until February 3, 1913. The Secretary of State certified its adoption February 25 (37 *Statutes at Large* 1785).[180]

The last states to ratify were Vermont, New Hampshire, and Massachusetts. Connecticut, Rhode Island, Pennsylvania, Virginia, Florida, and Utah either rejected the amendment or failed to take action. The action of each state legislature is shown in Table 6.

In most states there was little open opposition to the amendment. The argument of the Governor of New York has been discussed in the preceding section. The Governor of Connecticut, following the same argument, objected to it because he thought it would give the federal government power to tax income from state and municipal bonds. The legislature accepted his recommendation and rejected the amendment. The New York assembly rejected the amendment once, but when Governor Dix succeeded Governor Hughes the new assembly ratified it.[181] In Massachusetts a legislative joint committee on state and federal relations recommended no action for the same and other reasons, but despite this the legislature ratified it.

In Virginia the situation was different. The Governor favored the resolution, the Senate voted to ratify it, but the House of Delegates refused to order the engrossment of the bill. The arguments are interesting. Senator Bailey of Texas, who had been invited to

179 Probably no one can estimate accurately the amount of stimulus and influence that Professor Seligman's support gave to the income tax movement. Other economists also contributed articles and discussed the tax in professional societies. For later discussions of the meaning of the Sixteenth Amendment, see below, Chaps. XX and XXI, pp. 460 ff., 478 ff.

180 The Supreme Court has held that the effective date of ratification of an amendment is the date of ratification by the required number of states rather than the date of proclamation by the Secretary of State. *Dillon* v. *Gloss,* 256 U. S. 386 (1921).

181 Ratification of the amendment was one of the planks in the New York state Democratic platform in 1910.

Table 6

Ratification of the Sixteenth Amendment [a]

State	House			Senate			*Date of ratification*
	Yeas	*Nays*	*% of yeas*	*Yeas*	*Nays*	*% of yeas*	
Alabama......	81	0	100	23	0	100	Aug. 2, 10, 1909.
Arizona.......	33	0	100	Passed	....	100	Apr. 6, 3, 1912.
Arkansas......	54	2	96	24	6	80	Apr. 22, 17, 1911.
California.....	Passed	....	....	Passed	....	....	Jan. 31, 20, 1911.
Colorado......	63	0	100	30	3	90	Feb. 15, 7, 1911.
Connecticut ...	......	....	....	Rejected	....	....	....
Delaware......	27	0	100	Passed	....	....	Feb. 3, 1913.
Florida........	......	....	....	Rejected	....	....	....
Georgia.......	129	32	80	23	18	56	July 26, 11, 1910.
Idaho.........	Passed	....	....	Passed	....	....	Jan. 20, 1911.
Illinois........	80	8	90	41	0	100	Mar. 1, Feb. 9, 1910.
Indiana.......	93	0	100	48	1	98	Jan. 30, 17, 1911.
Iowa..........	81	0	100	45	3	93	Feb. 24, 22, 1911.
Kansas........	81	0	100	25	14	64	Feb. 18, Jan. 19, 1911.
Kentucky.....	Passed	....	....	Passed	....	....	Feb. 8 or 9, 1910.
Louisiana......	101	6	94	Passed	....	....	May 30, June 28, 1912.
Maine........	101	0	100	Passed	....	....	Mar. 31, 30, 1911.
Maryland.....	83	1	98	16	9	64	Mar. 21, Apr. 8, 1910.
Massachusetts..	Passed	....	....	Passed	....	....	Mar. 4, Feb. 27, 1913.
Michigan......	92	1	98	23	1	96	Jan. 24, Feb. 23, 1911.
Minnesota.....	89	0	100	49	5	90	June 6, 11, 1912.
Mississippi	85	51	62	28	2	93	Jan. 29, Mar. 7, 1910.
Missouri......	113	9	92	30	0	100	Mar. 16, 7, 1911.
Montana......	56	0	100	28	0	100	Jan. 30, 11, 1911.
Nebraska......	95	0	100	32	0	100	Feb. 1, 8, 1911.
Nevada.......	46	0	100	18	0	100	Jan. 24, 31, 1911.
New Hampshire	Passed	....	....	20	2	90	Feb. 18, 19, 1913.
New Jersey....	49	8	85	12	9	57	Jan. 27, Feb. 4, 1913.
New Mexico...	36	0	100	19	1	95	Feb. 3, 1913.
New York.....	81	42	65	35	16	68	July, 12, Apr. 19, 1911.
North Carolina.	Passed	....	....	Passed	....	....	Feb. 11, 1911.
North Dakota .	98	1	99	45	1	97	Jan. 24, Feb. 16, 1911.
Ohio..........	100	3	97	31	1	96	Jan. 19, 18, 1911.
Oklahoma.....	89	2	97	37	0	100	Mar. 4, 9, 1910.
Oregon........	45	8	84	25	2	90	Jan. 23, 18, 1911.
Pennsylvania...	......	....	....	......	....	....	....
Rhode Island..	Rejected	....	....	......	....	....	....
South Carolina.	101	4	95	22	11	66	Feb. 16, 19, 1910.
South Dakota..	100	0	100	41	0	100	Feb. 3, 1912.
Tennessee.....	82	3	96	24	4	85	Apr. 7, 6, 1911.
Texas.........	106	1	99	28	1	96	Aug. 16, 4, 1910.
Utah..........	Rejected	....	....	......	....	....	....
Vermont......	Passed	....	....	13	11	54	Feb. 19, 18, 1913.
Virginia.......	......	....	....	......	....	....	....
Washington ...	80	1	98	32	5	86	Jan. 26, 1911.
West Virginia..	73	0	100	30	0	100	Jan. 31, 29, 1913.
Wisconsin.....	92	0	100	21	0	100	Feb. 9, May 26, 1911.
Wyoming......	48	7	87	24	3	88	Feb. 3, 1913.

[a] 71st Congress, 3d Session, *Senate Document* 240, *U. S. Library of Congress, Legislative Reference Service, Data on Ratification of the Constitution and Amendments by States,* p. 10. Compiled from the records of the house and senate of each state. Footnotes of the original table are omitted.

address a joint session of the Virginia legislature on the income tax amendment, presented four reasons for its ratification, namely, (1) that the income tax was a just tax; (2) that there was no danger of a federal Congress abusing its power; (3) that a federal tax was necessary because Republican extravagance could not otherwise be supported; (4) that in the event of a Democratic victory, the Democratic party could not reform the tariff unless aided by the revenue from a federal income tax.

In reply to the Senator, Speaker Richard E. Byrd[182] said that nobody disputed his first argument; most people doubted the second; the third proposition hardly appealed to a Democrat, and the fourth might be "disputed upon very reasonable grounds." There were real objections to the proposal, according to Byrd. The ratification of the amendment would bring the individual into direct contact with the federal government, a contact of the most vital concern to the individual. It would mean that the state would give up a legitimate and long-established source of revenue and yield it to the federal government. It would mean even more, that the state actually invited the federal government "to invade its territory, to oust its jurisdiction and to establish a Federal dominion within the innermost citadel of the reserved rights of the Commonwealth." The amendment would go farther than the Fourteenth or Fifteenth Amendment in extending the power of the federal government, because it would reach the citizen in the ordinary business of life. He continued:

> A hand from Washington will be stretched out and placed upon every man's business; the eye of the Federal inspector will be in every man's counting house. . . The law will of necessity have inquisitorial features, it will provide penalties, it will create complicated machinery. Under it men will be hailed into courts distant from their homes. Heavy fines imposed by distant and unfamiliar tribunals will constantly menace the tax payer. An army of Federal inspectors, spies and detectives will descend upon the state. . . Who of us who have had knowledge of the doings of the Federal officials in the Internal Revenue service can be blind to what will follow? I do not hesitate to say that the adoption of this amendment will be such a surrender to imperialism that has not been since the Northern states in their blindness forced the fourteenth and fifteenth amendments upon the entire sisterhood of the Commonwealth.
>
> I am not willing by any voluntary act to give up revenue which the State of Virginia herself needs, nor to surrender that measure of States rights which. . . the construction of the Federal Courts have permitted to remain.[183]

[182] Father of Senator Harry F. Byrd and Admiral Richard E. Byrd.
[183] Richmond *Times-Dispatch,* March 3, 1910.

CHAPTER III

THE ACT OF 1913

THE FIRST MODERN FEDERAL INCOME TAX

THE POLITICAL SITUATION

During the three or four years in which the Sixteenth Amendment was being ratified by the state legislatures, an upset took place in the national political scene. The Insurgent Republicans who protested the tariff schedules of 1909 gradually increased in number and strengthened their position until they felt able to challenge the old line members in a nationwide contest for control of the party convention in 1912. Unsuccessful in this move, they formed a new party, the Progressive. This split in the Republican ranks enabled the Democrats to elect not only the President but also many national, state, and local officials. For the first time since 1897 and for the third time since the Civil War the White House was occupied by a Democrat. In the Sixty-third Congress the Democrats had an unwieldy majority in the House of Representatives and a majority of six in the Senate.[1]

Party feeling was much more harmonious among the victors at the beginning of President Wilson's administration than it was later, or than it had been during the previous Democratic regime, President Cleveland's second administration. On the whole members of Congress were friendly to the executive in 1913. The Speaker of the House, Champ Clark, was loyal to the President, although he never forgot that he had been "cheated" out of the Presidency by Bryan and his followers. Underwood, floor leader and Chairman of the Committee on Ways and Means, was also a loyal party man. On his committee were such future leaders as Kitchin, Garner, and Hull. At that time they were somewhat less experienced and less well-known than later but they did their share of the work in drafting legislation.

In 1913 the temper of the party was not ruffled by such bitter-enders as Hill, Cockran, and Gorman had been in the Fifty-third Congress, nor by such annoyingly clever opposition strategists as Aldrich and McMillan. Harmony was short-lived, however; before the Wilson administration was over Reed (Mo.) became a thorn in

[1] The party line-up was as follows:
House: Democrats, 291; Republicans, 128; Progressives, 15; Independent, 1.
Senate: Democrats, 51; Republicans, 44; Progressive, 1.

the flesh of the President and, on the Republican side of the Senate, Lodge (Mass.) was no less obstructive.

On the whole, the Democrats were in general agreement as to the extent of tariff reform desirable and, furthermore, the members of the House of Representatives had had the advantage of working together as the majority party in the last session of the Sixty-second Congress. In fact, of the 291 Democrats in the House, 184 had been in Congress before.

The income tax was almost certain to be accepted on a non-partisan basis, or, rather, on a bi-party basis. The Republicans had sponsored the Sixteenth Amendment and, although they had not mentioned the income tax in the party platform of 1912, they had favored it. This was clearly shown in the preceding session in the vote for a personal excise tax, which was as close an approximation to a general income tax as was then deemed feasible.[2] Even some of the more conservative Republicans had given support to the ratification of the amendment. Root's contribution, his able brief in reply to Governor Hughes' argument against the tax addressed to the New York legislature, has already been mentioned.[3]

ECONOMIC AND FISCAL CONDITIONS

The advent of the Democrats to power made "big business" very "jittery." Much of the campaign oratory of all three parties in 1912 had been directed against the trusts and monopolies, indicating that there was much popular support for such agitation. Business seemed to feel that Wilson would do more than talk about anti-trust legislation. As Governor of New Jersey he had made a name for himself as a critic of monopolies and trusts. One financial paper commented:

> The year 1913 was one of disturbing incidents and events. It marked the advent to control of the Federal Government of a most radical Administration — an Administration, too, that was determined to emphasize and to flaunt its adherence to radical doctrines. From beginning to end a propaganda of that kind was carried out. . . Everywhere iconoclasts were at work demanding change, destroying faith in everything that had long endured, questioning the soundness and the wisdom of every usage and of every practice and of every law that had stood the test of time. . .
>
> It was not so much what was done as the spirit in which it was done and conceived, not so much what was actually accomplished as what was

[2] This was to be a tax of 1% on individual income, after deduction of business expenses, losses, interest, taxes, and $5000. Provision was made for an adaptation of the British system of collection at the source. The bill was passed by the House by a vote of 253 yeas, 40 nays. The Senate also passed the bill but attached to it two extraneous amendments, neither of which the House was willing to accept. The Conferees were unable to reach an agreement hence the measure was left as unfinished business when the session ended. For House bill see *Cong. Rec.* 48: 9678.

[3] See above, Chap II.

proposed, not so much what was carried into effect as what was threatened. In a word, politics was the disturbing element.[4]

When the statistics of business for 1913 are analyzed it is seen that the year was one neither of serious depression nor of genuine prosperity. It was the last year not seriously affected by the upheaval of the World War. Bank loans and discounts showed an increase to $207.16 per capita in 1913, from $202.68 in 1912, and $186.46 in 1910. The Department of Commerce reported an all-time high in foreign trade.

On the other hand, there were several factors not so favorable. The index of food and crop production dropped from 93.67 in 1912 to 80.14 in 1913; total crop production from 92.66 to 81.81 for the same period, when the entire volume is considered, and from 118 to 99.49 on a per capita basis. These and other factors accompanied a noticeable increase in the cost of living, a fact which caused much discussion in Congress as well as in the press, and one that presented a talking point for the Democrats in their revision of the tariff. Net earnings of railroads declined primarily because of increased operating costs, chiefly wages. Building decreased so much that by the end of the year this industry was employing only about half the workers it had used when operating at full capacity. *Bradstreets* reported the greatest number of business failures since 1896, a number exceeded only in 1893.[5]

But the financial affairs of the United States Government were in good condition, according to the Report of the Secretary of the Treasury made in November 1912. The preceding fiscal year closed with an excess of receipts over expenditures amounting to more than $37,000,000.

THE FIRST INCOME TAX BILL DRAFTED BY THE COMMITTEE ON WAYS AND MEANS

President Wilson's program called for tariff and banking reform before the enactment of anti-trust legislation. In the 1912 campaign the Democratic party had stood for lower customs duties, its historic position. In his inaugural address the President had mentioned par-

[4] *The Commercial and Financial Chronicle,* 98: 8 (January 3, 1914). Later in the year this same journal reprinted the following open letter to the New York *Sun* (November 21, 1914):

Kind Words Can Never Die

To the Editor of the Sun: Sir—The kind words of the Administration to the business interests of the country remind me of the thrilling melodrama entitled "Nellie, the Beautiful Cloak Model."

In the early part of the play the villain pushed Nellie off the Brooklyn Bridge. Later he overthrew her from an Atlantic liner. Later still he thrust her under a descending elevator. The next time they met he said: "Nellie, why do you fear me?"

[5] Warren, George F., and Pearson, Frank A., *Prices*; 63d Congress, 1st Session, *House Report* 5.

ticularly the fact that the tariff then in force "cut us off from our proper part in the commerce of the world" and made the government "a facile instrument in the hands of private interests." [6]

The groundwork for extensive tariff revision had been laid in the preceding session of Congress, the "lame-duck" session, at the close of Taft's administration when the Democrats had a large majority in the House. It was then decided that when the recently elected Democratic Administration came in there should be a general reduction of import duties, particularly on items which entered into the cost of living, a reduction of those duties which had been so effective in encouraging the development of monopolies, and the complete removal of duties on several raw materials. The Committee deliberately planned for a reduction of revenue from the tariff.[7]

Shortly before the Sixty-second Congress adjourned, the Sixteenth Amendment to the Constitution was ratified by the thirty-sixth state,[8] so the Committee on Ways and Means agreed to use the income tax in order to make up the deficit that would result from the proposed tariff reductions. Details as to the extent of exemptions and height of rates were dependent on what commodities would be transferred to the free list.[9] Wool, hides, and sugar were most frequently mentioned in this connection but final decision on these highly controversial points was postponed until the Democratic administration came into office.

HULL DRAFTS INCOME TAX SECTION

When the new Congress convened in special session in March, immediately after the inauguration of President Wilson, the Committee on Ways and Means [10] apportioned sections of the revenue bill to

[6] *Cong. Rec.* 50: 3.

[7] Underwood, Oscar, *Drifting Sands of Party Politics,* p. 182.

[8] In fact, the 36th, 37th, and 38th states (Delaware, New Mexico, and Wyoming) ratified it Feb. 3, 1913.

[9] New York *World,* March 21, 1913.

[10] According to Senator Warren (Rep., Wyo.) most of the work was done by eight men, namely, Underwood, Shackleford, Kitchin, Dixon, Hull, Garner, Collier, and Stanley. (*Cong. Rec.* 50: 4437.) The complete membership of the Committee on Ways and Means was as follows:

Democrats	*Republicans*
Oscar W. Underwood (Ala.), Ch.	Sereno E. Payne (N. Y.)
Francis B. Harrison (N. Y.)	Joseph W. Fordney (Mich.)
Dorsey W. Shackleford (Mo.)	Augustus P. Gardner (Mass.)
Claude Kitchin (N. C.)	J. Hampton Moore (Pa.)
Henry T. Rainey (Ill.)	William R. Green (Iowa)
Lincoln Dixon (Ind.)	Sydney Anderson (Minn.)
Cordell Hull (Tenn.)	Victor Murdock (Kans., Prog.)
Winfield S. Hammond (Minn.)	
Andrew J. Peters (Mass.)	
A. Mitchell Palmer (Pa.)	
Timothy N. Ansberry (Ohio)	
John N. Garner (Texas)	
James W. Collier (Miss.)	
Augustus O. Stanley (Ky.)	

various members for more intensive and detailed work.[11] To Hull were assigned Schedule L, dealing with silk and its manufactures, and also Part II, the income tax. After he had completed his draft of the latter, a subcommittee composed of Underwood, Hull, Peters, and Palmer reviewed it but made little change in the original draft.

The sections most difficult to write were those that dealt with (1) the amount of personal exemptions, (2) the rates, and (3) the method of collection.[12] Although Garner was not on the subcommittee, he became very much interested in one phase of the law, namely, the graduation of rates. He became the chief proponent of the principle of graduation, a plan that was contrary to the ideas of expediency held at that time by Underwood and Hull.[13] Garner stated some years later that great pressure was brought upon the Committee from all parts of the country not to levy a progressive tax but that he and Shackleford resisted it successfully.[14] At the time he threatened to carry his fight to the party caucus if the Committee insisted on a flat rate.[13]

Hull favored a flat rate "primarily with a view to securing the validity of the tax sustained by the Court and also to get the law adjusted to the economic situation in as simple a way as possible, so that it would be less likely to be repealed." [15] Doubtless he was also influenced by the practical consideration that a graduated rate was incompatible with collection of the tax at the source, a British device that appealed to him as highly desirable.

The Committee, of course, was at a disadvantage in not having much statistical material upon which to base estimates of yield [16] and in not having results of any recent administrative experience in the United States except that connected with the rather limited corporation excise tax. On the other hand, the members were fortunate in having the benefit of the interest and thorough study which Hull

[11] At and prior to this time a federal revenue bill practically always meant a tariff bill. This was a natural connotation in view of the fact that the federal government depended almost entirely on revenues from customs duties prior to the Civil War and mostly on such duties, supplemented by excises on liquor and tobacco, from the Civil War to the World War. The income taxes of the Civil War, 1894, and 1913 were all thought of as supplementary revenues and were all sections of the tariff bills, the 1916 income tax being the first in a separate bill. Now, with the income tax the most important federal tax, a revenue bill is generally thought of as an income tax measure rather than as a tariff measure. In fact, customs duties have been relegated to third place or lower since tobacco, liquor and miscellaneous excises regularly exceed them in fiscal importance.

[12] New York *Times*, Washington *Star*, March 24, 1913.

[13] New York *World*, Washington *Star*, March 23, 1913. In 1928 Garner advocated graduation of corporation rates. See below, Chap. XI, p. 285.

[14] *Cong. Rec.* 65: 2431. This statement, however, gives a rather false impression of the position of those who favored a flat rate at that time for tactical reasons.

[15] Notation made by Secretary Hull on authors' manuscript.

[16] For example, it was thought early in the proceedings that a 1 per cent rate upon all income over $5000 would yield $100,000,000 of revenue. (The *Independent*, 74: 384, Feb. 13, 1913.)

had made over a period of years.[17] Furthermore, Democratic leaders recognized their responsibility not only for raising the necessary amount of revenue so that their plans for tariff revision would not "go awry" but also for writing the measure in such a way that it would not encounter popular opposition and "prove a political boomerang of the worst sort." [18]

At the end of March, the tariff schedules were sufficiently set so that the probable revenue could be computed. It was stated in the press that there would be a deficit of approximately $100,000,000 to be raised by an income tax. Inasmuch as the corporation excise tax had not produced over $33,000,000 in any previous year, the rates of the tax on individuals would have to be more than the flat 1% first advocated by Underwood and Hull in order to raise $100,000,000. Hence graduation was agreed upon, but the exact rates were left undecided at that time.[19] It was proposed early in April that the rates be made flexible and that the President should have the power to fix them at the end of each fiscal year when the Treasury needs were known.[20] There was, however, some question of the constitutionality of such a proposal and much doubt as to the willingness of the House to relinquish so much power to the Chief Executive.

Within the next few days the unsettled portions of the tariff sections of the bill, except the sugar schedule, were rapidly put into shape for presentation to the caucus and to the House; the sugar schedule was finally compromised at the very last moment.[21]

Since estimates of yield of the tariff were greater than they had been a month before, the estimated deficit to be met by the income tax was reduced from $100,000,000 to $69,000,000. The Committee, therefore, put the lowest income tax rate at 1% on incomes of $4000 or over, with an "additional tax" graduated as follows: 1% on that part of an individual's income which was over $20,000 and not over $50,000; 2% on that part of an individual's income from $50,000 to $100,000; and 3% on the excess over $100,000. The corporation income tax was left at 1%, as in the excise Act of 1909, but no exemption was allowed.

17 Champ Clark wrote in his memoirs, *My Quarter Century of American Politics* (II: 342), the following comment on Hull:

"In one branch of our financial system — income taxes — Judge Cordell Hull of Tennessee is considered the fountain head of information. He is a thorough master of that subject and is relied on implicitly as an authority by both the House and the executive departments."

18 New York *Times,* March 25, 1913.

19 New York *Times,* March 25, 1913. The rates were tentatively set to begin at ½ of 1% on incomes over $4000 and not over $10,000, and to increase to a maximum of 2% on incomes over $100,000. Garner wanted the rates to begin at ½ of 1% on incomes of $2500 and to reach a maximum of 4% on incomes over $100,000.

20 New York *Times,* April 3, 1913.

21 It was decided to make the duty on sugar one cent a pound for three years, at the end of which time it would be put on the free list.

The President followed every detail throughout the progress of the Ways and Means Committee's work.[22] He made it known to Congress that he preferred discussion, and such disagreement as would develop over the schedules, before they had gone too far along the legislative path.[23] Equally unusual was the interest shown in the bill by the Senate Finance Committee even before it was introduced into the House. Several conferences were held between the two committees and also between the representatives of the legislative body and the executive.[24]

THE INCOME TAX IN THE HOUSE OF REPRESENTATIVES

On April 7 Chairman Underwood formally presented to the House the majority report of the Committee on Ways and Means. This embodied their draft of tariff and income tax legislation.[25] Debate on this measure was delayed, however, for about two weeks. In the interim the Democrats, in caucus, went over the measure section by section and made some phraseological changes in the parts relating to the income tax.[26] On April 21 the bill was re-introduced; the following day it was read the first and second times, *pro forma,* and the minority report presented. On the 24th, Underwood introduced Peters who outlined briefly the chief points of each section.

Two days later Hull explained in detail Part II, the income tax section.[27] He prefaced his remarks by a summary of the general agitation and demand in almost every state in the Union and in almost every country in the world for intelligent, fair, and practical reforms and readjustments of tax systems, to the end that every citizen would be required to contribute to the support of the state or government in proportion to the revenue he enjoyed under its protection. He also cited the reports of several state officials and commissions. He spoke of the use of the income tax in other countries, particularly in England where Lloyd George had described it as the "center and sheet anchor" of their financial system.[28]

Hull then analyzed the proposed income tax law, explaining the

22 For example, the New York *Times* of March 26 carried this account: "Until the bill is returned from the White House, it is understood, the vote on this feature [the income tax rates] will be postponed. President Wilson, it was asserted at the White House today, had not decided whether he would prefer a flat tax or a graduated income tax. This must be decided by the Democrats of the Committee."

23 Washington *Star,* March 23, 1913; New York *World,* March 20, 1913.

24 New York *World,* April 5, 1913; New York *Times,* April 7, 8, 1913.

25 *Cong. Rec.* 50: 79, 300.

26 Almost all the amendments dealt with the taxation of insurance companies. New York *Times,* April 19, and April 21, 1913.

27 A synopsis of the bill as drawn up by the Committee on Ways and Means is in the *Cong. Rec.* 50: 516. The Committee report is in 63d Congress, 1st Session, *House Report* 5.

28 *Cong. Rec.* 50: 504-505.

meaning of each of its seven sections. Paragraph A defined those subject to the law: United States citizens living in the United States or abroad; residents, even if not citizens; and non-resident aliens receiving income from property or business in the United States. A year later he characterized its provisions as "almost as broad in its scope and meaning as the English law." [29] Paragraph B defined the net income of a taxable individual. Hull explained that it was not the intention to tax capital or principal but only "such gains or profits as may be realized from rent, interest, salaries, trade, commerce, or sales . . . or profits . . . from any source." Because of the difficulty of accurately interpreting these clauses the Committee expected that "the rulings of the Treasury Department and the decisions of the courts of this country with respect to the old income tax laws and also the English rules of construction, all essential portions of which will be embraced in the Treasury regulations, will make clear the distinction between taxable profits or income, on the one hand and capital or principal on the other." [30] It would seem that the author of the bill did not intend to tax capital gains, nevertheless, he was not entirely clear on the matter, as will be shown later in this chapter.[31]

Paragraph C defined such exemptions as those relating to state and municipal bonds and salaries of state and local officials. Paragraph D provided for three kinds of returns, namely, (1) that of an individual for himself; (2) that of a guardian or executor for the person for whom he acted; (3) that of a person or corporation required to withhold the tax and pay it to the government. Paragraph E provided for the time and manner of paying the tax. The new provision of this part of the law was a very broad application of the English principle of "stoppage at the source." Paragraph F provided penalties for failure to make a return or for making a fraudulent return. Paragraph G related to the corporation tax which was imposed at the rate of 1%, though a corporation was not allowed an exemption similar to that allowed an individual.

One of the unique features of the bill was the adaptation of the British method of collection at the source.[32] Some of the Civil War income tax laws had provided for the government to withhold the federal income tax from salaries of its employees and for certain other limited use of this method, and Hull had incorporated it in a proposed excise tax on individuals in 1912, but no previous attempt had

[29] *Proceedings of the New York State Bar Association,* Jan. 30, 1914, p. 124, quoted in *Cong. Rec.* 51: app. 103.

[30] For a discussion of the Regulations see below, pp. 99, 100; 500, note 70; 527 ff.

[31] See below, p. 82.

[32] As would be expected, British precedent exerted great influence on American income tax law, not only in 1913 but also before and since.

been made in the United States of such an extensive application of this administrative method. Whenever corporations paid out interest or dividends of any amount or when corporations or individuals paid out rent, interest, premiums, wages, or salaries or any such annual incomes amounting to $4000 or over, they were required not only to file returns giving information to this effect, but also to withhold the tax from the payee and to pay it directly to the government unless the taxpayer had filed, with the collector of Internal Revenue for the proper district, a return showing the deductions to which he was entitled. The original intention of the law was to provide for the assessment of this tax by the government after an individual or corporation had submitted a return, instead of self-assessment by the taxpayer; hence, it was thought important that the taxpayer should file his return in the same district as that in which the payer of his rent or interest filed returns showing tax withheld for the government.[33]

The author of the income tax section of the bill hoped that this method of collection would result in increased yield of revenue for the government at less cost, and that, at the same time, it would save the taxpayer much annoyance. It was realized, however, that such a system was not in harmony with the application of graduated rates because an agent who withheld the tax might have no information about income of the taxpayer from other sources. The Report of the Committee on Ways and Means cited in this connection the results of an investigation just completed by a British parliamentary commission on the relation of withholding the tax at the source to the graduation of rates. Its decision to retain the principle of withholding doubtless greatly influenced the Committee of the House.

Hull thought also that this method of collecting the tax would offset some of the inequities and inadequacies resulting from the poor assessment of intangible property by the states and, moreover, that it would reach non-resident citizens who had previously contributed little to the support of the government. He reminded his colleagues that many states already had laws to require banks to withhold and pay taxes for stockholders. He cited British practice, a "long-standing and well-understood and well-established and highly satisfactory method of enforcing this tax," and quoted from the report of the parliamentary commission mentioned above, which stated that this method of collection had resulted in doubling the amount of revenue with the same rate of tax; that it had almost en-

[33] This idea was not carried out in practice. From the beginning of the administration of this law the taxpayer completed the return and paid the amount he himself computed. This practice is commonly referred to as "self assessment" though, of course, the return is subject to audit by the Bureau of Internal Revenue which may assess additional taxes or grant refunds.

tirely removed the payers' objections to the annoyance of the tax, and claimed that this, "more than any other feature of the entire law," had contributed to the popular approval of the tax.[34]

There were many comments and questions, of course, and some criticism concerning this procedure of withholding which appeared rather complicated to members of the House. Hull had to explain several times how a taxpayer could secure an abatement or refund from the government if too much tax were paid or assessed at the source. There was some confusion in the minds of several members as to how the tax would be retained in the case of coupon bonds. It was shown that the tax would be withheld by the bank or whoever cashed the coupons, and that they would be taxable only once, regardless of the number of hands through which they passed.[35]

Graham (Rep., Pa.) objected to the plan of collection at the source, saying:

> It means that you are creating a horde of collectors who are not official; that you are constituting every man through whose hands passes a sum of money coming to you as income a collector to assess and withhold from you the amount of the normal tax, and he, not you, must pay it over to the collector.[36]

There was some criticism too of the sections relating to life insurance. The mutual companies wanted to be exempt from payment of the 1% normal tax. They sent letters to their stockholders claiming that they deserved the same treatment as fraternal and other exempt associations "operating for mutual protection . . . and paying no part of their net income to any stockholder or individual." Similarly they claimed that their so-called dividends were returns of premiums, not earnings, and were not properly subject to the tax.[37]

Hull answered these contentions immediately by statements to the press that this position of the companies was untenable in view of the language of the law, the statements of the companies to their policyholders, and the statements of authorized agents and sworn reports of the companies to various state authorities.[38] Two weeks later [39] he gave out a formal statement in which he showed that life insurance companies had made a practice of picturing to the public their large profits, but when the government proposed a tax of 1% on them, the companies abandoned these contentions. The word "surplus," he claimed, was "used as bait to catch policyholders . . . though the surplus is never divided and remains as a valuable asset."

34 *Cong. Rec.* 50: 1302.
35 *Cong. Rec.* 50: 508-513.
36 *Cong. Rec.* 50: 1300.
37 This question had, supposedly, been threshed out in connection with the corporation excise tax. See above, Chap. II, p. 56.
38 New York *Times*, April 16, April 19, 1913.
39 New York *Times*, May 5, 1913.

The proposed tax would apply "to any actual gains or profits arising from such investments. . ."

Many members of Congress were not satisfied with the wording of the law and proposed several changes when the draft was submitted to the caucus. As a result Hull compromised and, although he stated that the aim was to follow the 1909 law as closely as possible, in reality he admitted the contention that some of the dividends paid to policyholders represented return of premium. He said:

> We reduced it to a mixed question of law and fact as to what these dividends contain and not solely a question of law, if the contention of the gentlemen representing the insurance companies is correct, and that being so, if they return actual premium overcharges at any time by this method to the policyholders the fact would be disclosed and no tax would accrue. If, on the contrary, these dividends embrace actual profits . . . then the tax would fasten on it. . .[40]

On the floor of the house he introduced several amendments to clarify the meaning. For example, the law as first drafted by the Committee permitted insurance companies to deduct "the net addition, if any, required by law to be made within the year to reserve funds and the sums other than dividends or return of premium payments paid within the year on policy and annuity contracts." At the Committee's suggestion, this clause was amended so as to omit the words "return of premium payments" and to add "required reserves." Mutual fire insurance companies were given liberal treatment "on account of the hazards of the business." Such companies were authorized not to return as income any portion of the premium deposits returned to their policyholders, but to return as taxable income "all income received by them from all other sources plus such portions of the premium deposits as are retained by the companies for purposes other than the payment of losses and expenses."

The size of the personal exemption was debated at some length. Copley (Ill.) offered an amendment to increase the personal exemption to $5000 and to graduate the rates to a maximum of 68% on income in the highest bracket, that is, on those parts of an individual's income over $1,000,000. His reasons were that this would be the best way to equalize opportunities because, with the revenue which such a tax would bring, the government could carry on research in health, sanitary science, and medicine.[41] He advocated that part of the proceeds be returned to the states.

Gillett (Rep., Mass.) proposed that the rates begin at ½ of 1% on income in excess of $1000 so that the mass of people would have

[40] *Cong. Rec.* 50: 1240.

[41] *Cong. Rec.* 50: 1246. He was correct in predicting that "within ten years some such law will be written on the statute books of this country by the American Congress."

some appreciation of the costs of government.[42] One member proposed making the highest surtax rate 6%;[43] another 8%[44] and, in addition, one wanted to increase the exemption for a married person to $6000 with an additional $500 for each child.[45] Rogers (Mass.) offered an amendment to permit individuals to deduct "gifts to any corporation or association organized and operated exclusively for religious, charitable, benevolent, or educational purposes, no part of the net income of which inures to the benefit of any private stockholder or individual."[46] One or two members endeavored to insert clauses to tax the salary of the President of the United States, federal judges, and state bonds, but it was generally conceded that such taxes would be unconstitutional.[47] Needless to say, none of the above-mentioned amendments offered by members of the minority party was accepted.

Very little attention was paid to the question of allocating profits from sale of property acquired before 1913, probably because the problem was not generally understood. It was noted above that Hull emphasized the importance of distinguishing between income and capital. Some of the Committee members had privately informed their colleagues that all profits from such sales were to be reported as income for the year in which sold, regardless of the date of purchase. One Republican member protested against this interpretation but did not attempt to introduce an amendment to change it.[48] When this question had come up earlier, Hull stated that the corporation excise laws had been interpreted to mean that capital gains were to be prorated over the years the property had been held,[49] and after agreeing that profits would be the difference between cost and sales price he said:

> My judgment would be that as to an occasional purchase of real estate not by a dealer or one making the buying and selling a business this bill would only apply to profits on sales where the land was purchased and sold during the same year.[50]

This interpretation was not upheld by the Commissioner when the law was put into operation.

Debate on the income tax sections of the tariff bill was completed May 7, but no vote was taken at that time. The entire tariff bill was passed May 8 and sent to the Senate.

42 *Cong. Rec.* 50: 1247.
43 Murdock (Kan.) (*Cong. Rec.* 50: 1252).
44 Kelly (Penn.) (*Cong. Rec.* 50: 1251).
45 Britten (Ill.) (*Cong. Rec.* 50: 1254).
46 *Cong. Rec.* 50: 1259. Such deductions were allowed in the Act of 1917.
47 See below, Chap. XX, p. 460.
48 *Cong. Rec.* 50: 1262.
49 *Cong. Rec.* 50: 513.
50 For the text of the bill as passed by the House see *Cong. Rec.* 50: 1422-1424.

Throughout the discussion, no question was raised as to the desirability of an income tax and very little opposition was made to any of the sections. This was due in part, of course, to the overwhelming number of Democrats in the House. In part it was due to the general acceptance of the income tax principle. One of the minority members expressed his attitude as follows:

> The time for debate upon the question as to whether or not we shall have an income tax has long since passed. It is not necessary for one to express one's private views with reference to such a measure. The majority of this House have felt it to be their duty to present a bill upon this subject, and have asked the House to pass it. They have presented the one that is now under consideration, and it seems to me that it is the duty of the members upon this side of the House not to hinder, obstruct, or interfere with its passage, but to aid in making it such a measure as will give the question of an income tax a fair and full test by the American people when put in actual practice.[51]

AMENDMENTS OF THE SENATE FINANCE COMMITTEE

In this session of Congress the Senate Finance Committee [52] began work on the revenue bill as soon as it was introduced into the House. Indeed, Senators Simmons, Smith, Williams, and Hughes were in conference with Underwood even before that time. It was announced in March that there would be "no repetition of the Democratic fight over the Wilson-Gorman bill in 1893." [53] The House bill was reported in the Senate May 9, submitted to the Senate Finance Committee May 16, and reported back to the Senate July 11.

Although the Senate Finance Committee made over three hundred amendments to the tariff bill, they were, for the most part, changes that did not disturb the underlying principles of the House

[51] George S. Graham (Rep., Pa.) *Cong. Rec.* 50: 1299. The minority report of the Committee on Ways and Means made only the following short reference to the income tax: "In presenting this bill the committee is met with a threatened deficit in revenue of about $100,000,000, which it is compelled to meet by extraordinary methods of taxation used heretofore in time of war. As a revenue measure the committee at the very outset confess this bill to be a failure." (63d Congress, 1st Session, *House Report*, 5.)

[52] The members of the Senate Finance Committee were:

Democrats	*Republicans*
F. M. Simmons (N. C.), Ch.	Boies Penrose (Pa.)
William J. Stone (Mo.)	Henry C. Lodge (Mass.)
John S. Williams (Miss.)	Porter J. McCumber (N. D.)
Charles F. Johnson (Maine)	Reed Smoot (Utah)
Benjamin F. Shively (Ind.)	Jacob H. Gallinger (N. H.)
Hoke Smith (Ga.)	Clarence Clark (Wyo.)
Charles Thomas (Colo.)	Robert M. La Follette (Wis.)
Ollie James (Ky.)	
William Hughes (N. J.)	
Thomas Gore (Okla.)	

[53] New York *World*, March 20, 1913.

measure.[54] This was also the case with the modifications made in the income tax section by the subcommittee under the chairmanship of Williams and by the Finance Committee as a whole.

One of the first sections considered by the subcommittee was that dealing with insurance companies. It was decided to exempt from gross income dividends paid to policyholders by "genuine mutual insurance companies." [55] Next it was decided to fix March 1, 1913 instead of January 1, 1913 as the date from which the tax would be computed because the ratification of the Sixteenth Amendment was not certified until February 25.[56] At the request of representatives from certain large cities, a clause was inserted to exempt incomes from those corporations whose profits accrued to any state, municipality, or other unit of local government.[57]

Another important revision was made in the House bill to permit a corporation to deduct from gross income interest paid on an amount of indebtedness equal to the sum of one half of its combined bonded indebtedness and paid-up capital stock instead of on an amount equal to the capital stock.

One of the most important changes of this committee was the reduction of the personal exemption from $4000 to $3000 but an additional $1000 was allowed in case the taxpayer was married, and an additional $500 was allowed for each dependent child.[58] Simmons was very much opposed to these allowances for dependents, saying that for the sake of the effectiveness of the tax as a revenue producer there must be some limit to the amount of exemptions.[59]

The Committee rejected a plan submitted by Hitchcock (Dem., Neb.) to tax the tobacco trust out of business.[60] This was a plan to increase the tax rate according to the degree of the monopoly. The Committee learned that the President did not favor such a tax, hence

54 New York *Times,* June 21, 1913 said, "It is a safe generalization to say that the Senate amendments carry out the principles of the House bill more completely than the House did itself." For the Committee bill see *Cong. Rec.* 50: 2507-2515.

55 New York *Times,* June 4, 5, 6, 1913.

56 New York *Times,* June 5, 1913. See above, Chap. II, pp. 68 and 69.

57 This amendment was evidently first suggested by the controller of New York City who feared that the city might have to pay a tax on its share of the earnings of the Interborough Rapid Transit. Lewis (Ill.) presented the case of Chicago which received revenue from street car companies. (New York *Times,* June 10, 21, 25, 1913.)

58 New York *Times,* June 25, 1913. The allowance for dependents was eliminated in conference.

59 New York *Times,* July 1, 1913.

60 New York *Times,* July 1, 1913; *Cong. Rec.* 50: 2020. This was called the McReynolds plan because it was suggested by the Attorney General, later justice of the Supreme Court. The amendment provided that if the company produced or sold at least one-fourth and not more than one-third of the total amount of any line of production in the United States open to general manufacture or production, the tax would be five times the normal tax, or 5%; if the production were more than one-third and less than one-half the total amount, the tax would be ten times the normal tax; if the production were one-half or more of the total amount, the tax would be twenty times the normal tax.

gave it little consideration. The various amendments of the Senate Committee added $5,000,000 to the revenue expected from the income tax.

ACTION OF THE CAUCUS

The Democratic party had a majority of only six votes in the Senate when the Sixty-third Congress convened in April. For the tariff measure, this would certainly be cut down by the votes of the Louisiana members and possibly by those from Colorado, also, in both cases because the proposed revision put sugar on the free list. Before the debate on the bill was finished this slender margin was further reduced by the death of Johnston (Ala.). Therefore Senate leaders had to line up every vote. They were not sure about some of the opposition. Although some of the Republicans were "progressive" [61] so far as the tariff was concerned and, in general, favored the income tax, it was feared, early in May, that La Follette was prepared to criticize the income tax section because he thought it would not operate so well as the Wisconsin state income tax law which he had written.[62] This fear of La Follette's opposition proved groundless, however.

The Republican members of the Senate were troubled over the impending banking and currency legislation, so drew up their plans to delay everything, including the tariff, in the hope that they could gain assurances that the banking bill would be postponed until the next session.[63]

There was also a group of Democratic senators who were very independent, obstinate, or radical — the exact characterization to be applied depending on the point of view. These men — for example, Reed (Mo.), Vardaman (Miss.), and Ashurst (Ariz.) — became extremely critical of the President's program in his second administration. In 1913 they went along but even so their support did not appear to be entirely dependable. Furthermore the Senate never tolerated such discipline as Underwood maintained in the House.

Fearful lest the measure drawn up by the Committee might be radically amended on the floor of the Senate, the President requested

61 La Follette, Cummins, Borah, Bristow, Clapp, Crawford, Kenyon, Norris, and Gronna. Poindexter was the only Senator elected as a Progressive. (Washington *Star*, March 27, 1913.)

62 ". . . La Follette still has Presidential ambitions, and does not intend to place himself in the position of having helped to carry out the Democratic platform." (New York *Times*, May 26, 1913.)

63 New York *Times*, August 10, 1913. Even before the Sixty-second Congress adjourned, the President-elect gave several speeches which made financial circles nervous. For example, he said, that "the banking system of this country does not need to be indicted. It is convicted." After the banking and currency bill was introduced in July, the price of government bonds dropped. Secretary of the Treasury McAdoo accused the leading New York City banks of being engaged in a conspiracy to depress their price.

that the party members go over it in caucus, assuming that the decisions of such a meeting would be somewhat binding.[64]

By the first of July the caucus had finished many of the tariff schedules and so proceeded with the income tax section. The discussions were so lively that the leaders feared for a time that progress on the entire bill would be halted.[65] The first stumbling block was over the matter of personal exemptions, because many Senators thought the law should permit deductions for any number of children, and would have liked to include dependent parents and relatives as well. Simmons, however, was adamant against any such proposal, as he had been in the Committee. In fact, he said that unless the number of children to be benefited by the exemption was limited, he would advocate the restoration of the House exemption limit of $4000.[65] It was finally agreed therefore to accept the Committee limitation of two children for each of which the $500 exemption would be allowed.

The caucus vacillated on accepting the subcommittee's exemption of so-called "dividends," that part of the premium returned by mutual insurance companies to individual policyholders or credited to them on the companies' books. On one vote the exemption was struck out but on a later vote it was again inserted.[66]

The caucus accepted the Committee amendment to tax individual stockholders on the undivided profits of a corporation, although protests were made on the grounds that (1) it would be very difficult to ascertain such profits and (2) that, inasmuch as the stockholders would again have to pay taxes when the surplus was distributed as dividends, the same amount would be taxed twice.[67]

Hitchcock again made a fight for his tobacco trust tax amendment. Upon its defeat, by a vote of 23 to 18, he withdrew from the caucus, announced that he would not be bound by any of its decisions, and that he would offer his amendment again on the floor of the Senate.

This action of Hitchcock forced the leaders to try to bind party members to support the bill as drawn up by the caucus and to promise not to vote for any amendments proposed by Republicans.

64 Early in the session the President had taken a direct hand in the drafting by requesting each Senator to advise him personally just what amendments were desired. He would give them careful consideration and either explain that they did not meet with his approval or would request that they be incorporated in the bill. (New York *World*, April 10, 1913.) This was in great contrast to the "indirect" methods of President Taft.

65 New York *Times*, July 1, 1913.

66 New York *Times*, July 1, July 2, 1913.

67 New York *Times*, July 6, 1913. For a later adoption of this principle see Chap. XVII below.

Opposition to this pledge delayed the caucus for several days.[68] Finally the measure was agreed upon with six dissenting votes.[69]

In order to shorten debate on the floor of the Senate, a suggestion was made in the caucus that certain members be assigned to defend particular sections. This idea was first rejected because it was thought that "a Senator's right to speak could not be curtailed" but when the President urged that "something be done" the Finance Committee drew up a list of assignments. The income tax section was given to Williams and Hughes.[70]

THE INCOME TAX IN THE SENATE

The tariff bill was reported back to the Senate with committee amendments on July 18, but very little progress was made for more than a month because of the Republican filibuster and long speeches by Democrats whom the leaders were unable to restrain.[71] Attempted compromises which were offered proved of no avail. Unable to get a decision on about one hundred schedules Simmons finally decided to pass over those in dispute and to take them up after the income tax section had been considered.[72]

In accordance with this plan, Williams, on August 26, offered memoranda which had been prepared by Thurlow M. Gordon, an assistant to the Attorney General, Congressman Hull, and Senator Shields as answers to the contention of Senator Root that the income tax law could not constitutionally apply to income received before the passage of the law.[73] In July, Root had introduced an amendment that the tax be computed on incomes accruing from the time of the passage of the Act. The Senate Finance Committee had so far agreed with him as to make the tax apply to income received from March 1, 1913 instead of from January 1, 1913. Root argued that the income once accrued becomes principal, "and no law hereafter can tax it without apportionment, any more than we can tax now the income that was received 10 years ago without apportionment." [74] Hull's reply showed that previous income tax laws of the United States as well as those of England had applied to

[68] *La Follette's Magazine,* July 12, 1913, p. 11. Upon the withdrawal of Hitchcock, Simmons and Kern issued statements that the defeat of the tobacco trust amendment did not imply that the Democrats opposed it, but that the caucus did not consider it wise to deal with the trust problem in a tariff bill.

[69] Those who voted against it were Reed, Pomerene, Vardaman, Hollis, O'Gorman, and Hughes. The measure was "steam rollered" through the caucus according to La Follette. (*La Follette's Magazine,* Oct. 11, 1913.)

[70] New York *Times,* July 22, 1913.

[71] New York *Times,* Aug. 10, 1913.

[72] *Cong. Rec.* 50: 3770.

[73] *Cong. Rec.* 50: 3766 ; also printed as a separate, 63d Congress, 1st Session, *Senate Document* 171.

[74] *Cong. Rec.* 50: 2467.

income that had accrued before the act was passed, that even the Pollock decision did not hold the tax invalid because the income could become capital and escape the tax and that the United States Supreme Court had held that the tax was "payable by the person because of his income, according to its amount and without reference to the way in which it was obtained." The special assistant to the Attorney General stated in his memorandum that the definition assumed by Root's argument built up an unduly elaborate legal fiction, unwarranted by authority and very unfortunate in its results, for the following reasons: (1) that the word "income" does not necessarily imply *"a specific fund* from which the tax must be taken"; (2) that the word "upon" usually means "with reference to," or "based upon" or "measured by," not "carved out of"; (3) that courts did not go through an elaborate fiction to prove that the income is still income at the time the tax attaches and (4) "that the economic conception of an income tax is against Mr. Root's interpretation." [75]

No further action was taken on this matter and the Senate proceeded to the consideration of the amendments made by the Committee on Finance. When the secretary read that section of the law which stated the rates, Borah rose to say that while he would not introduce an amendment, he thought the rates should be increased in the higher brackets and that the surtax should begin on incomes in excess of $10,000 instead of $20,000. This started a very animated discussion, so that Borah did offer an amendment which three of his Republican colleagues – Lodge, Norris, and Bristow – revised. It would have made the surtax begin at 1% on income over $10,000 and not over $30,000 and reach the highest rate, 5%, on income over $100,000. The amendment was defeated by a vote of 17 to 47.[76] To the surprise of the majority leaders, nine regular Republicans joined the Democrats in opposing it.[77] The more radical members, however, were not discouraged by this action and the next day Bristow, a Progressive Republican, introduced an amendment to increase the rates so that the highest would be 10% on incomes over $100,000.[78]

As soon as this amendment was defeated, La Follette presented one with the same maximum rate but with different gradations. Williams endeavored to end the discussion because he did not want the caucus agreement broken. He told his colleagues that he declined "to let the question as to what shall be the points of demarcation in the graduation of the income tax be dignified into a great and important national issue," and that he was not convinced that the

75 *Cong. Rec.* 50: 3767-3768. President Wilson added a fifth reason, namely, that Root's interpretation would seriously impair the effectiveness of the tax as a war measure.

76 *Cong. Rec.* 50: 3773-3774.

77 New York *Times,* Aug. 27, 1913.

78 *Cong. Rec.* 50: 3805.

amendments would do otherwise than complicate the bill.[79] His effort was fruitless. The insurgent pressure from both parties was too strong. For the next two days no progress was made. Because of the high personal exemption, some of the conservatives, for example, Lodge, assailed the measure as the "pillage of a class." He favored the suggestion of McCumber for a small tax beginning with 1/10 of 1% on incomes of $1000 and stepping up as income increased so that every citizen would realize his responsibility to the government.[80] This day's session was the most exciting since the tariff bill was introduced and threatened a serious outcome for the regular Democrats unless matters were brought under control. Vardaman had "bolted" on the La Follette amendment, and three other Democrats — Ashurst of Arizona, Thompson of Kansas, and Reed of Missouri — "intimated that they only refrained from doing likewise because they hoped the Finance Committee would recommend increases." [81] These "radicals" boasted that they could secure from twenty-five to twenty-seven party members to vote for increases. The Republicans who favored higher rates — probably partly to embarrass the Democrats — were divided in about the same proportion.[82] The majority leaders did not wish to have a revolt on the floor, hence called a caucus for September 1.[83] As a result, they reached a compromise [84] which satisfied the Democratic insurgents and also met the approval of the President. It increased the surtax rates to a maximum of 6% on taxable income over $500,000. This practically ended this part of the discussion although on September 9, Bristow, La Follette, and Poindexter again insisted on introducing amendments to increase the rates. The Committee's amendment, which had been adopted on September 6 without a roll call, was retained.[85]

The much disputed problem of how to tax insurance companies equitably was settled by the elimination of all references to the exemption from gross income of dividends paid by mutual life insurance companies because it was thought that if so-called mutual companies were exempt, it would be necessary "to exempt all life insurance companies that issued a mutual participating policy" and the result would be a great loss of revenue.[86]

[79] *Cong. Rec.* 50: 3821.

[80] *Cong. Rec.* 50: 3839. Root also wanted the exemption lowered to $1000. (*Cong. Rec.* 50: 4068.)

[81] New York *Times*, Aug. 29, 1913.

[82] New York *Times*, Aug. 29, 1913.

[83] New York *Times*, Aug. 31, 1913.

[84] Reed tried to make the highest rate 10 per cent but O'Gorman (N. Y.) steadily opposed such radical increases. (New York *Times*, Sept. 6, 1913.)

[85] *Cong. Rec.* 50: 4379.

[86] *Cong. Rec.* 50: 4381. The Committee, however, introduced an amendment to permit mutual marine insurance companies to deduct from gross income amounts repaid to policyholders on account of premiums previously paid by them, plus the interest on such amounts.

When the administrative sections of the bill were debated, La Follette offered an amendment to permit officers of states having income taxes to have access to federal income tax returns of corporations. This was accepted, but when the Senator suggested that he would also like to extend this privilege to the examination of individuals' returns, Williams drew the line for the reason that he thought it would involve too great expense.[87]

Borah asked for a complete annual report by the Commissioner of full statistics of income showing the classification and distribution of income taxpayers by occupation, district, amount of tax paid, and other data such as were later specified in the Act of 1916. Williams replied that the Committee had considered a similar proposal but had rejected it because it did not seem necessary "to provide for such an expensive report that might not be read very widely." He dismissed the idea with the comment:

> We have all sorts of statistical bureaus all around everywhere, and we did not see any use of establishing another one.[88]

It is regrettable that Borah's suggestion was not carried out from the beginning of the income tax administration, instead of waiting till 1916.

The proposal to appoint new collectors and inspectors without regard to the Civil Service laws drew fire from several sources. Sherman (Ill.), who summarized the views of the minority on the bill as a whole, asked if it was necessary to make this exception. He called it "an assault on the civil service," a "legislative precedent," "the first break in the dam." [89] Protests were filed from several Civil Service Reform Associations and other organizations.[90] Lodge introduced an amendment to strike out this provision which he characterized as a perfectly unvarnished attempt to take all these offices out of the classified service and make them the subject of political appointment and personal favoritism.[91] Root, Gallinger, and Cummins also supported this amendment.

The Democrats endeavored to prove that the Civil Service examinations would not select men with necessary maturity and experience because "young men or young women from high schools would pass most flippantly and glibly an examination which others who for 40 or 50 years of our lives have been fairly successful in the transactions of business, who have led honest and sober lives, would find it impossible to pass." [92] Smith (Ga.) explained that the Committee

87 *Cong. Rec.* 50: 3869.
88 *Cong. Rec.* 50: 3872-3873.
89 *Cong. Rec.* 50: 3805.
90 *Cong. Rec.* 50: 3264, 3874, 3875.
91 *Cong. Rec.* 50: 3873.
92 Martine (N. J.). (*Cong. Rec.* 50: 3886.)

had not freed the clerical force from the Civil Service but had expressly distinguished between the clerical force and the field force which he compared to the "highest class and best-paid traveling men for big wholesale or manufacturing plants." [93] To this Lodge replied that there was "nothing very complicated about the duties of a deputy collector." Such a position, he maintained, was no more difficult to fill than a clerical position in any other branch of the service which required "honesty, character, intelligence, good common sense of a reasonable sort, and also a reasonable degree of education." [94]

Upon the defeat of Lodge's amendment, Gallinger presented one which substituted a provision requiring appointments to be made in accordance with the Civil Service Act and added "that hereafter when examinations are held for the positions of deputy collectors, agents and inspectors, the questions shall be so framed as to specifically test the capacity and fitness of the applicants for the several positions." This, too, was defeated.

The Senate did not vote on the income tax section separately from the rest of the tariff bill which was passed by a vote of 44 to 37. The Louisiana Senators were the only Democrats who voted against it. Two Progressive Republicans, Poindexter and La Follette, voted for it.[95]

From the point of view of future developments of income tax problems there were several interesting discussions. One was on the use of the corporate form of business to escape the surtax. The Finance Committee inserted in their draft of the bill a section that required individuals to include as income their share of the gains and profits, divided or distributed or not, of all companies whether corporations or partnerships. A similar phrase had been written into the Civil War laws of 1864 and succeeding years in defining taxable income. This wording was criticized by several Republican Senators, especially Root, who questioned whether a stockholder had a right "to demand a dividend from the profits of a corporation against the judgment of the directors or trustees of the corporation." Such profits, he maintained, "can not . . . be regarded as income of the stockholder until the directors of the corporation have declared a dividend on it." [96] Borah agreed, but pointed out that the Committee was trying to reach income that might otherwise escape taxation. As

[93] *Cong. Rec.* 50: 3881.
[94] *Cong. Rec.* 50: 3883-3884.
[95] *Cong. Rec.* 50: 4617. Fourteen members did not vote.
[96] *Cong. Rec.* 50: 3774. For an outline of later discussions along this line see Chapter XVII, "Revenue Act of 1936." In 1913 Williams said: "This clause gave us more trouble than anything in this bill. The Senate will see that unless we provide for this evil in some way men might escape . . . the additional tax by merely forming themselves [*sic*] or using a brother, wife, or somebody or an office boy." *Cong. Rec.* 50: 5318.

amended on the floor of the Senate the law stated that each taxpayer was to include, "the share to which he would be entitled of the gains and profits, if divided or distributed, whether divided or distributed or not, of all companies, whether incorporated or partnership, formed or fraudulently availed of for the purpose of preventing imposition of such tax through the medium of permitting such gains and profits to accumulate instead of being divided or distributed. . ." Accumulation of surplus was not to be construed as evidence of a purpose to escape the tax unless the Secretary of the Treasury certified that in his opinion such accumulation was unreasonable for the purpose of the business.[97]

Another interesting discussion was that on the concept of taxable income, a subject that apparently was no clearer to Senators then than now, as is shown by the following colloquy:[98]

MR. CUMMINS. If I understand this aright, if I have a farm and sell it for a thousand dollars, the money I would receive as the purchase price of the farm would be accounted as income ; but if anyone were to give me a thousand dollars during the year, or if I were to receive it by bequest . . . , that would not be accounted as income. . . If the one is income, why is not the other ? . . .

MR. SHIVELY. Mr President, if I understand the Senator correctly, he is inquiring, for the purpose of illustrating what he has in mind, whether the price of a piece of land sold during the year would be regarded as income. My answer is that it would not be. The price of that land would be principal. . .

MR. CUMMINS. But suppose 10 years ago I had bought a horse for $900, and this year I had sold him for $1000, what would I do in the way of making a return ? . . .

MR. WILLIAMS. . . That thousand dollars is a part of the Senator's receipts for this year, and being a part of his receipts, that much will go in as part of his receipts, and from it would be deducted his disbursements and his exemptions and various other things.

MR. CUMMINS. Would the price I paid for the horse originally be deducted ?

MR. WILLIAMS. No, because it was not a part of the transactions in that year ; but if the Senator turned around and bought another horse, that year, it would be deducted. . .

MR. BRISTOW. Mr. President, I desire to ask a question. . . As I understood the question of the Senator from Iowa, it was, if he bought a horse 10 years ago for $100.

MR. CUMMINS. Nine hundred dollars.

MR. BRISTOW. And sold it this year for a thousand dollars, whether or not that thousand dollars would be counted as a part of his income for this year, regardless of what he paid for the horse 10 years ago. Is that correct ?

[97] *Cong. Rec.* 50: 4380. A year later Hull commented on this section saying: "Although some of the Senators . . . expressed a contrary view, the fact should not be overlooked that the government has full power to impose and collect an income tax with respect to the undistributed profits of a stockholder." (*Cong. Rec.* 51: app. 103.)

[98] *Cong. Rec.* 50: 3775-3776.

MR. WILLIAMS. No; I did not say that. It would be part of his gross receipts for the year, of course, but it may not necessarily be a part of his net receipts, and therefore not a part of his income that is taxable.

MR. CUMMINS. But I asked the Senator from Mississippi specifically whether, in the case I put, the price that was originally paid for the horse could be deducted from the price received.

MR. WILLIAMS. The price paid 10 years ago? No; of course not. How could it? When a man puts in his return for his income of the previous year in order to be taxed he puts down everything he has received and everything he has paid out, subject to the exemptions and limitations otherwise provided in the bill. . .

Cummins objected to the idea that the capital of the individual must be preserved intact. He argued that the income tax was not concerned with capital but with the income that it earned. If the capital were lost, there would be a diminished income the following year upon which to levy the tax. He argued:

the taxable income should not be depleted by withdrawing from it a sum sufficient to maintain the capital unless the income arose out of a business in which the capital was employed.

He used as an example a loss of $20,000 from operations on the Board of Trade which offset $20,000 received from practice of a profession so that there would be no taxable income. He thought losses in trade should be confined to the trade or business out of which the profit or income was made. Brandegee, however, pointedly asked whether or not the Senator considered as taxable the profits made from speculation. To the answer, "unquestionably," he then asked why, logically, losses should not then be allowable deductions. "They should be," said Cummins, "if the business, being reckoned up at the end of the year, shows a profit. . . If it shows a loss, there would be no income arising from it, and it should not be taxed." The Senator continued his argument by protesting against the clauses which permitted allowance for depreciation but he made an exception for mines.

When Weeks asked if any deduction could be allowed for depreciation in the value of stocks and securities, Williams replied:

I have never thought about that, but I do not think that cuts any figure because the depreciation in the value of the stock is not like a depreciation by reason of the wear and tear arising out of the use of property. A man's income would still remain an income regardless of the value of his property. My plantation this year might yield me, say, $3000, and next year the same plantation might yield me $4000 or $2000; my income would be measured by what the plantation yielded me and not by the value of the plantation. Meanwhile, the property might go up in value or it might go down in value. That would have nothing to do with the income, nor would the value of your stock in the market have anything to do with the dividends which you receive upon your stock.[99]

Weeks was not satisfied, however, and presented the case of a sale of stocks at a loss. Williams thought that such transactions were mere changes of capital and principal from stocks into money. "It seems to me," replied Weeks, ". . . that it would be a shrinkage of my principal ; and, that under the reading of this bill, I am not sure but what that loss . . . could be deducted against my income. . ." The Senator was informed, however, that the depreciation clause could not possibly refer to stocks.[100]

Only one member mentioned the desirability of making a distinction between earned and unearned income. That was Crawford (S. D.). He offered an amendment to exempt earned income up to $20,000, that is, income which he defined as "earned in personal service, trade, and vocations where no property income is involved." He advocated making up the deficit which would result from this action by levying an additional income tax on large incomes from invested property and by an inheritance tax. The idea appeared to be understood by so few members that it was not pressed." [101]

THE CONFERENCE REPORT

There were not many obstacles to arriving at an agreement on the different proposals of the two houses. One of the most difficult sections, that relating to the personal exemption, was agreed upon, said Hull, "after protracted discussion and earnest controversy, hence as not infrequently occurs in such circumstances, the language of the paragraph is not clear nor is it quite in harmony with the assessment provisions of the law. . ." [102]

The rates accepted by the Senate at the close of their debate were the ones incorporated in the bill. The Conference adopted the Senate amendment limiting the amount of depletion of mines each year to 5% of the gross value of the output of the mine. The House provision requiring return of income for the entire year 1913 was

[99] *Cong. Rec.* 50: 3849.

[100] *Cong. Rec.* 50: 3849-3850.

[101] *Cong. Rec.* 50: 3815. The Senator later introduced a resolution that "the Committee on Finance be directed to investigate and ascertain the difference in character between income immediately and directly derived by an individual from the carrying on . . . of his profession, trade, and vocation, and income derived from property or investment in capital and to report an amendment which will make a just discrimination in the rate of levy in favor of incomes immediately . . . derived from the exercise of a profession, trade, or calling, as compared with income derived from property and capital investment." (*Cong. Rec.* 50: 3837.)

[102] *Proceedings of the New York State Bar Association,* January 30, 1914 ; reprinted in *Cong. Rec.* 51: app. 102. Although Hull was not one of the members of the Conference Committee he was consulted by them because he was regarded "as the ablest exponent of that question in Congress." (New York *Times,* Sept. 22, 1913.)

modified so as to include only income from March 1, 1913. Collection at the source was to begin November 1, 1913.

The Conferees agreed to permit computation of net income on an accrued or on a cash basis, whereas the corporation excise tax was based on cash transactions only. "Differences of opinion among members of the two Houses of Congress and expert accountants and others are responsible for the lack of harmony of terms prescribing in each instance the exact basis upon which the accounting shall be made," said Hull some time afterward.

The Senate provision for an appropriation of $1,200,000 for administration was reduced to $800,000.

The Conference Committee amended the Senate provision relative to appointment of employees without regard to Civil Service requirements by inserting the phrase "not including the clerical force below the grade of chief of division employed in the Bureau of Internal Revenue in the city of Washington, D. C."

The following excerpt from the report of the Conference Committee summarizes other important changes :

> The House provision which only exempted profits accruing to States and their political subdivisions from the operation of their essential governmental agencies is modified to the extent that all such profits accruing from public utilities shall also be exempt.
>
> The House provision exempting from tax, labor, agricultural or horticultural organizations, mutual savings banks, and fraternal beneficiary societies is extended to business leagues, chambers of commerce, or boards of trade not organized for profit and to civic organizations operated exclusively for the promotion of social welfare.
>
> Life insurance companies and mutual marine insurance companies are allowed exemptions to the extent of the actual premium overcharge returned or credited to policyholders.
>
> The House provision limiting deductions by corporations of interest paid on indebtedness to an amount not exceeding their paid-up capital stock is extended so as to permit such deduction to the amount of such interest paid on not exceeding one-half of the sum of the interest-bearing indebtedness of the corporation and its paid-up capital stock.
>
> The House provision imposing the income tax on corporations for the year 1913 is modified in that the existing excise law is continued in lieu thereof until March 1, 1913.
>
> The conference adopted the Senate amendment providing that no contract entered into after the act takes effect shall be valid in regard to any Federal income tax imposed on a person liable to such tax.[103]

The Conference Committee issued its report September 29, and President Wilson signed the bill October 3. The measure had been under consideration since April. It was in the House one month and in the Senate over four months.

[103] 63d Congress, 1st Session, *House Report* 86, p. 26.

SUMMARY OF THE LAW

Inasmuch as there has been much detailed discussion of the most important parts of the law in the preceding pages, the following summary will be brief.[104]

The law was written as Section II of the Act to Reduce Tariff Duties and to Provide Revenue for the Government, and for Other Purposes.[105]

A tax of 1% was levied on the taxable net income of every citizen of the United States, whether residing at home or abroad, and every resident of the United States, including the Philippine Islands and Puerto Rico.[106] In addition a surtax[107] with graduated rates was levied on the amount of taxable net income of individuals over $20,000. These surtax rates and brackets of income were as follows:

Rates of Surtax Per Cent	*Amount of Income ("Brackets")*
1	$ 20,000 — $ 50,000
2	50,000 — 75,000
3	75,000 — 100,000
4	100,000 — 250,000
5	250,000 — 500,000
6	500,000 —

Income was defined to include "gains, profits, and income derived from salaries, wages, or compensation for personal services . . . or from professions, vocations, businesses, trade, commerce, or sales, or dealings in property . . . also from interest, rent, dividends, securities, or the transaction of any lawful business carried on for gain or profit, or gains or profits and income derived from any source whatever including the income from but not the value of property acquired by gift, bequest, devise or descent."

Proceeds of life insurance and interest from state and United States bonds were exempt. The following deductions were allowed individuals : (1) necessary expenses incurred in carrying on any business, but not including personal or living expenses ; (2) interest paid within the year ; (3) federal, state, and local taxes, but not including taxes assessed against local benefits, that is, ordinary special assessments; (4) losses incurred in trade or from fires, storms, or shipwreck,

104 For a more extensive summary see Blakey, R. G., "The Revenue Act of 1913," *American Economic Review*, IV: 25-46 (March 1914).

105 38 *Statutes at Large* 166.

106 This act provided that in the Philippines and Puerto Rico the law should be administered by the internal revenue officers of those governments and that the revenue collected should accrue to those governments. The 1909 excise tax law applied to the United States only.

107 Then called "additional" tax.

and not compensated for by insurance; (5) bad debts actually charged off; (6) reasonable depreciation and depletion, limited in the case of a mine to 5% of the gross value of the output; (7) dividends from stock of a corporation taxable upon its net income (allowable only in computing normal tax) and (8) the amount of income on which the tax was paid at the source.

A personal exemption of $3000 of income was allowed each taxpayer, $1000 additional if married and living with husband or wife. Inasmuch as the law applied to only ten months of 1913, the exemptions from 1913 income were limited to 5/6 of this amount, or $2500 for a single person and $3333.33 for a man and wife.[108] The additional exemption for married persons was a departure from the Civil War and 1894 acts.

The law exempted compensation of state and local officials and of the President of the United States then in office during the term for which he had been elected and, also, compensation of federal judges for terms of office which began before the passage of the law.

In writing the 1913 law the authors profited by the litigation over certain sections of the 1909 excise tax law. The 1913 law did not impose the tax on the transaction of corporate business or on the privilege of doing business in a corporate capacity, but on the income of the corporation. It did not require that a company be engaged in business. The only requirement was that it should have a net income.

The rate of tax on corporations was made the same as that of the normal tax on individuals, 1% upon net income, but without any flat exemption such as that allowed by the 1909 law.

Deductions allowed to a corporation were: (1) all ordinary and necessary expenses paid within the year on the maintenance and operation of its business or properties; (2) all losses actually sustained within the year and not compensated by insurance, including a reasonable allowance for depreciation and, for insurance companies, the "net addition . . . required by law to be made within the year to reserve funds and the sums other than dividends paid within the year on policy and annuity contracts," and (3) interest on indebtedness, but not on more than "one-half of the sum of its interest-bearing indebtedness and its paid-up capital stock outstanding at the close of the year;" provided that in the case of indebtedness wholly secured by collateral the subject of sale in ordinary business of such corporation the total interest could be deducted; (4) taxes paid to the United States or any state or foreign government.

[108] The amount of exemption was discussed as much as any feature of the law. Hull, Cordell, "The Income Tax," *Proceedings of the New York State Bar Association* 1914; Blakey, R. G., "The Income Tax Exemption," *Outlook*, 106: 256-260 (Jan. 31, 1914).

The last section of the law repealed the corporation excise tax law but provided that it should be in effect from January 1, 1913 to February 28, 1913. The income tax law would apply to income received thereafter.

The normal tax on individuals was to be collected at the source as far as possible ; that is, a corporation, or employer, or agent, or other "source" of income was to deduct the tax, pay it to the government, and pay the remainder to the individual, providing the income was regular, definite, and amounted, generally speaking, to $3000 or more. In the case of interest on bonds, mortgages or deeds of trust issued by domestic corporations, or interest or dividends paid by foreign corporations the tax was to be withheld even if such income was less than $3000. Arrangements were made to prevent the collection of the same tax more than once.

The income tax returns of corporations were made "public records" but they were open to inspection only upon the order of the President under rules to be prescribed by the Secretary of the Treasury.[109] It was also provided that an officer of a state imposing an income tax could have access to federal corporation returns upon the request of the governor, "at such times and in such manner as the Secretary of the Treasury may prescribe."

Special provisions were made for insurance companies. They were permitted to deduct the "net addition . . . required by law to be made to reserve funds and the sums other than dividends paid within the year on policy and annuity contracts." Other allowances were granted to mutual insurance companies. They were not to include as income "any portion of any actual premium received from any individual policyholder as shall have been paid back or credited to such individual policyholder within such year."

Certain non-profit corporations were exempted, for example, labor or agricultural organizations, fraternal beneficiary societies, lodges, civic leagues, educational, religious, and scientific societies.

Foreign corporations were to compute taxable net income by deducting from gross income the amount of income from business in the United States, expenses of conducting business in the United States, and losses incurred in the United States, defined as for domestic corporations.

Partnerships *per se* were not taxed; each partner was taxed on his

109 The Secretary ruled that returns of corporations were open : (1) to the proper officers of the Treasury Department, (2) to officers of other departments of the Government upon written application to the Secretary of the Treasury, (3) to the courts, on certain conditions, and (4) to stockholders upon application in writing to the Secretary. Less severe restrictions were imposed upon the access to returns of certain corporations listed on a recognized stock exchange and corporations whose stock was advertised for sale in the press.

respective share of the profits, whether distributed or not, just as if it were individual income from some other source.

One section of the law stated that individuals were to return as income for the surtax their respective shares of profits, whether distributed or not, of all corporations formed or fraudulently availed of for the purpose of preventing the imposition of the tax through the medium of permitting gains and profits to accumulate. This provision was written to prevent the use of the corporation to evade the surtax by those whose incomes were large and whose tax would fall in the higher brackets. This section was long held to be unenforceable but, somewhat amended, it has been a part of every law since.

The administrative provisions required that an individual file his return on or before March 1, 1914, and that a corporation file its return the same date, or within 60 days after the close of its fiscal year. Returns were required of all individuals with net income of over $3000. The law specified in detail the information required from corporations. A maximum penalty of $10,000 was provided in case a corporation refused or neglected to make a return or made a false return. An individual who made a false return was guilty of a misdemeanor and liable to a fine not exceeding $2000.

There should also be considered, as part of the law, those sections of the Revised Statutes that related to the collection and assessment of internal revenue taxes. They empowered the Commissioner of Internal Revenue to prescribe forms and regulations for the collection of the tax, to authorize suits for recovery of taxes and penalties, to refund taxes illegally assessed or collected, and to compromise any civil or criminal case arising under the internal-revenue laws.[110]

Particularly important were the Commissioner's duties in drafting rules and regulations for the effective operation of the law. In 1913 many parts of the Income Tax Act were indefinite or contradictory and had to be interpreted by the Commissioner. The difficulties in regard to withholding at the source have been mentioned. Another uncertainty related to the handling of informational returns.

The Commissioner of Internal Revenue issued the first set of regulations October 25, 1913; the second set October 31, 1913, others from time to time, and in January 1914, a complete set of the rulings issued up to that time, under the title, *Regulations No. 33*. The latter was widely circulated in pamphlet form. It was written in non-technical language, for the most part, and was intended to be a synopsis of the law and Treasury Decisions "to assist both the tax-

[110] R. S. Sections 3173, 3176, 3179, 3213, 3214, 3215, 3220-3229. Similar authority had been granted to the Commissioner ever since the establishment of the office in 1862.

payer and the officers charged with its enforcement in complying with the requirements of this law." [111]

So important were the decisions of the Commissioner of Internal Revenue that one commentator wrote:

> It is to the regulations, quite as much as to the law, that the student of income-tax history in the United States will turn in the future, particularly when analyzing the effects of the provision for "collection at the source. . ." [112]

It should be noted, however, that these regulations had the force of law only so long as they were not overturned by the courts, or by other regulations of the Commissioner, or by new legislation. New rulings have been made frequently, in fact continuously, and comprehensive regulations are issued after every important revision of the income tax law.

THE ADMINISTRATION OF THE TAX

The income tax law went into effect October 3, 1913, except for the collection of the tax at the source which began on November 1. The tax applied to income received or accrued from March 1, 1913.

Fortunately the administrative features of the corporation excise tax were retained "in all essential respects." The Commissioner of Internal Revenue in referring to the corporation tax stated: [113]

> Because of the similarity in all essential particulars of the two laws, the merging of the administration of the old law into that of the new was accomplished with the least degree of friction or difficulty. In fact, the organization which had been built up for the administration of the special excise-tax law adjusted itself without interruption to an effective administration of the income-tax law.

There were, however, more corporations subject to the income tax than to the excise tax and there was greater taxability, first, because of the elimination of the flat exemption of $5000; secondly, because the new law applied to unincorporated associations hitherto untaxed; and, thirdly, because dividends received on stock of other taxable corporations had to be included in net income under the 1913 law, whereas they were exempt under the corporation excise tax.[114]

The administration of the personal income tax had to be newly organized. Many problems, described by the Secretary of the Treas-

[111] The history of these early Treasury regulations and rulings is given in Black, H. C., *A Treatise on the Law of Income Taxation*, 2d ed., Chap. II.

[112] "Washington Notes," *Journal of Political Economy*, XXII: 91 (Jan. 1914).

[113] *Report* 1914, p. 15.

[114] The Commissioner of Internal Revenue computed in 1914 that there had been 3.79% more corporate tax returns in 1913 than in 1912 with increase of taxable returns of 209.02% due almost entirely to the removal of the $5000 exemption.

ury as "intricate and difficult," were "involved in the initiation of a new law so far-reaching in its effects and so complicated in its operation." [115] This was particularly true of the section of the law which provided for deduction of the tax at the source. The Committee on Ways and Means, in introducing the bill, had advocated this method of collection in the expectation that it would save the taxpayer annoyance and at the same time practically double the amount of revenue the government would otherwise receive.[116] Those hopes were not borne out. For the Treasury Department as well as for the taxpaying public the plan appeared extremely complicated,[117] and difficulties were not lessened by the fact that only twenty-eight days elapsed between the passage of the Act and the date this provision went into effect. In the meantime the regulations had to be drawn up and promulgated.

The Commissioner of Internal Revenue did all that was possible to make enforcement of this part of the law feasible. His rulings and regulations simplified some of the complexities and reduced the number of forms from 19 to 10. Despite these efforts, individual taxpayers failed to submit properly executed exemption certificates or objected to disclosing their investments to others. Corporations that acted as collecting agencies were under a great burden of detailed labor. One railroad had to double the clerical force at its coupon and interest desk. It has been estimated that this system cost corporations from 10% to 20% of the amount of tax withheld for the government, and, if the tax was paid through a fiscal agent such as a bank or trust company, additional expense was involved.[118]

CONSTITUTIONALITY OF THE LAW

The act was declared constitutional January 24, 1916 in the case of *Brushaber* v. *U. P. R. R. Co.*[119] A stockholder of the railroad filed a bill to enjoin the corporation from complying with the income tax provision of the Tariff Act of October 3, 1913 because the provisions were unconstitutional. It was argued that the law violated the Sixteenth Amendment authorizing a tax upon incomes "from whatever source derived" on the grounds that some income of designated persons and classes was excluded; that it violated the amendment

[115] *Report of the Secretary of the Treasury* 1913, p. 5.

[116] 63d Congress, 1st Session, *House Report* 5, p. XXXVIII.

[117] The Secretary of the Treasury recommended, in December 1915, that the law be amended so that information at the source be substituted for collection at the source. (*Report* 1915, p. 19.) The Commissioner of Internal Revenue made the same request the following year. (*Report of the Secretary of the Treasury* 1916, p. 674.)

[118] Schiff, Mortimer L., "Some Aspects of the Income Tax," *Annals of the American Academy*, 58: 24 (March 1915).

See Chapter XXIII Administration, below.

[119] 240 U. S. 1.

in making its provisions apply retroactively; that it violated the Fifth Amendment of the Constitution on many counts, among which the following are examples: (1) the progressive tax and exempted amounts were based on wealth alone and therefore were repugnant to the due process clause; (2) the duty put upon corporations to collect the tax at the source was repugnant to the due process of law as taking of property without compensation; (3) the collection-at-the-source provision of the law discriminated against owners of corporate bonds in favor of individuals who did not own such property because bondholders were deprived of the use of money withheld during the interval between the deducting and paying of the tax on their bonds, and because, if a corporation that had once paid the tax should fail before turning it over to the government, the bondholder would have to pay the tax a second time; (4) "want of due process" resulted from: (a) the provisions that allowed "individuals to deduct from their gross income dividends paid them by corporations whose incomes were taxed, but did not give such right to corporations"; and (b) the provisions in the matter of personal exemptions that discriminated between a married and a single person, and also between husband and wife who lived together as compared with husband and wife who were separated.

The decision, which was unanimous,[120] was given by Chief Justice White. He said in part:

> So far as the due process clause of the 5th Amendment is relied upon, . . . there is no basis for such reliance since it is equally well settled that such clause is not a limitation upon the taxing power conferred upon Congress by the Constitution; in other words the Constitution does not conflict with itself by conferring upon one hand a taxing power and taking the power away on the other hand by the limitations of the due process clause.

Certain "numerous and minute" contentions were dismissed with the remark that their want of legal merit was at once apparent.

In interpreting the Sixteenth Amendment the Court held that it did not intend to confer power to levy income taxes in a generic sense because Congress already had such power. It did not intend to limit and distinguish between one kind of income tax and another. Its purpose was to relieve Congress from the necessity of apportioning the income tax among the states on the basis of their respective populations.

REVENUE

Receipts for the first ten months that the income tax was in operation, March 1 to December 31, 1913, were only about 40% of the

[120] Justice McReynolds took no part in the decision because of his previous connection with the law as Attorney General.

amount estimated by the Committee on Ways and Means; that is, $28,000,000 from individuals instead of $70,000,000. The total collections from both individuals and corporations were about $71,000,000. The poor estimate is not surprising since there were no adequate data for the original estimates. The experience of collecting the corporation excise tax, however, should have pointed to a low return from the first year's operation of the tax when administrative machinery was not working smoothly.

Not only was the yield much less than expected, but the number filing returns for the first year was smaller than estimated. Only 79,426 persons reported net income of more than $2500 and not over $3333; only 114,484 reported net income of more than $3333 and not over $5000; only 101,718 reported net income of more than $5000 and not more than $10,000. The total number who filed returns showing taxable net income was 367,598. The Committee on Ways and Means had estimated that there would be 425,000 returns.

Receipts for the year 1915 were somewhat more encouraging. The yield of the tax on individuals was $12,792,000 more than in the previous year. The corporation income tax, however, showed a decrease. The number who filed returns was approximately the same. The yield of the income tax for the first three years is shown in Table 7. The yield from 1914 to 1939 is shown in Table 39, in the Appendix below.

TABLE 7

INCOME TAX YIELD BY YEARS [a] — 1914-1916

Fiscal Year	*Individual*			*Corporation Income Tax*	*Total, Individual and Corporation*
	Normal Tax	*Surtax*	*Total Tax*		
1914	$12,728,038	$15,525,497	$28,253,535	$43,127,740[b]	$71,381,275
1915	16,559,493	24,486,669	41,046,162	39,144,532	80,190,694
1916	23,995,777	43,947,818	67,943,595	56,993,657	124,937,252

[a] U. S. Treasury *Statistics of Income* 1920, p. 30.
[b] Includes excise tax, $10,071,077, Act of August 5, 1909.

CHAPTER IV

REVENUE ACT OF 1916 – REVENUE FOR PREPAREDNESS

FISCAL SITUATION BETWEEN 1913 AND 1916

The outbreak of war in Europe, in August 1914, played havoc with both public and private finance even in America.[1] Importations from European countries fell off perceptibly and gradually reached very low levels, hence the revenue from customs duties was unexpectedly small. As anticipated, returns from the corporation income tax also declined because of the fall in business profits.[2] The tax on individual incomes yielded less than half of the amount estimated, as stated in the preceding chapter. Furthermore, receipts from the other internal revenue taxes showed the same trend due to decreased production of distilled spirits and fermented liquor and to the decreased manufacture of cigars and large cigarettes.[3]

The reduction in revenues was not accompanied by a corresponding reduction in appropriations. In addition to increased expenditures within the United States, the difficulties with Mexico and the war in Europe caused unexpected financial demands. In the spring and summer of 1914 the critical situation in Mexico had necessitated additional military funds which amounted to about $8,000,000. As soon as the European war broke out Congress appropriated almost $3,000,000 to bring home stranded Americans, over $5,000,000 to establish a war-risk insurance bureau for American business and $1,000,000 for our foreign embassies which were carrying on much of the business of the belligerents.

It was said by critics of the Administration that much of this extra spending was because of the enormous amounts for "rivers and harbors." Democrats defended themselves, however, by saying that not only were there the difficulties outside the United States which have just been referred to but, in addition, the Post Office Department had been enlarged by the creation of the parcels post system a few years before and this service was still in the developmental stage.

1 Fortunately for the government as well as for business, the Federal Reserve Act was passed in December 1913. Between that time and the outbreak of war the organization had been fairly well completed. As a result trade, banking, and credit were restored to normal conditions much more rapidly than would otherwise have been the case.

2 For the fiscal year ended June 30, 1915, there was collected $39,144,532; for the preceding year, $43,127,740. The returns from individuals showed an increase, perhaps because of improved administration.

3 The net decrease for the fiscal year 1915 as compared with 1914 was $25,906,292. By 1915, nineteen states had passed liquor prohibition laws, of which twelve were in effect before the close of 1915.

EMERGENCY INTERNAL REVENUE ACT OF 1914

Early in September 1914, shortly after the outbreak of war in Europe, President Wilson went before Congress to ask that an additional $100,000,000 be raised through internal taxes. The Administration measure, introduced almost immediately into the House, provided for revenues of $105,000,000 through excises on fermented liquors, wines, and gasoline, supplemented by stamp and other special taxes. There was no mention of increasing the income tax, in the first place, because the Administration thought this would not be wise so soon after the income tax law had been put into effect;[4] and, in the second place, because the Treasury wanted the funds to be available immediately. The bill was passed by the House September 25, by the Senate October 17, and signed by the President October 22. It was to be in force until December 31, 1915.[5]

Before the end of 1915 Americans became uncomfortably aware of the close interrelations of the nations of the world. The "emergency" for which this special legislation was passed in 1914 seemed a simple situation in comparison with the more serious developments later. Trade with Europe was completely dislocated and business in this country was correspondingly upset.

THE ISSUE OF PREPAREDNESS

The extensive use of submarines by the Germans and the consequent loss of American lives on the high seas brought home the realization that physical dangers could not be avoided more easily than economic ones. The civil war continued in Mexico despite American intervention. Villa and his followers became increasing nuisances on the border. United States troops and war-ships were dispatched to protect American property and, if possible, to catch Villa.

As a natural consequence of the general feeling of uneasiness, those who favored increased military expenditures found ample support even among those who were not ordinarily favorable to such policies. "Preparedness" became an issue. Ex-president Theodore Roosevelt was a prominent leader in the big navy group. Several propaganda organizations were formed, for example, the National Defense Society, the National Security League, and the Navy League.

Those who believed that the tactics of these organizations would only create more difficulties formed anti-militaristic societies. One

[4] There was some agitation for the repeal of the collection-at-the-source provision but Underwood served notice that it would not be considered. (New York *Times*, Jan. 30, 1914.)

[5] 38 *Statutes at Large* 745.

of the leaders of this so-called pacifist group was former Secretary of State Bryan who had resigned from the Cabinet in the spring of 1915 because of his disagreement with the President over the *Lusitania* notes.

President Wilson was on the side of the anti-militarists when he addressed Congress in December 1914, but became a more or less unwilling convert to the idea of preparedness as the German submarine warfare became threatening. In the fall of 1915 he made two speeches in which he preached the gospel of strong national defense and as time approached for the opening of Congress, worked out, with the approval of the Cabinet, an extensive program which involved greatly increased expenditures for the army and the navy. Once he took the step, his only hesitancy was over the problem of revenue. In order to avoid complicating the issue by controversy over tax measures, he wished to finance the plan by bond issues, but party leaders persuaded him to abandon this idea.[6]

"Adequate preparation for mobilization and defense" was the theme of the message which the President delivered to the 64th Congress on December 8, 1915. He explained in some detail the plans of the War Department for increasing the number in the standing army and for the development of a reserve of trained citizens. He outlined the navy building program and repeated his request for the passage of the ship purchase bill which had been killed in the Senate in the preceding session.

Squarely he faced the fact that such additional expenditures would be a heavy drain on the Treasury. Quoting a summary of the Report of the Secretary for the preceding year, which was about to be published, the President explained that although there was a surplus of $104,000,000 in June 1915, there would be a deficit of $177,000,000 in June 1916, if the preparedness program were carried out. He advocated the continuance of the emergency revenue act, estimated to yield $41,000,000, and of the duty on sugar,[7] which would provide $15,000,000 and requested, in addition, new revenue of $112,000,000.

His specific suggestions for sources of funds were four excise taxes: (1) one cent a gallon on gasoline and naphtha; (2) fifty cents per horse power on automobiles and internal combustion engines; (3) one cent on bank checks and, (4) twenty-five cents a ton on pig iron, fabricated iron and steel, in order that the government might draw more largely from the profits of the munitions industry. In addition to the measures above he proposed some feasible changes in the income tax, such as lowering the personal

6 New York *Tribune*, Nov. 23, 1915.
7 See above, page 76, note 21; also below, page 111.

exemptions and the minimum upon which the surtax was imposed.[8] The Secretary recommended more specifically (1) that the exemptions be reduced by $1000, that is, to $2000 in the case of a single person and to $3000 for a husband and wife, and (2) that the surtax begin at $10,000 or $15,000.[9]

DIVERGENCE OF VIEWS WITHIN THE MAJORITY PARTY

The preparedness program of the President was not accepted with unanimity by Congress, or even by the Democratic members. "Democratic solidarity is a reminiscence," said one member.[10] The Senate elected as president *pro tempore* James Clarke (Ark.) who had helped to block the ship purchase bill in the previous session and who belonged to the anti-preparedness group.[11] One faction was led by Gore (Okla.). He attempted to compel the adoption by the caucus of a partisan cloture which would be "certain to drive several senators from the support of the President's plan for an increased army and navy." [12] Another clique was led by Reed and Stone, both of Missouri, one or both of whom could almost always be counted on to be at odds with the other members of the party. "The preliminary struggle," commented one paper, "partook of the character of ward politics in a small town." [12]

There were several factions in the House also. The Bryanites led by Bailey (Pa.) were, of course, opposed to the President's idea of national defense. "I regard this preparedness hullabaloo as essentially a rich man's scare," he said.[13] The Tammanyites also were, of course, opposed to whatever the President advocated. Even Kitchin, the floor leader for the Administration, was unable to agree with the President on this issue as well as on some others.[14] In fact, he was regarded as the leader of those Democrats who opposed the President's efforts to secure legislation for national defense.[15] Before Congress opened he was quoted as saying:

> I believe if the people really knew the facts and the fabulous increase of appropriations which the programme demands and could contemplate the danger to our country and its institutions with which it is loaded, that not one disinterested person in a hundred would favor it, but on the contrary, would earnestly oppose it as I shall do in Congress.[16]

[8] *Cong. Rec.* 53: 98.
[9] *Report of the Secretary of the Treasury* 1915, pp. 48-50.
[10] New York *Tribune,* Nov. 28, 1915.
[11] New York *Tribune,* Dec. 5, 1915.
[12] New York *World,* Dec. 2, 1915.
[13] New York *Times,* Feb. 2, 1916.
[14] Washington *Star,* Jan. 26, 1916.
[15] New York *World,* Dec. 1, 1915.
[16] New York *World,* Dec. 1, 1915. Others who attacked the President's program were Saunders (Va.), Chairman of the House Democratic Caucus, Gordon (Ohio), Dies and Callaway (Tex.).

As one writer said: "While this subject is being discussed Mr. Kitchin cannot lead the House. He cannot even follow." [17]

On the other hand, the big navy and big army advocates in the House considered the proposals of the President quite inadequate. Thus the Administration was sorely in need of capable responsible leaders to whom it might entrust legislation. Even if the Democrats could have agreed, they were in none too strong a position because they had a majority of only twenty-three votes in the House of Representatives.[18]

THE EXTENSION OF THE EMERGENCY REVENUE ACT

A preliminary meeting of the Committee on Ways and Means before Congress assembled resulted only in the decision to postpone action until after the President's message had been delivered. It was rumored, however, that the Committee would follow the simple procedure of recommending an extension of the emergency tax measure and defer until later the framing of a new measure which was certain to arouse prolonged contention.[19]

The President's tax suggestions were received with as much divergence of opinion as were his views on preparedness. Those who wanted a heavy tax on the great profits of munition makers were keenly disappointed at the President's weak substitute, a tax on iron and steel products. On the other hand, nationwide organizations were formed to protest taxes on moving pictures, automobiles, gasoline, and other commodities.

Kitchin was particularly opposed to the idea of a stamp tax. He was sensitive to the effect of taxes on votes [20] and doubtless approved the remark of Tillman that "every time a man wrote a bank check he would have to lick a stamp and curse the democratic party." [21] Protectionist Republican leaders used every opportunity to ridicule the failure of the Underwood tariff to provide sufficient revenue and urged increased rates of custom duties.

Some of those who approved the President's policy thought that the extra defense costs should be paid for by bonds, the method used for financing the construction of the Panama Canal. Others "greeted the [President's] idea with joy, proclaiming that the rich should pay the cost of national defense because it is wealth that is to

17 *World's Work*, 31: 248 (Jan. 1916).

18 The membership of the House was as follows: Democrats, 229; Republicans, 197; Progressives, 6; Independent, 1; Socialist, 1. There was one vacancy.

19 New York *Times*, Dec. 8, 1915.

20 New York *Times*, Dec. 8, 1915; Jan. 17, 1916.

21 Washington *Star*, Dec. 11, 1915.

be defended – and incidentally because poverty has most of the votes." [22]

As it soon became evident that there was insufficient time before the Christmas recess to work out any new proposals, Chairman Kitchin and Secretary McAdoo announced, as the result of a conference, that immediate steps would be taken to extend the Emergency Internal Revenue Act, scheduled to expire December 31. The resolution to carry out this plan was passed by the House December 16 and by the Senate the following day. It was understood that a new measure would be written later.

THE WAYS AND MEANS COMMITTEE PREPARES A BILL

Immediately after the Christmas holidays the members of the Committee on Ways and Means [23] commenced their deliberations on a new revenue measure but had great difficulty in making any progress. This failure of leadership was characteristic of the handling of the whole Administration program in Congress that session. The blame for the stalemate was passed from one to another. Kitchin, who held the responsible position of Chairman of the Committee on Ways and Means as well as that of floor leader, said that the revenue measures might as well be held up until appropriation bills for the army and navy were ready so that the Committee on Ways and Means would know how much money would be needed.[24] On the other hand, few members of the House cared to vote for large expenditures for preparedness until they knew from what sources the money was coming.[25] In order to establish some good will among the leaders so that Congress would make some headway in the business at hand, Secretary McAdoo entertained the Democratic members of the Ways and Means Committee and some

[22] F. J. Haskins in the Washington *Star*, Feb. 7, 1916.

[23] Members of the Committee on Ways and Means were:

Democrats	*Republicans*
Claude Kitchin (N. C.), Ch.	Joseph W. Fordney (Mich.)
Henry T. Rainey (Ill.)	Augustus P. Gardner (Mass.)
Lincoln Dixon (Ind.)	J. Hampton Moore (Pa.)
Cordell Hull (Tenn.)	William R. Green (Iowa)
John N. Garner (Tex.)	Charles H. Sloan (Neb.)
James W. Collier (Miss.)	Ebenezer J. Hill (Conn.)
Clement C. Dickinson (Mo.)	Nicholas Longworth (Ohio)
Michael F. Conry (N. Y.)	George W. Fairchild (N. Y.)
William A. Oldfield (Ark.)	
Daniel McGillicuddy (Maine)	
Alfred G. Allen (Ohio)	
Charles R. Crisp (La.)	
John J. Casey (Pa.)	
Guy T. Helvering (Kan.)	

[24] New York *Times*, Jan. 17, 1916; Jan. 25, 1916; Washington *Star*, Jan. 21, 1916.

[25] New York *Times*, Jan. 17, 1916.

of the Cabinet officers at what the newspapers called "speed-up dinners," and he held many conferences with leaders of both houses. In spite of his efforts, however, the work dragged; in fact, it practically stopped.[26] The party strength seemed to be waning rapidly. The President's "own political fortunes were in the balance." [27]

Realizing that affairs were in a critical state, Wilson planned three tours to preach the gospel of Preparedness.[28] He hoped that he would not only impress Congress with the popular demand for action on the Administration bills, but also prove that he was the leader of the party. Only one of the three proposed trips was made. The President evidently decided that he could secure better results by staying in Washington in the hope of regaining the control he exerted over Congress in the preceding session. In that session, however, Underwood was in the House and Bryan was in the Cabinet and between them some party discipline was maintained. In the 64th Congress, Underwood was in the Senate and Bryan was at odds with the President.[29]

By the middle of February the Democrats themselves realized that Kitchin was leader in name only. It was decided that responsibility would be divided and various Administration measures, such as those for preparedness legislation, would be given to members who could enthusiastically support them and steer them through Congress, but the leadership of the revenue measure was finally left to Kitchin because he let it be known that he would push a bill if it consisted primarily of higher income tax rates.

Two motives seemed to be at the root of Kitchin's failure to take action. First, as mentioned above, he did not want to be responsible for an expensive preparedness program; secondly, he did not want to present any tax measure that would lose votes. He had his eye on the coming election. From this point of view one can understand why he favored increases in the rates of the higher surtax brackets and opposed lowering of the income tax exemptions.

Members of the Committee from eastern states opposed the changes which Kitchin approved and for somewhat the same reason

[26] "In spite of the presence of these Democratic leaders it was authoritatively asserted that last night's dinner was not productive of a revenue program. The dinner guests divided into groups and discussed the rather gloomy outlook but a concrete plan was not discussed." (New York *Times*, Jan. 17, 1916.)

[27] New York *Tribune*, Jan. 21, 1916.

[28] Letter of Wilson to Glass, New York *Tribune*, Jan. 22, 1916: "I do not think that the Congress quite realizes the genuine demand of the country for an adequate plan of preparation for national defense. I feel that it is my duty to explain this matter to the country and summon its support and that I ought to devote my whole energy, without turning aside, to the business of this session in which I want to be of assistance in every possible and legitimate way."

[29] New York *Tribune* of Jan. 21, 1916 stated: "The Bryan men declare that the present disorganization of Congress is due not to any direct efforts by the Commoner, but solely to his having taken his hand off the machinery."

— because the burden would fall on their constituents. Hull represented a group who wanted to broaden the base of the income tax as well as increase the surtax. The Committee seemed to unite in approval of a tax on manufacturers and others who were profiting from the war.[30] The suggestions of the President met with little consideration, except his proposal to repeal the free sugar clause of the Underwood-Simmons Tariff passed in 1913. It had been only a short time since this law was passed, indeed it had not even gone into effect,[31] and many members on both sides remembered the fine oratory and the eloquent pleas for the consumer that had accompanied its passage. Kitchin supported enthusiastically the measure for the repeal of the clause and it was passed by an overwhelming majority.

The Democratic caucus that was summoned to vote on the repeal of the free sugar clause used the opportunity to quiz the members of the Committee as to their plans for a tax program. Kitchin said that the largest amount would be raised by changes in the income tax and that the Committee would consider taxes on motion picture films, gasoline, automobile horse power, automobile tires, and graphophone records.[32] He made it clear, however, that he was opposed to lowering the income tax exemption below the existing $3000 minimum.[33]

In the midst of the deliberations of the Committee on Ways and Means came word of the unanimous decision of the Supreme Court in upholding the constitutionality of the Income Tax Law of 1913.[34] This heartened the supporters of the movement to extend its revenue producing possibilities. Hull commented:

> The Supreme Court's decision has unfettered the income tax. . . All doubt is removed and Congress is left much freer to act. I believe that Congress will take advantage of the opportunity to amend the law materially. Without any unusual or unjust changes it can be made to yield $185,000,000 to $195,000,000 as against $85,000,000 or $90,000,000 at present.[35]

It was currently reported that Hull was preparing amendments to reduce the income tax exemption, some said to as low as $600.[36] Data prepared by the Treasury Department indicated that these estimates of yield were somewhat over-optimistic, hence the Com-

30 Washington *Star*, Feb. 21, 1916; New York *Times*, Feb. 21, 1916.
31 The effective date of this provision was May 1, 1916.
32 Washington *Star*, Feb. 18, 1916.
33 Washington *Star*, Feb. 20, 1916.
34 *Brushaber* v. *Union Pacific Railroad Co.*, 240 U. S. 1, Jan. 24, 1916. See above, Chap. III.
35 New York *Times*, Jan. 25, 1916.
36 Washington *Star*, Jan. 25, 1916.

mittee began investigating the possibility of revenue from other sources.

Despite the President's program for legislation on numerous matters, coupled with a request for adjournment by June, progress was slow in both the House and the Senate. In March the House passed a bill to enlarge the army, but the Senate amendments for a force of 1,000,000 men involved such a large increase in funds that Kitchin again said he was unwilling to go ahead with any revenue measure until there was more certainty as to the amount that would be needed.[37] The Committee agreed that they would not try to introduce a bill prior to the party conventions.[38] Late in June the army appropriation bill and other appropriation measures had been passed, so the Committee began to put the revenue proposals in shape.

Hull submitted drafts of three bills for the Committee to consider, one for a surtax on income, estimated to raise $100,000,000; one for an inheritance tax, estimated to raise $50,000,000; [39] and one for a tax on munitions, estimated to raise $40,000,000. The Committee reduced the surtax rates somewhat but accepted Hull's ideas "in principle." Little objection was made to the other taxes except that many states were using the inheritance tax and it was feared that if the European war ended soon the munitions tax would not bring in much revenue!

Before the long-drawn-out work on the revenue bill was completed Treasury officials informed the Committee that $330,000,000 additional revenue must be raised instead of $150,000,000 as estimated earlier in the session. The new appropriation bill allotted the navy $164,000,000 more than that of the year before and included $130,000,000 to pay the cost of sending the "punitive" expedition into Mexico.[40] The critical relations with that country apparently furnished a sufficiently tense atmosphere to justify the expenditure. The Administration planned to raise about $125,000,000 from bond issues, but that left a large sum to be raised by taxation, particularly in an election year.[41] The Committee therefore put together an "omnibus" bill containing all the revenue suggestions, including Champ Clark's munition tax, and Hull's income and inheritance taxes.[42] Even the President's plan for a bi-partisan

[37] New York *Tribune*, April 3, 1916.

[38] New York *Tribune*, May 14, 1916.

[39] In 1913 Senator Norris (Rep., Neb.) had proposed a Federal inheritance tax but it was rejected by a large vote. (*Cong. Rec.* 50: 4423, 4469.)

[40] *Cong. Rec.* 53: 12954.

[41] After so many years of expenditures and deficits in multiples of billions it is difficult for present-day readers to view millions as did preceding generations.

[42] New York *Times*, May 22, 1916. Senator Stone (Mo.) also claimed credit for the idea of a tax on munition makers. There was precedent for such a tax in Canada as well as in several European countries.

tariff commission was included so that it would stand a better chance of passing. In fact, it was hoped that such a measure could be passed easily by a caucus as a party measure and rushed through under special rules, thus avoiding the risk of a fight on the floor. The Democrats had too small a majority to care "to become embroiled in a series of tariff fights." [43]

The measure reported by the Committee on Ways and Means provided for increased taxes on incomes of individuals and corporations; new taxes on estates and munition manufacturers; continuation of the excise taxes on manufacturers of tobacco, on theater managers, and on special articles such as alcoholic beverages. It repealed the duty on coal-tar crudes, reduced the duty on coal tar intermediates for a period of five years in order to encourage the dye industry, and created a tariff commission. Stamp taxes imposed by the Emergency Act of 1914 were repealed.[44]

The estate tax was an innovation in federal finance as a permanent feature, although the Act of 1894 had contained an inheritance tax clause, and there had been emergency war measures in 1867 and 1898. The 1916 law provided for a tax with rates graduated from 1% on net estates over $50,000 to 5% on those over $450,000. The Democratic textbook of 1916 spoke of this tax as one that offered the largest untapped field of revenue in this country. That it was not then considered a temporary tax was the opinion of Daniel C. Roper, who wrote sometime afterward that Congress approved it because it was a method of "acquiring permanent revenue which would not impose too great a burden on any." The writer continued:

> But revenue alone is not the sole reason for the enactment of the Federal death duty. There have been in this country for many years warm adherents to the belief that something must be done to discourage rapid growing fortunes, that some limit must be placed upon the possibility of a few individuals acquiring so much money that the Government itself is menaced by the power it brings them.[45]

The tax on munition manufacturers applied to companies that made a net profit in excess of 10%. The rates were graduated from 5% to 8% on gross receipts – not net – of manufacturers of gunpowder and other explosives; it was slightly less, 2% to 3%, for

[43] New York *Times*, Feb. 14, 1916.

[44] For the text see *Cong. Rec.* 53: 10662-10672.

[45] Roper, Daniel C., "Taxation Problems, II," *North American Review*, 222: 13 (Sept., Oct., Nov. 1925). Mr. Roper was secretary of the Committee on Ways and Means in 1916; Commissioner of Internal Revenue 1917-1920; Secretary of Commerce 1933-1939; United States Minister to Canada 1939–.

those manufacturing shells or firearms and for those smelting copper.[46]

The normal income tax rate was raised from 1% to 2% and the surtax rates increased from a maximum of 6% to 10% on incomes over $500,000. The personal exemption was made $4000 for a "head of a family," a broader provision than the previous law which had limited the allowance to a married man living with his wife. Other changes also were made in the text to clarify the law on the basis of the two years' experience. It was estimated that the yield of the new law from all taxes would be $197,000,000.

THE 1916 INCOME TAX BILL IN THE HOUSE

On July 5, the Committee on Ways and Means reported the bill to the House and, July 6, the Chairman of the Committee on Rules submitted a privileged resolution to "expedite the consideration and passage of this revenue measure." This was adopted. In presenting "this product of the best labor and best thought and judgment of the Committee" Chairman Kitchin gave a three hours' oration in which he stated to the amusement of the Republicans that they had been able to frame and present a bill to raise revenue which was absolutely "non-partisan" because there was not "an item of revenue in the bill that has ever been made a partisan question or a partisan issue," and because a majority of the Republican members had joined with the Democrats in voting for the enormously increased appropriations for the army and for fortifications. In fact he thought if it erred in favor of any party, the Republicans had the advantage, for some of the sections were too non-Democratic for him to accept. For instance, he could not approve of the establishment of the tariff commission, or the tariff on dye materials, and he never had been in sympathy with the appropriations for defense which necessitated the bill. These sections, he explained apologetically, he swallowed as he did a bad pill when he was a boy, all at once. If he began to nibble around and pinch off one piece at a time, he could not get it down.[47]

Fordney opened the argument for the opposition and criticized the measure because it did not provide for higher tariff rates.[48] Longworth (Rep., Ohio), who had signed the majority report, announced that he would support the bill because the Republican party was responsible for defense expenditures "even larger than the Demo-

[46] One of the arguments for the tax, as explained by Kitchin, was that it would provide the government with statistical information on the cost of munitions. Under the proposed act companies had to show the actual amount invested in plants, cost of raw materials, amount of wages, insurance, and overhead charges.

[47] *Cong. Rec.* 53: app. 1937-1950.

[48] *Cong. Rec.* 53: 10513-10520.

cratic party contemplated or desired." He objected, however, to the failure to lower the income tax exemptions.[49]

Hull explained the income tax provisions. By showing how heavily those in the lower income groups were already taxed by state and local jurisdictions, he defended the action of the Committee in maintaining the income tax exemptions, although it is known that he would have preferred to have them lowered. In this connection he said:

> I should not be very averse to lowering the exemption here, not so much for the revenue which would be small, but to remove the unjust prejudice against the law on account of the exemption.[50]

Few amendments were made in the House to the income tax section or, in fact, to any part of the bill. One introduced by the Committee at the request of Longworth provided for the taxation of stock dividends "to the amount of their cash value.[51] This was incorporated in the 1916 law but was declared unconstitutional by the Supreme Court in the far-reaching case of *Eisner* v. *Macomber* (252 U. S. 189, 1920). Another made a change in the computation of depletion.[52] Crosser (Rep., Ohio) introduced a schedule of rates to increase the surtax on incomes of over $60,000 to a maximum of 12%, but his amendment was defeated.[53]

James (Rep.), from the copper districts of Michigan, was one of the few who objected to the munitions tax. His position was that it singled out one metal, copper, for a heavy tax and that it would be much more fair to tax every person or corporation making net profits of over 10%.[54] Fordney proposed an amendment so that copper not used in the making of munitions would not be subject to the tax, but this was not satisfactory to James, who foresaw that it would be impossible to administer.

Some criticism was made of a federal estate tax because thirty-three states already had inheritance taxes. Hull answered this objection by recognizing the difficulties involved and by suggesting that an effort be made by the federal government to help the states improve the administration of their inheritance taxes and their income taxes also. In his estimation the possibilities of such co-operation were so great that he envisioned the abolition of the general property tax.[55]

On July 10 the measure was passed by a vote of 238 to 142.[56]

49 *Cong. Rec.* 53: 10529-10531.
50 *Cong. Rec.* 53: 10655.
51 *Cong. Rec.* 53: 10727.
52 *Cong. Rec.* 53: 10727-10728.
53 *Cong. Rec.* 53: 10764.
54 *Cong. Rec.* 53: 10759-10760.
55 *Cong. Rec.* 53: 10657.
56 *Cong. Rec.* 53: 10768.

THE BILL IN THE SENATE

The Senate Finance Committee[57] completed its work on the revenue bill early in August and reported it to the Senate on the 16th of the month. About ten days later the Senate took it up for consideration. Chairman Simmons presented the most recent estimates of appropriations for the session. They showed increases not only for the army and navy but also for rivers and harbors, the post office, and, in fact, for almost every item, a total increase for 1917 over 1916 of approximately $400,000,000.

The Finance Committee therefore presented a measure to increase the revenue even more than the House bill would. It did this by increasing the surtax rates, levying a new corporation tax on capital stock, increasing the rates of the munition tax, changing the computation to a net basis instead of gross, increasing the rates of the estate tax, and retaining the stamp taxes levied by the Emergency Internal Revenue Act of 1914.

For several days the leading majority and minority members made speeches on the bill, but for the most part they consisted of political generalities for home consumption. The Republicans took the occasion to blame the tariff policy of the Democratic party for the failure to raise adequate revenue but made no objection to the tremendous appropriations or, for the most part, to the revenue bill.

When the Senate was ready to begin work on the measure Williams, chairman of the subcommittee[58] on the income and inheritance tax section, presented the Committee amendments, many of which merely improved the wording of the law, but some of them made significant substantive changes. The first of importance was to increase the surtax rates to a maximum of 13% on an individual's income in excess of $2,000,000.[59] Another simplified the section which determined that gain from sale of property acquired before

57 Members of the Finance Committee were:

Democrats	*Republicans*
F. M. Simmons (N. C.), Ch.	Boies Penrose (Pa.)
William J. Stone (Mo.)	Henry Cabot Lodge (Mass.)
John Sharp Williams (Miss.)	Porter J. McCumber (N. D.)
Charles F. Johnson (Maine)	Reed Smoot (Utah)
Benjamin F. Shively (Ind.)	Jacob Gallinger (N. H.)
Hoke Smith (Ga.)	Charles E. Townsend (Mich.)
Charles F. Thomas (Colo.)	Robert M. La Follette (Wis.)
Ollie M. James (Ky.)	
Clarence D. Clark (Wyo.)	
William Hughes (N. D.)	
Thomas P. Gore (Okla.)	

58 The other members were James (Ky.) and Gore (Okla.). James had been one of the early advocates of an income tax. See above Chap. II.

59 *Cong. Rec.* 53: 13261.

March 1, 1913 should be computed on the basis of the market price or value as of March 1, 1913.[60]

As the section of the 1913 law providing for personal exemptions had not been entirely clear, the Senate Finance Committee rewrote it, but did not change the amount of the deductions. These were $3000 for a single person with $1000 additional in case of a married person living with husband or wife. Only one deduction of $4000 could be made. The subcommittee thought there would be great difficulty in administering the House provision which necessitated a definition of "head of a family," and that there would be no end to the number who would make claims of doubtful merit.

The section defining the amount of allowable depletion was completely rewritten. The law originally limited depletion for coal mines and oil wells to 5% of the gross value of the output for the year. It was amended to allow "a reasonable allowance for actual reduction in flow and production" of oil wells, "a reasonable allowance for the depletion of coal mines" and for timber stumpage.

During the public hearings which were held before the Senate Committee, several witnesses objected to withholding of the tax at the source and to the provision in the law regarding the tax-free clause in many bonds. Many organizations such as the American Bar Association had expressed the desirability of amending these sections.[61]

Although the Committee was not ready to abolish collection at the source it did introduce an amendment to prevent any future contracts for payment of interest without allowing for deduction of income tax.[62] Smoot feared that such a provision would give a great advantage to the marketing of securities issued by governmental agencies including the farm-loan banks and farm-loan associations. Williams explained that there was a difference between bonds that were tax-free by the act of the federal government and those made free by private contract entered into between two individuals. The amendment was adopted.

The allowances for losses were greatly liberalized. Whereas the 1913 law had limited deductible losses to those incurred in transactions connected with the taxpayer's business or trade, the House and the Senate amended the section to include losses incurred in other transactions to the extent of the gains. O'Gorman (Dem., N. Y.) endeavored to extend the allowance to cover all losses, but Williams stated his opposition to this because he feared it would open the way to evasion and fraud; for example, taxpayers would

60 *Cong. Rec.* 53: 13263.
61 *Proceedings of the American Bar Association*, XXXIX: 533 (Oct. 20-22, 1914).
62 *Cong. Rec.* 53: 13294. This section was taken out of the bill in conference.

deduct contributions to charitable organizations as "losses." He permitted, however, the insertion of the word "lawful" before "transactions."[63]

The Senate also gave partnerships the same rights as individuals in the reporting of non-taxable interest. By the Act of 1913, partnership earnings were subject to tax as parts of the incomes of the individual members of the partnership, but according to a ruling of the Treasury Department, interest from municipal bonds was held taxable if received by a partnership. There had been much discussion of the treatment of partnership income with respect to this and other points also before the Senate Finance Committee and outside of Congress.[64] The Senate therefore put partnerships on the same basis as individuals so far as this non-taxable interest was concerned but made no other change with respect to partnership returns.

Several members desired to decrease the personal exemptions. Underwood, who had refused a place on the Finance Committee,[65] proposed that it be reduced from $4000 to $3000 for husband and wife and from $3000 to $2000 for single persons and stated that he would gladly see it reduced still further, even to $1000 if he thought it would be adopted.[66] Stone agreed with him but did not press the matter because he had tried to persuade the Committee to accede to his point of view but had been unsuccessful. The Republicans, however, continued to urge the change. One member, for example, claimed that in compelling a few to bear the entire expense of the government, the electorate was being debased and

[63] *Cong. Rec.* 53: 13264-13266. The clause then read: "In lawful transactions entered into for profit, but not connected with his business or trade, the losses actually sustained therein during the year." Until 1924 the law made no distinction between current ordinary losses and losses from sales of capital assets.

[64] Protest against the unfairness of the treatment of partnerships was made before the Senate Finance Committee. For example, the special committee of the National Tax Association on the Federal Income Tax recommended that the law be amended so that partnerships "should file substantially the same kind of report as corporations are required to file and pay the normal tax as corporations do."

Speaking before the American Academy of Political and Social Science in March 1915, Mr. Mortimer Schiff called attention to the inconsistency of the law in regard to treatment of partnership income. (*Annals of the American Academy of Political and Social Science* 56: 27-29, March 1915.)

[65] Clark, *My Quarter Century of American Politics* (I: 372), gives the following explanation of Senator Underwood's refusal to serve on the Finance Committee:

"Shortly after he was translated to the Senate I asked him if he would be on the Finance Committee. . . I naturally supposed that he would desire that assignment. He replied by telling an apt anecdote. He said:

"Down in Kentucky there was a cobbler who unexpectedly inherited a large sum of money. He locked up his shop and went out in search of pleasure – in all sorts of wild dissipation. Finally he spent all of his money, and returned to his humble cobbler's bench. Not long afterward a lawyer went to his shop and informed the cobbler that he had inherited another fortune. He looked up from his bench and said: 'My God! Must I go through all that again?' And that's the way I would feel about another tariff bill!"

[66] *Cong. Rec.* 53: 13266. It was reported that the committees had voted early in August to reduce the exemption from $3000 to $2000. (Washington *Star*, Aug. 6, 1916.)

the way paved for "unwarranted extravagance." In fact, he went so far as to claim that the exemption of the small taxpayer was a direct bid for votes and in its effect was bribery.[67] Underwood's amendment was defeated.

As in every debate on the income tax, the issue of publicity of returns was brought up by certain Senators, usually by La Follette, who contended that it was necessary to have both individual and corporation income tax returns open to public inspection in order to prevent tax dodging. In the debate on the 1916 tax, Husting (Wis.) introduced an amendment to permit individual income tax returns to be open to inspection under the same conditions as corporation returns. Norris and Ashurst supported La Follette. The Committee believed, so Williams explained, that men's private affairs should be respected and doubted whether the much-talked-of "shining light of publicity" would be of much help in collecting the taxes.[68]

There was no objection in the Senate to the special munitions tax on corporations making articles of war; in fact, the companies themselves made no objection, but there was decided protest against taxing the raw materials that went into such finished products, for example, copper, as the House had provided.

THE CONFERENCE REPORT

The bill was passed by the Senate September 5,[69] revised by the Conference Committee within the next few days, and signed by the President September 8, the last day of the session.

The Senate amendments were retained for the most part, for example, those relating to the surtax rates, the estate tax rates, and the capital stock tax, but the House managers succeeded in cutting out the stamp taxes which the Senate had added. The tax on munition manufacturers was a compromise with respect to rates, but the Senate proposal for a net receipts basis instead of gross was adopted. The tax was made applicable to all types of business organizations, not to corporations only, as specified by the Senate.

SUMMARY OF THE LAW

The 1916 Revenue Act[70] was distinguished for several reasons: (1) For the first time an income tax measure was considered in Congress on its own merits, that is, not in connection with a tariff

[67] Oliver (Pa.) (*Cong. Rec.* 53: 13297). See also the speeches of Wadsworth and Weeks (*Cong. Rec.* 53: 13297, 13129).

[68] *Cong. Rec.* 53: 12293, 13852-13858.

[69] The vote was 42 to 16, 37 not voting. (*Cong. Rec.* 53: 13873.)

[70] 39 *Statutes at Large* 756.

bill; it was therefore written as a complete entity, not as part of a tariff bill; (2) it contained the first permanent estate tax, the first war-profits tax, and the first tax on corporation capital stock.

The law contained nine sections or titles: (1) income tax, (2) estate tax, (3) munition manufacturer's tax, (4) miscellaneous taxes, (5) tariff on dyestuffs, (6) removal of tariff on printing paper, (7) creation of the tariff commission, (8) unfair competition or anti-dumping provisions, (9) miscellaneous provisions.

Only the first three titles are closely related to the subject in hand. Important changes will be summarized here very briefly in view of the details of the work of Congress given in the preceding pages.[71]

Title I, the income tax, was completely rewritten, the arrangement greatly improved and the wording clarified. The rate of the normal tax was raised to 2% for both individuals and corporations. The surtax for individuals, applicable to income over $20,000, was increased from a maximum of 6% on income over $500,000 to a maximum of 13% on income over $2,000,000. Personal exemptions remained at $3000 for a single person and $4000 for a married couple.[72]

The list of exempt corporations (mostly non-profit) was increased to include specifically many which were included by inference in the previous law.

Deductions for losses were extended to make provision for those incurred in transactions outside of the taxpayer's regular trade or profession, but only to the extent of the profits arising therefrom.

Partnerships were put on the same basis as individuals so far as deductions were concerned.

Stock dividends were made taxable "to the amount of their cash value." [73]

In the definition of income the word "lawful" was omitted from the phrase "business carried on for profit."

The time for tax payments was advanced from June 30 to June 15 so that collections and statistics for the closing fiscal year could be handled more expeditiously.

March 1, 1913 was made the basic date for establishing value from which to calculate gain or loss from the sale of property acquired before that time.

The section defining depletion of mines was rewritten in more

[71] For more extended explanations of the other titles see Blakey, Roy G., "The New Revenue Act," *American Economic Review*, VI: 837-850 (Dec. 1916).

[72] See below, Chap. XXII, p. 509, for comparisons of rates and exemptions of various laws.

[73] This was held unconstitutional in the case of *Eisner* v. *Macomber*, 252 U. S. 189 (1920).

general terms, omitting the phrase "5% of the value of output at the mine."

Non-resident aliens were made subject to the tax on income from bonds with underlying assets situated in the United States.

Several new taxes imposed in 1916 were related to the income tax. A special additional income tax of 12½% was levied on the net profits of manufacturers of munitions, but profits from dynamite, blasting powder, cartridges and caps used for industrial purposes were excluded. The law was to be in force until one year after the close of the European War.[74] A capital stock tax on all corporations was levied at the rate of 50 cents per $1000 of fair value of the capital stock after allowing an exemption of $99,000.[75] A tax was imposed "upon the transfer of the net estate of every decedent . . . whether a resident or non-resident of the United States." Residents were granted an exemption of $50,000; for non-residents, the exemptions and deductions were in proportion to the amounts of their estates situated in the United States. The rates were graduated from 1% on amounts that did not exceed the exemption by $50,000 to 10% on amounts that exceeded the exemption by over $5,000,000.

The Act went into effect September 9, and applied to income received in the calendar year 1916.

[74] In 1917 Professor Bullock made the following comment on this tax:

"The tax on munition makers will make an interesting theme for the future historian of the war. It was levied before we got into the struggle, at a time when there was more or less talk about our wicked munition makers who had been manufacturing shells and sending them over to the Allies and had been coining money out of the terrible struggle in Europe.

"It was fortunate that having got into war we have a certain amount of preparedness . . . yet we have the special tax on munition makers who were singled out as an undesirable industry. . ." (*Proceedings of the National Tax Association* 1917, p. 155.)

[75] In estimating the value of capital stock, surplus and undivided profits were to be included. Munition manufacturers subject to special tax were allowed to deduct it as a credit against the capital stock tax.

CHAPTER V

REVENUE ACT OF MARCH 3, 1917 – THE FIRST EXCESS PROFITS TAX

THE FOURTH EMERGENCY

The first session of the 64th Congress came to a close September 8, 1916, the same day on which President Wilson signed the revenue measure that was drawn up to provide funds for national defense as well as for greatly increased civil expenditures.

Before the opening of the second session on December 4, the Treasury report indicated such a great decrease in the general fund and such rapidly mounting estimates of anticipated appropriations that the Revenue Act was considered inadequate almost before it could go into operation.[1] At the current rate of income and outgo the Treasury faced a deficit of over $280,000,000 by the end of the fiscal year, June 30, 1918. To meet the situation a new revenue bill was prepared, "the fourth emergency measure" since October 3, 1913, as Fordney described it.[2] It was laid before Congress in January of the short session and hurried through with little debate.

Even more promptly than its predecessor, it was destined to be replaced before it could be tried out, but it is of significance to income tax students because of the introduction of the principle of the excess-profits tax which was such an important feature of the fifth emergency measure, the War Revenue Act of October 3, 1917.

THE BILL IN THE HOUSE OF REPRESENTATIVES

Chairman Kitchin of the Committee on Ways and Means[3] faced a recalcitrant group among his own colleagues who disapproved of the militaristic trend of the Administration. This anti-preparedness bloc – mostly Southerners led by Page, Saunders, Bailey, and Keating – announced that they would not only fight the revenue bill which was occasioned by military expenditures but were prepared "to offer a resolution instructing the Military and Naval Committee

[1] Part of the difficulty was due to the outlay for the expedition into Mexico, which had cost more than was anticipated; part was due to the defense estimates which were again increased.

[2] *Cong. Rec.* 54: 2276. The three previous measures were the Emergency Internal Revenue Act of October 1914, the re-enactment of special excises in December 1915, and the Revenue Act of September 1916. See above, Chap. IV.

[3] The personnel was the same as in the first session. See above, Chap. IV, p. 109.

to reduce appropriations for preparedness." [4] There were about fifteen [5] whom Kitchin had to placate and he succeeded in winning them over by drawing up a revenue measure which would not hurt their constituents.

It was reported that he said in the party caucus which met to consider the revenue bill, "You can tell your people that practically all of this will go north of Mason and Dixon's line. The preparedness agitation has its hot bed in such cities as New York." [6] Appropriately, therefore, the tax burden would fall heavily on the wealthy classes and on those who had been clamoring for preparedness. Kitchin was severely criticized for this remark. He denied that he had used the expression "Mason and Dixon's line" when questioned on the floor of the House, but he confirmed it in these words:

> I will say now that this tax will go to pay appropriations practically all, or most of all, of which will go north of the Mason and Dixon line. . . I think most or the greater part of the tax will be levied north of the Mason and Dixon's line. . .[7]

That this remark did not cause more adverse feeling than it did is probably due to the fact that Congress did not anticipate a more serious situation; the country was prosperous and the tax rates were not severe. An editorial in the New York *Times* expressed the general sentiment in this way:

> The prolonged debate over the methods of meeting the Treasury's deficiency and need for $300,000,000 or more has had the happy result of determining that the emergency is temporary and that only temporary provision is necessary.[8]

Rainey (Dem., Ill.), who agreed with Kitchin that the expenditures for defense were exorbitant, foresaw that even other funds than those requested by the Treasury would be needed because, with the

[4] New York *Times*, Jan. 26, 27, 1917.

[5] The New York *Times* listed:

Samuel Taylor (Ark.)	Richard E. Olney (Mass.)
Oscar Callaway (Tex.)	Robert N. Page (N. C.)
Robert Y. Thomas (Ky.)	Percy E. Quin (Miss.)
Warren W. Bailey (Pa.)	Hubert D. Stephens (Miss.)
Martin Dies (Tex.)	John L. Burnett (Ala.)
Joseph B. Thompson (Okla.)	Robert L. Doughton (N. C.)
	Isaac R. Sherwood (Ohio)

To this list should be added Edward Keating (Colo.) and Edward Saunders (Va.).

[6] New York *Times*, Jan. 27, 1917. At this meeting the thirteen mentioned above were the only members who voted against accepting the Committee draft.

[7] *Cong. Rec.* 54: 2130. Kitchin's success is shown by the fact that in the final vote 13 of the 15 voted for the bill; two, Page and Doughton, did not vote.

[8] New York *Times*, Jan. 16, 1917.

continued spread of the prohibition movement, some new source of revenue would have to be found to supplant the $237,000,000 received from excise taxes on alcoholic beverages. He was dubious as to the possibility of securing enough money by taxation, for he thought that income tax rates had reached "the very highest notch." Even if the personal exemption were lowered to $1000, a prospect which he knew was not pleasing to the Democratic party, he did not think the enormous sums necessary could be raised.[9]

Apparently Rainey's remarks caused much cloakroom discussion and some talk of lowering personal exemptions to $1000 and $1500.[10] Kitchin later made a passing reference to the reasons for not increasing the income tax. He said that the additional revenue needed was so great that the normal income tax rate would have had to be doubled.[11] No mention was made of lowering the income tax exemptions. According to one New York paper, this was because of the fear that Congress, "for political reasons, for party reasons," was "much disinclined to bring home to the minds of a great number of new voters the fact that the defense of this nation is going to cost them something." [12]

Economic and fiscal as well as political considerations led party leaders to look elsewhere than to the small taxpayers for new revenue. The year 1916 had been a prosperous one in every part of the country and in every industry, particularly in those lines that profited from the war overseas.[13] Taxes on "big business" and an extension of the 1916 tax on munition manufacturers were logical developments. Furthermore, there were precedents in Europe where most of the governments had imposed war-profits taxes based on the excess of profits over those of prewar years. Kitchin explained that in Great Britain the rates of such taxes were 60%; in France and Russia, 40%; and in Germany something over 30%.[14] The rate of 8% selected for the United States looked small in contrast; moreover the Committee followed the Canadian system of basing the deduction on invested capital rather than on prewar profits.[15]

The measure submitted by the Ways and Means Committee con-

[9] New York *Times*, Dec. 10, 1916.

[10] New York *Times*, Dec. 21, 1916.

[11] *Cong. Rec.* 54: 2275.

[12] New York *Times*, Dec. 7, 1916. On the 24th of the same month this paper printed another editorial which urged improved income tax administration and quoted the *Annalist's* estimates of tax evasion to the extent of $5,000,000,000 of taxable income.

[13] New York *Times*, Dec. 31, 1916.

[14] *Cong. Rec.* 54: 2271.

[15] Adams, T. S., "The Excess Profits Tax," *Quarterly Journal of Economics*, 35: 364 (May 1921); Breadner, R. W., "The Canadian Business Profits and Income War Tax Acts," *Bulletin National Tax Association*, IV: 93, 116 (Jan., Feb. 1919).

tained four sections.[16] Title I was unusual in that it was a kind of prologue. It stated that all of the taxes collected from Title II and one-third of the yield from Title III were to be set aside as a special fund to be used for defraying the expenses of the army and navy and for fortifications.

Title II imposed a new tax of 8% on corporate and partnership excess profits above a flat exemption of $5000 plus 8% on "the actual capital invested." Incomes of partnerships from agriculture and personal services were not subject to this tax.

Title III amended the estate tax section of the Act of September 8, 1916 by raising the rates 50% so that the minimum became 1½% on the first bracket, the amount of a "net estate" not over $50,000, and the maximum 15% on the top bracket, the amount of a "net estate" over $5,000,000.

Title IV contained miscellaneous provisions such as authorizations of a bond issue of $100,000,000 and of the sale of the remainder of the Panama Canal bonds.

The House spent some time January 30 in general debate. The Republican opposition led by Fordney concentrated on the mistake of the Democrats in not trying to raise the needed funds by increasing the tariff.[17] On this matter Hamilton (Rep., Mich.) said that his party was opposed to all forms of direct taxation by the federal government. The Democratic answer was that in 1915 the Underwood Act with the income tax yielded as much as the Payne Act could have produced. The latter, in the best year, 1910, yielded only $326,000,000.[18] In addition it was emphasized that the $777,000,000 appropriation for defense alone was greater by $100,000,000 than the total amount raised from all sources in the best years of the Taft administration and the Payne Act.[19]

[16] *Cong. Rec.* 54: 2337. The House estimates of yield were as follows:

Estimated revenue under the present law:	
Customs	$230,000,000
Internal Revenue, ordinary	325,000,000
Total	555,000,000
[Additional]	
Estimated revenue under this bill:	
Tax on excess profits, corporations	170,000,000
Tax on excess profits of partnerships	56,000,000
Emergency revenues, receipts from munitions manufacturers, and estate taxes	134,000,000
Corporation income tax	133,000,000
Individual income tax	111,750,000
Sale of Panama Canal Bonds	222,000,000
3 per cent certificates to be issued by Sec. of Treas.	100,000,000
	$1,481,750,000

[17] *Cong. Rec.* 54: 2276-2282.

[18] *Cong. Rec.* 54: 2275.

[19] *Cong. Rec.* 54: 2411.

Green (Rep., Iowa) forecast the dispute of the House and Senate during the following session when he objected to the excess-profits tax, because it was based on profits in excess of certain percentages of invested capital rather than on profits in excess of those received in normal years.[20] Dillon (Rep., S. D.) forecast the tremendous problems of the next five years when he spoke on the administrative difficulties of establishing a proper valuation of capital. Bennet (Rep., N. Y.) thought the tax would bear so heavily on corporations that state revenues would suffer. He also considered the tax undesirable because the revenues from it could not be predicted with certainty, inasmuch as they would vary with the changing conditions of business.[21] No amendments were made on the floor. To Title III, Estate Tax, the only amendment offered was that of Green to exempt bequests for "public, benevolent, or charitable uses," in addition to the specific amount of $50,000. This was rejected.[22] When the last section, Title IV, was under discussion, Good (Rep., Iowa) attempted to insert an amendment providing for a tax on distilled liquors, but was unsuccessful. Fordney made a last-minute attempt to strike out Title II, the Excess-Profits Tax, but his motion to recommit was defeated by a party vote.[23]

The bill was passed by the House February 1 by a vote of 211 to 196.[24]

THE BILL IN THE SENATE

On the day before the House passed the revenue bill, the German government announced its intention to prosecute relentless submarine warfare. During the two weeks that the Finance Committee [25] spent revising the measure for consideration by the Senate, two American vessels were sent to the bottom of the sea by German submarines. The atmosphere in the Senate was not calm. La Follette and about a dozen of his colleagues resented the fact that the Administration was holding the appropriation bill so that it would have to be rushed through at the end of the session. They objected to the Armed Ship bill [26] because it meant war; they objected to the United States going into war; and furthermore, they objected to the "dictatorial powers" they expected the President to assume.

20 *Cong. Rec.* 54: 2324.
21 *Cong. Rec.* 54: 2418, 2419.
22 *Cong. Rec.* 54: 2437.
23 *Cong. Rec.* 54: 2440.
24 *Cong. Rec.* 54: 2442.
25 The personnel of this Committee was the same as in the first session. See above, Chap. IV, p. 116.
26 This measure was killed, hence the President was forced to call an extra session, the result desired by the La Follette group so that the President could not act without consulting them.

The tax bill was only one of many difficult problems; in fact, it was probably one of the less controversial matters. Chairman Simmons of the Committee on Finance was evidently not enthusiastic about any tax bill and wanted to substitute a bond issue.[27] This the Administration could not approve. Whether or not it was this issue that delayed the measure is not known, but the party caucus met several evenings without reaching a decision.[28]

Finally, on February 12, the revenue measure was accepted, almost as it was drawn up by the House. The minor amendments made by the Finance Committee were:

1. To limit the excess-profits tax to four years after the law went into effect.
2. To subject to the excess-profits tax partnerships as well as corporations engaged in agriculture.
3. To limit the tax on munition manufacturers to six months, instead of a year, after the close of the war.
4. To make the basis for the computation of invested capital the value of the property at the time of the investment instead of at the time of making the return.

The following day the bill was introduced into the Senate and a week later it was brought up for consideration in the Committee of the Whole.[29]

Simmons explained that there had been protests at the public hearings with respect to the computation of invested capital. Some corporations requested that a fairer basis would be "the cash value of the property at the time of the return of income for taxation, instead of at the time the property was turned over as part of the assets of the corporation." This, said the Senator, would have allowed a much greater exemption and "would have given them the benefit of the unearned increment, of good will, and so forth." [30] The amended basis was also thought to provide greater equality among taxpayers.

When objection was made to exempting individuals from the excess-profits tax, Simmons pointed out that they were subject to the surtax. In fact, the excess-profits tax might be looked upon as a method of taxing corporations as drastically as individuals. The tax on partnerships was not so easily justified, since the partnership with invested capital was subject to the excess-profits tax and in addition the partners paid income tax and surtax on their individual incomes including their respective shares of partnership profits.[31] The Sena-

[27] New York *Times*, Feb. 4, 1917.
[28] New York *Times*, Feb. 10, 1917.
[29] The bill as passed by the House is printed in the *Cong. Rec.* 54: 3674.
[30] *Cong. Rec.* 54: 3677.
[31] *Cong. Rec.* 54: 3678, 4274.

tor then defended those portions of the bill which had been subjected to most criticism at the hearings.[32]

Mutual life insurance companies protested that a war tax should not be imposed upon insurance for the reason that it was a class of business different from other businesses and should be given "higher and more preferential treatment because of the humanitarian and benevolent elements that enter into it." [33] The Committee rejected this plea also because there seemed to be no evidence that the policyholders would be adversely affected.

The munition manufacturers objected to being taxed both by the special tax of 12½% under the Act of September 8, 1916 and by the proposed excess-profits tax, particularly because the latter was made "retroactive," that is, it applied to sales already made; hence, as Simmons pointed out, they could not adjust their contracts so as to shift the tax to consumers. They asked exemption from the excess-profits tax for corporations that paid the 12½% special tax on munition manufacturers but the Committee was not impressed by their arguments and no exemption was granted.

La Follette strikingly illustrated the difficulties that would be experienced in enforcing the excess-profits tax because of the necessity of measuring invested capital. He used the example of the United States Steel Corporation to show how complicated if not impossible would be the determination of the actual cash value of assets "at the time of transference to the books of the company" of the hundreds of properties belonging to the many corporations that made up that big corporation.[34] He also sketched the tremendous work of the Interstate Commerce Commission with its large staff of experts in attempting to value railroad property.

As a substitute for the excess-profits tax and the proposed bond issues, La Follette proposed higher rates for the income and estate taxes, publicity of income tax returns, and the taxation of corporation dividends in the hands of individual recipients.[35] As long as he lived La Follette continuously fought for these changes as a matter of principle. In this session of 1917 he had other motives also. He wanted to keep Congress in session and used the income tax amendments as an excuse for a filibuster to delay proceedings as long as possible.

[32] Four subcommittees held public hearings February 6 and 7.

[33] *Cong. Rec.* 54: 3683.

[34] *Cong. Rec.* 54: 4495. This example was singularly appropriate and prophetic because the litigation that resulted from the necessity of determining the excess-profits taxes due from this company under the War Acts of 1917 and 1918 dragged on for years and finally was settled in 1928 with a refund to the company of over $50,000,000. See below, Chap. XXIII, p. 550.

[35] The Revenue Act of 1936 subjected such corporation dividends to the normal tax. See below, Chap. XVII, p. 424.

Few amendments were offered on the floor of the Senate by the Committee or others. Norris worked out a scheme for automatically increasing or decreasing the income tax rate according to the Treasury deficit or surplus, somewhat as suggested in 1913, but no interest was shown in it.[36] Lodge offered a rider which would have imposed the highest rate of duty in the tariff law on articles from foreign countries that were not manufactured in compliance with the child labor law passed in the preceding session.[37] This was defeated but a somewhat similar proposal was applied to domestic manufacturers in the War Revenue Act of 1917.

By the last of February the Democratic leaders agreed to some rather drastic measures to untangle the legislative snarl, for they were practically at the end of the session and only a few of the Administration measures had been enacted. In order to push the revenue bill through, the Senate was forced to pass it exactly as it was passed by the House. As one member of the Finance Committee said:

> We threw overboard some amendments because we found we had to take the House bill just as it came over, without dotting an "i" or crossing a "t." [38]

On February 28 the measure was reported to the Senate from the Committee of the Whole and, on the motion of Simmons, that body refused to concur in the amendments made in the Committee of the Whole. The Republicans did not vote on this motion. All the Democrats voted for it.[39] This saved the necessity of a Conference Committee.

Only one amendment was offered after that. Penrose attempted to have the bill recommitted and amended "so as to raise an equitable portion of the required revenue from a protective tariff." Upon the rejection of this motion the bill was passed. It was signed by the President March 3,[40] the last day of his first term, but before it could go into effect it was made obsolete by the declaration of war, a conflict which called for revenues far in excess of those contemplated by this bill.

36 *Cong. Rec.* 54: 4486.

37 *Cong. Rec.* 54: 4518.

38 64th Congress, 2d Session, *Hearings before the Senate Finance Committee on H. R.* 20573.

39 *Cong. Rec.* 54: 4523.

40 39 *Statutes at Large* 1000.

CHAPTER VI

THE WAR REVENUE ACT OF OCTOBER 3, 1917

FINANCING THE WAR

The second inauguration of President Wilson, March 4, 1917, was very different from the usually noisy, happy, jubilant affair; it was, on the contrary, marked with solemnity and anxiety over our being drawn into the European maelstrom. The ceremonies were scarcely permitted to interrupt the feverish efforts to prepare our people for what was impending. Not only Washington but the entire nation was very thoughtful, almost oppressed by the ominous proximity of war.[1]

A special session of the 65th Congress convened April 2 with members of the House of Representatives almost equally divided between the two parties[2] but when the vote was taken on the declaration of war April 6, it showed a united opinion. For war purposes the Secretary of the Treasury requested immediately about $3,500,000,000 in addition to the $240,000,000 appropriated by the House on April 5 and the $5,000,000,000 of the navy appropriation bill passed on the last day of the 64th Congress. Within a week after Congress opened the House Committee on Ways and Means authorized the issuance of $5,000,000,000 in bonds and $2,000,000,000 in certificates of indebtedness. Chairman Kitchin announced that as soon as this measure was out of the way the Committee would begin to work on the question of how the United States would pay for the war.

In his opening address of April 2, President Wilson had anticipated the difficulties that would arise in this connection and stated that his policy was to pay for the war while it was being waged, so far as possible. There was much wholesome argument on both sides of this question of borrowing versus taxing, by the public at large as well as at the Capital. The American Economic Association had spent some time discussing it at its annual meeting of the preceding December.[3] A large group of the members memorialized Congress, explaining the unfortunate economic effects of large bond issues and

1 New York *Times,* March 4, 1917.

2 There were 214 Democrats, 215 Republicans, and 5 Independents, enough of whom voted with the Democrats to re-elect Champ Clark speaker.

3 Sprague, O. M. W., "Loans and Taxes in War Finance," *American Economic Review,* VII: Supplement, 199-223 (March 1917).

recommending heavy taxes.[4] Various other groups also sent petitions and took part in the discussion by writing to the newspapers.[5]

CONSIDERATION BY THE COMMITTEE ON WAYS AND MEANS

Two preliminary questions of the Ways and Means Committee[6] were easily settled. First as to the method of procedure, it was agreed that majority and minority members were to work together. This was advantageous to both parties and certainly to the progress of legislation. It soon developed as the meetings continued that many disagreements were on other than party lines anyway. The declaration of war seemed to have brought about unanimity of purpose and harmony of action. Once the die was cast the anti-preparedness and anti-Wilson Democrats joined forces heartily with the Administration. Similarly the Republicans put aside partisan antipathies. According to Kitchin's somewhat euphemistic report the Committee work was distinguished by the fact that members even ignored such considerations as the effect of taxes on their constituents and "not one man . . . even hinted that this or that tax would bring disaster to his district or his State or to the industries of his State or district and therefore should not be imposed." [7]

The second question was how much of the money required should be raised by taxes and how much by bonds. The estimates of the

[4] *Cong. Rec.* 55: 2045. Only a few of the 187 signatures are listed in the Record.

[5] The Western Economic Society and the City Club of Chicago held a conference in Chicago, June 21, 1917. Seligman, Durand, and others, *Financial Mobilization for War* (pamphlet). (Many of the papers were also published in the *Journal of Political Economy.*) The American Academy of Political and Social Science held a Conference in November 1917 (*Annals,* Vol. 75). The United States Chamber of Commerce appointed a committee on methods of financing the war. The report was printed in the *Bulletin* of the National Tax Association, II: 216-220 (May 1917). The American Economic Association issued supplements on the subject in March 1918 and 1919. See also: Bogart, E. L., *Direct and Indirect Costs of the Great World War*; Blakey, Roy G., "The Effects of Bonds and Taxes in War Finance," *South Atlantic Quarterly,* XVI: 236-248 (July 1917); Bullock, C. J., "Conscription of Wealth," *North American Review* 205: 895-904 (June 1917); Sprague, O. M. W., "Conscription of Wealth Once More," *New Republic,* 11: 300-301 (July 14, 1917); Seligman, E. R. A., "Taxes versus Bonds," New York *Times,* April 15, 1917; editorials *New Republic,* 10: 93 (Feb. 24, 1917), 10: 292 (April 7, 1917). R. M. Haig made a special report on the British War Excess Profits Tax for the American Economic Association. *American Economic Review,* X: Sup. 108. (Dec. 1920.)

[6] The members of the Committee on Ways and Means were:

Democrats	*Republicans*
Claude Kitchin (N. C.), Ch.	Joseph W. Fordney (Mich.)
Henry T. Rainey (Ill.)	J. Hampton Moore (Pa.)
Lincoln Dixon (Ind.)	William R. Green (Iowa)
Cordell Hull (Tenn.)	Charles H. Sloan (Neb.)
John N. Garner (Tex.)	Nicholas Longworth (Ohio)
James W. Collier (Miss.)	George W. Fairchild (N. Y.)
Clement C. Dickinson (Mo.)	John A. Sterling (Ill.)
William A. Oldfield (Ark.)	
Charles R. Crisp (Ga.)	
Guy T. Helvering (Kan.)	

[7] *Cong. Rec.* 55: app. 483.

cost of the war were almost staggering. Of course, no one could tell how much it would cost, partly because no one could prophesy how long it would last. Early in April Secretary McAdoo gave out a figure of something less than $4,000,000,000 for the fiscal year 1918 of which approximately half might be raised by taxation and half by bonds. But, as Fordney stated in his opening speech on the revenue bill, this was only a fraction of the amount for the total was nearer $12,000,000,000 [8] and this, for only one year, was almost twice the cost of the Civil War which lasted four years.

The preliminary agreements of the Committees were: (1) not to impose consumption taxes, (2) not to interfere with the existing tariff, and (3) to follow Secretary McAdoo's suggestions so far as they were consistent with their other basic policies.[9] The Committee lived up to these principles fairly well, but before the measure was passed the House threw over most of them.

Secretary McAdoo recommended that the tax measure be drawn so as to yield $1,800,000,000. The means suggested were: (1) to reduce the personal exemptions of the individual income tax from $4000 and $3000 to $2000 and $1500; (2) to leave the normal rate at 2%; (3) to levy an additional special tax, in reality a retroactive tax, of 50% of the amount of tax due in June 1917 from corporations and individuals on 1916 income; and (4) to begin applying the surtax at $3000 and to increase the rates to a maximum of 40%. In addition he suggested import duties on many articles then on the free list and a long list of excise taxes on freight, amusement tickets, soft drinks, liquors, sugar, tobacco, automobiles, musical instruments, and other commodities.[10]

THE WORK OF THE SUBCOMMITTEE

As soon as the Committee received the Treasury requests and estimates Chairman Kitchin appointed a subcommittee of four to serve with him in putting the material into form for the Committee. At a preliminary meeting of the whole Committee some tentative agreements were made as to the contents of the measure.

The subcommittee was composed of Fordney, ranking Republican member on the Committee; Rainey, ranking Democratic member; Longworth and Dixon.[11] Kitchin seemed to have picked almost

[8] *Cong. Rec.* 55: 2125. It was estimated that, under existing laws, the tax receipts would be $1,570,000,000 and the new bill would bring in almost $2,000,000,000. Bonds of $790,000,000 were authorized at the preceding session and $7,000,000,000 at the opening of the 65th Congress.

[9] New York *World*, April 24, 1917.

[10] New York *Times*, New York *World*, April 16, 1917.

[11] New York *Times*, May 2, 1917.

the strongest-minded individualists on the Ways and Means Committee. Certainly if these five could get together there was a good chance that the rest of the Committee could be brought around to an agreement.

At the outset Fordney did not want to try to raise over one billion dollars in taxes, but he co-operated with the others in drawing up a bill to raise approximately $1,400,000,000. He wanted low income tax exemptions and high income tax rates [12] and no tax on automobiles.[13]

Longworth also wanted to widen the base of the income tax so as to reach more taxpayers. He remarked that the policy of placing the income tax burden on less than one-half of one per cent of the people did not encourage either patriotism or responsibility. In general this was the point of view of the Republicans. Most of them favored extending both the income and excess-profits taxes to those whom the tax had not affected theretofore rather than merely pushing up the rates of the tax as previously levied. Rainey favored confiscatory rates on all individual incomes over $75,000 or $100,000 but the others in the group thought 30 per cent or 40 per cent high enough.[14]

As to the excess-profits tax, Kitchin wanted to put as much as possible of the burden on manufacturers of the North and East whom he considered responsible for the war,[15] but he wanted the tax on a permanent rather than on a war basis.[16] One of the Republican members of the group wanted to abolish the tax altogether. Some one proposed to increase the rate to 20%, but this was considered much too high. Fordney and Kitchin disagreed radically on the method of determining invested capital. Kitchin approved of the method of the 1916 law, that is, to take the cash value of the assets of the date on which they were acquired. Fordney wanted to use "the fair price or market value" at the beginning of each accounting period for which the tax was to be computed, but Kitchin disapproved because such a basis would permit large deductions and thereby materially reduce the revenue.[17] Dixon seemed to be the only one who had no set views on the tax when the subcommittee started to work. Usually he and Longworth seemed to be in accord.

[12] New York *World*, May 1, 1917.

[13] Speaking of the 5% gross sales tax on automobiles Fordney said: "I quarreled and fought and sometimes came near using profanity, I took my hat and left the room three times but never went farther than the screen and then came back. I am black and blue from my head to my heels by the punishment the Committee has inflicted on me. . ." (*Cong. Rec.* 55: 2132.)

[14] New York *World*, April 7, 1917; New York *Tribune*, April 6, 1917.

[15] New York *World*, April 28, 1917.

[16] Adams, T. S., "Should the Excess Profits Tax be Repealed?" *Quarterly Journal of Economics*, 35: 364 (May 1921).

[17] *Cong. Rec.* 55: 2129-2130; 2142.

The report of these five members recommended that the measure be drawn so as to yield $1,400,000,000, an amount somewhat less than McAdoo had recommended. They made no change in the personal exemptions for the income tax, but raised the surtax rates so that the maximum became 30%, increased the normal tax rate for individuals and corporations from 2% to 4%, and the excess-profits tax from 8% to 16%.

THE REPORT TO THE COMMITTEE ON WAYS AND MEANS

After some discussion, particularly over the excess-profits tax section, the subcommittee presented a unanimous report on May 2 to the full Ways and Means Committee which accepted it, but only after a veritable storm of protest.[18] The first day of the meeting of the full Committee showed such violent disagreements that it did not look as if a majority would favor it, whereas the leaders talked of getting unanimous support. Secretary McAdoo also helped to disrupt the subcommittee's work by sending word that it was important that the bill produce several hundred million dollars more revenue than he had first requested.[19]

The first decision of the full Committee with reference to the subcommittee draft was to raise $400,000,000 more, that is, $1,800,000,000; the second was to raise the surtax rates from 30% on income over $1,000,000 to 33% on that over $500,000.[20]

The next issue was the rate of the excess-profits tax. A majority opposed the subcommittee's rate of 16% on the ground that it was much too high. After a seven-hour debate, 12% was set as a probable compromise.[21] Hull proposed to substitute a war-profits tax, such as the English had, based on an average of any three-year prewar period, taxing the excess of earnings of war years over those of previous years, but he won no support. The Committee feared his plan would prove too complicated.[22] Unfortunately Hull was ill during the first part of the session and unable to take much part in the writing of the bill.[23]

18 The subcommittee was accused of having taken upon itself too much authority, especially in decreasing the income tax exemptions too radically. New York *World*, April 30, 1917.

19 New York *Times*, May 2, 1917.

20 New York *World*, New York *Times*, May 2, 1917.

21 New York *World*, May 3, 1917; New York *Times*, May 4, 1917.

22 New York *Times*, May 3, 1917. For the debate in the Committee see New York *Times* and New York *World*, May 3-10, 1917. Green said on the floor of the House that each member of the Committee had read the English law and the opinion was that it was much too complicated. The Committee, however, had considered it somewhat favorably at first because the excess-profits tax could be evaded by corporations that were overcapitalized. The first plan of the Senate was for the war-profits tax. See below, pp. 139, 140, 144, 145, 147-149, 151, 152.

23 Holcomb, A. E., "Pending Federal War Revenue Taxes," *Bulletin National Tax Association*, 2: 245 (June 1917).

By May 7 the Committee almost agreed to disagree,[24] especially when estimates revealed that the measure lacked $300,000,000 of providing enough revenue. Harmony prevailed, however, when they decided to raise the excess-profits tax rate to the subcommittee's figure of 16% and put the corporation normal tax at 4% but, to the surprise of most of the members, the printed draft for some unknown reason showed rates of 14% and 5% respectively. They were restored to 16% and 4%,[25] just double those of the 1916 law. About this time the Senate Finance Committee announced that open hearings on the bill would be held before the House had finished.[26] That was interpreted to mean that the bill would be completely rewritten.[27] Then in the last afternoon session of the Committee several significant and surprising moves were made. Garner moved to increase all existing tariff rates by 10% and to subject all articles on the free list to duties of 10% [28] His motion was passed by the votes of one other Democrat and all the Republicans. The Committee raised the rates of the estate tax and lowered exemptions from $50,000 to $25,000. They adopted the long-resisted Treasury recommendation for a retroactive additional tax based on the amount of corporation and individual income taxes, exclusive of excess-profits tax, due in June 1916, but made the rate 33⅓% instead of 50%. So the bill as amended was expected to yield $1,800,000,000.[29] Thus the Republicans were mollified, the Treasury was somewhat gratified; and, even if not all the Democrats were happy over it, at least, they had a unanimous report to present and they could justify any inconsistencies with the argument that the Senate would not accept the bill in any case.[30]

The Committee bill as reported to the House, and with some slight exceptions, as passed by the House, was divided into 12 titles of which the first two are most pertinent to this study.[31] Title I —

24 New York *Times,* May 8, 1917, New York *World,* May 8, 1917.

25 New York *World,* May 8, 1917.

26 Many business representatives had tried in vain to present their protests to the Ways and Means Committee but as Longworth said, if they had yielded to their requests they would not have been able to write the bill so quickly.

27 New York *Times,* May 9, 1917.

28 New York *Times,* New York *World,* May 9, 1917. Garner had made a similar proposal when the Revenue Act of March 3, 1917 was being drawn up.

29 No mention has been made of the agreements on the excise taxes which are somewhat extraneous to this discussion. They were accepted practically as drafted by the subcommittee without much discussion. At the last afternoon session a few taxes were levied on articles of consumption, such as tea and coffee.

30 For example, Fairchild (Rep., N. Y.) fought the increases in the excess-profits tax from the beginning of the Committee meetings to the end and said he would carry his opposition to the Senate if necessary. (New York *Times,* May 10, 1917.)

31 65th Congress, 1st Session, *House Report* 45. The other titles were: III — Distilled Spirits; IV — Tobacco and tobacco products; V — Freight, express, pipe lines, advertising; VI — Automobiles, tires, and tubes; jewelry, sporting goods; VII — Admissions, dues; VIII — Playing cards; IX — War estate tax; X — War customs; XI — Virgin Island Products; XII — Postage rates.

the Income Tax, was written as an amendment to the 1916 law and an addition to it.[32] It imposed a new normal tax of 2% on single persons with net income of $1000 or over and on married persons with net income of $2000 or over. The 1916 rates remained in effect; therefore, a 4% rate applied to single persons with income of $3000 or over and to married persons with income of $4000 or over. In addition to the 1916 surtax rates (graduated from 1% on income of $20,000 and over to 13% on income of $2,000,000 and over) the Committee proposed a minimum surtax of 1% on income of $5000 or over, increasing by fifteen brackets to a maximum of 33% on income over $500,000.

The corporation rate was made 2% plus the 2% already in effect. There was no exemption of partnerships engaged in agriculture or personal service, as in the previous law. In addition corporations and individuals were to be subjected to an additional tax of one-third of the income tax due in 1917 on 1916 income.

Title II — Excess Profits, levied a tax of 8% on all corporation and partnership income in excess of a deduction ($5000 and 8% of invested capital [33]), in addition to the March 3 rate of 8%, making a total of 16%.

Title IX — War Estate Tax, imposed an additional estate tax at rates graduated from ½ of 1% of the amount of the taxable net estate not in excess of $50,000 to 15% of the amount by which the net estate exceeded $15,000,000. The Committee draft also proposed a lowering of the exemption from $50,000 to $25,000 and a tax of 1% on the amount of the estate over $25,000 and not over $50,000.

THE BILL IN THE HOUSE OF REPRESENTATIVES

Party lines were practically obliterated in the House, as in the Committee, when the war revenue bill was under discussion. Chairman Kitchin presented the Committee report in a five-hour speech which explained and praised the bill, not too enthusiastically to be sure, but with qualifications as was proper, for it was recognized as a compromise report.[34] Nevertheless, he said he would vote for it

[32] The law was written as an amendment to the 1916 law on the theory that after the war it would be easy to repeal the 1917 amendments and leave the earlier law practically unaffected.

[33] "Invested Capital" was defined as "(1) actual cash paid in, (2) the actual cash value of property paid in other than cash, for stock or shares in such corporation or partnership . . . , and (3) paid in or earned surplus and undivided profits used or employed in the business: *Provided* that the good will . . . is not to be included in the actual capital invested, unless the corporation or partnership made payment therefor specifically as such in cash or tangible property. . ."

In the preceding law Section 202 read: "actual cash value, at the time of payment, of assets other than cash paid in. . . ,"

[34] *Cong. Rec.* 55: app. 483-505.

"with his eyes shut." [35] Fordney was equally candid; he both criticized and eulogized the measure and gave as his reason for voting for it, "We need the money." [35] After their speeches the House seemed to understand that the passage of the bill, unamended, was a foregone conclusion and little interest was shown in the debate. As one commentator said, "The debate . . . was almost absolutely devoid of anything approaching a scientific treatment of the subjects." [36]

There were only two issues that were of much importance so far as the income tax was concerned. One was the excess-profits tax; the other was the surtax. Madden (Rep., Ill.) had a great deal to say about the injustice of the former because of basing the rate on invested capital.[37] Borland (Dem., Mo.) and Harrison (Miss.) agreed with Fordney that valuation of invested capital should be as of the date of tax assessment.[38] Borland introduced an amendment to have the Bureau of Internal Revenue value corporate stock as for the capital stock tax,[39] that is, at par. Good (Rep., Ia.) asked why the Committee had not followed the English plan of taxing corporations on the basis of prewar profits. This brought Green to his feet with a dissertation on the difficulties and complexities of the English law which he had learned by a diligent six-month study. For example, the law made no provision for corporations that were not in existence before the war or for those that showed losses. Canada, he said, had not followed the English practice.[40]

Several of the more radical members considered the Committee surtax rates much too low. Keating (Dem., Colo.) made the most extreme amendment which was to take all individual income over $150,000. Sherley (Dem., Ky.) and Sabath (Dem., Ill.) made various attempts to get small increases. They too were unsuccessful. Lenroot (Wis.) then took up the idea and pushed it. He favored an average increase of all the rates by approximately 25% and the addition of a new bracket to make the maximum 45% on income over $1,000,000 as against the Committee's 33% on income in excess of $500,000.[41]

[35] *Cong. Rec.* 55: 2124-2144.
[36] Holcomb, A. E., "Pending Federal War Revenue Taxes," *Bulletin National Tax Association,* II: 245 (May 1917). Probably the issues were too complex to be understood by many of the members. "The income tax section raised such a cloud of confusion that for a time the House resembled a class of higher mathematics with members of the Ways and Means Committee taking turns in expounding the intricate workings of the proposed schedule of percentages and super-percentages." (New York *Times,* May 11, 1917.) For over a quarter of a century the complexities of federal income tax laws have increased as rapidly as the education of the public and the legislators.
[37] *Cong. Rec.* 55: 2281.
[38] *Cong. Rec.* 55: 2130, 2545.
[39] *Cong. Rec.* 55: 2550-2551.
[40] *Cong. Rec.* 55: 2548.
[41] *Cong. Rec.* 55: 2419, 2420; 2474; 2815.

In the midst of the vote on this amendment Kitchin produced a letter received the preceding evening from Secretary McAdoo, which stated that the Treasury needs had been underestimated and that the revenue act should be written to produce $2,245,000,000 instead of $1,800,000,000. Kitchin did not approve of revising the bill to raise this entire amount but he was willing to accept Lenroot's amendment which it was estimated would yield an additional $55,-000,000. Thus the surtax rates were raised. This was the only amendment passed, with the exception of minor ones offered by the Committee to clarify the verbiage.[42]

On the 18th of May the debate on the first two titles was completed and the House passed on to the other sections.[43] On the 23d the entire bill was passed by an overwhelming vote, 329 yeas, 76 nays.[44] The tenor of the discussion, however, became less and less favorable to the measure as the debate progressed so it was not with surprise that the members saw the Senate begin to pick it to pieces, even before the House vote was taken.

REVISION BY THE SENATE FINANCE COMMITTEE [45]

The Senate Finance Committee evinced great haste in starting the revision of the revenue measure in May ; nevertheless, it was several months before it was reported to the Senate and six months before it became law.

On May 11 the Committee opened public hearings on the bill.[46] Only a part of the first day was devoted to the income and excess-profits tax sections ; the rest of the week was taken up by protests

[42] French (Rep., Idaho) offered an amendment to secure publicity of income tax returns by requiring lists of those subject to the income tax to be posted at a public place in the county of domicile. (*Cong. Rec.* 55: 2749.) It was rejected. The Treasury thought it could not be administered without great expense. (65th Congress, 2d Session, *Hearings before the Committee on Ways and Means,* I: 144.)

[43] One of the most controversial sections was that which levied 3 cents postage on first class mail and established a zone system, a proposal that called forth tremendous opposition from newspapers.

[44] *Cong. Rec.* 55: 2818-2819.

[45] Members of the Senate Committee on Finance were:

Democrats	*Republicans*
F. M. Simmons (N. C.), Ch.	Boies Penrose (Pa.)
William J. Stone (Mo.)	Henry Cabot Lodge (Mass.)
John Sharp Williams (Miss.)	Porter J. McCumber (N. D.)
Hoke Smith (Ga.)	Reed Smoot (Utah)
Charles Thomas (Colo.)	Jacob Gallinger (N. H.)
Ollie M. James (Ky.)	Robert M. La Follette (Wis.)
William Hughes (N. J.)	Charles E. Townsend (Mich.)
Thomas P. Gore (Okla.)	
Andrieus A. Jones (N. M.)	
Peter G. Gerry (R. I.)	

[46] 65th Congress, 1st Session, *Hearings and Briefs before the (Senate) Committee on Finance on H. R. 4280.*

directed towards the excise taxes on manufacturers and those on various commodities.[47] The first witness objected to the tax on stock dividends. Others pointed to the ambiguity of Section 202, which defined the basis for evaluating corporation capital for the excess-profits tax. The retroactive features of the bill were criticized also.

The Committee held informal meetings before the House measure was signed[48] but waited until May 24 to start rewriting the bill. From the outset the conservative majority of the Committee seemed to be harmonious and of one mind as to the goal. At the end of the first day's session it was agreed not to try to raise so much as the Treasury requested, not even so much as the House bill was expected to yield. The tentative amount set was about $1,250,000,000. It was also decided, at least for the time being, to substitute for the 16% excess-profits tax a war-profits tax based on an average of five prewar years, much as in the British plan, and to strike out the retroactive tax on individual and corporate incomes, the 10% increase in the tariff, and increases in the estate tax.[49] These changes, Penrose said, would go a long way towards restoring public confidence which was rudely shaken especially by the suggestion for the additional tax on 1916 income.

In the sessions immediately following, the Lenroot surtax rates were eliminated. That left the maximum surtax rate 33% on income over $500,000. Penrose and Lodge were the leaders in reducing income tax rates and would have liked even greater reductions on income in excess of $40,000.[50] La Follette and Gore made futile protests, not only because of the reduction in surtax rates but also because of the failure of the Committee to write a bill that would bring in a large amount of revenue. About the middle of June La Follette went to work on a substitute for the entire bill that would levy high income and surtax rates but abolish the excise taxes on necessities.[51] Whether or not his announcement had any influence is not definitely known, but soon after it came the Committee made tentative suggestions for increasing heavily the tax on war profits of large corporations by graduating the rates to the unheard of maxi-

[47] "It was a gloomy picture that interests opposing the war tax increases painted for the committee. Disorganization of industries, closed factories, discharged employees, reduced prices to producers, and destruction of retailers were among the predictions." (New York *Times*, May 12, 1917.)

[48] New York *World*, May 12, 19, 1917.

[49] New York *Times*, New York *World*, May 25, 1917. The Committee also eliminated the gross sales tax on certain manufacturers, but put taxes on coffee, cocoa, sugar, soft drinks, confectionery, and tobacco.

[50] New York *Times*, June 12, 1917.

[51] *La Follette's Magazine*, Aug. 1917, p. 12; Sept. 1917, pp. 1, 4-6; New York *Times*, June 11, 16, 1917. The House levied taxes on gas, electricity, telephone service, tea, and coffee.

mum of 75%,[52] but these rates were kept only temporarily, then lowered to a schedule with a maximum of 40%. The idea of graduating rates on corporation profits was new and was doubtless intended to make them correspond roughly with the surtaxes on individual income.

Most of the time of the Committee was spent on the war-profits tax section. Drafting it was a difficult task, for there were so many conflicting interests. The administration of a measure involving the determination of invested capital as proposed by the House would admittedly be a problem. Serious objection was made, however, to the British system of taxing war profits, for in this case it was necessary to establish base years of normal profits. Ever since the passage of the tax on profits of munition manufacturers there had been much pressure to extend it to others who had made profits from the war. The excess-profits tax that had been levied by the Act of March 3, 1917 and the one recently passed by the House were not considered adequate to reach such gains. The Committee was impressed by the advice of several financiers and economists that a war-profits tax would be more equitable than the excess-profits tax. It was influenced also by a study of the practice of European countries, particularly England. It will be recalled, however, that the House Committee had reached exactly the opposite conclusion after a similar study.

When the war-profits base was agreed upon, the years 1911, 1912, and 1913 were selected as those of normal profits, but only after much protest by business men that this had been a depressed period and hence was an unfair base.[53] Representatives of the railroads said the country would be much better off if they could use their surpluses for betterments and extensions rather than for taxes.[54] These arguments failed to influence the Committee and, after much consideration, the members decided to extend this war-profits tax also to individuals whose annual income from business exceeded $5000.[55] This attempt to spread the tax burden on all as equally as possible led to several complications. As the bill was passed by the House, the excess-profits tax upon corporations more or less roughly balanced the surtax on individual income. The Senate Committee proposal added undue burdens on some individuals. For example, it was applicable

52 New York *Times*, June 18, 1917. The fact that the war tax rate was made 80% in 1918 takes away the shock that the mention of 75% had in 1917. Even the English rate had not exceeded 60% at that time, although an 80% rate went into effect before the year was over.

53 New York *Times*, June 18, 1917. A representative of the Investment Bankers Association told the Committee that any other period would be more representative than this one.

54 New York *Times*, June 27, 1917.

55 New York *Times*, June 21, 1917.

to income from business, not to income from property, hence had the very reverse effect of that desired by many, namely, to tax "earned" income at a higher rate than "unearned" income.

Jones (Dem., N. M.) spent some time in attempting to help the Committee work out the nice problem of the equitable treatment of corporations, partnerships, and individuals in view of this new decision and also the problem caused by the common corporation practice of not distributing all earnings but of putting much back into surplus, thus relieving wealthy shareholders from the payment of surtax.[56] The latter method of reducing individual surtaxes was not available for partners or individuals not connected with corporations. Furthermore, corporations could deduct from gross income such items as salaries, whereas an individual in business could deduct only the salaries paid to others. The Senator's first suggestion was to treat corporate income like that of partnerships, that is, to tax it as if distributed whether actually distributed or not. This was not adopted, however, because it was feared that it would work a hardship on small stockholders who would have to pay a tax whether or not they received dividends. There was also the question of constitutionality.[57] It was then agreed to levy a 15% tax on undistributed earnings after permitting an exemption of 20% of net income.[58]

No sooner had this decision been made than protests poured in upon the Committee from corporations of all sizes, not only because such a measure would levy a third tax upon them but because it would seriously hamper them, particularly when, due to war demands, plant extensions were necessary and funds could not be easily secured because the government had "pre-empted the investment field" to a large extent.[59] The Committee agreed, therefore, to levy a penalty tax of 15% upon any surplus which the Secretary of the Treasury considered larger than required for the legitimate needs of the corporation. Before the bill was introduced, however, the rate was materially reduced.[60] As Jones was not at all satisfied that this would be equitable, he carried the fight to the Senate floor; and, in fact, he brought up the matter in connection with every tax bill thereafter until 1924 when it was accepted by the Senate, though later rejected by the Conference Committee.[61]

There seems to have been no opposition to the important substitution of information-at-the-source for collection-at-the-source, nor to the elimination of several of the House provisions, chiefly the retro-

56 See below, Chap. XVII.

57 *La Follette's Magazine,* Oct. 1917, p. 4; *Cong. Rec.* 55: 7474.

58 *Cong. Rec.* 55: 5966, 6004.

59 *Cong. Rec.* 55: 5966, 6004.

60 New York *Times,* Aug. 1, 1917. *Cong. Rec.* 55: 6165-6183.

61 See below, Chap. XVII and Exhibit 8, Appendix. In 1936 many thought the undistributed profits tax was a *new* proposal.

active 33⅓% tax on 1916 income, the 10% horizontal increase in tariff rates, the additional estate tax, and the special tax on munition manufacturers.

The Committee work was interrupted for about two weeks to await the result of the House vote on the liquor prohibition amendment to the Food Administration bill which, when passed, automatically killed one section of the tax bill.[62] Further delays were occasioned also by the "staggering and alarming" request of Secretary McAdoo late in June for $5,000,000,000 for the army and $2,000,000,000 for fortifications.[63] The war-profits tax rates were again raised, this time to 50%, which it was estimated would yield $505,000,000 more. Early in July, after six weeks' deliberation, the report was completed. It was estimated that the taxes recommended would yield $1,642,170,000, which was $150,000,000 less than the House bill and $228,000,000 less than McAdoo requested.

The report could not be taken up by the Senate immediately, however, for the leaders agreed that the Food Administration bill should take precedence over the revenue measure. Hence the revenue bill was withdrawn for about six weeks. In the interim wartime liquor prohibition became law, as part of the food conservation program, and the Treasury estimates of war needs were again raised, so the Finance Committee finally yielded to the pressure of Secretary McAdoo and revised the tax bill to produce more revenue. All income taxes were increased, including those on war profits, and, after much protest by Kitchin,[64] even those on individuals. Other changes were made also so that the estimate of the yield was put at $2,000,000,000.[65]

The Committee bill was then introduced for the second time.[66] Speaking editorially of the measure, the New York *Times* said :

> It is the greatest burden ever put upon any people, treble the amount paid by us before the war, double the amount paid by England now, and England raises a larger proportion of war expenses by taxation than any other country. These burdens would have been thought incredible, unendurable, but for the education through which the world has passed under German compulsion.[67]

62 New York *Times,* June 26, 1917 ; New York *World,* July 26, 1917.

63 New York *Times,* June 27, July 1 and 3, 1917. New York *World,* July 26 and 28, 1917.

64 Kitchin resented the "sweeping changes" made by the Senate. New York *Times,* June 11, 1917 ; New York *Tribune,* July 30, August 20, 1917.

65 "It [this announcement] seems to have a sobering effect upon those in the House and Senate who were disposed to criticize the Administration yesterday, and to bring to them a realization of the fact that the financing of the war devolves largely on the United States." (New York *World,* July 26, 1917.)

66 65th Congress, 1st Session, *Senate Report* 103.

67 New York *Times,* Aug. 8, 1917.

The minority report was signed by La Follette, Thomas, and Gore who wanted a larger percentage of total war expenses raised by taxes on corporate incomes, excess profits, and liquor rather than by taxes on small incomes or consumption.[66]

THE BILL IN THE SENATE

When the bill finally reached the Senate on August 15, Chairman Simmons, Senators Penrose, McCumber, and other members of the Finance Committee explained the differences between the House and Senate measures and why the changes were made.

Title I – the War Income Tax, provided for a normal tax on individual net income of 2% in addition to 2% already in effect, so that the total normal tax became 4%, the same as in the House bill. The Senate Committee reduced the maximum surtax from 62% to 50% but increased the bracket rates by 1% on incomes between $15,000 and $40,000 and raised the corporation rate, previously 4%, by 2% so that it became 6%. For the first time, therefore, the normal tax on corporate income was different from that on individual income. Simmons said there were two reasons for the increased corporation tax: first, because of the need for additional revenue due to increased army estimates and to the passage of the amendment for prohibition of liquor; second, because of the fact that the surtax made a discrimination against individuals and in favor of corporations, which was accentuated when the war-profits tax was extended to individuals.[68] Information-at-the-source was substituted for collection-at-the-source except for interest on bonds and for income of non-residents.[69] The Committee was impressed by the fact that of the $360,000,000 collected from the income tax in 1916, less than one-fourth was collected at the source. Furthermore, the Committee hoped that the information received as a result of the new requirement would be of real value to the Bureau of Internal Revenue in administering the complicated law.

In order to avoid double taxation the Senate Finance Committee exempted the dividends received by corporations from other corporations which had already paid the tax. As passed by the House this provision applied to the excess-profits tax, and the Senate extended it to the normal tax also.[70]

The Committee struck out the House provision for the additional tax of 33⅓% on 1916 income because it seemed "both morally and

[68] *Cong. Rec.* 55: 5966. The efforts of Jones to meet this situation are described above. See also *Cong. Rec.* 55: 5966 and Taussig, F. W., "The War Tax Act of 1917," *Quarterly Journal of Economics,* XXXII: 25, 29, 30, 34 (Nov. 1917).

[69] *Cong. Rec.* 55: 5967. See above, Chap. III.

[70] *Cong. Rec.* 55: 5967.

economically unsound and to deserve exclusion as retroactive legislation." [71]

Title II — the War Profits Tax, was the subject of much discussion. Why did the Senate depart from the excess-profits basis adopted by the House?

In the first place the Committee members were impressed by the statistics that showed corporations had made "war profits" of $3,000,000,000 in 1916. They thought the percentage of this amount that the House bill would take was much too small.[72] Secondly, the Committee agreed with many business men who testified at the hearings that the House bill was based on an inelastic and fallacious principle that everyone made the same percentage of profits before the war. "The standard," said Simmons, "must reflect the facts of the individual case and it must be equitable." Therefore the Committee substituted a principle "based upon the actual results of each man's business operations." That is, it allowed "a deduction of the average profits actually made during the three years immediately preceding the outbreak of the war." Another new principle was established by graduating the rates, much as in the case of the surtax on individuals, from 12% on income not in excess of 15% of normal profits to 50% on income in excess of 250% of normal profits. This followed European practice. The Committee thought that the flat rate as set by the House bill "would call for a greater sacrifice from the taxpayer who is making only a small additional profit than from one who is making an additional profit of from 100% to 200%." [73]

Furthermore, the House provision involved the determination of invested capital, which was difficult if not impossible to make. On one hand, there would be the problem of preventing the inflation of capital by "watering" the stock and by including intangible assets which could easily be made to appear as though they had been paid for. On the other hand, corporations might be legitimately entitled to include values of patents, trademarks, brands, and similar assets, which were valuable but for which no payment had ever been made.[74] So long as rates were low these difficulties were not serious, but with the immediate prospect of very high rates they appeared insurmount-

[71] 65th Congress, 1st Session, *Senate Report* 103.

[72] *Cong. Rec.* 55: 6497.

[73] *Cong. Rec.* 55: 5967. The difference in the tax under the House and Senate bills was shown in the Committee calculation of the amount due from 48 corporations on 1916 income. The following are a few examples:

	House bill	*Senate bill*
United States Steel Corporation	$21,685,000	$76,726,000
du Pont & Company	11,240,000	35,923,000
Anaconda Copper Company	5,817,000	14,512,000
Montgomery Ward & Company	476,000	638,000
Central Leather Company	1,894,000	2,164,000

[74] *Cong. Rec.* 55: 6001-6002; 65th Congress, 1st Session, *Senate Report* 103.

able. Another administrative advantage of a war-profits tax was the fact that the government already had records of prewar income of most corporations.

Another radical change was to make the war-profits tax apply to individuals, as has already been mentioned. This was done because the Committee wanted to make the tax "as embracing as possible." The House had already extended it to partnerships and the Senators thought it "but right and proper that the individual should also be included." The complications arising from this decision have already been noted.[75]

As in the House, opposition to the bill did not develop along party lines. The Senate lacked strong leadership to counteract the influence of several little cliques. One comparatively small group, nicknamed the "Obstructionists" because of their anti-war vote, wielded great influence. They were members of both parties, but more were Democrats than were Republicans. They opposed Wilson largely because they considered him a "college professor," not a politician. In this group were Stone and Reed (Mo.), and Vardaman (Miss.), men of dominant personalities.[76] There were those who wished to increase taxation on the rich, for example, Hollis (Rep., N. H.), Gore, Borah, Johnson (Cal.), La Follette and Norris. Several southern members, notably Underwood and Bankhead, led a coterie to make audible the distress of the cotton planter and manufacturer.

La Follette was the most determined fighter against the measure because he thought it a fundamental error to raise by taxes such a small percentage of the total war costs and to levy too small a proportion of the taxes that were imposed on those with large incomes. Gore and Thomas, who joined him in signing the minority report, took almost no part in the debate on the floor of the Senate.

La Follette's plan seemed to be to pursue the Senate with one amendment after another, even until the day the bill was passed. He started on August 22 with an amendment to increase the surtax but, doubtless to his surprise, before it came to a vote another somewhat similar one was voted on and passed.[77] This important break

[75] See above, p. 141. For further discussion of this controversy, see below, Chaps. VII and XVII.

[76] Vardaman was a negativistic person who demanded attention. One newspaper commented that his chief fear in life was that nothing would be said about him — "If you can't praise him he wants you to abuse him." "Jim" Reed was the gadfly of the Senate, annoying at most times, a wholesome critic of others, but liked by his colleagues. It was said that "the trouble with Reed is that he has been prosecutor so long that he can not get over it. The Senate is merely a court room to him. Every great question that comes up is merely a question to be tried. His job is to convict somebody." (New York *Times* Magazine, Aug. 19, 1917.)

[77] The press made much of the undercurrent of opposition to La Follette and the little group of "willful" men who fought against the Administration's armed neutrality bill, the declaration of war, and conscription of men for the army. (New York *Times*, New York *Tribune*, Aug. 24, 29, 1917.)

in the Committee measure was started by a Committee member, Gerry (Rep., R. I.), a wealthy young "would-be" radical, who prided himself on his study of war finance.[78] He thought the Committee bill "was not sound as regards big incomes" because the rates were not graduated above $500,000, so he proposed three brackets ($500,000 to $750,000, $750,000 to $1,000,000, and the excess over $1,000,000) to be taxed at 35%, 45%, and 50%, respectively. This change would add $40,000,000 to the yield. The author received support from such conservatives as Smoot and Lewis (Dem., Ill.) as well as from the "progressive" Borah and Johnson.

Kenyon (Rep., Ia.) was not to be outdone so he proposed rates reaching to 90%. Penrose sarcastically told his colleague that such rates made a total of 105% because he had overlooked the tax already in effect under the existing law. "It shows," said Penrose, "the profound investigation with which these amendments are offered." [79] Kenyon thereupon withdrew his amendment and that of Gerry was adopted without a dissenting vote.[80]

La Follette, still dissatisfied because the tax rates on the lower brackets were not changed by this amendment, introduced a substitute for the entire section. This was done while the Senate was working on the Committee amendments, with the result that there was more or less of a parliamentary snarl and the consumption of a great deal of time in speech-making. His amendment was defeated, but this did not prevent his introducing many more, each of which met the same fate.[81] Hollis, Johnson, and Hardwick joined the game with outwardly the same result, but the cumulative effort was successful. The Committee agreed to restore the Lenroot rates of the House bill and these were adopted by the Senate. The anomalous situation created by the adoption of this amendment in addition to Gerry's was straightened out by Simmons who proposed several amendments. The final Senate action was for a maximum surtax rate of 40% on income in excess of $500,000.

The corporation tax muddle was even worse than that surrounding the surtax. Bankhead, thinking of the cotton industry, was concerned about the company that had made small prewar profits and large war profits and which, therefore, would have large taxable earnings. He protested that the Committee had not followed the English practice as claimed because in that country the taxpayer could choose his prewar years.[82] Underwood, too, spoke in the same

[78] *Cong. Rec.* 55: 6220-6222; New York *Tribune*, Aug. 26, 1917.

[79] *Cong. Rec.* 55: 6237.

[80] *Cong. Rec.* 55: 6239.

[81] *Cong. Rec.* 55: 6542 (Sept. 3); 6624 (Sept. 5); 6662 (Sept. 6); 6720 (Sept. 7); 6872 (Sept. 10).

[82] *Cong. Rec.* 55: 6067-6097, 6446-6456. Cotton mill owners, especially in the South, "deluged" their Senators with protests over the Senate Committee plan. (New York *Tribune*, Aug. 28, 1917.)

vein. Simmons[83] and Lodge both defended the Committee action by showing the special provisions made for such cases, that is, corporations with subnormal profits during the prewar years were to have the tax levied "on the average profits made during six years by representative concerns in like business."[84]

Pomerene (Dem., Ohio) joined the opponents and argued that it was unsound to use prewar earnings as a basis, therefore the House bill was much more equitable in this respect. He showed that by allowing an exemption equal to prewar income, a corporation might entirely escape the war-profits tax. He said, for example :

> If a corporation has been making $1,000,000 per year during the years 1911, 1912, and 1913, and making $1,000,000 during the current year, in all good conscience I do not see any reason why that $1,000,000 should not contribute its share toward the maintenance of the government during this trying period of our history.

On August 25 Johnson, La Follette, Borah, and Kenyon conferred as to the most effective means of pushing through amendments for a higher tax on corporate profits.[85]

The majority members of the Committee were disturbed at the opposition to their bill because they did not want drastic increases in rates, yet felt they must find a compromise and do it speedily so as not to delay passage of the bill. They had worked on the principle that business must not be disturbed. The Administration, while desirous of getting revenue, considered that it was much more important to keep the wheels of industry going and not to bring on a panic. After all, the real goal was to win the war.[86]

The Committee members were admittedly impressed by the arguments of the objectors, particularly those of Pomerene, a conservative, and by the pressure put on them by the Senate, the temper of which was shown by the vote on the Gerry amendment. Simmons, therefore, with the approval of the Administration, perhaps at its instigation, presented to his colleagues a revised method of computing the war-profits tax, which was to limit the deduction with respect to prewar earnings to a minimum of 6% and a maximum of 10% of the invested capital as of January 1 of the taxable year.[87] In addition, the maximum rate of tax was increased from 50 to 60%.[88] This reversal from a strictly war-profits basis was a surprise even to some

[83] *Cong. Rec.* 55: 6449.
[84] *Cong. Rec.* 55: 6229.
[85] New York *Tribune,* Aug. 26, 1917.
[86] New York *Tribune,* Sept. 6, 1917.
[87] *Cong. Rec.* 55: 6433.
[88] *Cong. Rec.* 55: 6460-6461. A special provision was made for corporations in which the prewar profits were very low and for corporations that were not in existence in the prewar period, by basing the tax on profits of representative concerns in the same kind of business.

members of the Committee. Ten days before it would have been too radical for consideration. La Follette, for instance, said that he had supposed that it had been one of the principal aims of the Senate bill to avoid the question of capitalization. He told of the countless times in past weeks that the Committee had "solemnly decided that under no circumstances would the bill as reported impose upon the Secretary of the Treasury the necessity of ascertaining the capitalization of corporations."

The definition of invested capital again became important. The Committee called before it Professor Taussig of Harvard and other economists who did their best "to frame some definition which could be adopted by the committee and incorporated in this bill which would, so to speak, squeeze the water out of the overcapitalization of these corporations."

La Follette objected to this switch to the excess-profits basis because he favored a war-profits tax and because the Committee amendment allowed surplus to be counted as part of capital. He reproached the chairman because everything he had said in denunciation of the House plan applied equally well to that of the Senate.[89] Differences between La Follette and Simmons degenerated into a rather heated argument over the content of some tabular material. Borah intervened with the very pertinent remark :

> I am not at all interested in the intellectual combat going on between the Senator from Wisconsin and the Senator from North Carolina nor as to who shall win in the particular contest, but the thing that is perfectly bewildering to an onlooker in Vienna is why the committee did not discuss these facts during the eight weeks it was investigating the subject.[90]

To this Simmons replied, not very convincingly, that the Committee members had originally interpreted the sentiment of the country as favoring a distinctly war-profits tax, but later, Senators of both parties and many influential people outside of Congress had called to their attention the enormous requirements of the Treasury and that therefore the tax should be levied not as a war-profits tax but as an excess-profits tax.[90] Simmons estimated that these changes would add $500,000,000 to the revenue, a step that would have been almost inconceivable ten days earlier.[91] Then he announced a motion to invoke cloture, but this was withdrawn after La Follette's protest that the request was preposterous.[92]

[89] *Cong. Rec.* 55: 6524-6525. See also *La Follette's Magazine*, Dec. 1917.
[90] *Cong. Rec.* 55: 6538.
[91] New York *Tribune*, Aug. 29, 1917. Penrose and Smoot criticized the Treasury for sending in piecemeal estimates of expenditures. (*Cong. Rec.* 55: 6480-6481, 6562.)
[92] *Cong. Rec.* 55: 6437, 6462.

Bankhead also tried to combat the Committee's new plan by proposing an excess-profits tax based on invested capital with exemptions of 8% and with rates reaching a maximum of 75%. Underwood supported him. The majority, however, had successfully lined up their supporters and organized enough of a backing to defeat this amendment, the last of its kind.[92] With the acceptance of the Administration excess-profits tax section on September 5,[93] the biggest fight on the bill was over.

Then Jones brought forward his plan for taxing all undistributed corporation income, which the Committee had turned down. The Senate also objected to his plan, accepted the Committee's penalty tax of 10% on such earnings, and refused to eliminate the exemption for undistributed net income which was actually invested and employed in the business.[94] The Senate draft prevented evasion to some extent, however, by making dividends taxable at the rate in effect in the year when distributed so that corporations could not claim they were earnings of a previous year taxable at a lower rate.

Hardwick's amendment proposing a $50 bonus to members of the American forces serving in France stirred up a "stormy three-hour scene." [95] Another unsuccessful amendment was proposed by Owens (Okla.) to substitute the inheritance tax for the excise tax on articles of consumption.[96]

At four o'clock on September 10, according to previous agreement, the vote on the bill was taken, and only four negative votes were recorded, those of Gronna, Borah, La Follette, and Norris.[97]

ACTION OF THE CONFERENCE COMMITTEE

There were three main differences between the bills of the two houses, those respecting: (1) the income tax rates, (2) the excess-profits tax, and (3) the postage rates. Only the first two will be discussed here.

The Conference Committee spent several weeks working on the bill to reach compromises satisfactory to both sides. The House managers, particularly Kitchin, resented the Senate changes and seemed to try to exert a "determinative influence" that bordered on

93 *Cong. Rec.* 55: 6623.
94 *Cong. Rec.* 55: 6623. The section also contained a proviso that if the Secretary of the Treasury found that any portion of the amount so retained was not reasonably required in the business a tax of 15% should be levied. La Follette said at the time that it was wholly impossible of enforcement. (*La Follette's Magazine*, Oct. 1917.)
95 New York *Tribune*, Sept. 8, 1917.
96 *Cong. Rec.* 55: 6793.
97 *Cong. Rec.* 55: 6886.

"belligerency."[98] It was rumored that Underwood was called in to harmonize the divergent points of view.[99]

The Senate proposal for a maximum surtax of 50% on incomes in excess of $2,000,000 was accepted in lieu of the House maximum of 62%. The special tax on munition manufacturers was retained but the rate was reduced from 12½% to 10% and the tax was to expire December 31, 1917. The Conferees upheld the Senate in striking out the retroactive tax of 33⅓%, the increase in tariff rates, and the provision for collection at the source. The House estate tax was retained.

The Senate bill as finally passed was much more in line with the House bill than the one introduced into the Senate, so far as corporation taxes were concerned; but there were several points of disagreement, for example, with respect to the definition of invested capital, the amount of exemption, and the rates of the tax. The House managers were very insistent that their excess-profits plan be adopted but finally agreed to a compromise to limit the amount of deduction based on invested capital to a minimum of 7% and a maximum of 9%. The House draft was for 8%. An additional flat exemption of $3000 for corporations and $6000 for individuals was permitted. The latter was the Senate figure; the House figure had been $5000. The Senate plan for graduating rates was accepted but the minimum was increased from 12% to 20%.

Thus the bill, which was a compromise between divergent interests in each house of Congress, became even more of a compromise when revised by the Conferees. It is not strange that many inconsistent and complicated sections crept in. The general state of confusion in the minds of members of the House upon receiving the Conferees' report is exemplified in the following sarcastic comment of Congressman Cannon (Rep., Ill.):

> I put in an anxious day yesterday. I did not say my prayers or read a chapter in the Bible, or go to church. I tried to get outside the conference report. I went to bed at one o'clock this morning. I did not have any help present on Sunday, nor did I have any of the acts of Congress to which I could refer, but I arrived at the conclusion that I did not know how many law suits were to grow out of this bill, and that I did not know in many respects what it is to do. I hope it will produce a large amount of money, and I believe it will. I hope when another bill comes — and God knows, if this war does not close inside of 12 months another bill will come — I hope that that bill will be such that all of us experts and

98 "One member of the committee described the majority leader's attitude as a 'shame and a disgrace.'" "He has put stumbling blocks in the way of nearly every compromise suggestion made by other members of the Committee." "Members declared that his belligerency is prompted by his ambition to enter the United States Senate where Simmons stands in his way." (New York *Tribune,* Sept. 20, 1917.) Kitchin was, however, almost persecuted by the press. (Villard, O. G., *Fighting Years,* p. 308.)

99 New York *Tribune,* Sept. 22, 1917.

non-experts can see what it does. This bill harks back and refers to provisions in the Payne tariff law, the law of 1916, which is not repealed except in spots, the law of last March, which was repealed very largely, if not entirely. And I will confess that I do not believe that, unaided, I could get outside of it in three months. I wish that there had been time so that the bill could tell its own story upon its face, disregarding the law of 1916, the Underwood tariff law, the Payne tariff law, and the law of last March, repealing here and there a section or a clause or modifying it or amending it.[100]

Nevertheless, there was nothing for Congress to do but to accept it. The report was completed September 29, and the President signed the bill October 3, exactly four years after he had signed the first income tax bill.

The result, so far as estimated additional yield was concerned, was to increase it to $2,514,800,000, from $1,868,800,000 as drafted by the House, and $2,411,600,000 as drafted by the Senate.[101]

SUMMARY OF THE LAW [102]

The Act contained thirteen titles of which only three are pertinent to this study: I — War Income Tax; II — War Excess-Profits Tax; and XII — Income Tax Amendments. It must be borne in mind that the Act was written as an amendment to that of September 8, 1916, and not as a complete entity in itself.

Title I provided for a normal tax of 2% on net income of individuals, and 4% on that of corporations in addition to the 1916 rates, making the totals 4% for individuals and 6% for corporations. For the additional 2% tax the personal exemption of individuals was reduced from $4000 for heads of families and $3000 for single individuals to $2000 and $1000 respectively. A head of a family was allowed an additional exemption of $200 for each dependent.

The surtax, in addition to that already in effect (with maximum rate of 13%) was graduated from 1% on amounts by which income exceeded $5000 and did not exceed $7500 to 50% on amounts over $1,000,000, making a total of 63% on the highest bracket.

Title II provided for the war excess-profits tax, applicable to corporations, partnerships, and individuals, levied on the difference between the prewar normal profits and those of 1917. The basic "normal" years chosen were 1911, 1912, and 1913. A deduction was allowed of (1) an amount equal to the same percentage of invested capital for the taxable year which the average amount of the net in-

100 *Cong. Rec.* 55: 7594.

101 Details of the estimates of each title are shown in Blakey, Roy G., "The Revenue Act of 1917," *American Economic Review,* VII: 792 (Dec. 1917). The actual receipts from internal revenue taxes for the fiscal years 1916, 1917, and 1918 were $512,723,000, $809,383,000, and $3,698,955,000 respectively.

102 40 *Statutes at Large* 300.

come for the prewar period was of invested capital for the prewar period, but not less than 7 nor more than 9% of invested capital for the taxable year, and (2) $3000 for corporations and $6000 for individuals and partnerships.

If there was no income from business during 1911, 1912, and 1913, or if the relation of net income to capital was low in comparison to that of like concerns engaged in similar business, the Secretary of the Treasury was empowered to grant a deduction equivalent to the deduction granted such concerns. The definition of invested capital was much the same as in the House bill with the addition of more specific provisions as to patents, good will, trade marks, etc.

The tax rates were graduated as follows:

20% of the amount of net income in excess of the deduction and not in excess of 15% of the invested capital for the taxable year;

25% of the amount of net income in excess of 15% and not in excess of 20% of such capital;

35% of the amount of the net income in excess of 20% and not in excess of 25% of such capital;

45% of the amount of the net income in excess of 25% and not in excess of 33% of such capital; and

60% of the amount of net income in excess of 33% of such capital.

For business in which no capital or only a nominal capital was required, the tax was 8% of the net income in excess of a deduction of $3000 for a corporation or $6000 for a partnership or individual.

Contributions of individuals to educational and philanthropic organizations were allowable deductions but to an amount not in excess of 15% of taxable net income. Corporations and individuals were not permitted to deduct interest on "indebtedness incurred for the purchase of obligations or securities the interest upon which is exempt from taxation under this title."

A new penalty tax of 10% was levied on corporate earnings that were not distributed except such as were "actually invested in the business or . . . retained for employment in the reasonable requirements of the business," or invested in obligations of the United States issued after September 1, 1917, and, if the Secretary of the Treasury found that any portion of such surplus was "not reasonably required in the business," the tax was 15%. This was an attempt to prevent corporations from retaining their earnings, instead of distributing them so that shareholders whose incomes fell in the higher brackets would avoid the surtax. As predicted at the time this section was adopted, it was not enforced; the Treasury reported its administration impracticable.[103]

103 In drafting the 1918 Act Kitchin admitted that this section was absolutely inoperative because there was no way for the Treasury Department to get evidence whether the surplus was "reasonably required in the business." (*Cong. Rec.* 56: 10429.) See below, Chap. XVII.

A new section was added to require corporations, trustees, employers, and others who made payments of wages, salaries, interest, etc., of $800 or more in any taxable year to report the names of such employees or recipients and the amounts paid to them.

The first general criticism of the measure was that it would raise only about two and a half billion dollars, a small fraction of the funds needed for the war. Before the end of the calendar year 1917 Congress had appropriated about $19,000,000,000, including approximately $7,000,000,000 for loans to the "Allied and Associated Powers," and had provided means for raising only a little more than half of the requirements. Bond issues had been authorized to the extent of $5,000,000,000. Taxes from laws in effect before the declaration of war were estimated to yield about $1,300,000,000 and the new War Revenue Act was expected to produce a little more than $2,500,000,000 additional.

The enormity of the total war cost for the first year may be pictured somewhat more realistically when it is seen that the total cost of the federal government from 1791 to 1917 – including the War of 1812, the Mexican War, the Civil War, and the Spanish American War – amounted to $26,000,000,000. Furthermore, $19,000,000,000 was "more than all of the Entente Allies spent in either the first or second year of the war, four-fifths as much as Great Britain, the largest spender, has used in three entire years and . . . two-thirds of the combined expenditures of all the Central Powers in the same three year period." [104]

Students of finance showed very clearly that a policy of heavy borrowing was a very dangerous course to follow because of the economic consequences. In the first place, the burden of war could not be put entirely on the shoulders of the next generation ; secondly, the burden could not be met by "financial makeshifts" but demanded "unusual and stringent economy." Heavy borrowing would inevitably result in inflation, which in turn would bring about a rapid rise in prices, thus causing wholesale economic and social dislocations and serious hardship to wage earners, salaried employees, and those with fixed incomes.

On the other hand, there were those who thought that the tax bill had reached the "highest notch," and that any higher rates would injure business and destroy the source of revenue. It was also shown that the tax bill was the greatest burden that had ever been laid upon the American people and "heavier too than those made by any other country at a corresponding stage in the . . . great conflict." [105]

104 Blakey, Roy G., "Shifting the War Burden upon the Future," *Annals of American Academy of Political and Social Science,* 75: 90-104 (Jan. 1918).

105 Taussig, F. W., "The Financial Situation : A General Survey," *Annals of American Academy of Political and Social Science,* 75: 9 (Jan. 1918).

The most controverted part of the tax bill was Title II, the excess-profits tax. As Professor T. S. Adams said, when speaking before the American Academy of Political and Social Science :

> The excess profits tax law itself fairly bristles with legal and administrative difficulties. Section 210, for instance, considering cases in which the administrative authorities are unable satisfactorily to determine the invested capital, provides another and a satisfactory method of determining the deduction, but says nothing about the rates of taxation which depend, in a very important way, upon the amount of invested capital itself — which amount, this very section assumes it is impossible satisfactorily to compute. In other words, at this part of the law there is an open chasm. The law, as it were, starts to bridge a gulf but terminates abruptly when we are half way across.[106]

On the other hand, as Professor Bullock stated : "It was the sort of tax that Congress was bound to enact, and could not possibly avoid." The popular demand for taxation of those making money out of the war was too strong to overlook. And similarly there was insistence that all making large profits should contribute to the prosecution of the war.[107]

It has been shown above that the excess-profits tax was chosen in place of the war-profits tax because of the desire to establish the tax on a broader base. For a similar reason the tax was made to apply to partnerships and individuals in business unless there was practically no invested capital. These attempts to equalize the tax between different corporations and between corporations, individuals and partnerships were unsuccessful.

The first difficulty and one that proved insurmountable at that time was how to find a fair and practical basis for computing invested capital. To take original investment was inequitable. To quote Adams again —

> The original investment has no permanence. It changes inevitably. Durable assets, such as land and buildings, depreciate and appreciate. . . Intangible assets are built up and in turn disappear. The true capital, the true investment, changes with the shifting level of income and with future prospects based upon such income. Of course, if we take only the income of two or three years before the war, there is no necessary correspondence between such income and the true capital of the business. But what chanced to happen in the three years which preceded the outbreak of the war is not and should not be controlling in this connection. Even if we accept the pre-war profits standard, its logic requires that we ascertain pre-war earnings over a sufficient number of years to obtain a true or normal average ; and over such a series of years no industry, except a monopoly, can earn upon its true capital an abnormal rate of profits. In short, if we could satisfy in practice the logical requirements of both

[106] Adams, T. S., "Principles of Excess Profits Taxation," *Annals of American Academy of Political and Social Science*, 75: 147 (Jan. 1918).

[107] "War Finance," *Proceedings* National Tax Association 1917, p. 155.

methods it would make little difference in the vast majority of cases whether we employed the income or the capital basis.[108]

The Treasury had to consider the practicability of the definition of the invested capital from the standpoint of administration. That is, it might have been possible to have worked out a method of determining such a definition so as to be fair in each individual case, but it apparently was not possible to make it simple enough generally to be feasible. This was one of the reasons the tax was finally abandoned.[109] Another reason was the opposition and propaganda of many influential highly interested taxpayers.

The law prevented some but not all double taxation of incomes of corporations and individuals. It provided that corporations when computing the 4% normal tax might omit from taxable income dividends received from corporations that had paid the 4% tax, but did not extend this privilege with respect to the 2% tax under the Act of September 8, 1916. This had been allowed by the excise law of 1909 but not by the first income tax act of 1913. Individuals, including those doing business as partners, were permitted to deduct for the normal tax purposes all dividends received from corporations that had been subject to the tax.

Some doubt may be cast, also, on the equity of applying graduated rates to corporation incomes. Such a tax is, in the end, upon the stockholders and no schedule of rates can be graduated according to the several abilities of numerous shareholders, most of whom also have incomes of different amounts from other sources. This graduation of rates was dropped when the excess-profits tax was repealed by the Act of 1921, but another form of graduation was introduced in 1935.[110]

108 *Annals of the American Academy of Political and Social Science,* 75: 152-53 (Jan. 1918).

109 See below, Chap. VIII, pp. 189-222.

110 See below, Chaps. XV and XXII.

CHAPTER VII

REVENUE ACT OF 1918 – THE WAR ENDS

FINANCIAL AND POLITICAL SITUATION IN MAY 1918

When the Secretary of the Treasury made his annual report in December 1917, he estimated receipts for the fiscal year 1918 at slightly over $12,580,000,000 of which more than $8,000,000,000 would come from loans, $3,400,000,000 from income and excess profits taxes, and $220,000,000 from customs. For the same period, disbursements were estimated at $18,775,000,000. Of this amount only $1,593,000,000 was for "Civil Establishment" ; most of the remainder was for the war, including loans to foreign governments. Thus the Treasury anticipated for 1918 an unplanned-for deficit of $6,195,000,000 and for the fiscal year 1919 a deficit of a billion more.[1]

Kitchin favored the enactment of a new revenue measure early in the calendar year 1918, but he received no encouragement from the Administration ; [2] in fact, it opposed such legislation if it could be avoided. The President omitted any mention of it in the program of work which he submitted to Congress at the opening of the session. It should be said for the Treasury that tax receipts were more than had been anticipated. Nevertheless, expenditures increased even faster than revenues.

The second session of the Sixty-fifth Congress was an unusually busy one, with war problems constantly to the fore, but by May both houses had reached the stage for considering appropriation bills preparatory to an early adjournment before the oncoming election campaign.

During the first week of May the House Military Affairs Committee conducted hearings at which officers of the army presented their requests for funds. At this time Secretary of War Baker estimated that his department would need $15,000,000,000 for the next year. The Senate Naval Affairs Committee was about ready to report the naval appropriation bill with totals exceeding the sum provided by the House, and the Senate Military Affairs Committee prepared to increase and expedite the supply of munitions of war. The sundry civil service appropriations bill had reached the startling sum of $7,000,000,000, so that altogether the proposed appropriations for

1 *Report of the Secretary of the Treasury*, 1917, pp. 71-74.
2 New York *Times*, May 10, 1918 ; *Cong. Rec.* 56: 7163.

the year were approaching the unheard-of total of $33,500,000,000, exclusive of interest.[3]

Secretary McAdoo was not in Washington at the time but was stumping the country in the interests of the Third Liberty Loan. Nevertheless the New York *World,* May 6, said that a new tax bill would probably be necessary, and on May 10 quoted McAdoo as saying that the bill should be drawn so as to raise six or seven billion dollars and should be passed before the present Congress adjourned.

This press announcement was the first intimation of a tax bill according to Kitchin, who was highly displeased as well as surprised, despite his previous interest in such legislation. He said it was too late in the session and too near elections. He blamed the press lobbyists who had influenced someone in the Treasury Department, probably not the Secretary but someone in whom he had confidence, to say that a new bill should be enacted. According to Kitchin the press had been fighting the postal rates in the Act of 1917 ever since it had been passed and was determined that Congress should not adjourn until that section of the law was amended or repealed.[4] This pressure was, of course, denied by the Secretary.[5]

On May 10 Kitchin and Simmons each received a letter from McAdoo in regard to the tax bill ; but, as they both wished to protest the idea, they arranged for a conference to present their views in the hope that they could dissuade the Secretary and the President from pressing for legislation.[6]

On May 11 Fordney interrupted the debate on an appropriation measure to express his opposition to the advocacy of another tax bill. He protested because the United States was now paying more in direct taxes than any other nation in the world and because he considered it unnecessary to have more money that year.[7] Other members supported him. Garner agreed that the tax bill should be postponed until the next session. Senator McCormick (Rep., Ill.) caustically remarked that if it was time that Congress was to be asked for additional revenue legislation, "the request will be characteristic of the want of foresight and preparedness which has marked our policy

[3] The New York *Times,* May 12, 1918, published the following estimate of supply bills :

Army	$15,000,000,000
Fortifications and Field Artillery	6,000,000,000
Navy	1,500,000,000
Sundry Civil and Shipping	3,000,000,000
Ordinary Expenses	2,000,000,000
Loans to Allies	6,000,000,000
Total	$33,500,000,000

[4] *Cong. Rec.* 56: 7164.

[5] New York *Times,* June 1, 1918.

[6] Letter of McAdoo to Kitchin quoted in the New York *Times,* June 1, 1918.

[7] *Cong. Rec.* 56: 6389.

toward the war — before we entered it and since. It takes more than pep and agility to lay down the financial policy of the government." [8]

There was a great deal of talk in Congress of limiting appropriations "to the barest necessities," [9] for many members thought there was no point in providing funds that could not be expended in 1919. Senators Lodge and Smoot, the leading Republicans on the Finance Committee, thought legislation unnecessary because the Treasury would not receive much revenue until 1919 in any case. Their position was strengthened, so they thought, by two occurrences: (1) the May 15 report of the Secretary of the Treasury, which showed that revenues from the 1917 Act exceeded estimates,[10] and (2) the denial that the President supported a new tax bill.[11]

Leading the Democrats, Kitchin and Simmons first opposed a new revenue bill because it would mean keeping Congress in session until November; so they announced they would not agree to it until Secretary McAdoo could show the "imperative necessity for such legislation," and added that it would be most difficult to do so because proceeds of bonds and certificates of indebtedness were available to supply funds until the beginning of 1919. The President could call an extra session at that time if it were necessary. In the meanwhile it would be possible to authorize more bonds.

The Democrats not only disliked remaining in Washington during a hot summer with elections approaching; but they also disliked to present to their constituents new demands for taxes which would of course be at the heaviest rates that had ever been levied. In fact one correspondent wrote that "the injection of Secretary McAdoo's demand for another revenue bill into the situation has caused more dismay than anything that has happened since the Government came into the hands of the Democratic Party." [12]

In 1931 McAdoo wrote in his memoirs:

> The fear of some of the party leaders that this program of taxation, if adopted, would cause the Democrats to lose control of Congress was well founded. The November election took place while the revenue bill was still in Congress. The unpopularity of the bill with its proposal to increase taxes generally and to bear heavily on large corporate and individual incomes was undoubtedly the most potent factor in the defeat of the Democrats. We lost enough seats in Congress to give the Republicans a working majority.[13]

[8] New York *Times*, May 11, 1918.
[9] New York *Times*, May 13, 1918.
[10] *Cong. Rec.* 56: 6528.
[11] It was reported that he had not yet made up his mind but was impressed by the plea of Congressmen to get home as soon as possible. (New York *Times*, May 15, 1918.)
[12] New York *Times*, May 11, 1918.
[13] McAdoo, William G., *Crowded Years*, p. 412.

The conference between Congressional leaders and Secretary McAdoo only strengthened the opinion of each. Kitchin's and Simmons' chief argument was that a revenue bill should be deferred until after the election "to keep it from being a political football," [14] while McAdoo countered with the point that such a delay would be "injurious to the best interest of the government" because if the bill were postponed until the next regular session it could not be passed until the middle of March. The decision was to put the matter up to the President who conferred with them several times. At first he seemed inclined to agree with the legislators; but after McAdoo presented his case, Wilson agreed that it would be too great a risk to postpone tax legislation until the spring, that business should know before that time what its obligations were and that retroactive legislation should be avoided.[15]

Meanwhile the President received a letter from Hull in which he supported the Secretary of the Treasury's recommendation for a bill and offered suggestions that the inheritance taxes be increased, that heavy taxes be laid on luxuries, and that amendments be made to the income and excess-profits taxes. Kitchin is reported to have said that his position was not affected by this message.[16]

The President offered to compromise. If Congress would promise to have the bill completed by February 1, 1919, the Administration would be satisfied. In that way, Congress could adjourn about the middle of July, while the Committee on Ways and Means worked out a measure to be presented when it assembled after the elections. A poll of the Republican members of the Senate Finance Committee showed, however, that such a promise could not be made. Many of the Committee did not care to bind themselves to accepting in advance a measure which might prove very distasteful to them.[17] There was no alternative then but to request Congress for tax legislation immediately.

On May 27, the President addressed both Houses in a manner that called out warm praise. Never had a tax bill been requested in such high spiritual terms. He said, in part:

> The consideration that dominates every other now, and makes every other seem trivial and negligible, is the winning of the war. We are not only in the midst of the war, we are at the very peak and crisis of it. Hundreds of thousands of our men, carrying our hearts with them and our fortunes, are in the field, and ships are crowding faster and faster to the

[14] New York *World*, New York *Times*, May 21, 1918. Roper, Commissioner of Internal Revenue, Sherley, Chairman of the House Appropriations Committee, and Martin, Democratic leader of the Senate, were also present.

[15] New York *World*, May 25, 1918.

[16] New York *Times*, May 17, 1918.

[17] New York *World*, May 26, 1918.

ports of France and England with regiment after regiment, thousand after thousand, to join them until the enemy shall be beaten and brought to a reckoning with mankind. There can be no pause or intermission. The great enterprise must, on the contrary, be pushed with greater and greater energy. The volume of our might must steadily and rapidly be augmented until there can be no question of resisting it. If that is to be accomplished, gentlemen, money must sustain it to the utmost. Our financial program must no more be left in doubt or suffered to lag than our ordnance program or our ship program or our munitions program or our program for making millions of men ready. These others are not programs, indeed, but mere plans upon paper, unless there is to be an unquestionable supply of money.

That is the situation, and it is the situation which creates the duty, no choice or preference of ours. There is only one way to meet that duty. We must meet it without selfishness or fear of consequences. Politics is adjourned. The elections will go to those who think least of it; to those who go to the constituencies without explanations or excuses, with a plain record of duty faithfully and disinterestedly performed. I, for one, am always confident that the people of this country will give a just verdict upon the service of the men who act for them when the facts are such that no man can disguise or conceal them. . .

Have you not felt the spirit of the Nation rise and its thought become a single and common thought since these eventful days came in which we have been sending our boys to the other side? I think you must read that thought, as I do, to mean this, that the people of this country are not only united in the resolute purpose to win this war but are ready and willing to bear any burden and undergo any sacrifice that it may be necessary for them to bear in order to win it. We need not be afraid to tax them, if we lay taxes justly. They know that the war must be paid for and that it is they who must pay for it, and if the burden is justly distributed and the sacrifice made the common sacrifice from which none escapes who can bear it at all, they will carry it cheerfully and with a sort of solemn pride. I have always been proud to be an American, and was never more proud than now, when all that we have said and all that we have foreseen about our people is coming true. The great days have come when the only thing that they ask for or admire is duty greatly and adequately done; when the only wish for America is that she may share the freedom she enjoys; when a great, compelling sympathy wells up in their hearts for men everywhere who suffer and are oppressed; and when they see at last the high uses for which their wealth has been piled up and their mighty power accumulated and, counting neither blood nor treasure now that their final day of opportunity has come, rejoice to spend and to be spent through the long night of suffering and terror in order that they and men everywhere may see the dawn of righteousness and justice and peace. Shall we grow weary when they bid us to act?

May I add this word, gentlemen? Just as I was leaving the White House I was told that the expected drive on the western front had apparently begun. You can realize how that solemnized my feelings as I came to you, and how it seemed to strengthen the purpose which I have tried to express in these lines.[18]

[18] *Cong. Rec.* 56: 7114-7115.

The reaction in Congress was not on the same high level. Kitchin grudgingly remarked that the Commander-in-Chief had spoken and that the plain duty was to do as he requested, but in his speech on the floor of the House he made insinuating remarks concerning the influence of press lobbyists.[19] Penrose was puzzled as to the reason for this sudden demand for a tax bill and wanted to look carefully into the state of government finances. Longworth, too, regretted that the President thought a tax bill necessary; and Smoot proclaimed that "this does not mean that what the Secretary of the Treasury or anyone else happens to demand in the way of a bill is going to be swallowed. The revenue bill . . . will be a scientifically constructed one that won't have the flaws of the one passed at the last session." [20]

Moore (Penn.), another Republican on the Committee on Ways and Means, said the Committee would buckle down to work. This the Committee did. Immediately word went out that public hearings would be held in Washington beginning June 6.

THE BILL DRAFTED BY THE COMMITTEE ON WAYS AND MEANS [21]

The day before the Committee hearings were scheduled to start Secretary McAdoo wrote a letter to the chairman in which he gave an outline of the financial situation of the government and made a few recommendations as to the tax bill. If the rate of expenditures over the preceding year continued, the Secretary said, the Treasury would have to disburse about $24,000,000,000 in the coming year, of which about one-third should be raised by taxation. To rely upon $4,000,000,000, the estimated revenue from the 1917 law, would be "a surrender to the policy of high interest rates and inflation, with all the evil consequences which would inevitably flow therefrom and which would . . . bring ultimate disaster to the country."

As to the kind of taxes, he recommended the adoption of a war-profits tax, because many war contractors were making very great profits which the excess-profits tax did not reach; but he did not

19 See above, p. 157. An editorial of the New York *Times* (May 30, 1918) made the following comment: [Kitchin] "always speaks in the same tone, a tone of querulous protest, the protest of the balky horse forced to the trough and determined to spill as much water as possible over the driver and make him perspire as much as possible over the job. But in this latest speech, Mr. Kitchin goes beyond anything he has ever done and beyond all permissible bounds. He affects to believe that that speech of the President's which so warmed the hearts of true Americans . . . was dictated by a lobby . . . quite in harmony with all Mr. Kitchin's speeches . . . unhappy, disgruntled, querulous spirit. . ."

20 New York *Times,* May 28, 1918.

21 The membership of the Committee was the same as in the First Session with the addition of the following:

Democrats	*Republicans*
George O'Shaughnessy (R. I.)	Whitmell C. Martin (La.)
John F. Carew (N. Y.)	Willis C. Hawley (Ore.)
George White (Ohio)	Allen T. Treadway (Mass.)

advise the repeal of the excess-profits tax. In order that there might be a more equitable contribution to the financing of the war he urged an increase in income tax rates and a differentiation in the taxation of earned and unearned income, making the normal rate on the former 8% and on the latter 12%.[22]

The first informal meeting of the Committee found Kitchin with no definite plans. The consensus was that the Acts of 1916 and 1917 would be repealed and an entirely new bill written, that increased rates would be levied on those who had profited from the war, and that returns from the income and excess-profits taxes would be doubled. Fordney made known his desire for increased import duties but there was no general desire for a revision of more than one or two schedules, particularly because of the danger of injecting the tariff issue into the House discussion and possibly even into the election campaigns.[23]

The problems of the Committee were increased when it was learned that war profits would be less for 1919 than for 1918 because the government was fixing the prices of steel, copper, and other war materials, and wages had advanced.[24] The Committee heard others, from both the government and business, and decided to extend the hearings until June 20, and at that time they were extended again.

The reaction to the suggestions of Secretary McAdoo was favorable on the whole. Within two weeks the Committee had tentatively agreed to an alternative tax on corporations and to the higher tax on unearned incomes of individuals. Longworth was particularly zealous for the latter change which he said he had advocated for months. The Committee hoped to raise $8,000,000,000, of which a large percentage, $5,000,000,000, would come from war-profits and excess-profits taxes. In fact the Committee made such progress that Kitchin reported they could finish the bill by July 15 if the Treasury would submit the returns of income and excess-profits taxes that were received from the 1917 Act.[25] Nevertheless the preliminary work and the hearings delayed matters so that the Committee did not begin drafting the measure until July 16.

Congress became very much annoyed, not only at the lack of progress, but at the so-called secrecy of the Committee. Kitchin of course was the particular butt of criticism, so on July 20 he replied by putting the blame on the Treasury for not co-operating in the furnishing of requested information.[26] One of the Republi-

22 65th Congress, 2d Session, *Hearings before the Committee on Ways and Means on the Proposed Revenue Act of* 1918, I: 9-12.

23 New York *Times,* June 7, 1918.

24 New York *Times,* June 8, 1918.

25 New York *Times,* July 8, 1918.

26 New York *Times,* July 21, 1918.

can members defended the chairman by explaining the intricacies of the details of miscellaneous taxes and the income tax schedules.[27]

This difficulty with the Treasury Department did not smooth out the irritation that Kitchin had felt since the tax bill was forced upon him. When Treasury experts such as T. S. Adams suggested that corporations be divided into eight classes according to the percentage that income was to invested capital, Kitchin thought three classes would be a much better division.[28] He encouraged Committee members to work out counter proposals to the Treasury plan for corporation taxes. Instead of the existing rates on excess profits he proposed higher ones. He also wanted a rate of 18% for the normal tax on corporations with a 6% reduction on earnings that were distributed. In fact the Committee worked out four plans, none of which conformed to McAdoo's proposal because, so they said, his requests were too difficult of administration.[29] Meanwhile the House recessed to let the Committee draft the bill.

The Treasury did not approve the preliminary draft of the Committee so sent representatives to confer with them, but the results were only a series of clashes. Kitchin claimed that the Treasury plan would not yield enough revenue. The Secretary, at the end of July, ill and unable to be at his desk, became anxious about the legislative financial program which was not getting anywhere, and therefore telegraphed to the President asking that Kitchin expedite the tax bill. Kitchin telegraphed a reply that it would be ready by August 19; but when McAdoo learned that the bill was not written according to his suggestions he was not pleased and telegraphed to Kitchin August 4, urging the enactment of the war-profits tax at 80% and the excess-profits tax at the rates in force.[30]

Ten days later McAdoo appeared in person before the Committee and reviewed the whole matter. Kitchin said that the Committee had for some time agreed to the idea of an alternative tax plan; but, not certain they were convinced, McAdoo launched forth, reading a prepared statement which explained in much detail what he wanted and why.

The differences between the ideas of the two men can be boiled down to a few words, although they were difficult to harmonize. McAdoo wanted: (1) the excess-profits tax of 1917 retained, (2) a flat rate of 80% on war profits over certain deductions, (3) the

27 New York *Times,* July 21, 1918.

28 New York *World,* August 17, 1918. Professor T. S. Adams (Yale University) served as adviser to the Treasury Department from 1917. See below, Chap. XXIII, pp. 533 ff.

29 New York *Times,* July 24, 26, Aug. 18, 23, 1918.

30 65th Congress, 2d Session, *Hearings before the Committee on Ways and Means,* I: 25, 26, 85.

taxpayer to pay whichever was higher,[31] (4) a differentiation of 3% in the rates of taxes on earned and unearned incomes. Kitchin wanted the rates of the excess-profits tax raised. He did not object finally to the alternative scheme, although he did at first because he thought it would be extremely complicated, and thus frustrate one of his first ambitions which was to simplify the law. He objected, however, to the deductions for the excess-profits tax which the Treasury experts proposed.[32]

What were the bases of these differences of opinion between the Treasury and the Committee? The reader might recall here the fundamental differences between "excess-profits" taxes and "war-profits" taxes. The latter were taxes levied on profits presumably due to the war and measured by subtracting average profits of a prewar period from profits received during war years. Most information necessary for administration of such a tax was available from regular federal returns already required for the administration of corporation excise and income taxes for every year since 1909, hence this tax would be relatively simple and would cost relatively little extra to administer. The excess-profits tax, on the other hand, applied to profits received during the war period that were in excess of normal profits. The 1917 law designated 7%-9% on invested capital as normal profits for this purpose. This tax required the determination of all invested capital used each year in practically every business in the United States and, hence, was impossible to administer with any accuracy upon short notice, if ever, and very expensive and conducive to litigation, in any case, particularly when high rates are applied. Henry Ford was commonly cited as an outstanding example of one who made large prewar profits but who would pay little or no war-profits tax because he made little or no more during the war than in prewar years; hence, it was argued that large profits of Ford and others similarly situated could be reached by an excess-profits tax as they could not be by a war-profits tax.

The Treasury wanted a high war-profits tax so that "no one should profit largely by the war," particularly when the government was paying large prices for war materials in order to get them quickly. Corporations that entered into these contracts took risks and, as the Secretary said, they were not to be blamed for asking prices and terms accordingly. Nevertheless "when the risk has been liquidated by proper allowances, and the contract has

31 McAdoo's original proposal was for the war-profits tax to be superimposed upon the excess-profits tax but T. S. Adams preferred to have one as an alternative to the other.

32 *Hearings,* I: 50.

proved profitable, the Government should take back in taxes all profits above a reasonable reward." [33]

Such profits were not reached by an excess-profits tax which was based on the relation of income to capital. This tax, said the Secretary, "must rest upon the wholly indefensible notion that it is a function of taxation to bring all profits down to one level with relation to the amount of capital invested and to deprive industry, foresight, and sagacity of their fruits." He argued also that the excess-profits tax exempted capital and burdened brains, ability, and energy; it fell less heavily on big business than on small business, because big business was generally overcapitalized and small business was often undercapitalized.

Graduation of rates of the excess-profits tax was also held indefensible, because the burden fell on the stockholders without regard to their differences of income or ability to pay. Furthermore the tax was unfair to investors who bought shares of prosperous companies before the war. A war tax, on the other hand, would not burden such investors so heavily. In spite of these inequities the Secretary did not approve of repealing the tax because the government needed the revenue. If the rates were raised, however, the injustices would be increased.[34]

Assistant Secretary of the Treasury Leffingwell, in repeating the plea of the Secretary, said rather picturesquely when asked if the Administration plan would catch the war profiteers:

> I think that the proposed law would reach almost to the point of perfection the untaxed war profits, and I think the only thing we must be concerned about is so to guide ourselves in fixing the machinery for this new war-profits tax and in reconsidering the lower rates of the excess-profits tax . . . as to have in mind the fact that we are dealing with a buzz saw, and let us not monkey with it.[35]

Kitchin could not be brought around to see these arguments. He insisted on raising the rates of the excess-profits tax to 30%, 50%, and 80% [36] because he did not think it just to have such a spread between the rates of the excess-profits tax and the war-profits tax. He wanted "to catch the profiteers before as well as since the war began." This, he pointed out, was the reason the Senate changed from the House plan in writing the 1917 law.[37] The war-profits tax, on the other hand, would favor investors and companies that had made large profits and received large dividends before the war.

[33] *Hearings*, I: 15.
[34] *Hearings*, I: 16, 18, 31, 34-42.
[35] *Hearings*, I: 51. For evidence given by Leffingwell see pp. 55-85.
[36] *Hearings*, I: 79, 106. The minimum rate of the 1917 excess-profits tax was 20%, the maximum 60%.
[37] *Hearings*, I: 80, 87-88.

He cited examples of such corporations as the Ford Motor, Eastman Kodak, National Cash Register, Standard Oil of Indiana, American Tobacco, and others that would not be affected by the war-profits tax. "We insist that these corporations, who were wonderfully prosperous before the war and equally so now pay a part of the increased taxes." [38]

Garner frankly added another reason for wanting to maintain the 80% rate, namely, for the psychological, the political effect.[38] He looked forward to the time not far off when he and others of his colleagues would have to defend the bill on the floor of the House.

T. S. Adams undertook to harmonize the differences between the Treasury and the Committee. He told the members that, though doubtless there were many very profitable corporations such as those Kitchin had enumerated, there were a number that were "slipping back," that had no war profits, and, he continued:

> you will also find . . . a large number of corporations [in the higher tax brackets] who are there, not because they were fortunate but because they have not received a fair representation or measurement of their invested capital.[38]

Kitchin and McAdoo held several conferences and had some correspondence.[39] Even the President was asked to act as arbiter.[40]

About August 30, McAdoo and Kitchin again conferred and seemed ready to compromise. McAdoo was willing to abandon his demand for a differentiation between earned and unearned incomes because he said it was too complicated to be administered. Kitchin reduced the proposed maximum excess-profits tax to 70%. McAdoo, oddly enough, is reported to have been pleased that the rates were raised and thought them an improvement over those of the 1917 law.[41]

Later, when Kitchin introduced his bill in the House, Longworth asked about the differences between the Treasury and the Committee. The chairman assured the House that although there were a few differences of opinion they were discussed "in the most pleasant way," rather than "contested, conflicting, stubborn, fighting differences as the press would have the public believe." [42]

Even with all this apparent harmony the bill was not completed until the first of September. The Republicans cried, "Politics!" blaming the Democrats for trying to delay the bill until after the

38 *Hearings,* I: 106-108.
39 New York *Times,* Aug. 20, 1918.
40 New York *Times,* Aug. 27, 1918.
41 New York *World,* Aug. 28, 1918.
42 *Cong. Rec.* 56: app. 679.

election. Kitchin, in turn, blamed the Treasury, which had submitted fifty or sixty "brand new administrative suggestions," all of which required careful attention.[43]

THE COMMITTEE REPORT [44]

It was estimated that the bill proposed by the Committee would raise over $8,182,000,000, of which approximately $1,400,000,000 would come from the income tax on individuals; $894,000,000 from that on corporations; $3,200,000,000 from the excess-profits tax; $110,000,000 from the estate tax, and the balance from excises on transportation, telegraph and telephone services, admissions, beverages, and other commodities, services and transactions.

The Committee raised the normal tax of individuals to 6% on income of $4,000 or less, and to 12% on that in excess of $4000. In addition, the surtax rates were raised so that the minimum became 2% on income in excess of $5000, the maximum 65% on income in excess of $5,000,000, instead of 63% on income over $2,000,000. The personal exemptions, $2000 and $1000, were unchanged. Despite doubts of constitutionality, the tax was made applicable to income from obligations of states issued after the passage of the Act, the compensation of the President of the United States, the judges of the United States courts, and all other employees of the United States of America or of any state or political subdivision.[45] The first $3500 of salary of one serving in the United States forces abroad or at sea was exempt.

The normal tax on corporations was increased from 6% to 18%, but a new feature was introduced in permitting a lower rate, 12%, on earnings that were distributed. This was in order to stimulate the paying of dividends, first, for the benefit of the small stockholder and, second, "in order that the government may get the benefit of the surtaxes upon the distributed income." [46] An exemption of $2000 was permitted each corporation.

More liberal allowances than previously were permitted corporations in the deduction of interest. In the 1917 law interest could be deducted only on an amount equal to the sum of the capital stock paid in and one-half of the interest-bearing indebtedness. The Committee proposed that all interest be deducted in excess of tax-

[43] New York *World*, Aug. 29, 1918.

[44] 65th Congress, 2d Session, *House Report* 767.

[45] The Report stated: "Your Committee realizes that there is a great difference of opinion among the best legal talent with reference to the constitutionality of this provision, but feels that in all equity and justice such officials should be subject to income taxes and that, if necessary, this matter should be definitely decided by the courts." (p. 9.)

[46] This was not enacted into law at this time, but a similar proposal was the basis of the 1936 tax on undistributed profits. See below, Chap. XVII.

free interest received.[47] The tax was removed from dividends received from other corporations.

The excess-profits tax was made applicable to corporations only; individuals and partnerships were not included as in the 1917 law. In addition the Committee drafted a war-profits tax; the taxpayer was to pay whichever of the two was the higher. For the excess-profits tax the credit allowed was $3000 and 8% of invested capital for the taxable year. The tax was graduated as follows: on income of more than 8% but not over 15% of the invested capital the tax was 35%; on income that was over 15% and not over 20% of the invested capital the tax was 50%; and on the excess, the tax was 70%. Special provisions were made for corporations with invested capital of less than $50,000.

For the war-profits tax the rate was 80% of the corporate net income that was in excess of a specific credit which was $3000 plus the average net income for the three prewar years 1911, 1912, and 1913. If invested capital had been increased since the prewar period, the corporation could add an amount equal to 10% of the additional investment employed during the taxable year. In case the capital had been decreased since the prewar period, the exemption was reduced by an amount equal to 10% of the invested capital withdrawn. If the corporation had not been in existence during the prewar period or had no net income at that time, or if the prewar earnings were less than 10% of the invested capital of the taxable year, the specific exemption was $3000 plus 10% of the invested capital for the taxable year. In other words, as pointed out by the Committee, the "war-profits tax is not distinctly a war-profits tax since a minimum exemption of 10 per cent is allowed in all cases."

A section was inserted to allow for special amortization of buildings, machinery, or equipment acquired for war purposes after April 6, 1917 but the amount could not exceed 25% of net income.

In spite of some doubt as to its advisability, the Committee inserted a provision to prohibit consolidated returns.

A new administrative body, called the Advisory Tax Board, was created to take the place of the voluntary board that Commissioner Roper formed to help with the excess-profits tax. There were to be five members with salaries of $9000 each, to be appointed by the President with the consent of the Senate. They were to assist and advise the Commissioner of Internal Revenue with the interpretation and administration of the tax laws and were also to be at the service of taxpayers. That is, a taxpayer could demand that the Board consider a difference between himself and the govern-

[47] The allowance was made because borrowed money could not be included in computing invested capital for the purpose of the war-profits and excess-profits tax.

ment. The decision would then be left to the Commissioner, but it was expected that as a matter of practice he would accept the recommendations of the Board. It was provided that the Board would remain in existence for the period of the war and one year thereafter.[48]

Another important new step was the establishment of the legislative drafting service. For some time four specially trained men had been assisting Congress in this work as the result of a private endowment left to Columbia University with the hope that they would prove their worth to state legislatures as well as to Congress by getting laws into proper form.

Several other administrative changes were made, such as providing for installment payment of taxes, increasing the salary of the Commissioner, appropriating $7,500,000 for the collection of the internal revenue taxes and giving the Commissioner and the Secretary of the Treasury power to readjust salaries in the Bureau.

The estate tax rates were increased from a minimum of 2% to 3% and from a maximum of 25% to 40%. The exemption remained unchanged, $50,000.

THE BILL IN THE HOUSE OF REPRESENTATIVES

Chairman Kitchin presented the report of the Committee on Tuesday, September 3, gave notice that it would be called up for consideration the following Friday, and informed his colleagues that it was important that the bill be studied. On the specified day he addressed the House, speaking for five hours on the details of the measure, giving the reasons for proposed changes in the law, and estimating the revenue it would produce.[49] The total figure of $8,182,000,000 was indeed a tremendous one, twice the amount of taxes that the United States or any nation had ever attempted to collect in one year, three times the "gold value collections from taxes and bonds by this Government during the whole four years of the Civil War," $2,500,000,000 more than spent by both the North and South in the war. The Committee, he said, had worked with three fundamental aims in view: (1) to get the needed amount of money; (2) to place the burden as equally and equitably as possible; and (3) to co-operate with the Treasury Department in preparing a bill that would be supported, not only by the Committee and the House, but by the Administration and the Treasury as well.

On succeeding days other members of the Committee spoke for the bill – notably Fordney, Green, and Longworth – in spite of their

[48] See below, Chap. XXIII, for a more extensive discussion of administration.
[49] *Cong. Rec.* 56: app. 661-702.

individual differences of opinion as to certain phases of the measure.

Politics and sectionalism had been kept to a minimum in the deliberations of the Committee, but it was impossible to keep them out of the general debate. Moore (Rep., Pa.) emphasized how heavily the steel industry was taxed while cotton and corn were exempted, and in so doing aroused the southern members.[50] Crisp (Dem., Ga.) replied that cotton in manufactured goods, if a luxury, was taxed, but that so far as he knew coal was not taxed.[51] Caraway (Dem., Ark.) gave a pathetic account of the poverty of the cotton-growing section and involved the Food Administration in his criticism of the price fixed for seed.[52]

Longworth and Hull took the discussion from the plane of small sectionalism to that of broad consideration of the subject at hand, namely, the income and excess-profits taxes. Hull's general criticism was that the measure was complex, but perhaps necessarily so. As to specific changes desired, he named first the normal tax on individuals, which he thought might well be fixed at 15% with surtaxes starting higher. He was sure the Supreme Court would declare unconstitutional the sections which taxed instrumentalities and agencies of the states. He regretted that the Committee had not made a differentiation between earned and unearned incomes, the administrative difficulties of which did not appeal to him as serious.

He approved the principle of the war-profits tax, which indeed he had advocated and worked for since the war started, although he recognized that it was not "a scientific equitable method in the ordinary sense." The excess-profits tax, too, he considered a temporary war measure which had its chief support in the policy which no one could challenge, namely that "during the war the Government should demand and take over most of that category of abnormal profits which have arisen over and above normal profits of the prewar period and apply them to the expenses of the war." He preferred variable rates to the flat 10% deduction for the war-profits tax, criticized as too inflexible, and advocated giving greater discretion to the Treasury to make allowances for businesses that had lost heavily in previous years.[53]

Republican interruptions for the purpose of injecting the tariff issue did not disrupt the debate.[54] Hull, who was speaking when

50 *Cong. Rec.* 56: 10140. There were only two city members out of the twenty-three on the Committee, and only six or seven from the industrial states.

51 *Cong. Rec.* 56: 10141.

52 *Cong. Rec.* 56: 10159-10160.

53 *Cong. Rec.* 56: 10160-10168.

54 Fordney had made one attempt to introduce the tariff issue during the deliberations of the Committee on the grounds that extremely high taxation would injure business and that by increasing the tariff on luxuries the additional revenue needed could be raised easily and no one would object. (*Hearings,* I: 117.)

some of these questions were asked, agreed with the questioner that doubtless the tariff would come to be a greater producer of revenue when the war was over.[55]

The first amendment, proposed by Hardy (Dem., Tex.), was to substitute a new section for that which laid down the rule for the calculation of profits on the sale of property purchased before March 1, 1913. The law as written was objected to because it took no account of the general rise in the price level since 1913. The amendment would substitute the words "the fair market price or value . . . as of the date at the beginning of the year in which the sale is made." Fordney defended the original section chiefly on the ground that it was identical with that of previous income tax laws and because the proposed amendment would reduce the estimated yield of the tax by $2,000,000.[56]

The Committee offered very few amendments. One was to permit corporations to add to the amount of distributed income upon which the tax was reduced 6%, the amount paid for Liberty bonds. This started a discussion of the advisability of the proposed reduction in tax on distributed income. Chandler (Okla.) objected to it because conservative business practice required a certain amount of reserve. He preferred the previous law that permitted the Secretary of the Treasury to levy a 15% penalty tax when the amount retained was not used in the business. Longworth said the proposed differential should not be considered a penalty but a bonus for distribution. The individual income tax, he showed, had been tripled in the Committee draft; the normal tax on corporations was treated in the same way. He cited English practice as an example of encouraging distribution of corporate income, that is, by levying a tax of 30% on the amount retained as surplus and levying no tax whatever on the amount distributed in dividends.[57]

Fordney called this provision one of the most dangerous in the bill and the most objectionable to him. He stated that banks had to retain some of their undivided profits to care for bad accounts. If this section were enacted into law they would not do so, because they would not pay the extra 6%. Nevertheless he offered no amendment on the floor because he thought it useless to do so; he had fought the proposition all along the line in Committee and been defeated, but he looked forward to seeing it eliminated in the Senate.[58]

[55] *Cong. Rec.* 56: 10162.

[56] *Cong. Rec.* 56: 10422-10424.

[57] As a matter of fact, England taxes a corporation on all its profits and permits the company to deduct from dividends declared a proportionate amount of the tax paid, at the standard rate for the year in which the amount payable becomes due. Taxpayers are not subject to the income tax upon such earnings but are subject to the surtax.

[58] *Cong. Rec.* 56: 10423-10429.

Surprisingly little objection was raised to the war and excess-profits taxes. Madden (Rep., Ill.) and Stafford (Rep., Wis.) spoke against the excess-profits tax, because it discriminated against corporations that made less profit before the war than after, and in favor of corporations successful both before and after the war. Longworth called attention to the fact that there would be no discrimination against corporations earning less than 10%. Kitchin explained that Madden's argument was one of the reasons why the Committee insisted, over the protests of the Treasury, on increasing the excess-profits tax rates.[59]

The section taxing income of state officials was challenged by Montague (Va.) on constitutional grounds. Crisp admitted that when the Committee inserted the provision it had grave doubts as to its legality, but in view of the tremendous need for funds thought it only right that every state and federal official should be required to help raise them. "Let the gentlemen enjoying those salaries in this crisis, if they question it, take the matter to the courts and let the courts determine it," he suggested. Moore advised that the bill be left intact so that a test case could be made of it. Kitchin took the same stand. Montague's amendment was rejected and the Committee section remained as written. Montague then offered a similar amendment to prevent the taxation of bonds of states and their political subdivisions.[60] It met a similar fate.

Graham (Rep., Pa.) made an effort to strike out the section that limited the allowance for amortization of war plants and machinery to 25% of net income. Kitchin explained that the Committee had given the matter much thought and admitted that perhaps they should have accorded the Commissioner full power to determine amortization without restrictions. They feared, however, that if no limit were made, some of the munitions makers would take such large amortization deductions that it would absorb the total net income.[61]

The income and estate tax sections were finished on September 18. On September 20 the bill was passed with 349 favorable votes. No one voted against it, but 81 did not vote either way.[62]

59 *Cong. Rec.* 56: 10447-10450.
60 *Cong. Rec.* 56: 10372, 10409-10410.
61 *Cong. Rec.* 56: 10416-10417.
62 *Cong. Rec.* 56: 10548.

CONSIDERATION BY THE SENATE FINANCE COMMITTEE [63]

The House measure was reported to the Senate on September 21 and referred to the Finance Committee. Discussion of the bill on the floor of the Senate commenced immediately with an address by Thomas (Dem., Colo.), who attacked the very foundations of it, saying that eight billion dollars was far too large an amount to raise, for it would cripple industry; the idea of levying two taxes with radically different bases would just be the opening wedge to levying three or four or six. Furthermore the bill contained several sections that were probably unconstitutional.[64]

The Committee anticipated that it would not be long before their report would be ready, for in the first few days they found themselves in agreement on the House income tax rates. By the first of October this hope was shattered, for they decided to reconsider some of the fundamental principles of the law, such as the equalization of the taxation of corporations, partnerships, and individuals, and the gross versus the net basis of income tax reporting, as well as the amount of revenue to be raised.[65] La Follette proposed to make a thorough study of the law.

The constant urging of the Secretary of the Treasury for haste brought forth a statement from Lodge that the amount of revenue requested was alone enough to make the Committee pause and think. The requests were so large indeed that they might well "tend to reduce profits to a point which will dry up the sources" of the income tax, leaving the taxpayer in a position of having insufficient funds for reserves, little for dividends, and "their funds to take Liberty bonds will be so depleted as to have a very serious effect on placing the loans." The Senator reminded Secretary McAdoo that even he objected to the high excess-profits tax rates of the House.[66]

Although the statement above was issued in his name expressly as his own thought and not for the Committee it seemed to represent the viewpoint of a majority of the members. When the draft was completed early in November amendments resulted in reducing the estimated revenue to six and one-half billion dollars.

One of the first and most radical decisions was to change the reporting of income from a net to a gross basis, both for individuals and for corporations. By this plan every single person receiving at

63 The personnel of the Committee was the same as in the First Session except that William P. Dillingham (Rep., Vt.) took the place of J. H. Gallinger. See above, Chap. VI.

64 *Cong. Rec.* 56: 10627-10634.

65 New York *World*, Oct. 3, 1918.

66 New York *World*, Oct. 5, 1918.

least $1000 income and every married person receiving $2000 would make a return. From this information the Treasury officials would compute the taxable net income.[67]

Kellogg (Rep., Minn.) opposed on constitutional grounds the section which taxed income from state, county, and municipal sources. The Committee upheld him to some extent by taking out the section that levied a tax on interest from state and municipal bonds. The tax was left on all salaries without discrimination; the matter of legality would be for the courts to decide.

Much time and thought was devoted to the corporation taxes. In accordance with Secretary McAdoo's wish, the 6% differential normal tax on undistributed corporate earnings was removed although the Committee decided at one time to retain it. The statistician who assisted the Committee reported that it was common for corporations to retain reserves of about 40%, an amount which did not seem unreasonable. An example was given of one firm engaged in building a plant for the government that would be penalized a million dollars by this 6% differential tax. On the other hand, evidence was given to show that the retention of undistributed earnings offered an easy method of tax avoidance. The reply was that such corporations would be reached in other ways.[68]

After receiving assurance from the Treasury Department that the action would not result in loss of revenue, the House prohibition of consolidated returns was struck out of the bill and the Committee expressly authorized them. The reason for this action was to prevent tax evasion.[69] Affiliated companies, so they found, could distribute their income and invested capital to reduce their taxes. But the fundamental reason for the change was to permit business units to present their statements in such a way as properly to reflect their capital and income.

At the suggestion of the Secretary of the Treasury, the alternative excess-war-profits tax arrangement was discarded in favor of an excess-profits tax at lower rates upon which the war-profits tax was superimposed. This would relieve the Bureau of Internal Revenue from the necessity of using any discretion, and it would be simpler for the taxpayer to compute, but it probably would bring in less revenue.[70] There was also some question of the constitutionality of the House proposal.[71] As the law was revised, a corporation was allowed a specific exemption for the war-profits tax of $3000 plus

67 New York *World*, Oct. 5, 1918.
68 New York *World*, Oct. 5 and 19, 1918.
69 *Cong. Rec.* 57: 255. The House had prohibited consolidated returns for exactly the same reason.
70 New York *World*, Oct. 23, 1918.
71 65th Congress, 3d Session, *Senate Report* 617.

an amount equal to the average net income for the prewar period, plus or minus 10% of the difference between the average invested capital for the prewar period and for the taxable year. This was in addition to the excess-profits credit of $3000 plus 8% of invested capital. The rate of the war-profits tax was 80%. Therefore the total tax would be the sum of the following: (1) 30% of the amount of net income over the excess-profits credit and not over 20% of invested capital; (2) 60% on the amount of income in excess of 20% of such capital; (3) (the war-profits tax) the amount by which 80% of the net income in excess of the war profits credit exceeded the amount of excess-profits taxes, (1) and (2). Liberal allowances were granted for new corporations and those with small amounts of invested capital.

In view of the dissatisfaction with the 1917 law as applied to personal service corporations, the Committee voted to exempt them from the excess-profits tax and to treat their earnings as those of partnerships, that is, to subject the equity owners to the individual income tax and the surtax whether earnings were distributed or not.[72] The House normal tax rates were retained, but surtax rates were reduced on the smaller incomes and the number of brackets radically changed to 54 instead of 18.[73]

The House provisions relating to depletion of natural resources were liberalized by allowing discovery depletion, that is, by establishing the fair market value of the property on the date of discovery or twelve months thereafter as the basis for computing depletion for wells or mines discovered after March 1, 1913. The existing provisions relative to March 1, 1913 value as the basis for properties acquired prior to March 1, 1913 were retained. The Committee inserted a new section for determining taxable income in case of exchange of property. Prior laws had not specifically provided for such transactions and court decisions indicated that there might be tax liability even in cases of paper transactions. The substance of the new provision was that property received in exchange for other property was to be treated as the equivalent of cash to the amount of its fair market value, but when new corporation stock was received in place of other stock in connection with a reorganization, no gain or loss was deemed to have occurred from the exchange.

Instead of an estate tax, the Committee devised an inheritance tax, although there was little enthusiasm for either. Many members

[72] *Cong. Rec.* 57: 253. The term "personal service corporation" was defined as "a corporation whose income is to be ascribed primarily to the activities of the principal owners or stockholders who are themselves regularly engaged in the active conduct of the affairs of the corporation and in which capital (whether invested or borrowed) is not a material income-producing factor."

[73] New York *World*, Oct. 23, 1918.

thought that death taxes should be left to the states, except that they were considered important for fiscal reasons, especially in view of the probable loss in revenue following the prohibition of alcoholic liquors.[74]

As the bill was practically completed by the first of November, the Committee arranged for a recess until about the eighth, when they would put the finishing touches on it preparatory to introducing it November 12.[75]

THE ENDING OF THE WAR FORCES REDRAFTING OF BILL

Before this plan could be executed, however, the war came to an end with the signing of the Armistice on November 11, and the work on the measure was stopped until Simmons could confer with McAdoo and the President. It was reported that McAdoo was anxious not to give the impression that war expenses were at an end; nevertheless, he did not want to impose on the taxpayer any more than necessary. He was particularly desirous of retaining the war-profits tax.[76] Within a day or two the Secretary had worked out some preliminary estimates to accord with the suddenly changed picture. While there would be some decrease in expenditure, it would not be immediate nor at a very rapid rate. Pay for the army and navy forces at home and abroad would continue for some time; working capital for reconstruction would have to be furnished to the Allies. Probably instead of needing $24,000,000,000 for the fiscal year, $18,000,000,000 would cover expenditures. He recommended therefore a $6,000,000,000 revenue bill for 1919 and a $4,000,000,000 measure for 1920.

With reference to the character of the measure, he advocated retaining the war-profits tax, but reducing the rates of the excess-profits tax to those of 1917 and then making it payable only if it were greater than the war-profits tax. It should not be retained after 1919. He called attention to the importance of providing for amortization, for the conservative valuation of inventories and "the ascertainment of the minimum incomes which shall be exempted from tax on lines that will insure the taxpayer from injustice and avoidable injury." [77]

The Secretary personally attended a Committee meeting to explain his recommendations, but he met with rebuff on the part of the Republicans. They were so irate at his insistence on fixing rates

[74] New York *World*, Oct. 25, 1918; Roper, D. C., "Taxation Problems," *North American Review*, 222: 13 (Sept., Oct., Nov. 1925).
[75] New York *World*, Nov. 2, 1918.
[76] New York *World*, Nov. 13, 1918; New York *Times*, Nov. 15, 1918.
[77] Letter of McAdoo to Simmons, New York *Times*, Nov. 15, 1918.

for 1920 that the passage of the bill was threatened. Smoot said he would fight it to the last ditch. Penrose bluntly announced that the Republicans would fix 1920 taxes and that their plan would comprise a protective tariff. They also did not willingly accept the suggestion of the repeal of the excess-profits taxes. Switching from their demand for a small tax bill, they now wanted a large one, so that there would be ample funds in the Treasury when they became the majority party. They did not relish the thought of being compelled "to rig up any shortage . . . from the individual income tax." Such rates were high enough in 1918 and "any increase might be disastrous from a political standpoint." As one of the newspapers said, "The G. O. P. senators talk peace but think war." Many thought the only way to prevent McAdoo from getting his way was to delay the passage of the bill until after March 3 when the old Congress would expire.[78] This attitude of the Republicans should not have been a surprise in view of the results of the recent elections in which they gained a majority in the House.

The Finance Committee members were faced with the work of completely rewriting the bill and under much less favorable conditions than before, because of the recently developed Republican opposition. They therefore announced that they could not have the new draft ready for the present session, so Congress adjourned on November 21.[79]

When the Committee reassembled Simmons made the following proposals: (1) raise $6,000,000,000 for 1919 and $4,000,000,000 for 1920 as McAdoo had advocated; (2) for 1919 retain the income, excess-profits, and war-profits taxes without the 6% differential on undistributed corporate earnings; (3) eliminate the 20% excise tax on articles over certain prices; (4) retain the inheritance tax; and (5) for 1920, eliminate the war-profits tax, reduce the normal tax on individuals and corporations to 8% and reduce the excess-profits rate about one-third.[80]

In order to make some progress in a group that was apparently deadlocked, Simmons evolved a scheme to complete all of the 1919 section first, then to take up that for 1920.[81] When the time came, the Democrats had secured enough votes to override the Republican opposition, so 1920 rates were written into the bill in the face of threats of prolonged debate, numerous amendments, and other methods of causing delay in its course through the Senate.

78 New York *World,* Nov. 16, 17, 18, 19, and 24, 1918.

79 New York *Times,* Nov. 19, 1918. It will be recalled that this was before the adoption of the Twentieth ("lame-duck") Amendment to the Constitution (1933), therefore Congress convened regularly the first Monday in December.

80 New York *Times,* Nov. 22, 1918.

81 New York *World,* Nov. 23, 1918.

At this juncture Hull endeavored to heal the breach by issuing an unusual statement to the press. Congress, he said, was required by law to make appropriations covering all expenditures to June 30, 1920, likewise it was required to provide adequate revenues to meet these expenditures. He continued:

> To this end, the present proposal is to make the Revenue Bill produce a large yield to meet as far as possible the war expenditures of the fiscal year ending June 30, 1919, and at the same time to provide for a reduction of the revenues to $4,000,000,000 . . . for the year ending June 30, 1920. The chief portion of these revenues is now derived from income, war and excess-profits taxes, which are levied according to the calendar year, not the Government fiscal year.

He cited the example of other nations that invariably fixed rates a year before they went into effect and that "only emergencies such as the war conditions have caused deviations from this policy." [82]

Before long the Republican opposition to inserting 1920 rates had melted. Business sent a call, which could not remain unanswered, that the bill must be written so that tax obligations would be known.[83]

By the second drafting of the bill the normal 6% rate on the first $4000 of individual income was retained for 1918, but for subsequent years was reduced to 4%; the 12 % rate on income above that amount was retained for 1918 but reduced to 8% thereafter. For corporations the normal tax was reduced to 12% and 8% for 1919 and 1920 respectively. The excess-profits tax rates for 1920 were made 20% and 40% instead of 30% and 60% as first drafted. The inheritance tax was retained.

Three somewhat extraneous amendments were adopted at the last: one was to abolish the postal zone system, another to levy a tax on child labor, and a third to exempt the profits of gold mining from the excess-profits tax.

Estimates of the yield of the bill were six billion dollars for 1919, and four billion dollars for 1920.

There were three minority reports. One was signed by Penrose, Lodge, McCumber, Smoot, Townsend, and Dillingham; another by La Follette; and a third by Smoot. The chief criticism of the minority was of the inclusion of the 1920 taxes. They showed that it had been the part of wisdom to delay the bill thus far, although the Secretary had predicted dire results if the measure were not passed by September 28, 1918. Who knew what the situation would be in 1919, not to mention 1920? The argument that the taxpayers should know in advance what their taxes would be did

[82] New York *World,* Nov. 25, 1918.
[83] New York *Times,* Jan. 1, 1919.

not seem to them sufficient justification for "violating the methods of orderly legislative procedure." [84]

La Follette objected to the general plan of taxation, to raising too small an amount from taxation, and to permitting "war profits and excessive incomes to escape fair and reasonable taxation." He reserved his substitute proposals until the bill was reported to the Senate.

Smoot's report stressed his disapproval of the draft because it did not remove the "unworkable, unscientific and discriminatory provisions of the act of 1917." He would have liked a bill that was so plain "that any ordinary business man or individual could have understood it and would have had no trouble in making out a tax return." To that end he would have a flat tax on all corporations and individuals, one which would not involve the question of invested stock or bonded indebtedness, but he would have special treatment for those with invested capital of over $1,000,000 and those with undue profits. He disapproved also of the amount of revenue to be raised, for he considered it quite insufficient for the needs of the government, estimated at ten billion for 1920. His report commented also on the desirability of the substitution of a general sales tax for the nuisance taxes.[85]

THE REVISED BILL IN THE SENATE

The President devoted two paragraphs of his annual message, December 2, 1918, to the tax bill. He followed the same line of thought as that outlined by the Secretary of the Treasury, namely, that war expenditures would decline slowly, so that $6,000,000,000 would be needed for 1919 and $4,000,000,000 for 1920. He urged the incorporation of the much-debated 1920 provisions, saying:

> Any arrangements less definite than these would add elements of doubt and confusion to the critical period of industrial readjustment through which the country must now immediately pass. . . Clearly determined conditions, clearly and simply charted, are indispensable to the economic revival and rapid industrial development which may confidently be expected if we act now and sweep all interrogation points away.[86]

Chairman Simmons presented the revenue bill to the Senate on December 10, requesting that the formal reading be dispensed with so that immediate consideration could be given to Committee amendments, with the agreement that those to which Senators took

[84] *Cong. Rec.* 57: 542-543.

[85] The report is printed in the *Cong. Rec.* 57: 292 as well as in 65th Congress, 3d Session, *Senate Report* 617, Part 4. Smoot's interest in the sales tax was further demonstrated in 1921. See below, Chap. VIII, pp. 201, 212, 213, 216.

[86] *Cong. Rec.* 57: 14.

exception would be passed over. La Follette asked that they pass over almost all of the bill pertaining to the income, corporation, excess-profits, and inheritance taxes.[87] The progress of the bill was further delayed by a long political speech criticizing the President's trip to Versailles; so Simmons objected to yielding the floor for other members lest no headway be made in consideration of the task at hand. Merely the reading of the bill with the Committee changes took until December 15.

La Follette presented a substitute for the entire bill. His objections to the Committee draft were: (1) that the bill did not raise enough revenue and (2) that it did not distribute the tax burden fairly. As in the debate on the 1917 law, he regretted that the finances of the country were based to such a large extent on bonds. "We tiptoe around this question of taxing incomes," he said. The report of the new Secretary of the Treasury (Carter Glass)[88] put the figure for 1918 disbursements at over $21,800,000,000, which was $3,000,000,000 more than the estimate which Secretary McAdoo gave to the Finance Committee earlier in the year. "How is the Government going to float loans covering the next twelve months of from ten to twelve billion dollars of bonds, probably more, in addition to those already taken?" asked La Follette. We can, of course, pass this bill, wash our hands of the matter and hope that in the next few months something will turn up, or that the people will continue to buy bonds of the Government; but we must consider more than next year." He objected to the relief provisions also, especially the "cushion" of the reorganization section.[89]

Briefly summarized, La Follette's proposal was a normal income tax of 2% on individuals, with exemptions of $1000 and $2000; surtax rates rising from 5% on incomes over $5000 to 78% on those over $500,000. His corporation income tax rates, 18% and 12%, and his excess-profits tax were much as those in the House bill. He proposed an 80% war-profits tax without as many exemptions as the Committee draft. He estimated that his bill would yield $6,743,450,000 – over a billion more than he thought the Committee bill would produce.[90] Only five Senators voted with him for the substitute: Borah, Gronna, Norris, Nugent, and Vardaman.[91]

The most important issues were the remedial provisions inserted by the Committee to care for the sudden postwar changes, consolidated returns, and exemptions of income from bonds of states

87 *Cong. Rec.* 57: 293-312.
88 Secretary McAdoo resigned Nov. 23, 1918.
89 *Cong. Rec.* 57: 819-820, 828-829.
90 For La Follette's bill see *Cong. Rec.* 57: 799-818. The explanation and debate follow.
91 *Cong. Rec.* 57: 832.

and municipalities. Many Senators anticipated a serious deflation and were concerned over the possible effects of the proposed taxes on business. Lenroot, on the other hand, was an outstanding objector to some of the relief provisions, especially those which allowed losses to be carried over for three years.[92] Smoot upheld the Committee action in this case, showing that it had precedent in English law.[93] Gronna and Hitchcock were concerned lest the bill had not provided ample protection for reductions in inventories,[94] but they were finally satisfied with the Committee explanations and Gronna withdrew the amendment he had drafted.

Kellogg offered an amendment in regard to the consolidated returns of foreign corporations which the Chairman accepted. It allowed such corporations which were affiliated with domestic corporations to receive credit for taxes paid abroad.[95] Lenroot objected to permitting consolidated returns by domestic corporations in a case where "a corporation engaged in one line of business, making very large profits, may utilize the capital and returns of another corporation not making large profits to reduce the tax it pays to the government." His amendment permitting consolidated returns only when corporations were engaged in the same or a related business was accepted without a vote.[96] Another of his amendments was rejected. It aimed to prohibit consolidated returns in the case of individuals owning two or more corporations even though they were doing the same kind of business.[97] He thought the Committee provisions encouraged trusts and monopolies. Norris showed, however, that if Lenroot's amendment were passed the individual could incorporate and let the parent company rather than the individual own the stock of subsidiary companies. Lenroot agreed, but thought it could not be done in time to evade the law under consideration. As Kellogg pointed out, the question was a difficult one and he favored following the practice of the Treasury Department.

Jones (Dem., N. M.) also had a great deal to say about the bill. He proposed an amendment to limit individual or corporation exemption of interest on state and municipal bonds to that from a principal amount of $5000. Kellogg pointed out that this would subject income from such sources to the normal tax as well as to the surtax, but more important than that, the bonds were issued under the specific condition that they could not be taxed by the

[92] *Cong. Rec.* 57: 503.
[93] *Cong. Rec.* 57: 504.
[94] *Cong. Rec.* 57: 507-518, 548-549.
[95] *Cong. Rec.* 57: 668.
[96] *Cong. Rec.* 57: 719-721.
[97] *Cong. Rec.* 57: 721, 735-736.

federal government. Thomas argued that if the federal government could tax state securities, states could tax those of the federal government. Knox disagreed; he thought the war powers vested Congress with this right. Underwood thought it good public policy to maintain the present status.[98]

The excess-profits tax section was attacked by Jones and Smoot, as well as by La Follette.[99] Smoot had more to say than any other one member of the minority party. Some of his objections have been sketched in the summary of his report. On the floor of the Senate he took much time in criticizing the excess-profits tax which he condemned as discriminatory, unequal, and unjust.[100] Jones also thought the tax most inequitable and feared that the minimum flat exemption of 10% for the war-profits tax would aid well-established corporations, those with large capital, and hence it would operate to reduce the 80% tax by 10%. This had been admitted by the Committee on Ways and Means, and Jones was responsible for the Senate Committee remedial amendments such as those allowing new corporations the same exemption that representative concerns in a similar trade or business were entitled to have. He considered the excess-profits tax harmful to the industrial development of the country because it would destroy individual initiative. He said:

> It absolutely prevents the investment of money in some of the most essential industries of the country. It takes no reckoning of the difference between safe investments and hazardous investments.[101]

Thomas also offered a substitute for the excess-profits tax to obviate the difficulty of administration.[102] Gore proposed a new definition of taxable income for excess-profits tax purposes, and a new basis for computing excess-profits tax and war-profits tax: that the exemption or credit be deducted from net profits, and then the rates of the several brackets be applied to the remainder. This he thought would be more equitable between large and small corporations.[103] These amendments were rejected. Thomas did, however, win support for a tax of 100% on contributions of over $500 to political campaigns.

Doubtless to the relief of the majority party, the much disliked 1920 sections received little attention in the Senate. Penrose, Townsend, and McCumber made a few speeches, but the bitter

98 *Cong. Rec.* 57: 774-777, 10933-10941.
99 *Cong. Rec.* 57: 704.
100 *Cong. Rec.* 57: 491-500.
101 *Cong. Rec.* 57: 706-707.
102 *Cong. Rec.* 57: 713. In lieu of the excess-profits tax he proposed a war-profits tax on all individuals and corporations if prewar earnings were in excess of the average of representative concerns engaged in a similar business.
103 *Cong. Rec.* 57: 799.

feeling about them had died down. Borah said the actions of the Republicans were mysterious.

> The country was advised that this was such an injurious, unfair, improvident and unwise thing to do that the party coming into power felt constrained to defeat it even by the consumption of time, yet within a few hours after that position was announced, as a result of a conference of all the members of that committee upon the Republican side . . . the whole program was changed overnight. I do not understand it, except as the bill itself unravels the mystery. I think if you find that this bill, which purports to levy an 80% tax, in fact levies only a 48% tax, you will discover why the change took place.[104]

This statement started a rather animated discussion as to just how heavy the taxes would be. The estimates of the average effective rates varied from 48% to 60%.

The bill passed without a roll call on December 23 and the Presiding Officer appointed Simmons, Williams, Smith, Penrose, and Lodge as conferees to meet with those from the House.[105]

THE CONFERENCE REPORT[106]

When Congress convened after the Christmas recess the House appointed its conferees to meet with those from the Senate in order to reach an agreement on the 602 amendments which the Senate had made. Because of the desire of the Republicans for an extra session, which they hoped to get by preventing action on the appropriations, the Democrats decided to push the supply bills through first and then to take up the revenue measure. For this reason both Kitchin and Simmons remained at their homes for some days after Congress met in January 1919, and were in no hurry to begin work on the tax bill.[107]

Even before the Conferees met protests against the bill began to pour in upon them. The chairman of the Tax Committee of the Chamber of Commerce of the United States wrote that the proposed taxes were so high that they would injure business and restrict expansion at a time when the resources of the country should be used to permit the employment of men returning from war. Others asked why taxes could not be reduced since the war was over and government costs should be less.[108] Many congressmen, especially in the Republican ranks, held similar views.

Defenders of the measure showed, however, that the government was already involved to the extent of $31,000,000,000 for the fiscal

[104] *Cong. Rec.* 57: 742.
[105] *Cong. Rec.* 57: 834.
[106] *Cong. Rec.* 57: 2973-3003.
[107] New York *Times,* Jan. 6, 1919.
[108] New York *Times,* Jan. 1, 2, 1919.

year 1919, and that there would probably be additional expense; for instance, there was the loss from the guarantee to the farmers of $2.20 a bushel for wheat. Chairman Sherley of the Appropriations Committee busied himself in trying to find possible reductions in expenditure but to no avail. He stated January 31 that the government was still spending $50,000,000 a day.[109]

The main points of disagreement between the Senate and House managers related to: (1) the rates of the excess-profits tax, (2) depletion allowances for mines and oil wells, and (3) consolidated returns. There was almost a deadlock over the first point mentioned, and it was the issue last to be decided. Kitchin was very much opposed to the lower rates of the Senate bill because he feared that they would "not bring about a fair allotment of taxation" or provide the government with the money it needed.[110] The Senate had eliminated the 80% war-profits tax for 1920, but agreed to levy it in that year on any war contracts that remained. Kitchin finally surrendered and consented to the Senate plan for superimposing the war-profits on the excess-profits tax, with rates the same as those of the Senate in the first bracket, but higher in the second bracket by 5%. The House conferees also agreed to the Senate amendments covering depletion of mines and oil wells but the allowance for discovery depletion was based on value as of 30 days after acquisition, instead of twelve months.

The Senate amendment permitting consolidated returns of corporations in the same line of business was adopted after it was shown to be necessary to reach affiliated corporations that heretofore had been able to escape the tax.[111] Despite the assurance of T. S. Adams, Kitchin was convinced that the government would lose revenue by this provision, but the Senate conferees were very determined to have it.[112]

Senator Thomas' amendment for a tax of 100% on contributions over $500 to political campaign funds was not put into the final bill, although a few Senate conferees favored it.

The Senate members receded on the provision to have tax reports made on a gross instead of a net income tax basis. They accepted also the House provision for exempting the first $3500 of the income of a person in the army or navy. The Senate had not limited this exemption. The House provision to tax salaries of the President of the United States and judges of federal courts, which the Senate had eliminated, was restored, but the reference to state officers was

109 *Cong. Rec.* 57: 3015-3016.
110 New York *Times,* Jan. 17, 1919.
111 New York *Times,* Jan. 14, 1919.
112 *Cong. Rec.* 57: 3007.

omitted. The House estate tax was accepted instead of the inheritance tax.

On the floor of the House Fordney called the final draft a much better bill than the one first passed, inasmuch as it was more equitable to the taxpayers. Rainey, in summing up the measure just before the vote was taken, gave most thoughtful suggestions as to the future of taxation which he said must follow more simple principles.

> The numerous pages of this great revenue bill contain hundreds of carefully drawn but technical and complicated paragraphs. In our efforts to conceal taxes and make it apparently easier to pay them, we have inserted paragraphs relating to amortization, depletion, deductions, normal taxes, flat rates, war profits . . . and other complicated and technical paragraphs on other subjects.

He warned his colleagues that in the future it would take more money than ever to provide for the necessities of the national government and that more citizens ought to help contribute to its support.[113] The House vote for the Conference Report was 312 to 11.[114]

Penrose had the Conference Report read to the Senate; but, inasmuch as the House had yielded on a majority of the changes and it was lunch time, only four Republicans and three Democrats heard it. There was no roll call when the vote was taken.[115]

SUMMARY OF THE LAW [116]

Although the law became effective February 24, 1919, it was specifically provided that it be called the Revenue Act of 1918. The law was a complete entity, unlike the two Revenue Acts of 1917 which were amendments to a previous law. The Act contained 14 titles,[117] of which this study is concerned primarily with the first four and the last three.

The income tax sections were completely rearranged and rewritten. The normal tax rates on individuals for 1918 income were 6% on the first \$4000, 12% on the remainder. For each calendar year thereafter the rates were 4% on the first \$4000 and 8% on the remainder. Surtax rates began at 1% on income in excess of \$5000 and

[113] *Cong. Rec.* 57: 3034.

[114] *Cong. Rec.* 57: 3035.

[115] *Cong. Rec.* 57: 3271.

[116] 40 *Statutes at Large* 1057.

[117] These were: I – General Definitions; II – Income Tax; III – War-profits and Excess-profits Tax; IV – Estate Tax; V – Tax on Transportation and Other Facilities, and on Insurance; VI – Tax on Beverages; VII – Tax on Cigars, Tobacco, and Manufactures Thereof; VIII – Tax on Admissions and Dues; IX – Excise Taxes; X – Special Taxes; XI – Stamp Taxes; XII – Tax on Employment of Child Labor; XIII – General Administrative Provisions; XIV – General Provisions.

increased by 1% for each of most of the succeeding brackets until reaching a maximum of 65% on the amount over $1,000,000.[118]

For corporations, the income tax rate was 12% on income of the calendar year 1918 and 10% for each year thereafter. A special provision was inserted for railroads, then under federal control, so that their tax was 10% for 1918 and 8% for each year thereafter.

The war-profits and excess-profits tax rates, which applied to corporations only, were as follows for 1918:

Excess-profits Tax –
(1) 30% of the amount of the net income in excess of the excess-profits credit and not in excess of 20% of the invested capital;
(2) 65% of the amount of the net income in excess of 20% of the invested capital;
War-profits Tax –
(3) the sum, if any, by which 80% of the amount of the net income in excess of the war-profits credit exceeded the amount of the excess-profits tax computed under (1) and (2).

For 1919 the rate for the first bracket was 20%; that for the second bracket was 40%; the third bracket, the war-profits tax, was omitted.

In computing the excess-profits tax corporations could deduct $3000 and 8% of the invested capital for the taxable year. For the war-profits tax the credit allowed was $3000 plus an amount equal to the average net income for the prewar years 1911, 1912, and 1913, plus or minus 10% of the difference between the average invested capital for the prewar period and the invested capital for the taxable year, but not less than $3000 plus 10% of the invested capital for the taxable year. Income derived from gold mining was exempt from these taxes.

The definition of invested capital was much more detailed than in the 1917 law, permitting the inclusion of intangible property such as patents, copyrights, goodwill, etc., but not borrowed capital nor tax-exempt securities. There were many other definitions and special provisions which cover much space, showing the effort to arrive at some workable solution of this difficult problem.

Several sections were written to give relief in unusual situations which arose as a result of the war. One permitted liberal deduction for amortization of buildings, machinery, and equipment constructed or acquired after April 6, 1917, for the prosecution of the war. Another made special provision in case of substantial loss from depreciation in value of inventories.

The motive for enacting these sections was to assure justice to the

118 See Chap. XXII for individual and corporation rates and exemptions under different laws.

taxpayer but the practical results were unfortunate. The administration of them involved the Bureau in a maze of technical difficulties that appeared endless and almost resulted in the breakdown of administration and a big scandal.[119] As the Commissioner of Internal Revenue said:

> Certainty and simplicity are far more important in a tax measure than the abstract element of equity. . . The administrative machinery should not be burdened with the responsibility for distinguishing between taxpayers.[120]

In order to prevent the avoidance of the surtax by use of the corporate form of organization the law provided that a corporation created or used to prevent the imposition of the surtax upon its stockholders by permitting the accumulation of gains or profits would be taxed as a personal service corporation. This provision, like its predecessor, was unenforceable.[121]

Personal service corporations and partnerships were not subject to the corporation income or war-excess-profits taxes, though members of both of these kinds of organization were required to include in their individual income returns their respective shares of profits of such organizations, whether distributed or not.

The law removed some of the difficulties encountered in administering the preceding Act by simplifying the definition of a dividend. The Act of 1917 endeavored to determine the year in which the earnings were made; the law of 1918 stated:

> any distribution made in the year 1918 . . . shall be deemed to have been made from earnings or profits accumulated since February 28, 1913, or, in the case of a personal service corporation, from the most recently accumulated earnings or profits.

The allowance of $200 for a dependent was broader than that in the Act of 1917, which granted the exemption for a child only.

Taxpayers were permitted to make returns according to methods of accounting customarily used. Losses could be allowed even if not charged off within the year. Furthermore, if the loss exceeded the income for the year, the excess might be deducted in computing the tax for the next year. Allowances for depletion were increased, chiefly by permitting computation on the basis of discovery value. Provision was made for payment of the tax in quarterly installments.

Under certain conditions affiliated corporations were required to make consolidated returns.[122]

119 See below, Chap. XXII, and 69th Congress, 1st Session, *Senate Report* 27 (1926), "the Couzens Report." There is still (1939) litigation over 1917 and 1918 cases.

120 Roper, Daniel C., "Basis for Reform of Federal Taxation," *Annals of the American Academy of Political and Social Science,* 95: 164 (May 1921).

121 See below, Chap. XVII.

122 For a discussion of this subject see Staub, W. A., "Consolidated Returns," *The Federal Income Tax* (Columbia University Lectures 1920), pp. 188-222.

Even more than in previous Acts provision was made for a great deal of Commissioner-made law. The Advisory Tax Board and the Legislative Drafting service were established.

Title XII levied a special tax of 10% on the net earnings of any mine, quarry, factory, or other establishment that employed children under sixteen years of age. This title was declared unconstitutional in May, 1922.[123]

The most serious criticism made of the law was of its complexity. In discussing the measure in the House, Hull stated that "equity and simplicity should be the prime requisites of any law," but to secure equity it was necessary to insert numerous saving provisions, exceptions, and qualifications. These produce the complexities.[124] T. S. Adams, speaking before the American Economic Association in December 1919, said:

> There is an imperative need for immediate simplification in the system of internal revenue taxes. The unvarnished truth is that the income and profits taxes are so heavy and so intricate that a sufficient number of auditors and experts cannot be secured by the government to audit, assess, and settle old claims as fast as new claims are created.[125]

As to the definition of invested capital, critics pointed out that it was very defective because it laid too much emphasis on form, it permitted "undue advantage to be taken of the accident of reorganization or recapitalization prior to March 3, 1917," it was too arbitrary as to intangible assets, excluded "too much real capital and included too much apparent capital." [126] According to a report of a committee of the National Tax Association in 1919, old corporations and those capitalized conservatively were at a disadvantage in comparison with new ones, highly capitalized.[127]

123 *Bailey* v. *Drexel Furn. Co.*, 259 U. S. 20.

124 *Cong. Rec.* 56: 10161.

125 "Immediate Future of the Excess-Profits Tax," *American Economic Review*, X: Supplement, 15-18 (March 1920). See also the comments by Roper, D. C., "Basis for Reform of Federal Taxation," *Annals of the American Academy of Political and Social Science*, 95: 164 (May 1921); and Plehn, C. C., "War-Profits and Excess-Profits Taxes," *American Economic Review*, X: 283-98 (June 1920).

126 Holmes, George E., "The Excess-Profits Tax," *American Economic Review*, X: Supplement, 22 (March 1920).

127 "Report of the Committee on Federal Taxation," *Proceedings of the National Tax Association* 1919, pp. 315-367.

CHAPTER VIII

REVENUE ACT OF 1921 – REDUCTION OF WAR-TIME TAXES

POSTWAR PROBLEMS

The end of the war did not bring an end to government problems, least of all to fiscal problems. The President and the Congressional leaders, as well as taxpayers, knew that the tax burden was too heavy for peace times even though Treasury needs were not on a prewar level. Complexities in the law, particularly in the excess-profits tax section, called for careful revision. Changes were needed also to make the law more equitable; for example, as Secretary Glass and later Secretary Houston pointed out, some method was needed for prorating the income received from the sale of capital assets to the several years the assets were held. Most imperative of all was the devising of some plan for extricating the Bureau of Internal Revenue from the maze of tax claims.

The political situation, however, precluded any action until President Wilson's term expired. Both the House and the Senate of the 66th Congress were controlled by the Republicans. Many of the Democrats were almost as hostile to the President as were those of the opposition party. But legislation could hardly be postponed much longer after the Supreme Court, in *Eisner* v. *Macomber*,[1] declared unconstitutional the taxation of stock dividends and cast doubt on the validity of the existing method of taxing personal service corporations. The decision did not concern the status of the taxation of personal service companies but the Court clearly indicated that it would be invalid to tax stockholders on their shares of undistributed corporate net income. This was in effect what the law did in the case of a personal service company.[2] Estimates of the annual loss of revenue caused by this decision varied from $40,000,000 to $80,000,000.

Secretary Houston [3] urged immediate legislation, but his program did not appeal to Chairman Fordney of the Committee on Ways and Means. Moreover neither Fordney nor others of the House leaders wanted to sponsor measures that were just "patch work."

[1] 252 U. S. 189 (1920).

[2] In the 1918 law personal service corporations and their stockholders were treated essentially as partnerships and partners, respectively. See above, pp. 168 and 187.

[3] David F. Houston was Secretary of the Treasury from Feb. 6, 1920 to March 3, 1921.

THE CRUSADE AGAINST THE EXCESS-PROFITS TAX

Both political parties paid passing tribute to the tax situation in long platforms adopted in the summer of 1920. The Republicans called for a more just and simple system of taxation ; the Democrats "condemned the failure of the Republican Congress to respond to the President's demand for the readjustment of the tax laws to peace conditions." During the campaign the Republicans went so far as to declare that :

one of the chief needs of the country is the revision of taxation as one way to lower the cost of living, restore business confidence, and stimulate enterprise.[4]

The press commented on the need for new legislation. The issue was really pushed, however, by business men who began forming organizations to spread their ideas, chiefly in opposition to the excess-profits tax. One of the first of such groups was the Business Men's National Tax Committee which had as its goal the substitution of a sales tax for the excess-profits tax.[5] A similar organization was the Tax League of America. Other societies already formed set up committees to study the tax situation and to issue reports. An outstanding example of such efforts was the tax conference called in April 1920, by the National Industrial Conference Board at the instigation of the American Petroleum Institute and the American Mining Congress. Most of the speeches were devoted to criticism of the excess-profits tax.[6] A second conference was held in New York City in October 1920, at which the Tax Committee of the National Industrial Conference Board presented a report which rejected a sales tax proposal.

Other business men's groups opposing the sales tax were the National Association of Credit Men, the United States Chamber of Commerce, and the National Association of Retail Grocers.[7] Such well-established organizations as the National Tax Association not only discussed and debated divergent points of view, but also appointed committees of well-known tax authorities and economists to draw up recommendations to Congress as to changes needed in the 1918 law.[8] In fact, so intense was the campaign of business against

[4] *The Literary Digest*, Nov. 6, 1920, p. 9.

[5] "The Gross Sales, or Turnover Tax," *Proceedings of the National Tax Association* 1920, pp. 180-209 ; 67th Congress, 1st Session, *Hearings before the Senate Finance Committee on the Revenue Act of* 1921, pp. 43-63.

[6] National Industrial Conference Board, *Proceedings of the National Industrial Tax Conference, Special Report* No. 9, May 1920 (pamphlet).

[7] For a summary of the literature on the sales tax see the memorandum by K. M. Williamson, *Quarterly Journal of Economics,* 35 : 618-33 (Aug. 1921).

[8] *Proceedings of the National Tax Association* 1919, pp. 295-384 ; 1920, pp. 116-219 ; 1921, pp. 301-337. See also Haig, R. M., Friday, David, and others, "The Excess Profits Tax," *American Economic Review* X : Supplement, 1-32 (March 1920) ; *Annals of the American Academy of Political and Social Science,* vol. 95, (May 1921).

the excess-profits tax that it might better be described as a crusade. Representatives of farmers were the only ones who could be found to defend it.

What were the reasons for this united opposition to the tax? The injustice of the tax was undeniable, the variations in the tax burden were often too great because of the unjustifiable differences in invested capital reported by different corporations. At the same time, the known injustices of the tax were commonly used as pretexts to cover the chief real objection, namely, opposition to paying such heavy taxes. Moreover, Great Britain had set an example by repealing its excess-profits tax. One of the facts that could not be disregarded was a strong postwar deflationary price movement that started in the late spring of 1920 and was well under way by July. This depression accentuated the burdens of the high tax bills of corporations and in many cases made it difficult for taxpayers to find liquid funds with which to pay taxes on 1919 income. Thus there was a combination of pretext and real grievance motivating the business world.

Taxpayers rationalized that the excess-profits tax was the major cause of all their tax difficulties. It became the scapegoat, the symbol of all high taxes and, of course, of high government expenses, borne because of patriotic emotion during the war but now found unendurable. "The cause remains great," wrote one editor, "but the emotions it aroused evaporate more rapidly than the bills it left behind." [9]

Furthermore, there was a great deal of suspicion as to what it might lead to; for example, the passage of a soldiers' bonus bill might entail a higher tax rate or a more inequitable base. The following extract from a speech given before the National Industrial Tax Conference may be cited as an example of the fear psychology, or tax phobia, prevalent in the early spring of 1920:

> The present excess-profits tax is in a large measure responsible for the present high prices. Labor in turn made its demands, which further increased prices, and again called for further increases, and so the vicious circle turned. In all this we have been overlooking another class of people, large in numbers, who have hitherto been powerless to assert themselves or at least have declined to do so. I refer to people with set incomes who before the era of high prices had enough to live on, who could save a little and contribute to charity. Present conditions are grinding these people down, using up their savings, and rushing them to pauperism. What will be the result? Let me draw your attention to the recent elections in France. The "Reds" in that country are "redder" than ever, but in spite of this, since 1914 they have increased their numbers by better than half a million. . . This is the direct result of excessive taxation and it is the result of no other cause. In Russia the people have repudiated their national debt and therefore their taxes are nominal. . . With such examples as these before our eyes, shall we profit by them

[9] *New Republic*, 22: 47 (March 10, 1920).

while yet we may? For economic reasons, for patriotic reasons, and for the sake of unification of national thought and purpose, we must do away with the present law and substitute in its place another which will comprehend in its conception the whole subject of its effect.[10]

The argument that the tax was the cause of high prices was a very common one but not generally supported by economists. The latter showed that the rising price level started in July 1915 at 103 for wholesale prices (using 1900 to 1914 as 100); reached 214 in 1918, before the excess-profits tax was passed, and then rose very gradually to a maximum of 231 in 1920. Nevertheless, the high rates of tax no doubt encouraged extravagant expenditures for salaries, advertising, bonuses, and repairs on the assumption that the tax would later be reduced or repealed. Funds so used as well as taxes paid to the government were not available for re-investment in plant and thus future production of goods was somewhat reduced.[11]

The anxiety on the part of business men because the tax was shifted to the consumer was somewhat amusing. Probably most of their anxiety was really because they could not shift most of such taxes. As Secretary Houston pointed out, in many cases the desire to abolish the excess-profits tax was fundamentally a desire to substitute for the direct tax on business an indirect tax on consumption goods which would be borne by the masses.[12] In fact, one of the reasons why the excess-profits tax should be repealed, said one economist, was "that its inequalities and inequities are not rectified by a process of shifting and diffusion." [13]

There were, however, two arguments for the repeal of the tax that were not generally disputed: one was that the application of the tax was inequitable; the other, that the administration was impracticable. T. S. Adams, who saw the working of the tax at close range for a long period of time, described it as one of "intricacy and capricious inequalities." [14] It was inequitable in that it did not apply to partnerships, individuals, estates, or trusts. "Even among corporations it does not define excess-profits with accuracy or justice." As an example, he cited the fact that in 1918 the excess-profits taxes of four large corporations engaged in the same line of business constituted 5%, 11%, 18%, and 30% of their respective net incomes

[10] *Proceedings of the National Industrial Tax Conference* 1920, *Special Report* No. 9, May 1920, pp. 62-63.

[11] Friday, David, *Profits, Wages and Prices*; *Proceedings of the National Industrial Tax Conference,* May 1920, pp. 46, 62, 68; United States Chamber of Commerce, *Referendum* No. 34; p. 6; *New Republic* 22: 47, 74, 136, 263 (March 10, 17, 31, April 28, 1920). 28: 280 (Nov. 2, 1921).

[12] Houston, David F., "What You Need to Know about Federal Taxation," *World's Work* 42: 586 (Oct. 1921).

[13] Adams, T. S., New York *Evening Post,* Aug. 9, 1920.

[14] Adams, T. S., "The Excess Profits Tax," *Quarterly Journal of Economics,* 35: 369 (May 1921).

because of differences in organization. Secretary Glass wrote in 1919 that the tax encouraged wasteful expenditure; put a premium on overcapitalization and a penalty on brains, energy, and enterprise; discouraged new ventures, and confirmed old ventures in their monopolies.[15]

A representative of the National Association of Credit men charged that the tax caused inequities:[16] (1) between stockholders in the same enterprise; (2) between groups of stockholders owning competing enterprises but enjoying the same measure of prosperity; (3) between owners of an old-established business built up by them and purchasers of a business already developed; (4) between conservatively and loosely-managed businesses; and (5) between overcapitalized, fairly capitalized, and undercapitalized businesses.

A spokesman of the National Association of Manufacturers summarized his criticism as follows:

> It is an unsound tax economically and socially. It utterly disregards the essential relation between the risk of an enterprise and its return, a consideration which lies at the very foundation of all business investment and operation. It obviously discriminates against any business in exact proportion to its superior risk. It continues that discrimination by further disregard for comparative and superior quality of management in the conduct of the business, and thus penalizes the very efficiency that makes for success in industrial production and assures new sources of revenue. It of necessity discourages by its operation and by the demands which it makes for the cash necessary to pay taxes, the creation of adequate surplus, without which, particularly in times like these, general and special business risk is seriously increased.[17]

From the point of view of the government the tax was the most difficult it had ever tried to administer. Inasmuch as this phase of the tax is discussed elsewhere,[18] it will suffice here merely to summarize the difficulties. Most important was the problem of determining invested capital. The law contained several long, involved sections for computing invested capital, but Congress knew that these rules could not be applied universally. Hence the Commissioner was given the right of making special adjustments, where equity seemed to require them, so that the tax would accord with those of representative corporations in the same lines of business. These special exceptions greatly aggravated the administrative problems, particularly where there were, in any case, an enormous number of returns

[15] *Report of the Secretary of the Treasury* 1919, p. 23.

[16] Elliott, Ray G., Chairman of the Federal Tax Committee of the association. (*Proceedings of National Industrial Tax Conference,* May 1920, p. 68.) See also Rothschild, Meyer D., "The Gross Sales, or Turnover Tax," *Proceedings of National Tax Association* 1920, pp. 180-186.

[17] *Proceedings of the National Industrial Tax Conference,* May 1920, p. 9.

[18] See above, Chap. VII, and below, Chap. XXIII.

to be handled by a Bureau personnel in constant turnover. This unfortunate combination of factors made the auditing of the income and excess-profits tax returns a seemingly endless task. Furthermore, upon the promulgation or change of Treasury rulings or regulations, old cases were reopened so that claims for abatement and refund were apparently never finally settled.

The strain was such that it began to be feared that the income tax itself would be jeopardized. T. S. Adams, representing the Treasury Department before the Committee on Ways and Means, said in December 1920:

> We must use the larger portion of the force and all the brains we can get – and more if we can possibly get hold of them – to get through with the audit of tax returns now in the bureau for the calendar years 1917, 1918, and 1919. In other words, if the Bureau of Internal Revenue, with the favor of Almighty God and all the ability and talent it can possibly procure, gets through the next two or three years under any administration and under any party without a breakdown, I shall thank God.[19]

Commenting on the serious consequences of this situation in a series of articles in a New York paper, Adams said it was a surprise to him that the country had not awakened to the danger of the situation.

> Thousands of business concerns, particularly corporations, must some day be confronted with large additional tax bills for the war period. These "heavy but indefinable future obligations". . . hang like a suspended avalanche over American business, and in time they can hardly fail to create a political issue. If their settlement is protracted much longer, projects for a financial amnesty will inevitably be introduced . . . Some taxpayers are plainly counting on a shortening of the statute of limitations. . . Few things could be more unfair.[20]

Another reason for the interest of the Treasury in the repeal of the tax was that it had passed the peak of productivity as a revenue measure. From a maximum of $2,505,000,000 in 1918, it declined to $1,431,000,000 in 1919, to $988,000,000 in 1920, and to $335,-131,811 in 1921. The trend of receipts from corporation taxes is shown in Table 8.[21]

In view of the opposition of business to the tax, it is interesting to note the statistics as to the burden of the tax. In 1918 reports were received from 317,579 corporations, of which 115,518 showed a deficit and 202,061 showed net income of $8,361,511,249. The income taxes paid by such corporations amounted to $653,198,480; the war-profits

19 66th Congress, 3d Session, *Hearings before the Committee on Ways and Means on Revenue Revision,* Dec. 13, 1920, p. 38.

20 New York *Evening Post,* Aug. 4, 1920. See, also, issues of July 19, 21, 26, 28; Aug. 4, 9, 11, 16 and 18, 1920. These articles were later published in pamphlet form under the caption, *Needed Tax Reform.*

21 These figures do not include $350,000,000 received later as a result of government audit.

Table 8

Corporation and Individual Income Taxes, 1913–1922 [a]

Calendar Year	*Corporation Income Tax*	*War Profits and Excess-Profits Taxes*	*Total Corporation Taxes*	*Grand Total Individual and Corporation Taxes*
1913 [b]	$43,127,740 [c]	....	$43,127,740 [c]	$71,381,275
1914 [b]	39,144,532	....	39,144,532	80,190,694
1915 [b]	56,993,657	....	56,993,657	124,937,252
1916	171,805,150	....	171,805,150	345,191,844
1917	503,698,029	$1,638,747,740	2,142,445,769	2,937,826,707
1918	653,198,483	2,505,565,939	2,158,764,422	4,286,486,257
1919	743,535,888	1,431,805,690	2,175,341,578	3,444,971,682
1920	636,508,292	988,726,251	1,625,234,643	2,700,288,329
1921	366,443,621	335,131,811	701,575,432	1,420,962,538
1922	775,310,154	8,466,114 [d]	783,776,268	1,644,833,576

[a] United States Treasury, *Statistics of Income* 1922, p. 33. This table shows tax reported by corporations and individuals on income for the years indicated, hence does not correspond exactly with collections reported on the fiscal year basis by the United States Treasury in Table 39, below (Appendix).

[b] *Report of Commissioner of Internal Revenue* for fiscal year ended June 30 immediately following the year shown.

[c] Includes excise tax, $10,071,077, Act of Aug. 5, 1909.

[d] On net income earned from July 1 to Dec. 31, 1921, reported on fiscal year returns whose accounting period terminated prior to July 1, 1922.

and excess-profits tax, $2,505,566,000.[22] The distribution of these taxes by industries showed that practically two-thirds (66.9%) was paid by manufacturing concerns, 11% by corporations engaged in trade, 4.7% by transportation and other public utilities, 3.81% by financial, banking, and insurance companies. Of the manufacturing corporations, those engaged in metal and metal products paid almost one-third of that paid by all corporations (31.76%); the textile industry came next, with 12.46% of the total; food products and tobacco, 6.55%. The relative percentages were approximately the same for 1919, although in that year about 7000 more corporations filed returns, and the total tax paid was less. The relation of taxes to net income for 1918 is shown in Table 9.

If a study is made of the amount of tax relative to the size of the corporation, it will be noted that in 1918 one-third of the total excess-profits tax was paid by 180 corporations each showing net income of over $5,000,000; one-third by approximately 2000 corporations

[22] Statistics are not available for separation of the yield of the excess-profits tax and war-profits tax. The latter was collected for 1919 only.

TABLE 9

CORPORATION RETURNS DISTRIBUTED BY INCOME CLASSES, CALENDAR YEAR 1918 [a]

Income classes	*Number*	*Net income*	*Total, income, war-profits and excess-profits taxes*	*Average amount of tax*	*% of total tax to net income*
Reporting net income:					
0 to $2,000	68,973 [b]	$55,281,461	....	......	....
$2,000 to $5,000	49,397	162,073,156	$9,780,188	$198	6.03
$5,000 to $10,000	29,780	213,305,243	28,510,700	957	13.37
$10,000 to $50,000	37,053	800,570,917	204,015,955	5,506	25.48
$50,000 to $100,000	7,224	507,215,825	180,311,433	24,960	35.55
$100,000 to $250,000	5,383	838,508,564	329,237,965	61,163	39.26
$250,000 to $500,000	2,054	713,779,767	301,482,282	146,778	42.24
$500,000 to $1,000,000	1,171	815,090,903	348,693,637	297,774	42.78
$1,000,000 to $5,000,000	846	1,701,416,343	705,891,999	834,388	41.48
$5,000,000 and over	180	2,554,269,070	1,050,840,263	5,838,001	41.14
Total	202,061	8,361,511,249	3,158,764,422	23,734 [d]	38.03
Reporting no net income	115,518	689,772,361 [c]	....	......	.....
Grand Total	317,579	7,671,738,888	3,158,764,422	......	.....

[a] U. S. Treasury *Statistics of Income* 1918, p. 18.
[b] Excluding 3503 personal service corporations that were not subject to corporation taxes but were taxed as partnerships.
[c] Deficit.
[d] Average for returns reporting net income of $2000 and over.

each with net income of $500,000 to $5,000,000; and one-third by 199,000 corporations each with net income of less than $500,000.

Statistics of Income for 1918 does not classify corporations according to invested capital, but such figures are available in the report for 1919. The total income, war-profits and excess-profits taxes in that year for all corporations, represented an average of 23.24% of total net income. The taxes on corporations with invested capital between $150,000 and $300,000 were about 25% of net income; those on corporations with invested capital of $300,000 to $750,000 were 27%; those on the $1,000,000 to $4,000,000 group also were 27% of net income; those on the $90,000,000 to $1,000,000,000 group were 15.7%, practically the same as for those with invested capital of $20,000 to $40,000.[23]

THE OUTGOING ADMINISTRATION URGES TAX REVISION

When Secretary Houston reviewed the fiscal situation in December 1920, he urged modification or repeal of the excess-profits tax because of administrative difficulties and because of its inequitable burdens

23 *Statistics of Income* 1919, p. 15.

on a few corporations. He advocated the substitution of a tax on undistributed corporate earnings.[24] But the state of the Treasury did not warrant much reduction in the total tax yield. The continuing cost of the war was indicated in a table he presented, showing that 90% of the "ordinary" expenditures of the fiscal year just closed were for War Department, Navy Department, interest on the public debt, war risk insurance, pensions, purchase of obligations of foreign governments, and similar items.[25]

President Wilson's final message to Congress in December 1920 again reiterated the need for tax simplification and revision of the income and excess-profits taxes, but it was a perfunctory request because he knew he had insufficient support in Congress to get action. Even the pressure from business groups failed to move the Republicans, who were in no mood to carry out the requests of a Democratic Administration. Chairman Fordney of the Committee on Ways and Means took the position that it would be a waste of time to try to modify the revenue laws in accordance with Republican principles because Wilson would make his work useless, that is, would exercise his right of veto. The amount of revenue could not be reduced and what substitute could be found for the excess-profits tax?[26]

Nevertheless, the Committee on Ways and Means opened a series of public hearings on Revision of Revenue Legislation about the middle of December, although no bill had been prepared or was considered. The Committee was especially interested in finding a solution for the problem of tax-exempt income.

The first witness was T. S. Adams of the Treasury Department who explained the proposals of the Secretary for reducing the surtax, but his most impressive evidence was in connection with the administration of the excess-profits tax. He showed the great danger to the income tax in the piling up of work in the Internal Revenue Bureau, particularly where the work was seemingly endless. He asked the members of the Committee to do all in their power to secure passage of provisions similar to those introduced but not passed in the preceding session — provisions designed to allow final adjustment of taxes and to permit the adoption of regulations without retroactive effect. He urged that *Treasury Regulations* 41 governing the 1917 Act be made law so as to end litigation. He also explained how much administrative difficulty would result from a sales tax, a subject that interested most of the witnesses at the hearings.

Before Congress recessed for the holidays an emergency tariff bill

24 This was suggested by T. S. Adams. It is interesting chiefly as a historical antecedent of the main feature of the Revenue Act of 1936.

25 *Report of the Secretary of the Treasury* 1920, p. 48.

26 New York *Times*, Dec. 4, 1920.

was introduced into the House, a move that aroused the ire of the Democratic members of the Committee on Ways and Means. After the holiday recess the Committee resumed hearings but practically all attention was diverted from excess-profits taxes to customs tariffs. In the short session this emergency tariff bill was passed, only to be vetoed by President Wilson. It was said that Penrose was pleased; he thought the whole matter of federal revenue should be taken up before the new Congress convened in a conference between leaders of Congress and the incoming president.[27]

THE NEW ADMINISTRATION — TARIFF OR TAX REVISION FIRST?

The tariff issue which flared up just at the close of the Wilson administration became an important point of controversy between eastern and western Republicans at the opening of the 67th Congress, the first under the Harding regime. Western members were particularly conscious of the plight of the farmer, who suffered from the deflation of wartime prices of agricultural products, and from the burden of debts incurred for expensive land bought when it was expected that war prices would continue. The situation was made worse by the dumping of products from other countries.[28] Many farmers had long accepted the Republican doctrine of protection; now they wanted it applied to their products as well as to manufactured goods.

President Harding's inaugural address indicated that he was more concerned over the tax problem than about the tariff. He said:

> We can strike at war taxation and we must. We must face the grim necessity with full knowledge that the task is to be solved and we must proceed with the full realization that no statute enacted by man can repeal the inexorable laws of nature.

The great issue as to whether tariff or tax legislation should receive first attention could not be solved by House and Senate leaders. Senators Watson and Penrose, who were not particularly concerned over the plight of the farmer, favored beginning with taxation, stating that "the most important call on the Republican party is to relieve the producers and taxpayers of the burdens of war taxation." [29] Moreover they considered it inadvisable to pass a tariff bill until conditions became more normal. Fordney and Green, on the contrary, wanted an emergency tariff passed as soon as possible.[30]

27 New York *Times*, March 4, 8, 9, 1921.

28 Not only were countries anxious to sell goods at almost any price to pay war debts, but some, for example, Argentina and Australia, had piled up huge surpluses because they had been unable to ship grain and other commodities during the war.

29 New York *Times*, March 9, July 7, 1921.

30 Green, however, did not favor undertaking permanent tariff legislation at that time because he thought it would take two years to work it out.

They could see no reason for haste in reducing taxes when revenue was needed. Conferences between congressional leaders and the President ended in a stalemate. The President said that the decision would be left to the Committees on Ways and Means and Finance but he indicated informally that he preferred legislation in the following order : first, an emergency tariff, then a revenue measure, then a permanent tariff.[29]

Pressure groups then began their work. Western Senators informed Penrose that farmers must be given protection as soon as possible after Congress met.[31] The advocates of a soldiers' bonus announced that their scheme must form a part of the legislative program. The sales tax propaganda was gaining strength all over the country and business men were demanding the repeal of the excess-profits tax.

Just as it was generally conceded that Secretary Mellon had persuaded the Administration to act on the tax bills before taking up the tariff, a delegation of western Senators, distressed over the decision,[32] appealed to the President to use the wartime authority still vested in his office and declare an embargo on wool, hides, meat, butter, lemons, cottonseed oil, and cotton. Farmers in many parts of the country faced ruin, they said.[32] The Cabinet considered the situation. The farm bloc members in Congress openly charged eastern members with trying to "flim flam" the West. In two days they won their point. Harding telephoned to Fordney that an emergency tariff would take precedence over taxation.[33]

Fordney thereupon mapped out a legislative program for the session to open with the reconsideration of the emergency tariff bill which was much like the measure vetoed by Wilson but rewritten to include duties on farm products. This was to be followed immediately by an anti-dumping law, one to provide for the American valuation of imports, then by the preparation of a permanent tariff law ; and when these were passed, by the revision of tax measures.[34] The Republicans counted on forty Democrats to desert their party as they had in the last session in order to vote for the emergency tariff.[35]

Penrose, apparently not willing to admit defeat, announced that the Finance Committee would proceed with the tax bill while the

31 This was the beginning of the farm "bloc" whose leaders were : Senators Kenyon (Ia.), Poindexter (Wash.), Capper (Kan.), Stanfield (Ore.), Warren (Wyo.), Gooding (Ia.), and Cameron (Ariz.) ; Representatives Frear (Wis.), Young (N. D.), Timberlake (Colo.), Hawley (Ore.), and Hadley (Wash.).

32 When this news reached Fordney, he is reported to have said, "The West will raise hell !" New York *Times,* March 18, 1921.

33 New York *Times,* March 22, 1921.

34 New York *Times,* March 24, 29, 1921.

35 New York *Times,* April 4, 1921. This farm tariff bill was passed May 8.

House passed the emergency tariff, thus hoping to "renew confidence and instill hope in the business world." This action, he said, would not hinder the House but help it.

It is interesting that the western tariff proponents prevailed in spite of the propaganda of "big business," the wealth of the East, the determination of such leaders as Mellon, and the general agreement of the need of tax revision among members of Congress in both houses and in both parties.[36] Not only did the West hold the balance of power, but on this occasion its representatives were supported by the southern Democrats.

PRESIDENT HARDING CALLS A SPECIAL SESSION OF THE NEW CONGRESS

President Harding summoned the new Congress to a special session April 11, 1921, for the consideration of tax changes, a budget law, an emergency tariff, and plans for economy in expenditure. The Republican party controlled both executive and legislative branches of the government but the legislative session promised to be a difficult, even if a peaceful one, because of the problems which pressed for solution. The depression among the farmers has been mentioned. Business and industry of all branches were also suffering and calling for help.

The House elected Gillett (Mass.) Speaker and the minority chose Kitchin as their leader but, because of his illness, Garrett (Tenn.) was the real "Democratic war horse." The House lacked leadership. It was said at the time that the Speaker was supposed to be a great power, but he wasn't. Fordney, Chairman of the Ways and Means Committee, had "the semblance of great power rather than its actual possession." He was a man of wealth and correspondingly conservative, uneducated but shrewd, especially along political lines. Green, the real leader of the Committee, was a student of tax matters and personally friendly with all the members of the Committee. This Committee was one of the most powerful at a time when the House was governed by committees that were independent of the floor leader, the President, or anyone in the Administration. The radical farm bloc was led by Frear (Wis.) and Keller (Minn.).

In the Senate, Lodge was the jealous leader of the Committee on Foreign Affairs; Penrose was just as jealous of his prerogatives as Chairman of the Committee on Finance and was one of the most influential men in the Administration. It was to Penrose that Mellon was accustomed to go for information as to what the Senate would do. Although not so vigorous as he had been, he conducted

[36] William Allen White later traced to this revolt of western leaders "the political Johnstown flood" that swept Franklin D. Roosevelt into office. (New York *Times*, Nov. 8, 1936.)

business before Congress opened as actively from his apartment "office" as he did from the Finance Committee rooms in the Capitol.[37] Smoot was a member of the Senate Finance Committee but disagreed with most of his colleagues because of his opposition to the income tax and his determination to pass a sales tax law.

La Follette represented the radical group on the Committee but, strange to say, he had become somewhat mellowed and during this session was not so vocal as some of the Senators from the Far West. Altogether, as one commentator prophesied, "it promises to be a happy Congress – Harding wants peace with Congress and the prospects are that he will get it." [38] Whether or not it would be an effective Congress also was another matter.

The House plunged immediately into the emergency tariff, the Senate into foreign affairs, but Smoot was set to start off the session with his sales tax bill which he introduced on the first day. It provided for a 1% tax on all sales, modeled after the much touted law in effect in the Philippine Islands. There was no debate on the proposal, not even a speech by Smoot. It was brought up for consideration many months later, but as a 3% manufacturers' sales tax.[39]

THE FINANCIAL SITUATION AND SECRETARY MELLON'S RECOMMENDATIONS

By the end of April the way seemed to be clearing in the House for a consideration of revenue matters, so Fordney requested the Secretary of the Treasury to send up-to-date information as to the fiscal needs of the government. The reply told a story of expenditures at a "shocking rate," not only because of large appropriations for the army, navy, railroads, and interest on the public debt, but also by means of a trick used by Congress to spend large sums, in fact running into millions, without appropriating them, by "reappropriations of unexpended balances, revolving-fund appropriations and appropriations of receipts, and other indefinite authorizations. . ." [40]

Estimates of tax receipts for 1922 were lower than those for 1921 by $850,000,000 because of the business depression. Expenditures for ordinary purposes during the first three quarters of the fiscal year were $3,780,000,000, of which $2,600,000,000 were spent by the army, navy, and railroads and for interest on the public debt. At a similar rate the "ordinary" expenditures for 1921 would be about

[37] At one time Penrose weighed almost as much as Taft but he had "wasted away until many of his friends scarcely knew him." (New York *Times*, April 10, 1921.) He died in December of that year.

[38] New York *Times*, April 10, 1921.

[39] *Cong. Rec.* 61: 151, 7231, 7504.

[40] *Report of the Secretary of the Treasury* 1921, p. 351.

$5,000,000,000. Estimates for 1922 were correspondingly large. The military and naval departments asked for $1,100,000,000; the Director General of Railroads, $545,000,000. If such requests were granted, there was little chance of having a surplus with which to pay off the floating debt and, consequently, less possibility of reducing the tax load. The Secretary asked, therefore, that Congress take effective steps towards cutting expenditures. The following five recommendations were made for revision of the taxes of which three apply to the subject at hand, namely:

(1) substitute for the excess-profits tax a modified tax on corporate profits or a flat additional income tax on corporations and repeal the $2000 corporation exemption;
(2) lower the income tax rates so that the maximum normal and surtax rates would be 40% for 1921 and 33% thereafter;
(3) retain the miscellaneous sales and excise taxes;
(4) impose new taxes "of wide application" such as stamp taxes or license taxes on automobiles;
(5) adopt administrative amendments to simplify the work of the Bureau, such as giving the Commissioner power to make final determination of tax cases and providing for carrying forward of net losses for one year.[41]

Congress could easily agree to all of these suggestions except those for the reduction of the surtax and the imposition of additional taxes. Anticipating that objection would be raised to the reduction of the surtax on the ground that such action would benefit the rich, the Secretary presented some economic and fiscal reasons. He explained that the higher surtax rates had "already passed the collection point," that the rates were so high they drove income out of productive use into tax-exempt securities, in many cases prevented the sale of securities and other property, and destroyed business initiative.

Some discussion of the Secretary's proposals took place in both the House and Senate but neither body showed any haste or interest in pushing the revenue bill to completion. The Senate Finance Committee conducted hearings from May 9 to 27 during which time the sales tax was the chief item of consideration. A few witnesses spoke of the excess-profits tax, but it was assumed that it would be repealed. Penrose bluntly said that much of the testimony was a waste of time on subjects about which the Committee already knew.

In June the bill to establish a federal budget bureau was passed, an important aid to the proper management of federal finances, but little else was done to promote economy. A second bill for a bonus to veterans of the World War was introduced into the House in July. Harding appealed to the Senate to defer action on this bill and to proceed with matters that "were essential to the very beginning

[41] *Report of the Secretary of the Treasury* 1921, pp. 353-354.

of the restored order of things" such as revision of taxation, refunding of war loans and adjustment of foreign loans. House leaders hoped that a tax bill could be rushed through because it would then consist chiefly of provisions carrying out the recommendations of the Secretary but the representatives of the farm bloc were not so easily satisfied. They were the sole supporters of the excess-profits tax and high surtax rates and were prepared to fight to the end for the lost cause.

THE COMMITTEE ON WAYS AND MEANS CONSIDERS REVENUE MEASURES

Late in July the Committee on Ways and Means[42] held public hearings which, like those of the Senate, were devoted chiefly to consideration of the sales tax as a substitute for the excess-profits tax. The former was urged by several individuals and organizations including representatives of the Chamber of Commerce of the United States, although this latter group soon shifted its position and opposed such a method of raising revenue. Ogden Mills appeared to urge a "spendings tax," a modified income tax.[43]

On the whole the Committee was fairly liberal, although it had been selected to give the conservatives control. Fortunately for the liberals the conservative chairman was not well enough versed in taxation to be very influential. Green, the real leader, was upheld by Longworth, who was affable, excellent at winning compromises, and had liberal leanings. Hawley was moderately conservative; Frear strongly radical. Young was elected as a progressive but he generally yielded to Mellon. The other members were conservative but often followed Green. On the Democratic side, Kitchin, the ranking member, was too ill to be very active. Garner was com-

42 The members of the Committee were:

Republicans	*Democrats*
Joseph W. Fordney (Mich.), Ch.	Claude Kitchin (N. C.)
William R. Green (Ia.)	John N. Garner (Tex.)
Nicholas Longworth (Ohio)	James W. Collier (Miss.)
Willis C. Hawley (Ore.)	William A. Oldfield (Ark.)
Allen T. Treadway (Mass.)	Charles R. Crisp (Ga.)
Ira C. Copley (Ill.)	John F. Carew (N. Y.)
Luther W. Mott (N. Y.)	Whitmell P. Martin (La.)
George W. Young (N. D.)	Peter F. Tague (Mass.)
James A. Frear (Wis.)	
John Q. Tilson (Conn.)	
Isaac Bacharach (N. J.)	
Lindley H. Hadley (Wash.)	
Charles B. Timberlake (Col.)	
George M. Bowers (W. Va.)	
Henry B. Watson (Pa.)	
Alanson B. Houghton (N. Y.)	
Thomas A. Chandler (Okla.)	

43 67th Congress, 1st Session, *Hearings before the Committee on Ways and Means on Revenue Revision 1921*. Mills had recently been elected to Congress from New York. He was later Secretary of the Treasury.

mencing to be prominent. None of the others was especially active in the work of this Committee but went along with the party.[44]

When Secretary Mellon appeared before the Committee on August 4 with requested data, he showed that the total ordinary expenditures of the government for the fiscal year 1922 were estimated at slightly over $4,000,000,000, that public debt expenditures required by law (retirement of war savings certificates and certificates issued under the silver coinage act) amounted to over $550,000,000. The Secretary expected about $350,000,000 from such sources as the salvage of war materials and $370,000,000 from customs, hence estimated that about $3,830,000,000 should be provided from internal revenue. He emphasized the fact that the Treasury did not control nor supervise expenditures and that, if appropriations were made larger than those estimated, more revenue must be found. This total of $3,830,000,000 required from taxes was about $260,000,000 more than it was estimated would be forthcoming for 1921 from the existing law (Act of 1918), and House leaders bluntly replied that the amount was staggering. Congress could not provide that much money in such a year, they announced, implying that it was not necessary to have it and predicting the ruin of the party if such a plan were carried out.

The House leaders, Fordney and Madden, went to the White House to tell the President that Mellon's estimates were entirely out of the range of possibility.[45] Harding, doubtless at Mellon's suggestion, proposed as a compromise: (1) that total government costs be held at slightly over $4,000,000,000, partly by making economies and partly by redeeming war savings securities from "other public debt receipts," (2) that the surtax maximum rate be made 32% as of January 1, 1921 and 25% as of January 1, 1922, and (3) that the corporation tax be put at 12½ or 15%.

Secretary Mellon therefore presented a third estimate of government income and outgo showing a further estimated reduction of $350,000,000 in appropriations, achieved mostly by cutting the funds for the Department of Agriculture, the army, and the navy. He eliminated $170,000,000 for retiring certificates of indebtedness and increased his estimates of the proceeds of the tariff, hence the tax bill would need to yield only $3,000,000,000. The Secretary asked for authorization to issue additional Treasury certificates. In other words, the Administration was willing to borrow if necessary, but the tax rates had to be lowered.[46]

To help allay the suspicion, deep-rooted in the minds of many in Congress as well as among the general public, that the program

44 Interview with Judge W. R. Green, Jan. 1, 1937.
45 New York *Times*, Aug. 9, 1921.
46 *Report of the Secretary of the Treasury* 1921, pp. 369-371.

to repeal the excess-profits tax and reduce the surtaxes would relieve the rich, the President issued a statement of the "social and economic bearings of the new proposals," in which he stressed the fact that there had been no effort to relieve the rich of their share of the burdens. The basis of the program was economy in expenditure. The proposed taxes upon the rich man, he said, would yield about $1,800,000,000, while the balance would be distributed over the entire community, rich and poor. Like Mellon, he argued that the lower surtax rates were expected to produce more than higher ones, because the latter had prevented the transaction of business, had driven funds into tax-exempt securities, and led to fraud and evasion.[47]

The strategy of the Committee on Ways and Means was to find some concession to offer to the farm bloc members so as to win their support for the repeal of the excess-profits tax. Bacharach proposed that the income tax exemptions be raised from $1000 and $2000 to $1500 and $2500, and the allowance for dependents increased from $200 to $400. The Committee members were somewhat hesitant about raising the personal exemptions until it seemed advisable for tactical reasons.[48] Longworth eventually made a motion to make this change, saying that Treasury experts computed that by such a move the Treasury would lose only $50,000,000. The proposition seemed fair in view of the reduction allowed to those with large incomes. Since these concessions somewhat mollified the radical objectors on the Committee, the bill was drawn up much as sketched above, except that the corporation tax was placed at 12½%, the $2000 exemption for corporations was retained, and the maximum surtax rate was made 32%. Estimated receipts for 1922 were $3,570,000,000.

When the bill came before the party caucus it again met opposition at the hands of the farm bloc members who succeeded, with the aid of Mann (Ill.), and Fess (Ohio), in changing the effective date of the repeal of the excess-profits tax from January 1921 to January 1922. Forceful speakers, especially Mann, emphasized the point that manufacturers would make most of the profits for 1921, and pass the taxes on to the people before the pending bill would become effective. Fess succeeded in getting a separate vote on the extension

[47] *Report of the Secretary of the Treasury* 1921, p. 372.

[48] Judge Green stated to the authors (Jan. 1, 1937) that the exemptions were changed because it was the fair thing to do. The fact remains, however, that the changes were not made until some time after the Committee began to draw up the bill.

"Green conceded the necessity of the excess-profits tax in time of war but argued and showed by examples that it did not work out fairly between taxpayers and could not be made to do so. He stated it had been repealed by Great Britain and advocated its repeal by the bill and an increase in the tax on the net income of corporations to make up for the loss of revenue." (Statement of Green to the authors, Sept. 26, 1939.)

of time. With little other change the measure was introduced into the House on August 17.

MAJORITY AND MINORITY REPORTS

The first part of the Committee's report summarized its efforts towards reducing rather than shifting the tax burden as an essential basis for business recovery and explained the reasons for the abolition of the excess-profits tax, the reduction of the surtax, and other new features.[49]

One of the most radical changes recommended was a special tax of 15% in lieu of the regular income tax on profits from sale of property held over a period of years. Heretofore such gains were included with income from all other sources. The Committee was convinced that the high rates of war taxes imposed on such income had acted as a deterrent to the sale of farms, mines, and other properties; therefore, the special low rate would stimulate such transactions.[50]

Among other relief provisions were those for the carrying forward of net losses for two years, increasing the allowances for traveling expenses, exempting from the normal tax all dividends from all corporations, not only from those that were taxable, increasing the personal exemption by $500 for the head of a family and $200 for each dependent, and extending the list of deductible contributions.

New rules were made for the determination of gain or loss when property was exchanged for other property. The filing of consolidated returns was made optional; some corporations had found them very complicated to make out. Several administrative changes were made at the recommendation of the Treasury Department.

Frear set forth some "Additional Views," on the subject of the "well-organized nonpolitical effort . . . to stampede the American Congress into repealing the excess-profits tax, reducing high personal surtaxes, and imposing a turnover sales tax to relieve large business and financial interests from tax laws imposed during the war." He opposed the repeal of the excess-profits tax because, in his estimation, it was a tax based on ability to pay after allowing profits of 8% and other exemptions and, if the tax had been passed on to the consumer as often claimed, its repeal as of January 1, 1921 would be an "enormous gift to the corporations." Similarly he objected to the great reduction in the surtax rates and to the ignoring by the Com-

49 67th Congress, 1st Session, *House Report* 350.

50 The Committee later reduced the rate to 12½% to correspond with the tax on corporation income (*Cong. Rec.* 61: 5289).

mittee of Secretary Houston's proposal for a tax on undistributed corporate income.

In 1921 the Republicans returned to the prewar practice of not admitting minority members to the meetings of the Committee on Ways and Means while the revenue bill was being written. Kitchin dubbed these practices "the barred door, dark lantern methods." Nevertheless, the Democrats knew what was being proposed and had plenty of press space to report their opposition.[51]

The minority report, written by Kitchin from his sickbed, was devoted, in the main, to the issue of the repeal of the excess-profits tax and the reduction of the surtax.[52] He quoted data of the Commissioner of Internal Revenue for 1917 and 1918, from which he concluded that the repeal of the tax would not only be a gift to "the big profiteering corporations" but that it would involve an increased tax of 50% on the smaller corporations. He asked:

> Why in the name of right and justice should these big profiteering corporations and the millionaires and multimillionaires who filled their rapacious maw with these fabulous billions of blood money be relieved of taxation while we not only keep but actually increase the war taxes on hundreds of thousands of small and weak corporations and keep the war income taxes on millions of our fellow citizens who and whose sons went to the trenches in defense and protection not only of their country but of the profits and wealth of these same corporations and millionaires and multimillionaires. Not one of them made a sacrifice, braved a danger, endured a hardship financially or otherwise for their country during the war but was millions richer after the war than before, without a scar or scratch.[53]

Similar logic was used to defend the Democratic opposition to the surtax reduction. The argument used by the Secretary that the large incomes were driven into tax-exempt bonds was brushed aside as untrue. Even if it were so, he continued, were not funds secured by states, municipalities, and other local units from bonds used for the public good, such as for schools and eleemosynary institutions, "which benefit the people directly more than in spending the money from Federal taxes for large standing armies and big navies?"[54]

[51] See the New York *World's* daily Washington column, Aug. 1, 1921, and several days following.

[52] Kitchin's telegram to C. H. Englund of Aug. 14, 1921, read: "Wife just got your telegram. I am a little tired; just have finished my minority report. Have never felt better in my life and am now ready to take a good rest. I wrote on statistics too hard. . . Tell those who read the report of my relapse to read my report on the revenue bill and see if it sounds like that of a relapsed invalid. . ." (*Cong. Rec.* 61: 5237.) Kitchin's point of view was probably biased because he viewed the situation as it had been in the past; because the Democrats had introduced the excess-profits tax he felt bound to uphold it.

[53] 67th Congress, 1st Session, *House Report* 350, Part 2.

[54] 67th Congress, 1st Session, *House Report* 350, Part 2, p. 11.

THE BILL IN THE HOUSE OF REPRESENTATIVES

The Committee measure was introduced into the House of Representatives and was taken up for consideration on August 17. Any expectation the minority may have had of amending it was frustrated at the start by parliamentary procedure. The bill was considered under a special order and rushed through in four days.

Fordney presented the Committee report, which he probably did not fully understand, with a typical political harangue on the extravagances of the previous administration and a recital of the many attempts to repeal the excess-profits tax.[55] Garner replied for the minority on the same level.[56] Debate in the House was chiefly on the surtax and the excess-profits tax.

The Republican position was defended by Green. Bacharach also supported the bill and in addition expressed his approval of a tax on expenditures or sales which he predicted would be adopted within a few years.[57]

Frear gave a long explanation of his opposition to the bill, which is of interest because it represented the views of the powerful farmer-labor bloc. He first answered the charge that in postponing the repeal of the excess-profits tax until 1922 the Republicans were not keeping promises made in the campaign. Such promises, he said, had never been made. Then he pointed out the unfairness of the tax cuts. To lower the surtax would help some 4499 people, of whom 627 had incomes of $300,000 or over and 67 had incomes of $1,000,000 or over. Similarly, to repeal the excess-profits tax would relieve chiefly 1026 corporations, the number which in 1918 paid 55% of the total excess-profits tax. On the other hand, there were 10,000,000 farmers whose organized appeal to retain the tax was not a call to be disregarded; there were 1,000,000 miners, 4,000,000 domestics, and 4,000,000 laborers not on any classified list. Should Congress keep the faith with them or with the 4499 who paid heavy surtaxes? Farmers, to be sure, were not called on to pay large income taxes, but they were forced to pay "a tax on every bushel of grain and every pound of meat they get to market, taxes on what they eat and wear, taxes for schools for the county and state." But farmers were without a powerful press to insist on the repeal of their taxes.

He argued that from the point of view of revenue also the repeal of the tax appeared unwise. The excess-profits tax would bring in $450,000,000 for the year 1921 while the proposed substitute, an increase of 2½% in the flat tax on corporations, would probably bring

55 *Cong. Rec.* 61: 5125-5130.
56 *Cong. Rec.* 61: 5130-5134.
57 *Cong. Rec.* 61: 5136.

in less than one-fourth of that amount and, furthermore, it was inequitable. Smaller corporations would have to pay more tax than before while corporations with $500,000 capital or over making more than 10% would pay less. In reply to a question from a member as to the effect of the excess-profits tax on business, the speaker said that economic distress was a worldwide condition, it was not limited to the United States. War costs had not been paid off and taxes must be raised to meet them. Despite his objections to the bill, however, Frear said he would vote for it, since it seemed to be the best that could be drawn up under the circumstances.[58]

Hawley brought to the attention of the House a group of amendments to improve the administration of the tax, incorporating the chief features of the Treasury bills for settlement of tax cases which had failed at the last session, as well as several new proposals.[59] One of the most important was the provision for a committee to study means of simplifying the law and administrative procedure.[60]

The course of the bill through the House was rapid and smooth. The majority held such control that few non-committee amendments were proposed and none adopted.[61] Garner made a half-hearted attempt to recommit the bill in order to eliminate the surtax cuts. When asked why he did not include the excess-profits tax also, he said that he did not want members from Iowa, Nebraska, Missouri, and other farm districts to be able to sidestep questions from their constituents by saying that they voted against the motion because something else was in the bill. His motion was defeated by 230 to 169; 50 Republicans voted for it and 1 Democrat against it.[62] The only Committee amendment that was not adopted was one to appoint a committee for the study of tax-exempt securities.[63] It was estimated that the bill would yield $3,240,000,000.

In the final vote, August 20, three Democrats joined 271 Republicans for the measure and 9 Republicans voted with the Democrats against it.[64]

[58] *Cong. Rec.* 61: 5139-5145.
[59] *Cong. Rec.* 61: 5201-5203.
[60] See below, Chap. XXIII.
[61] The leaders and their party reaped a harvest of ill will by these domineering methods. Before the next revenue bill was introduced (1924) the radicals succeeded in bringing about a drastic change in the House rules. See below, Chap. IX, p. 225.
[62] *Cong. Rec.* 61: 5358.
[63] *Cong. Rec.* 61: 5354.
[64] *Cong. Rec.* 61: 5359. The three Democrats were Campbell (Pa.), Dupre and Lazaro (La.). The nine Republicans were Beck, Nelson, Voight and Lampert (Wis.), Clague and Keller (Minn.), Michaelson (Ill.), Sinclair (N. D.) and Woodruff (Mich.). It is interesting to note the geographical concentration.

REVISIONS BY THE SENATE FINANCE COMMITTEE

Soon after the House passed the revenue measure Congress recessed, while the Senate Finance Committee [65] worked on its revision under an agreement to have the bill ready on the first day the Senate met.

Chairman Penrose's ambition was to rewrite the bill so that it would be understood by every taxpayer; in other words, so that it would be unnecessary "to hire a lawyer to find out what it means." He also wanted to carry out Harding's request to repeal the excess-profits tax as of January 1, 1921.[66] The Committee support for such a move was very uncertain, however, because government expenditures showed little sign of decreasing; in fact, there seemed to be some evidence that they would amount to $5,000,000,000 for the fiscal year.[67] Smoot and other sales tax advocates took advantage of this situation to urge such a tax for at least two years, and this idea received some favorable comment.

Secretary Mellon made six recommendations to the Senate Committee: (1) repeal the excess-profits tax and the capital stock tax as of January 1, 1921, the most important step the government could take to revive industry; (2) reduce the maximum surtax rates to 25% on January 1, 1922; (3) raise the corporation tax to 15%; (4) reduce the transportation tax by 50% for 1922 and repeal it for 1923; (5) retain the personal exemptions adopted by the House; and (6) repeal the tax on proprietary medicines as of January 1, 1922. The only change from the recommendations made to the House was that he favored retaining the high surtax rates for 1921 and cutting them to a maximum of 25% for 1922. If these suggestions were followed it was estimated that the bill would raise $3,200,000,000.

The older Senators, chiefly Penrose and Watson, favored accepting these suggestions, but they were opposed by the tremendous pressure of the farm-labor group to such an extent that the main objective of the Committee became the writing of a bill that would be quickly accepted even by these members.

65 The members of the Committee were:

Republicans	*Democrats*
Boies Penrose (Pa.), Ch.	Furnifold M. Simmons (N. C.)
Reed Smoot (Utah)	John Sharp Williams (Miss.)
Robert M. La Follette (Wis.)	Andrieus A. Jones (N. M.)
William P. Dillingham (Vt.)	Peter G. Gerry (R. I.)
George P. McLean (Conn.)	James A. Reed (Mo.)
Charles Curtis (Kan.)	David I. Walsh (Mass.)
James E. Watson (Ind.)	
William M. Calder (N. Y.)	
Howard Sutherland (W. Va.)	

66 Harding is said to have informed the Committee that it would be a political mistake and an economic blunder to raise the amount levied in the House bill. (New York *Times*, Sept. 7, 1921.)

67 New York *Times*, Sept. 3, 1921.

The administrative sections were considered first because they were the least controversial. Although most of the House provisions were adopted, the Committee objected to the sections to exempt from the income tax the compensation of the President of the United States and the federal judges, to exempt dividends of the first $500 invested in building and loan associations, to permit more liberality in allowances to traveling men, and to permit corporations to deduct contributions to charities. A change was made also in the method of handling gains and losses from sale of capital assets. The House bill levied a special flat rate of 12½% on such income [68] but the Senate Finance Committee proposed a different method, namely, that only 40% of such gains be considered for income tax purposes. A new provision was inserted which required the filing of a return by an individual whose gross income was $5000, even if the net income was less than the personal exemption.

It was more difficult to secure agreement on the amount of levies. All the Republicans except La Follette agreed to the repeal of the excess-profits tax as of January 1, 1922. The Democrats did not vote on this question. The corporation tax was made 15%, the capital stock tax was repealed as of July 1, 1921, and, to make up for the loss in revenue, some of the transportation taxes were retained in spite of the opposition of the farm bloc. The surtax rates on individual income were reduced by 1% on those between $20,000 and $30,000, but for income over those amounts the House rates were retained, that is, the maximum was 32%. Depletion allowances for mines were restricted so that the deduction based on value at time of discovery could not exceed net income.

At the suggestion of the chairman, a new section was adopted which required the government to pay interest of ½% a month on refunds to taxpayers. This radically new idea was promulgated in the hope that it would give some incentive to the Treasury to settle refund claims more promptly. The Committee took no action on the sales tax proposals, preferring to let that matter be thrashed out on the floor of the Senate. It was estimated that the bill as reported to the Senate would raise $3,326,000,000 for 1922, about $14,000,000 less than the House bill.

Over one-half of the minority report was devoted to protesting that the bill did not give to the taxpayer the reform and fiscal relief that had been promised by the majority party. Even though some

[68] *Cong. Rec.* 61: 5289.
Green said: "When the bill was originally prepared the Committee fixed the maximum amount which ought to be allowed for either capital gain or capital loss at 15%. Subsequently in order that an individual or a copartnership might not be compelled to pay more than a corporation which under the change in the corporation rate was made 12½%, we changed the maximum of gain or loss as provided in the next paragraph from 15% to 12½%."

tax reductions were made, they were possible only because of the fact that the Treasury would borrow, rather than because of economy in expenditure. The Democrats objected especially to the repeal of the $2000 exemption for corporations, the lowering of the surtax to 32%, the repeal of the capital stock tax, and the failure to remove taxes on transportation.[69]

THE BILL IN THE SENATE

When Congress re-assembled on September 21, Chairman Penrose presented the report of the Finance Committee without the customary speech of explanation. Reed (Dem., Mo.) said that its sponsors dropped it like an illegitimate baby on the public doorstep and ran! In order to expedite matters, Penrose requested that consideration be given first to the uncontested amendments such as those of a technical nature and those relating to administration which were drawn up mostly by Treasury experts rather than by the Committee. He also asked that Senators refrain from making speeches of "an academic nature." [70]

Almost immediately Gerry (R. I.) and Walsh (Mass.), both Democrats, introduced two amendments, one of which would reduce the normal taxes on individual income to 2%, 4% and 6%; the other would substitute for the excess-profits tax a graduated tax of 10%, 15% and 20% [71] on corporate net income. They were rejected. Within a week, Smoot presented his sales tax substitute which he had introduced on the first day of the session.[72]

The Democratic point of view was presented by Simmons,[73] who reviewed the changes made just after the close of the war by which the war-profits tax was repealed and the excess-profits tax rates were reduced. Most of the reduction then as in 1921 was in favor of corporations. The Act of 1918 did not change the so-called "nuisance taxes" except the stamp taxes. The 1921 bill under consideration was also one-sided, since it gave almost no relief to the great body of consumers.

Simmons admitted that he disliked the excess-profits tax in times of peace but he did not favor its repeal until some fair substitute was found. The proposed bill would relieve corporations of excess-profits taxes to the amount of $600,000,000, and of capital stock

[69] 67th Congress, 1st Session, *Senate Report* 275.

[70] *Cong. Rec.* 61: 5711, 5807, 6918-6920.

[71] *Cong. Rec.* 61: 5731-5732, 6868.

[72] His program was: (1) repeal the taxes on excess-profits, transportation, insurance, beverages, admissions, and dues; (2) levy a 3% tax on sales of commodities by manufacturers and producers. *Cong Rec.* 61: 5891, 6212-6220.

[73] *Cong. Rec.* 61: 5892-5900.

taxes of $81,000,000. For this there was substituted only a 15% tax, which it was estimated would yield $260,000,000. Furthermore, Treasury statisticians reported that at least half of the $90,000,000 reduction in tax on individuals with income over $66,000 (the bracket on which the surtax became the maximum, 32%) would be realized by recipients of corporate dividends. So Simmons added another $45,000,000 benefit to corporations, and noted also that by these tax reductions corporations would be permitted to pay out more dividends than in previous years.

He objected also to the surtax reductions because they relieved chiefly those with large incomes; for example, a taxpayer with income of $1,000,000 paid $583,000 under the 1918 law, but would pay only $308,780 under the proposed bill; whereas one with income between $5000 and $6000, or one with income between $32,000 and $68,000 would be helped only to the extent of $10. A taxpayer with income of $72,000 would get a reduction of $70 and one with income of $90,000, a reduction of $1330. Furthermore there were many more taxpayers with incomes of less than $66,000 than with larger incomes. In 1919 there were 578,731 taxpayers below the $66,000 level and 11,077 above it. Thus the proposed law would reduce taxes for 11,077 people by $90,000,000, and for 578,731 people by $18,000,000.

Simmons emphasized also the disparities in the treatment of corporations, individuals, and partnerships which the 1917 law tried to correct by levying the excess-profits tax on them all. He feared that if the excess-profits tax were repealed, and no additional tax were placed on corporations, the burden on individuals would again be disproportionately heavy. He scored the so-called economies of the Administration which apparently would result in necessitating loans for current expenditures.[74]

Reed (Mo.) then continued the attack on the measure in his inimitable sarcastic vein. He was followed by others, notably by Robinson, McKellar, Underwood, and Harrison on the Democratic side, and by Lenroot for the radicals.[75]

These expected critical speeches of the minority were, however, accepted as a matter of course. Real worry was caused by the concealed opposition to the bill that was crystallizing among members of the majority party. There were two powerful groups; one led by Smoot was for the sales tax; the other was the farm bloc whose

[74] He said: "There is no difficulty in the administration exercising its discretion, and in this way eliminate as much from the estimates as they may see fit, in order to accomplish a political purpose or make a showing of extraordinary economy and retrenchment in expenditure of the people's money." (*Cong. Rec.* 61: 5894.)

[75] *Cong. Rec.* 61: 5902, 5959, 5973, 6066, 6076, 6229.

members were as much opposed to the Smoot plan as to the Committee bill.

The farm bloc had long been opposed to the repeal of the excess-profits tax and to the great cut in the surtax maxima but, inasmuch as the bill had passed the House safely, the "Old Guard" Republicans erroneously assumed that it would pass the Senate also. The agricultural group, however, conscious of the lack of harmony in the party, became encouraged to try to repeal the transportation taxes at least, then perhaps to prevent the passage of the bill. They flirted with the idea of accepting the Democratic invitation to join them in rewriting the bill. It was even suggested as a first step that Smoot's sales tax proposal be passed as a substitute for the Committee bill, then count on Republican support to defeat it on the final vote. The feasibility of the plan was the subject of a meeting called by McNary for the night of October 5. During the day, Republican leaders conferred with the President; as a result the conservative Lodge, oddly enough, was sent to carry a message of conciliation to the meeting of the western Republicans held at the home of Capper. Fearful of a split which was all too reminiscent of 1912, even the conservatives conceded that the tax bill would have to be amended.[76]

Penrose, ill and irritable, gave out a surprising statement that the bill was only a temporary measure. Simmons replied that this idea was contradictory to the understanding of all during the framing of the measure and called attention to the fact that the remark was not made until the bill was shot to pieces.[77]

Some suggestion of the latent power of the farm bloc had been shown earlier in the session in the insistence for an agricultural tariff.[78] In the Senate one of the important considerations was the fact that of the sixty Republican members, thirty-three came from states bordering on or lying west of the Mississippi; five came from Ohio, Indiana, and Michigan; twenty-two from New England and West Virginia. Most of the western members had come from states that were Democratic under the Wilson Administration; in other words, it was the West that gave the Republican party the control of the Senate. The "Old Guard" was shrewd enough to see that

[76] Washington *Post,* Oct. 4-9, 1921.

[77] *Cong. Rec.* 61: 6074.

[78] "Penrose and his all prevailing finance committee have been compelled to bend the knee to the so-called agricultural bloc. Time was when Penrose at the crack of the whip could have formed all Republican senators into line and trained them in a chorus of 'ayes' which would have put through any form of tax or tariff legislation he desired. But that time is no more. The West has risen. The West is feeling its strength. The West has plainly told the East that it was the West which gave the Republican party control of the Senate, that it was the West which produced nearly all new Republican senators for this session." (Washington *Post,* Oct. 7, 1921.)

party harmony was more important than tax details. As one editor wrote, it was like General Forrest's philosophy, "If you can't lick 'em, jine 'em." [79]

These western members wanted to increase surtaxes to 50%, to restore the capital stock tax, to increase tax rates on estates over $10,000,000, and to repeal the transportation taxes.[80] The Finance Committee thereupon prepared several amendments to carry out these demands. But not all the Senators bowed so meekly as did Lodge to the demands of the Westerners. Moses (Rep., N. H.) was utterly scornful of "that division of the invisible empire which seems now to be ruling us and which may be styled . . . the Ken-Cap [Kenyon-Capper] Klan." [81]

When McCumber presented the revised amendments for a surtax maximum of 50% on income in excess of $200,000 instead of 32% on income in excess of $66,000, Simmons agreed to this rate although he had stated that he stood for a surtax maximum of 52%. The changes made in the lower brackets (income under $66,000) made that part of the bill acceptable to him.[82] Hitchcock made an effort to re-instate the 65% maximum of the 1918 law but failed.[83] The 50% maximum was adopted.

When the Senate reached the section on corporations, Reed (Mo.) moved to retain the excess-profits tax, but his amendment was defeated. He then introduced a proposal to make the rates about half those of the 1918 law, explaining that he did not offer the amendment "out of a mere desire to make a record," but because Congress was following exactly the wrong policy : it was cutting down on the revenue, whereas it should be increasing it. His proposed tax would bring in $200,000,000, which would do a lot of things; for example, it would pay the soldiers' bonus.[84] He chose an opportune time to make this reference to a bonus because the American Legion was then meeting in Kansas City, his home town.

Watson (Rep., Ind.) replied that the Republican party had already given the answer, that even the appeal for a soldiers' bonus would not fool the public. The excess-profits tax, he argued, was passed on to the consumer. Caraway (Dem., Ark.) and a few others came to the defense of Reed but his amendment was defeated,

[79] The Wall Street *Journal*, October 10, 1921, called it a "holdup," a "pusillanimous surrender," "a cowardly retreat before a gang of demagogues, euphemistically called an agricultural bloc."

[80] Washington *Post*, Oct. 6, 1921.

[81] *Cong. Rec.* 61: 6471.

[82] *Cong. Rec.* 61: 6585-6587.

[83] *Cong. Rec.* 61: 6646.

[84] *Cong. Rec.* 61: 6736-6744.

as was another he introduced immediately to tax corporations at the rate of 20% of net income in excess of 50% of the invested capital.[85]

After the Committee amendments for the repeal of the excess-profits tax had been adopted, Jones (Dem., N. M.) presented to the Senate his proposal for the encouragement of the distribution of corporate surpluses by a tax on the amount undistributed. This idea, his "hobby," he had tried to impress upon the Senate in two previous sessions. Smoot replied that when the excess-profits tax applied to individuals and partnerships as well as to corporations there was some justification for the Senator's complaint that there was discrimination against individuals. But Smoot thought the answer of the Senate to Jones in 1918 was conclusive — that answer was to relieve individuals from paying the excess-profits tax.

Simmons supported Jones to some extent by showing that with the repeal of the excess-profits tax there was discrimination in favor of corporations, but he would not go so far as his colleague in removing all the normal tax from corporations, even if all earnings were distributed.[86]

Upon the defeat of this motion McKellar proposed a revised version of an amendment he had introduced earlier for the Secretary of the Treasury to secure from foreign governments the amounts due to the United States, but Penrose objected to complicating and delaying the revenue bill by the problem of foreign debts.[87]

The controversial subject of the sales tax was injected into the debate November 3 when Smoot brought up his amendment for consideration.[88] He added fat to the fire by suggesting that such a tax might be used to provide funds for a soldiers' bonus. The opponents of the sales tax were the agricultural bloc plus the "Old Guard," so there was little chance of its passage. Smoot was not to be downed by one vote, however. He presented another amendment, which was also defeated, but he came within five votes of a majority.

La Follette did not have so much to say as in previous sessions, although he introduced a few amendments. One was to make returns open to public inspection. Another was to levy an additional estate tax upon securities that had not been subject to income

85 *Cong. Rec.* 61: 6745, 6786-6787, 6790-6800. Later he again made a futile effort to push through his amendment (*Cong. Rec.* 61: 7301, 7421.)

86 *Cong. Rec.* 61: 6833-6865.

87 *Cong. Rec.* 61: 6865.

88 *Cong. Rec.* 61: 7231. He had reduced the rate from 3% to 1% to overcome some of the objections of the farm bloc, and had changed his earlier general sales tax proposal to one for a tax on manufacturers' sales.

tax during the life of the owner.[89] Neither was adopted. The Senate did, however, double the maximum estate tax rate.

In the long final night session of November 7, Walsh, supported by La Follette and Jones, brought up unexpectedly an amendment to tax gifts in order to prevent evasion of income and inheritance taxes.[90] Thirteen radical Republicans again broke away from party lines to insure its passage. The soldiers' bonus was brought up twice, only to be rejected each time. At 1:35 A.M. the Senate passed the bill by a vote of 38 to 23 with 35 members not voting.[91] After the passage of the tax bill, Pomerene introduced his bill to create a Federal Court of Internal Revenue Appeals which was referred to the Committee on the Judiciary.[92]

Although there were more than 800 amendments to consider, the Conferees completed their work in about ten days. On the most controversial point, the surtax rates, the House managers receded, but not until there had been some stirring debate on the floor of the House. For some reason Fordney neglected to include a provision to instruct the House conferees when they were appointed, hence the minority leader offered a resolution on November 17 that the House accept Senate amendment 122. By this means the minority and the radicals forced the House acceptance of the Senate higher surtax rates despite the opposition of the majority leaders and a letter from the President.[93] The Senate managers accepted the House method for taxing capital gains, but omitted any reference to capital losses and made the provision applicable to corporations as well as to individuals. The House conferees then revised the section to state that the total tax for individuals on this special income plus other income should not be less than 12½% of the total net income. The Senate managers introduced the two-year limitation in the definition of capital asset. Neither the House nor the Senate debate on the Conferees' report was important. The President signed the measure on November 23.

SUMMARY OF THE LAW [94]

Former Commissioner of Internal Revenue, Daniel C. Roper (Dem., S. C.) wrote in the spring of 1922:

> The new Federal income tax is disappointing to most people who have looked forward to a thorough revision of the 1918 Act. It was hoped that a comprehensive measure, complete in itself, would be the result of the

[89] *Cong. Rec.* 61: 7491.
[90] *Cong. Rec.* 61: 7485. This amendment was thrown out by the Conference Committee.
[91] *Cong. Rec.* 61: 7524.
[92] *Cong. Rec.* 61: 7526. This was the origin of the Board of Tax Appeals.
[93] *Cong. Rec.* 61: 7860-7889.
[94] 42 *Statutes at Large* 227.

work of Congress. After the debate proceeded, however, it became clearer that Congress could not be brought to any such fundamental accomplishment. The new law is merely a collection of patches on the old act and both must be read and interpreted together to arrive at the existing situation.[95]

The disappointment over the new law was almost universal; it seemed to please no one. Business was annoyed because the excess-profits tax was not repealed as of January 1921. Not only men of wealth but others thought it a mistake to maintain such a high schedule of surtaxes. Most of all there was irritation that the law was not simplified. There was cause for both relief and annoyance that the Act was admittedly only a temporary measure so that the government as well as business would probably soon be distracted again by making adjustments to a new tax.

As Mr. Roper said:

> What we need is a simplified structure which will stand the test of a decade, permitting the lowering or raising of rates in accordance with the fiscal demands of the government without requiring changes in fundamental principles.

Hull said:

> It was most unfortunate that the attempted revision legislation of 1921 degenerated measurably into a wrangle between champions of large income taxpayers and those of the smaller taxpayers, each striving to see which could unload the largest amount of taxes first. The legislative situation thus became so confused and demoralized that but scant opportunity for the consideration of comprehensive, scientific tax revision was afforded. . . The tax reductions under the act of 1921 amounted to $800,000,000. It is interesting to look back at the different tactics resorted to by the larger taxpayers whose deliberate purpose was as speedily as possible and step by step, if necessary, to wipe out all graduated income taxation, and it may be noted that this has since been and still is the objective of a majority of these persons.[96]

What did the new law accomplish? Briefly, it eased the tax burden by reducing the rates of the surtax, eliminating the excess-profits tax after 1921, permitting a carry-over of net losses for two years, granting an option to file consolidated returns and by other similar liberal provisions. The new treatment of capital gains and losses was an important innovation, the principle of which was followed until 1932. Congress made a gesture toward the solution of administrative problems by providing for a committee to survey the Bureau of Internal Revenue, the Tax Simplification Board.

The technical sections, such as those involving exchanges, re-

[95] Roper, Daniel C., "Administrative Problems in United States Internal Taxation," *South Atlantic Quarterly* XXI: 97-108 (April 1922).

[96] *Cong. Rec.* 67: 563-564.

organizations, etc., were put in much better form than in previous laws. The income tax had become such a complicated law from the point of view of Congress as well as from the point of view of the Bureau of Internal Revenue and of the taxpayer that it was necessary to have expert advice at every step of the legislative path.

There were thirteen titles of which Title II — Income Tax Rates, Title III — War-profits and Excess-profits, and Title XIII — General Administrative Provisions are of particular importance in this study.[97]

No change was made in the rates of the normal income tax which were 4% on net income of $4000 or less and 8% on income in excess of that amount. The personal exemptions for those with income of $5000 or less were increased from $2000 to $2500 for a head of a family and for a married couple, but remained at $1000 for a single person. The exemption for dependents under eighteen years of age was increased from $200 to $400. For 1922 and thereafter, the maximum surtax rate was reduced from 65% on income in excess of $1,000,000 to 50% on that in excess of $200,000. For 1921, the Act of 1918 rates were retained; in this law the rate on income in excess of $200,000 was 60%.

In order to make the law conform to the decision of the Supreme Court in the case of *Eisner* v. *Macomber* (252 U. S. 189, 1920), it was specifically stated that a stock dividend was not subject to tax. A general rule was established as to distributions in liquidation and all other distributions otherwise than out of earnings accumulated since February 28, 1913. This rule was that such distributions were to be treated as a partial or full return of cost of stock or shares to the distributor; and, if the stockholder received more than the cost of his stock, he was taxable upon the excess in the same manner as though the stock had been sold. Gains that accrued before March 1, 1913 were not taxable.

In order to prevent evasion of tax by gift of property that had appreciated in value, a new rule was established, namely, that the basis for determining gain and loss in case of property acquired by gift after December 31, 1920 was to be the same as if the last preceding owner had sold it.

An important new section made special provision for the taxation of capital gains. Profits from sale of assets held over two years could be separated from other income and taxed at 12½%

[97] The other titles were: IV — Estate Tax; V — Tax on Telegraph and Telephone Messages; VI — Tax on Beverages; VII — Tax on Cigars, Tobacco, etc.; VIII — Tax on Admissions and Dues; IX — Excise Taxes; X — Special Taxes on Miscellaneous Occupations; XI — Stamp Taxes; and XII — Tax on Employment of Child Labor. They are discussed by Blakey, Roy G., "The Revenue Act of 1921," *American Economic Review,* XII: 75-108 (March 1922).

instead of at the regular tax rates if the taxpayer so wished, provided that the taxpayer did not pay less than 12½% upon his entire net income. This limitation restricted the benefit of the option to those with net incomes of at least $29,000. No provision was made for limitation of the amount of capital loss that could be deducted. Inasmuch as the excess-profits tax was repealed as of the date when this new capital gains tax went into effect and the tax on corporations was 12½%, there was no object in applying the special rate of 12½% on capital gains of corporations, so it was expressly stated to be inapplicable to them.

This compromise treatment of capital gains did not prove to be satisfactory to the government. In his report for 1922 the Secretary of the Treasury wrote:

> capital losses may entirely cancel real income, while capital gains will not be realized at all, or, if realized, are taxable at only 12½ per cent. Under the present system the Government is being whipsawed, and the Treasury therefore strongly urges that the existing provision as to capital gains be made to apply conversely to capital losses and that the amount by which the tax may be reduced on account of losses from the sale of capital assets should not exceed 12½ per cent of the amount of the loss. . . . The alternative is to refuse to recognize either capital gains or capital losses for income tax purposes, and if the present situation were allowed to continue there is no doubt that it would save revenue to adopt this course. . .[98]

Another provision, meant to prevent hardship, injustice, and administrative difficulties, but later used for the evasion or avoidance of taxes, was the very complicated section which permitted the transfer of property from one corporation to another or to a new corporation upon reorganization without tax liability under certain conditions, to wit: (1) if it could be shown that the property did not have a "readily realized market value;" (2) even if it had such value, if it was held for productive use, not for sale, and was exchanged for property of a like kind or use; (3) when stock or securities in the re-organized corporation were exchanged for securities already owned; or (4) when other property was transferred for property or stock of substantially the same value. Congress did not intend to exempt from tax securities acquired in reorganizations, but merely to postpone the reckoning until a sale or other definite transaction took place.[99]

The 1921 law contained also a new provision for the calculation of depreciation which specifically stated that the basis should be cost or, in the case of property acquired before March 1, 1913, fair

[98] *Report of the Secretary of the Treasury* 1922, p. 14.

[99] 68th Congress, 1st Session, *Statement of Changes Made in the Revenue Act of* 1921 *. . . and the Reasons Thereof* (Gregg Report).

market value of the property on that date. This was to clarify the situation rendered somewhat doubtful by two court decisions which seemed to indicate that depreciation should be based on cost even in the case of property acquired before March 1, 1913.[100] In cases of mines, oil and gas wells, and other natural resources, depletion allowance based on discovery value was limited to the amount of the net income. This section was productive of much administrative difficulty.[101]

More generous provisions were made also in the allowance of deductions. Net losses could be carried forward to the following two years, but this benefit was permitted only with respect to losses resulting from the operation of the taxpayer's regular trade or business. Traveling men were permitted to deduct the entire amount expended for meals and lodging while away from home. Previously the rulings of the Commissioner permitted only a fraction of such expenditures to be deducted.

The law attempted to remedy the discrimination in favor of building and loan associations which were doing more or less of a general banking business, a situation of which banks had complained for some time. The exemption permitted to building and loan associations was limited to those whose business was confined to making loans to members.

The corporation tax was raised from 10% to 12½% partially to compensate for the loss of revenue resulting from the repeal of the excess-profits tax, effective January 1, 1922. A flat exemption of $2000 was allowed to corporations with net income of $25,000 or less. Consolidated returns of affiliated corporations were permitted but, once the option of making consolidated or separate returns was exercised, all returns thereafter had to be on the same basis unless permission to change was granted by the Commissioner.

The treatment of insurance companies, except mutual companies, was radically changed by the 1921 law, so that they were taxed on the basis of "their investment income from interest, dividends and rents, with suitable deductions fairly chargeable against such investment income." In the case of life insurance companies this tax was to take the place of all federal taxes levied against corporations, so that for 1921 they were relieved of the excess-profits tax and the capital stock tax. In the case of other insurance companies the new tax took the place of all other taxes for 1922 and succeeding years. The rate of tax was made 12½%, the same as for other companies.[102]

100 *Goodrich* v. *Edwards*, 255 U. S. 527; *Walsh* v. *Brewster*, 255 U. S. 536.

101 69th Congress, 1st Session, *Senate Report* 27 (The Couzens Report).

102 The subject of the taxation of insurance companies is a very technical one. The details of the 1921 law and the amendments made in 1924 are explained in Holmes, G. E., *Federal Taxes*, 6th ed., pp. 318-349.

Another important change was in the manner of taxing personal service corporations. It will be recalled that the 1917 Act taxed at 8% income of partnerships and individuals in business with only a nominal invested capital, if any. By the 1918 law such "personal service corporations" were treated as partnerships. The 1921 law followed the 1918 practice for the income of 1921, but for 1922, and years following, such organizations were to be taxed as corporations. Because of the doubt cast on the constitutionality of these sections of the 1918 law by the Court decision in the case of *Eisner* v. *Macomber* a "safety," or alternate provision, was written into the 1921 law which stated that if the sections just referred to relating to personal service corporations were declared invalid by final adjudication such companies were to be taxed as other corporations.[103]

Several important administrative changes were made. Chief among them was the provision for a final settlement of income tax cases upon the written agreement of the Commissioner and the taxpayer. One of the reasons for the "administrative jam" was that "the taxpayer was never through." [104] Claims once settled were reopened upon the presentation of new evidence, and even more often after a new ruling by the Solicitor or the courts. The new section stated that such rulings could be made without retroactive effect. Such a provision had been requested by the Treasury Department for years. Another important new section provided for the payment of interest by the government on taxes improperly collected.

In order to work out further improvements in the law and its administration the Tax Simplification Board was established. It was to be composed of six members, three of whom would represent the public, and three the Bureau of Internal Revenue. It was continued under the 1924 Revenue Act and was very helpful in suggesting administrative improvements as well as desirable legislation, but could not check the pace of rapidly accumulating complexities in the law, much as that was desired.

103 See above, pp. 187 and 189.
104 See below, Chap. XXIII.

CHAPTER IX

REVENUE ACT OF 1924 — REDUCTION OF SURTAX RATES

THE MELLON PLAN OF TAX REDUCTION

In November 1923, about a month before the 68th Congress was to convene, the Secretary of the Treasury sent a letter to Chairman Green of the Committee on Ways and Means, in which he described the excellent financial condition of the United States Treasury and the consequent possibilities of tax reduction. The years 1922 and 1923 each closed with a surplus of about $310,000,000 above ordinary expenses including the sinking fund requirements. For the forthcoming fiscal year the Administration hoped to reduce ordinary expenditures by $170,000,000 to a total of $3,500,000,000 of which about $500,000,000 would be allocated for debt retirement. Taking account of the expected receipts from customs as well as from internal revenues, the Secretary recommended the following twelve-point program of tax reduction and revision : [1]

1. Grant a 25 per cent tax reduction on income that is earned.
2. Reduce normal taxes from 4 per cent and 8 per cent to 3 per cent and 6 per cent.
3. Reduce the surtax rates so that they will begin to apply at $10,000 instead of $6000 and make the maximum rate 25 per cent on income of $100,000 and over instead of 50 per cent on income of $200,000 and over.
4. Limit the deduction of capital losses to 12½ per cent of the amount of the loss, as the tax on capital gains was limited to 12½ per cent.
5. Limit the deductions for interest paid during the year and, for losses not of a business character, to the amount that the sum of these items exceeds the tax-exempt income of the taxpayer.
6. Tax community property income to the spouse having control of the income.
7. Repeal the tax on telegrams, telephones, and leased wires.
8. Repeal the tax on admissions.
9. Repeal some of the miscellaneous nuisance taxes, at least, those not productive, if the condition of the Treasury does not warrant repealing all of them.
10. Amend the act to eliminate tax avoidance.
11. Establish a Board of Tax Appeals to hear cases involving internal revenue taxes.
12. Amend the law to simplify the administration of the income tax.

Most of the suggestions will be considered in connection with the drafting of the bill. The third suggestion, however, should be

[1] *Report of the Secretary of the Treasury* 1923, pp. 6-11.

explained in some detail for it was the heart of the plan and became the most controverted item. What was the philosophy back of the suggestion? The Secretary believed that the heavy surtax was an emergency war measure, not to be retained as a permanent part of the fiscal system in peace times. He argued that it had become unproductive because the rates were so high that taxpayers had sought escape in tax-exempt securities instead of investing in industry, and that the result was not only loss of capital for business enterprises but loss of initiative on the part of business men.[2] A similar but much stronger statement was contained in an open letter to Chairman Green "and to the friends of the Progressive Income Tax in Congress" by T. S. Adams, formerly of the United States Treasury.[3]

Few of the Secretary's suggestions were new. Congress had discussed many of them several times. Mellon had urged the cut in surtax rates ever since he took office, and the matter of tax avoidance was as old as the income tax, in fact, as old as government itself. Nevertheless, the letter of the Secretary was almost dramatic. The merits and faults of his program, the political aspects, and the fiscal aspects made it one of the most talked-of issues of the day. During the year the Secretary elaborated his thesis in a book entitled *Taxation: The People's Business.*

To appreciate the background, it must be remembered that 1924 was an election year. Mellon knew that political capital would be made of some of the material. In justifying the surtax reduction he said, "The readjustment . . . is not in any sense a partisan measure." Nevertheless it was charged that the Mellon plan was political. The Republican party, as a matter of fact, could not afford to overlook any bids for popularity. The avalanche of investigations into the Veterans' Bureau, the Bureau of Engraving, Tea Pot Dome, ship subsidies and other questionable matters was not the best of advertising for the party. In Congress the Republicans had rather narrow margins which were weakened by the possible defection of recalcitrant "progressives." Republicans numbered 275 out of a total House membership of 485, but 17 were "radicals" or "insurgents" who might at any time join the 207 Democrats. Only three had third party labels, two Farmer-Laborites from Minnesota, and one Socialist from New York. In the Senate 51 had been elected on the Republican ticket, 43 on the Democratic, and 2 on the Farmer-Labor. In reality, however, there were 46 Republicans, 43 Democrats, and 7 La Follette followers.[4]

[2] *Report of the Secretary of the Treasury* 1923, p. 8.

[3] *Bulletin of National Tax Association,* IX: 131-132 (Feb. 1924).

[4] Howell and Norris, Neb.; Ladd and Frazier, N. D.; Brookhart, Ia.; and Johnson, Minn., in addition to La Follette who was unable to attend the Senate until very late in the session because of illness.

Nelson (Wis.) led a House radical bloc which urged the revision of the inflexible rules so that the Progressives would have more influence in legislation. The committees really ran Congress, they said; all that was necessary was to have a majority of 21 on each of the four major committees. They complained that on the important Ways and Means Committee the radicals had only one representative, Frear. For a time this group held up the organization of the House, but Longworth conceded a place on the Rules Committee to one of their supporters and added three minority members to the Committee on Ways and Means.[5] Early in the session a coalition of Democrats and Progressives had scrapped the Underwood rule that required amendments to the bills to be germane. Small wonder that the Republicans feared the Progressives more than they did the Democrats!

Another division in the 68th Congress was caused by the soldiers' bonus advocates. A measure had been passed in the preceding session, but not enough votes had been secured to pass it again over the President's veto. The demand was to be insistent in 1924. Some of its proponents accused Mellon of issuing his tax letter "as a smoke screen to fight adjusted compensation." [6]

At the outset it looked as though the great contest in the forthcoming session would be over the soldiers' bonus and/or tax revision. As a matter of fact, the bonus was accepted as inevitable.[7]

The Democratic position on tax revision was also outwardly nonpolitical. Garrett (Tenn.), minority House leader, gave out a statement before Congress assembled that the party would consider tax legislation solely from the point of view of the public good.[8] It was no secret that the Democrats had been caught napping when the Mellon proposal was published. The very suggestion of tax revision was bound to strike a responsive chord with most Congressmen as well as with their constituents. The Republicans had "scooped" the Democrats. What position would their opponents take? [9] Certainly they would not be against tax reduction even though they might be for a soldiers' bonus.

The first reaction throughout the country was decidedly favorable to the Mellon plan. The Republicans in Congress accepted it at the beginning of the session as a clever move. The President took

5 New York *Times*, Dec. 4 and 5, 1923.

6 Commander Quinn of the American Legion, quoted in the New York *Times*, Jan. 24, 1924.

7 New York *Times*, Dec. 2, 1923. Before the month was over all bonus bills were taken from the jurisdiction of the Committee on Ways and Means.

8 New York *Times*, Nov. 26, 1923.

9 "The Republicans are counting upon such a powerful reaction among the taxpayers, irrespective of political affiliations, as to compel the minority to consider taxation and the bonus non-partisan issues." New York *Times*, Dec. 8, 1923.

it up as one of the major Administration measures. Great applause followed his reference to the plan in his message at the opening of the session. In order to clinch the favorable public opinion aroused by the program, a campaign of publicity and propaganda was undertaken, the like of which had not been seen before. Members of Congress suddenly found their desks almost buried under piles of letters from their constituents, individuals, business firms, railroads, and organizations of various kinds, urging their representatives to cast a favorable vote for the Mellon plan. Some of the writers obviously did not know just what the Mellon plan meant.[10] It was not long before members began to suspect that this "popularity" was really propaganda.

THE COMMITTEE ON WAYS AND MEANS DIVIDES ON THE MELLON PLAN

By 1924 drafting of a revenue act was admittedly a technical piece of work — too technical for Congress to handle. The Treasury began work on the measure in the summer of 1923, and by enormous effort a draft was ready for the Committee on Ways and Means by December. It was said at the time that the proposed changes could be divided into three parts: (1) political, (2) structural, (3) administrative.[11] The political changes were those dealing with rates, the imposition of such new taxes as the gift tax, and the publicity provisions. These were in the province of Congress to determine. The structural changes involved those to permit a freer flow of business and those to prevent tax avoidance. These changes will be discussed in connection with the analysis of the law.

The Committee on Ways and Means accepted the Treasury draft of the structural changes with almost no debate except the sections dealing with community property, the creation or use of corporations to evade the surtax on individuals, and the definition of "capital asset." The last was an attempt to tax stock dividends of corporations. Similarly the administrative sections were adopted as the Treasury wrote them except for the provisions in regard to the Board of Tax Appeals. The discussions in Congress, therefore, were centered almost exclusively on the rate structure.

Although Frear was the only out-and-out radical on the Committee

[10] *Cong. Rec.* 65: 643-653, 939-941, 977, 2463, 3359; *New Republic* 37: 242, 329 (Jan. 30, and Feb. 20, 1924); New York *World*, Jan. 3, 1924.

[11] Winston, Garrard B., "Changes Made by the Revenue Act of 1924," *Proceedings of the National Tax Association* 1924, p. 267.

on Ways and Means,[12] the Republican members held the most divergent views on the extent of desirable tax reduction. Chairman Green was a middle-of-the-road independent westerner who thought Mellon's plan for lowered surtax rates favored the rich and who preferred a policy of debt retirement to one of tax reduction. Mills, a new member, supported Mellon, in fact it was reported that he had been selected with that in view.[13] Enough others sided with him to make it appear that the Committee was stacked against the Chairman. Longworth, formerly on the Committee, was the majority leader, in sympathy with Green's point of view, and of great service as a conciliator both in the Committee and in the House.

On the Democratic side the Committee was strengthened by the return of Rainey and Hull, although the latter could give little time to tax bills because of his added duties as Chairman of the Democratic National Committee. Garner's influence had increased with his years of service.

After some delay caused by opposition threats to force action on the bonus issue prior to that on the tax bill, the Committee settled down to work late in December. By that time each member had the results of a detailed preliminary study of technical sections by the Legislative Drafting Service and a copy of the Treasury tax bill that embodied most of the Secretary's twelve-point program as well as explanations of changes by Mr. Gregg, then special assistant to the Secretary of the Treasury.[14]

The first section, which was devoted to administrative features, was passed over *pro forma*. Next, attention centered on the stock

[12] The entire membership of the Committee was as follows:

Republicans	*Democrats*
William R. Green (Ia.), Ch.	John N. Garner (Tex.)
Willis C. Hawley (Ore.)	James W. Collier (Miss.)
Allen T. Treadway (Mass.)	William A. Oldfield (Ark.)
George M. Young (N. D.)	Charles R. Crisp (Ga.)
James A. Frear (Wis.)	John F. Carew (N. Y.)
John Q. Tilson (Conn.)	Whitmell P. Martin (La.)
Isaac Bacharach (N. J.)	Peter F. Tague (Mass.)
Charles B. Timberlake (Colo.)	Henry T. Rainey (Ill.)
Henry W. Watson (Pa.)	Cordell Hull (Tenn.)
Ogden L. Mills (N. Y.)	Clement C. Dickinson (Mo.)
James C. McLaughlin (Mich.)	John J. Casey (Pa.)
Charles C. Kearns (Ohio)	
Carl R. Chindblom (Ill.)	
Frank Crowther (N. Y.)	

[13] The Mellon tax plan was occasionally called the New York plan.

[14] A. W. Gregg drafted a detailed report explaining the more technical sections of the proposed measure that is of great importance in understanding not only the 1924 Act but also succeeding measures. It was published as a government document, unnumbered, not by the Treasury. *Statement of Changes in the Revenue Act of 1921 . . . by H. R. 6715 and the Reasons Thereof.* Also published in the New York *Times*, Jan. 5, 1924.

dividend problem. Rainey asked Treasury experts to draw up a plan to tax gain from sale of stock dividends held two years at regular income tax rates instead of as capital assets. Mr. Gregg replied that one way would be to except stock dividends in the definition of capital assets; but he did not recommend such a plan because it could be easily evaded by some corporations and would be unfair to others.[15] Therefore the Committee dropped it. The Committee refused to accept the Treasury suggestion for the elimination of the section permitting the carrying over of net losses for two years, but agreed to accept the amendment long desired by the Treasury to limit deductible capital losses to 12½% of the amount of the loss. The harmony with which the Committee worked at the beginning of its sessions, that is, until about the middle of January, was only a calm before the storm.

Discussion of the Secretary's proposed reduction of the surtax began long before the Committee reached the sections relating to it. This proposal was an issue not only in the House and Senate but in the press. One Democratic member aptly remarked:

> The battle of the rich started early, a little too early, I am disposed to think, because the boomerang returned to plague and destroy them.[16]

Meanwhile the Democrats were working out their reply to the Mellon plan. They decided on more general tax reduction so that it would affect more taxpayers, in other words, "to go the Republicans one better." The normal tax rates proposed were 2%, 4%, and 6%, but the maximum surtax rate was reduced to 44% rather than to 25%.[17] Personal exemptions were raised to $2000 and $3000 and the definition of earned income was made much broader than Mellon proposed. This was the Garner plan.

The Democrats challenged the claims that the Mellon surtax reductions would: (a) make the nation prosperous, (b) increase the amount of capital available to industry, (c) result in any additional revenue to the Treasury, or (d) save the administration of the tax from collapse. As for political considerations, the Democrats admitted they too were out for votes, but denied that this proved their plan had no merit.

Then the "radical" tax bill was laid before the Committee by Frear. Like the Democratic plan it reduced the tax on small incomes, but left the maximum surtax at 50% and in addition, proposed a restoration of the excess-profits tax with rates graduated from 10% to 75% in order to raise funds for a soldiers' bonus. The most significant part, however, was the denunciation of Treasury

15 New York *Times,* Jan. 4, 1924.
16 *Cong. Rec.* 65: 2463.
17 New York *World,* Jan. 7, 1924.

secrecy. "No one in Congress or in fact in the country knew what went on behind the closed doors of the Treasury," said Frear, "except as it filtered out meagerly and impersonally." The new administrative body proposed by the Secretary was criticized as open to this objection. The members were to be appointed by the Secretary, outside the civil service, the salaries were to be almost as high as those of the justices of the Supreme Court, and to be tax-exempt. When it organized, this new "Treasury oligarchy" would sit in secret behind closed doors.[18] This protest did not go unheeded.

Frear also had a new idea for the taxation of hitherto exempt government securities. He objected to the idea of a constitutional amendment to prevent future issues of such tax-exempts because it would take too long to secure ratification. His plan was to write a bill to tax the securities already issued, worded in such a way as to prevent the Supreme Court from overturning the law except by a vote of 8 to 1. Mellon, to whom Frear submitted this idea, asked that the author drop it on the grounds that it was unsound and unfair. The Secretary admitted a constitutional amendment was not a complete remedy because it would not reach the $11,000,000,000 of securities already issued, hence his proposed reduction in the surtax rates in order to make such investments less alluring.[19] Frear did not follow the Secretary's advice but was unsuccessful in getting favorable action on his amendment.

The pressure of opposition to the Mellon plan became so great by the middle of January that Green began casting about for a compromise. Not only were the Democrats and the Progressives solidly against it, but some Republicans such as Senator Couzens were bitterly opposed; in fact, many of the rest were only lukewarm. Green's position was the more uncertain because, by the change in the House rules forced by the Democrats and Progressives, a bill could easily be killed by amendments on the floor of the House.[20] It became essential, therefore, for the bill to be assured of passage before it reached the House. Longworth and other party leaders[21] agreed with Green that the surtax rates proposed by Mellon would be entirely unacceptable to the House. President Coolidge was not so easily persuaded. For some time he maintained his original position that if the Treasury bill were seriously altered he would veto it.[22]

Despite Mellon's continued attacks on the Garner plan, Green

[18] New York *Times*, Jan. 8, 1924.
[19] New York *Times*, Jan. 9, 1924.
[20] That is, the Underwood rule, which forbade amendments to a bill unless they were germane, was abolished.
[21] Crowther, Chindblom, Watson, and even Mills (New York *Times*, Jan. 13, 1924).
[22] New York *Times*, Jan. 5, 26, 1924; New York *World*, Jan. 26, 1924.

refused to support the Mellon surtax rates and apparently saw no more feasible outcome for the predicament in which he found himself than to accept the Garner rates.[23] Before giving up completely, however, he asked Garner if the Democrats were determined to stand by their published plan or if they would compromise. Garner replied by asking if Green intended to stick by the Mellon bill as a partisan measure. The "horseplay" was transferred to the House and even to the Senate. So progress on the bill was stalled until Green decided to keep the Democrats out of the future meetings of the Committee and to present the bill as a party measure.[24] By this time the administrative sections had been written, the public hearings[25] had been held, and the portion that remained dealt chiefly with the rate structure, "the real sticking point."

The Republicans alone in Committee could arrive at no decision on this point so Green finally made a bargain. Since Mills and ten of his followers insisted on the Mellon rates, they could write the report if they would accept four changes in the Mellon plan: first and most important of all, give everyone who paid an income tax in 1924 a rebate of 25% of the amount of tax due;[26] second, define as earned income all income under $5000 but in no case permit it to exceed $20,000;[27] third, have the members of the proposed Board of Tax Appeals appointed by the President instead of by the Secretary of the Treasury; fourth, eliminate other nuisance taxes beside those on telephone and telegraph messages.

The Republicans on the Committee issued three reports. One signed by Green, Timberlake, and McLaughlin emphasized the tax reduction features of the bill but merely mentioned the surtax rates. It explained at some length the clarification of the law, the improved administrative machinery and the closing of legal means of avoidance wherever possible. A second was signed by eleven members who supported the Mellon rates, that is, by all the rest of the Republican members except Frear. This report emphasized the reasons for reducing the surtax rates "to a point where the temptation to avoid . . . will, at least, be less compelling." The third report, by Frear, stated that the tax rates submitted by Mellon were "discriminatory and unjust to the great majority of income taxpayers."

[23] New York *World,* Jan. 15, 18, 20, 1924.
[24] New York *World,* Jan. 24, 1924.
[25] Jan. 14-19. Most of the witnesses appeared to protest the excise taxes.
[26] On the floor of the House, O'Connor (Dem., N. Y.) stated that Green probably got this idea from Gov. Alfred E. Smith who proposed a similar cut in New York state taxes on Jan. 1, 1924. (*Cong. Rec.* 65: 2518.) Senator Copeland also claimed credit for it because on Jan. 24 he introduced a resolution that the Secretary of the Treasury present to Congress some plan for a reduction of tax on returns due in 1924, in view of the reported surplus. (*Cong. Rec.* 65: 4020.)
[27] This would care for the broader definition of earned income demanded by the minority party and the radicals.

He proposed a 50% cut in normal tax, no reduction in surtax, and the enactment of an excess-profits tax. His proposals were later explained in detail to the House.

The Democratic report was short. It advocated lower normal rates, objected to the surtax rates which "cast a cloud of suspicion over any so-called tax reduction program," and expressed the fear that the Secretary of the Treasury still had too much discretionary power.

The bill as drafted by the Committee provided for two forms of tax reduction: (1) "temporary and immediate relief" by a 25% reduction of income tax due in 1924 on 1923 income; (2) permanent relief by the reduction of rates of certain taxes and the repeal of others. The normal income tax rates were reduced from 4% and 8% to 3% and 6%, respectively. The surtax rates applied to incomes of $10,000 and over instead of starting at $6000, and the maximum rate was 25%, instead of 65% on income over $5,000,000. The 1921 rate on income in excess of $100,000 was 48%. A new feature was the recommended 25% reduction of tax on earned income not in excess of $20,000. This was an adaptation of English practice and was intended to relieve taxpayers whose income was from personal services, salaries and wages, in contrast to those whose income was from investments.

The non-political or structural changes of special importance were: (1) limitation of the amount of deductible loss from sale of capital assets so that the tax was not reduced by more than 12½% of the loss; (2) allowance of deduction for interest on indebtedness (other than that incurred in connection with trade or business) and for non-business losses only to the extent that the sum of these two items exceeded the tax-exempt income of the taxpayer; and (3) revision of the reorganization section so as to prevent its use to increase the basis for determining gain or loss or to increase the basis for depreciation or depletion.

An important new feature was the establishment of a Board of Tax Appeals, to be composed of not more than 28 nor less than 7 members appointed by the President, with salaries of $10,000 a year. The Board was to be outside the Treasury. Its function was to hear taxpayers' appeals from deficiency levies of the Bureau before the payment of income, excess-profits, war-profits, or estate taxes. Divisions of the Board were to conduct hearings in different parts of the United States so that taxpayers would be relieved of the necessity of going to Washington.[28]

[28] 68th Congress, 1st Session, *House Report* 179.

THE BILL BEFORE THE HOUSE OF REPRESENTATIVES

February 14 Green did his duty as chairman by explaining the Committee report, but he made no recommendations. He emphasized the points on which all of the members agreed, such as the 25 per-cent reduction to all taxpayers and the administrative improvements.

Garner presented the Democratic viewpoint. After some chiding of Green for his easy susceptibility to the pleas of Mills and the other Mellon-plan supporters he showed why the Democrats opposed the low surtax maximum of 25% ; next he announced that he would sponsor an amendment to broaden the definition of earned income ; and finally, he asked for some provision for publicity of income tax returns so that committees of Congress, at least, could have access to them.

The Garner substitute amendments were introduced on the same day. They provided for : (1) normal taxes of 2% on income not in excess of $5000, 4% on income in excess of $5000 and not over $8000 and 6% on the remainder ; (2) surtax rates beginning at 1% on income in excess of $12,000 and increasing to 44% on income in excess of $92,000 ; and (3) personal exemptions of $2000 for a single person and $3000 for a husband and wife or head of a family. The chief defender of the minority proposal aside from the author was Rainey, who labeled the Mellon rates "a distinct political proposition," inasmuch as they were written into the bill by the Republicans alone. In addition to criticizing the Treasury statistics he criticized the Secretary's attitude towards the bonus.[29]

Then Frear introduced his amendment which provided for normal taxes of 2% on the first $4000 of taxable income, and 4% on the remainder ; surtaxes beginning at 1% on income over $6000 and increasing to a maximum of 50% on income in excess of $200,000.

For four days the House wrangled over the Committee draft and the two substitutes and also over the estimates of their effect on the revenue. The conservative Republicans stated that the Garner plan would result in a net reduction of $511,977,000, so much less revenue than the existing law would yield that by 1927 it would result in a deficit of $300,000,000, whereas, the Mellon rates would result in a net reduction of $233,400,000. Garner replied that this comparison was unfair because no one knew what business conditions would be by that time and that the Treasury experts had informed him that

[29] *Cong. Rec.* 65: 2431-2440. Comparative amounts of tax due at different income levels under the Mellon, Garner, and Longworth plans are shown in tabular form in a report of the Senate Finance Committee (68th Congress, 1st Session, *Senate Document* 62).

his plan would bring in $100,000,000 more revenue for 1924 than the Mellon plan. The main differences were that the Garner plan decreased the tax more on small incomes and less on larger incomes than did the Mellon plan.

The temper of the debate showed clearly that, even if the Mellon surtax rates were accepted by a majority of the Republicans on the Committee on Ways and Means, the House would not accept them. On February 16 it was announced that no attempt would be made to take a vote on the proposed 25% surtax maximum.[30] In fact, the radicals served notice that if these rates were not raised they would vote with the Democrats.[31] Longworth, who seemed to have taken upon himself the role of harmonizer, began casting about for a rate high enough to get sufficient votes.

Green, it will be remembered, was never favorable to the Mellon rates. Doubtless he would have compromised with Garner during the Committee meetings if he could have had his way. The contest then became a series of bargains conducted outside the House. At first the Republicans stood out for a 35% maximum surtax but admitted that if necessary they might increase it slightly. On February 16 the Republican insurgents agreed to accept 40% if normal rates were cut in half. At that time Longworth flatly refused to consider such a proposition, but later, after the prolonged debate in the House and its acceptance of much higher rates, he looked upon 40% (the Senate rate) as highly desirable. In February, however, he would not consider 40%. As a concession Republican leaders offered 37½% but that was refused, even though the President's Secretary appealed to the radicals to join the party.[32] So the House in Committee of the Whole adopted the Garner substitute by a vote of 221 to 196,[33] and then proceeded with the reading of the bill and consideration of the Committee amendments.

One of the important amendments was to eliminate the phrase "for profit or investment" from the definition of capital assets. Green pointed out that as originally written gains from sale of the taxpayer's home would be taxed at regular rates.[34] Garner offered an amendment to add the words "but not including stock received as a stock dividend by the taxpayer," so that the profits from the sale of such stock would be taxable at regular income tax rates, not at the special 12½% rate applicable to sale of capital assets. This was accepted

[30] Washington *Post,* Feb. 16, 1924.
[31] New York *Times,* Feb. 17, 1924.
[32] New York *Times,* Feb. 20, 1924.
[33] *Cong. Rec.* 65: 2794.
[34] *Cong. Rec.* 65: 2842-2845. The 1921 Act defined capital assets as "property acquired and held by the taxpayer for profit or investment for more than two years (whether or not connected with his trade or business), but does not include property held for the personal use or consumption of the taxpayer. . ."

despite the previous Committee action and the opinion of the Treasury.

The usual discussion of publicity of income tax returns was injected into the debate by Frear. His amendment to make returns public records was defeated, but the House passed one to permit certain committees of Congress to call on the Secretary of the Treasury for returns or for data contained in returns.

Oldfield (Dem., Ark.) attempted to take out all of the section relating to capital gains, because he considered it unfair to taxpayers to "divide and specify and set aside different sorts of income, and make sacred a certain kind of income." [35] Green explained that the section had been put into the 1921 law because many of the larger taxpayers held their property instead of selling it at a profit because of the tax, but on the other hand they sold property so as to take their losses which were deductible. The proposed amendment would cause the government to lose $25,000,000 in revenue. Furthermore, it seemed unfair to tax at regular income tax rates capital gains that had been realized over a period of years. The House acceded to Green's request that the amendment be rejected.[36]

Several members were concerned over the definition of earned income. Garner wanted to be assured that small farmers and merchants could take advantage of the 25 per-cent reduction permitted to those earning their income.[37] Another member objected that the whole section was arbitrary. Mills defended it on the authority of T. S. Adams, who said that the only way to avoid the difficulty of a definition was to adopt an arbitrary limitation of some amount such as $5000. Garner's proposal was considered absolutely impossible from an administrative point of view. Chindblom proposed that the limit be made $7500.[38] Tilson also offered an amendment to add to Garner's the words: "but not exceeding 20 per cent of the net profits of the taxpayer from the business in connection with which his personal services are rendered." Thus the amendment was passed.[39]

The ever present problem of finding some method of taxing obligations of states and their subdivisions received some attention. Black (Texas) proposed an amendment that would require taxpayers to include in gross income all interest from such securities in excess of that received from a principal amount of $5000. Oliver (Rep., N. Y.) countered with two constitutional amendments: (1) to give

[35] *Cong. Rec.* 65: 2846.
[36] *Cong. Rec.* 65: 2847, 2849.
[37] *Cong. Rec.* 65: 2849-2850. His amendment read: "Earned income also means reasonable compensation or allowance for personal services where income is derived from combined personal services and capital in the production by unincorporated persons of agriculture or other business."
[38] *Cong. Rec.* 65: 2851.
[39] *Cong. Rec.* 65: 2854-2855.

Congress power to collect taxes on securities issued after the ratification of the amendment and (2) to return to the states the revenue collected by the federal government from the tax on income from such securities. Neither amendment was passed.[40]

During the discussion of the allowable deductions an amendment was proposed to encourage building of low-cost houses[41] but, as it had not been submitted to the Committee and because of its unusual content, it was not taken very seriously.

Very little time was given by the House to the matter of taxing the undistributed income of corporations. Frear drafted an amendment to levy an additional tax of 5% on undistributed corporate earnings above a certain minimum, and not in excess of $20,000 and 10% of the amount of such surplus in excess of $20,000. It was rejected because few if any of the members of the House knew what the fiscal or economic effects of such a provision would be.

The House defeated also Frear's plan for raising funds for a soldiers' bonus by an excess-profits tax on corporations.[42] After some disagreement as to whether or not the amendment was germane, the House spent only a short time in discussing it. The Committee had previously turned down the proposition, but this did not trouble the author of the amendment. Hill argued that if this were germane to the bill then the same could be said of his amendment for a soldiers' bonus. Blanton supported Frear, but otherwise there was no enthusiasm for this proposal and it was voted down by a large majority.[43]

When the income tax sections were practically completed, Ramseyer (Rep., Iowa) succeeded in putting through an amendment to increase the rates of the estate tax to a maximum of 40% instead of 20% on the amount of an estate in excess of $10,000,000.[44] The author stated that he had made a study of the yield of inheritance taxes of other countries and was convinced that there were great possibilities for the United States. Mills argued that the federal government should not impose such a tax, but when Garner asked him if he wanted to strike the section out of the bill he said he did not. The House accepted Frear's amendment providing that a credit of 25% of the federal tax be given when an estate pays a state inheritance tax. The purpose was to equalize the estate taxes of the various states.

[40] *Cong. Rec.* 65: 2859. Shortly before the bill was introduced the House defeated a resolution introduced by Green to submit to the states a constitutional amendment to forbid future issues of tax-exempt securities.

[41] McKeown (Dem., S. C.) proposed that there be deducted from taxpayers' income "25 per cent of all income derived from cheap sanitary dwellings rented to families having two children under 16 years of age. . ." (*Cong. Rec.* 65: 2859.)

[42] *Cong. Rec.* 65: 3003-3007. Green anticipated this move and expected it to receive some support (*Proceedings of the National Tax Association* 1923, p. 299).

[43] 78 ayes, 156 nays (*Cong. Rec.* 65: 3007).

[44] *Cong. Rec.* 65: 3350.

He preferred a rebate system and suggested it be on a 50-50 basis, but as others interested in the estate tax did not agree with him he accepted the credit plan.[45]

Following consideration of the sections dealing with the excise taxes and some of the administrative matters the debate centered on the surtax rates. Hawley tried unsuccessfully to push through the Mellon rates.[46] Longworth and Green continued their daily conferences with the radical leaders [47] in an effort to win them over.[48] Various compromises were offered, but reduction in normal rates was insufficient to interest them. Finally Longworth agreed to cut the normal rate from 3% to 2% and to make the maximum surtax 37½%. He was not given much assurance that this would be accepted, but three radicals were agreeable and the time had come when he had to take a chance – the House had about reached the point of the closing vote. On February 29 Longworth did get enough votes to pass his substitute for the Garner plan, so that the agreed surtax maximum became 37½%; [49] therefore Green dropped his plan to substitute the Committee's exemptions of $1000 and $2000 for those of Garner, which were $2000 and $3000.[50] The House accepted Green's amendment to impose a gift tax at the same rate as the estate tax.[51] So on February 29 the House passed the bill by a vote of 408 to 8.[52]

Estimates of revenue reduction by the various proposed measures were somewhat inconsistent and, as has been shown, were subjected to much political banter.[53] Table 10 shows the Treasury estimates at the time of the passage of the House draft.

SECRETARY MELLON PROPOSES IMMEDIATE REDUCTION

Within a week after the passage of the bill by the House, Secretary Mellon proposed that Congress pass a joint resolution to make effective at once the 25 per-cent reduction in income tax payable in 1924 on 1923 income. He wanted this part of the law made a separate measure so that it could apply to the first installment of the tax due March 15. People were confused, the Secretary said, and the income tax payments were not coming in as they should. If the measure

45 *Cong. Rec.* 67: 707.
46 *Cong. Rec.* 65: 3347.
47 Chiefly La Guardia, Woodruff, Cooper, Clague, and Nelson.
48 New York *Times*, Feb. 17, 1924.
49 *Cong. Rec.* 65: 3349.
50 *Cong. Rec.* 65: 3350.
51 The Senate in 1921 had adopted a similar amendment.
52 *Cong. Rec.* 65: 3354.
53 This controversy started the Couzens-Mellon "feud." See below, Chaps. X and XXIII.

TABLE 10

COMPARISON OF TAX PLANS [a]

Estimated Net Loss of Revenue

	Losses		
	Longworth (House bill)	*Garner (Democratic plan)*	*Mills (Committee on Ways and Means)*
Normal tax.............	$130,000,000	$227,000,000	$91,600,000
Surtax.................	150,000,000	171,000,000	101,800,000
Unearned income credit..	90,000,000	85,000,000	89,500,000
Miscellaneous...........	126,000,000	126,000,000	108,040,000
	$496,000,000	$609,000,000	$390,940,000
	Gains		
Non-taxable income including capital losses..	$50,000,000	$50,000,000	$49,500,000
Net Total Loss...........	$446,000,000	$559,000,000	$341,400,000

[a] New York *Times*, March 4, 1924.

were passed later the Treasury would have to make more confusing computations in working out the refunds.[54]

Green called a meeting of his Committee and notified Smoot, who placed the matter before the Senate Finance Committee. Both agreed that such a resolution as the Secretary proposed would be desirable but the parliamentary situation was complicated. Inasmuch as an agreement had been made that the bills regarding Muscle Shoals and the soldiers' bonus would be considered immediately, it would require unanimous consent to consider any other measure. On the Republican side Mills, Treadway, Tilson, and Bacharach, the "die-hard Republicans," were so anxious to push the resolution through they said they would put up a fight for it.[55] Longworth flatly opposed it.[56]

The Democrats saw in the proposition a trick to take out of the bill the real tax reduction feature, so that Coolidge could veto it without

[54] New York *Times*, March 7, 1924.
[55] New York *Times*, March 8, 1924.
[56] New York *Times*, March 9, 1924.

embarrassment should the surtax rates be higher than the Administration approved. Crisp very pointedly remarked that the refund would amount only to a bonus at a time when the Administration claimed there was insufficient surplus to provide a bonus for soldiers.[57] Therefore the Committee on Ways and Means did not sponsor a resolution, but Porter (Rep., Pa.) introduced one on March 8. In spite of the efforts of the few Republicans who favored it, and a special message from the President to Congress,[58] the resolution received no backing from House leaders. Longworth announced that it was dead and Coolidge was so informed.[59]

THE SENATE FINANCE COMMITTEE ADOPTS THE MELLON PLAN [60]

The attempt to rush through the resolution for immediate tax reduction was taken as an indication that the Administration was going to do all in its power to reduce the surtax rates below those written into the bill by the House. A majority of the Republicans on the Senate Committee on Finance were very conservative and approved of the Mellon rates. McCormick and La Follette did not agree with them, but when the Committee began its work in March, both these men were absent ; the former was busily campaigning, and the latter was ill. The Committee had no hope of winning La Follette to their point of view on this matter. If McCormick also joined the seven Democrats, the Republicans would be outvoted.

The first two weeks were spent in going over the sections on administration. The rates were decided upon later. March 24 the Committee secured a vote of 8 to 7 for the Mellon rates. At this meeting only five Republicans were present, but they cast proxies for four absentees, to the great indignation of McCormick. In fact, he notified his colleagues that he would confer with the Republicans from the Northwest and the Middle West and get their support for pushing through much higher rates, at least, those favored by Longworth.[61]

57 New York *Times,* March 7, 1924.
58 *Cong. Rec.* 65: 3938.
59 New York *Times,* March 11, 12, 13, 1924.
60 The members were :

Republicans	*Democrats*
Reed Smoot (Utah), Ch.	Furnifold M. Simmons (N. C.)
Robert M. La Follette (Wis.)	Andrieus A. Jones (N. Mex.)
George P. McLean (Conn.)	Peter G. Gerry (R. I.)
Charles Curtis (Kan.)	James A. Reed (Mo.)
James E. Watson (Ind.)	David I. Walsh (Mass.)
David A. Reed (Pa.)	Pat Harrison (Miss.)
Davis Elkins (W. Va.)	William H. King (Utah)
Medill McCormick (Ill.)	
Richard P. Ernst (Ky.)	
Robert N. Stanfield (Ore.)	

61 New York *Times,* March 26, April 9, 1924.

The Democrats claimed to be highly pleased at this decision because they wanted a chance to debate the issue on the floor of the Senate. The position of the minority was not very clear, however. At one time their leader, Robinson (Ark.), said their proposal would be for a bill along entirely new lines,[62] but eventually they contented themselves with amendments. Robinson stated that they would start out with a demand for a maximum surtax of 44% for trading purposes.[63]

Members of both parties complained that the Treasury had not been frank in its explanation of the fiscal situation of the country. At one time it reported a surplus; at another, insufficient funds for a soldiers' bonus.[64] More than one member of Congress stated that in 1923 the President had vetoed the bonus bill because of a billion-dollar error in estimates. The Senate Finance Committee claimed that when estimates of certain Treasury statisticians differed from those of the Director of the Customs Service or the Commissioner of Internal Revenue, the Treasury took the lowest.[65] The Secretary, his special assistant, Gregg, and other Treasury experts appeared before the Committee for several days to untangle the technicalities of the estimates. The conclusion seemed to be that the Treasury expected to have a surplus of $395,000,000 for the fiscal year 1925;[66] but if the House bill should become law there would be a deficit because it would result in less revenue than the 1921 law by $450,000,000. It was estimated that the bill as proposed by the Senate would result in a deficit of $75,000,000. Furthermore, bills with aggregate appropriations of $3,600,000,000 that had not been included in the budget were then pending in Congress. Smoot was favorable to enacting some additional taxes but, at a White House conference, the President let it be known that he was opposed to any new taxes.[67]

The Committee therefore concluded its sessions and submitted its

62 New York *Times*, March 28, 1924.

63 New York *Times*, March 6, April 7, 1924.

64 Senator Simmons to Undersecretary Winston:

Senator Simmons: Those things you did not consider in your first estimate, did not anticipate in your first estimate, and the result was that the difference between your estimate in July and in November was $700,000,000, and the difference in your estimate and the actual result shown in July, 1923, changed this $600,000,000 deficit to a surplus of $313,000,000.

Mr. Winston: Yes; you will recall business conditions when these estimates were first made. We were just getting out of a slump.

Senator Simmons: As a matter of fact, you can not always anticipate what business conditions are going to be? (68th Congress, 1st Session, *Hearings before the Committee on Finance . . . U. S. Senate on H. R.* 6717, p. 131.) See also *Cong. Rec.* 65: 2433.

65 New York *Times*, March 21, 1924.

66 Testimony of Secretary Mellon, 68th Congress, 1st Session, *Hearings before the Senate Committee on Finance on H. R.* 6715, p. 60.

67 New York *Times*, April 5, 1924.

draft of the bill. For individuals the maximum surtax rate was made 25% on income over $100,000, the normal income tax rates were 3% on the first $4000 of income and 6% on the remainder, just as Mellon requested. For corporations the rate of net income was raised from 12½%, as set by the House, to 14%, but the capital stock tax was repealed. These rates were put into the bill at the suggestion of Reed (Pa.), who estimated that the Treasury would gain some twenty million dollars in revenue, would be saved the work of administering the capital stock tax, and corporations would be saved the annoyance of making out so many returns.[68] The third important change was in the section relating to the estate tax. The Committee took out the gift tax, probably at the request of the Treasury because Mellon thought it was of no value from the point of view of revenue, incapable of effective administration, and a further levy upon capital.[69] The Committee also reduced the estate tax rates from 50% to 25%, those of the 1921 law, and eliminated the credit for state inheritance taxes.

The minority report, which was not submitted until almost two weeks after that of the majority, protested the changes made, particularly the acceptance of surtax rates which had been repudiated by the House.

THE BILL BEFORE THE SENATE

April 24 Smoot explained the majority position as stated in the report of the Finance Committee. Most of his speech was devoted to a defense of the low surtax rates, chiefly on the grounds that the reductions would help not only the wealthy, as had been claimed by opponents of the Mellon plan, but the small taxpayer as well. From available statistics, the Senator concluded that more than 60% of the reduction in income taxes would go to those with taxable income of $10,000 or less, representing 88% of the national income, and 20% would go to those having taxable income in excess of $100,000, representing 3% of the national income. The arguments as to the disastrous effect of high surtaxes were those that Secretary Mellon had used in advocating their reduction; namely, that they discouraged business transactions and were impossible to collect.[70]

Jones replied for the minority of the Committee that the program advocated by the Republicans had been repudiated in 1921 by both the House and Senate and again by the House in the bill just passed. Adequate statistical evidence as to the effect of the high surtax rates

68 New York *Times*, April 5, 7, 1924; *Cong. Rec.* 65: 7067.

69 New York *Times*, April 7, 1924; *Cong. Rec.* 65: 7068. Mellon's objections are set forth in the *Report of the Secretary of the Treasury* 1924, p. 14.

70 *Cong. Rec.* 65: 7064-7070.

was admittedly lacking. A study of 251 estates that had reported to the Bureau of Internal Revenue showed that the average amount of tax-exempt securities held was only 6.8% of the gross estate.[71] A more important means of tax evasion, according to the Senator, was through the corporate form of organization. Yet neither from the Secretary of the Treasury nor from other "responsible Republican source" had there been heard any remedy for preventing the use of the corporate form for evading the surtax. Simmons made a very short speech ; then the Senate began the reading of the bill. Most of the general debate had occurred before the measure was formally introduced.[72]

The first amendments were accepted without any question. They eliminated the House provisions for taxing at normal rates gains from the sale of stock received as dividends that had been held more than two years. The Senate thus restored the provisions of the 1921 law for taxing such gains at a special rate of 12½%. The Senate then rejected the House amendment which was inserted at the request of the Treasury to limit capital losses to 12½%.[73] The House definition of earned income was amended so as to make an arbitrary maximum limit of $10,000 instead of $20,000 to the amount of income subject to the 25% reduction in tax.[74]

When the Senate reached the section which dealt with the corporation income tax, McKellar opposed raising the rates.[75] Smoot replied that corporations did not object to the raise because they were gratified at the repeal of the capital stock tax. Dial (S. C.) also opposed the change because the capital stock tax yielded $85,000,000, was administered with a minimum of friction, and was collected from all corporations, whether or not they made a profit ; thus it reached holding companies such as those with undeveloped natural resources that otherwise would pay only when they disposed of their properties.[76] King admitted that the Committee had not been unanimous on this matter ; in fact, several of the members were somewhat dissatisfied with the change. In answer to a question from Glass as to the effect of the proposed amendment, Smoot showed that corporations making less than 6⅔% profit would be benefited by the amendment while those making over 6⅔% would have to pay more if

[71] *Cong. Rec.* 65: 7072-7076.

[72] For example, the speeches of Brookhart (Ia.), Jones (N. M.), Copeland (N. Y.), and Ashurst (N. C.). (*Cong. Rec.* 65: 585, 591, 690-694, 743-740.)

[73] *Cong. Rec.* 65: 7123.

[74] *Cong. Rec.* 65: 7125.

[75] *Cong. Rec.* 65: 7211. He thought that there should be "a uniform and, as nearly as possible, a relatively equal reduction of taxes all along the line, on corporations as well as individuals of high and low degree."

[76] *Cong. Rec.* 65: 7338.

the Senate bill were passed. The Senate finally accepted the Committee's proposal.[77]

The Democrats proposed three amendments: (1) the Garner normal rates of 2%, 4%, and 6%; (2) a personal exemption of $2500 regardless of the amount of income instead of the Committee's proposal to limit this amount to those with incomes of $5000 or less; (3) a 40% surtax maximum.

It was acknowledged by everyone that the biggest fight would be over the surtax rates. Smoot was prepared to substitute 30% for the 25% maximum set by the Committee and then, if necessary, to go higher. On May 5 Simmons presented his amendment for a 40% maximum, made a speech on the propaganda for the Mellon bill, then yielded the floor to Jones. When he had spoken just a few moments, Simmons whispered something in his ear; Jones then said he was ready to vote on the substitute offered by the Senator of North Carolina.[78] The Republican leaders were taken completely by surprise and tried to find some way to postpone the vote. Lodge, Watson, and Reed hastily conferred, but there seemed no way out of the dilemma.[79] The Democratic rates were adopted by a vote of 43 to 40 in Committee of the Whole; 7 Republicans and one Farmer-Laborite joined 35 Democrats to pass the amendment. Two Democrats, Bruce and Edwards, voted against it. Smoot gave notice he would ask for a separate vote on this section when the bill reached the Senate.[80] Three days later he presented an amendment for a maximum surtax rate of 32% but it was rejected,[81] and so the Simmons rates were voted into the bill.[82]

Strange to relate, the Senate adopted without any objection the amendment of Norris to provide publicity of income tax returns, and that of McKellar that "all claims for abatement and refund of taxes shall likewise be public property subject to inspection under similar rules."[83] This was amended before its passage so as to include the publicity of Treasury decisions on such claims.

Jones again brought up his proposal for lessening tax avoidance by taxing undistributed corporate earnings. Early in the session the Senator succeeded in getting favorable action on a resolution to require the Secretary of the Treasury to furnish information as to corporate earnings for the year 1922, classified as to the percentage distributed and that undistributed to stockholders.[84] The Secre-

[77] *Cong. Rec.* 65: 7342, 7449.
[78] *Cong. Rec.* 65: 7848.
[79] New York *Times*, May 6, 1924.
[80] *Cong. Rec.* 65: 7849.
[81] *Cong. Rec.* 65: 8195.
[82] The vote was 46-39 (*Cong. Rec.* 65: 8196).
[83] *Cong. Rec.* 65: 7692.
[84] *Cong. Rec.* 65: 591.

tary's report stated that 108,611 corporations reported taxable net income for 1922, of which 78,923 submitted complete returns showing net income, amount and kind of dividend distribution. There were 48,875 corporations that paid out cash dividends and 30,048 that paid no dividends. Of those that paid dividends 39,294 paid out 30% or more of their net income in cash dividends; 9581 paid out less than 30%. The 30,048 corporations that paid no dividends reported net income of $1,196,000,000 and accumulated surpluses of nearly $4,000,000,000. The corporations that submitted incomplete returns, and therefore could not be classified with respect to percentages of cash dividends and stock dividends, reported net income of $1,197,000,000 and paid out dividends of $249,000,000. The total paid out to stockholders by all corporations was $2,763,000,000 in cash and $2,547,000,000 in stock.

Jones computed that from 1916 to 1922 the total net incomes of corporations amounted to approximately $56,000,000,000. The total income and excess-profits tax was $10,798,000,000. There remained for distribution therefore $45,296,000,000, but corporations distributed only slightly over $18,000,000,000. The Senator then went on to say that because the law did not require distribution, these corporate earnings were subject only to the normal corporation income tax of 12½%. The stock dividends could not be taxed in the hands of individuals and, furthermore, corporations owned large amounts of Liberty Bonds upon which they paid no tax, since interest on bonds of the first issue was exempt from all taxation and that of subsequent issues was subject to the surtax only. A third injustice was that of favoring the holding companies which were not taxed on dividends received from other corporations. According to the statistics of income in 1922 such dividends amounted to $500,000,000.

The solution advocated by the Senator was that which he had proposed at almost every session of Congress that had considered tax legislation since 1918, namely, a tax graduated according to the amount of corporate net income that was undistributed. He would, however, lower the normal tax on corporate net income from 14% to 9%. It was estimated that such a corporation tax would bring in only $6,000,000 a year but would increase the individual surtax yield by $300,000,000.

Edge opposed the amendment. He thought it would weaken the financial structure of corporations because it would force them to pay dividends when it was perhaps unwise to do so. Caraway wanted to know if a better solution would not be to find some way of taxing stock dividends. Smoot quoted figures of corporate distribution to show that from 1910 to 1916 dividends amounted to 53½% of the net profits; that, although complete figures for the years from 1917 to 1922 were not available, 141 of the largest corporations paid out dividends that averaged 65% of the profits and for 1922 cash dividends of all corporations "constituted more than 53% of the profits available for distribution." He thought the proposition of Jones was therefore unnecessary; and, in addition, he considered that the effect would be detrimental to business prosperity, in fact, he prophesied that it would be "disastrous." Business, he said, needed to accumulate reserves for growth and expansion.[85]

Jones' amendment was adopted by a vote of 43 to 21.[86] Although it was deleted by the Conferees, its acceptance by the Senate was a great victory after the Senator's long years of fighting for a principle which has influenced income tax legislation down to the present time.[87]

Reed (Pa.), a personal friend of Mellon, made an effort to include an amendment to tax future issues of securities, whether issued by the United States or any state or a political sub-division thereof. This matter had been thoroughly thrashed out in many sessions but the constitutional objections and other considerations were gone over again. Walsh was the only member who gave the proposition much support.[88]

Walsh proposed to reinstate the House gift tax with rates from 1% on gifts not in excess of $25,000 to 36% on gifts over $5,000,000. Simmons supported the proposal on the ground that gifts were a frequent means of tax evasion. When it was made clear that provisions had been made for exemption of gifts to religious, educational, and scientific organizations, the amendment was accepted.[89]

The Senate also accepted the proposal of Walsh to substitute an inheritance tax for an estate tax. He said that most states had decided that an inheritance tax was more just than an estate tax, both Republican and Democratic members of the Senate had favored an inheritance tax in 1918, and the administration of the inheritance tax would not be more difficult than that of the estate tax.[90]

The Senate examined carefully the provision establishing the Board of Tax Appeals.[91] No one denied the necessity of settling the old tax cases from the points of view of both the Bureau of Internal Revenue and the taxpayer. There were differences of opinion only as to method. Should the Board members be lawyers? Should the

[85] *Cong. Rec.* 65: 8011-8020.
[86] *Cong. Rec.* 65: 8033.
[87] It was one of the main issues in the contests over the 1936, 1938, and 1939 tax bills. See below, Chaps. XVII, XIX, and XX.
[88] *Cong. Rec.* 65: 8200-8216.
[89] *Cong. Rec.* 65: 8094-8097.
[90] *Cong. Rec.* 65: 8034-8047. The estate tax was and still is retained (1940).
[91] *Cong. Rec.* 65: 8109-8115. See below, Chap. XXIII.

Board be a court of law? Should a taxpayer have the right to appeal to a court of law when an additional assessment was determined by the Board? Several amendments passed by the Senate to change radically the Committee provision were thrown out by the Conferees. One that was written into the law was that of Jones to provide that the hearings be open to the public and that the testimony taken at the hearings be reduced to writing.[92] This was to correct the secrecy of the Treasury Department in adjudicating cases, which, according to the report of minority members of the Committee, afforded an opportunity for "favoritism, arbitrary action, fraud and collusion."

The final vote on the bill was 69 yeas, 15 nays, 12 not voting.[93]

REPORT OF THE CONFEREES

There were six "material differences" between the House and the Senate bills, namely those relating to: (1) the normal tax rates, (2) surtax rates, (3) the size of personal exemptions, (4) corporation taxes, (5) publicity of returns and (6) an estate versus an inheritance tax.

The real stumbling blocks were the tax on undistributed corporate earnings and the provisions for publicity. Jones' proposal was unacceptable to the House managers. The Senate managers were doubtless not entirely convinced of its desirability, hence receded. As a substitute the Conferees re-enacted Section 220 for a tax on net income of corporations formed to avoid the surtax although even the Secretary of the Treasury said that it had been ineffective.[94]

As to publicity of returns, the House draft permitted public inspection only under the rules prescribed by the Secretary and approved by the President but added that special provision should be made for certain committees of Congress to have access to such returns, especially the Ways and Means Committee of the House and the Finance Committee of the Senate. The Senate had voted complete publicity. The Conferees followed the House bill for the most part, but added that each collector should prepare and make available for the public a list containing the name, address, and tax of each person making an income tax return.[95]

[92] *Cong. Rec.* 65: 8132.

[93] *Cong. Rec.* 65: 8268.

[94] Letter of Secretary Mellon to Senator McKellar, Feb. 8, 1924, quoted in *Cong. Rec.* 65: 4014.

[95] While the Conferees were deliberating Herbert Hoover, then Secretary of Commerce, issued a statement that publicity of returns would do much harm to business, particularly to the small trader because competitors could find out too much. He referred to the publicity of the income tax returns in the years 1867 to 1872 which he said contributed to the industrial and financial chaos of the times. (New York *Times*, May 17, 1924.)

When the report was read in the Senate, Norris opposed it. He was particularly disappointed at the rejection of his amendment for the publicity of income tax returns. He was sure that if the members of the House of Representatives had had a chance to vote on the proposition it would have been written into the bill. Walsh went further and objected to the system by which legislation was enacted in secret, "behind closed doors." This he characterized as "star-chamber" government, which he thought would ultimately lead to "widespread protest from the American people." Jones had much the same to say as to the deletion of the tax on undistributed income.[96]

In the House, objections were made to certain amendments but, on the whole, the comment was favorable.[97] Even the obstructionist Frear had something good to say about the measure, chiefly because it was better than the Mellon plan.

The bill was estimated to yield $3,437,000,000 as compared with $3,459,000,000 by the Mellon plan and $3,798,000,000 actually yielded by the Revenue Act of 1921.

Secretary Mellon, of course, was not pleased with the rate schedule, or the gift tax. He was further displeased because the Senate passed a bill for a soldiers' bonus over the President's veto, just before the Conferees reported the tax bill. He announced that tax cuts were thereby imperiled. Rumors were current that President Coolidge would veto the measure.[98]

Although the President signed the bill June 2, 1924, he did so reluctantly and issued a statement objecting to: (1) the height of the surtax rates, (2) the failure to pass a resolution for a Constitutional amendment to abolish tax-exempt securities, (3) publicity of income tax returns, (4) the change of the Board of Tax Appeals from an administrative body to a judicial body and (5) the high estate tax rates.

SUMMARY OF THE LAW [99]

The Revenue Act of 1924 was written as a complete entity, not as amendments to previous laws. It was probably the most carefully drafted of all revenue acts up to that time because of the professional work done by experts in the Treasury Department and in the Legislative Drafting Service. As explained above, the technical sections were presented to Congress in good form and were not changed except in minor degree.

96 *Cong. Rec.* 65: 9403-9409.
97 The final House vote on the Conference report was 377 to 9. (*Cong. Rec.* 65: 9543.)
98 New York *Times,* May 20, 1924. It was rumored that Congressional leaders knew that the Treasury surplus was much larger than the published estimate.
99 43 *Statutes at Large* 253.

Although much of the discussion in Congress centered on the rate structure, the law is of interest to tax students because of the "structural" changes, those made to prevent the tax laws from hindering business and those made to prevent tax avoidance. The 1924 Act may be looked upon as laying down fundamental principles as to rules for computing gain or loss in corporate reorganization, in exchange of property for other property, in treatment of capital gains and losses, and in creation of trusts. It may be rather straining the meaning of the term "fundamental" to use it in connection with income tax laws that have been revised every two years from 1924 to 1934 and, from then on, every year. Nevertheless, some of the provisions of the 1924 Act just referred to remained unchanged until 1932, some until 1934, and others have not been changed except in minor details.

The Revenue Act of 1924 was made up of 13 titles of which Titles II, III, VII, IX, X, and XII are of special concern in this study.[100] They will be briefly summarized.

Title II – Income Tax. The normal tax on individuals was graduated: 2% on the first $4000 of taxable income, 4% on the next $4000 and 6% on the remainder. The personal exemptions were $2500 for head of a family, $1000 for a single person, and $400 for a dependent. The surtax was graduated from 1% on net income in excess of $10,000 to 40% on that portion of the net income in excess of $500,000. In the 1921 law the surtax began on incomes in excess of $6000 and reached a maximum of 50% on income in excess of $200,000. The 1924 act contained a provision that had been frequently discussed in Congress but not previously adopted, namely, the reduction of tax rate by 25% in favor of "earned" income. The first $5000 of an individual's taxable income was assumed to be earned, and therefore granted the lower rate. This favorable differentiation was not permitted, however, to income in excess of $10,000.

The tax rate on corporate net income of 12½% and the capital stock tax of one dollar for each $1000 of par value were retained, as in the 1921 law.

Allowance for discovery depletion was reduced from 100% of net income to 50%.

The 1921 plan of taxing capital gains and losses was retained in 1924 with amendments to limit the amount of deductible loss. Inasmuch as this section of the law was re-enacted in the Acts of 1926, 1928, and 1932, it may be explained in some detail. The term "capital assets" meant property held by the taxpayer for more than

[100] The other titles were: I – Definitions; IV – Tax on Cigars, Tobacco and Manufactures thereof; V – Tax on Admissions and Dues; VI – Excise Taxes; VIII – Stamp Taxes; XI – General Provisions, including a section changing the name of the legislative drafting service to that of legislative counsel.

two years (whether or not connected with his trade or business), but did not include stock in trade of the taxpayer, or property that would be inventoried if on hand at the close of the taxable year, or property held by the taxpayer primarily for sale in the course of his trade or business. If the taxpayer so chose, he might separate gain from sale of capital assets from other income and pay a tax of 12½% on such income. In case of loss, the taxpayer might deduct from his tax on ordinary net income an amount not exceeding 12½% of his loss. The total tax due could not be less than if this provision regarding loss were disregarded.

At the time opinion differed as to whether or not this method was an improvement. Some writers commented on the advantage of the low rate.[101] Nevertheless, this new provision opened up a paradoxical situation. As illustrated by T. S. Adams:

> A bond [held for more than two years] sold at a loss would reduce the ordinary tax by only twelve and one-half per cent, but if the bond became a total loss it could be deducted in full as a bad debt under Section 214 (a) (7).[102]

That it was fairly satisfactory must be implied from the fact that it remained in force ten years.

The fact that the United States income law regarded capital gain, that is, increment in value of property, as income, introduced many complexities into the law. For example, sales or exchanges of real estate, corporate reorganizations and other business transactions would be almost completely stopped if the rule were followed inflexibly. Therefore it became necessary to draft exceptions. These provisions are among the most complicated in the law. The basic theory was explained in 1924 by the Undersecretary of the Treasury in these words:

> We have drawn it upon this theory : that you can go through any kind of a reorganization which the necessities of the particular business require, provided the stockholders get no money out of the transaction or no different property than they had before. That is, you can take two corporations and merge them into one, and give the stockholders of the two the stock in the single corporation. You can take a single corporation – and this is a most important change in the new law – and split it into two corporations and give the stock of each corporation to the original stockholders. If, however, in doing this, the stockholders realize additional cash, such cash is taxed to the proper parties in the proper way. That is, if it is in effect a dividend, it is taxed as a dividend ; if it is in effect a capital gain, it is taxed as a capital gain. If you just get other pieces

101 *National Income Tax Magazine* II: 210 (July 1924).

102 Adams, T. S., "The Economic and Social Basis of Tax Reduction," *Proceedings of the Academy of Political Science,* XI: 30 (May 1924). This remained true until the 1938 Act was passed.

of paper, and no more than you had before, then the original value attaches to those pieces of paper, and when you dispose of those and realize your gain, you are taxed, as if the reorganization had not taken effect.[103]

Another section that remained unchanged for some years (until 1932) was that defining income from revocable trusts. Before 1924 a taxpayer could "avoid" the income tax by creating trusts with the right to revoke the trust in favor of himself. The Treasury felt that gifts so well tied with strings were not a real parting with the income, and therefore the 1924 law made the income taxable as though the trust had not been created. Similarly, trusts were created for the purpose of paying insurance premiums. The 1924 Act provided that in such cases the part of the trust income applied to paying insurance premiums must be reported as gross income of the grantor.[104] This section also remained unchanged in the Acts of 1926 and 1928.

Discussion of methods of preventing individual surtax evasion by taxation of corporate surpluses ended in merely a re-enactment of the unsatisfactory Section 220. This provided that, if a corporation were created or used for the purpose of investing earnings, or if the surplus were larger than needed for the ordinary needs of the business, there would be imposed a special tax of 50% of the net income. The provision was strengthened by the clause that if a corporation were a mere holding company, or investment company, the fact would be considered *prima facie* evidence of a purpose to escape the surtax. Theretofore, the section had been ineffective because (1) it was impossible to decide what the ordinary needs of a company might be, and (2) net income subject to tax did not include dividends from other companies. The 1924 law attempted to overcome these difficulties by defining net income for this purpose as ordinary net income plus (1) dividends paid by corporations, and (2) interest on government obligations which would be taxable in the hands of an individual owner. These changes, however, proved inadequate.

A new provision was enacted that required posting the names of income taxpayers and the amount of tax paid. The Treasury Department did not like it and did not expect much from it.

Title III — The Estate Tax. Rates were graduated from 1% on the bracket in excess of $50,000 to 40% on the bracket in excess of $10,000,000. The maximum in the 1921 law was 25%. Both laws permitted an exemption of $50,000. The 1924 law permitted a tax credit of the amount of death taxes paid to states, but not in excess of

103 Winston, Garrard B., "Changes made by the Revenue Act of 1924," *Proceedings of the National Tax Association* 1924, p. 267. Detailed explanations of changes were made in the Gregg report cited above.

104 Legal interpretations of these sections are explained in Magill, *Taxable Income*, pp. 236-267.

25% of the federal estate tax. The 1924 law had a new provision to prevent tax evasion, the gift tax, at the same rate as the estate tax.

Title VII — Capital Stock Tax. The rate was the same as in the 1921 law, namely, one dollar per $1000 par value of capital stock.

Title IX — Board of Tax Appeals. This title described the membership and functions of the new Board of Tax Appeals, a quasi-judicial body to hear appeals in cases of additional assessment of income and estate taxes. The members, seven in number permanently (but for two years there might be as many as twenty-eight), were to be appointed by the President with consent of the Senate. The work of the Board is described in detail elsewhere in this study.[105]

Title X — General Administrative Provisions. This title was entirely rewritten to clarify many uncertainties of the previous law, such as a definition of control for the requirement of filing a consolidated return and the period of limitation upon claims, suits, and proceedings by taxpayers. A requirement was inserted for a report of the amount of the tax-exempt securities held by the taxpayer.

One new provision stated that:

> No taxpayer shall be subjected to unnecessary examinations or investigations, and only one inspection of a taxpayer's books of account shall be made for each taxable year unless the taxpayer requests otherwise or unless the Commissioner, after investigation, notifies the taxpayer in writing that an additional inspection is necessary.

Another provision amended the 1921 Act so as to bring about a closing of cases upon written agreement between the taxpayer and the Commissioner. In order to prevent a review of cases by the United States Comptroller, a section was enacted that forbade the review of a claim by any other administrative officer after it had been decided by the Commissioner.

Title XII — Reduction of Income Tax Payable in 1924. This title provided for a 25 per-cent rebate or reduction of the tax on 1923 income due under the 1921 Act and payable in 1924.

The effective date of the Act was June 2, 1924, but the income tax title went into effect as of January 1, 1924, the excise taxes thirty days after the law went into effect.

105 See below, Chap. XXIII.

CHAPTER X

REVENUE ACT OF 1926 – REDUCTION OF THE ESTATE TAX

In view of the major differences between the tax bill sponsored by the Administration in 1924 and the one passed by Congress it was inevitable that a Secretary of the Treasury as forceful as Mellon would not be content until the law was revised. To that end he used every influence. His efforts started at the time of the enactment of the 1924 law. The President, as has been stated, signed the Act with much reluctance. Doubtless at the instigation of Mellon he issued a formal apologia, a public statement, in which he enumerated his reasons for disapproving the Act.[1]

This was a period when big business was in the saddle. One of the wealthiest men in the country had been Secretary of the Treasury five years, the President's friends were those of wealth and his sympathies were with them and the property-owning class.[2] In Congress there was much the same point of view. The radical members were few and of little influence. The general dormant state of the public conscience was seen in the lack of indignation over the scandals in the government of the Harding Administration. In 1926 the same inertia was reflected in the Senate action on the estate tax.

ATTENTION FOCUSED ON THE ESTATE TAX

In his public protest against the 1924 Act, the President objected to the surtax maximum rate of 40%, the provisions for publicity of the proceedings of the Board of Tax Appeals, the publication of the amount of income tax paid by each taxpayer, but most of all to the increased rates of the federal estate tax, and the imposition of the gift tax, which he characterized as "a further invasion of the rights of the citizen."

In view of the interest of the states in inheritance taxes, the President suggested that it would be advisable to call a conference of their representatives and representatives of the United States Treasury before the next session of Congress to consider the possibilities of separation of sources of federal and state revenues and the prevention of overlapping and unfair taxes.

[1] *Report of the Secretary of the Treasury* 1924, pp. 4, 264-267; 1925, p. 346. Coolidge was not a student of taxation and knew little about it. He was chiefly interested in economy of expenditure.

[2] The Administration was described as "flat and dull," with less life and color and sparkle in Congress or in the Cabinet than for years. *New Republic* 46: 169 (March 31, 1926).

TABLE 11

FEDERAL AND STATE DEATH- AND GIFT-TAX COLLECTIONS, 1915–1939 [a]

Year	Federal		State	
	Collections	*% of total taxes and customs*	*Collections*	*% of total tax revenue*
1915	....	....	$28,784,000	7.9
1916	....	....	30,748,000	8.4
1917	$6,077,000	0.6	40,038,000	9.8
1918	47,453,000	1.2	41,432,000	9.0
1919	82,030,000	2.0	47,889,000	9.0
1920	103,636,000	1.8	64,647,000	9.2
1921	154,043,000	3.1	65,703,000	9.0
1922	139,419,000	3.9	70,503,000	8.2
1923	126,705,000	4.0	75,193,000	8.2
1924	102,967,000	3.1	83,697,000	8.2
1925	108,940,000[b]	3.5	91,171,000	8.2
1926	119,216,000[b]	3.5	96,052,000	7.6
1927	100,340,000	2.9	112,191,000	8.3
1928	60,087,000	1.8	132,599,000	8.8
1929	61,897,000	1.7	148,592,000	9.2
1930	64,770,000	1.8	180,794,000	10.1
1931	48,078,000	1.7	182,653,000	10.3
1932	47,422,000	2.5	143,746,000	8.8
1933	34,310,000	1.8	126,359,000	8.4
1934	113,138,000	3.8	92,240,000	5.3
1935	212,112,000	5.8	100,783,000	....
1936	378,840,000	9.7	....	....
1937	305,548,000	5.8	....	....
1938	416,874,000	6.7	....	....
1939	360,716,000	6.5	....	....

Year	Federal	
	Estate tax	*Gift tax*
1933	$29,693,000	$4,617,000
1934	103,985,000	9,153,000
1935	140,441,000	71,671,000
1936	218,781,000	160,059,000
1937	281,636,000	23,912,000
1938	382,175,000	34,699,000
1939	332,280,000	28,436,000

[a] 75th Congress, 3d Session, *Hearings before the Committee on Ways and Means on Revenue Revision* 1938, p. 133; and special reports for 1938 and 1939.
[b] Includes gift-tax collections amounting to $5,718,000 in 1925 and $3,175,000 in 1926.

Table 12

Number of Taxable Federal Estate-tax Returns Filed, by Net Estate Classes, for Years 1927–1935 [a]

Net estate classes, before exemption (000 omitted)	*Year filed*								
	1927	1928	1929	1930	1931	1932	1933	1934	1935
Under $100..........	......	......	......	......	......	......	2,644	4,037	4,522
$100 to $150..........	2,690	2,184	2,288	2,258	2,154	1,869	1,485	1,567	1,624
$150 to $200..........	1,232	1,026	1,189	1,236	1,112	893	729	714	696
$200 to $300..........	1,259	1,067	1,132	1,235	1,100	899	688	686	713
$300 to $500..........	837	884	998	1,006	908	701	467	450	534
$500 to $700..........	350	326	414	425	353	267	172	198	201
$700 to $900..........	181	167	221	257	198	147	83	109	112
$900 to $1,100........	105	110	137	132	110	86	63	53	63
$1,100 to $1,600.......	135	136	149	190	178	99	57	86	86
$1,600 to $2,100.......	55	67	79	98	86	49	29	26	33
$2,100 to $2,600.......	26	44	41	57	43	22	18	19	16
$2,600 to $3,100.......	19	23	29	35	26	17	6	8	15
$3,100 to $3,600.......	15	19	12	13	19	10	5	5	11
$3,600 to $4,100.......	16	11	14	16	14	9	2	12	8
$4,100 to $5,100.......	8	16	14	28	18	9	8	5	5
$5,100 to $6,100.......	12	12	10	8	13	7	4	1	7
$6,100 to $7,100.......	8	7	7	7	8	7	1	......	3
$7,100 to $8,100.......	1	3	3	7	4	2	1	3	2
$8,100 to $9,100.......	2	4	3	4	2	4	2	......	2
$9,100 to $10,100......	3	2	2	1	1	1	......	......	......
$10,100 and over......	7	8	16	15	17	6	......	2	2
Total.............	6,961	6,116	6,758	7,028	6,364	5,104	6,464	7,981	8,655

[a] 75th Congress, 3d Session, *Hearings before the Committee on Ways and Means on Revenue Revision* 1938, p. 133.

Two conferences were held, at one of which the President spoke. The general tenor of the discussion at the first one indicated that the federal government would probably not be persuaded to retire from the estate tax field as easily as the President and perhaps some of the states had hoped. Advocates of the tax commended its social as well as its fiscal purposes. (See Table 11.) Many states that needed revenue from their inheritance taxes were perturbed at the action of Florida in trying to lure men of wealth by passing a constitutional amendment to prohibit income and inheritance taxes in that state.[3]

In order to spread propaganda against the federal estate tax an organization was formed, first known as the American Bankers' League (presumably not connected in any way with the American Bankers' Association), later called the American Taxpayers' League. This association organized "tax clubs" in every state, but was particularly zealous in Iowa and Texas, possibly in order to influence

[3] *Proceedings of the First Conference on Inheritance and Estate Taxation,* Washington, D. C., Feb. 1925; *Proceedings of the Second Conference on Inheritance and Estate Taxation,* New Orleans, Nov. 1925, under the auspices of the National Tax Association.

or embarrass Green and Garner, the leading Congressional advocates of the estate tax. The membership of these clubs was made up of prominent business men, newspaper men and others supposed to have influence. The obvious intention was to bring pressure upon the Committee on Ways and Means, especially to induce the chairman to withdraw his support of the estate tax. Plenty of funds seemed to be available to organize tax clubs, hold banquets, and secure speakers. Sizable delegations were sent to Washington and entertained at the best hotels. The most ardent individual worker was Frank Mondell, at one time member of Congress from Wyoming.[4] He traveled extensively, had his speeches printed in attractive form for wide circulation, went to Washington to lobby before the Committee on Ways and Means and even appeared on the floor of the House. Apparently, however, he had small influence with that body. On the floor of the House Blanton congratulated Chairman Green on the way he "spanked him." "Mr. Mondell tried to create a spell over the Committee and Chairman Green simply made a monkey out of him." [5] Many of these lobbyists were state legislators. Members of Congress were almost shocked at the way they jammed the corridors of the House Office Building and the Committee rooms. Much of the force of their objections to the tax was weakened by their methods and by the testimony that their expenses to Washington were paid by the League.[6]

THE COMMITTEE ON WAYS AND MEANS STARTS TO WORK

Fortified with information from inheritance tax conferences and from public hearings as well as reports of the Administration, the Committee on Ways and Means [7] proceeded to draw up the Revenue

[4] Mondell was said to be acting especially for the estate of Senator Clark of Montana.
[5] *Cong. Rec.* 67: 948.
[6] In October 1927, the organizer of the League, J. A. Arnold, testified before the Committee on Ways and Means that his salary was $1000 a month.
[7] Members were:

Republicans	*Democrats*
William R. Green (Ia.), Ch.	John N. Garner (Tex.)
Willis C. Hawley (Ore.)	James W. Collier (Miss.)
Allen T. Treadway (Mass.)	William A. Oldfield (Ark.)
Isaac Bacharach (N. J.)	Charles R. Crisp (Ga.)
Lindley H. Hadley (Wash.)	John F. Carew (N. Y.)
Charles B. Timberlake (Col.)	Whitmell P. Martin (La.)
Henry W. Watson (Pa.)	Henry T. Rainey (Ill.)
Ogden L. Mills (N. Y.)	Cordell Hull (Tenn.)
James C. McLaughlin (Mich.)	Clement C. Dickinson (Mo.)
Charles C. Kearns (Ohio)	Robert L. Doughton (N. C.)
Carl R. Chindblom (Ill.)	
Frank Crowther (N. Y.)	
Harris J. Bixler (Pa.)	
Charles L. Faust (Mo.)	
Richard S. Aldrich (R. I.)	

Act of 1926. The members were much more unified in purpose than they had been for years. They agreed that there must be tax reduction for all brackets of income. The chief differences were over the surtax rates and the retention of the estate tax but the extreme conservatives, the followers of Secretary Mellon, were not so influential as in 1924. For example, Bacharach had swung from the side of Mellon to that of Green and, in view of their harmony of purpose, suggested that the Democrats and Republicans work together on the bill. This idea was carried out. It should be mentioned also that the extreme radical group was no longer represented on the Committee. Republican leaders did not invite to the party caucus those who had been followers of La Follette. In other words, they read them out of the party, so Frear was not given a place on the Committee on Ways and Means.[8]

The Democratic opposition to the Mellon plan was not very evident even before the Committee met, and after the compromises offered by the Republicans it completely evaporated. Senator Reed (Mo.) was almost the only member of the party to protest at the surrender of Democratic principles and only the radical press decried the loss of character of the party. Others looked upon the coalition of the parties as a desirable evidence of harmony.

THE ADMINISTRATION PROGRAM

As in previous years the Secretary requested first a reduction in surtax rates. This, so he stated, would be not only a means of tax reduction but a rational basis of tax reform, and a method of stimulating business. He repeated his belief that surtax reduction would eventually result in increased tax receipts.[9]

The aim of the tax system, according to the Secretary, should be to find the lowest rate that was consistent with adequate revenue. Such a point, "at which the most revenue could be derived with the least disturbance to business," had been variously placed at 10% and 15% but certainly it should not be over 25%. On the basis of a maximum surtax of 20% and a normal tax of 5%, which he recommended, the estimated loss in revenue would be $140,000,000 for the fiscal year 1927 and $100,000,000 for 1928.

Secondly, the Secretary asked for repeal of the federal estate tax for the reasons that (1) there was "no logical basis for the federal government collecting this tax" ; (2) it was essentially an emergency tax ; (3) the states needed the revenue more than did the federal

[8] Frear said he considered himself a member of the Committee but the chairman forgot to notify him of the meeting. He went to the hearings, at least, on the opening day, but only as a listener.

[9] 69th Congress, 1st Session, *Hearings before the Committee on Ways and Means-Elect*, pp. 6-7 ; *Report of the Secretary of the Treasury* 1925, pp. 346-355.

government; (4) the federal tax added to the "muddle" resulting in some cases in taxes of over 100% of the estate.

In the third place, the Secretary asked for repeal of several other taxes, chiefly the gift tax and excises on automobiles, admissions, and jewelry. The gift tax, he said, had proved to be not very remunerative and had resulted in the opposite social effect from that of the estate tax which it was intended to supplement. The latter was designed to break up large estates while the former tended to prevent that result. Opportunities for escape from taxes might not be so coveted if the surtaxes were lower, he concluded.[10]

The fourth recommendation was for a revision of the provisions for publicity of income tax returns. This section seemed to have resulted in no additional revenue, in the opinion of the Treasury, and had proved of no administrative value according to the reports of internal revenue collectors and other officials. On the contrary, publicity encouraged tax evasion, in Mr. Mellon's opinion.

Other matters covered by the Secretary related to the differentiation of the income tax rates on earned and unearned income, the rights of the states to render ineffective the federal graduated tax rates by community property laws, the most efficient number of members of the Board of Tax Appeals and the need of a Constitutional Amendment for abolition of tax-exemption of government securities.

When this report was made public, the press generally supported the Administration. Most of the papers had been behind the Mellon plan from the first and, since 1924, the prestige of both Mellon and Coolidge had increased. One correspondent commented on the fact that the original Mellon bill "had swung the newspapers to the support of Coolidge with a solidity that had not been shaken since." [11]

TAX REDUCTIONS PROPOSED BY THE COMMITTEE

The Ways and Means Committee program was, first, to decide how much tax reduction was possible. The Secretary had estimated $250,000,000 to $300,000,000. The Committee was skeptical of his estimates of tax yield which were proverbially low and, at the public hearings, had listened to requests for reductions of items that totaled $700,000,000. Although there was much talk of making reductions of $350,000,000, the Committee compromised on $325,000,000. It was then decided to reduce the surtax rates on individual incomes to a maximum of 20%. Garner had earlier expressed himself as

[10] According to Judge Green, men of wealth looked upon the gift tax as the most obnoxious tax on the statute books, except the estate tax. (Interview with the authors.)
[11] *New Republic* 44: 330 (Nov. 18, 1925).

favorable to a 25% maximum and agreed to the lower amount when the Committee, after some hesitation, accepted the Democratic proposal for increasing the personal exemption.

The next controversial issue to be settled was the fate of the estate tax, against which there had been so much propaganda. The Secretary of the Treasury did everything he could to have the Committee repeal it.[12] Chairman Green took issue with him on this point and, supported by public opinion as shown in the Delano report, and with the aid of Garner, put up a successful fight to retain it.[13] There was a general agreement to the reduction of rates from a maximum of 40% to one of 20%.

This victory was a tremendous one in view of the extensive and well-paid propaganda that had descended upon Congress and indeed upon the country, as described above. Green knew that the members of Congress from states of wealthy constituents — especially New York, Pennsylvania, and Massachusetts — wanted the tax repealed. He decided, therefore, to make a great concession to the states by increasing the credit for state death taxes paid from 25% to 80% of the amount of the federal tax. This strategy was successful.

The chairman succeeded also in killing a proposal for a rebate to be given to estates for taxes paid under the 1924 law, which was once adopted by the Committee but dropped when protests were received from the general public. The chairman failed, however, in his attempt to retain the gift tax, one of his own suggestions which had been adopted in the previous revenue act. At the time no one had much good to say for it. Even the author admitted that the original bill was not well drafted. From the fiscal point of view the yield had been small; but Green was doubtless correct in stating that the effect would be to increase the yield of the estate tax, in fact, the estate tax could easily be evaded without it. From an administrative point of view the Treasury disliked it, but this attitude may have been a reflection of Mellon's personal antipathy to it. Although the defeat of this measure was not pleasant for Green he did not feel that his position was materially weakened because of important amendments that were secured to close the loopholes

12 *Cong. Rec.* 67: 651. When Ramseyer (Rep., Iowa) appeared before the Committee a question arose in regard to estates over $10,000,000. The following colloquy took place:

Ramseyer: I have appeared here before you before, and I have urged you to ask the Treasury Department to furnish you all this information. I can not get it.

Garner: Mr. Ramseyer, in that connection, it is a little difficult, it seems, for the Treasury Department to furnish information that is not in accord with its views. That is the difficulty that I have had, and I think others have had the same difficulty. (69th Congress, 1st Session, *Hearings before the Committee on Ways and Means* 1925, p. 407.)

13 *Proceedings of the Second National Conference on Inheritance and Estate Taxation,* New Orleans, Nov. 1925, under the auspices of the National Tax Association.

in the estate tax law.[14] He had the satisfaction of seeing the gift tax restored some years later, that is, in the 1932 Revenue Act.

When the corporation section was reached, the Committee tried to find some way of giving relief to small companies especially ; so a sub-committee was appointed to consider the advisability of permitting certain corporations to file as partnerships and, on the other hand, to allow certain partnerships to file returns as though they were corporations. This provision was not adopted by the Committee, however.

The existing allowance of 50% of net income for discovery depletion was retained, but some additional restrictions were drafted to define a "proven area."

To improve the administration of the income tax the Committee recommended the establishment of the new office of Special Deputy Commissioner of Internal Revenue. Treadway had the same purpose in mind when he suggested the establishment of a joint group to study the operation, effects, and administration of the internal revenue taxes. The Committee adopted this idea and provided that the personnel of such a committee was to be made up of five members from the Senate, five from the House, and five from the general public. This proposal was somewhat of an answer to a very critical report of the condition of the Bureau of Internal Revenue made by Senator Couzens, a report that was discredited officially but one which could not be ignored.[15]

THE BILL IN THE HOUSE OF REPRESENTATIVES

Because of the prompt action of the Committee on Ways and Means as well as the desire of the Administration to have the measure enacted as soon as possible, the draft was ready for the House at the opening of the session. As customary, the House centered its attention on the more political phases, in this case the rate structure and the estate tax, accepting the prepared draft of technical sections.

Chairman Green's speech in reporting the bill was not merely an official report as in 1924 but a positive recommendation that the House adopt it. He explained first the changes in the income tax. The rates of the normal tax were reduced from 2%, 4%, and 6% to 1½%, 3% and 5%, respectively. Personal exemptions were increased to $1500 for single persons and to $3500 for married persons.

[14] The bill provided that all transfers made within two years of the decedent's death without payment of fair consideration would be included in the gross estate regardless of whether or not they were made in contemplation of death.

[15] This suggestion was enacted into law but has served a very different function from that which the author intended. The Joint Committee on Internal Revenue Taxation is now primarily a research organization to assist Congress in drawing up tax legislation. See below, Chap. XXIII.

The maximum surtax rate was reduced from 40% to 20%. A credit of 25% was allowed for earned income, and the maximum amount of income that could be considered "earned" was increased from $10,000 to $20,000. No change was made in the rate of the corporation tax (12½%).

Next the chairman explained the changes in the estate tax which were probably more numerous than those in any other section of the bill. When defending the action of the Committee in retaining the tax, he explained the pressure brought by organized groups to repeal the tax. Nevertheless, because of the competition started by certain states to attract wealth by reducing inheritance tax rates, the federal government could not withdraw from that field of taxation without throwing state systems into chaos. Furthermore, there was a strong element of justice in the fact that in most cases wealth was not derived from any one state but usually from many.

The next matter of importance discussed was that of administration of the income tax law. The chairman had spent the preceding summer in England studying administrative procedure and came home with the conviction that the English system was much superior to ours.

Much time was spent by the Committee and also by the House on changes in the section of the law that related to the Board of Tax Appeals. As the chairman confessed, many members of Congress had been somewhat reluctant to establish this Board, yet the testimony of accountants, attorneys, and economists at the public hearings was not only favorable but enthusiastic over the work of the Board since its organization. Despite the objection of several Committee members, the bill proposed life tenure and a salary increase from $7500 to $10,000.

During the general debate from December 9 to December 12, the most suggestive and critical comments were made by Rainey, Hull, La Guardia, and Frear who showed they had not been "steamrollered" into acceptance of the Committee report, which they did not hesitate to call the Mellon Plan, although it followed the Secretary's proposals in only a few matters. La Guardia frankly could not join the "feast of mutual admiration" on the bill nor could he justify the failure of the minority party to set up an effective opposition to the policy it had always stood for instead of acquiescing in a bill that was chiefly to relieve the rich. He scored the Committee particularly for repealing the publicity provisions.

Frear also enjoyed himself, not only in pointing out the weak spots in the bill but in chiding the Committee for having neglected to let him know of its meetings and in poking fun at the subsidized Texas and Iowa tax clubs that did their best to embarrass the Representatives from those districts. He was seriously concerned because there was no effective opposition to Administration proposals, with the result that the House was becoming "a rubber stamp."

Although it was generally conceded that the House would make no important amendments to the Committee bill, Lozier (Dem., Mo.) tried but failed to secure adoption of an amendment to restrict allowance for discovery depletion in order to correct abuse resulting from the lenient allowances. This "leak" had been disclosed in the recently published report of the Senate investigation of the Bureau of Internal Revenue which showed that oil companies had withheld from the government at least $25,000,000.[16] Lozier thought that Couzens, chairman and "promoter" of the study, had not "scratched the surface." Garner and Mills defended the Committee proposals as adequate to remove 90% of the administrative difficulties in this matter, inasmuch as they were based on the views of geologists and recommended by the Treasury.[17]

Rainey made an unsuccessful gesture to raise the maximum surtax rate to 25% on incomes in excess of $150,000 in order that the stamp tax and the excise taxes on automobiles might be removed.[18] Before the vote was taken, La Guardia offered an amendment to make the maximum 30% on incomes in excess of $500,000, but it received only 24 favorable votes.[19] Rainey's next step was to try to limit the personal exemptions to those with incomes of $45,000 or less.[20] The reason he offered this, so he said, was to see if the "Mellon Machine" was "so well oiled" that he could not break into the bill "at any point along the line." [21]

Ramseyer, who had been so successful in 1924 in getting the House to accept his estate tax proposal, could see no reason for the Committee reduction of the maximum estate tax rate in 1926 from 40% to 20%; conditions had not changed much in the year. He was, however, willing to compromise on a maximum of 30%, and introduced an amendment to that effect. He hoped to see the estate tax a permanent part of the federal tax system with rates left unchanged over a period of years. Mills led the debate in opposition to it. Although more discussion took place over this than over any other amendment, it too was rejected.[22]

16 69th Congress, 1st Session, *Senate Report* 27. The report was a severe criticism of the methods of the Bureau especially in determining depletion of oil wells and amortization of property purchased for war purposes. Although the study was started as a Senate Committee project it was monopolized by Couzens. Jones, King, Ernst, and Watson, the other members, took very little part. See below, Chap. XXIII.

17 *Cong. Rec.* 67: 773-777.

18 *Cong. Rec.* 67: 778, 791.

19 *Cong. Rec.* 67: 783.

20 *Cong. Rec.* 67: 887.

21 *Cong. Rec.* 67: 892-893.

22 *Cong. Rec.* 67: 941-943; 956-957.

Frear endeavored to secure re-enactment of the gift tax at the same rates as the estate tax but was unable to arouse any interest in his amendment.[23] Green (Fla.) went to the other extreme and introduced an amendment to strike out the entire section enacting the estate tax.[24]

The Committee amendments to the section on the Board of Tax Appeals drew forth some criticism. Many members of the House disliked the provision for life tenure; some objected to the increase of salary from $7500 to $10,000; others to the number of members and to the strict rules as to who might practice before the Board.[25] On the last day of debate the Committee, therefore, revised the bill so as to make the tenure of office fourteen years, but to make the terms overlap; the first appointees would have the following terms: four members, eight years; four members, ten years; four members, twelve years; and four members, fourteen years.[26]

On the 18th of December the amendments were completed and the House passed the bill by the tremendous majority of 390 to 25,[27] although Rainey fought to the last to increase the surtax rates and finally to recommit the bill.

THE SENATE FINANCE COMMITTEE MAKES FEW CHANGES

In contrast to the procedure in many sessions, the Senate Finance Committee[28] did not rewrite the House bill but contented itself with making very few amendments. This was expected inasmuch as it was a conservative bill, one that was satisfactory to the Administration except as to the estate tax, which it wanted to repeal. La Follette and McCormick who had been the chief objectors to Chairman Smoot's theories were no longer in the Senate.[29] Their places on the Committee were filled by conservatives.

23 *Cong. Rec.* 67: 1006.
24 *Cong. Rec.* 67: 959-968.
25 *Cong. Rec.* 67: 655, 731, 1127, 1129.
26 *Cong. Rec.* 67: 1125.
27 *Cong. Rec.* 67: 1164.
28 The members were:

Republicans	*Democrats*
Reed Smoot (Utah), Ch.	Furnifold M. Simmons (N. C.)
George P. McLean (Conn.)	Peter G. Gerry (R. I.)
Charles Curtis (Kan.)	Andrieus A. Jones (N. M.)
James E. Watson (Ind.)	Pat Harrison (Miss.)
David A. Reed (Pa.)	William H. King (Utah)
Richard P. Ernst (Ky.)	Thomas F. Bayard (Del.)
Robert N. Stanfield (Ore.)	Walter F. George (Ga.)
James W. Wadsworth, Jr. (N. Y.)	
William B. McKinley (Ill.)	
Samuel M. Shortridge (Cal.)	

29 Both La Follette (Prog., Wis.) and McCormick (Rep., Ill.) died in 1925.

Of the Democrats, King was almost the only one who made much opposition. The minority party, to be sure, held several parleys with Treasury statisticians to find out whether or not more tax reduction was possible than the House bill provided and in general they objected to the low surtax rates. On the whole, however, the opposition was not very vigorous. As if further to suppress any minority opposition, the national chairman of the Democratic party warned Simmons that the tax bill must not be delayed, and Glass (Va.) and Bruce (Md.) let it be known that they did not "sympathize with any campaign which would place their party in an undesirable light." [30]

More as a matter of form than with any hope of getting acquiescence, the minority members presented at one of the first meetings of the Committee the following "demands": (1) cut the surtax rates on incomes from $22,000 to $100,000, (2) repeal the capital stock tax, and (3) abolish the 10% levy on admissions. They were each rejected by a strict party vote, but the Committee later did accept the second proposition. At the same time, however, the corporation tax was raised by ½% of 1%; that is, to 13%, as of January 1, 1926 and by 1%, to 13½%, as of January 1, 1927.[31] Insurance companies were exempted from the increase.

It should be noted that the Democrats made no mention of the estate tax. It was common knowledge that most of them agreed with Smoot and Mellon on the undesirability of such a tax. The chairman was given support by several outside the Committee,[32] especially by the two Senators from Florida and by Overman (N. C.), who was openly trying to get relief for the Duke estate. So eager were they, and others, to abolish the estate tax that they won over the Committee, not only to recommend its repeal but to make a retroactive cut; therefore, the 1921 rates would apply to all estates that had been probated since that law went into effect, despite the provisions of the Act of 1924. It was reported that this inexcusable and uncalled-for rebate of about $80,000,000 was the price that the Democrats asked for their acceptance of the Coolidge-Mellon bill.[33] Apparently the price was very willingly paid; King was the only member of the Committee to vote against the proposition.

Just after this vote was taken, Chairman Green went to see Smoot to object to this serious amendment of the House bill, not only because of the fiscal loss but because it would kill the inheritance tax as a state tax. He thought that in ten years all the states would be forced to follow the example of Florida. Among the Senators, a few

[30] New York *Times*, Jan. 14, 1926. [31] New York *Times*, Jan. 12, 1926.

[32] Even before the Committee on Ways and Means met, there was published in the New York *Times* (Oct. 12, 1925) a list of thirty-two Senators who would vote for repeal of the tax. Twenty were Republicans; twelve, Democrats.

[33] *New Republic* 46: 71 (March 10, 1926).

such as Norris, La Follette, Jr.,[34] McNary, and Dill promised to fight against the repeal. McNary said he was sure they would be successful because he could not conceive of a western Republican daring to vote for the repeal of the tax.[35]

While the Committee was in session Senator Couzens published his completed report of the investigation of the Bureau of Internal Revenue.[36] The Finance Committee could not completely disregard its findings but in reality they paid very little attention to it. The counsel for the investigation appeared before the Committee and A. W. Gregg, Solicitor for the Bureau of Internal Revenue, testified as the representative of the Bureau. The Treasury successfully discredited the report on the grounds that most of the information had been procured from discharged and disgruntled Bureau employees and because of the personal animosity between Couzens and Mellon. The public had practically no interest in it.

Depletion of natural resources was almost the only part of the Couzens Report discussed by the Finance Committee. Some possibility of working out a new basis of taxing oil, gas, and other mining companies was considered, but eventually the percentage method was retained. The Committee was impressed, however, by the need for continuous study of the work of the Bureau of Internal Revenue, much as suggested in the House proposal for a joint committee of representatives of senators, congressmen, and the public. Couzens was very scornful of the paltry appropriation of $25,000 for the work and could see no benefit in having on the committee representatives of the public. He recommended, also, that the membership be reduced to ten, with five from each house of Congress, and that authority be granted to employ engineers, accountants, and other needed experts.[37] His suggestions were incorporated in the bill.

As a result of four important court decisions the Treasury requested the Committee to make many revisions of a technical nature.[38] Several amendments were made also in the administrative

34 Robert M. La Follette, Jr. was appointed to fill his father's seat.

35 New York *Times*, Jan. 19, 1926.

36 See below, Chap. XXIII.

37 New York *Times*, Jan. 16, 1926.

38 The United States Supreme Court in the case of *U. S.* v. *Robbins*, 269 U. S. 315, Jan. 4, 1926, held that in view of the legal interest of a wife under California Community Property Law, the husband was, under the federal income tax act, taxable on the entire income from community property and from his personal earnings. The Supreme Court also ruled on the year of accrual of the munitions tax for purposes of determining the year of its deductibility in computing net income. (*U. S.* v. *Anderson, U. S.* v. *Yale and Towne Mfg. Co.*, 269 U. S. 422, 1926). The Board of Tax Appeals "questioned the validity of the provisions in the income tax regulations which permit dealers in personal property on the installment plan to defer payment of tax until the cash is actually collected from installment sales" (Appeal of B. B. Todd, Inc., B.T.A. 762). The Court of Claims ruled in the case of *Toxaway Mills* v. *U. S.* (61 Ct. Cl. 363, 1925), that taxes collected by the United States after the statutory period had expired could not be recovered by a claim for refund for that reason alone.

sections as written by the House. The terms of office for the Board of Tax Appeals were decreased so that four members were to be appointed for four years; four for six; four for eight; and four for ten years. Almost the last act of the Committee was to accept the Democratic plea for a reduction of surtax rates in the middle brackets, that is, on incomes between $24,000 and $100,000.[39]

When the draft was completed, members of both parties claimed the victory. It was reported by the Committee that the reduction in taxes would amount to $352,500,000. Green did not agree. He charged that this estimate should be increased by $115,000,000 because the loss resulting from the repeal of the estate tax would be $110,000,000 instead of $20,000,000, and the loss from the capital stock tax would be $93,500,000, not $68,000,000.[40]

The Senate Committee report was in two parts. One was signed by the ten Republicans. The other was signed by King who expressed in some detail his own objections.[41] In the first place he pointed out that reductions for governmental expenditures had not been so great as "propaganda statements" had made out, that instead of economy, the demands of many departments were inordinately large. Secondly, he advocated "a rational, scientific, and democratic revenue system" that should be built upon the income tax, customs, and excise taxes upon tobacco. Sales taxes, justified for war needs, should not be imposed in times of peace. Neither the House nor the Senate bill went so far as the Senator thought desirable in repealing these excise and stamp taxes, a course that was possible if real economy were practiced. The Senator also opposed the repeal of the estate tax, the gift tax, and the publicity sections of the income tax. He did not approve of the distribution of reductions in the surtax rates or of the increase in the corporation tax. He thought twelve members were sufficient for the Board of Tax Appeals, that $7500 was a large enough salary, and that it was unnecessary to create eight new positions for the General Counsel of the Bureau of Internal Revenue. His report concluded with this statement:

> This bill carries no sufficient provision to correct the evils found and reported by the select Committee which has investigated the Bureau of Internal Revenue. The bill perpetuates the structural defects of the present law. The work of reforming the revenue act will have to begin where this bill ends.[42]

[39] New York *Times*, Jan. 17, 1926.
[40] New York *Times*, Jan. 25, 1926.
[41] Simmons made it clear to his colleagues that this was King's report for himself, not for the minority members. King was known as a chronic objector.
[42] 69th Congress, 1st Session, *Senate Report* 52, Part 2.

THE SENATE CONSIDERS THE REVENUE BILL

Chairman Smoot hoped that the Senate as a whole would act as speedily in accepting the report as the Committee had in writing it and announced, when the debate began on January 28, that he expected to have the bill passed not later than February 10.

Before the chairman could start his opening speech of explanation, amendments were offered and general discussion began. The Progressive group, now reduced to a few members led by Borah, Norris, and Couzens, drew up a plan of campaign to secure important amendments, chiefly to re-enact the federal estate tax and to impose higher surtax rates than those proposed by the Committee. Smoot was very much afraid they would delay the bill by a filibuster but Norris promised they would not do so "unduly."[43] Nevertheless, they did not want to be limited as to time. If it looked as though they could not finish it by the date requested by the chair, he thought it would not be difficult to insert a sentence that would permit the postponement of income tax payments from March 15 to April 1. Smoot need not have been concerned about the strength of the opposition. The Democrats agreed with the Republicans on most issues. Not even Couzens and Norris could make a stir. The general apathy of the members was typical of that of the country as a whole.

For one day there was some general discussion. The following day the Committee began to introduce its amendments. Except for several controversial sections that were passed over, most of them were accepted immediately without a roll call.

The debate, however, was not entirely without its exciting moments. One was occasioned by an amendment that clarified the law as to payment of interest by the government in case of refund of income tax. This opened an opportunity for Glass to call attention to a case in which the Bureau of Internal Revenue notified a taxpayer of an overpayment of $4065 but refused to grant interest except from the time a claim was filed for refund. The Senator launched forth on a terrific attack upon the Bureau and its methods. McKellar, bitterly antagonistic to the Bureau, agreed that its procedure was open to much criticism. He opposed the amendment to give the Treasury four years in which to make reassessment of tax, much more time than necessary. Two years should be enough, he thought. Chairman Smoot disagreed. There followed some very critical comments on the failure of the Bureau to finish reviewing cases that dated back to 1917, also on the secrecy that surrounded refunds and rulings. Reed (Pa.) reminded his colleagues that Congress

[43] *Cong. Rec.* 67: 2866.

should bear its share of the blame for passing laws that were so difficult to administer.[44]

Attention was again centered on the Bureau of Internal Revenue a few days later when Ernst presented the minority views of himself and Watson on the Couzens' report of the investigation of the Bureau of Internal Revenue. As stated above, the Finance Committee had received the report early in January but had paid little attention to it. Ernst was given time to explain some of the reasons for his objection to the report; for instance, representatives of the Bureau had answered many of the charges to the satisfaction of the minority members; in other cases the Bureau had not had opportunity to answer. The Senator reminded his hearers that when the amortization sections were written both Kitchin and Smoot warned Congress that greater discretion and power had never before been given to the Commissioner of Internal Revenue and the Secretary of the Treasury. Was it fair, then, to criticize them for exercising this power?[45] Couzens announced that he would reply to the Senator from Kentucky as soon as he had read his criticism. Smoot promised to give him time. Such an opportunity was never found, however, and Couzens created great excitement by charging Smoot with bad faith in failing to do so.[46]

Meanwhile, Couzens, McKellar, and Norris joined forces in delaying progress on the bill while they discussed for five hours the desirability of permitting publicity of income tax returns. Several interesting amendments grew out of this discussion but none was accepted. For example, McKellar proposed that exclusive jurisdiction be conferred upon the district courts of the United States to pass on claims for refund in which the sum involved exceeded $10,000, all claims for depletion and abatements, and all claims for additional taxes assessed by the government when the amount exceeded $10,000.[47]

The "well oiled machinery" of the majority rendered futile the efforts of King to make any change in the surtax rates decided upon by the Committee. The Senator reported much protest from taxpayers in these middle groups of income, $20,000 to $60,000, because they had been granted reductions of from 9 to 21%, while those with incomes from $60,000 to $100,000 were given reductions of 20 to 32%. Simmons, who was doubtless in sympathy with King's amendment,

[44] *Cong. Rec.* 67: 3014-3018. Green said some years later that the lack of system of the Bureau during the Mellon administration was well known. Subordinates stood in fear of the wealthy and were cautious in making adverse decisions affecting the large income taxpayers. This was not true before that time and it was not true afterwards. (Interview with the authors.)

[45] *Cong. Rec.* 67: 3414-3421.

[46] *Cong. Rec.* 67: 3526.

[47] *Cong. Rec.* 67: 3367.

explained why it could not be adopted. He said he had proposed to the Committee a plan by which the income brackets would be rearranged so that the spread between them would be $4000 instead of $2000, but the Committee wanted to avoid any unnecessary complications. Norris, too, was critical because the rates stopped at 20% and he notified the Senate that he would introduce an amendment to make the maximum 25%. Lenroot and Howell (Neb.) introduced similar amendments. Couzens agreed that the bill was not equitable. These few were, however, unable to break the domination of the Administration and all such amendments went down to defeat.

The vote on the Norris amendment for publicity of returns was not taken for several days after it was introduced, and every effort was made by both sides to get out adherents. The defeat was a blow to the Progressives.[48] McKellar had prepared an amendment to restore the provisions of the 1924 law on this matter but realized that there was no use in presenting it.

The next question debated was that most controversial matter, the estate tax. Fletcher (Fla.) made a long speech upholding the Committee action in repealing the tax and substituting the 1921 rates for estates subject to the 1924 tax. Simmons was particularly clever and subtle. He said that he was not actuated by the principle of relieving wealth. He considered the estate tax a proper source of revenue that had been fruitful to the government in the emergency, but since the emergency was over, the states should have it. Of course, he favored the retroactive reduction.

Caraway opposed a federal estate tax and also the principle of giving credit to the states. He even went so far as to say that he considered it "vicious" for the federal government to coerce a state. King offered an amendment to continue the tax but reduce the credit from 80% to 25%. He preferred a federal tax with low rates and with no credit to the states but he knew such a proposition would receive little favor.[49] But Lenroot, Norris, La Follette, and Borah supported him. The strongest speech of the day was by Norris, who named many large estates that would profit by the retroactive provision of the Committee amendment, especially the Duke property which Overman and Simmons were particularly anxious to protect.[50] Except for Norris the public would not have known of this outright

48 The vote was 32 yeas and 49 nays.

49 *Cong. Rec.* 67: 3601.

50 Some of the larger estates that would profit by this reduction, according to Norris, were those of: Frank E. Anderson, $5,727,000; Fred F. Ayer, $10,463,000; Anne H. Benjamin, $15,448,000; William A. Clark, $41,000,000; Mai Rogers Cole, $16,238,000; James B. Duke, $75,000,000; Isabella Gardner, $11,753,000; D. Herbert Hostetter, $10,844,000; A. D. Huntington, $22,163,000; Victor F. Lawson, $19,550,000; Jennie Woolworth, $59,738,000 (*Cong. Rec.* 67: 3669).

gift to the heirs of at least twenty millionaires. Nevertheless, the public was not seriously interested. Even the press was silent. So far as is known only one periodical protested the Senate action.[51] The rebate to the Duke estate was justified, according to Simmons, on the grounds that much of it had been left for educational and charitable purposes.

After the acceptance of the Committee decision to make the retroactive reduction in the estate tax rate, the Senate took up the sections on the admissions tax, at which time the chairman said it was necessary to retain the tax for fiscal reasons. Norris was perturbed and disgusted. The government had plenty of money, he said, when the majority wanted to relieve large taxpayers of death duties or when it came to considering publicity provisions that might bring in millions of dollars; but when it came to tickets for ball games and theaters the government needed money, and so the appeal must be made "to the poor people to give up their nickels and put them in Uncle Sam's vest pocket." [52]

Glass was successful in securing passage of an amendment which prevented appointment of former employees of the Bureau of Internal Revenue to the Board of Tax Appeals until two years after they had severed connections with the Bureau. This action illustrates the suspicion if not hostility with which many members of Congress viewed the Bureau of Internal Revenue.

The very technical subject of depletion deductions for natural resources occupied the attention of Senators for a short time. The Finance Committee had amended the House sections radically by abolishing discovery depletion for oil and gas wells and re-enacting the existing provisions so far as mines were concerned. "In the interest of simplicity and certainty in administration" the Committee proposed that taxpayers be allowed depletion deduction of 25% of gross income from oil and gas wells, but not over 50% of net income from the property.

Couzens proposed an amendment to exclude from computation of depletion such intangible values as were due to taxpayer's manufacturing ability, good will, or selling ability. Smoot explained that such allowances were not made under existing law and therefore the amendment was unnecessary; furthermore, the Treasury did not want it. The amendment was rejected, although Couzens insisted that the Bureau was not carrying out the law in that respect.[53]

51 *The New Republic* 46: 55, 71 (March 10, 1926).

"When the bill went to conference, Green strongly opposed the retroactive provision but was deserted by all the other House conferees, both Democrats and Republicans." (Statement of Judge Wm. R. Green to the authors, Sept. 26, 1939.)

52 *Cong. Rec.* 67: 3697.

53 *Cong. Rec.* 67: 3761-3777.

In the closing hours of the debate many individual amendments were offered but not accepted. Reed (Mo.) endeavored to raise the limitation on earned income from $20,000 to $50,000. McKellar proposed an estate tax of low rates. Shipstead introduced an amendment to prevent the sale of a taxpayer's homestead to satisfy federal taxes,[54] and Norris one to raise the maximum surtax rate to 25%.[55]

Democratic opposition was even less in evidence than when the Committee was drafting the bill. King received no support in his efforts to reduce the number of members on the Board of Tax Appeals, or to strike out the Committee recommendation for the creation of six assistants to the General Counsel. Only two party measures were proposed. One was to repeal the stamp tax on capital stock issues.[56] The other was to prevent the increase of the corporation tax from 12½% to 13½%. Neither was carried, though neither was of great consequence.[57] Just before the final vote was taken on February 12, Norris flayed the measure in short, cryptic sentences. It passed, however, by a vote of 58 yeas to 19 nays.[58]

THE REPORT OF THE CONFEREES

The differences between the House and Senate bills were very unimportant so far as the tax rates and most of the administrative provisions were concerned. The real battle was over the retention of the estate tax. On this matter the Senate yielded to the House and the tax was retained. An exemption of $100,000 was agreed upon, the rates were graduated to a maximum of 20%, but the Senate won approval of the retroactive reduction in spite of Chairman Green's objections to it. As a result the 1924 estate tax rates were also reduced so that the maximum for the years 1921-1926 became 25% as in the 1921 Act. On the whole, Green was very successful in securing acceptance of the House provisions except on this item. He said some years later that as he looked back upon that report he realized that he was fighting a great organized propaganda and that those who disagreed with him let him have almost everything else to force his acceptance of this Senate amendment. He had to make the report to the House as a matter of duty but he did so without recommending its adoption. The Progressives were asleep. Only one member of the House protested. Newton (Rep., Minn.), who was a conservative

54 *Cong. Rec.* 67: 2022, 3871.

55 *Cong. Rec.* 67: 3887.

56 *Cong. Rec.* 67: 3868, 3892.

57 Simmons stated that the minority had won every point it wanted except those just mentioned; in fact, that the Democratic party should have credit for writing practically the entire bill, although, he might have added, they would not get it. Never in his career, he said, had he, a representative of the minority party, achieved such a victory!

58 *Cong. Rec.* 67: 3896.

on most matters, denounced the amendment in severe terms as a gift of millions to the rich. No one could deny the truth of his statement, yet no one supported him. The work of the American Bankers' League and the rest of the propaganda had been fairly effective. The Conference Report was adopted by an overwhelming vote. The press gave further support to the statement made at the beginning of this chapter that "Big Business was in the saddle." Almost no protest was made.[59]

SUMMARY OF THE LAW [60]

The law was divided into twelve titles, of which I, II, III, X, XI, and XII dealt with the income and estate tax rates and administration.

The first title defined a few of the terms used in the Act. The second described the income tax. The rate of tax on individual income was reduced to 1½% on the first $4000 of taxable income, 3% on the next $4000 and 5% on the remainder. The surtax rates began at 1% on income in excess of $10,000 and increased to a maximum of 20% on income in excess of $100,000. The personal exemption for a single person was increased from $1000 to $1500, and for a head of a family or a married person living with husband or wife, the exemption was increased from $2500 to $3500. The $400 allowance for a dependent was unchanged. Earned income was permitted a 25% credit in tax rates and the upper limit of the amount considered earned was made $20,000 instead of $10,000.

The tax on corporation capital stock was repealed, and as an offset the tax on corporation net income was raised from 12½% to 13% for 1925 and to 13½% thereafter except for insurance companies. They had never been subject to the capital stock tax, hence the tax

[59] One exception was the *New Republic,* whose Washington correspondent wrote (March 10, 1926): "There is, as I see, less excuse for this refund to the twenty-odd great estates enumerated by Congressman Newton in his House speech . . . than for any other action of Congress in a good many years. The defense was lamentably poor and evasive. It was a weak and wanton thing to do and it ought to be kept fresh in the minds of the people, one way or another. But it won't be. Already it has practically passed out of the public memory and even at the time it made no real impression.

"This is probably the only political period in our history in which such a thing could be so easily done with so little protest and publicity. It was the most unashamed and complete surrender to great wealth that has taken place in my recollection. . . There were two particularly astonishing features of this retroactive federal inheritance tax action. One was that it was completely unnecessary. There was no demand for relief, no claim that an injustice had been done any group, no contention that there had been overpayment. . . The other extraordinary thing about this feature of the law was the coalition of Republicans and Democrats who got behind it, pushed it steadily through and by shrewd parliamentary tactics on the House side and a tacit and effective if informal understanding in the Senate, kept the names of the chief beneficiaries — the Duke, Clark, Begg, Woolworth and Fleishman estates — almost entirely out of the debate."

[60] 44 *Statutes at Large* 9. The other titles were: IV — Tobacco; V — Admissions and Dues; VI — Excise Taxes; VII — Special Taxes; VIII — Stamp Taxes; IX — Distilled Beverages.

on them was left at 12½%. The flat corporation exemption remained $2000 if the net income was $25,000 or less.

As in the 1921 and 1924 laws, affiliated corporations were permitted the option of making separate returns or consolidated returns, whichever they preferred. But once the decision was made, all future returns must follow the same practice unless permission to change was granted by the Commissioner. The 1926 law retained the 1924 provision that concerns were deemed to be affiliated when (1) one corporation owned at least 95% of the stock of the other, or (2) if at least 95% of the stock of the two or more corporations was owned by the same interests, but added the proviso that for 1926 and each year thereafter the term "stock" did not include non-voting stock which was limited and preferred as to dividends.

The law retained Section 220 which imposed a tax of 50% on net income of corporations that were formed or used to permit gains to accumulate beyond the reasonable needs of the business. Modifications were made so that the penalty would not apply if the stockholders reported in their individual returns the distributive shares of net income for the taxable year, whether distributed or not.

The section defining depletion was rewritten to restrict the deduction based on discovery value of mines to an amount not exceeding 50% of the net income of the taxpayer from the property. Oil and gas wells were allowed depletion, but not over 27½% of the gross income, and not over 50% of the net income of the taxpayer from the property.

As in the 1924 law, net losses could be carried forward two years. The method of computing capital net gains and losses remained as in the 1924 Act, but the 1926 law was much more explicit in defining the period for which the property was held. New provisions were made for determining gain or loss in case of sale of property received as a gift or in exchange for other property. Express provision was made in the definition of net income for reporting installment sales.

The list of exempt corporations was increased by the addition of "farmers' or other mutual hail, cyclone, casualty, or fire insurance companies or associations . . . the income of which is used or held for the purpose of paying losses or expenses." Stricter limitation was made of the exemption of farmers', fruit growers', and similar co-operative marketing organizations.

Many changes were made in the administrative sections, most of which were too technical to be of interest to the general reader. Among the more important ones was the amendment to the section on publicity of returns so that the Secretary of the Treasury was permitted to submit data contained in any return to certain committees of Congress, such as the Committee on Ways and Means of the

CHART 1

FEDERAL ESTATE TAXES * 1926-1936

Total Taxes Before Credit for State Inheritance Taxes
and Net Taxes Received by Federal Government.†

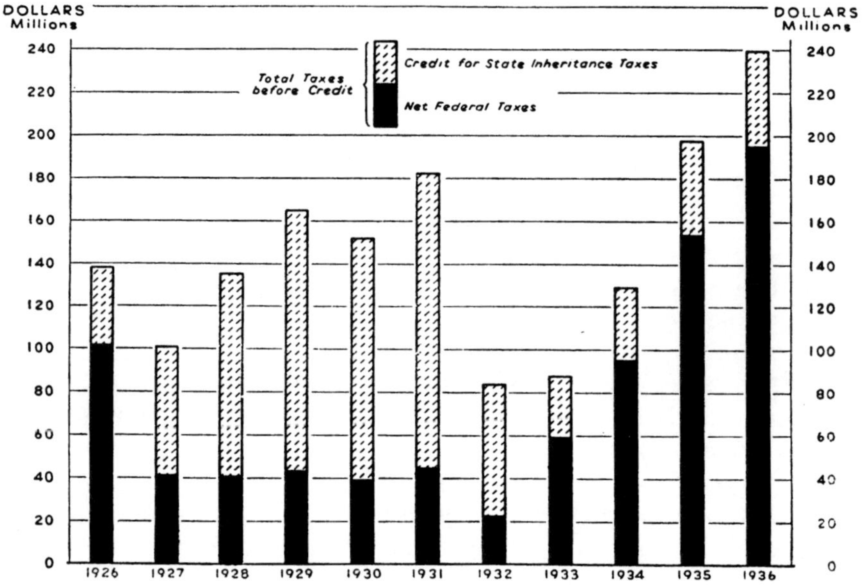

* Based on tax liabilities reported in Statistics of Income.
† 75th Congress, 3d Session, *Hearings before the Committee on Ways and Means on Revenue Revision,* 1938, p. 131.

House, the Finance Committee of the Senate and special investigating committees of either House "sitting in executive session," and it permitted such a committee to inspect returns "at such times and in such manner as it may determine." Certain officers were also permitted to inspect corporation returns, or an abstract of them. Collectors in each district were required to make available to public inspection the names and addresses of taxpayers but not, as in 1924, the amount of tax paid.

Slight changes were made in the additional assessment procedure. As under the 1924 Act, when the Commissioner determined that additional tax was due, a notice of such deficiency was to be sent to the taxpayer by registered mail. Within sixty days the taxpayer could file with the Board of Tax Appeals a petition to have the amount re-determined. The 1926 law specifically stated that, except when the Commissioner considered collection in jeopardy, no assessment of a deficiency could be made nor could any court proceedings to collect the tax be started until the expiration of the sixty-day period or after petition until decision of the Board became final. The

CHART 2

FEDERAL ESTATE TAX RATES

Effective Rates of the 1926 Act and the 1935 Act *

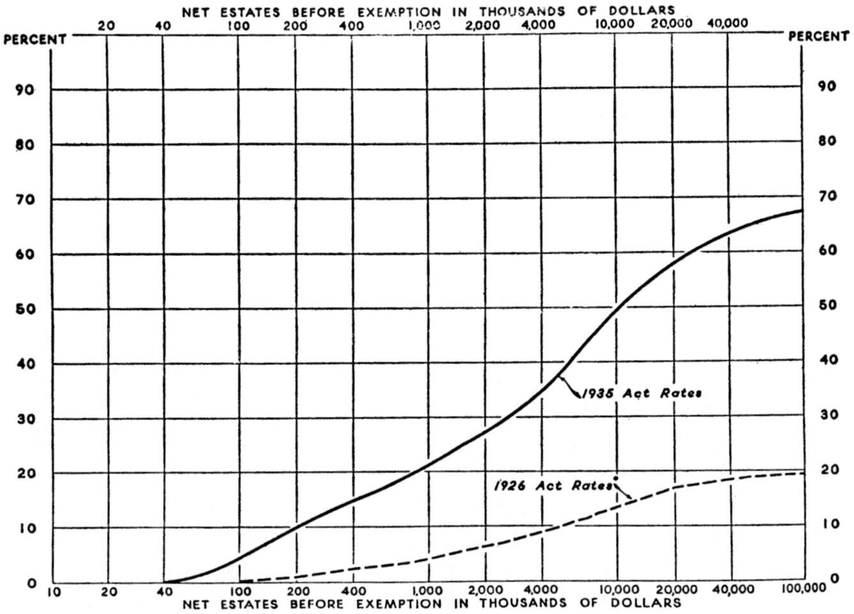

* 75th Congress, 3d Session, *Hearings before the Committee on Ways and Means on Revenue Revision,* 1938, p. 129.
Rates under 1926 Act are used to determine credit for state inheritance taxes.
(The 1935 law is still in effect, Jan. 1, 1940.)

Board was given power in the 1926 Act to determine the correct amount of the deficiency, even if the re-determined amount was greater than that of which the Commissioner notified the taxpayer. After the deficiency letter had been mailed the Commissioner had no power to determine any additional deficiency for the same taxable year except in case of fraud. The 1926 law reduced the period within which additional assessment of taxes must be made to three years, in contrast to four years for 1921 to 1924. The period of limitation had been five years for taxes under earlier laws.

Title III—The Estate Tax—increased the exemption from $50,000 to $100,000 and decreased the rates not only for 1926 but for estates subject to the 1924 law. As passed the rates of the latter were graduated from 1% to 40%. The 1926 law retroactively reduced them so that the maximum rate on estates over $10,000,000 was 25%. For estates of decedents who died after the 1926 law went into effect, the maximum tax was 20%. Each estate was permitted a credit for death duties paid to states, but not in excess of 80% of the amount of the federal tax. The 1926 law strengthened the provision of the 1924 law that transfers of property without consideration made within two years of death would be considered to have been made in contemplation of death. The gift tax was repealed.

Title IX — The Board of Tax Appeals. The Act reduced the number of members from "not more than twenty-eight" to sixteen, approximately the number that had been appointed. The salary of each was increased from $7500 to $10,000. The terms of all members then in office were ended June 1, 1926. The new tenure of office was twelve years, but, for the new appointees, four had six-year terms; four, eight; four, ten; and four, twelve-year terms. The 1926 Act removed the prohibition that former members of the Board could not practice before the Board for two years after leaving office. A fee of $10 was established for the filing of each petition. It was determined that all hearings should be stenographically reported and that reports should be made in writing in all cases except those dismissed, not only with respect to those involving $10,000 as specified in the 1924 law. Rules were laid down concerning the review of decisions. Appeals could be taken to the Circuit Court of Appeals for the circuit of which the individual taxpayer was a resident or in which the corporation had its principal place of business, or to the Circuit Court of the District of Columbia. The judgment of such court was to be considered final except that it was subject to review by the Supreme Court.

Title XI — Administrative Provisions — contained no changes of general interest. Title XII — General Provisions — created two new administrative organizations. One was the office of General Counsel for the Bureau of Internal Revenue in the Treasury to care for the duties hitherto performed by the Solicitor of Internal Revenue in the Department of Justice.

The other new organization was the Joint Committee on Internal Revenue Taxation, intended to be permanent, made up of five members from the Committee on Ways and Means and five from the Senate Committee on Finance. The law specified that the members from each house were to be chosen from both parties, three from the majority party, two from the minority party. The duties were:

(1) To investigate the operation and effects of the Federal system of internal-revenue taxes;
(2) To investigate the administration of such taxes by the Bureau of Internal Revenue or any executive department, establishment, or agency, charged with their administration;
(3) To make such other investigations in respect of such system of taxes as the Joint Committee may deem necessary;
(4) To investigate measures and methods for the simplification of such taxes, particularly the income tax;

(5) To publish, from time to time, for public examination and analysis, proposed measures and methods for the simplification of such taxes, and to make to the Senate and the House of Representatives, not later than December 31, 1927, a definite report thereon, together with such recommendations as it may deem advisable ; and

(6) To report, from time to time, to the Committee on Ways and Means and in its discretion to the Senate or the House of Representatives, or both, the results of its investigations, together with such recommendations as it may deem advisable.[61]

The income tax sections of the law took effect as of January 1, 1925; excise and other special taxes became effective at various stated times but, in general, February 26, 1926.

[61] The first report was made in the winter of 1927-1928. See Chap. XXIII below.

CHAPTER XI

REVENUE ACT OF 1928 – REDUCTION OF CORPORATION TAXES

THE SEVENTIETH CONGRESS

During the political campaign of 1926 tax matters were not an issue between the two parties. Secretary Mellon guardedly remarked in October that if there should be a business boom there might be some chance for tax reduction, but he did not expect a boom because business was then already very good.

Much surprise was expressed, therefore, at the remark of President Coolidge to press representatives on November 5 that there might be a rebate or refund of income taxes paid in 1926 on 1925 income amounting to 10%, 12%, or even 15% if the surplus reached $350,-000,000. He thought it might be desirable for Congress, soon after it met, to pass a joint resolution to go into effect before the next income tax installment was due. This remark, apparently made without consulting Mellon, was loaded with political dynamite. Both the Republican and Democratic leaders criticized the suggestion and the way seemed to be opening for much discussion of tax revision, a matter that Coolidge thought his plan would avoid.

The annual report of the Secretary of the Treasury showed that, despite the lower tax rates of the Act of 1926, receipts from the income tax were greater for 1926 than for 1924. Expenditures also seemed to be increasing because of aid to highways, public buildings, and the soldiers' bonus. Therefore the Secretary was very canny as to the estimates of surplus for the ensuing fiscal year ; and he stated that, even if there were a surplus, its existence would not assure the government of sources of revenue in excess of normal needs. He recommended, however, that Congress allow taxpayers a credit of 30% of half the year's taxes due in 1927 on income received in 1926.

In his opening message to Congress in December 1927, President Coolidge followed Secretary Mellon's cue and touched very cautiously on tax reduction. Admittedly the surplus would be large for the current fiscal year, about $383,000,000, and if it were feasible he would welcome some permanent tax reduction. There were, however, circumstances which made such a step impractical. It was estimated that the revenues for 1928 would be very little more than needed, the experience under the 1926 Revenue Act had been short, and much of the current surplus had been derived from nonrecurring items such as additional income taxes for prior years. He recommended, therefore, that both parties agree on a bill granting temporary tax relief.[1]

Green and the other Republicans on the Ways and Means Committee were doubtless relieved that the President had not used stronger language in urging his tax reduction plans. They saw the partisan political controversies that were latent in tax proposals; they knew the difficult legislative program that had already been agreed upon, and the session was a short one. On December 11, the Republican members voted unanimously against the original proposal of Coolidge for a 10% refund, against the Mellon plan for a tax credit, and they also refused to set a date for consideration of Garner's proposals. He stood for tax reduction of $300,000,000 to $400,000,000 by lowering the corporation rate to 11% and repealing the excises on automobiles, admissions, and club dues.[2]

This cut the ground out from under the militant Progressives who had expected to hold up tax relief until they had their say about farm relief. The Democrats, however, decided to press their bill regardless of Committee action by filing a petition to take it from the Committee. Such a procedure would require the signatures of a majority of the Representatives.[3] When this failed in the House, several Democratic Senators attempted to introduce amendments for tax reduction plans, chiefly to get on record the Republican vote against tax relief.

Norris proposed the following innocuous substitute:

> That it is the sense of the Senate that any surplus be applied to the reduction of the national debt.[4]

The resolution, adopted by a vote of 46 to 33, represented the final action of Congress for tax reduction in that session.

TAX REDUCTION AGAIN UNDER CONSIDERATION

As soon as the income tax collections for March 1927 were tabulated, it was seen that the Treasury surplus for the fiscal year would be a large one; in fact, as June approached, the estimate was as high as $600,000,000. The press reported that the Committee on Ways and Means would have a revision bill ready as soon as Congress opened.[5] There was even some talk of a special session. News of the large surplus was taken as an invitation by all groups to publish tax plans. Smoot came out for a corporation tax of 12%, a 50%

1 *Cong. Rec.* 68: 29.
2 New York *Times,* Dec. 12, 1926.
3 New York *Times,* Dec. 14, 1926. This was an old plan, but one rarely used.
4 *Cong. Rec.* 68: 2926.
5 *National Income Tax Magazine,* V: 140 (April 1927).

reduction of the tax on automobiles, elimination of the excise tax, and reduction of surtax rates on incomes between $15,000 and $60,000.[6] Senator Reed (Pa.) announced that the Administration measure would cut $300,000,000 from corporation income, inheritance, and nuisance taxes.[7] Democrats said they would re-introduce the Garner bill which had not even gotten out of committee in the preceding short session.[5] Undersecretary of the Treasury Mills came out for a repeal of the estate tax.[8] Fearful lest tax reduction once set in motion might run away into dangerous territory, Coolidge took the opportunity presented at the thirteenth meeting of the "Government's Business Organization" [9] to warn the nation that tax reduction must not go too far. He stated that, although the surplus for 1927 was about $600,000,000, that for 1928 would be not much more than half as large. In any case, such funds should be used for debt reduction.[10]

Chairman Green also gave out a statement to curb too great expectations of tax cuts. Both the President and the Secretary of the Treasury, he said, had pointed out that much of the surplus was made up of nonrecurring items. Furthermore, every indication pointed to heavy appropriations. The Senate had failed to pass the Second Deficiency bill at the previous session. This $20,000,000 would have to be cared for out of 1928 revenue. He anticipated large appropriations for flood control. If any reductions were possible, he thought that corporations had the strongest claim for consideration because their tax rates had not been reduced in 1926. Nevertheless, he warned that every one per-cent cut in the rates reduced the revenues of the government by $100,000,000. In fact he thought the government would follow a much wiser program by reducing the public debt which would distribute the benefit to all taxpayers and put the government in a strong position to care for any emergency that might arise in the future.[11]

Another setback to hopes for large tax reductions came from the report that the President had approved tentatively a budget of $3,316,000,000, exclusive of deficiency appropriations, relief for farmers, flood control, and additional expenditures for the navy. On the basis of the budget presented there would be a surplus of only $215,000,000.[12]

6 New York *Times,* April 24, 1927.
7 New York *Times,* May 29, 1927.
8 New York *Times,* April 3, 1927.
9 Sponsored by the Bureau of the Budget.
10 New York *Times,* June 11, 1927.
11 New York *Times,* June 23, 1927; interview of the authors with Judge Green, Feb. 1937.
12 New York *Times,* Aug. 14, 1927.

THE ADMINISTRATION ADVISES THE COMMITTEE ON WAYS AND MEANS

On the authority of a joint resolution that passed the House in the closing days of the Sixty-ninth Congress, Green summoned the members-elect of the Committee on Ways and Means to meet in October 1927, in advance of the opening of the Seventieth Congress even though the Senate had not approved the resolution.[13] The motion was similar to that passed in 1925 and, in the light of the importance of the revenue measure, the chairman did the expedient thing. The dates for public hearings also were set.

On October 31 the Committee had its first session with all members present except three Democrats.[14] The first witness was the Secretary of the Treasury who asked Undersecretary Mills to read his prepared statement. The opening sentence of the report cautioned the members to remember that, in drawing up the tax reduction program, it was necessary to consider not only the current fiscal year but the one succeeding also. Then he warned them not to be too enthusiastic about the amount of the surplus. Cautiously he admitted that there had been previous underestimates by his department, but they had not been made deliberately. Actually they were overstatements, because much of the increase was accounted for by collections of back taxes; without these items the estimates would have been too high.[15] In spite of the elimination of 2,000,000 taxpayers and reductions in maximum surtax rates from 40% to 20%, there was not a loss in revenue from the income tax, but a gain of $30,000,000. The Secretary used these facts to vindicate the theory he had repeatedly expounded, namely, that lower rates would be more productive than higher ones. He admitted that some credit must be given to the fact that business had been very prosperous in the preceding year. Mills interrupted his reading of Mellon's report to express his opinion that much of the tax increase was due to the sale of capital assets by taxpayers.

The Secretary laid before the Committee this five-point program:

1. Reduce the corporation tax from 13½% to 12%.
2. Permit small corporations, that is, those with incomes of $25,000 or less and with not over ten stockholders, to file returns and pay taxes as partnerships or corporations as they prefer.
3. Readjust the surtax rates on individual incomes from $10,000 to $70,000.

[13] The resolution was passed by the Senate March 4, 1927, but Harrison (Miss.) moved to reconsider the vote. This motion was under consideration when the Senate adjourned.

[14] Except for two Republican places, unfilled, the members of the Committee were the same as in 1926. Crisp, Rainey, and Carew, Democrats, were out of town.

[15] Treasury underestimates of tax collections and amount of the surplus had come to be expected. Mellon was naturally conservative and he and Coolidge would have been pleased to have had some surplus to apply on the debt. (Interview of the authors with Judge Green, Feb. 1937.)

4. Repeal the estate tax.
5. Exempt from taxation "income derived from American bankers' acceptances held by foreign central banks of issue."

He explained in some detail the basis for his program. Corporations, he said, had not shared in recent tax reductions equivalent to those of individuals; in fact, they had had little relief since 1922 when the excess-profits tax was repealed. Defending his renewed suggestion that the surtax rates be modified, the Secretary showed that the effect of the 1926 Act had been to benefit the large taxpayers and the small taxpayers, but not those in the middle brackets. Relief could be spread more evenly to all classes by the simple expedient of adjusting the rates so that they would rise uniformly, increasing 1% for each additional $4000 of income from $10,000 to $70,000.

The fourth recommendation, that for the repeal of the estate tax, was also a repetition of a request of previous years. Again the Secretary endeavored to show: (1) that this tax belonged to the states, (2) that it was an emergency source of federal revenue for war purposes, and (3) that the fiscal loss would be small if the tax were repealed. The Treasury logic was that, inasmuch as 80% of the tax was credited to the states in 1929, repeal would cost the federal government only $7,000,000. Questioning from the Committee on this point brought out the fact that from previously enacted laws the tax would produce about $75,000,000 for the fiscal year 1928, $65,000,000 for 1929, and gradually decline in five years to $20,000,000 annually.

The Secretary knew that there would be little sympathy for his proposal merely to reduce the tax on the sale of automobiles rather than repeal it. Two arguments were advanced in support of his position: (1) the federal government was granting large amounts for aid to state highways, and (2) the automobile was the chief competitor of the railroads which were very heavily taxed.

The fifth point, that relating to income from bankers' acceptances, was of concern to comparatively few. The Act of 1926 was not consistent in its treatment of foreign bank surpluses. It taxed at 13½% income of foreign central banks of issue received from bankers' acceptances but did not tax other income, such as that derived from surplus on deposit or from funds invested in short-time government securities. As a result, such banks were withdrawing funds from the American market and investing them abroad. In other words, it tended to force American merchants to finance their transactions abroad rather than through dollar acceptances.[16]

16 Interim 69th-70th Congress, *Hearings before the Committee on Ways and Means-Elect on Revenue Revision* 1927-1928, pp. 2-42; 70th Congress, 1st Session, *House Report* 960.

THE COMMITTEE ON WAYS AND MEANS REJECTS THE SECRETARY'S PROPOSALS

As usual, the Committee listened for several days to business men, manufacturers, representatives of organizations, clubs, chambers of commerce, and even of state governments, who wanted large tax cuts and also to representatives of farmers who wanted none. Then the members went into executive session to thrash out a bill that had to be ready in three weeks for presentation to Congress.

Chairman Green started with the presumption that the estate tax would remain, that corporation taxes would be slightly reduced, that there would be no surtax reductions for the middle brackets of income, and that the total reductions would be about $25,000,000 more than the limit suggested by the Secretary.[17] Speaker Longworth wanted a $300,000,000 reduction.[18] The Democrats accepted this program as a basis for a bill but disagreed on some details, especially as to the maximum surtax and the amount of total reduction.

The Democratic demands were reinforced by the Chamber of Commerce of the United States which issued a report, the result of a questionnaire to its members, asking for tax reduction of $400,000,000. They wanted corporation taxes cut to 10%, all war excise taxes and the estate tax repealed.[19] The President resented this interference and issued a reply. The condition of the Treasury was not such as to warrant such a reduction, he said, and if it were made there would be a deficit. He noted that the Chamber had failed to point to any measures of economy, but on the contrary were advising various departments how to increase their expenditures. The only result of their efforts would be to offer encouragement to the Democrats, and he implied that an organization with so many Republican members should know better. Green also resented the Chamber's demands.[20] The effect on the Democrats was precisely as the President stated. Rainey forthwith said he would like to see the adoption of the Chamber's program for a $400,000,000 tax cut. He charged the Treasury with deliberately stalling off tax reductions so that they might be made annually for political purposes.[20]

In the Committee sessions, both parties worked together. The differences were on details, not fundamentals, that is, on (1) the total amount of reduction, (2) whether the corporation tax rate should be 11% or 12%, and (3) whether or not cuts should be made in the so-called "nuisance" taxes. Work on the bill should have proved much

17 New York *Times*, Nov. 1, 5, 13, 15, 1927.

18 New York *Times*, Nov. 18, 1927.

19 Interim, 69th-70th Congress, *Hearings before the Committee on Ways and Means-Elect on Revenue Revision* 1927-1928, pp. 63-94.

20 Baltimore *Sun*, Nov. 26, 1927; New York *Times*, Oct. 10, 12, Nov. 26, 1927.

simpler for the Committee in 1927 than in previous years because the Committee did not intend to rewrite the bill completely, and also because of the usual Treasury draft of the technical sections and the helpful material at hand in the preliminary report of the Joint Committee on Internal Revenue Taxation.[21] Nevertheless, when even a few sections were changed many others were involved.

As in previous years the sections that evoked little partisan discussion, those that made structural and administrative changes, were considered first. Some time was given to the discussion of earned income. Collectors reported that about 10% of the errors made in individual income tax returns were those made in computing the credit for earned income. Several remedies were considered by the Committee. One was to reduce all the rates slightly and abolish the differentiation between "earned" and "unearned" income. This proposal was rejected because it would give a disproportionate amount of help to those in the upper income groups, a policy directly contrary to the purpose of the provision. Furthermore the Committee did not believe that Congress was ready to abandon the principle of differentiation between earned and unearned income. If there was any dissatisfaction, it was because the application had not been carried far enough.

With respect to the differentiation in favor of earned income the Joint Committee recommended substituting a 10 per-cent deduction from the tax base (net income) for the existing 25 per-cent credit against the tax, but this proposal was rejected by the House Committee because, although simpler to compute, it would favor large taxpayers and result in smaller revenue for the government,[22] while giving the general impression that the amount of credit had been reduced. With the assistance of Treasury experts Chairman Green worked out a simple table for computing the deduction on incomes in excess of $5000, which could be printed on the form filed by the taxpayer, but some members objected to putting anything more on the return. Some thought that insufficient time had been given to the consideration of the idea. Others hoped that perhaps in the

[21] This committee was appointed under the authority of the Revenue Act of 1926 to report to Congress in 1927 but was delayed in getting organized. When completed the Report was of three parts: (1) needed revisions in the law, (2) rearrangement of the law, and (3) a survey of the administration of internal revenue taxes. (See above, Chap. X and below, Chap. XXIII.)

The Committee on Ways and Means did not accept this report at its face value but carefully scrutinized the probable effect of each change. It was, however, more and more evident that Congress could not write the law in the last analysis, but must rely on expert draftsmen who were versed in the technicalities. In any case, the chief function of Congress is to formulate policy.

[22] Variously estimated at $15,000,000 to $50,000,000. The plan is explained in the *Report of the Joint Committee on Internal Revenue Taxation* (1927) 1: 31-39.

course of time taxpayers would become accustomed to computing the deduction as the law was written in 1926. The consensus therefore was to leave this section of the law unchanged.

The Committee on Ways and Means accepted, however, the suggestion of the Joint Committee to eliminate the privilege of filing consolidated returns after 1928 and to substitute a provision by which a member of an affiliated group of corporations might offset a net loss against the gain of another. This change was recommended to improve administration.

These phases of the law were only two items in a large program for simplification that was much talked about by taxpayers as well as by members of Congress. In view of the enormous amount of work involved, the shortness of time at the disposal of the Committee and the House, as well as the knowledge that the Joint Committee was at work on the problem – all these facts led the Committee on Ways and Means to decide against a general revision, much as it was needed.

From the discussion of the administrative sections the Committee proceeded to the more controversial and political part, the rate structure. The press announced that there would be a "big fight" because of party differences. Nevertheless, Green had the situation well in hand and there were no "radicals" or Progressives on the Committee to upset his calculations. By a strict party vote, Garner's proposal for tax reduction of $300,000,000 was defeated.[23] The same fate met his motion for a reduction of $275,000,000, but on this, one Republican voted with the Democrats. The amount agreed upon was approximately $250,000,000.

By a vote of 17 to 6 the Committee refused to repeal the estate tax, and by a vote of 21 to 2 refused to revise the surtax rates. The rates of miscellaneous taxes were reduced in most cases; a few were repealed, such as the stamp tax on sale of produce on exchanges, and the small tax on cereal beverages. The corporation tax rate was made 11½%. No change was made in the rates of the individual income tax because they had been gone over very carefully in the last revenue bill.[24] Garner wanted the effective date of the lowered corporation tax made March 15, 1929, instead of a year earlier. He believed, apparently, that as a general rule corporations had passed the tax on to the consumer, so that the proposed tax reductions would amount to a bonus of $166,000,000 to the corporations. During the hearings, Green and Mills tried to convince him that as a rule the tax could not be passed on to the consumer but came out of corporate

[23] Baltimore *Sun,* Nov. 22, 1927.
[24] *Cong. Rec.* 69: 403.

earnings and hence fell on the stockholder. Garner, unconvinced, replied that he would offer an amendment on the floor of the House.[25]

The Committee rejected the Treasury recommendation that small corporations be given the option to file their returns as corporations or partnerships because the members thought that relief should be granted not only to corporations that were small, in the sense that they had few stockholders, but also to those that had small profits. Therefore they decided to allow an extra exemption of $1000 (a total of $3000) to a corporation with a net income of less than $25,000.

The net result of the Committee draft was the acceptance of only one of the Secretary's recommendations, that for tax exemption of American bankers' acceptances held by foreign banks of issue. No minority report was filed.

THE HOUSE OF REPRESENTATIVES REWRITES THE COMMITTEE BILL

When Chairman Green reported the bill to the House on December 9, he stated that the Committee had been guided by three principles, namely:

(1) To keep reductions within bounds so that there would not be a Treasury deficit,
(2) To distribute the reductions "where relief seemed to be more necessary and advisable,"
(3) To give special attention to those taxes that had not been reduced since the war.[26]

Detailed explanation of the first point, that is, the decision to grant reductions of about $250,000,000, was made to the House by Hawley (Ore.). On the second and third points Green argued that corporations were entitled to much consideration. The war-time corporation tax of 10% had not been reduced, but on the contrary had been increased to 13½%, although the total burden had been reduced by the repeal of the excess-profits tax and the capital stock tax. The Committee proposed not only a reduction in the rate from 13½% to 11½% but also an additional $1000 exemption.

The members of the House showed much interest in the revision of the wording of the law made by the Joint Committee for convenient reference and also for the purpose of simplification.

Oldfield (Ark.) was selected by Garner to present the case for the minority party. Instead of making a long critical speech as might have been expected at that point, he enumerated the amendments that would be submitted, one of which would be for a further cut in corporation tax rates. He scoffingly alluded to the Republicans' fear of a deficit and recalled the annual underestimates made by the

25 Interim 69th-70th Congress, *Hearings before the Committee on Ways and Means* 1927, p. 36; New York *Times*, Dec. 3, 1927.

26 *Cong. Rec.* 69: 402.

Secretary of the Treasury in the past five years. Jacobstein (Dem., N. Y.) then explained his original plan for an automatic sliding scale of reductions of the corporation tax according to the amount of the Treasury surplus. This ingenious suggestion was not taken very seriously, because, for one reason, it delegated to an administrative officer an important function of Congress, namely, the decision of what the rate of tax should be.[27]

In a speech bristling with statistical data Hull showed that the current surplus was not due to the much-vaunted Coolidge economy but to numerous other forces, many of which were set in motion by the Democratic party. For example, the Federal Reserve system, the War Finance Corporation, and the farm loan system had been outstanding factors in stabilizing money, credit, and business, and the modernized sinking-fund law had been an important factor in reducing the debt. As for expenditures, the speaker showed that they had fluctuated comparatively little since 1922 but had increased about $150,000,000 within the past fiscal year and almost $600,000,000 a year since 1924. The most significant remark of the speaker, however, was that friends of direct taxation should take warning that there would be a fight on the income tax principle within the next few years much as there had been in 1921. He added that there could be no complete or permanent tax relief until tariff rates were lowered.[28]

After two days of general debate that raised few fundamental questions the House worked on amendments in Committee of the Whole. Just as the Committee on Ways and Means disregarded the Treasury proposals, so the Democrats made merry with the Committee proposals. One of the first and most radical changes was acceptance of Garner's plan to graduate the tax on corporations as follows :

(1) 5% on net income of $7000,
(2) 7% on net income over $7000 and not over $12,000,
(3) 9% on net income over $12,000 and not over $15,000,
(4) 11½% on the remainder.

Treasury experts estimated that this schedule would reduce the federal revenue by $24,000,000. Garner submitted the amendment because he was dissatisfied with the Committee treatment of small corporations. Green explained that he had been just as eager as Garner to do something for the small corporations but he wanted to do "something logical," something that would not "plague us in the future." The idea of graduating a corporation tax did not strike him as logical. In spite of his protest the amendment was adopted by a

27 *Cong. Rec.* 69: 425-430.

28 *Cong. Rec.* 69: 432-435. Hull thus forecast the fight for a sales tax and for additional tariff in the tax debates of 1932.

close vote.[29] Green explained some years later that this feature appealed to those who thought that some corporations were getting too large for the good of the country.[30]

Garner succeeded also in securing a majority vote for his surprise amendment to strike out the section relative to affiliated corporations. The Committee draft prohibited the filing of consolidated returns after 1927 and substituted a provision by which certain corporations could take advantage of affiliations to deduct net loss of one from net profits of another. Many members felt this gave undue advantage to large corporations, for example, to the United States Steel Corporation and the Standard Oil Company. Green, caught off his guard by this move of Garner,[30] tried to show that these large corporations did not favor this substitution but preferred the former law. Black (Tex.), among others, was incredulous. He claimed that if the Committee proposal were enacted into law a company could "hunt up an affiliated company that had losses and take advantage of these losses upon their own corporate return," an advantage that would redound to the benefit of chains and other large groups that already were making serious competition for the independent company. No one supported Green by speaking for the measure, so another Committee amendment was rejected.[31]

When the estate tax sections came up for discussion, Merritt (Conn.) introduced an amendment to repeal the tax, but was not successful in having it adopted. Green (Fla.) spoke at some length in favor of it on the grounds that the federal estate tax "had wrought havoc in Florida," and resulted in that state's paying an undue proportion of the tax and causing great resentment against the federal government's policy of trying to force the states into a uniform tax system. Rainey replied that the member from Florida had given the best possible reason for maintaining the tax, namely, that a millionaire's estate paid the same tax wherever it was located. He characterized the fight to repeal the tax as "the last charge of the tax dodgers' brigade." [32]

Garner called attention to the Committee substitute for Section 220 of the 1926 law to prevent surtax evasion by use of the corporate form of organization. He stated that the Treasury had been uninterested in enforcing this provision because the Secretary was not in sympathy with it. It had been a subject of discussion in every session of Congress that had considered a tax bill and would become more serious in later years. The Joint Committee, after devoting some time to a study of the matter, came to a conclusion in 1927

[29] *Cong. Rec.* 69: 501-504. The vote was 136 yeas, 132 nays. There was no roll call.
[30] Interview with Judge Green, Feb. 1937.
[31] *Cong. Rec.* 69: 601-605.
[32] *Cong. Rec.* 69: 615-616, 626-629.

that the House Committee would not accept, namely, that the tax should be graduated according to the amount of income withheld from distribution. Garner wanted this plan adopted but Green explained that it did not seem to be a solution because it would penalize those who were honestly trying to build up legitimate surpluses.[33] The Committee decided to retain Section 220, and to add a new section which made a distinction between personal holding companies and other corporations, and to impose an additional tax of 25% upon net income if such a company permitted its undistributed profits to exceed 30% of the sum of its net income, dividends, and tax-free interest. Green admitted he was not entirely satisfied with the Committee proposal, but no one seemed to be able to offer anything better. The House accepted it without any objection.[34]

On the last day of debate, Chairman Madden of the Appropriations Committee offered an amendment to strike out the section to give the Secretary of the Treasury authority to increase compensation of certain of the men in the higher ranks of the Bureau of Internal Revenue. He feared that the Committee proposal would lead to the creation of an "aristocracy" in the Treasury where, he claimed, employees had been favored already. Garner assured the House that there was need of some action to give the Treasury an adequate force to settle the 19,000 cases still pending. Green explained that so far as salaries were concerned only $70,000 was involved, a mere "flyspeck," but in reality a much larger sum was involved, $550,000,000, the amount at stake in cases before the Board of Tax Appeals. He showed that any cases that could be settled before they were sent to the Board saved money for the government, and that cases could not be settled by $3000-a-year auditors. The Committee recommended the appointment of twenty-three assistants to the General Counsel at $7500 each, twenty-six administrative or technical employees at $7500 each and fifty administrative or technical experts at $6000 a year each. The House sustained the Committee proposal.[35]

There were a few rejected amendments of some interest. As in 1925, Mrs. Norton (Dem., N. J.) tried to secure favorable action on a proposal to increase the exemption of married persons from $3500 to $5000 and that of single persons from $1500 to $3000.[36] McSwain (S. C.) presented an amendment to permit the deduction of medical and funeral expenses "not exceeding $1000." [37] La Guardia intro-

[33] This matter was to be debated many times in subsequent sessions, especially in 1936. See below, Chap. XVII.

[34] *Cong. Rec.* 69: 518-521.

[35] *Cong. Rec.* 69: 712-713. The average salary then was between $4500 and $5000; only three employees received over $6000.

[36] *Cong. Rec.* 69: 511.

[37] *Cong. Rec.* 69: 508.

duced an amendment to add one more bracket to the surtax rates so that the tax on income over $1,500,000 would be 30%.[38]

On the last day devoted to the bill, December 15, Chairman Green made a futile effort to reassert his leadership. He demanded separate votes on three of the amendments voted in the Committee of the Whole : the graduated tax on corporation net income, the repeal of the section on affiliated corporations, and the repeal of the tax on automobiles. To his mortification all amendments were again passed. So changed was the bill from that presented by the Committee that Republican leaders tried to recommit it.

On the final vote the bill received 366 yeas and 24 nays.[39] Garner asked that representatives of the Democratic party be selected to confer with the Senate "in view of the fact that the minority had predominated in the consideration of this bill."

THE SENATE FINANCE COMMITTEE DELAYS CONSIDERATION

It was estimated that the bill as passed by the House would reduce taxes by about $290,000,000, a much greater sum than the Administration had recommended. Undersecretary of the Treasury Mills, addressing the American Institute of Bankers on December 19, scored the House bill as a serious menace to the balancing of the federal budget. He said that taxes were not an unbearable burden, that there had been several reductions since 1921, and hence there was no conceivable excuse for incurring the risk of an unbalanced budget which would mean "the serious interruption of a reasonable and moderate program of debt reduction." [40] Coolidge also disapproved of the bill and Smoot agreed with him.

Using the excuse that, if the Senate Finance Committee [41] waited

[38] *Cong. Rec.* 69: 500.

[39] *Cong. Rec.* 69: 717. Of the 24 who voted against the bill, 21 were Republicans, one a Democrat, one a Socialist, one a Farmer-Laborite. A Washington correspondent wrote : "It was an amazing performance, one of the most remarkable exhibitions of lack of administrative strength and party leadership given by an administration remarkable for the absence of both. The minority became the majority and the administration bill was simply shot to pieces. . . I do not recall, however, any instance where, with his own party in control by a clear twenty-eight votes a President has been so contemptuously treated by the House." *New Republic,* 53: 191 (Jan. 4, 1928).

[40] New York *Times,* Dec. 20, 1927. See also his speech before the Chicago and Cook County Bankers' Association, March 29, 1928. (*Report of the Secretary of the Treasury* 1928, pp. 291-296.)

[41] The members of the Committee were :

Republicans	*Democrats*
Reed Smoot (Utah), Ch.	Furnifold M. Simmons (N. C.)
George P. McLean (Conn.)	Andrieus A. Jones (N. M.)
Charles Curtis (Kan.)	Peter G. Gerry (R. I.)
David A. Reed (Pa.)	Pat Harrison (Miss.)
Samuel Shortridge (Cal.)	William H. King (Utah)
Walter E. Edge (N. J.)	Thomas F. Bayard (Del.)
James Couzens (Mich.)	Walter F. George (Ga.)
Simeon D. Fess (Ohio)	David I. Walsh (Mass.)
Frank L. Green (Vt.)	Alben W. Barkley (Ky.)
Charles S. Deneen (Ill.)	

until later to take up the measure, the Treasury would have more adequate data on which to base estimates of tax receipts, the chairman agreed to postpone action until after March 15. It was charged that this delay was arranged in order to sidetrack tax cuts, but the Democrats were unable to line up any Republican support to defeat the motion to defer action when it was voted upon in the Committee.

On the floor of the House, Garner made several charges that the delay in the action of the Senate was due to the fact that the Mellon interests would have to pay much heavier taxes if the provisions for consolidated returns were repealed; [42] but these personal remarks were discounted and, as a matter of fact, many Democrats were pleased because they did not want the reductions applicable to corporation taxes due in 1928 on income received in 1927. Treadway labeled such talk as "too low demagogism to bear." [43]

Early in April Secretary Mellon published reduced estimates of the amount of possible tax reduction on the basis of income tax returns of March 15. He recommended tax cuts of $181,000,000 or perhaps of even $201,000,000, an amount less than in the preceding fall because of increased expenditures. He gave his approval to the following House provisions: (1) increasing the corporation exemption to $3000, (2) increasing the exemption on tickets of admission, (3) repealing the beverage tax, and (4) reducing the tax on wines. He disapproved the graduated corporation tax and the repeal of the automobile tax.

On the basis of a surplus of $212,000,000 he recommended that: (1) the corporation tax be reduced to 12%; (2) the surtax be reduced in the income brackets between $14,000 and $75,000; (3) the federal estate tax be repealed; and (4) income from American bankers' acceptances held by foreign banks of issue be exempt from tax.[44] The fact that it was an election year predisposed Congress to reduce taxes but there were certain opposing factors that had to be taken into consideration. The business recession of 1927 was certain to reduce the tax yield. Furthermore, Congress had not taken final action on a billion-dollar naval bill or on smaller appropriations for agricultural relief, flood relief, public buildings, or the public works program for unemployment relief.[45] On the other hand, there were indications that the Democrats and Progressives would combine to force as great tax reductions in the Senate as in the House.

Some evidence that the Administration was uneasy over the outcome of the bill is seen in the removal of Chairman Green from the

42 *Cong. Rec.* 69: 1531-1532. The House bill provided for the abolition of consolidated returns after 1928.

43 *Cong. Rec.* 69: 1604-1606.

44 *Report of the Secretary of the Treasury* 1928, pp. 296-304.

45 *National Income Tax Magazine*, 6: 102 (March 1928).

House of Representatives. Green was from the Middle West but was not one of the radical Republicans. He was, nevertheless, independent in his thinking and in his actions. He favored higher taxation on large incomes and while he was chairman of the Committee his influence was so strong with the House that it was impossible to obtain the repeal of the estate tax as desired by the President and Secretary Mellon. He was a strong believer in upholding the prerogative of the House to initiate revenue measures. In 1924 particularly he had steered his own bill through the legislative maze, a bill that was not exactly what the Administration wanted. In 1928, as has been shown, the House bill was also very different from that which the Administration had requested. Apparently the President and Secretary Mellon thought that the chairmanship of the important Committee on Ways and Means should be in "safe" hands. In February the President tendered Green an appointment to the United States Court of Claims. Green had not solicited the position but he had become tired of the constant conflict with the Administration and also was somewhat disappointed at the failure of the Republicans on the Committee to support him when votes were taken in the House, as he thought they should. Consequently, he accepted the appointment, which was promptly confirmed by the Senate.

The news that Green was leaving the House was particularly unwelcome to those who opposed the repeal of the estate tax. Perhaps, however, it revived their alertness. It was said at the time that the Senate Finance Committee was made conscious of the danger to which the whole bill would be exposed if the estate tax were repealed.[46]

Early in April the Finance Committee began the revision of the House bill. The members were much more favorable to Mellon than those of the House Committee had been. By the first vote the rate of the corporation tax was placed at 12½%, practically that requested, and the Democrats' motion for an 11 per-cent rate was defeated.[47] Then the Committee began to undo the work of the House on other sections. The surtax rates in the middle brackets were reduced ; the Garner plan for a graduated income tax on corporations was turned down as "unsound and without justification from either a theoretical or practical point of view" ; the privilege of filing consolidated returns was restored ; the new section for an additional tax on personal holding companies was eliminated, and many of the retroactive administrative provisions of the House were either amended so as to apply only to the future or were struck out altogether.[48]

[46] *National Income Tax Magazine,* 6: 184 (May 1928).
[47] New York *Times,* April 5, 1928.
[48] 70th Congress, 1st Session, *Senate Report* 960.

The Committee did not follow Secretary Mellon's requests entirely, however ; for example, the estate tax was not repealed, largely because of Couzens' efforts and the pressure from the House.[49] The tax on automobiles was repealed. The total reduction, $210,000,000, was, however, approximately that recommended by the Treasury.

THE BILL IN THE SENATE

The majority party in the Senate was in the uncomfortable position of not having a majority ! Due to the fact that Smith (Ill.) and Vare (Pa.) were refused seats because of corrupt election practices only 47 Republicans were present. There were 46 Democrats and one Farmer-Laborite. The Democrats had been asked to organize the Senate but they had the political sagacity to refuse.

Fortunately, tax reduction was not a party issue in the Senate ; both sides wanted it, just as in the House. Indeed, the Democrats wanted greater cuts than the Republicans. There were, however, two other matters that were likely to cause trouble for the Republican leaders, the tariff and farm relief. It was rumored that sponsors of these measures were planning to attach riders to the tax bill. It was also current gossip that such riders might be added for the very purpose of getting the President to veto the bill if the conservative element tried to defeat tax reductions.[50] The regular Republicans on the Senate Finance Committee exacted a promise from the Democratic members to oppose such riders, particularly those dealing with the tariff.[51] This agreement, however, did not prevent other members from raising the issue.

Chairman Smoot reported the bill out of Committee May 1 [52] and called it up for consideration on May 3. Before he could make his usual speech of explanation, King asked if it were not true that a majority of the Committee were in favor of repealing the estate tax even though they had not voted that way. Smoot disregarded the question and proceeded with his explanation of the bill. Brookhart (Ia.), one of the most zealous of the farm bloc members, questioned the advisability of any tax reduction, even if the surplus was $212,000,000, inasmuch as appropriations were at least $3,642,000,000,

49 New York *Times,* April 25, 1928. King said on the floor of the Senate that a majority favored repealing the tax but "certain considerations led them to take a different course." (*Cong. Rec.* 69: 7704.) On April 27 it was reported that Hawley and Bacharach of the House, who would be on the Conference Committee, informed Senate leaders that under no circumstance would the House agree to the repeal of the estate tax. To insist upon it would be to jeopardize the entire bill (New York *Times,* April 27, 1928).

50 *National Income Tax Magazine* 6: 102 (March 1928).

51 *Cong. Rec.* 69: 9304.

52 *Cong. Rec.* 69: 7501.

a sum that did not take into account a farm bill of $400,000,000, which, to be sure, had not passed. The Senator indulged in a long declamation against the moneyed interests that preyed on agriculture and protested against further reduction of taxes "on the millionaires of the country who have gained their profits from the farmers of Iowa." [53]

As Simmons did not care to make a set speech, Harrison presented the Democratic criticism of the debt reduction policy of the Treasury and of the Treasury estimates of surpluses. This subject could always stir up political controversy as to the accuracy of official forecasts. Harrison thought the condition of the Treasury warranted a tax cut of at least $325,000,000. He advocated debt reduction "in an orderly certain way," but not so fast as the Treasury planned because it was not fair to American taxpayers to load them down with heavy taxes just to pay off the debt sooner.[54] It was amazing how interested Congress was in the technical problem of debt reductions, in fact, how much discussion there was by the general public as well as by legislators. This subject led very naturally to discussions of the repayment of foreign loans and appropriations for the United States army and navy.

After two days of general debate the Senate, in Committee of the Whole, considered amendments to the bill. According to common practice, those on which there was no disagreement were passed and those that were controversial were postponed.

The strength of the Democratic party was shown in the passage of the amendment to reinstate the House provision for the graduated tax on corporate income. Simmons' argument for it was that it would help the small corporation. Smoot called attention to the Committee's reasons for striking out this tax. He said that, while graduated rates were justified as a correct measure of ability to pay on the part of individuals, the size of corporation income did not reflect its ability to pay because it did not take into account the amount of invested capital. He pointed out that the employment of a tax system that involved the determination of invested capital would mean a return to the excess-profits tax, which had certainly not been a success. There was little discussion of the proposal but it secured a bare majority of votes.[55]

When the Senate reached the section which made the corporation tax rate 12½%, instead of 11½%, as provided in the House bill, the Democrats made a fight for the latter figure. Smoot insisted that the Treasury could not stand such a cut in addition to the other reduc-

[53] *Cong. Rec.* 69: 7704-7711.
[54] *Cong. Rec.* 69: 7793-7799.
[55] *Cong. Rec.* 69: 8501-8504.

tions already voted. Harrison quoted the figures of the United States Chamber of Commerce to show that Smoot was underestimating the Treasury surplus. The Republicans were successful, however, in securing forty votes for agreement to the Committee rate.[56]

The most controversial matter was the estate tax. Borah expressed the feeling of many when he requested that those who wanted to repeal the estate tax should desist from trying to do so at that time. He said that debate on the issue would occupy three or four days, that some of his colleagues did not care whether or not there was any tax reduction; but if an attempt was made to repeal the tax, it might change their attitude.[57] This speech did not deter Bingham (Conn.) from introducing his amendment for repeal.[58] The Senator argued on the basis of state rights that the estate tax was a state rather than a federal matter. King opposed him, saying that the federal tax did not force the states, and that the movement for repealing the federal tax was part of a much larger drive for repealing the state inheritance taxes. Bingham denied knowing of any such drive. He was supported by Metcalf (R. I.), Fletcher (Fla.), and Reed (Pa.). As has been stated, Reed was an intimate friend of Mellon and was looked upon as his spokesman in the Senate. Nevertheless, Bingham's amendment was rejected. He immediately produced another to reduce the federal rates to one-fifth of those in the 1926 law and to repeal the provision granting the 80 per-cent credit for state death taxes. Borah insisted that there were really two propositions in this motion and that there should be two votes. Both of these amendments were rejected.[59] No better success awaited Reed's proposal to end the 80 per-cent credit for state inheritance taxes. Fletcher then made a futile effort to secure the adoption of an amendment to permit executors to institute suits to enjoin the collection of the federal estate taxes if the suit were brought solely on the ground that the tax was invalid because of the provision for credit against the federal tax for state inheritance taxes up to 80 per-cent of the amount of the federal tax, and if the state of which the decedent was a resident joined as a petitioner. This amendment was intended to enable taxpayers again to raise the issue disposed of in a recent decision of the Supreme Court.[60]

[56] *Cong. Rec.* 69: 8518.
[57] *Cong. Rec.* 69: 8695.
[58] *Cong. Rec.* 69: 8709, 9149.
[59] *Cong. Rec.* 69: 9177-9178 (1927).
[60] *Florida* v. *Mellon,* 42 Sup. Ct. 265. This unusual case was a request made by the state of Florida to the Supreme Court for leave to file a bill against the Secretary of the Treasury to restrain him from enforcing the Federal estate tax in Florida. The interest of the state was based on two claims:

(a) "That the State is directly injured because the imposition of the Federal tax, in the absence of a State tax which may be credited, will cause the withdrawal

Although there was much discussion over some of these amendments, others that evoked much comment in the House went through without any remarks. Such was the case with the Committee amendment to strike out Section 104, which levied a special tax on personal holding companies that accumulated unduly large surpluses. Simmons admitted that the plan to re-enact Section 220 of the law of 1926 was not a satisfactory solution of the problem of evasion of surtax by incorporation, but the Committee was unable to suggest anything better. It was hoped that as the surtax rates were reduced there would be less incentive to evade the tax.

Because of recent decisions of the Supreme Court the Committee introduced an amendment to the section on gross income so as to tax the salary of the President of the United States taking office after the enactment of the law. The important phrase was "taking office after enactment of the law." The 1926 law stated that gross income included "in the case of the President of the United States the judges of the Supreme Court and inferior courts of the United States and all other officers and employees, whether elected or appointed, of the United States, Alaska, Hawaii . . . the compensation as such." [61] This was very similar to the section of the 1918 law that had been declared unconstitutional in 1925. In that case the Supreme Court had ruled that, inasmuch as the law applied indiscriminately to judges appointed previous to the enactment of the law and also to those appointed subsequently, and inasmuch as the Constitution prohibited the reduction of salaries of federal judges and the President during the terms for which they were elected or appointed, the provision in the revenue act for taxing all judges was unconstitutional.[62] Certain Senators, especially Reed (Pa.), thought this decision might be extended to the President, so he advocated the amendment stated above, to which Smoot agreed. It was accepted by the Senate without a record vote but was rejected by the Conference Committee.

---

of property from the State, with the consequent loss to the State of subjects of taxation; and

(b) that the citizens of the State are injured in such a way that the State may sue in their behalf as parens patriae."

The Court decided that it had no jurisdiction in the case, that there was no authority to file a petition to test the validity of this provision of the estate tax law because, for one reason, the Revised Statutes (Sec. 3224) forbade any suit being brought to enjoin the collection of the tax; however, the Court then, strange to say, decided that the estate tax was constitutional. See Machen, Arthur W., Jr., "The Strange Case of *Florida* v. *Mellon*," *Cornell Law Quarterly*, April 1928, quoted in *Cong. Rec.* 69: 7966-7974.

61 The House had omitted these phrases on the ground that the Constitution permitted the taxation of these officers under the general definitions of income.

62 *Evans* v. *Gore*, 253 U. S. 245 (1920); *Miles* v. *Graham*, 268 U. S. 501 (1925). In the latter case the judge was appointed after the income tax statute had been enacted. See below, Chaps. XX and XXI.

Simmons presented an amendment to reduce the surtax rates much more than the Committee schedule on incomes under $20,000 and not to lower the rate on incomes over $70,000. He claimed that his schedule would benefit 225,000 taxpayers, in contrast to the 125,000 who would have their taxes reduced by the Committee schedule, and would help those who needed it rather than the very rich. In supporting the amendment he quoted the recommendation of the Secretary of the Treasury for the reduction of the surtax in the middle brackets. Smoot disliked the proposition. He reminded his colleagues that when the Secretary made that recommendation he had not counted on the repeal of the automobile tax, which reduced the Treasury revenue by $66,000,000, or the reduction of the admission taxes, which reduced it $17,000,000, both of which measures had passed the Senate. Simmons' amendment was defeated.[63]

In order to overcome the criticism against the refunds made by the Bureau of Internal Revenue the Committee introduced the amendment to require the Joint Committee to approve all income tax refunds and credits in excess of $75,000 each, before they could be paid, and to report to Congress annually the amount of refunds and the names of persons and corporations to whom made.

The Senate rejected a proposition of the Committee to make the lower surtax rates applicable to 1927 income. This would have been equivalent to a rebate of $25,000,000 to those who paid the surtax, a comparatively few taxpayers. Thomas (Dem., Okla.) showed that it would cost the Treasury over a million dollars more than that because it would necessitate letters to the 125,000 taxpayers affected. No one spoke for the Committee plan. The vote was 28 to 54 against it.[64]

On the evening of May 18, when many of the Senators had gone home, a surprise amendment for publicity of income tax returns was rushed through by Norris, with the support of La Follette, Reed (Mo.), McKellar, and Couzens. Shipstead used this opportunity to be critical of the Bureau of Internal Revenue. He wanted to know if the amendment would permit publicity of records that were concerned with refunds and the settlement of claims. Reed (Pa.) opposed Norris' resolution because it was not wanted by the Administration. He reminded his colleagues that it had been tried once and in his opinion resulted in the creation of "sucker lists," in the inspection of returns by the curious or those seeking alimony. Nevertheless the amendment was adopted.[65]

[63] *Cong. Rec.* 69: 8610-8614, 8622.
[64] *Cong. Rec.* 69: 8622, 8624.
[65] *Cong. Rec.* 69: 9059-9064, 9069, 9073-9082.

Copeland (Dem., N. Y.) also succeeded in getting favorable action on an amendment to insert the word "profession" in the section that specified the deductions allowed to those in business, so that doctors could deduct expenses incurred in attending conventions. Smoot was opposed to the change, saying it meant that a doctor could deduct his expenses whenever he was called anywhere, even to a neighboring city or state, even for months while he studied, in fact, for any length of time.[66]

Smoot hoped to reach a final vote on the bill on May 19, but late that afternoon the farm relief advocates carried out their threat to filibuster. Shipstead introduced a group of amendments for tariffs on agricultural products. Pittman explained at some length his amendments rejected by the Committee for tariffs on hides and silver. Johnson (Cal.), fearful lest this delay hinder his bill for Boulder Dam, which was next on the calendar, also used up time in defending his project and refused to agree to a plan of the Republicans to stop all proceedings Saturday and continue on Monday.

In this chaotic condition Senators listened to personal attacks on Herbert Hoover, the leading Republican aspirant for the presidency, and other extraneous matters. Smoot managed, however, to line up enough votes to reject several of these agricultural tariffs; but he was unable to prevent the adoption of Howell's (Neb.) amendment that all claims for tax refund in excess of $10,000 be audited by the General Accounting Office. At about 3 o'clock Sunday morning the Senate adjourned until the following day, agreeing to vote on the bill then.[67]

When Smoot again secured control of the situation on Monday, the 21st, his aim was to get a change of vote on the amendment for the graduated corporation tax. He did not attempt to get another vote on the publicity provision, doubtless knowing he could have it rejected in conference. By a clever bit of strategy he was successful in having the Senate reject Simmons' amendment for the graduated corporation tax. When the first vote was taken to sustain the amendment made in the Committee of the Whole, the vote was 35 for it and 27 against. Nye called attention to the fact that Blease (S. C.), who had voted for the amendment, was really paired with Frazier (N. D.). Blease asked that the vote be reconsidered. A new vote was called for, and this resulted in a tie, 33 – 33. Vice-President Dawes, slapping his hand on the desk, then cast a loud vehement negative vote, so that the amendment was rejected.[68] After one more amendment was voted on, the bill was passed without a roll call.

66 *Cong. Rec.* 69: 9053-9056. It was deleted in Conference.
67 *Cong. Rec.* 69: 9178-9203.
68 *Cong. Rec.* 69: 9322-9340. New York *Times,* May 22, 1928.

THE CONFERENCE REPORT

The chief differences between the bills of the House and Senate related to: (1) the amount of tax reduction, (2) surtax rates, (3) consolidated corporation returns, (4) the tax on personal holding companies, and (5) publicity of returns. There was no difficulty over the differences in the tax year to which the new rates should apply because the Senate had not passed the bill before March 15 as the House had intended, so the rates were effective for the taxable year 1928.

The total reduction agreed upon was $222,495,000, a sum closer to that of the Senate bill than to that of the House bill. The difference was due chiefly to the lowered rates of the normal corporation tax, special reductions for corporation taxpayers with income of less than $15,000, and the lowering of certain excise taxes.[69]

The Senate managers receded on the change in surtax rates in the middle brackets but the House agreed to the Senate amendment for increasing to $30,000 the amount of earned income upon which a 25 per-cent tax credit would be permitted. The House managers agreed to the elimination of the special tax on personal holding companies.[70]

The Conference Committee was deadlocked for some time because the Senate insisted on retaining the section for publicity of income tax returns, despite Administration objection. Then it was decided to have a separate vote on the proposition in the Senate. When the matter came up for a vote Couzens explained that the press had given to the country an entirely false idea of the content of the amendment. It merely stated that "returns should be open to inspection as other public records"; it did not give permission to anyone to publish the private affairs of taxpayers. Robinson (Dem., Ark.) said he did not think there was much demand for publicity of returns, although the matter had been agitated for many years. Contrary to what might have been expected, Reed (Mo.) advocated yielding to the House, although personally he preferred the amendment, because he thought they would not get anywhere by insisting on retaining it. Smoot finally succeeded in getting a favorable vote to recede from the amendment.[71]

The Conferees threw out the Senate amendment sponsored by Copeland to permit traveling expenses of professional men because the House was unwilling to make any more exemptions than already

[69] Tabular estimates of the loss in revenue that would be occasioned by the Senate and House bills and the Act of 1928 are given in the *Congressional Record* 69: 10133-10134.

[70] Such a tax, however, was enacted in 1934. See below, Chap. XIV.

[71] *Cong. Rec.* 69: 9843-9854.

existed in the law. They also rejected Howell's amendment to have all tax refunds of $10,000 audited by the Controller General, inasmuch as there was already in the bill a provision that no refund of $75,000 and over be paid until approved by the Joint Committee on Internal Revenue Taxation.

The Senate had eliminated a section passed by the House to provide for higher salaries to certain of the technical staff of the Bureau of Internal Revenue without regard to classification under the Civil Service Act. The Conferees secured an agreement that at least fifteen assistants to the General Counsel, fifteen of the administrative and technical employees, and fifty employees of the Bureau of Internal Revenue would be classified. It was also agreed to accept the Senate amendment for a maximum salary of $7500 for collectors of the internal revenue. The House bill maximum was $6000.

The Senate receded on its amendments to tax the salary of the President of the United States and to permit the deduction from income of all expenses incurred in contesting liability for any tax, federal, state, municipal, or otherwise.[72]

SUMMARY OF THE LAW [73]

The Revenue Act of 1928 contained five titles: I — Income Tax; II — Miscellaneous Taxes; III — Amendments to the 1926 Income Tax; IV — Administrative Provisions; V — General Provisions.

As in 1926 the law was a complete entity in itself and was much better arranged than any previous law, because of the work of the Joint Committee on Internal Revenue Taxation. The use of typographical devices, indentations, marginal notes, and a good table of contents all combined to make the law much more easily read. In general, however, the law made few changes, either in the rates or in the structural sections.

Title I — Income Tax. The normal tax and surtax remained as in the 1926 law, that is, the normal rate was 1½% on the first $4000 of net income, 3% on the next $4000 and 5% on the remainder; the surtax began with 1% on income in excess of $10,000 and increased by steps of 1% till it reached 20% on income in excess of $100,000.

The personal exemptions remained at $1500 for a single person, $3500 for the head of a family or married person living with husband or wife, and $400 for each dependent. A credit of 25% of the tax was allowed for "earned" income, as in the previous law, but the maximum amount that could be considered earned was increased from $20,000 to $30,000.

[72] *Cong. Rec.* 69: 10123-10131.

[73] 45 *Statutes at Large* 791.

One of the most important changes was the reduction of the corporation tax from 13½% to 12% of net income. A flat exemption of $3000 was allowed if the annual net income was $25,000 or less.

There was no change in the provision for taxing capital net gains. An individual taxpayer, not a corporation, could separate capital gains from other income and have such income taxed at 12½%, provided his total tax was not less than 12½% of his entire net income. Capital net losses could also be separated and a tax credit of 12½% of the net loss taken but the total tax could not be less than the tax would be when computed at normal and surtax rates if the capital net loss were deducted from ordinary net income.

A new section was added to permit employers who established a pension reserve fund to transfer reserves to a pension trust and to deduct this amount from gross income. Earnings of the fund were taxable to the individual who received them when distributed. Other corporations added to those exempt from income tax were real estate boards not organized for profit, teachers' retirement fund associations, and financing corporations organized by marketing associations.

In computing net income, a taxpayer could carry forward net losses until the third succeeding year.

As in the previous law, affiliated concerns were given the option of making separate or consolidated returns. Corporations were deemed affiliated if one corporation owned at least 95% of the stock of the other corporation or if at least 95% of the stock of two or more corporations was owned by the same interests. Returns for the year 1928 were required to be on the same basis as for 1927 unless the Commissioner gave permission to change. An insurance company could not be included with another kind of company in making a consolidated return.

As in the 1926 law, a corporation "formed or availed of for the purpose of preventing the imposition of the surtax" by accumulating its income as surplus instead of distributing it to stockholders was made subject to an additional tax of 50 per cent of the net income.

Title II – Miscellaneous Taxes. This title dealt with the estate tax, taxes on admissions and dues, automobiles, liquors, cereal beverages, narcotics and foreign built boats. Most of the excises were reduced. The tax on automobile manufacturers was repealed. A few taxes were increased – those on foreign-built yachts and on admissions to prize fights. The estate tax was retained at the same rates as in the previous law.

Title III – Amendments to the 1926 Income Tax. This dealt chiefly with the statute of limitations.

Title IV – Administrative Provisions. This title contained many important changes, but they are too technical to be of general interest. Some of those that applied to the Board of Tax Appeals will be considered in the chapter dealing with administration of the income tax laws. The most significant were those that gave the Commissioner power to close cases by agreement with the taxpayer and those that permitted the Commissioner to apply new regulations without retroactive effect. Another important change was to put the burden of proving fraud in tax proceedings on the government. In the previous law the burden was on the petitioner before the Board of Tax Appeals.

Title V – General Provisions. This title was concerned mostly with retroactive provisions of several sections of the law, for example, those relating to the estate tax, installment sales, taxability of trusts, and contributions to charity. A retroactive provision permitted individuals to deduct contributions to trusts organized for religious, charitable, scientific, or educational purposes in computing taxable income for 1923 if the taxpayer gave substantially the same amount to the same trust in 1924. The maximum allowable deduction was $50,000.

A new section required that no refund or credit of income, estate, or gift taxes in excess of $75,000 each be made until after the expiration of thirty days from the date upon which a report was submitted to the Joint Committee on Internal Revenue Taxation. This Committee was to report to Congress annually the names of persons and corporations to whom such refunds were made and the amounts of the refunds.

The Act became effective May 29, 1928, the day the President signed it, except for the income tax sections which were effective as of January 1, 1928.

CHAPTER XII

REVENUE ACT OF 1932 – THE BOTTOM OF THE DEPRESSION

TAX REDUCTION 1929

The prosperous 1920's were nearing an end when the Revenue Act of 1928 was passed, but the boom did not reach its climax for another year. The financial crash came in September and October of 1929, though neither the extent of the reversal, nor the severity and length of the ensuing depression was anticipated then.

In December 1929 the Secretary of the Treasury recommended that Congress pass a joint resolution to reduce the normal tax rates for 1929 from 1½%, 3% and 5% to ½%, 2% and 4%, respectively; the corporation tax from 12% to 11%. He reported that the Revenue Act of 1928 had produced more revenue than the law it replaced, although it was intended to relieve the taxpayer. The Treasury receipts for the two succeeding years were expected to be greater than for 1929, and expenditures not much more, so a surplus of over $225,000,000 was anticipated.[1] A resolution to give effect to these reductions for one year was passed by both houses of Congress without delay. In the House, Ramseyer (Ia.) was almost alone in calling it an unsound measure, "lacking in statesmanship and in the long run . . . politically unsound"; in the Senate it was questioned only by La Follette and Couzens.

A year later the Secretary gave out a warning that, because of the continued downward trend of business and upward trend of government expenditures, this temporary decrease in income tax rates could not be continued. Further than this he did not recommend that rates be increased. Congress paid no attention to tax matters that session and adjourned March 4, 1931, seemingly little concerned about the fiscal state of the nation.

Tax returns for the first quarter of 1931 showed a tremendous decline in income. Receipts from the income tax were 40% less than for March 1930 and government expenditures were $300,000,000 greater than estimated. Hence there loomed a Treasury deficit of about three quarters of a billion dollars. Nevertheless, President Hoover still maintained that it would be unnecessary to increase taxes in the coming year if Congress would keep appropria-

[1] *Report of the Secretary of the Treasury* 1929, pp. 22-26.

tions within the budget recommendations and postpone "sectional and group demands for Federal assistance." [2]

House and Senate leaders pledged their co-operation in keeping taxes down. Apparently on the supposition that the depression would soon be over they relied on the assurance that Secretary Mellon would pull the country out of difficulty by short-term loans. They knew that it would be impossible to reduce appropriations. The Administration was responsible for this point of view because Treasury experts had said that the government could carry on without any embarrassment by borrowing and by reducing the amount applicable to debt retirement.

THE DEFICIT BECOMES MORE SERIOUS

Addresses by Secretary Mellon and Undersecretary Mills in May 1931 forecast the sales tax controversy in Congress about six months later. They stressed the lack of flexibility in the tax system because so much reliance was placed on the income tax and because comparatively few paid this tax. The income tax, source of about two-thirds of the federal tax revenue, was subject to the great fluctuations of business conditions; these were increased by the way capital gains and losses were treated. Secretary Mellon referred to the fact that the Treasury had long been aware of this defect and had warned Congress three years before that it was a mistake to repeal the excise taxes. A deficit was a matter of grave concern and was not viewed with complacency, he said.[3]

Borah criticized the speech on the ground that the Secretary wanted to lower the exemptions. He said the result would be similar to lowering wages, which President Hoover was trying to avoid. Hull too criticized the Administration for not seeing what was happening to the government's fiscal structure.[4] The June and September tax collections offered little hope for avoiding tax revision. Nevertheless, neither the President nor the Treasury came out flatly for increasing taxes until every other means had been exhausted. One of the uncertain factors was the amount that would have to be used for federal construction in order to care for the unemployed. If local relief agencies throughout the country had successful drives in the fall the federal government might not have to appropriate funds for public works to keep up employment.[5] Another uncertainty in the fiscal situation related to payment of loans by foreign governments. The Administration had no desire to increase taxes

2 New York *Times,* April 1, 1931.
3 *Report of the Secretary of the Treasury* 1931, pp. 351-358, 396-401.
4 New York *Times,* May 26, 1931.
5 *Cong. Rec.* 74: 35; Baltimore *Sun,* Sept. 2, 1931.

in 1932, an election year, and therefore carefully surveyed the situation to determine whether or not it would be possible to manage for another year by borrowing.[6]

Congressional leaders were as divided as the members of the executive department. Watson, Senate floor leader, did not want any new taxes; Bacharach, influential member of important House committees, advocated extensive changes in the direction of heavier taxes on inheritances, luxuries, and incomes over $100,000. The most unexpected pronouncement, however, was by Reed (Pa.) who advocated a sales tax of one-half of 1%, repeal of the capital gains and loss provisions in the income tax law, higher rates for the estate tax but not for the income tax. He estimated that the sales tax would yield two billion dollars, nearly half of the government's annual expenses, and would not be hard on the consumer.

Such an announcement was looked upon as of much greater significance than statements of many members. Reed's personal friendship with Mellon and close contact as his advisor, lent importance to his proposal which was viewed as probably inspired by the Administration to test out popular reaction to a sales tax, a "trial balloon," as it were.[7] Smoot had long advocated such a tax, but most of the members doubtless thought that the issue had been fought out in 1921.[8]

The independents in Congress, represented by La Guardia, sponsored a plan not very different from that of Bacharach, namely: (1) increased taxes on larger incomes, estates and stock transfers; (2) new taxes on luxuries and on gifts, and (3) higher postage rates.[9]

On the Democratic side also there was some diversity of opinion. Byrns, the minority leader, declared that higher taxes should be levied, that the situation was too serious for playing politics. He thought that necessary additional levies should be placed on estates, on incomes over $50,000, and on gifts.[10] Rainey was much opposed to a sales tax but favored increases in other taxes.[11] Glass thought that expenditures could be curtailed but if more taxes were necessary, he wanted increased income tax rates.[12] Harrison favored slowing up on debt retirement.[13]

6 Baltimore *Sun*, Sept. 2, 3, 1931; *The Tax Magazine*, 10: 145 (April 1931).
7 Baltimore *Sun*, Sept. 11, 1931; New York *Times*, Sept. 26, 1931.
8 See above, Chap. VIII.
9 Baltimore *Sun*, Sept. 2, Oct. 5; New York *Times*, Oct. 5, 1931.
10 Baltimore *Sun*, Sept. 18, 1931.
11 New York *World Telegraph*, Dec. 9, 1931.
12 Baltimore *Sun*, Sept. 6, 1931.
13 New York *Times*, April 29, May 29, Sept. 12, 1931.

SHOULD CONGRESS INCREASE TAXES OR LET THE TREASURY BORROW?

The 72d Congress convened in December 1931. Any faint hope of the temporary nature of the depression that may have been cherished earlier had now vanished. All signs pointed to a continuing downward trend of economic conditions. Discouragement was accentuated by the many failures of banks and other business concerns. Whatever policy of legislation was adopted as to expenditure or taxation was a matter of grave concern. Comment has already been made relative to the divergence of opinion among members of both parties as to the wisest path to follow. Vacillating as the Administration pronouncements of fiscal policy had been during the summer and fall, the conclusion had finally been reached that tax increases were inevitable.

The decision was more difficult because the Administration did not control the House. There were three more Democratic than Republican members, and therefore important committee chairmanships were held by Democrats. In the Senate there were 48 Republicans, 47 Democrats and one Farmer-Laborite, so the Republicans controlled the committees if not always the votes. Party lines, however, divided members less than blocs based on local interest. The power of these small groups was realized when they succeeded in forcing extraneous tariff schedules into the tax bill. Doubtless there was cheer in the announcement that, at any rate, Watson and Speaker Garner would lay aside politics.[14]

For the first time since the war, members of Congress were faced with a huge problem of financing a deficit, a much less agreeable task than enjoying a surplus and reducing tax rates, particularly when an election was approaching. Instead of receipts of $2,813,000,000 from the income tax, as estimated at the beginning of the fiscal year 1930-1931, they were $1,860,000,000 in spite of the fact that the returns for six months (June to December 1930) were based on 1929 earnings.[15] Receipts from customs also showed a great decrease, and so did those from miscellaneous sources. Total ordinary receipts were $861,000,000 less than in 1930. The government was also deprived of almost $250,000,000 by reason of the moratorium on debt payments granted to foreign governments. Hence, instead of the estimated deficit of $180,000,000, there was actually a deficit of slightly over $900,000,000 for 1931 and it was estimated that it would be over $2,000,000,000 for 1932.

The Secretary recommended certain provisions for additional revenue on the theory that it was fundamental to maintain public

[14] Baltimore *Sun*, Nov. 20, 1931.

[15] In 1930 the receipts from income taxes had been $2,411,000,000.

credit. He laid down two basic principles to be observed: (1) that the sinking fund for the retirement of public debt must be maintained and (2) that "over a period of years revenues must be equal to expenditures." [16]

The President's annual message delivered to Congress early in December 1931, contained no specific proposals for tax measures but pointed out the big deficit anticipated for the fiscal year 1932 and recommended that steps be taken to reduce expenditures and to raise additional revenue in order to balance the budget for the fiscal year 1933.

THE COMMITTEE ON WAYS AND MEANS PROPOSES A SALES TAX

No action on tax matters was taken by Congress until after the Christmas recess. On January 7, 1932 the Committee on Ways and Means [17] voted to begin public hearings on January 13 and continue them until January 25.

The first witness on the opening day was the Secretary of the Treasury, as was customary. Mr. Mellon brought a prepared statement which he asked Undersecretary Mills to read. The fundamental principle of it was that the budget should be balanced for the fiscal year beginning in July 1932, so as to end further increase in the public debt. Such a goal would involve not only self-denial, he said, but "some measure of sacrifice." Every unnecessary expenditure should be curtailed, every economy practiced, and every available resource tapped for increased revenue.

The Secretary pointed out the great fluctuations in the income tax, as contrasted with the comparative stability of the yield of miscellaneous taxes, especially the tax on tobacco.[18] From these

[16] *Report of the Secretary of the Treasury* 1931; p. 27.

[17] The members of the Committee on Ways and Means were:

Democrats	*Republicans*
James W. Collier (Miss.), Ch.	Willis C. Hawley (Ore.)
Henry T. Rainey (Ill.)	Allen T. Treadway (Mass.)
Charles R. Crisp (Ga.)	Isaac Bacharach (N. J.)
Robert L. Doughton (N. C.)	Lindley H. Hadley (Wash.)
Heartsill Ragon (Ark.)	Chas. B. Timberlake (Colo.)
Samuel B. Hill (Wash.)	Henry C. Watson (Pa.)
Harry C. Canfield (Ind.)	James C. McLaughlin (Mich.)
Thomas H. Cullen (N. Y.)	Carl R. Chindblom (Ill.)
Christopher D. Sullivan (N. Y.)	Frank Crowther (N. Y.)
Morgan G. Sanders (Tex.)	Richard S. Aldrich (R. I.)
Edw. E. Eslick (Tenn.)	
John W. McCormack (Mass.)	
Clement C. Dickinson (Mo.)	
David J. Lewis (Md.)	
Fred M. Vinson (Ky.)	

[18] Individual income tax receipts declined from $1,061,000,000 in 1930 to $730,000,000 in 1931, and were estimated at $370,000,000 for 1932. The actual receipts for 1932 were $351,000,000. Tobacco tax receipts were $450,000,000 in 1930, $444,000,000 in 1931, $398,000,000 in 1932, and $402,000,000 in 1933.

facts he concluded that the federal revenue system rested on too narrow and fluctuating a base. Anticipating the pressure there would be to put heavy taxes on those with large incomes, the Secretary warned the Committee that in times of depression large incomes fall a greater percentage than smaller ones. He recommended some increase in both the surtax and the normal tax rates but also wanted the law revised so that many more would pay income taxes than previously.

On the basis of a study of the manufacturers' sales tax in Canada,[19] the Secretary opposed the adoption of such a tax in the United States because it would be very difficult to administer and because it would add to the cost of living, but he selected certain miscellaneous articles and services which might bear sales taxes, for example, tobacco, automobiles and accessories, radios, checks and drafts, telephone, radio and telegraph messages, and transfers of capital stock. He suggested also that the estate tax be increased and that postal rates be raised. Such a program of retrenchment of expenditure and increase of taxation would spread the burden, balance the budget in the next fiscal year, 1932-1933, and thus invigorate the entire credit structure of the country.[20]

Except for the representatives of the Farm Bureau Federation, and a few others, the Committee heard nothing but protests. Manufacturers of automobiles, electricity, gas, beauty parlor supplies, and tobacco, theatrical managers, musicians, managers of bus companies and hotels, florists and bankers — almost the whole range of American industry and business — sent representatives to convince the legislators that the taxes proposed would ruin them. The printed volume of hearings was over 1200 pages in length.

Snell, Republican House leader, optimistically forecast at the close of the hearings that the Ways and Means Committee would put aside politics, draft a measure that would get the Treasury out of the red, and be passed by March 15.[21] The first part of his prophecy proved correct. The Committee adopted a non-partisan attitude under the leadership of Crisp who took over the chairmanship when the illness of Collier forced his absence. The Republicans were invited to join with the Democrats in writing the bill. Speaker Garner, the real leader of his party, helped the situation by his re-

[19] In the fall of 1931 about fifty Congressmen and four Senators visited Canada at the expense of William Randolph Hearst to observe the operation of the manufacturers' sales tax. About the same time T. S. Adams and E. C. Alvord went at the request of the Treasury. Neither group recommended that such a tax be adopted in the United States. (72d Congress, 1st Session, *Hearings before the Committee on Ways and Means* 1932, pp. 30-36, 239-267.)

[20] 72d Congress, 1st Session, *Hearings before the Committee on Ways and Means on Revenue Revision* 1932, pp. 1-8.

[21] Baltimore *Sun*, Jan. 27, 1932.

quest early in the month that Democratic members refrain from discussing tax matters until the party policy was framed.[22]

At the start the Committee made three objections to the Treasury program. The first was to the excises on certain articles. The numerous and forceful protests by manufacturers of these products, not only at the hearings but in the press and directly to Committee members, made such an impression on them that one of the first decisions was that the so-called "nuisance" taxes should be avoided. Instead they considered "widely distributed consumption taxes," such as one-half cent per kilowatt hour on electricity, one cent a gallon on gasoline, five cents on stock transfers, ten cents a month for the use of telephone instruments, increase in surtaxes and estate taxes.[23]

The second objection raised by the Democrats to the Treasury program was that it was inequitable to make the increases retroactive, that is, to make the new rates effective on income received in 1931 and reported in 1932. The Republican members agreed. In vain the Treasury experts challenged such a use of the word "retroactive." Mills made a personal appeal to his friend Garner to make the tax apply to 1931 incomes so that the budget could be more nearly balanced. The third objection was that the Committee had no control over appropriations which the Treasury wanted curtailed nor over postal rates which the Treasury wanted raised.

Early in February Mills informed the Committee that the November estimates "had gone bad," that the deficit for 1933 would probably reach $1,241,000,000 in place of $920,000,000 and that the receipts from the taxes proposed would probably not exceed $786,000,000.[24] The Secretary[25] requested further reductions in expenditure and an additional half-billion dollars of revenue, which he advised raising by increasing further the rates of the corporation tax, the surtax, and the tax on transfers of capital stock, and by imposing new taxes on the sale of gasoline and on the domestic consumption of gas and electricity.[26]

Crisp laid the matter before the House. On February 11 he told his colleagues that the Committee on Ways and Means was up against the most difficult situation that any Committee had ever faced, much more difficult than raising war taxes, for at that time

22 New York *Times*, Jan. 1, 1932. Garner said on the floor of the House in March that the Democrats on the Committee decided it would be better to prepare a non-partisan bill in view of the small Democratic majority in the House. (*Cong. Rec.* 75: 7028.)

23 Baltimore *Sun*, Oct. 25, 1931; Jan. 27, 1932; New York *Times*, Jan. 25, 27, 1932.

24 Baltimore *Sun*, New York *Times*, Feb. 10, 1932.

25 Ogden L. Mills had been Acting Secretary of the Treasury for some months after Mellon was appointed as Ambassador to the Court of St. James's but he did not become Secretary until February 11, 1932, when Mellon became Ambassador.

26 *Report of the Secretary of the Treasury* 1932, pp. 270-271.

business was prosperous, no one complained, the income taxes on individuals and corporations yielded tremendous amounts of revenue. Moreover, war psychology covered taxes with a glamor of patriotism.

In contrast with war days was the 1932 situation when business was depressed, people generally were discouraged and income taxes failed to produce enough to balance the budget. Hence it was argued that some form of sales tax or excise tax must be levied. Crisp stressed the importance of raising enough funds even though it was difficult and unpopular to do so, and appealed to the House to remember, when appropriating funds, that taxes would have to be levied to pay for them. In closing, he said that he was willing to go ahead and levy sufficient taxes to balance the budget regardless of political consequences:

> Now, my friends, I want you and the country to gird yourselves with stamina, with backbone and with courage to meet this emergency.[27]

In order to make progress, the Committee was divided into small groups to study various phases of the tax situation. Rainey was made chairman of the subcommittee on the sales tax.[28] Despite all the arguments presented against the sales tax by those who had studied Canadian experience, and despite Rainey's long and well-known opposition to it, the subcommittee voted to write it into the bill. The full Committee accepted this recommendation and voted to make it the main feature of the tax bill.[29] No adequate explanation of this move has ever been made. The only excuse seems to have been that the Committee members thought that there would be less protest if a tax were put on all manufacturers than if only a few were selected, and that enough of the necessities of life could be exempted to relieve consumers in the lower income groups. The committee was seemingly at a loss as to any other means of raising so large an amount of revenue as such a tax was expected to yield.[30] Rainey predicted that $600,000,000, about half of what the Treasury requested, could be raised by this small sales tax on everything except food.[31]

The Committee called before it the special auditor of excise taxes for the Canadian National Revenue who told the members that Canada had found the manufacturers' sales tax a satisfactory one.[32] Fortified by his assurance, the Committee went ahead. Other sub-

27 *Cong. Rec.* 75: 3772-3773.

28 The other members were Eslick (Tenn.), McCormack (Mass.), Cullen (N. Y.), Hawley (Ore.), Bacharach (N. J.), and Hadley (Wash.).

29 New York *Times*, Feb. 18, 22, 1932.

30 Baltimore *Sun*, Feb. 24, 1932.

31 New York *Times*, Feb. 18, 1932.

32 Baltimore *Sun*, Feb. 25, 1932.

committees worked on the technical and administrative sections, especially with a view to closing loopholes which might be used for tax avoidance, such as the provisions relating to capital losses and gains, consolidated returns, and income earned abroad.[33] After these changes had been made and the new tax provisions drafted, the Committee still needed to raise $200,000,000. The source chosen, temporarily, was a consumption tax on gas and electricity, gasoline and oil.[34] This plan was abandoned, however, before the report was completed.

Mills was not willing to have the Treasury plan thrown over without some protest, so he went to the Committee and listened to their criticisms of his failure to modify the program in the light of what they considered a "more practical situation." In Mills' presence the members voted twenty-three to one against the "retroactive" income tax. Nevertheless, the Secretary maintained his position that the tax should apply to 1931 incomes.[35] The Committee, however, did accept one or two Treasury recommendations – it did not abolish consolidated returns, because it was feared that a change would hinder business recovery. It increased the corporation and individual income tax rates and lowered the exemptions much as Mills had suggested, but adopted a gift tax which he opposed.

Shortly before the bill was completed, it was decided to request the Committee on Post Offices and Post Roads to increase parcel post rates so as to reduce the postal deficit of $25,000,000, and to substitute for the consumption taxes on gas and electricity, taxes on malt sirup, grape concentrate, and other essentials of "home brew" and, as a result of pressure from a bloc of western and southern Democrats and a Republican, taxes on gasoline and oil imports, although the members realized that these taxes would evoke a great deal of controversy. Four members were particularly opposed to inserting tariff provisions but they were won over by the plea that such items would win at least forty votes for the sales tax.[36]

As completed, the Committee draft proposed the following taxes: (1) a manufacturers' excise tax at 2¼%; (2) increase of the corporation tax from 12% to 13%, increase of the individual normal income tax rates from 1½%, 3% and 5% to 2%, 4% and 6%, respectively; increase of the surtax from a maximum of 20% to a maximum of 40%; (3) increase of the estate tax from a maximum of 20% to one of 40% and enactment of a gift tax with a maximum rate of 30%;[37] (4) a tax of 10% on admissions of 25 cents and over;

33 Baltimore *Sun*, Feb. 19, 1932.
34 New York *Times*, Feb. 22, 1932.
35 New York *Times*, Feb. 22, 1932.
36 The Committee divided 14 to 9 on this tax (*Cong. Rec.* 75: 6965).
37 A gift tax was imposed by the Act of 1924 but not re-enacted in 1926.

(5) increase of the stock transfer tax from 2 cents to 4 cents; (6) excises of 4 cents a gallon on lubricating oils; 35 and 40 cents a gallon on malt sirup and grape concentrate, respectively; 5 cents on telephone, telegraph, and radio messages costing less than 50 cents, and 10 cents on those costing over that amount; and 1 cent per gallon on imports of gasoline, gas oil, fuel oil, and crude oil.

The report of the Committee pointed out that, even with the drastic increase in the income tax, the additional revenue from that source would be only $168,000,000, leaving an amount of over a billion dollars to be procured from some other source in order to balance the budget.

Considerable space in the report was devoted to the following arguments in defense of the manufacturers' excise tax: (1) every other conceivable source had been considered and found discriminatory against some business or industry; (2) the tax was proposed for a two-year period only; and (3) it did not seriously violate the principle of ability to pay, because the rate of tax was so small that even if the entire tax were passed on, the effect would be negligible, and in many cases the manufacturer would assume the tax. However desirable a tax on luxuries might be from the point of view of equity, the estimates showed that from a fiscal point of view it was inadequate. The report concluded with these words:

> Your committee submits that there is no other source of revenue which will yield the amount imperatively required with as little protest, as little annoyance, and as little disturbance to business as a manufacturers' excise tax.[38]

It was estimated that the bill would raise $1,121,000,000 additional revenue, of which over half was expected to come from the manufacturers' sales tax. Increased income tax rates on both corporations and individuals were expected to yield $133,000,000; the estate and gift taxes, $35,000,000; admissions taxes, $90,000,000; the tax on sirup, $50,000,000; and administrative changes, $100,000,000. The Committee counted on savings of $25,000,000 by reduction in expenditures, hence their estimates showed a total of $1,246,000,000 from taxes and expenditure reductions, which was $5,000,000 more than was considered necessary to balance the budget.

A group of three "wet Democrats," two of whom were from New York, seized the opportunity to present some "Supplemental Views" on the possibilities of raising at least $350,000,000 by a tax on 2.75% beer. It would be only a matter of time, so these gentlemen argued, until the Volstead Act would be modified and, in view of the fiscal emergency, it would seem expedient to change the law as

[38] 72d Congress, 1st Session, *House Report* 708, p. 10.

promptly as possible. They pointed out that the Committee had recognized bootlegging by placing a tax on malt sirup, wort, and grape juice and, if $50,000,000 could be raised by taxing the illegal product, would it not be more equitable, honorable, and moral to make the business legal, and at the same time raise a great deal more revenue? This proposed injection of the prohibition issue was not relished by the other members of the Committee, for passage of the sales tax alone would probably require all the strategy that the leaders could command.

Crisp did his best to prepare the nation psychologically for the bill. On March 1, shortly before the Committee report was completed, he broadcast an appeal to every citizen to give earnest thought to the emergency financial situation and to be willing to bear additional tax burden for the coming two or three years so that the federal budget could be balanced.[39]

THE HOUSE OF REPRESENTATIVES REJECTS THE SALES TAX

The Committee draft of the revenue bill was introduced into the House on March 10 by Chairman Crisp, who was not allowed to proceed uninterrupted in his explanation of the proposed taxes. Questions on the sales tax came from members of all parties. The chairman was asked to compare the proposed rates with those of Canada and Australia to show how much lower the Committee had made them; to list the exemptions; to tell what taxes the Treasury recommended as a substitute for the sales tax. Frear asked about the exemptions for food. Cannon (Dem., Mo.) asked about the taxation of schoolbooks and Bibles.[40] The chairman was followed by Hawley, ranking Republican member of the Committee, who emphasized the non-political character of the bill and the efforts of the Committee to find equitable and remunerative sources of revenue. Treadway also pointed out some of the good points; for instance, that pyramiding of the tax was eliminated.[41]

It was evident from the outset that the sales tax would have much opposition, yet the leaders anticipated no trouble in securing its passage. Speeches in opposition to the tax continued and increased in intensity. One Democrat, Lozier (Mo.), tried to pin the blame for it on Mellon who had said that he was opposed to it, to be sure, but—

> The plain facts are that the Republicans have outsmarted the Democrats, and by pretending to favor a little different plan have adroitly maneuvered the Democrats into the dangerous position of proposing a

[39] New York *Times*, March 2, 1932.
[40] *Cong. Rec.* 75: 5688-5697.
[41] *Cong. Rec.* 75: 5697-5703.

sales tax. Some of my Democratic colleagues, who, in their perplexity are seeking a way out of this Republican abyss, may imagine that they hear the voice of Jacob, but I warn them that the guiding and controlling force behind this bill is the hairy, yet adroit, hand of Ogden "Esau" Mills, who, if he succeeds in putting over this sales tax, will have successfully accomplished the most far-reaching political 3-shell game since Esau deceived the half-blind Jacob. . .[42]

Johnson (Dem., Okla.) challenged the conclusions of the pro-sales tax speakers as to the effect of the Canadian tax on the consumer. He had gone to Canada the preceding fall with other members of Congress to find out how the tax worked and he had concluded that the Canadians were anxious to sell the idea of the success of the tax. They said that the tax was painless, but the evidence seemed to show that such was not the case. He learned that manufacturers and jobbers had added as high as 16% to the cost of goods and that the tax offered "not only an opportunity but a temptation for graft and corruption." He was sure that the Canadian people were not ignorant of the fact that the tax was passed on to the consumer, and hence he thought it could not honestly be said that the people were satisfied with the tax.[43]

While the southern members hammered away at the sales tax, eastern members objected to the tax on oil imports.[43] They showed that it was, to all intents and purposes, a tariff, and that Congress had refused to pass such a measure in 1930 and 1931 when oil imports were larger than in 1932. The tax would be particularly hard on the Atlantic seaboard where most of the imported oil was received, and where freight costs on oil from the western part of the United States made its use uneconomical. The claim was made before the Committee that the proposed tax would help the independent producers and increase employment in the oil fields of California and Texas.[44]

On the last days of general debate, criticism was again concentrated on the sales tax. Cannon (Mo.) spoke for fifteen minutes on the indefensible features of the tax and expressed his fear that, once adopted, it would never be abandoned. He proposed several substitute taxes, such as a tax on "wash" sales of stock, taxes on sales of futures on produce exchanges, much higher inheritance taxes, an excess profits tax, and heavier taxes on incomes in the higher brackets.

This devastating pounding away against the main feature of the tax bill created no little anxiety on the part of the Administration, as well as of the Committee. The Democratic leaders used every

[42] *Cong. Rec.* 75: 5812.
[43] *Cong. Rec.* 75: 5718.
[44] *Cong. Rec.* 75: 6020-6031.

resource to line up their colleagues. Even Raskob, chairman of the National Democratic Committee, and Jouett Shouse, chairman of the party's Executive Committee, exerted their efforts to hold the ranks because the Democrats had promised to see that the budget was balanced by June 1933. This party disagreement was, at the same time, a matter of concern to the Republicans. As one of the papers said, they were robbed of any pleasure they might have had at seeing the threatened Democratic split because they wanted to see the bill passed.[45] Mills, too, did what he could to support the measure for, in spite of the fact that it differed in many respects from what he recommended, he gave it his blessing. On March 12 he broadcast an explanation of the necessity for a balanced budget and his reasons for supporting the bill.[46]

These efforts were unsuccessful in blocking opposition. Not only were there many Democrats against it, but the Progressives led by La Guardia had even gone so far as to draw up a substitute bill. The Committee, however, still thought its draft could be passed if the list of exemptions to the sales tax was somewhat extended to include more articles of food.

On the evening of March 16, about fifty Democratic members of the House gathered under the leadership of Doughton to plan the strategy of their attack on the sales tax. Earlier in the day about twenty-six members, both Republicans and Democrats, mostly the former who called themselves the Allied Progressives, met with La Guardia for the same purpose. Neither group emphasized substitute plans.[47]

To counteract these defections and save the sales tax, both the Republican and Democratic leaders in the House "brought their heaviest artillery into play." Rainey, described as one of the "heavy batters," a picturesque character with his tousled white hair and flowing windsor tie, took the floor. With all the force and fire for which he was famed he defended the tax for one hour and forty minutes. Very diplomatically he started out by expressing his understanding of the position of those who opposed the sales tax, for he had been a vigorous opponent of it for years; in fact, even in the preceding fall he had refused to join the party that went to Canada to study it. Then the Committee hearings took place. Each industry that would have been affected by the proposed excise tax made such a plea, such an "absolutely air tight defense," that all together they convinced the Committee of the unfairness of selecting a few industries, and forced them to the conclusion that it would be more

[45] New York *Times*, March 12, 1932.
[46] *Report of the Secretary of the Treasury* 1932, pp. 258-262.
[47] New York *Times*, Baltimore *Sun*, March 17, 1932.

equitable to spread the burden over as wide a base as possible. Twenty-four of the twenty-five members agreed. Only one (Doughton) disagreed, and that was the reason why the bill was not unanimously supported.

Rainey conceded that the Committee had made a tactical error. But, he asked, suppose the Committee had proposed taxes on radios, automobiles, tobacco, checks, etc., such as the irritating war taxes, what about the opposition to them? There would have been a storm of protest, and then it would have been necessary to substitute the sales tax. To give an idea of the current fiscal trends, which he did not claim to be complete justification, he showed that practically every state imposed sales taxes on gasoline, most of them on cigarettes, and that West Virginia had developed a very complete system of such taxes. He forecast that nobody would feel the sales tax after it was put into operation, for it had been drawn up to avoid the mistakes of the sales taxes of other countries, and he tried to discount the extent of the opposition by blaming most of it on organized lobbyists.

The last part of Rainey's defense of the tax was an explanation of the financial situation of the government. He predicted the worst panic in all the history of the world if Congress failed to take immediate and effective steps to balance the budget.[48] In reply Doughton and his supporters occupied the floor for an hour in an exciting evening session.

On the following day the House, in Committee of the Whole, commenced reading the bill for amendments. Crisp asked consent for blanket authorizations for the clerk to make changes when the bill was engrossed to save the necessity of securing permission for individual changes. La Guardia facetiously remarked:

> The gentleman from Georgia has certainly displayed foresight in anticipating changes.

Thereupon the wrecking of the Committee bill commenced in a stormy, noisy session. The Democrats stamped and shouted that the rich should bear wartime taxes. La Guardia secured the floor for some speechmaking, then introduced an amendment to raise the normal tax on income over $8000 from 6% to 7%. This amendment was adopted.[49] Canfield (Dem., Ind.) then offered an amendment to increase the surtax rates to a maximum of 50%,[50] but Swing (Rep., Cal.), one of the group that was working to defeat the sales tax, moved to increase the maximum surtax rates to 65%, wartime rates.[50] Crisp tried to block the tide of opposition by asking

[48] New York *Times,* Baltimore *Sun,* March 18, 1932; *Cong. Rec.* 75: 6353-6359.
[49] *Cong. Rec.* 75: 6469-6470.
[50] *Cong. Rec.* 75: 6471.

the House to consider carefully what the effect of such an amendment would be. "Dollars are sensitive," he said. He did not question that the tax rate could be pushed so high that men would not risk their funds in business but would put them in tax-exempt securities. If this were the result, if much business were suspended, would that not increase unemployment? La Guardia replied that the highest rate, 65%, applied only to incomes of $5,000,000 and over, so he did not think the House needed to be exercised over that. The Swing substitute rates were adopted by a vote of 153 to 87.[51]

The sponsors of the bill then held their lines in preventing the adoption of three amendments to the corporation tax,[52] but on the following day the opponents succeeded in getting a majority for an amendment to strike out a section that allowed corporations and individuals to have credit for taxes paid to foreign countries and to possessions of the United States.[53] When the vote was announced the House yelled a veritable shout of triumph, and stamped and cheered.

The success of this opposition and the feelings engendered thereby brought Crisp to his feet. He realized that the situation had got beyond his control. With jaw set and fist clenched, he told members that he did not believe the House was in the proper frame of mind to legislate and thought it would do everyone good to cool off and to think. He moved that the Committee of the Whole arise.[54]

Rainey again tried to defend the Committee, but Doughton supported the objectors. He said he realized that the House was in no frame of mind to legislate, and that there had been some intemperate remarks. Nevertheless, the important question was the duty of the members. Those who opposed the sales tax did so because they considered the tax unjust, unfair, and unreasonable, not because they were opposed to balancing the budget.[55]

Crisp was uncertain as to his next move. Should he let the House rewrite the bill or should the Committee revise it? Hopeful that added exemptions would make the bill more palatable, the Committee set to work on amendments. On Wednesday, following the eventful adjournment of Saturday, the House again went to work on the bill. Crisp reported that he had seen Snell, Republican leader, and that Doughton, Rankin (Miss.), and La Guardia had conferred with him as to the possibility of working out some agreement to expedite

51 *Cong. Rec.* 75: 6475-6477.

52 A capital stock tax, an increase of the net income tax to 15% and a tax of 2% on corporation surpluses. (*Cong. Rec.* 75: 6478, 6480, 6481.)

53 *Cong. Rec.* 75: 6497-6511.

54 *Cong. Rec.* 75: 6512.

55 *Cong. Rec.* 75: 6513.

the measure. It was suggested that the House first consider the estate tax, then the sales tax question. This was acceptable to all.[56]

No sooner had the estate tax section been read than an amendment was proposed by Lewis (Dem., Md.) to increase greatly the yield of this tax by changing the brackets and by reducing the exemption. Ramseyer, who had been an advocate of high estate taxes for years, also proposed a similar amendment but his rates were not so high as those of Lewis. He said that he was in an unusual situation for he had often sought increased rates, but now he cautioned the House against making them excessively high.[57] The Ramseyer amendment was adopted. It provided for a maximum of 45% on parts of estates over $10,000,000 but less steeply graded than those proposed by Lewis, who wanted the maximum of 40% to apply to parts of estates over $500,000.

Crisp then presented Title IV, the controversial manufacturers' excise tax, with a number of concessions to the opponents. The new amendments exempted food, wearing apparel, agricultural machinery, medicine, insecticides used for agricultural purposes, and malt sirup in containers of not less than fifty pounds each used by bakers for making bread.[58]

Soon after this Cullen (Dem., N. Y.) introduced his amendment for a tax of 3 cents a pint on beer and other non-intoxicating beverages containing not more than 2.75% alcohol. This amendment did not come up for discussion for several days. An effort was made to prevent its consideration as being out of order, but the chair ruled otherwise. In spite of the offer of the "wets" to "drink up the deficit," the amendment was rejected. If a discussion of the Eighteenth Amendment were started, even the sales tax would sink into insignificance.[59]

The same evening, Doughton broadcast an address explaining his opposition to the sales tax. The first reason he objected to it was because it was a tax on consumption, imposed without any regard for the principle of ability to pay. The Democratic party had always stood for this principle, he said. He quoted able economists as opposed to a sales tax. The tax before Congress was characterized as one of the worst that could have been written because it exempted only certain kinds of food, and taxed everything else, education, transportation, arts and sciences and amusements. Furthermore, he did not think his opponents used a sound argument when they said that the tax was needed to balance the budget. Taking into account the reductions in expenditures, the additional income that could be

56 *Cong. Rec.* 75: 6659.
57 *Cong. Rec.* 75: 6661-6681.
58 *Cong. Rec.* 75: 6684.
59 *Cong. Rec.* 75: 6687, 6827-6846. "Many wets realized that the suggestion was in the realm of visions." (New York *Times*, April 3, 1932.)

provided by raising income tax rates, the possibility of levying some taxes on luxuries from all these sources, he was sure that wealth could carry the burden. He reminded his hearers that not even in the war days was the situation so serious as to demand a tax on those with small incomes such as the Committee proposed in the midst of a depression.[60]

Not even the modifications proposed by the Committee were enough to save the sales tax. It was reported that La Guardia was somewhat inclined to accept these amendments but after conferring with the "bitter enders" agreed to continue to fight.[61] On March 24 the House almost went wild in wrecking the bill by offering countless amendments for exemptions of all possible commodities, such as harness, crates, baskets, boxes used for handling, packing, and shipping fruit and vegetables, turpentine or resin, ice, artificial limbs, coal, fuel used in the home, and the American flag ! [62] Then Doughton moved to strike out the paragraph under consideration ; this would be tantamount to eliminating the sales tax provision.[63]

As Rainey said, this was the crucial point in the sales tax proposition. He, Byrns, Crisp, and Hawley tried to save the measure. It was useless. By a vote of 223 to 153 the sales tax was killed.[64] Only forty Democrats stood by the chairman. The House broke into pandemonium.

Crisp addressed his colleagues. He said he had no criticism of anyone who disagreed with him, but as he had been turned down three or four times on the very heart of the bill, he thought he had no right to manage it further. He expressed his willingness for any member of the opposition to take charge. Cries came back, "No! No!" So he consented to pilot the bill through the House as well as he could.[64] He called a meeting of the Committee on Ways and Means for the following Saturday.

The press made many prophecies that the public had lost confidence in the Democratic party, that it would be the undoing of Garner, that it was ridiculous for the Democratic party to scuttle its own bill and other comments that proved to be erroneous.[65] It could not be denied, however, that Crisp was the hero, though defeated. Through the whole debate he had been fair in giving time to his opponents and had maintained his sense of proportion.

While the Committee struggled over possible substitutes to raise

[60] *Cong. Rec.* 75: 6731.
[61] New York *Times,* March 22, 1932.
[62] *Cong. Rec.* 75: 6797-6808.
[63] *Cong. Rec.* 75: 6809.
[64] *Cong. Rec.* 75: 6816.
[65] New York *Times,* Baltimore *Sun,* March 25, 1932. In the latter were printed many comments from other papers.

the necessary $363,000,000, the House engaged in a tariff battle that became very bitter. As one of the members said, the proposal to put a duty on oil was an invitation to put a tariff on many other articles, such as butter, matches, lumber, bananas, chemicals, and other products. Some eastern Republicans led by the Pennsylvania delegation succeeded in winning support of high tariff Democrats for a duty on coal to prevent the importation of Russian coal "mined by forced labor." Despite the curious temporary alliance of Crisp, La Guardia, and Doughton, the amendment was passed. As predicted, many other tariff amendments were offered immediately, but none of them was passed.[66]

On the 29th, Garner exerted all his personal persuasiveness and political ingenuity in a plea to the House to put aside their bickerings and to balance the budget. He asked the members of his party to be brotherly, as far as possible, "not to throw brick bats" ! In true revivalist style, he invited those of his hearers who wanted to stand by him to rise ! Snell also addressed the House, asking that members of both parties work together in the interest of the country. Crisp then summarized the new Committee proposals.[67] The combination of the Speaker's plea and the new tax program turned the hitherto unmanageable house into a docile, harmonious group, in fact, "a veritable love feast" ensued, according to one correspondent.[68]

Briefly outlined, these proposals were as follows : (1) Begin the individual income surtax at $6000 instead of $10,000 ; (2) reduce the corporation exemption to $1000 instead of $2000 ; (3) repeal the provision permitting the carry-over of net losses ; (4) tax dividends even if paid out of earnings or profits accumulated prior to March 1, 1913 ; (5) revise the depletion allowance ; (6) tax sales of stock one-fourth of 1% but not less than 4 cents a share ; (7) tax bond transfers one-eighth of 1% ; (8) tax issues of capital stock and bonds 10 cents per hundred dollars ; (9) increase the tax on produce for future delivery sold on exchanges from 1 cent to 5 cents for each $100 value ; (10) increase the exemption for theater admissions from 25 cents to 45 cents and (11) impose a group of new excises on such articles as furs, jewelry, sporting goods, beverages, radios, mechanical refrigerators, automobiles, and yachts.[69] As these suggestions were given the stamp of approval by La Guardia and Doughton, the House proceeded to adopt most of them. In fact, the docility was such that they rejected

[66] *Cong. Rec.* 75: 6824-6826, 6846-6859, 6867-6883, 6961-6967 ; New York *Times,* April 3, 1932.

[67] *Cong. Rec.* 75: 7027-7029.

[68] Baltimore *Sun,* March 30, 1932.

[69] *Cong. Rec.* 75: 7029-7030, 7034-7044. The changes were made by a subcommittee of Ragon, Canfield, and Vinson, Democrats ; Hawley and Treadway, Republicans.

even the Swing surtax rates that had been adopted in the first exciting days of the revolt in the Committee of the Whole.[70]

Crisp also presented some additional Committee amendments to increase the tax yields. One that proved to be somewhat controversial was for an additional tax of 1½% in case affiliated concerns filed consolidated returns. Many of the Democrats did not want corporations to have this privilege. Garner was the leader of this group. He explained that he could see no defense for consolidated returns and had succeeded in having the House abolish them in 1928, but the Senate thought otherwise. He still disapproved of such returns but was willing to agree to the Committee's proposal for a "penalty" tax of 1½%. In this way, a record could be kept over a series of years to see what the results were. The expected additional revenue of $14,000,000 or more was also an argument in favor of the new plan.[71]

Crisp explained that if affiliated and consolidated returns were not permitted, a great many short line railroads would probably be "junked" because their rates were fixed by public utilities commissions and hence the tax could not be passed on. Cannon (Mo.) was hopeful of increasing the additional tax to 2½%, not only to bring more revenue into the Treasury but also to help the independent corporation by taxing more heavily the chain corporations. His amendment was rejected and that of Crisp was accepted.[72]

Probably as an answer to a last-minute Treasury request for more funds, Crisp presented an unexpected amendment that he admitted was considered rather drastic, namely, to apply the normal tax to dividends received by individuals from corporations with gross income of $25,000 or over. It was a surprise to the minority members of the Committee on the morning of the day it was brought up. Treadway drew up a substitute amendment to exempt taxpayers with incomes of $10,000 or less from this provision, but it was rejected. Crisp's proposal was accepted.[73]

One last effort was made by Crisp to re-enact the manufacturers' sales tax, but it failed by a vote of 236 to 160.[74] The House also affirmed its former action in accepting the Ramseyer rates on the estate and gift taxes.[75] The bill was passed on April 1 by a vote of 327 to 64.[76]

70 *Cong. Rec.* 75: 7325.
71 *Cong. Rec.* 75: 7127.
72 *Cong. Rec.* 75: 7124-7130.
73 *Cong. Rec.* 75: 7299-7310. This was deleted in Conference.
74 *Cong. Rec.* 75: 7324.
75 *Cong. Rec.* 75: 7326.
76 *Cong. Rec.* 75: 7329.

SUMMARY OF THE HOUSE BILL

The bill as finally drafted by the House was estimated to yield $856,000,000 additional revenue, of which approximately one-fourth was expected from increased rates of the individual income tax; about the same from miscellaneous taxes on telephone and telegraph messages, admissions and stamp taxes; slightly more from excise taxes on the sale of lubricating oil, brewer's wort, malt sirup, toilet preparations, furs, jewelry, automobiles, and a tariff on coal and oil; and about $160,000,000 from increased corporation taxes and changed administrative provisions. Even this large amount would be insufficient to balance the budget unless government expenditures were reduced by $200,000,000.

The rates of the individual normal income tax were made 2% on the first $4000, 4% on the next $4000 and 7% on the remainder. The surtax rates were graduated from 1% on income in excess of $6000 to 40% on income in excess of $100,000. Dividends received by individuals from corporations with gross income of $25,000 and over were subject to the normal tax. Personal exemptions were decreased from $1500 to $1000 for a single person and from $3500 to $2500 for married persons and for a head of a family. Earned income was granted a deduction from net income rather than a credit against the tax.

The rate of the corporation tax was increased to 13½% and the exemption reduced to $1000 but allowed only in case the net income was $10,000 or less. An additional tax of 1½% was levied on corporations that filed consolidated returns.

The privilege of carrying over net loss from one year to the next was abolished; deductions of losses from sales of securities were limited to the amount of the gains from such transactions and the allowance for depletion reduced. The "wash sales" provision was clarified to show that the section applied to sales and repurchases occurring on the same day.

Estate tax rates were increased to a maximum of 45% on amounts of estates over $10,000,000 and the exemption was reduced to $50,000. A gift tax was enacted with rates graduated from three-fourths of 1% on amounts not over $10,000 to 33½% on amounts over $10,000,000.

ACTION OF THE SENATE COMMITTEE ON FINANCE

The Senate Finance Committee [77] met to line up its work soon after the House bill was passed. Smoot promised that the budget would be balanced and that the tax measure would be drawn up in such a way as to minimize its offensiveness to business and to the country as a whole. Almost immediately the members became involved in a tariff wrangle. A few Democrats, especially Walsh, Tydings, and Hull, tried to prevent the interjection of the tariff issue, but Connally and Gore, whose constituents were interested in oil, opposed them. Tydings interrupted the business of the Senate on April 8 to attempt to secure support for a resolution that would instruct the Committee to strike from the revenue bill all tariff matters. He made his request on the ground that it was important to have the bill passed. He did not need to tell them that, inasmuch as the oil and coal duties were already in the bill, efforts would be made to levy tariffs on a number of other commodities and the consequent discussion might delay matters for months.[78] This resolution was not voted on, but an understanding was supposedly reached among members of the Committee that tariff proposals would be considered last.

At the public hearings in April the Secretary of the Treasury summarized the causes of the financial situation, especially the decline in large incomes, and analyzed the recently-passed House bill. He held that its great merit was the amount of revenue it would raise, but he disapproved of a number of the principal sections. He considered the corporation tax rates too high, especially when 1½% was added for the privilege of filing a consolidated return, a feature which he thought unfair. He disapproved of the application of the normal tax to dividends from large corporations, the abolition of the provision for carrying forward net losses, the amount of the stock transfer tax and the rates of the estate tax.

Several of the Committee, especially Harrison, ranking Democratic member, were not satisfied with the negative comments ; they wanted specific constructive suggestions. When the Secretary advocated a

[77] The members of the Senate Committee on Finance were:

Republicans :	*Democrats :*
Reed Smoot (Utah), Ch.	Pat Harrison (Miss.)
David A. Reed (Pa.)	William H. King (Utah)
Samuel M. Shortridge (Cal.)	Walter F. George (Ga.)
James Couzens (Mich.)	David I. Walsh (Mass.)
Henry M. Keyes (N. H.)	Alben W. Barkley (Ky.)
Hiram Bingham (Conn.)	Tom Connally (Tex.)
Robert M. La Follette, Jr. (Wis.)	Thomas P. Gore (Okla.)
John Thomas (Idaho)	Edward P. Costigan (Colo.)
Wesley L. Jones (Wash.)	Cordell Hull (Tenn.)
Jesse H. Metcalf (R. I.)	

[78] *Cong. Rec.* 75: 7735.

bill very much like the one he had originally presented to the Ways and Means Committee the preceding December, the Senator became very irritated. The Secretary replied rather caustically that he would rewrite the bill, if that was what the Committee desired, but he could not take out one item of which he disapproved and substitute another. This difference of opinion between the Secretary and the Democratic members made an unfortunate break in the non-partisan attitude of the Committee towards the bill.[79] It soon developed, however, that differences of opinion were not along party lines.

The ambition of the Committee to make speed in preparing the bill was also dampened somewhat by the opposition to the House excise taxes expressed by numerous witnesses at the hearings. In two weeks the Committee was bombarded with objections to all parts of the House bill.[80]

When the hearings were completed and the Committee retired into executive session, two extremely complicated issues divided the members. One was the sales tax. Back of a move to restore the House provisions for a manufacturers' sales tax were Reed on the Republican side and Walsh (Mass.) on the Democratic, with sympathy from Smoot, the Chairman. Reed said on the floor of the Senate that he used every possible opportunity to press his case with all the vigor he had.[81]

The other issue was tariff protection. As has been stated, La Follette and Hull foresaw the almost endless time that would be consumed in the discussion of schedules and the "log-rolling" that would result, once the topic was introduced. To prevent this La Follette moved that all tariff items be eliminated. Only five Democrats and two Republicans, an insufficient number, supported him.[82] The Committee then proceeded to vote on the various schedules. The House provisions for import duties on coal and oil were retained, but not until several votes had been taken. The vote for a duty on copper was a tie. This seemed to end the tariff discussion for the time being.

So the Committee settled down to a slightly less controversial subject — the income tax rates. The issues here were very different from those that were involved in the tariff sections. Couzens was the leader for high rates, apparently because he wanted sufficient revenue

79 New York *Times*, April 14, 1932.

80 The published transcript of testimony covers over 1400 pages.

81 *Cong. Rec.* 75: 10259.

82 On the second vote on the resolution seven Republicans and two Democrats voted against it and four Republicans and six Democrats for it. According to La Follette, the tariff advocates, in order of persistence, were: Smoot, Watson, Reed, Shortridge, Couzens, Bingham, Thomas, and Jones. Couzens' votes, however, were not so consistently pro-tariff as the others. On one occasion he voted to strike out the oil tariff from the bill, and another time voted to strike out the coal tariff.

from the income tax to obviate the necessity of certain excise taxes, especially on automobiles.[83] With Couzens on this issue were La Follette and most of the Democrats, but not Harrison. Other Republicans, especially those close to the Administration, did not want such high rates on large incomes.

At the start the Committee seemed to favor rather drastic provisions. The high tax advocates succeeded temporarily in almost doubling the normal rates,[84] in pushing the maximum surtax rate to 45% and the corporation tax rate to 14%.[85] Many exemptions were eliminated, such as that hitherto allowed for veterans' pensions and for income received by non-resident American citizens employed by the United States government. The Committee made the tax applicable to salaries of the President of the United States and members of the federal judiciary taking office after the enactment of the law.

On a few points the Committee accepted the proposals of the Treasury. For example, it decided to abolish the 1½% additional tax for consolidated returns and to restore the exemption of dividends from the normal tax. Before the month was over, however, the 1½% tax was restored. In spite of these few concessions, the Treasury became somewhat alarmed at the trend of the Committee measure, so Mills made a point of being present very frequently or of sending Undersecretary Ballantine to represent him.[86]

Again Couzens attempted to have the income tax rates increased to those of 1918, but he was unsuccessful. The rates of 1921 were then proposed and these too were rejected. Connally then secured, temporarily, adoption of the rates of the 1921 Act applicable to 1922 — 4% on the first $4000 of taxable income, and 8% on the remainder with surtaxes reaching to 55%. Then the deduction for earned income was eliminated.[87]

On the following day the high tariff advocates seized control and re-opened many schedules. La Follette reported afterward that fully 30% of the time of the Committee was spent on the tariff issue.[88]

In the midst of the Committee deliberations a message came from the White House. Apparently both alarmed and annoyed, perhaps

83 New York *Times,* April 28, 1932; 72d Congress, 1st session, *Hearings before the Committee on Finance, United States Senate, on the Revenue Act of 1932,* p. 59.

84 The 1929 rates were 1½%, 3% and 5%. The Committee voted for 3%, 6% and 9%.

85 Couzens wanted wartime rates restored, so voted against these rates.

86 New York *Times,* May 1932.

87 *Cong. Rec.* 75: 10748.

88 *Cong. Rec.* 75: 10750. A new coalition developed, a kind of closed corporation. The men who wanted tariffs on coal, oil and copper decided that after they had gotten their duties written into the bill no more would be permitted. The lumber interests succeeded in getting a tariff on certain products but not on shingles or logs. Then the gates were closed. The advocates of tariff on butter, casein, manganese and numerous other commodities were turned down amid confusion caused by the pressure from many interests. (New York *Times,* May 5, 1932.)

also disgusted with the slowness of the Committee that seemed to amount almost to dilly-dallying, President Hoover sent word to Congress that the most essential factor to economic recovery was the restoration of confidence; but certain events in Washington had spread fear and alarm through the country. Of these events he listed first the manner in which the House of Representatives had rejected not only the revenue program of the Treasury,[89] but also that reported by the Committee on Ways and Means. Next he criticized the vast appropriations, which virtually destroyed a program of economy. He recounted the decrease of federal revenues by an amount of $1,700,000,000 below those of 1929, causing a situation which necessitated "inexorably" a broader basis of taxation, prompt enactment of a revenue bill, and "a drastic reduction of expenditures in order to balance the budget." [90]

The message called forth some sharp remarks that the Treasury had been responsible for the failure of Congress to balance the budget because estimates of tax yields were constantly changing and because expectations of tax yields were based on hoped-for improvement in business conditions that had failed to materialize. Robinson (Ark.) criticized the President for having failed to give specific suggestions. Reed (Pa.) defended the Administration but won no good will by his remark that what the country needed was a Mussolini.

In the Committee the excise tax debate became the battleground on which the sales tax issue was fought out. Reed in particular believed that if he could strike out the automobile tax or any other of the sales taxes he could get a general manufacturers' sales tax. The Committee agreed to eliminate certain excise taxes and reduce the rates of others so that the estimate of what the bill would be expected to yield was reduced by $20,000,000. Seventy-seven million was still needed to balance the budget. To the dismay of sales tax advocates the Committee turned to increased income taxes to fill the gap. They accepted the rates proposed by Connally, which had been adopted once before, that is, 4% and 8% normal taxes, a surtax maximum of 55% on income over $1,000,000, and a reduction of the personal exemption for married persons to $2000 where the net income was $5000 and over. Reed then made his last attempt to get support for a sales tax and, being unsuccessful, said he would carry the fight to the floor of the Senate.[91] Smoot was not at all pleased with Connally's rates. Indeed it was reported that he was very angry,

89 This charge seemed somewhat unfair because the House had not entirely rejected the Treasury proposals.

90 *Cong. Rec.* 75: 9640; New York *Times*, May 6, 1932. Arthur Krock commented: "The President's message . . . is the most effective move he has made in his dealings with the parliamentary bodies of the nation . . . It was a bull's eye, and the cries of the wounded were instantly forthcoming."

91 New York *Times*, May 6, 1932. The vote on the Connally Amendment was 11 to 9.

that he pounded on his desk and said that he would summon the Secretary for the next morning's session.[92]

Promptly at ten o'clock Mills arrived in a determined mood. One of the members described him as a litigant who wanted to compromise, and was willing to compromise if you would give him the judgment.[93] The Secretary bargained back and forth across the Committee table "as if trading merchandise across a counter," according to one correspondent.[94] He wanted the income tax rates lowered, the extra 1½% for consolidated returns deleted, and many of the excise taxes abolished. To compensate for these losses he requested a tax on checks, an import duty of 5 cents a pound on rubber, increased sales taxes on automobiles and a tax on theater admissions of 10 cents and over.[95]

The Committee members were worn out. They were not entirely satisfied with the results of their work, which seemed more or less of a hodge-podge, and most of them welcomed anyone who wanted to "father the bill"; [96] nevertheless, a few were unwilling to "have the Committee blandly succumb to the voice of authority," and to have the work of a month reduced to chaos. In thirty minutes the Secretary had secured most of his requests, including lowered income taxes and even the application of the admission tax to tickets of 10 cents.

The vote on the redrafted bill resulting from Mills' visit was thirteen yeas and four nays.[97] From a fiscal point of view the bill was inadequate, $32,000,000 short of what the House bill would produce, and lacked $231,000,000 of balancing the budget. Mills was quoted as having optimistically said that economies could be found! [98]

During the next few days the bill was again revised but essentially it represented Mills' wishes. By May 11 it was in shape to be reported. The main features were as follows:

1. The normal income tax rates were 3% on the first $4000, 6% on the second $4000, and 9% on the remainder of net income. The exemptions were placed at $1000 for a single person and $2500 for a married couple. No deduction or credit was allowed for earned income. Compensation for personal service in excess of $75,000 could not be deducted as a business expense.

[92] *Cong. Rec.* 75: 10306.
[93] *Cong. Rec.* 75: 10281.
[94] New York *Times,* May 7, 1932.
[95] *Cong. Rec.* 75: 10258, 10282, 10306, 10308.
[96] *Cong. Rec.* 75: 10281.
[97] For the bill: *Republicans* — Smoot, Watson, Reed, Shortridge, Jones, Keyes, Bingham, Metcalf, Thomas; *Democrats*—Harrison, Walsh, King and George. Against the bill: *Republicans* — Couzens, La Follette; *Democrats* — Hull and Connally. (Baltimore *Sun,* May 7, 1932.)
[98] Congress had not shown much interest in economy. The appropriations for road building had been increased by $132,000,000, additional non-service-connected benefits had been granted to veterans and the House had failed to authorize the reduction of government bureaus and commissions.

2. The surtax rates began at 1% on income in excess of $6000 and reached 45% on income in excess of $1,000,000.

3. The corporation rate was 14%. The exemption previously allowed to small corporations was eliminated and no additional tax was levied if consolidated returns were filed.

4. The estate tax and gift tax rates were the same as those passed by the House.

5. Import duties were imposed on oil, coal, lumber, copper, and rubber.

6. Sales taxes were imposed on certain selected articles but not nearly so many as in the House bill.

7. Postage rates were increased on first and second class mail.[99]

A minority report was filed by five Democrats : Harrison, Costigan, Walsh, George, and Hull. They dissented from the majority report especially because of the tariff duties on oil, coal, copper, and lumber. The inclusion of these duties was characterized as "utterly indefensible," unsound in principle, and dangerous in practice. They pointed out that the arguments for such tariffs were presented in Congress when the Smoot-Hawley Tariff Act was written in 1930, but they were rejected ; no new arguments were presented in 1932 except that the industries were in greater need of relief than ever, but that situation was not limited to these few, it applied to every industry in the country.

Walsh (Mass.) also submitted a report entitled "Personal Views" in which he explained his reasons for favoring a manufacturers' excise tax and announced that he would submit an amendment for such a tax when the bill was before the Senate.

THE SENATE BECOMES INVOLVED IN A TARIFF WRANGLE

Chairman Smoot formally laid the tax bill before the Senate on May 12,[100] and on the following day explained it briefly.[101] His speech was interrupted by the introduction of a host of amendments, some of which were filled with political dynamite. For example, Tydings proposed a tax on 2.75% beer, which he advocated because it would raise half of the billion dollars needed ; the people would not protest against it ; in fact, it would be only just. Why, he asked, should honest industry be taxed while bootleggers and racketeers become rich and contribute nothing whatsoever to the government ? [102]

Couzens, who was especially perturbed about the effect of the manufacturers' tax on the automobile industry, then renewed his

99 72d Congress, 1st Session, *Senate Report* 665, Part 1.
100 *Cong. Rec.* 75: 10073.
101 *Cong. Rec.* 75: 10082-10084.
102 *Cong. Rec.* 75: 10103-10106.

effort to increase the income tax rates to those in effect in 1918. Long (La.) had previously introduced an amendment with similar rates,[103] but both of these plans had been rejected by the Finance Committee. Couzens' proposition was that if the income tax rates were increased it would be possible to raise sufficient revenue so that taxes need not be levied on production and consumption. The latter taxes, explained the Senator, were imposed whether there was a profit or a loss. An income tax, on the other hand, was imposed only if there was a profit. In fact, as the Senator pointed out, much of the sales tax propaganda was pushed by those who were large income taxpayers, to relieve them of the burden and to push it off on consumers of necessities. As in previous struggles for high income taxes, opponents argued that the tax could be evaded by investment in tax-exempt securities, but Couzens had an answer to that. The experience of the Treasury Department indicated that only about 12% of the total assets of $2,700,000,000 of estates of $3,000,000 and over that had filed returns from September 1928, to January 1932, were invested in tax-exempt bonds ; if all estates for that period were considered, 5.7% of all the assets were in tax-exempts.

Walsh (Mass.) replied to Couzens that his proposal implied the departure from the accustomed program of levying taxes because all previous laws had included some excises on manufactured commodities and miscellaneous taxes such as those on admissions to theaters, athletic events, etc. Another argument was that Couzens' proposal was unfair because it would increase twelve times the tax on incomes of $5000, but no millionaire's income tax was increased nearly that much.[104] The debate then went off on a sales tax discussion which some thought not germane since there was no sales tax in the bill. Norris pointed out the connection when he said that there would be one before they were through if incomes were not adequately taxed.[105] Couzens' amendment was discussed for three days, but in spite of support from Borah, Norris, La Follette, Costigan, and many other Progressives it was defeated by a vote of 31 to 49.[106]

Connally then offered an amendment to restore the 1922 rates of the 1921 Act which the Committee had adopted before Mills forced them to be lowered. Smoot, of course, was much in favor of the lower rates. He would not admit that the Secretary of the Treasury had, at one time, advocated the rates of 4% and 8% which Connally proposed.

[103] *Cong. Rec.* 75: 10108.
[104] *Cong. Rec.* 75: 10108-10121.
[105] *Cong. Rec.* 75: 10189.
[106] *Cong. Rec.* 75: 10276. Of those who voted for the amendment, 15 were Republicans, 15 Democrats and one Farmer-Laborite. Of those against it, 24 were Republicans and 25 Democrats.

Long took up the cudgel for the higher income tax rates, which he espoused as an important feature of his campaign, "Share-Our-Wealth." He wanted the Senate to consider the income tax provisions and settle them, then decide upon a sales tax before the excise tax sections were reached. Smoot tried to secure the consent of the Senator to limit the time of speeches, but Long protested that he could not agree to a proposal that did not allow him to be heard after his colleagues had had an opportunity to be influenced by Mills. So he began a filibuster to keep the Senate in session until it would be too late to see Mills. "I hope," he said, "that the Senators will understand that I am undertaking to save them from themselves." [107] For over three hours he held the floor, and Senators who had come to conduct business that evening were left to walk the floor or listen to the oratory. Long's speech was an exhibition of his mannerisms and gyrations. He laughed at his own performances and winked and smiled at his colleagues. Sticking remarkably close to the subject of taxation, he kept up his flow of words until ten o'clock, the time for adjournment.

On the following day, Connally's amendment was voted on and defeated.[108] Thereupon Long offered his proposal for heavier surtaxes, starting at income of $10,000 or over instead of at $6000 and reaching a maximum of 65% instead of 55% on income of $1,000,000 and over. This proposal also was rejected.[109] With the defeat of the amendment Long gave up his hard fight and, as a result of this decision, the Senate seemed to feel a unity not seen before in the tax debate. The income tax titles were read and, one after another, seventy-two Committee amendments were adopted in less than three hours.[110]

This harmonious interlude was short. Trouble began when the Senate reached Title IV — Manufacturers' Excise Taxes. It was known that Walsh (Mass.) would propose a restoration of the tax proposed by the House Committee on Ways and Means. Advocates of farm relief measures and tariffs on oil and other commodities were ready with amendments of many kinds. Harrison tried in vain to get unanimous approval to eliminate all these tariff sections but protectionist Republicans secured enough help from special-interest tariff Democrats to pass the oil schedules, then those relating to coal, copper, rubber, and lumber, and, finally, those providing duties on copra, cocoanut oil, olive oil, and other ingredients of oleomargarine.

107 *Cong. Rec.* 75: 10298. See below, Chap. XV.

108 The vote was 31 yeas, 46 nays. The party division was as follows: For — 15 Republicans, 15 Democrats, one Farmer-Laborite; against — 24 Republicans, 22 Democrats. (*Cong. Rec.* 75: 10389.)

109 *Cong. Rec.* 75: 10400.

110 *Cong. Rec.* 75: 10400-10417.

When the sections on malt and wort taxes were reached, Tydings introduced his amendment for a tax of 1% on alcoholic beverages containing 2.75% alcohol,[111] the proceeds of which would be put into a fund to pay interest on a $1,500,000,000 issue of bonds for a public works employment project. Smoot's reaction was expressed in the simple question, "Does the Senator really insist upon a vote upon his amendment?" To this, Tydings replied that he was sincere. The tax, he said, would yield half of the billion dollars needed by the Treasury, it would be paid without protest, and it would be a step towards the ending of bootlegging and racketeering. Senate leaders did not care to have the prohibition issue interrupt the tax bill, much as they may have sympathized with both the means and purpose of the amendment. With less discussion than might have been expected, it was defeated by a vote of 23 to 60.[112]

The discussions went far afield from matters of taxation, even to relief for agriculture.[113] Tydings implored the President to speak out and to end the impasse,[114] but no word came for several days.

Then the Senate returned to the question of excise taxes. The Committee amendment to increase the rates set by the House on automobiles was rejected. So, too, was Couzens' amendment to strike out the tax. Again the tariff became the subject of debate. Shipstead's amendment for a duty on copra and other Philippine products brought up the subject of Philippine independence. Following the agreement to postpone the vote on this proposal,[115] the Senate proceeded to accept the Committee amendments to strike out the taxes on jewelry and furs.[116] Then snags were struck once more. Bingham brought up again the tax on 2.75% beer, Vandenberg and Couzens tried to remove the tax on automobiles. They failed in this but succeeded in preventing the tax on trucks from being increased from 2% to 3%, as the Committee proposed.[117] Again a majority of members upheld the Committee action, made at the Treasury's request, to strike out the House taxes on boats, mechanical refrigerators, firearms, matches, cameras, chewing gum, soft drinks, candy, tooth paste, and jewelry.[118] After several days' consideration of these smaller

[111] *Cong. Rec.* 75: 10425. Under the Volstead Act, the legal limit of alcoholic content was ½ of 1%.

[112] *Cong. Rec.* 75: 10435-10519. "We have taxed almost everything from which we can pluck a feather in the whole United States. We have gone over it with a fine tooth comb."

[113] Norris introduced his amendment for an export debenture plan such as had been considered and rejected in 1930. (*Cong. Rec.* 75: 11014.)

[114] New York *Times*, May 21, 1932.

[115] Shipstead's amendment was later amended to omit all reference to the Philippines, then defeated. (*Cong. Rec.* 75: 11094, 11113-11116.)

[116] *Cong. Rec.* 75: 11023.

[117] *Cong. Rec.* 75: 11037, 11139.

[118] *Cong. Rec.* 75: 11146-11152, 11264-11283, 11300.

excises, the general manufacturers' excise tax was brought up again by Walsh (Mass.) who, it will be recalled, had issued his "Personal Views" on the subject when the Finance Committee issued its report.[119] Before it was voted on the Senate disposed of amendments to the postal rates and to the estate tax provisions.

Then rumors began to circulate that the President and his advisors were about to advocate the enactment of a sales tax.[120] Harrison made a long speech condemning this indirect method of "browbeating" the Senate into undoing its work. Smoot denied that he had said that the sales tax movement was growing as the press had reported him, or that he and the President had discussed the sales tax. Nevertheless, Harrison was not convinced that propaganda on the tax was not being vigorously pushed and he asked for an immediate vote.[121] Couzens agreed with him. He reported that thirty-nine newspaper publishers had been pledged to the sales tax and that others were about to endorse it.[122] To offset this propaganda, a group of those opposed to the tax began some "backstage" work for their side. They circulated two "round-robin" petitions, each of which read: "In order to expedite the passage of a revenue bill to balance the Budget and to prevent unnecessary prolongation of debate thereon, the undersigned now declare that they will at this time vote against any and every form of a sales tax on the pending bill." [123]

Walsh scored this action as a method of indirection, "un-American," "undemocratic," and "an attempt to restrict open and free discussion." [124] Vandenberg defended the circulation of the petition as a means of expeditiously clearing the track for final action on the bill, "in a situation where time is so utterly the essence of our desperate problem." He urged that the bill be passed and that no further consideration be given to the sales tax. Reed, however, wanted a sales tax. He thought it preferable to the miscellaneous taxes on selected articles that the Senate had favored. Even with these taxes and the proposed economies to save $300,000,000, the budget would not be balanced. The proposition was voted on three days later, shortly before the last vote on the bill, and was defeated.[125]

On May 31 the long-expected message of the President was received. He spoke of the continued downward trend of business, of the "run on the dollar" by foreign countries, and of the decrease in government revenues. He asked the Senate for drastic reduction in

119 *Cong. Rec.* 75: 11361.
120 Baltimore *Sun*, May 28, May 29, 1932, New York *Times*, May 29, 1932.
121 *Cong. Rec.* 75: 11488-11490.
122 *Cong. Rec.* 75: 11492.
123 One was signed by 35 Democrats, the other by 20 Republicans (*Cong. Rec.* 75: 11563, 11564).
124 *Cong. Rec.* 75: 11564.
125 *Cong. Rec.* 75: 11567-11568.

expenditures and passage of adequate relief legislation. Specifically he recommended "the extension for a limited period of the many special excise taxes to a more general manufacturers' excise tax with exemptions of food and clothing." He explained in some detail that the latter was not to be confused with a general sales tax that could be pyramided. Such a tax had never been approved by the Administration. He showed that the bill as it stood would raise less than the House bill and that, even with increased income taxes, it would not raise enough to "cover the gap in our revenues." [126]

There is no evidence that the Senate paid the slightest attention to the President's request for a general sales tax. The debate continued on the bill at hand. The Finance Committee then held a special meeting and decided to make several changes. One was to increase the income tax rates to those of 1922, as sponsored by Connally and adopted by the Committee before Mills urged their reduction. The Senate incorporated them into the bill by a vote of 86 to 3.[127] Another change was to impose a tax of 5% on electrical energy, to be paid by the consumer,[128] and a third was to tax gasoline at the rate of one cent a gallon.

Howell (Rep., Neb.) had previously offered an amendment to tax the gross income of power companies at the rate of 3%, but the Senate Finance Committee had taken no action on it. He offered it again on the floor of the Senate as a "proper and just tax" on an industry that had scarcely felt the depression and would bring in about fifty million dollars. Then the Committee became interested in the idea and proposed a substitute so that the tax would be on both electricity and gas and would be paid by the domestic consumer. The Senate rejected the Committee proposal. Walsh then offered a substitute amendment to have the tax paid by both industrial and domestic users. This too was rejected. Then Howell's proposal was accepted after eliminating an amendment to add the words "payable from net income." [129]

The tax on gasoline was accepted at the rate advocated by the Committee, although an attempt was made to reduce it and to substitute a provision by which state governments could borrow from the Reconstruction Finance Corporation.[130]

In the closing hours of the debate attempts were made to reconsider some of the tariff amendments that had been inserted earlier, but time was pressing, in spite of the fact that the Senate had spent

[126] *Cong. Rec.* 75: 11596-11598.
[127] *Cong. Rec.* 75: 11588.
[128] *Cong. Rec.* 75: 11603.
[129] *Cong. Rec.* 75: 11591, 11603-11616. This amendment would have limited the tax to those companies that had a net income for the year.
[130] *Cong. Rec.* 75: 11616-11623. Several Senators thought the states needed the revenue from a gas tax as much if not more than the federal government.

many an evening session on the bill. Walsh's proposal for a manufacturers' sales tax was voted on under these conditions and rejected.

Just before the final vote on the bill was taken, Tydings explained that he could not support it because of the "indefensible" tariff items, and because, with the defeat of the sales tax, the bill would not yield enough to balance the budget. Glass gave a similar explanation, but made no reference to the sales tax. There were few other speeches. The final vote, on May 31, was 72 yeas, 11 nays.[131]

THE REPORT OF THE CONFEREES

The Conference managers for the House and Senate composed their differences in twelve hours. The Senate had made comparatively few changes in the House bill and they were mostly in the excise and tariff sections. As completed, the Conference measure was estimated to yield additional revenue of $1,118,500,000, as compared with $856,000,000 expected from the House bill or $1,117,000,000 from the Senate bill.[132]

SUMMARY OF PRINCIPAL CHANGES MADE BY NEW LAW [133]

The law was composed of nine titles as follows: I — Income Tax; II — Additional Estate Tax; III — Gift Tax; IV — Manufacturers' Excise Tax; V — Miscellaneous Taxes; VI — Estate Tax Amendments; VII — Tax on Transfers to Avoid Income Tax; VIII — Postal Rates; IX — Administrative and General Provisions. A brief outline will be given of changes made in titles pertinent to this study.

Title I — Income Tax. This title provided for a normal tax of 4% on the first $4000 of taxable net income of individuals and 8% on the remainder. The surtax started at 1% on net income in excess of $6000 and increased by 1% steps to a maximum of 55% on net income in excess of $1,000,000.[134] There was no allowance for a lower rate on earned income, as in the immediately preceding laws. The personal exemptions were reduced to $1000 for a single person and $2500 for a married couple or a head of a family, but the allowance for dependents remained at $400. The rate on corporation net income was increased from 12% to 13¾%, and there was no flat deduction for small corporations as in the 1928 law. If affiliated corporations chose to make consolidated returns, they might do so upon payment of an additional tax of ¾ of 1%.

131 *Cong. Rec.* 75: 11666.
132 The details of estimated yield of each Title are tabulated in the *Cong. Rec.* 75: 12069.
133 47 *Statutes at Large* 169.
134 For a comprehensive table of rates, see below, Chap. XXII.

Several changes were made to tighten the law. Interest incurred for purchasing or carrying an annuity was not deductible. No loss was deductible from gross income if it had been claimed for estate tax purposes. Non-resident employees of the United States were subjected to the income tax. The $300 exemption for dividends from building and loan associations was eliminated.

Stricter limitations were placed on the losses arising from the sale or exchange of securities that had been held two years or less. Such losses were deductible only for the year in which they were sustained and only to the extent of gains derived from such sales, but losses disallowed in one year (to an amount not in excess of the net income) could be carried over to the following year.[135] Salaries of presidents of the United States and federal judges taking office after June 6, 1932 were made subject to the tax.[136] Information returns were required respecting payments of $1000 or more. In the 1928 law the minimum was $1500.

The reorganization provisions also were amended to prevent evasion. The existing law permitted a corporation, by means of a reorganization, to distribute tax-free to its shareholders stock or securities in another corporation, a party to the reorganization. Thus a corporation could distribute stock as a dividend without any tax upon the shareholder. The new provision was enacted to make stockholders liable for tax upon receipt of such dividends.

The sections relating to "wash" sales were revised to show clearly that the provisions applied to sales and re-purchases occurring on the same day. A new paragraph was added to the capital gains provision to include stock purchased in a wash sales transaction, and to restrict losses from sale of such property to the 12½% limitation.

Rules for depletion deductions were revised for sulphur, coal, and metal mines so that they were no longer allowed discovery depletion. Coal mines were allowed a depletion deduction of 5% of the gross income of the property; metal mines, 15%; sulphur, 23%; oil and gas wells, 27½%. In no case, however, could the allowance exceed 50% of the net income of the taxpayer from the property. For the tax years 1932 and 1933 the taxpayer had the option of choosing the greater of the deductions, either (1) the percentage depletion allowance, or (2) an allowance computed on an adjusted basis, according to cost or March 1, 1913 value with adjustments. In the return for 1933 the taxpayer was required to state which basis he elected to follow for succeeding years.

135 This provision relating to the carrying forward of such losses was repealed, before it became effective, by the National Industrial Recovery Act of 1933.

136 The Supreme Court upheld the validity of this section May 24, 1939, *O'Malley* v. *Woodrough*, 59 Sup. Ct. 858.

Title II — Estate Tax. A graduated tax on estates was imposed in addition to the tax imposed by the Act of 1926 so that the total rates were more than doubled. The additional tax equaled the excess of the amount of a tentative tax over the tax computed under existing law prior to the allowance of the 80% credit. The "tentative" tax rates started at 1% on net estates not in excess of $10,000 and increased to 45% on parts of net estates in excess of $10,000,000. The flat exemption with respect to the new additional tax was $50,000; in the previous law it had been $100,000. The credit of 80% for death taxes paid to states was not allowed for the new additional estate tax. With the exception of these changes in exemptions the allowable deductions were the same as in previous laws.

Title III — Gift Tax. A tax was imposed at rates graduated from 3/4 of 1% on net gifts not in excess of $10,000 to a maximum of 33½% on amounts in excess of $10,000,000. A flat deduction of $50,000 was permitted; also exempt were gifts made to the United States, to any state or political subdivision thereof for public purposes; to corporations, trusts, or foundations organized for religious, charitable, scientific, or educational purposes; and to organizations of war veterans.

Title IX — Administrative Provisions. This title covered several matters, such as new rules that (1) in case of installment sales the tax was to be collected on each payment; (2) in case of overpayment of excise taxes, refunds and credits were allowed, but not interest thereon. The regulations as to period of limitation for prosecution for internal revenue offences were clarified. The Act went into effect when signed, June 6, 1932, but applied to income received in the tax year of 1932. The excises became effective at various dates specified in the law.

CHAPTER XIII

NATIONAL INDUSTRIAL RECOVERY ACT TAX SECTIONS

DISAPPOINTING YIELD OF THE ACT OF 1932

Most of the excise provisions of the Act of 1932 went into effect on June 21 of that year. Despite the increased rates of old taxes and the levying of new ones the collections for the succeeding months of the year were much less than had been anticipated. The total receipts from all sources were $97,000,000 less than for the same period of the preceding year. Secretary Mills' report to Congress in December 1932 showed that estimates of receipts for the fiscal year 1933 would be materially reduced as a result of these smaller tax collections, that is, he then expected receipts of $2,624,000,000 instead of $3,098,000,000, or $474,000,000 less than previously estimated.

The decline, according to the Secretary, was due partly to the continuing depression in business, partly to large sales of commodities in advance of the effective date of new excise taxes, and partly to difficulties "which inevitably hamper in the administration of a variety of scattered levies." Inaccuracy of the estimates could be partly accounted for also by the lack of adequate basic data.[1] Whatever the extenuating circumstances, government receipts were falling, expenditures increasing, and the federal debt becoming larger. On July 1, 1931, the total gross debt was $16,801,000,000. A year later it was greater by $2,685,000,000.

THE ADMINISTRATION'S DEFLATIONARY POLICY

Again the country heard both from Secretary Mills and from President Hoover that it was essential to have the budget balanced.[2] Their theory was that only by this action would the credit of the United States be maintained. Extensive federal borrowing would tend to lower the price of government securities, and this in turn would affect the solvency of banks and tend to depress private bonds.

In order to balance the budget, government expenses must be cut to the bone and taxes increased. An analysis of the expenditures showed that the first part of this program would be impossible to carry out. The debt service required about 20% of the federal budget in 1932; national defense, about 12%; veterans, 20%, and

[1] *Report of the Secretary of the Treasury* 1932, p. 25.
[2] *Cong. Rec.* 76: 52; *Report of the Secretary of the Treasury* 1932, p. 28.

outlays occasioned by the depression, 28%. Non-functional[3] and departmental expenditures were less than 20% of all expenses, and of this somewhat more than half was for the departments.[4] In other words, if all the salaries of all the government employees were cut 50% and if the other expenses of the departments were similarly reduced, the saving would be only 7% of the five-billion-dollar budget. This policy of saving also implied the reduction of funds for public works, relief, the Reconstruction Finance Corporation, and other agencies established to fight the depression.

The other side of the Administration's policy was equally futile. It was perhaps simple to urge Congress to pass more tax bills but Congress was not so inclined. The income taxes were not yielding sufficient revenue because business was still in the doldrums; the excise taxes were a disappointment, even though they had not been in effect a year. A general sales tax seemed to be the only solution. So the President recommended this tax, one that had been thrown out by the House less than a year before and had not gained any congressional goodwill since. Another objection to it was that it was being adopted very generally by the states.

THE LAME DUCK SESSION

The elections of November 1932 reflected the popular discontent with the economic as well as the political situation. The Democrats were not voted in so much as the Republicans were voted out.

Because of the unfortunate system of waiting until March for the newly-elected members of Congress to take their seats and for the new President to be inaugurated, this last session of the 72d Congress was one composed of the lamest of "lame ducks." [5] In the House were 98 Republicans who had not been re-elected and in the Senate there were twelve. Even before the election the Democrats had a majority of five in the House and a slight majority in the Senate, due to the fact that two Republicans were ineligible for some time.[6]

[3] For example: refund of taxes, purchase of securities, payments in settlement of war claims.

[4] *Report of the Secretary of the Treasury* 1932, pp. 14, 15.

[5] This was the last "lame duck" Congress. The Twentieth Constitutional Amendment, ratified in a remarkably short time, went into effect October 15, 1933. Thereafter the term of office of Representatives and Senators began at noon January 3, and that of the President and Vice-President January 20; Congress convened January 3, each year unless a different day was established by legislation. Therefore the short session, beginning in December, was abolished.

[6] Before the election there were 48 Republican Senators, 47 Democratic and one Farmer-Labor. At the opening of the session, Davis (Pa.) did not take his seat because of charges of corruption in the election and Schuyler (Colo.), who was appointed to fill a vacancy, was not accredited for some days.

The situation was somewhat similar to that of 1919 and 1920, when a discredited Democratic President presided over a hostile Republican Congress with the result that nothing could be done. President Hoover was probably even in a much more depressing situation than President Wilson had been because of the irritation created throughout the country by economic conditions. Business grew worse each month, and banks were failing rapidly throughout the country while the government looked on helplessly. The President lost what little leadership he had once possessed; indeed his veto was almost his only remaining evidence of authority. His annual message recommending a sales tax was just another scrap of paper.[7] In the House there were almost no sales tax advocates, although in the Senate there were a few.

Chairman Collier dutifully called the Ways and Means Committee to consider possible new taxes. Perfunctorily they discussed the President's proposals. Rainey offered a beer tax as his solution. Garner forecast that there would be no new tax bill until the Senate Finance Committee had made its recommendations.[8] He might have gone farther and predicted none until after March 3, 1933.

The Democratic leaders, especially Garner, were in constant touch with President-elect Roosevelt. Many conferences were held in New York as a result of which the decision was reached to kill the proposed sales tax.[9] For a time it looked as though the Democrats would push a bill for increased income tax rates and lowered exemptions so that the incoming President would not have to call an extra session immediately after his inauguration.[10] This idea of heavier income taxes was, however, soon rejected, as involving too unpopular a step.[11] The impasse was thus characterized by a Washington correspondent:

> Since the conference of Democratic leaders with Mr. Roosevelt a week ago, the complete futility of the present Congress has become more firmly assured. As things appear now, literally nothing will be done. The Democrats having scuttled their own proclaimed program of income-tax increases, are at the moment utterly devoid of any legislative plan whatever, and are united only in opposition to Hoover's budget-balancing

7 New York *Times*, Dec. 9, 1932.

"The wild outburst of Mr. Rainey and other Democratic House leaders when the Honorable Ogden L. Mills appeared before the Committee to back up Hoover's budget-balancing sales tax and veteran reduction recommendation was an indication of the temper of the House. They shrieked at Mr. Mills and Mr. Mills shrieked back. It is quite clear that except under the strongest kind of pressure Hoover's proposals for economy and taxation will be thrown into the discard. . ." (*New Republic* 73: 185, Dec. 28, 1932.)

8 New York *Times*, Dec. 25, 1932.

9 New York *Times*, Jan. 1, 4, 1933.

10 New York *Times*, Jan. 7, 1933.

11 New York *Times*, Jan. 10, 1933.

recommendations, which include the manufacturers' sales tax and a reduction in the cost of veteran compensation.[12]

Consequently, practically no tax measures of any kind were introduced by the House Committee in the final session of the 72d Congress. Even the beer revenue measure was discarded.

Secretary Mills, even at the eleventh hour, was not disposed to have his recommendations so lightly heeded. Over a nationwide hook-up he broadcast on January 16 a plea for balancing the budget and warned his listeners that the President intended to "bear down" on Congress for revenue legislation. He showed that economies alone, however desirable, would be inadequate, for even cuts in expenditures to the extent of $500,000,000 would not suffice. Therefore, new taxes were necessary. He explained that at one time he had opposed a sales tax, but he had come to think of it as preferable to a great variety of taxes; after all, the excise taxes already on the statute books were in reality taxes on consumption. The time had come to balance the budget, he repeated, and he blamed the political situation for making it impossible to settle the huge fiscal problem, a problem that would otherwise be "comparatively simple" ! [13]

The President then submitted a special budget message. One editor commented: "Mr. Hoover continues to act as though no election had taken place and he were to remain in office indefinitely." [14] Congress, however, paid no more attention to these pleas than it had to others earlier in the session.[15] The much-discussed plans for reorganizing the government, direct relief, bank reform, prohibition repeal — in fact, practically all bills — were lost in the maze of filibusters.[16]

THE NEW DEAL

Public interest in an inauguration has usually been keen, but on March 4, 1933, it was tense. Just two days before, the Governor of Michigan ordered the closing of all banks in the state because of the failure of large banks in Detroit. This was followed by similar action in other states. On the morning of March 4 practically all banks in the country were closed. The new President ordered them to remain closed for a time. Someone felicitously called it a "bank holiday." People took it well, on the whole. Thus the depression reached its lowest point. The long-feared worst was now known.

[12] *New Republic* 73: 293 (Jan. 25, 1933).
[13] New York *Times*, Jan. 17, 1933.
[14] *New Republic* 73: 280 (Jan. 25, 1933).
[15] New York *Times*, Jan. 19, 1933.
[16] The New York *Times* (Feb. 12, 1933) computed that from December 3d to February 11th the speeches in Congress had cost $4000 a day and that not even one appropriation bill had passed. (In 1939 this cost does not strike the reader as unusually excessive !)

With the coming of the new President, the new party, and new theories of government, perhaps prosperity would venture out from "around the corner."

Certainly it was cheering on that cold gray day to see a charming smile from the President-elect in contrast to the lugubrious face of his predecessor. Was it a symbol of a new era for the "forgotten man" or merely a will o' the wisp?

A special session of Congress was summoned to convene March 9. In contrast to the lack of administrative leadership in the preceding session, President Roosevelt asked for and received such dictatorial power that it "almost stunned the statesmen on the hill, but it apparently pleased nearly everyone else." [17] In contrast to the inertia and pessimism of the preceding Administration, there was energy and hope. In the face of the emergency Congress ceased playing politics for a time.

A different theory of national policy was the order of the day. Economy and budget balancing had been preached during the campaign and at the very beginning of the new Administration a drastic reduction in federal expenditures was authorized. But not for long was budget balancing and economy to mean less expenditure of public funds. The Administration worked out a scheme for a double budget, one for ordinary current expenses, one for the emergency that might be considered for capital or extraordinary purposes.

Banking and "recovery" measures claimed the attention of Congress but, as a temporary expedient, it was decided to rush through a measure to continue the three-cent first class postage rates, except for drop letters, and the taxes on gasoline and electrical energy that would expire on June 30. General tax revision could be postponed for another year.[18] The few other necessary tax changes could be made a part of the National Industrial Recovery Act then being drafted. This bill contained a plan for a $3,000,000,000 public works project and taxes were proposed to raise the amount necessary for interest and sinking fund requirements of the bond issue involved.

The President was very much concerned about the main features of the Act and saw to it that they were drawn up as he wished. It was expected that he would dictate the tax sections also. Strange to say, there was a little talk of a manufacturers' sales tax to be dis-

[17] *New Republic* 74: 156 (March 22, 1933).

[18] This measure was passed by the House April 20 (*Cong. Rec.* 77: 2050) and by the Senate, May 12 (*Cong. Rec.* 77: 3330). Before the Conferees considered the measure (June 9), however, the Congress passed the NIRA in which was incorporated an additional tax of ½ cent a gallon on gasoline, so the section of the excise tax bill containing the gasoline tax was eliminated. This bill was signed June 16. (*Cong. Rec.* 77: 3318, 3329.)

guised as a "re-employment tax," [19] and of a breakfast table levy on coffee, cocoa, etc.,[20] but a few thought such taxes would be levied. Roosevelt, however, finally came to the conclusion that he would let Congress decide this point. Douglas, the director of the Bureau of the Budget, came forward immediately with the following four suggestions: (1) a general manufacturers' sales tax of 1⅛% with no exemption; (2) sharp increases in the normal income tax rates; (3) the application of normal income tax levies to corporation dividends, and (4) miscellaneous levies, such as on tea, coffee, cocoa, telephone messages, admissions, and gasoline.[21]

The chairman of the finance committee of each house immediately began hunting for some means of avoiding the sales tax. When the bill was ready, Doughton called a meeting of his Committee on Ways and Means [22] to find taxes that would fill in the gap of $220,000,000, the President giving them a week in which to do it — quite a different procedure from that usually followed.

The Committee voted to increase the normal income tax rates and to apply them to corporation dividends, to levy a tax of three-fourths of a cent per gallon on gasoline, to extend the stamp taxes and the special excises on imported articles. It was estimated that this program would raise $700,000,000. They decided, however, to impose such additional taxes only until the repeal of the Eighteenth Amendment, by the ratification of the Twenty-first Amendment.

THE MORGAN DISCLOSURES

The day before the bill came up in the House the scene changed. The testimony of J. P. Morgan before the Senate Committee on Banking and Currency that he and his partners had paid no income

19 New York *Times,* May 13, 14, 1933.
20 New York *Times,* May 12, 1933.
21 New York *Times,* May 19, 1933.
22 The members of the Committee were:

Democrats	*Republicans*
Robert L. Doughton (N. C.), Ch.	Allen T. Treadway (Mass.)
Samuel B. Hill (Wash.)	Isaac Bacharach (N. J.)
Thomas H. Cullen (N. Y.)	Frank Crowther (N. Y.)
Christopher D. Sullivan (N. Y.)	James A. Frear (Wis.)
Morgan D. Sanders (Tex.)	Harold Knutson (Minn.)
John W. McCormack (Mass.)	Daniel Reed (N. Y.)
Clement C. Dickinson (Mo.)	Roy O. Woodruff (Mich.)
David J. Lewis (Md.)	Thomas A. Jenkins (Ohio)
Fred M. Vinson (Ky.)	William E. Evans (Cal.)
Jere Cooper (Tenn.)	Thomas C. Cochran (Pa.)
Ashton C. Shallenberger (Neb.)	
Charles West (Ohio)	
John W. Boehne, Jr. (Ind.)	
James V. McClintic (Okla.)	
Claude A. Fuller (Ark.)	

taxes in 1932 startled the country.[23] The public was given to understand by the press that, in spite of large incomes, these bankers had found "loopholes" by means of which they could legally avoid the income tax.[24] Little publicity was given to the fact that tremendous capital losses had been sustained in the depression and that, while in Great Britain these same firms had paid taxes continuously because capital gains and losses were not treated as ordinary income in computing taxable net income, the amount of tax paid there in the years of prosperity was much less than it would have been if there had been a tax on capital gains like that of the United States.[25]

The public reaction to these "disclosures" of the Pecora investigation forced the Ways and Means Committee to consider changing its program. Much as the members desired to modify the income tax law so as to stop flagrant evasion, they did not want to delay consideration of the National Industrial Recovery Act.[26] The tax proposals in the bill were, therefore, the same as those the Committee had originally decided on, namely: (1) increase of the normal income tax rates to 6% on the first $4000 and 10% on the remainder, (2) application of the normal tax to corporate dividends in the hands of stockholders, (3) increase of the gasoline tax from 1% to 1¾%. It was estimated that the income tax increases would yield $46,000,000; the tax on dividends, $83,000,000; and the increased gasoline tax, $92,000,000 additional revenue.[27]

When the bill came before Congress the docility towards Administration proposals almost vanished, largely because of the tax sections. By a small margin, House leaders secured passage of a special rule for consideration of the measure.[28] Objection to the bill was based on the complaint that it was manifestly unfair to increase the tax burden on those with small incomes, "the butcher, the baker,

23 The firm of J. P. Morgan wrote off a loss in depreciation of securities of $21,000,000 as of January 2, 1931 at the time of the reorganization of the partnership upon the admittance of S. Parker Gilbert. The partnership filed an income tax return for these two days, January 1 and January 2. This return, as well as others, had been examined and approved by representatives of the Bureau of Internal Revenue. (73d Congress, 1st Session, *Hearings before the* [Senate] *Committee on Banking and Currency on Stock Exchange Practices* 1933.)

24 The 1932 law permitted the taxpayer to deduct from ordinary income his losses from sale or exchange of securities which had been held two years or less only to the extent of the gains. These disallowed losses could be carried forward for one year but only to the amount of the net income. Dealers in securities, incorporated banks, and persons carrying on a banking business were not subject to these restrictions.

25 *Journal of Accountancy* 56: 1-2 (July 1933). In 1927, 1928, and 1929, the partners paid $22,000,000 in taxes. (73d Congress, 1st Session, *Hearings before the* [Senate] *Committee on Stock Exchange Practices* 1933.)

26 New York *Times*, May 25, 1933.

27 The Republican members did not agree to the tax sections of the bill. (*Cong. Rec.* 77: 4329.)

28 To limit the debate to six hours and to forbid any amendments except by the Committee on Ways and Means.

the storekeeper," while allowing the millionaires to escape. The Committee capitulated to the extent of amending the law so that losses from sale of stocks and bonds held less than two years could be deducted only for the year in which they occurred; that is, losses could not be carried forward to later years.[29]

Because of parliamentary rules, very few amendments were made. By special agreement an effort to impose a manufacturers' sales tax was brought up but it was defeated by a vote of 265 to 137.[30]

THE NIRA IN THE SENATE

The Morgan disclosures influenced also the Senate Committee on Finance.[31] Chairman Harrison urged amendments to the House bill so as to tighten the provisions that applied to partnerships and private bankers. For instance, he wished to exclude private bankers from the privilege of deducting unlimited stock losses as permitted to banks and security dealers, and to prevent members of a partnership deducting from their individual income the distributive share of stock losses disallowed to the partnership.

He reasoned that stockholders of a corporation could not deduct any of the corporation losses from their individual incomes, so it did not seem unfair to take the advantage away from partners. Such a program, he said, would force some of the private banking corporations to incorporate, or would force some of the private banking concerns "to pay a fair proportion of our tax burden." From the point of view of revenue also the proposal was advantageous, according to the author, because it would eliminate the need for increased normal taxes or surtaxes.

In addition to these administrative changes, Harrison proposed a capital stock levy of $1 per $1000 of declared value to raise $80,000,000, similar to levies of 1916-1926, and a levy on corporation dividends to raise $70,000,000. When Committee members questioned the feasibility of arriving at a fair value of capital stock, the

29 *Cong. Rec.* 77: 4188-4197.
30 *Cong. Rec.* 77: 4372.
31 The members of the Committee were:

Democrats	*Republicans*
Pat Harrison (Miss.), Ch.	David A. Reed (Pa.)
Walter F. George (Ga.)	James Couzens (Mich.)
David I. Walsh (Mass.)	Henry W. Keyes (N. H.)
Alben W. Barkley (Ky.)	Robert M. La Follette, Jr. (Wis.)
Tom Connally (Tex.)	Jesse H. Metcalf (R. I.)
Thomas P. Gore (Okla.)	Daniel O. Hastings (Del.)
Edward Costigan (Colo.)	Frederick C. Walcott (Conn.)
Josiah Bailey (N. C.)	
Bennett C. Clark (Mo.)	
William G. McAdoo (Cal.)	
Harry F. Byrd (Va.)	
Augustine Lonergan (Conn.)	

chairman evolved a clever scheme for an excess-profits tax based on the amount of income in excess of a certain percentage of adjusted declared value of the stock of the corporation, "the primary purpose of which was to induce corporations automatically to declare a fair value of the stock" for the capital stock tax. The secondary purpose was to prevent litigation by allowing a corporation to choose its own capital value. A third purpose was to levy a somewhat higher rate of tax on profits that were large in proportion to the capital of the corporation.[32]

This program met with the instant approval of most of the Committee. Connally agreed to drop his scheme for a 10% additional tax to be paid on all returns due March 15.[33] The sales tax advocates, however, demanded a vote on their proposition for a general manufacturers' sales tax; in fact, there were two votes. Each was unfavorable by a small margin.[34]

The bill presented to the Senate, therefore, provided for the following taxes: (1) a capital stock tax of $1 for each $1000 of the declared value of the capital stock of corporations; (2) an excess-profits tax of 5% on the portion of the net income which was in excess of 12½% of the declared capital stock value; (3) an additional gasoline tax of one-half cent per gallon; (4) a 5% tax on dividends to be deducted at the source by corporations but to be borne by the stockholder; and (5) administrative changes to secure more taxes from private bankers and partnerships.

There were many features of the NIRA that provoked more discussion in the Senate than the tax sections, but the Administration saw to it that the whole bill was pushed through with little change.

The sales tax advocates carried out their threat to take their fight to the floor but did not secure much support.[35] Ashurst asked Reed if he would accept an amendment to tax income from federal securities issued thereafter, an amendment which he was sure would win votes for his sales tax proposal. He and Hill had presented a similar amendment in the preceding session but, like most legislation, it had made no progress. Ashurst pointed out that if the government could find some way of taxing income that was then tax-exempt it would prevent the feeling that a certain class of citizens were not

32 73d Congress, 1st Session, *Senate Report* 114. Litigation over capital valuations for the war excess-profits tax had been disastrous to the administration of the tax. By allowing a corporation to choose its own capital value this difficulty was avoided. By linking the capital stock tax with the excess-profits tax, tax evasion was prevented. That is, if the value of the capital stock was made low, the excess-profits tax would be higher when large profits developed.

33 Connally presented this plan late in May. (New York *Times*, May 30, 1933.)

34 The first vote was ten to eight; the second ten to nine. (New York *Times*, June 4, 5, 6, 1933.)

35 The amendment was offered by Reed (Pa.) on behalf of himself, Walsh (Mass.), and Byrd (Va.). It was rejected by a vote of 28 yeas, 57 nays. (*Cong. Rec.* 77: 5416.)

bearing their just share of the burden of government.[36] After the defeat of the sales tax proposal, Clark (Mo.) offered an amendment similar to that suggested by Ashurst, which he believed would "close the greatest gap in our income tax system with the possible exception of the gap which now occurs through the capital-losses provision of the present income tax law." [37]

Clark's amendment was to tax income from all future securities "including obligations of the United States or its possessions, and of any State, Territory, or any political subdivision thereof, or the District of Columbia." There was no debate on the amendment. It was agreed to by the Senate [38] but not accepted by the Conferees. It was then considered of doubtful constitutionality. Harrison later charged the author with offering it, not exactly to obstruct the NIRA to which Clark was opposed, but knowing that it would not promote the measure.

La Follette also secured a favorable vote on his proposal to permit income tax returns to be public records. He reminded his colleagues that in 1924 the Senate adopted an identical amendment which was greatly changed by the Conference Committee so that the law as enacted stated that merely the amount of tax paid by the taxpayer should be a matter of public record.[39]

Only one other amendment to the tax section was offered,[40] and no others to any other part of the measure were accepted. So the bill passed June 9.[41]

THE CONFERENCE REPORT AND SUMMARY OF NEW PROVISIONS

On the morning of June 10 the managers of both houses met in conference and reached an agreement before the day was over.

Treasury representatives appeared before them to ask that the Senate amendment to tax state securities be eliminated. Members agreed that it would not be fair to the states to enact such a law. On the floor of the Senate Clark protested this rejection, Harrison replied that he was surprised, for he did not know that the Senator was so serious about it.

The Conferees objected also to the La Follette amendment to give publicity to income tax returns, so qualified it by adding a phrase to make it read:

36 *Cong. Rec.* 77: 5415.
37 *Cong. Rec.* 77: 5420.
38 Yeas, 45; nays, 37. (*Cong. Rec.* 77: 5421.) See below, Chap. XX.
39 *Cong. Rec.* 77: 5419.
40 A technical question relating to the definition of a jeweler for the excise tax section. (*Cong. Rec.* 77: 5422.)
41 Yeas, 58; nays, 24. (*Cong. Rec.* 77: 5424.)

all returns made under this act . . . shall constitute public records and shall be open to public examination and inspection to such an extent as shall be authorized in rules and regulations promulgated by the President of the United States.

La Follette was very much annoyed. He thought that the Conferees had not made a determined enough effort to secure the amendments passed by the Senate, by a two-to-one vote. He objected to the Conferees' amendment because it was practically a re-enactment of the existing law. It gave the President the right to determine what portion and how much, if any, of an income tax return might be examined and inspected. Norris supported La Follette. Inasmuch as the House had already agreed to the Conference Report they were helpless to make any change or even to move that it be referred to the Committee.[42]

For the most part the Senate amendments were adopted. The income tax rates were unchanged. A tax of 5% was levied on corporation dividends received by individuals. The tax rate upon net income of corporations that filed consolidated returns was increased by three-fourths of 1% for the taxable years 1932 and 1933, and by 1% for 1934 and 1935.

Somewhat reminiscent of war years, a tax was imposed upon corporations, at $1 per $1000 of the fair value of capital stock and, partly as a check on the valuation of stock, an excess-profits tax of 5% was imposed on the net corporate income in excess of 12½% of the adjusted declared value of the capital stock.

Several changes were made to limit the amount of deductible losses. One repealed a section that had been a part of the income tax law since 1919, by which taxpayers could carry forward net business losses from one year to the succeeding year. Another repealed the privilege of carrying forward losses from sale of stocks and bonds held less than two years. Under the 1932 law, such losses could be carried forward to the following year. A new provision was added which prevented partners from deducting from their personal income losses from sale of stocks and bonds disallowed the partnership. Private bankers were no longer given the same exemption as other bankers from limitation of gain and loss from sales of capital assets; that is, deductions of losses incurred by private bankers from the sale of stocks or bonds held less than two years were limited to the gains from similar transactions and could not be used to reduce income from other sources.

The section that provided for a 50% penalty tax upon accumulation of excessive surplus was broadened in order to prevent individuals from evading any internal revenue tax, not merely the surtax.

42 *Cong. Rec.* 77: 5620-5621 (House debate); 5766-68, 5849-5861 (Senate debate).

An unusual section was included to provide for terminating certain of these taxes. It stated that when the total receipts of the federal government exceeded its total expenditures (excluding public debt receipts and expenditures), or when the Eighteenth (Prohibition) Amendment was repealed, the capital stock tax was to be repealed. The gasoline tax would be reduced and the tax on dividends would be repealed on the first day of January following the President's proclamation of either of these eventualities. The bill was signed June 16. The gasoline tax went into effect the next day. The income tax sections were effective as of January 1, 1933.[43]

[43] 48 *Statutes at Large* 195.

CHAPTER XIV

REVENUE ACT OF 1934 – PRESSING FOR MORE REVENUE

SPENDING FOR RELIEF AND RECOVERY

As a result of the ratification of the Twentieth Amendment ("Lame Duck"), the second session of the 73d Congress did not convene until January of 1934. At the close of the preceding session much dissatisfaction was expressed with the internal revenue taxes, even more than usual complaint over this perennial subject. There were criticisms that the burden of the taxes was inequitable, that the new taxes were difficult to administer, and that the income tax receipts were especially inadequate in periods of business depression. Therefore the House instructed the Committee on Ways and Means to use the long interim to study the situation.

The Report of the Secretary of the Treasury in December 1933 for the fiscal year 1933 showed a decline in income tax yield of $311,000,000 from that of 1932, and this was not quite compensated for by the additional excise taxes imposed by the Act of 1932, which were not then fully effective. Expenditures for the depression emergency were $163,000,000 more than for the preceding year; but expenditures for other purposes had decreased so that the total expenditures for 1933 were slightly less than for 1932, that is, $5,143,000,000 instead of $5,154,000,000. The deficit for 1933 was $2,602,000,000.[1]

In the budget message to Congress in January 1934 the President set forth in some detail his plan of spending for relief and recovery which he had outlined a few days before in his annual message. He estimated that total expenditures would reach almost $10,000,000,000 for 1934, of which over half would be for the emergency created by the depression. The deficit for the fiscal year was estimated at over $7,000,000,000.

The President suggested that additional revenue might be secured from liquor taxes,[2] for which a bill had already been drafted, and by tightening the administrative sections of the income tax law.[3]

[1] *Report of the Secretary of the Treasury* 1933, pp. 1-8. In later Reports (1935 and thereafter) the amount of expenditures was revised to include all expenditures of the Reconstruction Finance Corporation so that the total for the year 1933 was placed at $5,889,249,118. The revised amount of deficit was $3,068,266,874.

[2] The Liquor Taxing Act of 1934 was drafted to tax alcoholic liquors as soon as the Twenty-first Amendment repealing the Eighteenth (Prohibition) was effective. It was introduced into the House January 3 and passed January 5, reported to the Senate January 10 and passed the same day. The President signed it January 11. It was estimated it would yield $600,000,000. (*Cong. Rec.* 78: 91-132, 141-59, 321-29.)

[3] *Cong. Rec.* 78: 30.

STUDIES OF TAX AVOIDANCE

Meanwhile the subcommittee on tax revision had made its report to the Committee on Ways and Means. This subcommittee had been instructed to investigate: (1) methods for the prevention of evasion of the internal revenue laws, (2) ways of simplifying these laws, and (3) feasible new sources of revenue. Hill (Wash.) was made chairman of the subcommittee.[4] The research was done by the Joint Committee on Internal Revenue Taxation. The report published in December 1933 was in two main parts: I, Major Problems, and II, Minor Problems.

The major problems were: (1) tax-rate structure, (2) depreciation and depletion, (3) capital gains and losses, (4) personal holding companies, (5) exchanges and reorganizations, (6) dividends out of earnings accumulated before March 1st, 1913, (7) foreign tax credit, (8) consolidated returns, and (9) partnership losses. For each of these matters the committee offered some solution. In addition there was listed a group of six problems that were "passed over," namely, earned income, intoxicating liquors, tax-exempt government securities, joint returns of husband and wife, excessive salaries of corporation officers, and the effect of the statute of limitations.[5]

The minor problems were more numerous, thirty for which the subcommittee made some recommendations, and nine[6] that were "passed over."

THE COMMITTEE ON WAYS AND MEANS CONSIDERS PROPOSALS

This extensive report of the subcommittee was the basis for the public hearings conducted by the Committee on Ways and Means[7] late in December 1933 and early in January 1934. It indicated more independence and initiative on the part of Congress than for some years past, and much more than was shown in drafting subsequent measures for some years; however, the 1934 bill was modified in line with Treasury requests before it was enacted.

On the opening day of the hearings, Secretary of the Treasury

[4] The other members were: Cullen, Vinson, and Cooper, Democrats; Treadway, Crowther, and Frear, Republicans. The Senate also appointed a committee but no report was published. The members were: King, Barkley, and Byrd, Democrats; La Follette and Reed, Republicans.

[5] The subcommittee report was published as a House Document (unnumbered) 73d Congress, 2nd Session, *Prevention of Tax Avoidance.*

[6] These were: taxation of annuities, interest on money borrowed to purchase tax-exempt securities, deduction of death and gift taxes from net income, gambling losses, dividends from foreign corporations, losses between members of a family, accrued income and deductions for estates, casual sales on installment basis, sales of mines and oil or gas wells.

[7] The Committee members were the same as in the preceding session. See above, Chap. XIII.

Morgenthau started to read a formal statement, but before long handed his manuscript to Mr. Magill,[8] a recent appointee to the Department who was better equipped to discuss the more technical phases of the law.

It soon became evident that the Treasury did not approve several of the Committee's recommendations, yet was not prepared to offer substitutes in all cases.[9] The Republicans, especially Treadway, ranking minority member, made much of the failure of the Administration to give specific suggestions and of the plea that the Treasury Department needed more time for further study.

The subcommittee had recommended starting the surtax at $4000 instead of at $6000, but permitting the personal exemption to be used as an offset against the surtax as well as normal tax. The Treasury, however, "doubted the wisdom" of thus extending the use of the personal exemption. The purpose back of this additional allowance was to assist those whose incomes were small. If the exemption were deducted from the surtax it would reduce the income in the highest brackets, thus giving a greater advantage to those with large incomes than to those with small. The Treasury suggested, as a substitute, that the surtax rates might begin at a higher point than that recommended. Until the Budget had been made out, however, the Treasury was not prepared to say what the exact tax rates should be.

The Treasury also disagreed with the subcommittee on proposals for handling depreciation and depletion, which were to reduce deductions for 1934, 1935, and 1936 by 25% of the amount allowed for depreciation and depletion by the Bureau under the existing law. The Committee thought such a scheme would prove a test of this section of the law, would be advantageous from the fiscal point of view, and would not be unjust to the individuals or corporations concerned. The Treasury experts objected to this proposal as unfair and as probably unconstitutional also. Depreciation and depletion, they pointed out, were intended to remove from gross income such amounts as in fact represented an allowance to the taxpayer for loss of a portion of his capital investment; they represented just as much a cost of business as cost of goods in the case of a merchant. If a taxpayer were forced to reduce his depreciation deductions by 25%, as suggested, his income would not be accurately shown. Therefore,

[8] Roswell Magill, Professor of Law, Columbia University, Adviser to the Treasury 1934-1936, Undersecretary 1936-1938.

[9] The Treasury memorandum was published under the title, *Statement of the Acting Secretary of the Treasury, regarding the Preliminary Report of a Subcommittee of the Committee on Ways and Means* 1933. The most important sections of the report were published in 73d Congress, 2nd Session, *Hearings before the Committee on Ways and Means, House of Representatives, on Revenue Revision* 1934. The Secretary's statement was published in the New York *Times*, Dec. 16, 1933.

if these deductions were not permitted, the taxpayer could justly contend that he was subject to a tax on his capital. Furthermore, in a period of rising prices depreciation reserves were more likely to be too small rather than too large. The Treasury advocated adjustments of the regulations and other changes in the administrative procedure, not a hard and fast rule of a flat percentage cut.

Members of the Committee found it difficult to be convinced that the Treasury point of view was correct. They were impressed with the fact that corporations had reported net income for 1930 of over $9,295,000,000 before taking depreciation. After deducting depreciation and depletion to the amount of almost $2,867,000,000 net income was $6,428,000,000. Of the corporations that reported a deficit for 1930, the depreciation and depletion deductions were $1,582,000,000, making the total deficit of these companies after depreciation and depletion, $4,877,000,000. Thus, in the case of companies showing a profit, the net income was reduced 31% by these allowances and in the case of companies showing a deficit, the deficit was increased by 48%. Frear skeptically asked Magill if the Treasury fully appreciated the importance of these deductions. The matter of discovery depletion allowance, however, was different. The Treasury did disapprove the provisions of the existing law on the ground that they granted more or less of subsidy to a limited number of taxpayers.

The third section of the subcommittee report on capital gains and losses covered a controversial issue of long standing and one which had also received much publicity at the time of the Hearings of the Senate Banking Committee. After some study, the subcommittee decided to accept the following recommendations of the Joint Committee for the taxation of profits and the deduction of losses from the sale of capital assets: (1) segregate such gains and losses for tax purposes; (2) recognize such gains and losses in percentages varying from 100% to 20% according to the length of time the asset had been held; (3) tax such gains so recognized at the ordinary normal and surtax rates; and (4) disallow any net loss.

The Secretary approved of this plan, in general, although he commented on the fact that it discriminated against earned and business income and in favor of invested income, and would put a greater brake upon sale of capital assets than did the existing law.

Chart 3 indicates the fiscal effects of including capital gains and losses in the taxable income of individuals. Note that this inclusion reduced income tax collections in only three of the ten years shown (1930-1932) and increased collections very much in four of the years (1926-1929).

Section 4 of the subcommittee report dealt with the personal

CHART 3

INDIVIDUAL INCOME TAXES,* 1926-1935 [1]

Total Taxes and Taxes on Income Other than Capital Gains and Losses †

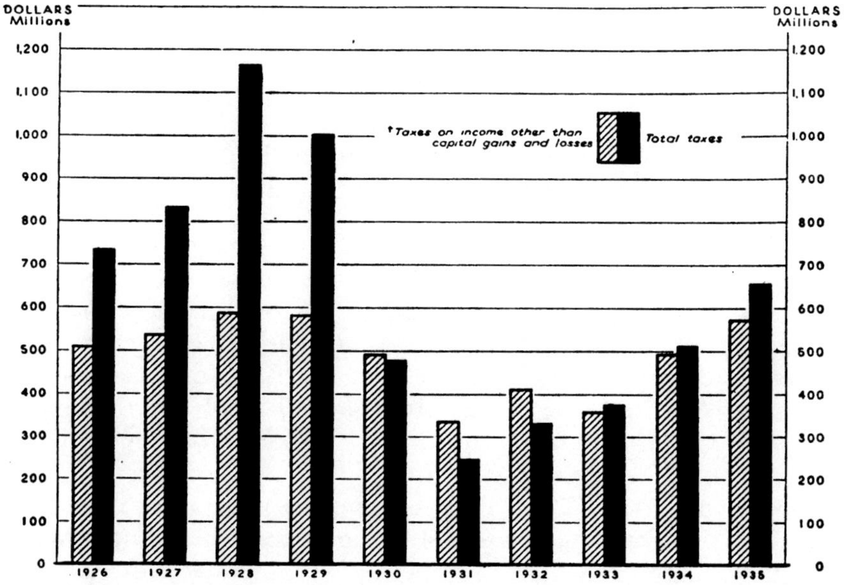

[1] 75th Congress, 3d Session, *Hearings before the Committee on Ways and Means on Revenue Revision* 1938, p. 117.
* Based on tax liabilities reported in Statistics of Income.
† As defined by 1936 Revenue Act.

holding company as a prevalent method used by individuals to avoid taxes. The existing law contained a penalty provision to prevent the accumulation of profits for the purpose of evading surtaxes, but it seemed to have proved inadequate. The Committee recommended that this section be divided and that a special tax be levied on the undistributed earnings of personal holding companies. The Treasury admitted that personal holding companies had frequently been used to reduce income taxes; nevertheless, the Department did not believe that the subcommittee plan was desirable for the reason that it was "overspecific legislation," because "legal ingenuity" could probably devise some other form of company and evade the tax. Mr. Magill, however, had no substitute provision to offer.

The fifth section covered the matter of determination of gain in cases of exchange of property and reorganization of corporations. The subcommittee recommended the elimination of all the exchange and reorganization provisions of the existing law except, that, in cases where the payment of tax on gain from an exchange or reorganization worked an undue hardship on the taxpayer, the Treasury should be authorized to extend the time "for payment of that portion of the tax attributable to such gain for a period of not in excess of two years." There would be two advantages of such elimination, according to the subcommittee: (1) it would abolish one of the most prevalent methods of tax evasion, and (2) it would simplify the law by removing one of its most complicated provisions.[10] From the fiscal point of view, this change was estimated to bring in $25,000,000 additional revenue directly or indirectly.

Mr. Magill, summarizing the Treasury memorandum on this point, disagreed with the report. He thought the new plan would not be of any advantage so far as any additional revenue was concerned. On the contrary, the abolition of the sections might result in a loss of revenue, because depreciation and depletion for thousands of corporations were computed under the reorganization provisions. If these were abolished, taxpayers could, with justice, claim largely increased amounts of such deductions. Furthermore, because of the fact that reorganizations generally involved insolvent corporations, the abolition of the reorganization provisions would permit thousands of bondholders and stockholders to establish losses.

There was also a difference of opinion between the subcommittee and the Treasury on the matter of foreign tax credit. The committee favored placing taxes paid to foreign governments on the same basis as state income taxes, that is, to permit their deduction from gross income, not as a credit against the income tax. The Treasury wanted the credit plan maintained.

The Treasury and the subcommittee also disagreed on the matter of consolidated returns. The subcommittee concluded, after their study of the problem, that the privilege of filing consolidated returns was of special benefit to large groups of corporations, that it resulted in reducing and postponing the tax. It was estimated that if the privilege were abolished, there would be an annual increase of revenue of $20,000,000 in the first few years. The Treasury argued for the justice of consolidated returns and thought the suggested amount an overestimate because:

> presumably the intelligent lawyers who advise large corporations will see to it that the intercompany transactions are arranged in such a way that the group will suffer as little loss as possible by the change in the law.

[10] The study made by the staff of the Joint Committee on Internal Revenue Taxation proposed three alternative measures: (1) abolish the exchange and reorganization provisions of the present law; (2) abolish all the exchange and reorganization provisions except those permitting an individual to incorporate his business without being subject to tax; (3) "to require gain to be realized and the tax determined in accordance with plans (1) or (2) but not to require the payment of the tax (A) within two years from the date the tax is due, or (B) within six months after the property received is sold, whichever date is the earlier."

The Treasury memorandum, discussed by Magill, showed that consolidated returns were necessary in order to secure a correct statement of income from affiliated corporations. In fact, the Treasury had requested Congress to write into the 1918 law the provision requiring consolidated returns for affiliated corporations in order to prevent evasion. Magill agreed, however, that the Committee might carry out the plan of the existing law by requiring a slightly higher tax for filing a consolidated return and might even increase the differential. In reply to questions it was brought out that there was no statistical material as to the effect of the increased tax on the number of affiliated concerns that had filed consolidated returns.

A study not available at that time throws some light on the fiscal effects of eliminating consolidated returns, though it contains no estimate of the offsetting effects that such action has on changes in corporate accounting and other practices. The extent to which the law permits the carrying forward of losses from one year to following years would be quite important also. From an analysis of nearly 6000 consolidated returns for the years 1930 and 1933 there has been ascertained the amount of the losses which subsidiaries deducted from the net profits of the several affiliated groups for those years that could not have been deducted under the Act of 1934. On the bases of these rather large and representative samples it has been estimated that the total extra revenue which would have been received if the Act of 1934, which eliminated consolidated returns, had been in force would have amounted to $118,402,500 for 1930 and to $58,525,000 for 1933, assuming that corporations had not changed their forms of organization, accounting, etc. For summary, see Appendix Tables 42 and 43.

Another matter that had evoked some discussion since the somewhat sensational publicity of the rise and fall of Morgan tax payments was that of partnership losses. The subcommittee recommended that no partner be allowed to deduct from personal income his share of the amount of loss sustained by the partnership. The Treasury did not believe such a drastic policy was equitable, consistent, or legal, because partnerships were not regarded as legal entities, and because income and losses should be treated consistently. The losses deductible under the existing law were not fictitious, nor did they represent evasion or avoidance.

The Treasury and the subcommittee agreed on the principle of permitting a reduction of tax on earned income but the subcommittee hesitated to recommend it until revenue needs of the government were known.

THE REPORT OF THE COMMITTEE ON WAYS AND MEANS

The draft of the new revenue measure as presented to the House was a compromise between the recommendations of the subcommittee and those of the Treasury. The measure was not intended, at the outset, to be a general revision of the entire law, but to tighten the provisions so that there would be fewer legal means of evasion and, in this way rather than by increased rates, it was expected to bring more revenue into the Treasury. Before the draft was completed, however, the law was rather completely revised.

The Committee recommended one normal tax at 4% instead of two, as had been the practice for some years, and a revision of the surtax rates to begin at 1% on income of $4000–$6000 and rising by steps to 59% on income in excess of $1,000,000. A new arrangement was made for the deduction of the personal exemption and credit for dependents for computation of the surtax as well as the normal tax. The credit for earned income was restored, but at a rate of 10%. The maximum amount that could be considered as earned was $8000 but all income not in excess of $3000 was considered earned.

One of the most interesting provisions was that for the taxing of capital gains and the deduction of capital losses according to the length of time the assets had been held. The following table shows the percentages of gain or loss that could be taken into account for tax purposes by individuals, not by corporations:

100% if the asset had been held for not more than one year;
80% if the asset had been held for more than one year but not more than two years;
60% if the asset had been held for more than two years but not more than five years;
40% if the asset had been held for more than five years.

If losses taken into account in this way exceeded the gains, the excess loss could not be deducted from other income.

Another new section imposed a tax of 35% of the undistributed adjusted net income of personal holding companies that were formed to accumulate earnings and thus aid individuals in avoiding the surtax. This was aimed at the so-called "incorporated pocketbook." Such a company was defined as

> any corporation 80 per cent of whose gross income for the taxable year is derived from rents, royalties, dividends, interest, annuities and gains from the sale of stock or securities, and whose voting stock to the extent of more than 50 per cent is owned by not more than five individuals at the close of the taxable year.

Other corporations improperly accumulating a surplus were subject to a penalty tax of 25%.

In view of the Treasury opposition to the abolition of the provisions for exchanges and reorganizations, it was decided to retain them but to make certain restrictions so as to prevent as much tax avoidance as possible.

Similarly the Committee changed its position as to the elimination of the provision for consolidated returns. As the Treasury requested, affiliated corporations were granted the privilege of filing consolidated returns, but the additional tax for so doing was made 2% instead of 1%, as enacted in the tax provisions of the NIRA.

After much study of partnership tax evasion by the Committee on Ways and Means as well as by the subcommittee on tax avoidance, it was decided to follow the suggestions of the Treasury instead of the subcommittee and make very few changes in the law as it applied to them. The report showed that in years of prosperity individual members of a partnership had paid large income taxes on their profits and in most cases the taxable profits had far exceeded the losses. The proposed treatment of profits and losses from sale of capital assets according to the length of time assets had been held would safeguard much of the revenue in the future. The changes proposed would also make more definite the provisions of the law already in force respecting sale of property that had appreciated in value. Because of these amendments the Committee did not re-enact the provision of the NIRA by which partners were not allowed to deduct from personal income stock losses disallowed to the partnership.

The Committee voted also to recommend a 5-cent tax on imported coconut oil and copra but made no comment on this section. They also agreed to terminate the 2-cent check tax December 31, 1934, instead of June 30, 1935, as provided in the existing law. The other changes dealt with the administration of taxes on gasoline and lubricating oil.

The report was unanimously agreed upon, but Frear and Crowther presented some additional views. Frear thought the law should contain a provision to demand the filing of joint returns by husband and wife so as to prevent the loss of revenue, claimed to be from $40,000,000 to $60,000,000, resulting from the community property laws of a few states, and he wanted greater publicity of income tax returns. He objected to the excise tax on imported coconut oil and to the 3-cent rate on first class postage. Crowther limited his "Views" to a statement of his preference for a general sales tax in place of the numerous "nuisance" taxes.

THE BILL PUSHED THROUGH THE HOUSE UNAMENDED

On February 14 Bankhead, Chairman of the Committee on Rules, called up the House resolution by which the debate on the tax bill was limited to sixteen hours and amendments were restricted to those proposed by the Committee on Ways and Means. The Chairman quoted Thomas B. Reed's remark that in presenting this "gag" rule he was bringing forth "another outrage." [11] Snell sarcastically thanked his colleague for permitting a motion to recommit. O'Malley (Rep., Wis.) asked why there was to be any debate at all; [11] Byrns remarked there was nothing to do but to adopt the rule,[12] and he might have added "and pass the bill."

Chairman Doughton explained the new theory upon which the bill was drawn up, namely, to increase the tax yield by preventing tax avoidance rather than by increasing tax rates. The three fundamental tax principles of equity, consistency, and certainty were the guiding principles of the Committee. It was hoped that the new bill would bring in $258,000,000 additional revenue. This sum apparently had no relation to need, but it was all they thought they could get.

The debate was centered almost entirely on the tariff sections which imposed an excise tax on coconut oil and copra. Doughton admitted that such items had no place in the tax bill and even objected to their being called taxes. Shallenberger (Neb.), who took the responsibility for the section, explained why he did not consider it a tariff measure.[13]

There was less discussion of the fundamental income tax sections than on any similar occasion. The few speeches made were in explanation of the changes. Perhaps the amendments were of such technical nature that they were not readily understood. Perhaps the members thought it futile to debate in view of the stress that had been placed on the profound study made by the subcommittee. Certainly, after the passage of the gag rule, there was no point in offering amendments. Treadway's motion to recommit was lost by a vote of 271 to 133. The bill passed on February 21, by a vote of 390 to 7.[14]

FEW CHANGES MADE BY THE SENATE FINANCE COMMITTEE

Early in March the Senate Finance Committee began to revise the House bill. Contrary to the practice that had been followed for some years, Secretary Morgenthau did not appear at the public hear-

11 *Cong. Rec.* 78: 2503.
12 *Cong. Rec.* 78: 2508.
13 *Cong. Rec.* 78: 2513, 2528-2530.
14 *Cong. Rec.* 78: 3005.

ings but was present at executive sessions of the Committee. He informed the members that he approved of the House bill except for minor details.[15]

The public hearings opened a week later. No representatives of the Administration appeared. Most of the testimony was on the extraneous tariff sections, although a few witnesses asked for a more generous allowance for the carrying over of losses to succeeding years, for allowance of corporation deductions for charitable contributions, and for elimination of the proposed taxation of annuities.[16]

At the conclusion of the three-day hearings the Committee again resumed executive sessions and completed the measure in two weeks. Chairman Harrison objected to the House bill because he feared it would have an unfavorable effect on business. Therefore he planned to substitute for all the excise taxes three measures: (1) continuance of the excess-profits tax that expired in January 1934; (2) continuance of its companion measure, the capital stock tax that was due to expire in July because of the repeal of the Eighteenth Amendment (by the ratification of the Twenty-first); and (3) increase of estate tax rates to a maximum of 60% and reduction of the exemption from $50,000 to $15,000. As time went on, however, such a plan did not seem feasible. Most of the excise taxes were retained because of the need for revenue, but three minor ones were repealed; those on soft drinks, clocks, and certain fur articles. The date for repeal of the tax on bank checks was left July 1, 1935, as in the existing law.

The Committee agreed to the House income and surtax rates and to the graduated percentages of recognized taxable gains and losses from the sale of capital assets, but added one bracket to care for assets that had been held over ten years. They revised the definition of capital asset to exclude "property held by the taxpayer primarily for sale to customers in the ordinary course of his trade or business" and extended the amount of deductible capital losses to include $2000 of the amount of excess of loss over gain. They also approved the House plan for taxing personal holding companies that were formed to evade taxes but changed the proposed flat rate of 35% to graduated rates: 30% of the first $100,000 of the undistributed adjusted net income and 40% on the amount over $100,000. One important amendment of the House bill was the re-enactment of the capital stock tax and its adjunct, the excess-profits tax.

A few changes were made in the allowances for deductions. The Senate Committee struck out the following House sections: (1) the

[15] New York *Times*, March 7, 1934.

[16] 73d Congress, 2d Session, *Hearings before the (Senate) Committee on Finance on H. R.* 7835.

disallowance for income tax purposes of gift and inheritance taxes; (2) the limitation of gambling losses to the amount gained in similar transactions, and (3) the provision that banks could not deduct from taxable income the interest on debt incurred to procure tax-exempt securities.

THE SENATE INCREASES TAX RATES

On March 27 Harrison reported the bill to the Senate [17] but it was not brought up for debate until April 2.[18] The chairman explained that the Committee had revised the measure so that it would bring in about $330,000,000 additional revenue, approximately $70,000,000 more than the House bill. Most of the difference was due to the continuance of the capital stock and excess-profits taxes. The following outstanding features of the bill were pointed out: (1) new treatment of income from sale of capital assets; (2) special taxation of personal holding companies; (3) capital stock tax; (4) limitation of partnership losses; (5) amendments to the reorganization sections; (6) taxation of dividends from surplus accumulated prior to March 1, 1913; and (7) imposition of an additional tax equal to 50% of the income tax on citizens and corporations of a foreign country if such country imposed discriminatory taxes on taxpayers of the United States.

After the Committee had secured acceptance of many of its changes on April 2 and 3, La Follette offered an amendment to increase the normal tax on individual income to 6% and to increase the surtax rates so that the minimum became 5% on income not in excess of $8000 and the maximum 71% on income in excess of $1,000,000.[19] Norris and Long were the chief supporters of these increased rates; indeed, Long thought they did not go "a fourth far enough." [20] Most of the members, however, thought that the proposed maximum of 59% was sufficiently severe, so rejected La Follette's amendment.[21]

Two other amendments to change the rates of the income tax were pending. One was by King to reduce somewhat the Committee rates of the surtax on incomes from $4000 to $18,000, but to increase the rates on larger incomes so that the maximum surtax rate would be 65%,[22] and the other by Couzens, for a flat 10% increase of both the normal tax and surtax payable on income for the taxable year 1934. Both were rejected. The vote on the latter proposition was almost

[17] *Cong. Rec.* 78: 5472.
[18] *Cong. Rec.* 78: 5845.
[19] *Cong. Rec.* 78: 5772.
[20] *Cong. Rec.* 78: 5988.
[21] *Cong. Rec.* 78: 6091.
[22] *Cong. Rec.* 78: 6241, 6298-6300

a tie, 44 yeas, 46 nays.[23] On the following day, however, Couzens secured a reconsideration of his amendment, and on the second vote it was passed.

The next controversial matter was the tax on capital gains. Murphy (Dem., Iowa) who had at one time been connected with the Bureau of Internal Revenue, objected to the Committee plan. He thought that abolition of the 12½% tax as in the existing law would "make a present of one billion dollars to taxpayers with incomes of $100,000 or over." He worked out a plan to give relief to those taxpayers a large part of whose income was from the sale of capital assets, so that the tax would approximate the amount that would have been paid "if the gain had been realized in equal annual amounts" over the period in which the assets had been held.[24] His plan was very complicated and for that reason had previously been rejected by the Committee. There was very little support for it on the floor of the Senate. La Follette alone spoke for it. If the only argument against it was complexity of administration, he said, and if the enactment of such a law would prevent a great deal of evasion by large taxpayers, it would seem that there was ample justification for attempting a new method. The consensus appeared to be, however, that the matter had been thoroughly studied by the Joint Committee on Internal Revenue Taxation, by the House Committee on Ways and Means, as well as by the Senate Finance Committee; so Murphy's amendment was rejected[25] and the Committee proposal for a plan only slightly different from that of the House was accepted.

The sections on discovery depletion then occupied the attention of the Senate for a short time. McKellar, for years a bitter opponent of the Bureau of Internal Revenue, objected to the existing law because he thought that the oil companies received unusual benefits, hence he wished to strike out the section that permitted percentage depletion for oil and gas wells, and substitute a new method.[26] Gore, who came from an oil state, defended the deductions. He pointed out that these sections had evolved out of the experience of years, and were originally designed to give some concessions because of the risk of the industry. He showed how the method of computing depletion had changed in the course of the years so that the results were very different from those stated by the Senator from Tennessee.[27] He explained that the discovery depletion section no longer applied to oil wells and that the oil industry paid tremendous taxes, even in

[23] *Cong. Rec.* 78: 6300, 6306.
[24] *Cong. Rec.* 78: 6099.
[25] *Cong. Rec.* 78: 6176-6177.
[26] *Cong. Rec.* 78: 6178.
[27] *Cong. Rec.* 78: 6211-6213.

the most depressed period. McKellar's amendment was rejected as Gore requested.[28]

McKellar then proposed an amendment to limit the amount that corporations could deduct for salaries by providing that "no allowance for salary or compensation in excess of $50,000 shall be considered reasonable." Couzens explained that the Senator had a legitimate object in view but that his amendment would defeat its own end if it were put in effect because, although the government would get 13¾% from the corporation, it would lose the individual income surtax which was much higher.[29]

La Follette offered several interesting amendments; one for the publicity of income tax returns had come to be an expected part of every income tax debate. He recalled previous votes by which the Senate had adopted provisions for such publicity. Norris, of course, supported him, as did one or two others. There was little opposition and the amendment passed by a vote of 41 to 32. As in previous years, the provision was amended by the Conferees but the results this time were much more in line with the wishes of the author than had previously been the case.

An amendment of La Follette to increase the estate tax rates was also adopted.[30] The maximum he proposed was 60% on parts of estates in excess of $10,000,000, whereas the Committee draft was for a maximum of 50%. La Follette succeeded also in reducing the exemption from $50,000 to $40,000. Corresponding changes were made in the gift tax.[30]

Borah succeeded in getting enough support to pass his amendment to eliminate the privilege of filing consolidated income tax returns.[31] He considered this provision a great advantage to holding companies because it enabled them to save enormous amounts of taxes. Norris agreed that such companies were parasites, "organized for the purpose of deceiving the public," and cited the case of Kreuger and Toll and the ramifications of various electric companies. Harrison objected because he thought it was necessary for some companies to file consolidated returns, for example, the railroads. Furthermore, many states required incorporation as a condition of doing business. The Committee, he said, had gone much further than ever before in requiring a 2% additional tax if a consolidated return was filed.[31]

[28] *Cong. Rec.* 78: 6240.

[29] *Cong. Rec.* 78: 6243-6245. The amendment was defeated. Earlier in the session, Gore offered an amendment to tax at the rate of 80% the amount of compensation, salary, and bonuses that exceeded $75,000 per annum and provided that such excesses should not be deductible by corporations in computing income liability. This amendment was made immediately after the publication in the press of the report of the Federal Trade Commission on salaries and bonuses. (*Cong. Rec.* 78: 3371.)

[30] *Cong. Rec.* 78: 6411, 6461, 6462.

[31] *Cong. Rec.* 78: 6464-6466.

Couzens agreed that there were cases when a consolidated return was justified but "the viciousness" of the matter was that it permitted the filing of consolidated returns "for other than allied industries" and thereby promoted "an unfair competitive condition." He therefore supported Borah's amendment because, if passed, a new provision could be worked out in the Conference Committee.

Another debatable matter of long standing was that of tax-exempt securities. As in previous sessions, Clark presented an amendment to tax interest on obligations of the United States, and of any state or political subdivision thereof.[32] McKellar took the heart out of the proposed measure by amending it so that state obligations were excluded. Thereupon Clark withdrew his amendment.[33]

In order to draw attention to his study of the causes of war and their relation to war taxes and profits, Nye (Rep., N. D.) introduced an amendment that in the event of war, taxes should be increased 100%. He realized that this was a matter for study and not for immediate consideration. Therefore he did not ask for a vote, but presented instead a resolution that a special committee be appointed to investigate the munitions industry. This was agreed to.[34]

On the last day of the debate Ashurst proposed an increase to 10 cents a pound in the excise tax on imports of copper. Clark remarked that inasmuch as he wanted to remove the four-cent excise tax altogether and as neither he nor his colleague could succeed, he was perfectly willing to have the amendment come to a vote! [35] There was no other discussion of the excise taxes. No one mentioned the fact that Congress had just passed a Philippine Islands independence bill that contained a provision to admit free 448,000,000 pounds of coconut oil annually. The revenue bill was then passed by a vote of 53 to 7, 36 not voting.[36]

THE REPORT OF THE CONFEREES

The chief differences between the House and Senate bills were in regard to the surtax rates on incomes of $32,000 or less, the maximum amount of earned income to be allowed credit, the rates of tax on personal holding companies formed for the purpose of surtax avoidance, publicity of income tax returns, consolidated returns, the estate tax rates, capital-stock and excess-profits taxes, the processing tax on oils, and the 10% increase in tax rates for 1934.[37]

32 *Cong. Rec.* 78: 6561.
33 *Cong. Rec.* 78: 6572.
34 *Cong. Rec.* 78: 6472-6479.
35 *Cong. Rec.* 78: 6573.
36 *Cong. Rec.* 78: 6574.
37 *Cong. Rec.* 78: 7815-7985.

By May 1, that is, within about two weeks, the Conferees reached an agreement on all of the issues except the Couzens amendment for the 10% tax increase for 1934; so that section was not included in the Conference Report but was considered separately. Of the fifty most important amendments, the House receded on eighteen, the Senate receded on five, and a compromise was reached on the remainder.

On the question of publicity, an entirely new plan was proposed. The Conferees were fearful that, under the broad terms of the Senate provision to require the President to open all returns to public inspection, trade secrets would be disclosed, the value of the returns as evidence in litigation would be weakened, and the Treasury would be subject to excessive expense and annoyance. The Conferees therefore adopted a suggestion that was offered in the House by Patman (Tex.) [38] but not introduced in the form of an amendment; namely, to have the taxpayer file an additional statement of identifying information and amount of tax. Such a statement would be available for public inspection in the collector's office.

When the report was submitted to the House the chief interest was in the excise sections. The Couzens amendment for increasing the income tax due in 1934 by 10% was brought up but rejected.

The Senate discussion of the report was very short, because the only interest was in the elimination of perilla oil [39] from the list of articles that were granted an excise on imports. Tydings called attention to the fact that the Philippine legislature had accepted the bill that granted them independence, yet almost before the ink had dried the United States had changed its whole attitude, "the whole tenor and purpose and import of our agreement with those people." The excise taxes, he said, would deprive that country of 40% of its trade. He appealed to the Senate to reject the Conference Report, but in vain. The report was then accepted and the bill signed by the President May 10, 1934.

SUMMARY OF THE ACT [40]

The Revenue Act of 1934 contained seven titles: I — Income Tax; IA — Additional Income Tax on Personal Holding Companies; II — Amendments to Estate Tax; III — Amendments to

[38] *Cong. Rec.* 78: 2601.

[39] An oil used in paint for drying purposes. Late in May the President sent a special message to Congress asking that the excise tax on coconut oil be reconsidered for the reason that it violated the spirit and intent of the Philippine Independence Act and worked a hardship on thousands of families in the Philippine Islands. He requested that the proposal be studied until January. The matter was referred to the Committee on Ways and Means but the members thought it was too late to do anything about it. (*Cong. Rec.* 78: 9682, 9757; New York *Times*, May 29, 1934.)

[40] 48 *Statutes at Large* 680.

Prior Acts and Miscellaneous ; IV — Excise Taxes ; V — Capital Stock and Excess-Profits Tax ; VI — General Provisions.

Title I — Income Tax. This Title levied a single normal rate of 4% on income of individuals. The surtax rates were graduated from 1% on income over $4000 and not over $6000 to 59% on income in excess of $1,000,000. For the normal tax only a credit of 10% was allowed for earned income not in excess of $14,000. The first $3000 of income from any source was assumed to be earned. Such allowance had not been granted since the expiration of the 1928 law.

The rate on corporation income remained unchanged at 13¾%. Railroads alone were permitted to file consolidated returns, and for this privilege an additional 2 per-cent tax was imposed.

A new method was arranged for taxing capital gains and losses of individuals. The following percentages of gain or loss from sale of capital assets were to be recognized for income tax purposes :

100 per cent if the asset had been held for not more than one year ;
80 per cent if the asset had been held for more than one year but not more than two years ;
60 per cent if the asset had been held for more than two years but not more than five years ;
40 per cent if the asset had been held for more than five years and not more than ten years ;
30 per cent if the asset had been held for more than ten years.

Capital gains so computed were to be included with other net income and taxed at the full normal and surtax rates. Capital losses could be deducted only to the amount of the capital gains of the same tax year plus $2000.

A tax was imposed upon the improperly accumulated surplus of any corporation formed or availed of by individuals to evade the surtax, but the rates were put at 25% on the amount of adjusted net income not in excess of $100,000 plus 35% of the amount of the adjusted net income in excess of $100,000. This tax was in lieu of the penalty tax that had been imposed by previous income tax acts but rarely enforced.

Several amendments were made to restrict deductions. Estate, inheritance, and gift taxes could not be deducted from gross income. Deductions could not be allowed for contributions to organizations if a substantial part of their activity was "carrying on propaganda or otherwise attempting to influence legislation." Expenses of earning wholly exempt income other than interest were not deductible. Deductions of losses from wagering transactions were limited to the amount of the gains. No loss could be taken on a sale or exchange of property between members of a family or, except in case of liquidation, between an individual and a corporation in which he owned directly or indirectly more than 50% in value of the outstanding stock.

The provision for exclusion of annuities from gross income was revised so that a taxpayer was required to include in gross income amounts received under an annuity or endowment contract except that there could be excluded the excess of the amount received in the taxable year over an amount equal to 3% of the aggregate premiums paid until the aggregate amount excluded equaled the total premiums paid.

An additional tax at double the ordinary rate was imposed upon corporations or citizens of foreign countries that imposed discriminatory taxes against United States citizens and corporations. The tax could not, however, exceed 80% of the net income of the taxpayer.

The provisions as to basis for realization of gain were clarified to prevent tax avoidance by partners. If property was acquired by a partnership after February 28, 1913, the basis for determining gain or loss in case of sale was made the same as it would have been in the hands of the transferor, "increased in the amount of gain or decreased in the amount of loss recognized to the transferor upon such transfer under the law applicable to the year in which the transfer was made."

The reorganization provisions were tightened by omitting the section that permitted a corporation by means of a reorganization to distribute to its shareholders stock or securities in another corporation without any tax to the shareholders. The definition of reorganization was revised so as to conform more closely to corporation law requirements for continuity of interest.

The provision for publicity of income tax returns required the taxpayer to make out a slip giving his name, address, total gross income, total deductions, net income, total credits, and tax payable. Failure to file this so-called "pink slip" subjected the taxpayer to a penalty of $5.[41]

Title IA – Personal Holding Companies. This was a new section, imposing a surtax on undistributed net income of personal holding companies, "incorporated pocketbooks." A personal holding company was defined as any corporation other than a bank or trust company in which (a) at least 80% of its gross income for the year was derived from royalties, dividends, interest, annuities and from the sale of stock or securities and (b) more than 50% of its stock was

[41] This famous "pink slip" provision was repealed in April 1935, after only one collection of the tax under the 1934 Act. In 1935 public opinion was very much aroused against this publicity of private affairs and much pressure was put on Congress. Many House members were sympathetic with the taxpayers' viewpoint, but the Senate was firm for the original provision and gave out warning that if the publicity provisions were repealed they would pass the La Follette amendment. (*Cong. Rec.* 79: 3398-3412, 4441, 4614, 5428.)

owned by not more than five individuals. The rates were graduated: 30% on undistributed net income not in excess of $100,000, after certain adjustments; 40% on such income over $100,000.

Title II — Amendments to Estate Tax. The rates of estate taxes were increased to a maximum of 60% on parts of net estates in excess of $10,000,000. The exemption was $50,000. Corresponding increases in the gift tax were placed in Title III.

Title III — Amendments to Prior Acts. This title covered changes in regard to overpayments found by the Board of Tax Appeals, the statute of limitations, and other administrative matters. This Title also created the office of General Counsel for the Department of the Treasury. The General Counsel was to be appointed by the President and to receive compensation of $10,000 a year. An Assistant General Counsel was also to be appointed by the President at a rate not to exceed $10,000 a year. This office had charge of all legal matters for the Treasury, including the Bureau of Internal Revenue.

Title IV — Excise Taxes. Processing taxes — in reality tariffs — were levied on imports of coconut and other edible oils, including whale and fish oil. The revenue from the tax on coconut oil was to be put in a separate fund and paid to the Philippine Islands.

The tax on soft drinks was repealed.

The act continued the tax on gasoline at the rate of one cent per gallon, increased the tax on colored matches and on cigarettes over 6½ inches in length, and levied a tax of $\frac{1}{10}$ of a cent per barrel to be paid by producers of crude petroleum.

The stamp tax on sales of produce for future delivery was reduced from 5 cents to 3 cents per hundred dollars. The date for termination of the tax on bank checks was made January 1, 1935, instead of July 1, 1935, but the 3-cent rate on postage was extended to July 1, 1935, instead of terminating on July 1, 1934, as provided in the previous Act.

Title V — Capital Stock and Excess-Profits Tax. This title reenacted the capital stock tax at $1 for each $1000 of the adjusted declared value of the capital stock of every taxable corporation. In order to prevent this value from being placed too low, a tax of 5% was levied on the amount of net income in excess of 12½% of the "adjusted declared value" of the stock.

Title VI — General Provisions. This title defined many terms used in the Act, and stated the effective date. Most of the Act went into effect when signed. The income tax sections were effective for the taxable year beginning after December 31, 1933.

CHAPTER XV

REVENUE ACT OF 1935 — SHARE THE WEALTH

THE POLITICAL ATMOSPHERE

On June 19, 1935, two days after the House passed the joint resolution to extend the expiration date of the excise taxes [1] and while the Senate was debating the Social Security Act, the President sent a surprise tax message to Congress. On the basis of studies of the Treasury and of the Joint Committee on Internal Revenue Taxation, he offered several suggestions for important changes in the basic policy of the federal tax system. The introductory part of the message contained these words :

> Our revenue laws have operated in many ways to the unfair advantage of the few, and they have done little to prevent an unjust concentration of wealth and economic power.

As this sentence was read, Senator Huey Long of Louisiana happened to be walking directly in front of the rostrum, with his hands in his pockets. He stopped abruptly, made a grimace, raised his eyes and almost waltzed.[2] When the clerk had finished he alone had a remark to make for the Record :

> Mr. President, before the President's message is referred to the Committee on Finance, I wish to make one comment. I just wish to say "Amen !" [3]

From that moment the Senator from Louisiana had much satisfaction in telling his colleagues that he was the actual originator of the wealth distribution plan. The idea was of course much older than the regime of Huey Long, nevertheless there was much truth in his remark. As the benevolent despotic Governor of Louisiana, he had abolished the poll tax, increased educational facilities, highways, and state institutions, and he had also rolled up a state debt of $150,-000,000.

His tremendous popular following was built up and welded together by his magnetic personality and his clever techniques, for example, radio speeches, papers, and circulars delivered within a few hours to almost every house in the state by highway police. Most important of all, however, was his closely-knit organization, the

[1] The Revenue Act of 1934 provided that certain excise taxes would expire June 30, 1935, for example, those on lubricating oil, gasoline, automobile trucks, passenger automobiles, motorcycles, jewelry, oil, copper, etc. The three-cent rate on postage was to be reduced to two cents the same date.

[2] New York *Times*, June 20, 1935.

[3] *Cong. Rec.* 79: 9659.

"Share-Our-Wealth-Club: Every Man a King," with the following objectives:

1. Limitation of poverty to a minimum of a $5000 family estate.
2. Limitation of wealth to a maximum of $10,000,000.
3. Free higher education for all, with a mental test instead of a tuition test . . .
4. Employment of all by the shortening of hours.
5. Full compensation for veterans.
6. Old-age pensions.
7. Great national development programs to absorb the unemployed.[4]

On the day after the President's tax message, Will Rogers wrote:

I would sure liked to have seen Huey's face when he was woke up in the middle of the night by the President who said, "Lay over, Huey. I want to get in with you."[5]

Senator Long was not the only advocate of economic equality. In California Dr. Townsend, a physician almost seventy years old, distressed by the predicament of many people of his age, worked out a pension plan for a payment of $200 a month each to all unemployed over sixty, on condition that it be spent in the United States within thirty days. As in Louisiana, clubs were formed, but the Townsendites paid 25 cents to sign the register of membership. These registers were in the form of petitions to Congress asking for the enactment of the plan. It is said that 25,000,000 such signatures were secured. In any case, the movement became nationwide and doubtless influenced the terms and passage of the Social Security and Revenue bills.

Another advocate of social change was Charles E. Coughlin, a priest of the Roman Catholic Church in a small parish near Detroit, Michigan. Broadcasting every Sunday afternoon, eventually over his own twenty-six station hook-up, he inveighed against economic inequality and against the international bankers in particular. Popular response to his "sermons" was enormous. His ambition was fired also to form an organization. This he called "The National League for Social Justice," with sixteen planks in the platform, among which were "LIBERTY OF CONSCIENCE AND OF EDUCATION," "A LIVING ANNUAL WAGE," "CONTROL OF PRIVATE PROPERTY FOR THE COMMON GOOD," "CONGRESSIONAL CONTROL OF COINAGE," "STEADY CURRENCY VALUE," "SOCIAL TAXATION" and "SIMPLIFICATION OF GOVERNMENT." The strength of his leadership was demonstrated at the time of his opposition to the World Court. The Senate vote on the resolution that the United States join the World Court was defeated after one of

[4] Smith, Gerald L. K., "Or Superman?" *New Republic* 82: 15 (Feb. 13, 1935). In February 1935 the membership of the clubs was said to have been 326,000 in Louisiana, 3,000,000 in the United States.

[5] New York *Times,* June 21, 1935, quoted in *Cong. Rec.* 79: 9907.

Coughlin's broadcasts against it, although a preliminary count of votes the day before indicated that it would be carried. Senators could not vote "yea" in the face of the unprecedented flood of telegrams sent by the priest's followers. These well-organized efforts for pensions opened the way for many smaller groups and even individuals to hope for "handouts" via the Social Security or the relief bill.[6]

The Administration could be neither blind nor deaf to this surging movement for social justice, with its political as well as its economic aspects. Coughlin sometimes supported the President and sometimes he did not. The New Deal patronage in Louisiana was controlled by Long's enemies, and there was plenty of talk of "Huey Long in the White House in 1936." There were other indications of the strength of pressure groups and of the weakness of the Administration. One editor commented:

> The handwriting is on the wall and is growing more distinct every day. President Roosevelt should take the trouble to read it.[7]

In Congress the debates on the Social Security bill and the labor disputes bill gave evidence of a strong left-wing opposition to the President. Long mastered every parliamentary device to undermine the Administration forces in the Senate. He taunted the President for his failure to live up to his promises to redistribute wealth and stated that he would make a nationwide tour in the summer spreading his gospel of Share-Our-Wealth. Others criticized the President for partiality to rich friends such as Vincent Astor.[8] There were press comments of the waning popularity of the New Deal.

Perhaps the President read the signs and decided to send his surprise tax message of June 19. In the annual message to Congress in January he had stated that no new taxes would be needed.[9] In April the possibility of levying taxes to provide funds for a soldiers' bonus was mentioned, but the idea was not pressed. Early in June the President was reported to have said that he had given the matter no more thought.[10]

The President's supporters denied, however, that he drew up the message hurriedly or that he was influenced by Long's or other

[6] *New Republic* 82: 267 (April 24, 1935).

[7] *New Republic* 82: 267 (April 24, 1935). For example: Lundeen (Farmer-Labor, Minn.) forced his unemployment insurance bill out of the committee and succeeded in getting the necessary 218 names for a petition to secure its consideration. It practically "guaranteed a minimum standard of living to industrial and agricultural workers."

[8] Washington *Post,* June 21, 1935; New York *Times* Jan. 10, 1935.

[9] *Cong. Rec.* 79: 95. His words were: "While I do not consider it advisable at this time to propose any new or additional taxes for the fiscal year 1936, I do recommend that Congress take steps by suitable legislation to extend the miscellaneous internal revenue taxes which will expire next June. . ."

[10] New York *Times,* June 8, 1935. This announcement did not quiet the rumors.

"Share-Our-Wealth" propaganda. The idea, they said, had been basic with the President since 1929 and had been worked out in a series of conferences sponsored for the most part by the Treasury.[11] Borah defended the Administration program, but objected to calling it "soak-the-rich" or "share-the-wealth"; he preferred to label it "share-the-burden." He considered it sound morally as well as economically "to take care of our vast expenditures to a larger degree through heavier taxes," but as a distribution-of-wealth program he called the Administration plan a "fake." [12]

These remarks gave Long an opportunity to say that his suspicions were confirmed. He therefore wanted to know whether the President was really sincere in saying that he wanted to distribute the nation's wealth or whether his message was a "sop" to the left-wingers. That there should be no misunderstanding he addressed a letter to the President that closed with these pointed questions:

1. Do you wish the Congress to limit the amount of wealth one man should be permitted to own, and what is the outside limit you would set?
2. Do you wish the Congress to provide for such a redistribution of wealth as would give to every man a homestead where they may have the fair comforts of life up to not less than one-third the average family wealth in America free of debt?
3. Do you wish the Congress to provide that every family shall have such a share of our national income to live on as will give to every family not less than one-third the average family earning?
4. Do you wish to limit the size of inherited fortunes and of incomes; and, if so, what are the limits you suggest?
5. Would you favor the money being also used to secure every child in a full right to education and training, including the professional or vocational education and training in college?
6. And would you allow this money for the redistribution of wealth to be used so that all those above 60 years of age who have not a fair earning can draw a pension and in what amount would you fix such a pension? [13]

Long embarrassed the Administration leaders also by announcing in the press that he would swing his 20,000 Share-Our-Wealth clubs to the support of the President if the tax bill as finally enacted really carried out the plan suggested in his recent message.[14]

DID THE PRESIDENT WANT A TAX BILL IMMEDIATELY?

When the tax message was heard on June 19, Congressional leaders were not sure what was meant. The President departed from Washington almost immediately to be away for several days but left

[11] New York *Times*, June 20, 1935.
[12] New York *Times*, June 24, 1935.
[13] *Cong. Rec.* 79: 9906.
[14] New York *Times*, June 20, 21, 23, 1935.

no instructions about a bill. Chairman Doughton of the Committee on Ways and Means hopefully thought that the President did not intend to insist on a new tax measure that session. Moreover, he did not subscribe to the "soak-the-rich" idea. He advocated avoiding extremes. La Follette proposed that the new tax bill be written as an amendment to the joint resolution for extending the expiration date of the excise taxes that had already passed the House and was then before the Senate Finance Committee. Harrison and Doughton both thought the time much too short to do this, as less than ten days remained before these taxes expired.[15] McNary, Senate minority leader, had much the same opinion. Hastings (Rep., Del.) said that the President's message gave the distinct impression that the tax situation did not need attention immediately, that Congress was "tired, sick and sore and in confusion." He might have added that hot weather was upon them. He quoted from the speech to show that the President was demanding a bill that would bring forth social reform. He continued :

> I assumed it was a political gesture intended to offset the great public alarm and the very great interest in the share-the-wealth movement which is so evident in our country.[16]

It was pointed out that the President had sent the Social Security bill at the end of the session in order that it might be studied over the vacation. Other messages contained such phrases as "Before the termination of this session of Congress I believe that it is important that definite action be taken. . ."[17] but there was no such recommendation to pass the tax bill immediately. Word came from someone at the White House that the President would not insist on a measure along the lines of his message, but that he was anxious to have steps taken to permit the taxation of government securities.[18]

This news was not welcome to the Progressives. La Follette, Borah, Norris, and Johnson wanted a new bill at that session. For years they had advocated higher taxes on the wealthy, both on incomes and on bequests. In April of 1935 La Follette announced over the radio that the Progressives would make the best fight they could for drastic increases in income and estate taxes.[19] On June 18, the day before the President's speech, news was published concerning their plan to amend the pending excise bill so that it would yield $500,000,000 new revenue from these sources.[20] The President's message "espoused

15 New York *Times*, June 20, 21, 1935.
16 *Cong. Rec.* 79: 10271.
17 For example, the message requesting a bill to forbid suits against the United States by holders of gold clause bonds.
18 New York *Times*, June 23, 1935.
19 New York *Times*, April 29, 1935.
20 New York *Times*, June 18, 1935.

their cardinal political philosophy" and they were prepared to stay all summer to enact the Administration proposal.[21] Speaker Byrns also interpreted the message to mean that the President desired to have at least inheritance, gift, and corporation taxes enacted at the present session, and approved of the idea of tying them to the excise tax joint resolution. He could not see why time was needed for study, as Harrison and Doughton had argued, because these taxes had been studied for years. This was particularly true of the inheritance tax.

While the Democrats vacillated, the Progressives began to take action. In the Finance Committee, La Follette made every effort to attach at least part of the President's plan to the excise tax resolution. He was defeated temporarily, however, when Harrison said the President did not want it done that way.[22] Then the Progressives circulated a petition asking for immediate action on the new tax proposals and expressing their willingness to stay in session "until action is taken upon this vitally important question."

Nye said that there were two reasons for the petition : one was to get the desired legislation, the other was to test the President's sincerity. In view of the current comment that the message was only a gesture, the Progressives wanted to find out whether they could have faith in him. Upon his action on the proposed tax plan would depend their decision as to whether or not they would support him in the coming election.[23]

The pressure from Long, the Progressives, and, indirectly, from the Republicans who accused the President of insincerity, apparently forced the Administration to take action. The President was "put on the spot." On Monday following the tax message (June 24) he summoned House and Senate leaders to a conference where he argued for three hours that a bill must be passed immediately. When Speaker Byrns and majority leader Robinson supported the President in a direct reversal of his previous stand, Doughton and Harrison reluctantly consented to amend the joint resolution then under consideration before the Senate Finance Committee. If such a plan were carried out, it would mean that the bill must be rushed through in five days, or else the excise taxes would expire, and the government would lose over a million dollars a day.[24]

Harrison, therefore, published a draft of changes, described as

21 New York *Times*, June 22, 1935.

22 New York *Times*, June 21, 1935. Inasmuch as there was no draft of a bill under consideration, La Follette proposed his own rates.

23 New York *Times*, June 22, 1935.

24 New York *Times*, June 25, 1935. Mr. Moley marks this event as the beginning of the split in the Democratic party. "Heaven or Bust," *Saturday Evening Post*, Aug. 19, 1939. [This chapter was written before Mr. Moley's article appeared.]

"rough and tentative." He proposed: (1) an inheritance tax, in addition to the existing estate tax, at 4% on legacies from $300,000 to $500,000, graduated to 75% on bequests of over $10,000,000, (2) gift taxes at three-fourths of the foregoing rates, (3) higher surtax rates, graduated from 60% on income of $1,000,000 to $1,500,000 to 80% on income over $10,000,000, and (4) a graduated corporation tax at a minimum of 10¾% on income less than $2000 and increasing to a maximum of 16¾% on income above $20,000,000.[25]

The Senate Finance Committee met that same afternoon and, in spite of pressure from the President and Majority Leader Robinson, the members refused to be "steam rollered" to "jam" the bill through, but insisted on an opportunity for hearings.[26] This protest was only the beginning of a revolt. Long thought the rates much too low, and delivered a clever, sarcastic denunciation of the proposal.[27] The Progressives pointed out that the estimated yield of $100,000,000 would be of little help in reducing the deficit or in redistributing the nation's wealth. Other Senators thought there was "unseemly haste."[28] House members objected because they saw the Senate usurping powers delegated to them by the Constitution and the Administration trying to "ram a bill down their throats" at the end of a session within a period of five days.[29] The press had nothing good to say of the plan. Typical editorial comment was as follows:

> The procedure which Mr. Roosevelt has chosen to jam this policy through is intolerable. No milder word will serve.[30]

Nevertheless, at nine o'clock Monday evening work began on the drafting of a bill. A Senate Finance Committee meeting scheduled for Wednesday was postponed on the ground that the experts were not able to finish their draft. On the floor of the Senate that afternoon Harrison explained that, because of certain developments, he would not call up the joint resolution for the extension of the excise taxes as previously announced. While Harrison wavered between finishing the legislative program for quick adjournment, as he wished, and carrying out his obligation to the President, La Follette prepared tax amendments but agreed to withhold them when Harrison reluctantly promised a tax bill that session.

25 New York *Times*, June 26, 1935; *Cong. Rec.* 79: 10033.
26 *Cong. Rec.* 79: 10272.
27 *Cong. Rec.* 79: 10145-10150.
28 *Cong. Rec.* 79: 10033.
29 *Cong. Rec.* 79: 10084-10183; New York *Times*, June 26.
30 Washington *Post*, June 26, 1935. See also Washington *Daily News*, June 24, 25, 1935; New York *Times*, June 26, 1935; New York *Sun*, June 25, 1935; Baltimore *Sun*, June 26, 1935; New York *Herald Tribune*, June 26, 1935, with editorials headed "Vengeance or Virtue," "The New Hysteria," "Shooting from the Hip," "No Time for the Bum's Rush," "How Not to Do It."

Doughton agreed to do his part in keeping Congress in session until a bill was passed if the Senate would pass the resolution to extend the excise taxes without further amendments. This plan was more agreeable to House leaders and also to Harrison and Senate Progressives than attaching a hastily drawn measure to the excise bill. So the "rush order" was canceled. The President asked press representatives on Wednesday why they ever thought that a bill would be rushed through by Saturday!

The Senate passed the joint resolution to extend the excise taxes and the House Committee prepared to draft a measure to carry out the new proposals.[31]

THE COMMITTEE ON WAYS AND MEANS ATTEMPTS TO CARRY OUT THE PRESIDENT'S REQUESTS

In his message of June 19 the President made three specific recommendations: (1) a federal inheritance tax in addition to the estate tax and a gift tax to prevent evasion, the proceeds from which should be applied to the reduction of the national debt; (2) increased taxes on the larger incomes, that is, on those over $1,000,000; (3) a corporation income tax graduated from 10¾% to 16¾%, instead of the flat rate of 13¾% then in effect and; (4) to prevent evasion of this tax by formation of affiliates, a tax on dividends received by corporations.[32]

On July 4 Chairman Doughton of the Committee on Ways and Means,[33] and members of the subcommittee in charge of the bill,

[31] *Cong. Rec.* 79: 10143-10150, 10152-10157, 10270-10277. The members of Congress as well as the press commented on Harrison's good sportsmanship in bearing the brunt of criticism for the change of plans, and taking the blame from the President's shoulders. "His unbroken record as a keeper of promises is one of the factors that have made him the best 'horse-trader' in the Senate." (New York *Times*, July 16, 1935.)

[32] *Cong. Rec.* 79: 9658.

[33] The members of the Committee were:

Democrats	*Republicans*
Robert L. Doughton (N. C.), Ch.	Allen T. Treadway (Mass.)
Samuel B. Hill (Wash.)	Isaac Bacharach (N. J.)
Thomas H. Cullen (N. Y.)	Frank Crowther (N. Y.)
Christopher D. Sullivan (N. Y.)	Harold Knutson (Minn.)
Morgan G. Sanders (Tex.)	Daniel A. Reed (N. Y.)
John W. McCormack (Mass.)	Roy O. Woodruff (Mich.)
David J. Lewis (Md.)	Thomas A. Jenkins (Ohio)
Fred M. Vinson (Ky.)	
Jere Cooper (Tenn.)	
John W. Boehne, Jr. (Ind.)	
Claude A. Fuller (Ark.)	
Wesley E. Disney (Okla.)	
Arthur P. Lamneck (Ohio)	
Frank H. Buck (Calif.)	
Richard M. Duncan (Mo.)	
Chester Thompson (Ill.)	
J. Twing Brooks (Pa.)	
John D. Dingell (Mich.)	

met Treasury experts at the White House.[34] There was much discussion of the advisability of starting the increased surtaxes on brackets lower than $1,000,000. The Treasury advocated such a move in order to get more revenue. Doughton was very optimistic as to the speed with which the measure could be drafted. He thought that the increased surtaxes and the graduated corporation taxes would not take much time but that there might be discussion on the inheritance tax, which proposed a radical departure from the existing practice.[35] He was confident, too, that once the measure was introduced into the House it would be passed promptly. Press commentators were not so sure; the Capitol had not yet been air-conditioned against Washington's depressing heat; [36] the controversy over the President's demands in the recently debated utility bill showed that the majority of the members were conservative and independent, worn out, irritable, and resentful. From Senate ranks came warnings by Vandenberg (Mich.) that Congress should go slowly. The Federal Treasury, he said, was "racing merrily towards potential insolvency day and night" but the President's tax plan was "not even a good soap box formula." [37] Hastings (Del.) introduced a resolution that Congress adjourn until November.[38] Nevertheless, the Committee proceeded to work out a bill and gave no hint of letting up on the plan to rush the bill through before adjournment.

Although no bill had been drafted when the hearings opened on July 8, Hill, chairman of the subcommittee, presented twenty-eight schedules so that Treasury experts might estimate the yields. The Secretary of the Treasury went through the formality of being the first witness, but he had no suggestions or recommendations. He said he was present in order to analyze the schedules that had been submitted, not to tell the Committee how much money should be raised. Republican members asked pointed questions as to the amount of the federal debt and what taxes Congress should levy. Crowther offered a five-year plan for balancing the budget. Vinson rescued the Secretary from an embarrassing position by remarking:

This is one time in the history of our country when the Executive relies upon this committee, as they have relied upon it throughout this

[34] The subcommittee members were Vinson, Hill, Cooper and Cullen; Treasury representatives, Oliphant and Haas. L. H. Parker, of the Joint Committee staff, and Charles West, recently appointed Under-secretary of the Interior and "contact man" between the President and Congress, were also present.

[35] New York *Times*, July 5, 1935.

[36] Arthur Krock said: "When Washington dogs chase Washington rabbits in summer, both of them walk." (New York *Times*, July 14, 1935.)

[37] New York *Times*, July 8, 1935.

[38] *Cong. Rec.* 79: 11611.

administration, and as the Executive should have always relied upon this committee, under the Constitution.[39]

L. H. Parker of the research staff of the Joint Committee on Internal Revenue Taxation was much more helpful, particularly with respect to the difficult problem of drafting the federal inheritance tax provision which the President had requested.

Representatives of the business world who testified before the Committee were concerned over the prospects of a graduated corporation tax. Their protests seem to have had some effect; the bill drawn up by the Committee proposed only two rates, but opposition was made to even this slight graduation. At the same time the President let it be known that he did not approve of abandoning the graduation of rates. As a compromise measure the majority members proposed an extension of the excess-profits tax. They estimated that, inasmuch as the existing tax had brought in over $5,000,000 for eleven months, it would be easy to raise the amount expected from the proposed graduated corporation tax ($67,000,000 to $100,000,000) by reducing the exemption from the excess-profits tax to 10% of net profits and by increasing the rate on all profits over that minimum. Doughton favored substituting this for the normal corporation tax, but the President protested. Therefore, the Committee kept both taxes, despite Treasury objections that the excess-profits tax would be difficult to administer and was not so fair as the normal tax.[40]

By June 25 the Democratic members of the Committee completed the draft of a bill which it was estimated would produce $150,000,000. The new surtax rates commenced at $150,000 and were graduated till they reached 75% on income in excess of $10,000,000. A graduated corporation tax was kept only "in principle," that is, the rates were made 13¼% and 14¼%; the excess-profits tax was retained, with lowered exemptions, and rates increased to 20%. There were added also an inheritance tax with rates to reach as high as 75% and a gift tax with rates three-fourths of those of the inheritance tax. There was no provision for earmarking the revenue from this tax for the public debt and there was no provision for taxing dividends received by corporations. Before this preliminary work was completed changes were made in the additional surtax rates so that they would begin at a lower bracket.

It was reported that the majority members agreed to stand together in support of the bill. This gave Doughton more confidence in

[39] 74th Congress, 1st Session, *Hearings before the Committee on Ways and Means on Proposed Taxation of Individual and Corporate Incomes, Inheritances and Gifts*, p. 14.

[40] New York *Times*, July 16, 20, 23-26, 1935; 74th Congress, 1st Session, *Hearings before the* [Senate] *Committee on Finance*, pp. 26, 227-233.

holding the House to the measure as written and in preventing extraneous amendments being tied to the bill, for example, inflation, soldiers' bonus, and farm mortgage financing amendments.[41]

The Republican minority voted against the Committee report because, according to their published statement,

> That it is nothing but a political gesture seems to be universally conceded. That it will fail to raise any appreciable amount of revenue cannot be denied.

The Republicans had not had much time to analyze the measure, so their criticisms were of a general nature. They recalled the warnings of previous Secretaries of the Treasury that tax rates might be pushed so high that they would cease to be productive. They objected to the principle of a graduated corporation tax because its purpose was obviously to break up the large corporations, not to raise revenue; because small stockholders were disregarded; and because the bill did not take into account the fact that the amount of profit a corporation earned was not necessarily in proportion to the size of the corporation.

The minority disapproved also the increased burden from the excess-profits tax that would fall on corporations; objected to the omission of an exemption for corporations from income tax on contributions made to charitable organizations; and disapproved the proposed inheritance taxes.[42]

THE HOUSE ACCEPTS THE COMMITTEE DRAFT

Chairman Doughton reported the bill July 30 and debate commenced August 1. The minority attempted to delay House action by demanding that the bill be read and by making numerous requests for roll calls.[43] Hill, chairman of the subcommittee in charge of drafting the measure, explained and defended the changes from the existing law. Treadway presented the arguments of the minority, that the bill was not in any way a "soak-the-rich measure" but rather a "bill to save the face of the President." Most of the speeches on both sides of the House were political. The debate was completed in two days.

Few amendments were offered and only one was adopted. This permitted corporations to deduct gifts to charitable organizations.

41 New York *Times*, July 29, 1935.

42 74th Congress, 1st Session, *House Report* 1681.

43 *Cong. Rec.* 79: 12288. For the House debate see pp. 12299-12406, 12418-12449, 12499.

This amendment was offered by McCormack, a friend of the bill, although it had been vigorously opposed by the President. McFarlane (Tex.) proposed a 1% increase in surtax rates applicable to all incomes above $2000 and a confiscatory tax of 99½% on incomes over $100,000. This was rejected. Truax (Ohio) offered an amendment to graduate the corporation tax from 13¼% to 16½%, in accordance with the President's recommendations of June 19. It was rejected after Cooper's defense of the Committee, in which he said:

> the Committee on Ways and Means gave perhaps more extensive consideration to this provision of the bill than to any other provision in it. . . It is felt by the committee that the provision as it now stands in the bill is far preferable to the provision contained in this amendment, and the committee asks that the amendment be voted down.

In his testimony before the Senate Finance Committee, Parker of the Joint Committee staff explained that the House Committee considered the excess-profits tax a fairer tax than the graduated corporation tax but were willing to adopt a mild form of the latter as an experiment.

The bill was passed by a vote of 282 to 95. Of those who favored the measure 254 were Democrats, 18 were Republicans, 7 were Progressives, and 3 were Farmer-Laborites. Eighteen Democrats joined 77 Republicans against the bill.

As passed by the House, the bill increased surtax rates on individual net income in excess of $50,000, graduated so that a maximum rate of 75% was reached on income in excess of $1,000,000. The corporation tax was increased from a flat rate of 10% to rates of 13¼% on the first $15,000 of net income and 14¼% on the remainder. In place of the 5% tax on profits in excess of 12½% of the value of the stock, there was substituted an excess-profits tax with rates graduated in five steps: 5% on the portion of the net income in excess of 8% and not in excess of 12½% of the value of the stock to 20% on the portion of the net income in excess of 25% of the adjusted declared value. Corporations were not permitted to make a new declaration of capital stock value. An inheritance tax at rates graduated to a maximum of 75% was imposed in addition to the federal estate tax.

THE SENATE FINANCE COMMITTEE MAKES RADICAL CHANGES

Before the House had passed the tax bill, the Senate Finance Committee [44] held its public hearings. Secretary Morgenthau was as noncommittal as when before the House Committee ; in fact, his attitude was very annoying to the chairman, who wanted an analysis of the House bill from the point of view of the Administration. The Secretary replied that such a request was embarrassing.[45] The chairman persisted in his questions, particularly as to the provision for only 1% graduation in the corporation income tax, because he wanted to know whether such a procedure was approved by the Treasury Department. The Secretary would not answer this question even after conferring with some of the Treasury experts in the room. Harrison's wishes were to draw up a bill that followed the President's suggestions more closely than the House bill had done, but he received no help towards this end from the Secretary. Robert Jackson, Assistant General Counsel of the Treasury Department, and L. H. Parker, of the Joint Committee, bore the brunt of the burden of explaining the technicalities of the bill.

The hearings were concluded August 8, and the Committee reported the bill August 13. In the intervening four days the House bill was radically revised. Harrison succeeded in securing assent to several provisions that he considered closer to the President's wishes as expressed in the tax message, for example, with respect to a graduated corporation tax. He was unable, however, to prevent the substitution of an increase in the estate tax for the proposed inheritance tax.[46] This was a disappointment to the chairman who saw the bill becoming merely a revenue measure.

[44] The members were:

Democrats	*Republicans*
Pat Harrison (Miss.), Ch.	James Couzens (Mich.)
William H. King (Utah)	Henry W. Keyes (N. H.)
Walter F. George (Ga.)	Robert M. La Follette, Jr. (Wis.)
David I. Walsh (Mass.)	Jesse H. Metcalf (R. I.)
Alben W. Barkley (Ky.)	Daniel O. Hastings (Del.)
Tom Connally (Tex.)	Arthur Capper (Kans.)
Thomas P. Gore (Okla.)	
Edward P. Costigan (Colo.)	
Joseph W. Bailey (N. C.)	
Bennett Champ Clark (Mo.)	
Henry Flood Byrd (Va.)	
Augustine Lonergan (Conn.)	
Hugo L. Black (Ala.)	
Peter G. Gerry (R. I.)	
Joseph F. Guffey (Pa.)	

[45] 74th Congress, 1st Session, *Hearings before the Senate Finance Committee on H. R. 8974*, p. 96.

[46] The vote was eleven to eight to reject the inheritance tax. Those who supported Harrison were Barkley, Connally, Costigan, Black, and Guffey, Democrats ; La Follette, Progressive ; and Capper, Republican.

La Follette, as was expected, pushed for higher surtax rates and lower personal exemptions. The Committee agreed to reduce the personal exemptions from $2500 to $2000 and from $1000 to $800, and to begin the application of the surtax at $3000 instead of $4000. Borah and Norris protested this additional tax on small incomes, so two days later the Committee reversed its action.[47]

As introduced into the Senate the bill provided for: increased surtaxes on incomes in excess of $1,000,000; a tax on corporations graduated from 12½% to 15½%; an excess-profits tax of 6% and 12%; an increased federal estate tax; a tax on inter-company dividends; and increased rates on personal holding companies.[48] Two of the minority members, Metcalf and Hastings, signed a separate report.[49] They objected to the Committee bill because: (1) it was not a revenue producer but was supported only because the President wanted it; (2) it violated every sound principle of taxation; (3) the majority party evidenced "an utter disregard for obvious inequities and patent absurdities." They made the following recommendations:

(1) Adjourn Congress immediately.
(2) Leave business alone. . .
(3) "Eliminate extravagance and waste in Government expenditures and let us have a Budget showing a sincere and sound program for restoring a balance between expenditures and receipts. . ."
(4) If additional revenues are required, give adequate opportunity for studying the operation of the present laws, the distribution of existing tax burdens, the relation between taxpaying ability and the innumerable other measures exacting tremendous sums from our citizens, including particularly producers and consumers.
(5) Then enact a comprehensive and sound revenue measure based upon the foregoing studies and surveys and upon actual facts.

THE BILL IN THE SENATE

Harrison was eager to prevent undue delays in the consideration of the measure that might result from extraneous amendments, particularly from soldiers' bonus advocates. An agreement was therefore reached between the committee chairmen concerned that a vote on immediate cash payment of a bonus would be promised early in the following session.[50] There was no such simple solution to keep La Follette from proposing increased tax rates, a move that Harrison feared unduly.

On August 13 Harrison explained the development of the bill in response to the President's message, the House bill, and the Senate

[47] New York *Times*, August 11, 12, 13, 1935.
[48] 74th Congress, 1st Session, *Senate Report* 1240, Part I.
[49] 74th Congress, 1st Session, *Senate Report* 1240, Part II.
[50] New York *Times*, Aug. 7, 1935.

Committee changes. Vandenberg, Steiwer (Ore.), and Hastings stated the case for the minority.[51]

One of the first amendments offered was that of La Follette to increase the surtax rates on income over $8000, although his proposed maximum rate was no higher than the 75% set by the Committee. He did not change the personal exemptions. The Senate rejected his proposal by a vote of 32 to 56 [52] but, when the Committee rates were under discussion, he urged that they be rejected and the higher rates of the House bill be accepted. He estimated the additional revenue would be $41,000,000 more than from the Senate Committee amendments. After the Senate accepted the Committee rates, La Follette offered, merely for the record, his amendment to reduce the personal exemptions from $2500 to $2000 and from $1000 to $800.[53] It was estimated this would bring in $40,000,000.

Borah received support for his amendment to tax interest from future issues of federal bonds. Harrison was in sympathy with the aim of his colleagues, namely, to establish a policy for doing away with tax-exempt securities, and was willing to have the amendment go to conference.[54] This was almost the only noncommittee amendment adopted.[55]

A few unsuccessful attempts were made to introduce extraneous matters, such as amendments for a cash payment to world war veterans [56] and an excise tax on importation of poultry and eggs.[57] The debate was completed much sooner than even the friends of the bill anticipated and, August 15, the measure was passed by a vote of 57 to 22.[58]

THE CONFERENCE REPORT

The divergence between the House and Senate bills was such that it would have been difficult for the Conferees to have reached a decision if they had not been in a hurry to adjourn. The major differences related to the inheritance versus the estate tax, taxation of intercorporate dividends, and surtax rates.

Because of advice from the Treasury that the inheritance tax would be extremely difficult to administer, the House managers receded on that point and accepted the Senate increases in the estate tax. Senator Borah's amendment to tax interest from federal securities was dropped.

51 *Cong. Rec.* 79: 13044-13049.
52 *Cong. Rec.* 79: 13213.
53 *Cong. Rec.* 79: 13223.
54 *Cong. Rec.* 79: 13240.
55 There was adopted also an amendment for reducing the producers' tax on crude petroleum from 1/10 of a cent per barrel to 1/25 of a cent. (*Cong. Rec.* 79: 13246.)
56 *Cong. Rec.* 79: 13245.
57 *Cong. Rec.* 79: 13250.
58 *Cong. Rec.* 79: 13254. Ten Democrats voted against it.

The House accepted the principle of taxing intercorporate dividends but reduced the portion taxable to 10% of those received. Both the House and Senate bills were estimated to produce about $255,000,000 additional revenue.

Three Republican members did not sign the Conference report because they did not wish "in any way to be a party to the final enactment of this legislative absurdity." [59] They objected to the measure on the ground that it was passed merely because the Administration wanted it, not for revenue reasons, and they protested particularly the graduated corporation tax which they claimed was unfair, unjust, violated the principle of ability to pay, and was in the bill merely to satisfy a whim of the President. The bill was signed by the President on August 30.

SUMMARY OF IMPORTANT CHANGES MADE BY THE ACT [60]

The Revenue Act of 1935 contained five titles: I — Income and Excess-Profits Taxes; II — Amendments to Estate Tax; III — Amendment to Gift Tax; IV — Miscellaneous Provisions; V — General Provisions. The law was written as an amendment to the Revenue Act of 1934, not as a complete entity or as a substitute for the existing law. The changes made by it were relatively few.

Title I — Income and Excess-Profits Taxes. The normal tax and exemptions of the 1934 Act were unchanged. The surtax rates were changed only in the brackets of income of $50,000 and over. The new rate on income in excess of $50,000 and not in excess of $56,000 was 31% instead of 30%; the maximum rate was 75% on income over $500,000 instead of 59% on income over $1,000,000. The tax on net income of corporations was graduated as follows:

Upon net income not in excess of $2000, 12½%;
Upon net income in excess of $2000 and not in excess of $15,000, 13%;
Upon net income in excess of $15,000 and not in excess of $40,000, 14%;
Upon income in excess of $40,000, 15%.

Corporations were permitted to deduct from gross income 90% of dividends received. The penalty surtax imposed on corporations improperly accumulating surplus was left at 25% and 35% of retained net income, but to conform to the increased surtaxes the rates of tax on personal holding companies were increased to the following:

(1) 20 per centum of the amount of the undistributed adjusted net income not in excess of $2000; plus

[59] Senator Metcalf, Representatives Treadway and Bacharach. (*Cong. Rec.* 79: 14265.)
[60] 49 *Statutes at Large* 1014.

(2) 30 per centum of the amount thereof in excess of $2000 and not in excess of $100,000 ; plus

(3) 40 per centum of the amount thereof in excess of $100,000 and not in excess of $500,000 ; plus

(4) 50 per centum of the amount thereof in excess of $500,000 and not in excess of $1,000,000 ; plus

(5) 60 per centum of the amount thereof in excess of $1,000,000.

New provisions were drafted to define tax-free exchanges of property received by a corporation in liquidation of another corporation.

For the first time corporations were permitted to deduct gifts made to charitable organizations but not in excess of 5% of the amount of net income. The capital stock tax was increased from $1 to $1.40 for each $1000 of the declared value of the stock. The new excess-profits tax rates were 6% of net income in excess of 10% and not in excess of 15% of the adjusted declared value of the stock; 12% of the net income in excess of 15% of the adjusted declared value.

Title II — Amendments to Estate Tax. The estate tax rates were increased so that the maximum was 70% on estates in excess of $50,000,000. On these additions there was no credit allowed for death taxes paid to states, as in the 1926 law.[61] The amount of exemption was reduced from $50,000 to $40,000.

Title III — Gift Tax. The rates of the gift tax were increased to 1½% on gifts in excess of $10,000 to 52½% upon gifts in excess of $50,000,000. The exemption was decreased from $50,000 to $40,000.

Title IV — Miscellaneous Provisions, dealt with : administrative regulations as to the excise taxes on sale of manufactured articles, oils, crude petroleum, and liquor; interest on delinquent taxes; and penalty for failure to file any internal revenue tax return required by law.

Title V — General Provisions, defined certain terms and stated effective dates. The law took effect upon its enactment on August 30, except that the income tax amendments were applicable to taxable years beginning after December 31, 1935.[62]

[61] See Chap. X for tables and graphs pertaining to estate and gift taxes.

[62] The income tax sections were amended by the Revenue Act of 1936 before they went into effect. For tax rates and exemptions under various acts, see Chapter XXII, below.

CHAPTER XVI

TAXES FOR SOCIAL SECURITY

THE ACT OF 1935: THE CABINET COMMITTEE

When the first session of the 74th Congress convened in January 1935, the President devoted his annual message to the following three-point program for economic and social security which he said was ready for legislative action:

> First, the security of a livelihood through the better use of the national resources of the land in which we live;
> Second, security against the major hazards and vicissitudes of life;
> Third, the security of better homes.[1]

The second item of this program was covered by the Wagner-Doughton-Lewis bill for an extensive program of (1) federal grants to the states for old-age assistance, benefits for dependent children, child welfare, child and maternal health services and increased public health services, and (2) a system of old-age annuities and unemployment insurance [2] to be financed by payroll taxes. This bill was based on the report of the President's Cabinet Committee on Economic Security appointed in 1934.[3] This group, made up of four members of the Cabinet and Relief Administrator Hopkins, served as a steering committee for numerous other advisory and technical committees which made a thorough study of social insurance.[4]

Such an extensive subject, especially involving the complications of federal-state relationships, cannot be discussed here.[5] The financing of the program is the part that is germane to this study. The basic fiscal problem was, of course, how extensive and expensive a program should be undertaken. Once this was decided, how should costs be allocated (1) between the federal and state governments and (2) between governments, employees, and employers? [5]

For constitutional and political reasons the Cabinet Committee followed as far as possible a federal-state organization plan. It was obvious, however, that federal grants for protection of the aged and unemployed would involve a tremendous drain on the United States

1 *Cong. Rec.* 79: 95.

2 In 1934 Wagner and Lewis had introduced a somewhat similar measure designed to encourage state unemployment insurance plans.

3 *Report to the President of the Committee on Economic Security*, Jan. 1935. Published as a separate document; summarized in the New York *Times*, Jan. 18, 1935.

4 A list of committees is printed in 74th Congress, 1st Session, *House Report* 615.

5 Much has been published on this subject; see especially Douglas, Paul, *Social Security in the United States.*

Treasury. Therefore, the Committee proposed a federal old-age insurance system with compulsory contributions and, for financing of unemployment insurance, a tax remission plan somewhat similar to the federal estate tax credit plan for state death taxes.[6] For financing outright assistance or pensions to the needy aged, services to dependent children, and aid for maternity and child health, the Committee recommended that the federal government match state contributions. This system of matching grants had been used for many years to encourage construction of highways, teaching of vocational subjects in the schools, and for other purposes, and had been upheld by the courts.[7]

In order to finance unemployment insurance the Committee recommended : (1) a uniform payroll tax on those who employed four or more persons for a reasonable length of time, and (2) financing and supervising of state administration of federal grants.

The permanent tax rate suggested was 3%, but only 1% or 2% might be imposed for 1936 and 1937 if the Federal Reserve Board's index did not indicate that economic recovery had progressed "satisfactorily." No industries were to be excluded, but separate systems were favored for railroad employees and maritime workers.

It was proposed that the employers' payroll tax should be credited, to the extent of 90% of the tax, for contributions made to a state system of unemployment insurance, if the state met certain conditions for the administration of unemployment compensation. In order to encourage adequate and efficient state administration, it was proposed that the revenue from the portion of the tax paid to the federal government be used for grants to the state "under conditions designed to insure competence and probity." The states were to have freedom in determining benefit rates, maximum benefit periods, and waiting periods.

For contributory old-age annuities the Committee recommended a compulsory system applicable to all manual workers and non-manual workers earning less than $250 per month, except those in the government and railroad services already covered by pension plans.[8] Both employers and employees were to be subject to a tax of ½% each for the first five years the law was to be in effect; 1% for the

[6] The Supreme Court had upheld the validity of the federal estate tax credit in *Florida* v. *Mellon,* 273 U. S. 12 (1928).

[7] *Mass.* v. *Mellon,* 262 U. S. 447 (1922).

[8] After the Railroad Retirement Act was declared unconstitutional in 1935 (*R. R. Retirement Board* v. *Alton R. R. Co.,* 55 Sup. Ct. 748), a new retirement act for railroad workers was enacted in the same year. Railroad employees were, therefore, excluded from the federal old-age insurance system. Since there was no unemployment compensation system for railroad workers, states were permitted to cover them. In 1938 the Railroad Unemployment Compensation Law was enacted, and the railroad employees were removed from coverage by the states on July 1, 1939.

second five years; 1½% for the third five years; 2% for the fourth five years and 2½% thereafter. The employer's tax was to be based on payroll, the employee's on wages. It was suggested that the federal government make no contribution so long as the income from the taxes exceeded payments from the fund, but that it guarantee to make contributions sufficient to maintain the reserve at the level of the last year in which income exceeded payments. It was estimated that this reserve would be maintained at about $15,250,000,000.

No benefits were to be paid until the system had been in operation for five years, or to a person who had not made at least 200 weekly contributions, or before he had reached the age of 65 and retired from gainful employment.

As a supplement to the compulsory system just outlined the Committee proposed that the government sell to individuals on a cost basis deferred life annuities similar to those of commercial companies, with premiums as small as $1 per month and with maximum annuities of $50 per month.

The plan to impose payroll taxes was not adopted by the Committee without serious consideration of other methods. Critics of the payroll tax argued that wages of workers were generally inadequate and should not be further reduced by taxation. It was also claimed that the taxes paid by the employers would be shifted to the employees in the form of decreased wages, or in the form of increased prices. Another argument was that the tax would cause shifts in industry, if not unemployment, because of the advantage that mechanized industries would have over those using many employees.

One of the other methods considered by the Committee for raising at least part of the costs was an additional general income tax on individuals with incomes in the higher brackets. Such a tax could not be shifted. The reasons for the rejection of this plan are not known. It has been suggested that the Administration was opposed to any new levies on wealth.[9] If that is the case, there was a radical shift in the next few months, because in June the President demanded a tax program to bring about a distribution of wealth.

THE WAGNER BILL BEFORE THE COMMITTEE ON WAYS AND MEANS

The Wagner-Lewis bill based on the Cabinet Committee report was introduced in both the House and the Senate on January 17, 1935. It was referred to the Committee on Ways and Means in the House and to the Committee on Finance in the Senate, because of the taxation features that were the responsibilities of these Committees. It was suggested also that there was perhaps some fear that

[9] Douglas, Paul, *Social Security in the United States*, p. 68.

the more logical sponsors, the committees on labor, would be more liberal and extend the provisions more than the Administration desired.[10]

Public hearings were begun by the House and the Senate Committees January 21 and 22, respectively. The Administration members did what they could to push the measure along by limiting the time of the witnesses, in the hope that the bill could be passed while state legislatures were in session. Criticism was directed against the principle of the measure by certain business and industrial groups, against certain features of the bill and in favor of more liberal and very different plans such as the Townsend plan and that sponsored by Congressman Lundeen.[11]

Most surprising was the testimony of the Secretary of the Treasury, who asked for radical changes in the bill so that the financing of contributory old-age insurance would be put on a self-supporting basis and that federal contributions would be eliminated. To this end he recommended that payroll and earnings taxes should be increased to 2% for the first three years, 3% for the next three, thence increasing by 1% until a maximum of 6% was reached in twelve years (1949). This change meant that a huge reserve would be built up in the Treasury, about 47 billion dollars by 1980.[12] The Secretary asked also that the administration of the law be simplified by exempting certain classes of laborers such as those in domestic service and agriculture, as well as transient or casual laborers.[13]

Because of these requests and also because the bill needed more careful drafting, the Committee had to rewrite the measure.[14] The most important changes from the original draft were: (1) to establish a central federal reserve account; (2) to change the terms "payroll" tax to "excise tax" and "earnings" tax to "income" tax "with a view to constitutionality"; (3) to accept the Secretary's suggestion as to tax rates; (4) to remove the Social Security Board from the Department of Labor; (5) to base benefits to insured workers over 65 on total income during their insured lifetime; and (6) to abolish the power of the federal government to set personnel standards for state administration. The minority approved of the purpose of the bill in a half-hearted fashion but objected seriously to the provisions for compulsory old-age insurance. Knutson (Rep., Minn.) was more

10 *New Republic* 82: 3 (Feb. 13, 1935); Douglas, Paul, *Social Security in the United States*, p. 85.

11 January 3, Lundeen (Farm.-Lab., Minn.) succeeded in introducing his bill for payments during involuntary unemployment at the prevailing local rate of wages with a minimum of $10 per week plus $3 for each dependent.

12 74th Congress, 1st Session, *Senate Report* 628. (See Table 13, below.)

13 74th Congress, 1st Session, *Hearings before the Committee on Ways and Means on H. R.* 4120, pp. 897-941; New York *Times*, Feb. 6, 1935.

14 New York *Times*, Feb. 14, 1935.

opposed than the others, however, and he stated that he could not vote for the bill because the payroll taxes would retard business recovery by driving many industries into bankruptcy or by forcing them to close down altogether.

It soon became evident that the measure could not be rushed through as quickly as the President had originally desired. The Committee members were hampered by their divergent views, by the complexity of the measure, by the strength of the Townsend-Lundeen demand for more liberal payments, and by a "well-organized opposition." [15] As the legislative session progressed, Congress seemed to become somewhat apathetic to the measure, so the combination of circumstances led the Committee to postpone final action until the World War veterans' bonus issue was settled. Mrs. Greenway (Dem., Ariz.), who was known to be very close to the President, suggested that at least the section on old-age assistance be separated from the rest of the bill and passed, in view of the pressure from radical groups for some action on that matter, and that the less urgent unemployment compensation provisions be postponed until fall.[16] But somehow the obstructions were cleared away and the Committee completed the draft by March 24.

THE HOUSE OF REPRESENTATIVES BILL

The revised bill introduced into the House contained ten titles, namely: (I) Grants-in-aid to the states for old-age assistance to dependent persons of sixty-five years of age or over, the federal government to match the funds raised by the states within certain limits; (II) Old-age benefits to be measured by wages, first payable in 1942 to those who had reached sixty-five years of age, regardless of the needs of the recipient; (III) Grants-in-aid to the states to pay the administrative costs of state unemployment compensation systems; (IV) Grants-in-aid to the states for aid to dependent children, the federal government agreeing to contribute one-third of the total amount, within certain limits; (V) Grants-in-aid to states for work in maternity and child welfare, including services to crippled children and vocational rehabilitation; (VI) Grants-in-aid to the states for developing their public health research work; (VII) Establishment of a Social Security Board of three members as an independent agency in the executive branch of the government; (VIII) An income tax levied on certain groups of wage earners measured by their wages, an excise tax on employers, the funds to be deposited in the United States Treasury and invested in government bonds yielding not less than 3% interest; (IX) An excise tax on certain employers of ten

15 *The Survey* 71: 110 (April 1935).
16 New York *Times*, March 20, 1935.

or more employees, measured by wages payable but allowing credit for contributions paid to state unemployment funds under state unemployment compensation acts; and (X) Definitions and miscellaneous provisions.

Titles II, III, VIII, and IX will be described briefly. Title II provided that old-age benefits would be paid after January 1, 1942 to employees in the United States, including Alaska and Hawaii, except the following: agricultural labor, domestic service in a private home, casual labor not used in the employer's regular business, employees of a state or the United States government, employees of institutions operated for religious, charitable, literary, or scientific purposes, or employees upon vessels documented under the laws of the United States. The conditions for receipt of old-age benefits were: (1) that the recipient be at least 65 years of age; (2) that he had received not less than $2000 total wages after the title became effective and before he reached 65; (3) that wages were paid to him on some day in each of five years after the title became effective and before he reached 65. Monthly benefit payments were based on percentages of wages: ½% of the first $3000, 1/12% of the next $42,000 and 1/24% of all over $45,000. Table 14, below, illustrates how this would work out.

Funds for the payment of these benefits were to be derived from taxes, provided in Title VIII, levied on both employers and employees. The rate schedule was as follows: 1937-1939, 1% on total payroll of employer and income (wage) of employee; 1940-1942, 1½%; 1943-1945, 2%; 1946-1948, 2½%; 1949 and thereafter, 3%.

Title III provided for grants to the states for administering their unemployment insurance systems. The funds for the benefits to unemployed were expected to be derived from an excise (payroll) tax on employers (Title IX) of which 90% would be credited to state taxes levied for the purpose. The remaining 10% was to be used for federal aid to the states in establishing efficient administration of their unemployment insurance systems.

It should be noted that the provisions defining the benefits and the sources of revenue were separated and that there was no reference in one to the other. This was done for the purpose of preventing a taxpayer from bringing the issue of the validity of the tax before the courts.[17]

[17] See *Frothingham* v. *Mellon,* (262 U.S. 447, 1923). The adverse decisions of the Court on the railroad pension act (*Railroad Retirement Board* v. *Alton R. R.*, 55 Sup. Ct. 748), while the Social Security Act was being drafted and on the A. A. A. (*U. S.* v. *Butler,* 297 U. S. 1, 1936) soon after the Social Security Act went into effect, gave much uneasiness to sponsors of the measure. One of the cases which had caused doubt was that of *Bailey* v. *Drexel Furniture Co.* (259 U. S. 20, 1922). This child labor case was cited as indicating the Court's insistence that a tax must have some revenue features and could not be wholly regulatory. The Social Security Act was upheld by the Supreme Court in *C. C. Steward Machine Co.* v. *Davis* (301 U. S. 548, 1939).

The House passed the measure on April 19 by an overwhelming majority. The minority contented themselves with a few speeches. The Townsend plan was discussed and the Lundeen bill offered as an amendment, but the majority leaders were able to prevent the measure from being changed except for two Committee amendments offered on the floor.[18]

AMENDMENTS BY THE SENATE COMMITTEE ON FINANCE

The House bill was amended by the Senate Finance Committee as indicated below.[19] An additional condition was imposed in regard to the receipt of old-age insurance; namely, that the recipient must not be regularly employed. This was to prevent persons who continued at work from receiving benefits. It was thought that this restriction would reduce the cost. The Senate Committee also put back into the bill the provision for the sale of annuities to those not eligible for old-age insurance.

The Social Security Board was again put under the Department of Labor because of the close relationship between the functions of the Board and this Department. It was pointed out that such types of legislation in other countries were almost invariably under the direction of the labor department or one with similar functions. Furthermore, administrative costs might be reduced by so doing. The Senate Committee also changed the coverage of the tax on employers in Title IX to those with four or more employees for 13 weeks during a year. A new title was added to provide federal aid to states for services to the blind.

Administration of the grants-in-aid to the states for aid to dependent children was placed in the Children's Bureau instead of the Social Security Board. The House requirement that state unemployment compensation funds should be of the "pooled" type in which all funds are mingled and undivided as a condition to qualify for the credit against the federal tax under Title IX was stricken. Two new sections were inserted to give additional credit to employers who, under state laws, are permitted to lower their rates of compensation because of favorable employment experience.

SENATE AMENDMENTS AND REPORT OF THE CONFEREES

The Senate made 113 amendments, about five of which made up the group involved in the changes sponsored by Clark (Mo.). He proposed that employers be permitted to retain their own pension

[18] *Cong. Rec.* 79: 5467, 5528-6070.
[19] 74th Congress, 1st Session, *Senate Report* 628.

systems instead of contributing to the state-federal system [20] but the House conferees refused to accept this change. The Senate conferees would not recede; so the matter had to be considered again. The House voted against it after a good deal of discussion and it was not written into the bill. Some concession was made, however, by the agreement to appoint a committee of five members from each house to study the proposition and to report at the next session.

In addition to the Clark amendments there were about six other important changes made by the Senate. One, introduced by Russell (Ga.), was a provision requiring the federal government to contribute $15 per month for two years for each person qualified to receive an old-age pension if he lived in a state that had a constitutional prohibition of a state pension plan, or if he lived in a state that was financially unable to contribute to an old-age pension fund. This was not accepted by the Conferees.

Another Senate change was to put the Social Security Board under the Department of Labor instead of making it an independent body. The Senate receded on this amendment so the House provisions were accepted. A third change provided for a pension of $30 a month to needy Indians. This was not accepted by the Conferees because it contained many provisions that seemed hastily and poorly drawn. A fourth change was the La Follette amendment to permit states to adopt either a pooled fund system for unemployment compensation or an individual employer reserve system. This was acceptable to the House conferees. The fifth change was to add a title providing for aid to the blind. This was acceptable to the House. The Conferees compromised on a coverage of employers with eight employees for twenty weeks or more.

The Senate did not debate the Conference Report to any great extent.[21]

Inasmuch as the House provisions have been stated in such detail, no further summary of the law [22] appears necessary at this point.

CRITICISM OF THE ACT OF 1935

The provisions of this Act were severely criticized on several grounds: (1) the separation of the needy into categories, (2) the amount of the benefits of the contributory schemes, (3) the omission of provision for widows and dependent children in the old-age in-

[20] Clark was supported by George (Ga.) and Tydings (Md.) on the Democratic side and McNary (Ore.) on the Republican. The three Democrats were not enthusiastic New Deal followers and were among those marked by the President for defeat in his 1938 "purge." One of their arguments against the Social Security bill was that it would set up a tremendous bureaucracy in Washington.

[21] *Cong. Rec.* 79: 11307, 12793.

[22] 49 *Statutes at Large* 620.

surance scheme, (4) the fiscal arrangements and (5) the economic effects of the payroll taxes. These will be briefly summarized, but most attention will be given to the financial sections.

Because of the divisions set up in the law between the needy who are (1) old, (2) children, or (3) blind, the way is open to bring pressure on state legislatures for special or increased amounts of aid. This results in the most vocal or the most effective lobbying groups getting the largest amount of assistance. Colorado may be cited as an example of a state where persistent pressure has been brought by the aged, even to the extent of getting a provision for a $45-a-month payment written into the state constitution. Such a financial burden appears to be greater than the state can afford now, consequently other needy groups suffer and other services of the state, such as education, are seriously handicapped.

The provisions for compulsory contributory old-age insurance were criticized because the benefits were small in comparison with the free grants to the needy. By 1942 a worker who was earning $100 a month would retire on an annuity of $17.50 a month; in 1947, he would receive $22.50; in 1952, $27.50; in 1957, $32.50. These were smaller sums than many states granted the aged who contributed nothing. The Act made no provision for any other members of a worker's family such as an aged wife, or a young widow with dependent children, except for a lump sum payment equal to 3½% of wages earned by the husband in covered employment.

The fiscal provisions for old-age insurance were the subject of attack from the time they were passed. As pointed out above, they were not the provisions recommended by the technical experts but were forced into the measure by the Administration. Criticism centered chiefly on the provisions for the large reserve. It was pointed out that if this reserve were built up it could be easily squandered. In fact, these funds have been "borrowed" and used for current government expenses, as authorized in the Act. Even if not squandered it would be difficult to invest such a reserve properly without disturbing the money market. The required return of 3% interest was more than some government bonds were paying currently, hence the difference would have to be made up by the taxpayer. It has been argued, too, that even if the reserve fund were kept intact it might not be sufficient to pay all benefits required by 1970, hence taxes from other sources would have to be imposed by that time. The accompanying table shows appropriations, benefit payments, and reserves as estimated at the time of the passage of the act.

The economic effects of payroll taxes have also been the subject of controversy. The taxes are of course added burdens to employers and act as deterrents to hiring additional workers. To what extent

TABLE 13

ESTIMATED APPROPRIATIONS, BENEFIT PAYMENTS, AND RESERVES UNDER TITLE II [a]

(In millions of dollars)

Fiscal year ending June 30—	*Appropriation for reserve*	*Interest on reserve*	*Benefit payments*	*Balance in reserve*
1937	255.5	0	1.9	253.7
1938	513.5	7.6	7.2	767.5
1939	518.5	23.0	14.5	1,299.5
1940	662.2	38.8	22.0	1,973.6
1941	807.2	59.2	29.7	2,810.3
1942	814.8	84.4	52.8	3,656.6
1943	970.0	109.8	94.2	4,642.1
1944	1,126.6	139.3	142.9	5,765.1
1945	1,137.0	173.0	191.2	6,883.9
1946	1,291.4	206.5	249.2	8,132.7
1947	1,447.1	243.9	314.5	9,509.2
1948	1,460.1	285.2	377.4	10,877.0
1949	1,621.1	326.3	442.1	12,382.4
1950	1,783.3	371.5	505.5	14,031.7
1955	1,861.2	615.8	887.8	22,115.7
1960	1,939.1	844.2	1,379.9	29,543.9
1965	2,016.9	1,040.9	1,844.0	35,898.5
1970	2,094.8	1,210.9	2,303.5	41,366.7
1975	2,172.7	1,341.8	2,872.1	45,368.3
1980	2,180.5	1,406.0	3,511.3	46,942.7

[a] 74th Congress, 1st Session, *Senate Report* 628, p. 9.

they hinder employment, however, is not known. Some economists maintain that the taxes are all borne by labor, in the form of either lower wages or higher living costs, and that the taxes encourage mechanization of industry and therefore tend to reduce employment of workers. Another criticism relative to the hindrance of business recovery is that large amounts of money that might be used for the purchase of goods go into the United States Treasury for taxes.

In view of some of the criticisms of the Act, steps were taken to work out improvements. An Advisory Council was appointed in 1937 by a Social Security Subcommittee of the Senate Committee on Finance [23] and the Social Security Board to study the old-age insurance features of the Act. The twenty-five members of the Ad-

[23] Senators Harrison, Byrd, and Vandenberg.

visory Council were selected to represent three groups: employers, employees, and the general public. Their report, submitted December 18, 1938, by the Chairman, Professor J. Douglas Brown of Princeton University, recommended enlarging the scope of the benefits, expanding the system to cover a larger proportion of the population, and improving the financial program.[24]

As to the benefits, the report pointed out that under the existing law there was no provision, except on the basis of the means test, for supplementary protection to wives of annuitants, aged widows, widows with young children, or surviving children of deceased wage earners. Therefore it was recommended that supplementary benefits be provided in such cases. The Council recommended also that seamen and bank employees be included at once, that the Act be extended to include employees of non-profit-making, charitable, religious, and educational institutions, and, by 1940, farm employees and domestics.

The financial recommendations were, in brief: (1) that the federal government contribute eventually a share equal to that of the employers or the employees, that is, each would contribute one-third; (2) that the reserve fund be kept at a much lower figure than provided for in the existing law; (3) that the reserves be put into a special fund with trustees to supervise the investments; (4) that the increase in tax rate go into effect in 1940 as planned, but that those scheduled for later years be held in abeyance until further study could be made. If these changes were made it would be possible to increase the benefits in the earlier years of the program, to redetermine the tax rates, and to readjust the taxes in relation to benefits. The plan of the Council included the maintenance of a small contingent reserve, so that the payments of benefits would not be dependent on quick Congressional action.

The report emphasized the increasing cost of old-age insurance. In 1900 there were 3,080,000 persons 65 years of age and over representing 4.1% of the population. In 1930 there were 6,634,000 persons 65 years of age, representing 5.4% of the population; in 1939, 8,180,000 persons in that age group, representing 6.3% of the population. It is estimated that by 1980 there will be over 22 million, representing 14% to 16% of the population. At the end of July, 1939 there were 45,154,355 registered under the federal old-age program of whom over 5,000,000 were in New York State. Studies of the Advisory Council indicated that 65% of all persons of 65 years of age or over were wholly or partially dependent.

The original act provided for monthly benefits ranging from a minimum of $10 to a maximum of $85. It was estimated that by

[24] 76th Congress, 1st Session, *Sen. Doc.* 4; New York *Times*, Dec. 19, 1938.

1942 the average would be $17, on the same basis. In contrast to this $17 average payment, the Council cited the following payments under the old-age assistance program of Title I. In 1938 federal, state, and local governments contributed $380,000,000 for the needy aged. The average grant in September 1938 was $19.21. The amounts ranged from a minimum of $6.37 in Mississippi to a maximum of $32.39 in California. Approximately 35% of those receiving assistance were paid less than $15 a month; over 50% between $15 and $30, and nearly 15% over $30.

Anticipating the criticism that the Council's program for federal contribution would necessitate additional taxes, Senator Vandenberg, a member of the special Senate Committee, pointed out that under the existing act the federal government eventually would have to pay interest on the full reserve anyway.[25]

The Administration seemed to have been influenced by this report, for it reversed its stand and indicated a willingness to recommend additional federal support from general tax sources. Professor Brown was "borrowed" by the Treasury to make a special study of needed fiscal legislation.[26] In March 1939 the Secretary of the Treasury appeared personally before the Committee on Ways and Means asking for radical changes in the fiscal provisions of the Act. He advocated abandonment of the full reserve principle and stated that in times of "incomplete business recovery like the present" contributory old-age insurance should be financed so as to have the least possible deterring effect on business. The Secretary offered the following three alternatives as substitutes for the payroll tax rates then in effect:

1. Increase tax rate on employers and employees from 1% to 1¼% in 1940; to 1½%, 1941; to 1¾%, 1942; and maintain the existing schedule thereafter.
2. Increase the rate from 1% to 1⅙% in 1940; to 1⅓% in 1941; to 1½% in 1942; then follow the existing schedule.
3. Omit increase from 1% to 1½% for 1940 but step up rates in 1943 and follow the present schedule thereafter.

He recommended also that the reserve be retained at an amount not more than three times the highest prospective annual benefit payments in the ensuing five years; that taxes be named "contributions" so as to improve public understanding of the purpose for which the funds were collected and that there be created a board of trustees composed of the Secretaries of the Treasury and Labor De-

[25] New York *Times*, Dec. 19, 1938.

[26] New York *Times*, Feb. 6, 1939. "For the first time the President has completely assented to a major New Deal law revision which is simultaneously a candid admission of error and a cooperative move for business recovery." (New York *Times*, March 8, 1939.)

partments and the Chairman of the Social Security Board "to make it clear to the public that the fund is for the benefit of those who have contributed to it." [27]

Later in the month Chairman Altmeyer of the Social Security Board also suggested to the Committee on Ways and Means extensive changes in the law so as to broaden the coverage and increase the benefits. By eliminating the lump sum payments savings could be effected to finance partially those changes. Mr. Altmeyer made it clear that eventually a government contribution would be required to carry the additional cost. He pointed out also the need of additional federal aid to states for administration of unemployment compensation provisions because of the rapid growth in the number of states that had established approved unemployment insurance plans.[28]

AMENDMENTS TO THE ACT 1939

Congress was forced to give unusual attention to the needy in the spring and summer of 1939 because of the measures introduced to reorganize and cut appropriations for WPA and to inaugurate the Townsend pension plan. Moreover, important parts of the routine appropriations were for relief.

Soon after the defeat of the Townsend plan, Chairman Doughton published the report of the Committee on Ways and Means on Amendments to the Social Security Act. The report was agreed to by members of both parties, although the minority members added a supplementary statement which was largely devoted to reminding the Democrats that they had at last come around to accepting Republican suggestions of several years past.[29]

June 6, Doughton explained the outstanding amendments although only fifty or sixty members of the House were present. Immediately a group of Southerners commenced attempts to break down the 50-50 plan of federal-state contributions so that those receiving old-age assistance in states with poorer resources could have more aid. The trend of this move was frankly stated by Taylor (Tenn.) when he said:

> In my judgment we will never have a satisfactory old-age pension law until the pension is paid direct from Washington.[30]

The Administration forces were, however, able to defeat all such amendments. The only change in the bill as introduced was made by Jenkins (Ohio), whose proposal to increase the maximum federal

[27] New York *Times*, March 25, 1939; 76th Congress, 1st Session, *Hearings before Committee on Ways and Means on Social Security*, Feb.-April, 1939, III: 2111 ff.
[28] New York *Times*, March 30, 1939.
[29] 76th Congress, 1st Session, *House Report* 728.
[30] *Cong. Rec.* (June 6, 1939).

grants in aid to the blind to equal those to the aged ($20) was accepted by the Committee. The changes made in the existing law by this Committee bill were in the sections dealing with financing, benefits, and coverage of old-age insurance, appropriations for vocational rehabilitation, administration, and finance of unemployment compensation. (See Table 14.)

TABLE 14

ILLUSTRATIVE MONTHLY BENEFITS, OLD-AGE INSURANCE [a]
1935 Law and 1939 Amendments

Basic Monthly Benefits Payable Under 1939 Amendments [b]

Average Monthly Wages	Old-Age			Current monthly benefits to widows with—		
	Single	Married	Widow	1 Child	2 Children	3 Children
$50	$20	$30.00	$15.00	$25.00	$35.00	$40
100	25	37.50	18.75	31.25	43.75	50
150	30	45.00	22.50	37.50	52.50	60
250	40	60.00	30.00	50.00	70.00	80

Monthly Old-Age Retirement Benefits under 1935 Law and 1939 Amendments

Years of Coverage	1935 Law	1939 Amendments		1935 Law	1939 Amendments	
		Single	Married		Single	Married
	(Average monthly wage of $50)			(Average monthly wage of $100)		
3	c	$20.60	$30.90	c	$25.75	$38.63
5	$15.00	21.00	31.50	$17.50	26.25	39.37
10	17.50	22.00	33.00	22.50	27.50	41.25
20	22.50	24.00	36.00	32.50	30.00	45.00
30	27.50	26.00	39.00	42.50	32.50	48.75
40	32.50	28.00	40.00	51.25	35.00	52.50
	(Average monthly wage of $150)			(Average monthly wage of $250)		
3	c	$30.90	$46.35	c	$41.20	$61.80
5	$20.00	31.50	47.25	$25.00	42.00	63.00
10	27.50	33.00	49.50	37.50	44.00	66.00
20	42.50	36.00	54.00	56.25	48.00	72.00
30	53.75	39.00	58.50	68.75	52.00	78.00
40	61.25	42.00	63.00	81.25	56.00	84.00

[a] 76th Congress, 1st Session, *Hearings before the Committee on Ways and Means on Social Security*, p. 2165, corrected by a member of the Social Security Board staff to conform with the law as enacted. It is assumed that an individual earns at least $200 in each year of coverage and $50 in the requisite number of calendar quarters to secure an insured status. If this were not the case, the benefit would be somewhat lower, if not entirely eliminated. This table is not strictly accurate in rounding off fractions of a cent.

[b] These basic benefits are increased by 1% for each year of coverage with a maximum limitation of: (1) twice the primary benefit, or (2) $85, or (3) 80% of the average monthly wage, whichever is the least.

[c] Benefits not paid until after 5 years of coverage.

TABLE 14 (Continued)

Monthly Widows' and Orphans' Benefits under 1939 Amendments

Years of Coverage	Widow with— No Children (A)[d]	Widow with— 1 Child (B)[e]	Widow with— 2 Children (C)[e]	Widow with— No Children (A)	Widow with— 1 Child (B)	Widow with— 2 Children (C)
	(Average monthly wage of husband, $50)			(Average monthly wage of husband, $100)		
3	$15.45	$25.75	$36.05	$19.31	$32.19	$45.06
5	15.75	26.25	36.75	19.69	32.81	45.94
10	16.50	27.50	38.50	20.63	34.38	48.13
15	17.25	28.75	40.00	21.56	35.94	50.31
20	18.00	30.00	40.00	22.50	37.50	52.50
25	18.75	31.25	40.00	23.44	39.06	54.69
	(Average monthly wage of husband, $150)			(Average monthly wage of husband, $250)		
3	$23.18	$38.63	$54.08	$30.90	$51.50	$72.10
5	23.63	39.38	55.13	31.50	52.50	73.50
10	24.75	41.25	57.75	33.00	55.00	77.00
15	25.88	43.13	60.38	34.50	57.50	80.50
20	27.00	45.00	63.00	36.00	60.00	84.00
25	28.13	46.88	65.62	37.50	62.50	85.00

[d] Payable only in the event that the widow is age 65, whether or not such age had been attained at the death of her husband. It is then payable for life, or until remarriage.

[e] Widow with children receives benefit until last child attains age 16 (or 18 if in school). In both cases widow receives benefit shown in column A upon attainment of age 65 or her own old-age benefit, whichever is greater.

The tax on both employers and employees for old-age insurance was "frozen" at 1% for the three years 1940, 1941, and 1942 as against the 1½% rate of existing law. States were ermitted to reduce their contribution for unemployment insurance if certain reserves and minimum benefits were retained. Taxes for unemployment compensation would henceforth be paid only on the first $3000 of an employee's salary, instead of on the total amount. Provision was made for refunds and abatements to employers who paid their unemployment insurance contributions for 1936, 1937, and 1938 too late to receive the 90% credit. It was estimated that these changes would save employers and employees $1,710,000,000 for the years 1940 to 1942.

About 1,400,000 more persons were brought under the old-age insurance system and about 200,000 more under unemployment insurance by extending the benefits of the former to seamen, bank employees, and employed persons of age 65 and over, and by extending the benefit of the latter (unemployment insurance) to bank employees. Some restrictions were made in coverage by excluding certain incidental employments where the tax was a nuisance. Agricultural labor was re-defined to extend the exemptions materially.

Old-age insurance benefits were liberalized by (1) providing monthly survivor benefits to widows, children, and aged dependent parents in lieu of the flat-sum payments to estates of deceased; (2) changing the benefit base from total accumulated wages to average wages so as to provide larger benefits in the early years; and (3) providing additional benefits where the annuitant had an aged wife. The date for beginning payment of benefits was advanced from January 1, 1942 to January 1, 1940.

Radical changes were made in the financial framework of the old-age insurance system. The old-age reserve account was changed to a federal old-age and survivor trust fund with the Secretary of the Treasury, Secretary of Labor, and the Chairman of the Social Security Board acting as a board of trustees. No large reserve fund will be built up. Funds not needed for current claims or administrative purposes will be invested as provided in the original law for unemployment insurance funds. That is, they will be invested so as to earn "the current average rate of interest borne by all outstanding interest-bearing obligations composing the public debt," instead of the 3 per-cent rate required previously.

A provision was adopted by which statewide contributions to unemployment compensation funds would be reduced if state funds reached a certain amount.

The Committee report pointed out that future development of the system depended on many contingencies such as changes in average wages, death rate, birth rate, and shifts between insured and uninsured groups. If future payroll tax collections were inadequate to meet payment of benefits it would be necessary to increase the tax rate or provide for the deficiency out of other taxes, or both.

Additional appropriations were made to the states for vocational rehabilitation. Federal grants for the states' assistance to the aged were increased so that the total allowance on a 50-50 matching basis could be $40 a month instead of $30. Aid to dependent children was, also, placed on a 50-50 matching basis, whereas formerly, the federal government had paid only a third of the cost.

CONSIDERATION OF AMENDMENTS IN THE SENATE

The Senate Finance Committee members quickly approved the House amendments to "freeze" old-age insurance taxes at existing levels for the next three years and adopted the whole insurance benefit program. They rejected the House extension of definition of employee to cover salesmen working on commission and the proposal for permitting statewide reduction of contributions for unemployment compensation if state funds reached a specific amount. The House amendments were accepted to tighten the personnel requirements of state agencies receiving and administering federal funds for old-age assistance and services to the blind, and dependent children.

Pressure for increased federal aid for old-age assistance was continued after the passage of the House amendments and was powerful enough to affect Senate action when the bill was brought up on July 13. Aided by a coalition of Southern members and certain New Deal followers, Connally won support for a revision so that henceforth the federal government would contribute twice as much as the states on pensions for the needy aged up to $15 a month, and one-half the cost of pensions over that amount to an additional $10. More radical measures were proposed and rejected, such as that of Lee (Dem., Okla.) for a pension of $40 a month to everyone over 60, and that of Bilbo (Miss.) for a pension of $30 to everyone eligible under the existing law. The Senate also materially liberalized the qualifying requirements for old-age insurance benefits so that more old persons could qualify in the early years ; and also, to this end, made taxes for those over 65 retroactive to January 1, 1939.

These extensions of federal aid were opposed by Vandenberg (Rep., Mich.) and Byrd (Dem., Va.), who warned of the tremendous expense of the program. The latter estimated that about $750,000,000 had already been added to social security costs by other Senate amendments, and estimated that this extension would cost $200,000,000 a year eventually. The estimates of Chairman Altmeyer of the Social Security Board were from $63,000,000 to more than $100,000,000, according to Senator Connally.

Almost before this amendment could be printed, however, Johnson (Colo.) rushed through a qualifying amendment compelling every state to pay from its own funds $10 to each recipient of old-age assistance in order to qualify for federal aid. Barkley, Harrison, and George led a futile protest to this provision, which meant that some states would pay three times as much as they were then paying and would require all but 17 states to increase their payments. Johnson's amendment was deleted by the Conferees.

Wagner (Dem., N. Y.) won support for amendments to create (1) an advisory council on unemployment insurance for the study of various phases of the problem and (2) an advisory council on disability insurance. The bill passed by a vote of 57 to 8 on July 13, and was sent to the House for consideration of changes.

REPORT OF THE CONFERENCE COMMITTEE

The Conference Committee became deadlocked until the day before Congress adjourned, chiefly because of the (Senate) Connally amendment for old-age assistance and the (House) McCormack amendment for reducing contributions for unemployment compensation if state funds reached a specified amount. Both these amendments were rejected, and the Committee stated that further study should be given to such proposals. The Committee modified slightly the power given the Social Security Board to require personnel standards on a merit basis by state administrations co-operating with the federal government under the Social Security Act.

The following House provisions for employers' and employees' excises on taxes for old-age insurance were adopted:

(1) 1 per cent with respect to payroll of employer and wage of employee for calendar years 1939 to 1942.
(2) 2 per cent, for calendar years 1943 to 1945.
(3) 2½ per cent, for 1946 to 1948.
(4) 3 per cent after December 31, 1948.

The provisions for payment of benefits were those of the House bill, examples of which are shown in Table 14.

The measure was signed by the President, August 10, 1939.[31]

[31] 53 *Statutes at Large* 1360.

CHAPTER XVII

REVENUE ACT OF 1936 – UNDISTRIBUTED-PROFITS TAX

THE REQUEST OF THE PRESIDENT

When President Roosevelt delivered his annual message to Congress, January 3, 1936, he said that except for the item of relief the budget was "in balance" and therefore no new taxes were requested at that time. Three days later the Supreme Court declared the Agricultural Adjustment Act unconstitutional.[1]

This decision affected the budget in an amount of over $1,000,000,000; it eliminated an important source of revenue, the processing taxes, estimated to yield over $500,000,000, and it necessitated a change in the farm relief program that would cost a little less than $500,000,000. Within a month Congress passed over the President's veto the bill for the payment of the soldiers' bonus in 1936 instead of in 1945, which added an annual charge of $120,000,000 for nine years, in addition to the $160,000,000 already in the budget.

On March 3 the President addressed a special message to Congress in which he called attention to the unexpected change in the fiscal situation, and asked (1) for the next nine years additional revenue of $620,000,000 annually, and (2) within the next two or three years a sum of $517,000,000. Although he stated explicitly that he wished to leave to "the discretion of Congress the formulation of the appropriate taxes for the needed permanent revenue," he suggested consideration of a tax on undistributed corporate income, accompanied by a repeal of the 1935 corporate income tax, the capital-stock tax, and the excess-profits tax. For the temporary revenue he suggested (1) a tax on the "windfall" enjoyed by processors who had shifted to others the taxes collected under the Agricultural Adjustment Act, and (2) a temporary excise tax at low rate on the processing of a large number of agricultural products.

By means of the new form of corporation tax, which would be graduated according to the amount of earnings withheld from distribution, the President expected to accomplish an important tax reform, the removal of two inequalities in the tax system and the prevention of "leaks" in surtaxes.[2] These reforms should accomplish

[1] *U. S.* v. *Hoosac Mills*, 297 U. S. 1.

[2] The President quoted Treasury estimates that over 4½ billion dollars of corporate income would be withheld from stockholders in 1936, thus depriving the Treasury of individual surtaxes amounting to over $1,300,000,000. (*Cong. Rec.* 80: 3119.) The Commissioner's statement shows, however, that the repeal of corporation income, capital stock, and excess-profits taxes was a prerequisite to the accumulation of the 4½

a fairer distribution of the tax load on business profits, (1) whether derived from unincorporated enterprises or incorporated businesses and (2) whether distributed to real owners or withheld from them. On the subject of surtax evasion he said:

> The accumulation of surplus in corporations controlled by taxpayers with large incomes is encouraged by the present freedom of undistributed corporate income from surtaxes. Since stockholders are the beneficial owners of both distributed and undistributed corporate income, the aim . . . should be to seek equality of tax burden on all corporate income whether distributed or withheld from the beneficial owners.

He advocated a rate that would yield approximately the same revenue as would be yielded if corporate profits were distributed and taxed in the hands of stockholders. Such a revision, he said, would simplify tax procedure and corporate accounting and improve understanding of the whole subject by the citizens of the nation.

To ask Congress to levy additional taxes in an election year seemed, on first thought, to be an unpopular and a courageous thing to do. But the cleverness of the President's suggestion was soon apparent. The reform aspect of the suggestion, making the tax more equitable, would certainly be acceptable to all, except perhaps to those whose tax burdens would be increased. The burden of the tax would fall on corporations that wished to retain large proportions of their surpluses rather than to pay dividends, and on individual taxpayers who would receive the dividends, presumably those whose incomes would fall in the higher brackets. There would probably be little extension of the number of taxpayers. As currently reported, the Administration favored levying a simple tax of 33⅓% on undistributed corporate incomes, subjecting dividends to the normal tax and repealing the 1935 corporation income, capital-stock, and excess-profits taxes.

It was not long, however, before criticism of such radical ideas began to appear in the press. One correspondent compared the much-talked-of "simplicity" to that which would "improve the shoe business by making everybody wear size 8½B." [3] Business again looked askance at New Deal proposals which seemed contrived to dictate management and policy.[4]

It was stated that the Treasury wanted the President to advocate this radical change in the tax system in 1935 along with his other

---

billion dollar surplus. (74th Congress, 2d Session, *Hearings before the Committee on Ways and Means*, pp. 25-37.)

[3] Quoted in the Washington *Post*, June 2, 1936.

[4] *Commercial and Financial Chronicle*, March 14, 1936. The Chamber of Commerce of the United States summoned its Committee on Federal Taxes and Expenditures to meet. "The Chamber's Weekly Washington Review termed the President's proposal 'the use of a revenue measure to impose reform of important financial practices of business management.'" (New York *Times*, March 8, 1936.)

"left" proposals, but some of his close advisors counseled him against it. In 1936 persuasions from the Treasury were effective. Evidence seems to indicate that the President accepted the idea without thinking through all of its implications and without consulting some important members of the government who were in a position to give him advice.[5]

TAX AVOIDANCE BY INCORPORATION

Much publicity was given to this "new" proposal. Accusations were frequent that it was invented by such "leftist" advisors as Mr. Herman Oliphant, General Counsel of the Treasury, and Mr. Rexford Tugwell of the AAA, and adopted by the Administration as a scheme to "soak" corporations and their "economic royalist" directorates. A review of past legislation shows, however, that it was not a new idea but had been proposed at one session after another since 1917 by those who could not be characterized as "radicals."

Doubtless there has always been some tax avoidance on the part of individuals with large incomes by allowing earnings to accumulate in surpluses of corporations they control. The problem was recognized when the first income tax law was drafted, and it has become increasingly important and complicated in direct proportion to the height of surtax rates.[6] The difficulty arose largely because of the discrepancy in treatment of the income of individuals as compared with that of corporations. If there were no personal exemptions so that everyone paid a tax, if there were no surtax, or if all corporation income were distributed as earned, it would be a simple matter to reach practically all taxable income in the course of time by levying a tax on individuals only. Corporation income could thus be taxed as received by individuals in the form of dividends or interest.[7]

The corporation tax rate and the normal tax rate for individuals have been the same in only two federal income tax laws: 1% in the Act of 1913 and 2% in the Act of 1916. When the corporation rates were made 4% and the maximum surtax rates were increased from 13% to 65% by the 1917 law, it was hoped to equalize the tax burden approximately as between individuals and corporations by imposing

[5] Arthur Krock in the New York *Times*, May 17, 1936; Moley, Raymond, "Heaven or Bust," *Saturday Evening Post*, Aug. 19, 1939.

[6] Much of the historical material on this subject is summarized in 74th Congress, 2d Session, *Hearings before the Committee on Ways and Means on the Revenue Act of 1936*.

[7] This was the original plan of Senator Cummins who proposed an income tax in 1909, but he was forced to abandon it because of criticism of his colleagues that large flourishing corporations would be relieved of all taxes. It was also discussed by one of the present authors before the American Economic Association in 1927. (*American Economic Review* 18: Sup. 102-119, March 1928.)

on business an excess-profits tax and by subjecting stock dividends to tax in the hands of individual recipients. But the excess-profits tax soon proved impracticable of administration under the conditions then existing and the tax on stock dividends was declared unconstitutional by the Supreme Court.

Every income tax law since the ratification of the Sixteenth Amendment has contained some section designed to prevent the evasion of the surtax by the use of the corporate form of business. In fact, each Civil War Act from 1864 to 1870 contained a provision that in estimating taxable income there should be included "profits, whether divided or not, of all companies and partnerships. . ." In drafting the 1913 law this phraseology was followed very closely in the House bill, but it was amended in the Senate because of constitutional objections.[8] As finally adopted, the law subjected to the surtax all income to which a taxpayer was entitled, whether divided or not, of all corporations "formed or fraudulently availed of for the purpose of preventing the imposition of such tax through the medium of permitting . . . gains and profits to accumulate." This section was carried over into the laws of 1916, 1917, and 1918, with minor changes. Later laws imposed an additional tax on corporations that were used by stockholders to avoid the surtax, but, like the earlier sections, they seemed to be ineffective.[9]

There were several reasons for the failure to enforce this section. Not only was it difficult if not impossible to prove that a corporation was "formed or availed of for the purpose of preventing the imposition of such tax," but, according to the laws prior to 1924, corporations were not required to include as taxable income dividends received from other corporations that paid the normal tax or income from government securities.[10] By the very nature of the case the income of companies formed to evade the tax was often largely from dividends, so this almost automatically made the law a dead letter.[11]

[8] The validity of this Civil War provision was upheld in 1870 (*Collector* v. *Hubbard*, 12 Wall. 1), but the Court did not follow this precedent in later cases. In 1890 the Court held that "Money earned by a corporation remains the property of the corporation, and does not become the property of the stockholders unless and until it is distributed among them by the corporation." (*Gibbons* v. *Mahon*, 136 U. S. 549.) The Civil War precedent was also overruled in *Pollock* v. *Farmers' Loan and Trust Co.*, (157 U. S. 429; 158 U. S. 601, 1895). The culminating decision was *Eisner* v. *Macomber* (252 U. S. 189, 1920) in which the Court emphasized the necessity of "separation" and "realization" of corporate gains and profits in the hands of stockholders before they could be considered taxable individual income.

[9] These penalty sections are summarized in the Appendix, Exhibit 8. See also Chapter VI above, footnotes 56 and 61.

[10] Corporations generally were not required to include in gross income dividends from stock of other companies until 1935, but the 1924 and succeeding laws required the inclusion of such income for the purpose of this additional tax imposed as a penalty for accumulating unreasonable surpluses.

[11] Letter of Secretary of the Treasury Mellon to Senator McKellar (Dem., Tenn.). *Cong. Rec.* 65: 7355.

A suggestion that the problem be met by imposing a tax on the undistributed earnings of all corporations was first advocated in 1917 by Senator Andrieus Jones (Dem., N. M.). This idea became a hobby with him, so he said. Certainly he persisted before the Finance Committee and the Senate for the next seven years. In 1917 he won some little encouragement from the Finance Committee, but only temporarily, and when the law was finally enacted the only relic of his idea was a penalty tax of 15% on corporations that retained surplus not "actually invested and employed in the business. . ." In 1924 he won Senate approval of his amendment, but it was rejected by the Conferees.[12]

In 1919 T. S. Adams, then a special adviser to the Treasury, advocated much the same proposal, but for a different purpose, namely, as a substitute for the excess-profits tax that was proving to be so difficult to administer. Doubtless on this advice, Secretary of the Treasury Houston in 1920 devoted considerable space in his annual report to the inequities of the income tax as between individuals and corporations and offered as a remedy the substitution for the excess-profits tax of a flat rate "on profits in excess of the distributed earnings." [13] In 1928 the Joint Committee on Internal Revenue Taxation proposed a similar tax, but Congress was not convinced that it would be desirable. Members were afraid to make such a radical change — it was feared that penalties might be inflicted on small businesses, that many corporations would be relieved of all taxes if they distributed their earnings, and that the revenue yield would be less than under the usual tax on net income.

In succeeding Revenue Acts Congress merely re-enacted the penalty sections, although in 1934 an additional tax was imposed on the undistributed income of personal holding companies.

Testimony before the Committee on Ways and Means in 1936 indicated that there is no very satisfactory way of judging the efficacy of these penalty sections. The indirect effect may have been greater than is realized.[14] Nevertheless, it is evident that prior to 1934, at least, they were generally ineffective. Several extenuating reasons have been offered for non-enforcement of this part of the law. First of all, the wording was vague. This defect was due to the fact that the law had to be flexible enough to cover a great variety of situations, hence it was necessary to use general terms. Consequently much discretion was left to the administrator. For example, the Commissioner must decide what were the legitimate needs of the business;

[12] See above, pp. 141, 216, 242-246.

[13] *Report of the Secretary of the Treasury* 1920, p. 32. See also Houston's letter to Fordney, New York *Times*, March 18, 1920.

[14] 74th Congress, 2d Session, *Hearings before the Senate Committee on Finance*, p. 263.

he must prove that the corporation was used for the purpose of evading the surtax and, after 1921, had to decide when a corporation was "a mere holding or investment company." The Bureau did not automatically receive the information to determine whether or not the section was applicable, inasmuch as the income tax returns did not show the nature of the corporation's investments. Aside from the wording of the law and other extenuating facts, it was generally believed that the Secretary of the Treasury was not interested in enforcing this section.[15] Many comments to this effect were made in Congress. Further evidence is offered by the Report of the Joint Committee on Internal Revenue Taxation in 1927, in which it was stated that there was an entire lack of published rulings and decisions relating to the interpretation of this Section 220 and, up to October 1927, only five cases involving it had been filed with the Board of Tax Appeals.[16] In February 1930 the *Internal Revenue News* reported that 3 cases were pending in the courts, 38 in the Board of Tax Appeals, 38 in the Attorney General's Office, and 65 in the Income Tax Unit. The General Counsel's office had disposed of 385 cases.[17]

The subcommittee on tax evasion reported to the Committee on Ways and Means in January 1938 that these penalty provisions had proved very troublesome to enforce. "The barrier of effective enforcement has been found to be chiefly in the difficulty of proving the intent to avoid surtaxes." The surtax on personal holding companies had worked fairly well, according to the subcommittee, but the corporations subject to this title (IA) form a very limited class. It was thought that operating companies "with closely held stock ownership and net incomes of substantial size were commonly used to avoid individual surtaxes." [18]

15 Judge Green to the authors, Jan. 1, 1937; *Cong. Rec.* 65: 7353-7361.

16 *Report of the Joint Committee on Internal Revenue Taxation,* I: 48-56.

17 Reprinted in *National Income Tax Magazine* 8: 104 (March 1930).

18 75th Congress, 3d Session, *Hearings before the Committee on Ways and Means on Revenue Revision,* pp. 27-30.

THE COMMITTEE ON WAYS AND MEANS PREPARES A BILL

Late in March 1936 the Committee on Ways and Means [19] opened public hearings to get views on a bill of which only the framework was drafted. The subcommittee, of which Hill was chairman, had sketched in outline a bill for: taxes on incomes of corporations, graduated according to the ratio of undistributed net income to adjusted net income; the eventual repeal of corporate income, excess-profits and capital stock taxes; a tax of 80% on "unjust enrichment" resulting from the shifting of the federal excise taxes on processing; and a tax on those who held, on January 1, 1936, floor stocks of articles subject to the processing tax — substantially the President's requested program.

Uneasy suspicions that reform rather than revenue was the essential reason for the measure were not allayed by the testimony of the first witness who represented the Treasury Department, Mr. Helvering, Commissioner of Internal Revenue. He explained that the primary reasons for change in method of taxing corporate income were:

> First, to eliminate the present inequalities in our taxation of business profits as between incorporated and unincorporated business; second, to remove a very important source of tax avoidance that inheres in our present income tax laws; and third . . . to increase the Federal revenues . . .

He explained that the existing income tax laws discriminated against the individual taxpayer and in favor of the corporation in several respects. Corporations could distribute dividends when they chose, pay them out when other income of the stockholders was small and thus prevent application of high surtax rates. Individual businessmen and partnerships did not have this privilege. Furthermore, a corporation which had re-invested its earnings and subsequently

[19] The members of the Committee on Ways and Means were:

Democrats	*Republicans*
Robt. L. Doughton (N. C.), Ch.	Allen T. Treadway (Mass.)
Samuel B. Hill (Wash.)	Isaac Bacharach (N. J.)
Thomas H. Cullen (N. Y.)	Frank Crowther (N. Y.)
Christopher D. Sullivan (N. Y.)	Harold Knutson (Minn.)
Morgan G. Sanders (Tex.)	Daniel Reed (N. Y.)
John W. McCormack (Mass.)	Roy O. Woodruff (Mich.)
David J. Lewis (Md.)	Thomas A. Jenkins (Ohio)
Fred M. Vinson (Ky.)	
Jere Cooper (Tenn.)	
John W. Boehne, Jr. (Ind.)	
Claude A. Fuller (Ark.)	
Wesley E. Disney (Okla.)	
Arthur P. Lamneck (Ohio)	
Frank H. Buck (Cal.)	
Richard M. Duncan (Mo.)	
Chester Thompson (Ill.)	
J. T. Brooks (Pa.)	
John D. Dingell (Mich.)	

CHART 4

ESTIMATED POTENTIALITIES OF UNDISTRIBUTED-PROFITS TAX *

Additions to Taxable Incomes of Individuals, Assuming All 1936 Estimated Corporate Earnings Were Distributed

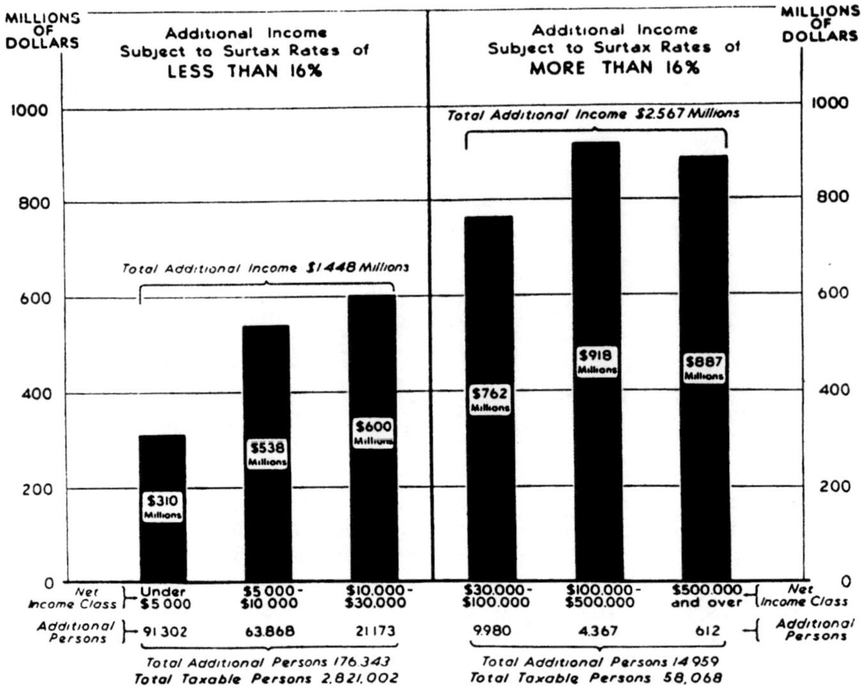

* 74th Congress, 2d Session, *Hearings before the Committee on Finance on H. R. 12395 (Revenue Act of 1936)*, p. 27.

suffered a loss would not pay income tax for the poor years, but an individual would have paid a tax already on income received in good years.

The difference in the application of the tax laws to corporations and to individuals also permitted considerable tax avoidance. Corporations could retain much of their earnings as surplus which, if distributed to shareholders, would be subject to individual income taxes. On the other hand, all the earnings of an individual or partnership in excess of personal exemptions were taxable, whether they were re-invested in the business or not.

In answer to the increasing criticism voiced in the press, the Commissioner stated that there had been a great deal of misapprehension in regard to the effect of the proposals upon the accumulation of corporate reserves; first, because the tax would not apply to existing surpluses; second, because there would be no change in the laws

TABLE 15

RATIO OF CASH DIVIDENDS PAID TO NET INCOME, TO NET INCOME INCLUDING DIVIDENDS RECEIVED, AND TO ADJUSTED NET INCOME, CORPORATIONS, 1923-1935 [a]

[Amounts in millions of dollars]

Year	*Net income* [b]	*Net income including 100% of dividends received*	*Adjusted net income*	*Cash dividends paid*	*Ratio of cash dividends paid to —*		
					Net income	*Net income including 100% of dividends received*	*Adjusted net income*
1923	$8,322	$8,992	$8,055	$3821	45.9	42.5	47.4
1924	7,587	8,291	7,409	3995	52.7	48.2	53.9
1925	9,584	10,568	9,398	4817	50.3	45.6	51.3
1926	9,673	10,917	9,687	5530	57.2	50.7	57.1
1927	8,982	10,286	9,155	5785	64.4	56.2	63.2
1928	10,618	12,213	11,029	6585	62.0	53.9	59.7
1929	11,654	13,843	12,649	7842	67.3	56.6	62.0
1930	6,429	8,193	7,481	6841	106.4	83.5	91.4
1931	3,683	4,536	4,137	3872	105.1	85.4	93.6
1932	2,153	2,590	2,305	2320	107.8	89.6	100.7
1933	2,986	3,426	3,010	2386	79.9	69.6	79.3
1934	4,275	5,216	4,628	3853	90.1	73.9	83.3
1935	5,165	6,657	5,947	4651	90.0	69.9	78.2

[a] 75th Congress, 3d Session. *Hearings before the Committee on Ways and Means on Revenue Revision* 1938, p. 126.

[b] Statutory net income as tabulated in the Statistics of Income for these years.

governing the deduction from net income of operating reserves such as for depreciation ; and third, because, under the committee's proposals, many corporations could retain a fairly substantial surplus without increasing their taxes over those of 1935. For example, a corporation with income of less than $10,000 could put back into surplus 30% of its adjusted net income and be subject to a tax of only 7½% of its net income. Larger corporations, that is, those with incomes of over $10,000, could retain 30% and be subject to a tax rate of 15%. Within three years, the Commissioner stated, such accumulation would amount to almost 100%, hence he considered that adequate provision was made for a cushion. "It is not a feather bed, but it is a cushion, and I think a very reasonable one." [20] In spite of the Commissioner's insistence that there was "no intention to interfere with the internal management of business enterprises," he had to admit to critics on the minority side that the new law would undoubtedly tend to exert pressure upon them.

Mr. McLeod, statistician of the Treasury Department, explained the data upon which the Administration based its computation of yield under the proposed plan of taxing undistributed corporate income. Placing the statutory corporate net income for 1936 at $7,200,000,000, and deducting therefrom capital stock and excess-profits taxes, and payments of cash dividends, the Treasury estimated that over $4,700,000,000 of dividends would be withheld as a result of which the Government would fail to collect $620,000,000 that might be collected from individuals if all earnings were distributed.

It became increasingly evident, as the hearings progressed, that the Administration proposals were the result of the research carried on by the staff of the Commissioner of Internal Revenue and other divisions of the Treasury. Mr. Oliphant, General Counsel for the Treasury, explained the historical development of the government's efforts to prevent tax evasion and avoidance by taxpayers through the use of the corporate form of organization. Commissioner Helvering also pointed out that Congress had made many efforts of this kind, but the administration of these sections had proved very difficult, and it was generally agreed they were ineffective.

The minority members of the Committee were skeptical of the motives of the Administration, of the need for additional revenue, and of the effect upon business of such radical proposals. At the hearings these members took every opportunity to be facetious, to disparage the practical wisdom of the Treasury spokesmen, especially of those who bore the title of "professor," and they tried to associate the origin of the idea with the so-called visionary members of the Administration, especially Mr. Tugwell. His book, *Industrial Discipline*, was quoted to show that he favored a re-allocation of capital which could be accomplished by forcing corporate surplus into the open market by means of the taxing power.[21]

The serious criticisms which were heaped upon this proposed drastic change in corporate taxation by representatives of business made more than the usual impression upon the Committee because of the realization that big business was not complaining. Apparently companies with well-established reserves stood to gain. Several witnesses expressed the fear that the extreme reduction of reserves likely

[20] 74th Congress, 2d Session, *Hearings before the Committee on Ways and Means on Revenue Act of* 1936, p. 38.
[21] *Hearings*, p. 42.

to result from the proposed measure would accentuate booms and depressions and would make employment more precarious, the very reverse of what the government was endeavoring to accomplish through the Social Security Act. Others pointed out that it would intensify the fluctuations in stock and bond prices and thus affect the collateral behind loans. The Administration seemed unable to meet satisfactorily the objection that small corporations would be seriously handicapped in building up sufficient reserves to expand and meet the competition of large corporations. Thus companies with large reserves already accumulated would be favored and monopolies would be fostered. The effect of such a proposal on companies carrying large bank loans was also considered serious, for such corporations could pay their debts only out of earnings and would have only small sums for dividend payments. In fact, the criticisms indicated that the proposals would have the tendency to discourage small companies, encourage monopolies, "freeze" business at its present status, and create an atmosphere of uneasiness among business men generally — quite opposite results from those which the President desired to achieve.

Nevertheless, in the face of these serious attacks upon the Administration's basic ideas, the Committee drew up a bill to carry them into effect.

THE MEASURE BEFORE THE HOUSE OF REPRESENTATIVES

The bill drawn up by the Committee on Ways and Means was accepted by the House of Representatives with little debate and passed with only three amendments which were introduced by the Committee.

When Chairman Doughton introduced the measure on April 23, he admitted that taxes were never popular, but for this bill no apologies were in order. It had at least four merits: (1) it would remove great existing inequalities in the taxation of incorporated and unincorporated businesses; (2) it would permit a nearer approach to taxation on the basis of ability to pay; (3) it would increase Federal revenues mainly by removing important sources of tax avoidance rather than by increasing tax rates or imposing new taxes; and (4) it appeared, in general, to be greatly superior to any alternative proposal.[22] The chairman was followed by Hill, Vinson, and other Democratic members of the subcommittee on tax revision, who explained the details of the bill which was written in such strange, new, complicated terms that all members were confused.

Treadway and Crowther led the discussion of minority objections,

[22] *Cong. Rec.* 80: 5978-5989.

based on the arguments that had developed at the hearings, namely that the measure was socialistic, unsound, and unworkable. "The President," said Treadway, "made you enact his pet graduated income tax on corporations last year and now he has left you 'holding the bag' by abandoning the scheme even before it went into operation. How do you know he will not abandon this unsound scheme before adjournment and suggest some other experiment?" [23]

Taber (Rep., N. Y.) spoke at length on the possibilities of avoiding new taxes by reducing appropriations. He cited examples of the "fake soil conservation bill" of $440,000,000 and of unnecessary reclamation projects of $62,000,000. The Department of Agriculture could save at least $10,000,000, he thought, by "cutting down on some of these tremendous increases for many projects which do not have any merit at all" and the items for river and harbor improvements in the War Department appropriations could be reduced from $150,000,000 to $90,000,000.[24]

Reed (N. Y.) attacked the bill because he considered the tax on undistributed earnings a plan of industrial control, and a

> hasty, superficial, undigested substitute for the present corporation method of taxation, which, with all of its defects, is nevertheless something to which the business of this country has become adjusted and which is providing steadily increasing revenue.[25]

The vote on April 29 was 267 to 93; it was on party lines except that eleven Democrats voted against the bill and four Republicans for it.[26]

THE HOUSE BILL

The salient feature of the bill as passed by the House was the tax on corporate earnings, graduated according to the proportion of corporate income withheld from distribution. Two new refinements of the meaning of net income were introduced. One, "adjusted net income," was defined to mean net income, plus inter-corporate dividends received (hitherto permitted as a deduction), minus interest on Liberty Bonds and obligations of government corporations.[27] The second, "undistributed net income," was defined to mean "adjusted net income," minus the sum of (1) taxable dividends paid during the taxable year, and (2) the tax computed under the new schedule.

[23] *Cong. Rec.* 80: 5989-5993.
[24] *Cong. Rec.* 80: 6182.
[25] *Cong. Rec.* 80: 6317.
[26] *Cong. Rec.* 80: 6367.
[27] The Act of 1934 used the term "adjusted net income" in connection with the surtax on corporations improperly accumulating surplus to mean "net income computed without the allowance of the dividend deduction otherwise allowable, but diminished by the amount of dividends paid during the taxable year." The term was also used in connection with the surtax on personal holding companies with somewhat different meaning.

For corporations with adjusted net income of $10,000 or less, the rates were graduated from a minimum of 1% of the adjusted net income, if the undistributed net income was not over 10% of adjusted net income, rising to a maximum of 29.5% of the adjusted net income if the undistributed net income was 70% or more of the adjusted net income. For corporations with adjusted net income of more than $10,000 the rates were graduated from a minimum of 4% of adjusted net income, if the undistributed net income was not more than 10% of adjusted net income, rising to a maximum of 42.5% if the undistributed net income was 57.5% or more of adjusted net income. In any case there would be no tax on corporate income of the year if it was all distributed during the year.

Special treatment was accorded certain corporations. Banks, domestic insurance companies, and corporations in receivership were subject to a flat tax of 15%. A special rate of 22½% was provided for foreign corporations, for corporations which, prior to the passage of the law, had made contracts not to pay dividends, and for corporations which lacked sufficient accumulated earnings to distribute dividends because of nondeductible losses or deficits from prior years. In case the accumulated earnings and profits of the corporation were less than the adjusted net income, the tax was to be a combination of: (1) 15% of "the excess of the adjusted net income over such accumulated earnings and profits," and (2) a tax on the remainder of the adjusted net income . . . computed "under the usual method as if the adjusted net income were equal to the amount of such remainder so reduced."

The capital stock tax was reduced from $1.40 to 70 cents per $1000 for the year ending June 30, 1936, and repealed as of June 30, 1936. The excess-profits tax was repealed, effective June 30, 1937. The normal corporation tax was repealed as of December 31, 1935.

Individual income tax rates were left as in the 1935 law, but corporate dividends received by individuals were made subject to the normal tax of 4%.

A "windfall" tax of 80% was imposed on the income representing the "unjust enrichment" resulting from refunds and shifting of processing taxes,[28] but the law did not include the substitute processing tax that the President suggested.

The estimated revenue yield of the tax on corporations was somewhat less than that requested by the President, and it developed at the hearings that not all of it would be immediately available because some of the additional amount would come through the surtax

[28] This tax would apply to two classes of persons: (1) those who were supposedly liable for the tax and shifted its burden to others, but who did not pay the tax or who paid it and obtained a refund, and (2) dealers who included the tax in price of goods sold but were subsequently reimbursed by their vendors for the amount of the tax.

paid by individuals on dividends from corporations and not directly from the corporations.

THE SENATE FINANCE COMMITTEE DRAFTS A NEW MEASURE

Even before the measure reached the House it was evident that the more conservative Senate Finance Committee [29] would not accept the so-called "radical and complicated" Administration measure as unquestioningly as had the Committee on Ways and Means.

The hearings before the Finance Committee brought out the extreme hostility of business to the House measure. Approximately one hundred witnesses appeared before the Committee, practically all of whom opposed the measure, except those representing the Administration. The Secretary of the Treasury, who had been resting at a southern resort at the time of the hearings before the Ways and Means Committee, appeared perfunctorily before the Senate Finance Committee with a short plea for the bill, based chiefly on the equity of the proposals. Unfortunately he overstated the estimate of corporation earnings which would be transferred to surplus in 1936. Much was made of this error by a later witness and the Secretary finally wrote to Chairman Harrison that his statement might be misunderstood, but it did not affect the estimate of the total amount of tax from such source.

TESTIMONY OF TREASURY SPOKESMEN

The Administration's defense of the change in tax methods was drawn up at a conference in the Treasury and presented by Herman Oliphant, General Counsel, and George C. Haas, Director of Research and Statistics.

Mr. Haas answered the four main arguments against the new tax. The first objection he considered was that big corporations with

[29] Members of the Senate Finance Committee were:

Democrats	*Republicans*
Pat Harrison (Miss.), Ch.	James Couzens (Mich.)
Wm. H. King (Utah)	Henry Keyes (N. H.)
Walter F. George (Ga.)	Robert M. La Follette, Jr. (Wis.)
David I. Walsh (Mass.)	Jesse H. Metcalf (Del.)
Alben W. Barkley (Ky.)	Arthur Capper (Kan.)
Tom Connally (Tex.)	
Thomas P. Gore (Okla.)	
Edward P. Costigan (Colo.)	
Josiah W. Bailey (N. C.)	
Bennett C. Clark (Mo.)	
Harry F. Byrd (Va.)	
Augustine Lonergan (Conn.)	
Hugo L. Black (Ala.)	
Joseph F. Guffey (Pa.)	
Peter G. Gerry (R. I.)	

ample surplus reserves would not face much competition if such a plan were in force because small corporations would "be prevented from growing into big ones." The Treasury representatives thought this result would not occur because (1) much lower tax rates were provided for corporations with incomes of $10,000 or under, and (2) capital funds could be obtained from the sale of shares to investors generally as well as to their own stockholders. In fact, he thought that small corporations would have a substantial advantage over large ones in this matter of securing new capital for the reasons that the compactness of the organization would result in more direct and informal action and a greater proportion of the earnings of small corporations than of large ones would be available for re-investment.

The second objection considered was that all corporations would "be prevented from securing sufficient capital for expansion and other legitimate purposes." The reply was much the same as to the first objection.

The third objection was that individuals with large incomes would be encouraged to invest in tax-exempt securities. The main part of the reply was that (1) "the aggregate amount of tax-exempt income available constitutes only a small fraction of the total amount of corporate income and (2) the larger part of it already goes to individuals subject to the higher surtax rates who, therefore, would possess little motive for selling their tax-exempt securities to others."

In answer to the fourth objection, namely, that the bill failed to make adequate provision for corporate reserves needed for "the maintenance of solvency and of employment during depressions," Mr. Haas showed that the House bill allowed the usual reserves for depreciation, depletion, and bad debts, and permitted the accumulation of reserves upon the payment of less tax than the 1935 normal income tax. He maintained, moreover, that during the depression corporate surpluses were not used to keep up payrolls,[30] but in many cases they served to stimulate overextension of plants and speculation in the stock market in the boom that led to the depression, hence they may have assisted materially in causing the depression.

The theme of his testimony may be summarized in the concluding paragraph of his formal statement :

30 A Treasury study of income tax returns for 1931-1933 showed that all corporations reported net income of $14,147,000,000 for the years in question before making valuation deductions of over $20,000,000,000 for depreciation, depletion, bad debts, and loss from sale of capital assets which left a net deficit of over $6,000,000,000. Cash dividends for those years were a little over $13,000,000,000. From these data Mr. Haas concluded that "dividends, wages, and other payments came out of current receipts, primarily, and not from accumulated 'liquid surpluses.' The book surpluses . . . were indeed reduced, but they were reduced, in the aggregate, not by actual cash disbursements, but by the writing down of assets on the books of the corporation."

I should like to state my conviction that the economic arguments advanced in opposition to the proposed change in corporation taxation rest very largely upon misapprehension and misinterpretation of the facts . . . In my opinion, the proposed change in our system of corporate taxation is one that, in addition to its productivity from a revenue standpoint, would improve the character of our economic organization as a whole.[31]

TESTIMONY OF REPRESENTATIVES OF BUSINESS

The testimony of Mr. E. C. Alvord may be taken as typical of the evidence presented by business men [32] to the Committee. Mr. Alvord, formerly special assistant to the Secretary of the Treasury, appeared as a representative of the Committee on Federal Finance of the Chamber of Commerce of the United States. He recommended that the bill "be scrapped in its entirety" and that "no revenue legislation be undertaken until a sound fiscal program embodying control over expenditure as well as raising revenues has been prepared. . ."

From the point of view of revenue, the witness showed that according to the statement of the Secretary of the Treasury only $310,000,000 could be expected from the corporation tax for the fiscal year 1937, not $620,000,000 as the President requested. This amount, $310,000,000, could be "secured much more readily and at much less risk by retaining the present law."

From the point of view of equity, as well as revenue, the witness thought the 1935 tax law not far out of line. The inequality which the Administration emphasized was because of the difference in rates applied to corporations and individuals, because partnerships were not taxed at all and because individuals were taxed upon their distributive shares of partnership income and upon the dividends which they received from corporations. This inequality was shown to be a theoretical, not a practical one. If the differences were serious, a partnership or individual could incorporate. Furthermore, few partnerships or individuals carried on businesses in competition with large industrial corporations. The disparity in the existing law between corporations and individuals which resulted from the flat rate tax of 15% upon corporations, regardless of the amount of income of their various stockholders, was partly cared for by personal exemptions.

31 74th Congress, 2d Session, *Hearings Before the Committee on Finance, United States Senate, on H. R.* 12395, pp. 34-65.

32 Others of prominence who appeared were: George O. May of Price, Waterhouse and Company, accountants; Roy C. Osgood of the First National Bank of Chicago; Fred R. Fairchild of Yale University, representing the Manufacturers' Association of Connecticut; and Arthur Ballantine representing the Merchants' Association of New York City. Mr. Alvord had served in the Treasury under Secretary Mellon; Mr. Ballantine, under Secretaries McAdoo, Mellon, and Mills.

As to the proposed measure the witness discussed the difference between "adjusted net income," as defined in the law, and earnings and profits from which dividends could be paid. For example, he explained how a corporation might show a net income of $100,000 but at the same time incur a loss of $100,000 on securities, hence there would be no earnings and profits out of which to pay dividends but, nevertheless, the tax would be $42,500 under the proposed bill.

He outlined the differences in dividend-paying ability among four classes of corporations: (1) those subject to legal limitations in payment of earnings such as banks, trust, and insurance companies; (2) those that could not pay dividends (a) because the payments might impair their capital, or (b) because the payments would render them insolvent; (3) those prevented from paying because of business policy; and (4) those that could distribute without limitation. The new tax policy would give tremendous advantage to one of this last class, because it could pay out all of its earnings and thereby avoid any tax. He emphasized the complexities of a tax policy that would be required to cover all such exigencies which were not covered in the House bill although it was a highly complex measure. In fact the bill specified five different computations of earnings and profits.

Almost scathingly he described the confusion in administering the laws then on the statute books and added:

> But I shudder to contemplate the consequences of a virtually complete uprooting, in a few weeks' time, and the substitution of new statutory provisions, in an unknown and unexplored field, piled upon the present complexities of computing taxable net income, and with the Government and the taxpayer sharing dollar for dollar in the error.[33]

OBJECTIONS BY COMMITTEE MEMBERS

For some time in April members of the Finance Committee had been receiving instructions from Treasury tax experts, "dress rehearsals," Couzens called them,[34] so that opposition of Committee members unfriendly to the bill had been thoroughly aroused by the time the hearings opened. Testimony of witnesses at the hearings made the bill look even less desirable.

King, who was next to Chairman Harrison in point of seniority, led the revolt. He objected to departing from the fixed principles of corporation taxation as established by all former laws and proposed, as a substitute, increased rates on corporate and individual income.[35] Byrd, who at one time favored "any tax measure that would help bring revenues into line with expenditures,"[36] became a critic of

33 *Hearings*, pp. 252-293.
34 Washington *Post*, April 30, 1936.
35 New York *Times*, May 2, 1936.
36 New York *Times*, May 8, 1936; Washington *Post*, May 11, 1936.

the House measure on the ground that many large corporations would be unduly favored by the plan. He said that the figures submitted by the Treasury proved his point, for they showed that of the 600 corporations with incomes of over a million dollars each in 1934, 238 would have had their taxes reduced at least 50% and 138 would have paid no taxes if they had been levied only on undistributed profits. As this list was of a confidential nature, submitted by the Secretary at an executive session of the Committee, Byrd was not at liberty to publish it. Nevertheless, in a letter he sent to Morgenthau requesting further information he enumerated the following corporations that would pay either no tax or very small taxes if the proposed plan were adopted: [37]

Examples of corporations that would pay no tax:

American Telephone & Telegraph Co.
American Tobacco
American Smelting & Refining Co.
General Electric
Goodyear Tire and Rubber
International Harvester
National Biscuit Co.
National Dairy Products
Ohio Oil Co.
R. J. Reynolds Tobacco Co.
Texas Co.

Examples of corporations that would pay less than 5% of net income:

Air Reduction Co.
Allied Chemical & Dye Corporation
Corn Products Refining Co.
Curtis Publishing Co.
E. I. DuPont Co.
Firestone Tire & Rubber Co.
General Foods
Great Western Sugar
Imperial Oil Co.
Liggett, Myers Tobacco Co.
Parke, Davis Co.
Pennsylvania Railroad Co.
U. S. Smelting & Refining

Examples of corporations that would pay less than 10% of net income:

American Can Co.
Armour & Co. (Del.)
Eastman Kodak Co.
General Motors
Great Atlantic & Pacific Tea Co.
International Stove Co.
J. C. Penney Co.
Procter and Gamble
Socony-Vacuum Oil Co.
Standard Oil of California
Standard Oil of Indiana
Standard Oil of New Jersey
Texas Gulf Sulphur Co.
United Fruit Co.
F. W. Woolworth

Byrd therefore proposed that the Committee limit its activities to raising needed revenue and that more thorough study of permanent measures be made later by a joint congressional committee.[37] He was supported by George and Clark.

[37] New York *Times*, May 9, 11, 15, 1936. The request for more complete data for 1935 was not granted as the data apparently were not available.

Connally, who was said to have written more amendments to tax bills in the past four years than probably any other Senator,[38] feared that the bill would bear unfairly on the small stockholder and would tend "to freeze business at present levels and prevent small concerns from expanding." [39] He presented a compromise plan for a combination of the method already established and that proposed by the Administration. In fact, it looked for a while as though each member of the Committee was completely engrossed in working out a bill of his own.

Strength was given to the conservative forces on the Committee by a letter to Harrison from Chairman Jesse Jones of the Reconstruction Finance Corporation which contained the statement that:

> if substantial concessions could be made that would encourage modernization, new plant construction and new buildings to replace old ones, new equipment for railroads and industry of all kinds, including allowances for new debts created for these purposes, the employment situation and business generally, would in all probability be greatly helped, and society much better served.[40]

At the same time Chairman Eccles of the Federal Reserve Board also wrote to Harrison proposing a combination of a flat rate (15%) on corporation net income and, after exempting $15,000, a tax on withholding at the rate of 60% if less than half the earnings were distributed, and 40% if more than half were distributed.[41] These letters were apparently interpreted to mean that the Administration was not so united in its plan as Congress had been led to believe.

By the end of May the conservatives were clearly dominating the Committee and Harrison became so alarmed over the strength of the Byrd group that he threatened to withdraw and write his own bill if the Committee refused to accept at least the principle of taxing undistributed corporate income. La Follette thought the Chairman would do well to carry out his threat and take the fight to the floor of the Senate. Byrd yielded, however, when it was agreed to retain the normal tax and add the tax on undistributed earnings as a surtax. Barkley, one of the most ardent Administration followers and almost the sole Democratic member to want the House bill, also agreed to compromise.[42]

During the next ten days harmony was temporarily interrupted by the attempt of the Treasury to present more drastic schedules and by the efforts of the President to get more revenue than the Committee bill seemed to provide for but, by June 1, the reports

[38] New York *Times*, May 8, 1936.
[39] Washington *Post*, May 9, 1936.
[40] *Hearings*, p. 887.
[41] Washington *Post*, May 16, 1936.
[42] New York *Times*, May 22, 1936.

were ready. The majority report, signed by all but three members, explained at some length each section of the bill, and in many instances gave reasons for the Committee action.

Two minority reports were filed. Black and La Follette were determined to put up a fight for the Administration proposals. This left the President in the ludicrous position of being supported by only one Democrat and one Progressive. In their report, they protested against the Committee bill because it did "not provide for any effective incentive for the reasonable distribution of dividends" but, by adding to the present corporation rates, exaggerated the existing unjust treatment of the small income taxpayer and the small corporation. They proposed a simplified schedule, part of which was as follows :

1. Exempt the first $15,000 of adjusted net income from the undistributed-profits tax.
2. In addition to the present corporation tax, impose no additional tax upon the first 20% of corporate adjusted net income.
3. Impose 20% tax on that part of the undistributed adjusted net income in excess of 20% and less than 40% of such income.
4. Impose 30% tax on the remainder of the undistributed net income.[43]

Hastings wrote the second minority report. In it he protested against the extravagance of the Administration and the consequent bad effect on business conditions. "Corporations," he said, "dare not spend more than necessary when they know the Administration is endeavoring to punish them. There should be no tax bill at this time. . . When a tax bill is proposed it should be submitted to careful study . . ." [44]

The Committee proposed (1) a tax of 7% on undistributed corporate net income; (2) a graduated tax on all corporate net income with rates 3% higher than under the 1935 Act ; (3) the capital stock and excess-profits taxes at 1935 rates ; (4) 1% increase in the surtax on individual net income between $6000 and $50,000 ; (5) subjecting dividends received by individual stockholders to the normal tax ; (6) a tax of 80% on unjust enrichment arising from shifting to others the burden of the processing taxes, but with certain amendments of the House provision "to relieve hardship . . . and to provide for simpler and more equitable determination of tax liabilities."

This measure bore little resemblance to the House bill, or to the President's requested program. The reasons for rejecting the House plan for a single corporation tax were these : (1) the proposed system was untried and uncertain as to revenue yield ; (2) it would penalize

[43] 74th Congress, 2d Session, *Senate Report* 2156, Part 2, p. 5.
[44] 74th Congress, 2d Session, *Senate Report* 2156, Part 3.

many corporations in order to reach a few that had been formed or used to avoid surtax; (3) it would prevent the growth of new corporations because they would be unable to build up reasonable reserves; (4) it would retard business expansion and seriously affect employment; (5) it would penalize corporations that were small or had insufficient reserves; and (6) it tended to transfer "the corporate control from the officers and directors of the corporation to the legislative branch of the Government." [45] It is rather significant that the report was written by King and not by Harrison, who was ill.

It was estimated that this bill would bring in $751,000,000 additional revenue, of which $215,000,000 would come from the graduated tax on corporations; $217,000,000 from the 7% tax on undistributed profits; $90,000,000 from the normal tax on dividends; $50,000,000 from increasing the surtax.

THE BILL IN THE SENATE

Impatient to adjourn for party Conventions, and delayed by several unforeseen events, Senate leaders introduced the bill on June 1, and pushed it through at a more or less frenzied night session on June 5 with a vote of 38 yeas and 24 nays.[46] In order to speed action on the last night majority leader Robinson himself took the chair. Countless amendments, several of which dealt with tariff proposals, that might have delayed action unduly, were accepted on the theory that they would be thrown out in conference.

When La Follette learned, as the result of an informal poll, that his amendment for a more severe tax on undistributed earnings had no chance of being accepted, he withdrew it at the suggestion of Robinson in order that it might have more chance of adoption by the Conferees. The Senate also defeated Adams' (Dem., Colo.) amendment to carry out the suggestion of Chairman Jesse Jones of the Reconstruction Finance Corporation to exempt from the undivided profits tax funds spent for plant expansion. One amendment which was adopted reduced from $1,000,000 to $250,000 the amount of insurance that could be used tax-free to pay estate taxes.

The debate was very unusual; most of the opposition was from the majority (Democratic) side. Almost the only speakers for the Administration's original plan were La Follette, Norris, and Black — one a Progressive, one a Republican, and one a Democrat.

[45] 74th Congress, 2d Session, *Senate Report* 2156, p. 5.

[46] One Republican (Norris) and one Progressive (La Follette) voted for the bill; nine Democrats voted against it (Adams, Brown, Bulkley, Copeland, Donahey, Holt, Moore, Murphy, Tydings) *Cong. Rec.* 80: 9110. For the debate see pp. 8526, 8647, 8666-8808, 9041, 9051.

THE REPORT OF THE CONFERENCE COMMITTEE

When the members of the Conference Committee were chosen, Couzens and Keyes declined to serve because of their opposition to the bill. The Senate was represented by King, George, Walsh, Barkley, Connally, and La Follette ; the House by Doughton, Hill,[47] Cullen, Vinson, and Cooper. Because of the divergence of opinions of the two houses, the President called the Committee to meet with him and certain representatives of the Treasury in order to press his views.

In contrast to the simple tax structure which the President advocated in March, the compromise bill of June developed into the most complicated income tax measure that Congress ever passed.

The House managers retained the Administration principle of taxing corporations according to their undistributed profits, but agreed to lower the rates, while the Senate won the principle of continuing the normal tax on corporation net income. The increased surtax rates on individual income were abandoned, but corporation capital stock taxes, excess-profits taxes, penalties for "improperly" accumulating surplus and graduated taxes on personal holding companies were retained. The Conferees retained also the normal tax on dividends received by individuals, a provision inserted when the House proposed to tax corporation income when distributed. The Senate receded on the amendment to permit a deduction from the net estate of proceeds of life insurance policies not in excess of $250,000 for payment of death taxes.

Three reports were filed by Committee members who did not agree to the Conferees' report and, in addition, the Chamber of Commerce of the United States issued a statement.

A statement by a group of Republican members of the House explained that their refusal to sign the Conference report was due, in the first place, to the fact that the bill had "all the objectionable features of the original House bill" ; secondly, to the fact that they were opposed to any new taxes until the Administration "made an honest effort to reduce expenditure and eliminate waste and extravagance." Furthermore, "the primary purpose of the original House bill was not to raise revenue but to give effect to the Tugwellian philosophy of forcing the distribution of corporate earnings. . ." The compromise bill was in some respects more objectionable to them than either the House or Senate bill, because it penalized (1) the accumulation of necessary rainy day reserves, (2) the payment of debt, and (3) the re-investment of earnings for purposes of rehabilitation or expansion.

[47] This was almost the last act of Hill as a member of Congress. He was appointed to the Board of Tax Appeals on May 18.

Walsh and George issued a minority report in which they explained that they refused to sign the Conference Report because the bill provided for a tax which "the Senate had never approved." They repeated the fundamental objection to the plan for taxing undistributed corporate earnings, cited their belief in the need for corporate reserves, questioned the alleged amount of tax avoidance and listed business concerns which would be discriminated against; for example, those that had no reserves, "those whose taxable income may be merely increases in their inventories" and those prohibited by state laws from making distributions of dividends if it would impair their capital. Byrd's statement repeated the charges made previously in the Senate, that the tax on undivided earnings would entrench monopolies and destroy competition.

The Chamber of Commerce of the United States gave out a statement that the compromise revenue measure embodied a destructive theory of taxation which "would retard recovery and discourage re-employment," and advised business interests to take immediate steps to prepare for consideration by the next session of Congress a "comprehensive plan of carefully devised expenditures and revenues, looking toward progressive improvement of the fiscal condition of the Government." [48]

THE PASSAGE OF THE ACT

The House accepted the Conference Report on a very hot day at the hectic end of the session without even having a copy of the printed bill before it. Members voted on the strength of Chairman Doughton's outline of the measure, knowing that the President had given orders that a tax bill must pass. The vote was almost on party lines. Twenty-two Democrats opposed it, however, in contrast to eleven when the House voted in April.

The report came before the Senate on the last night of the session. The vote showed independence, however. Of the 29 against the measure, 18 were Democrats and 11 Republicans. For three hours the bill was discussed. Byrd called it a "mongrel hybrid" measure which would "do damage to many and be an important issue in the coming campaign." Barkley supported it on the grounds that the revenue was needed and the bill under consideration was "the fairest and most sincere and the most just that we have been able to bring out in the confusion" between the conflicting ideas of the House and the Senate. Connally admitted that the bill would not suit those who would pay more taxes or who did not want any tax bill;

[48] New York *Times*, June 20, 1936.

but he cited the need for funds, which none could deny. He defended the compromise because it would give the Treasury some experience in administering the new tax on undistributed profits, yet it did not give up an old tried plan.

SUMMARY OF IMPORTANT CHANGES MADE BY THE NEW LAW

The Revenue Act of 1936 [49] was divided into nine titles: Title I – Income Tax; Title IA – Additional Income Taxes; Title II – Capital Stock and Excess-Profits Tax; Title III – Tax on Unjust Enrichment; Title IV – Export, Charitable, etc., Refunds and Floor Stocks Adjustment under AAA; Title V – Amendments to Taxes on Certain Oils; Title VI – Miscellaneous Provisions; Title VII – Refunds of Amounts Collected under the AAA; Title VIII – General Provisions. Titles I, IA, II, and VIII are most pertinent in this income tax study.

Title I – Income Tax. The normal tax of 4% and the surtax rates on individual income were retained as in the 1935 law, but corporation dividends received by individual shareholders were subjected to the normal tax as well as the surtax.

The normal tax on corporations was imposed on "normal-tax net income" at the following rates: 8% on income not over $2000; 11% on the amount over $2000 and not over $15,000; 13% on the amount over $15,000 and not over $40,000; 15% on the excess over $40,000. The rate for banks and insurance companies was 15%.

The term "normal-tax net income" meant net income minus the sum of (1) interest on obligations of the United States and (2) 85% of the dividends received from corporations subject to tax. Mutual insurance companies were not allowed this second deduction but were allowed a credit for dividends paid.

A new surtax was imposed on corporations with the intent of inducing them to distribute their profits. The rates were graduated by five steps rising from a minimum of 7% of the amount of "undistributed net income" not in excess of 10% of "adjusted net income" to a maximum of 27% of the portion of the undistributed net income which was in excess of 60% of the adjusted net income. If the adjusted net income was less than $50,000, a specific credit was granted, equal to the portion of the undistributed net income which was in excess of 10% of the adjusted net income and not in excess of $5000. If a corporation was entitled to the credit, the tax due was equal to the sum of (a) the tax computed as for other corporations on the amount of the undistributed net income reduced by the

[49] 49 *Statutes at Large* 1648.

CHART 5

CORPORATION INCOME TAXES *

Effective Rates of Tax Under the 1936, 1935 and 1934
Revenue Acts Using 1936 Net Incomes †
By Net Income Classes

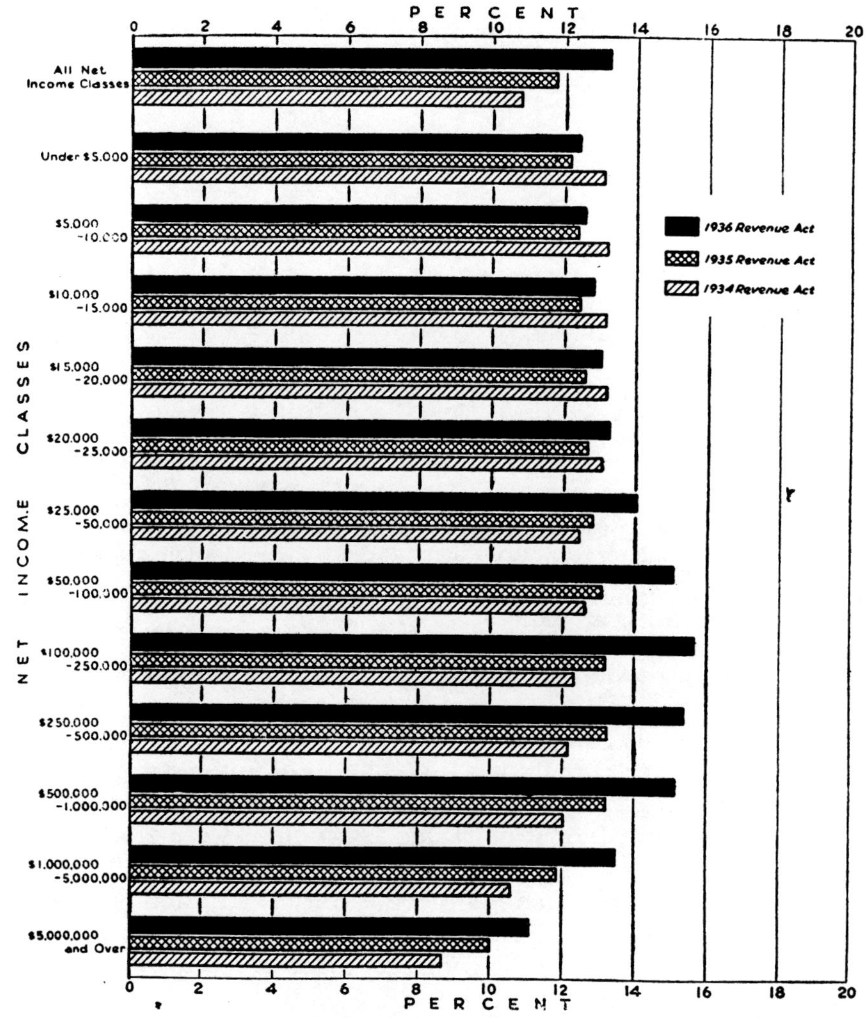

* 75th Congress, 3d Session, *Hearings before the Committee on Ways and Means on Revenue Revision* 1938, p. 123. Based on Table 16.
Normal tax and surtax, 1936 Act; normal tax, 1934 and 1935 Acts.
† Returns filed through Aug. 31, 1937.

TABLE 16

EFFECTIVE RATES OF CORPORATION INCOME TAXES UNDER THE 1936, 1935, AND 1934 REVENUE ACTS, BASED ON 1936 NET INCOMES[a]

Net income classes (thousands of dollars)	*Average tax as a percentage of average net income*[b] *under—*		
	1936 *act*	1935 *act*	1934 *act*
Under 5	12.41	12.17	13.12
5 to 10	12.57	12.39	13.20
10 to 15	12.83	12.44	13.19
15 to 20	13.05	12.60	13.21
20 to 25	13.29	12.68	13.08
25 to 50	14.03	12.83	12.97
50 to 100	15.06	13.12	12.64
100 to 250	15.64	13.23	12.32
250 to 500	15.39	13.27	12.16
500 to 1,000	15.14	13.24	12.04
1000 to 5000	13.52	11.88	10.60
5000 and over	11.10	10.02	8.68
Total	13.23	11.76	10.80

[a] 75th Congress, 3d Session, *Hearings before the Committee on Ways and Means on Revenue Revision* 1938, p. 122. Taxes under the Act of 1936 include normal tax and undistributed-profits tax; under Acts of 1935 and 1934, normal tax only. Net incomes are those shown in returns filed through August 31, 1937.

[b] Before excess-profits tax deduction.

amount of the specific credit, and (b) 7% of the amount of the specific credit.[50]

The term "adjusted net income" was defined to mean net income minus the sum of (a) the normal tax, and (b) interest from obligations of the United States and its instrumentalities. Holding company affiliates and national mortgage associations were granted additional special credits.

The term "undistributed net income" meant adjusted net income minus the sum of (1) dividends paid during the taxable year, and (2) certain credit because of contracts made prior to May 1, 1936 restricting the payments of dividends.

The following corporations were exempt from the surtax: (1) banks, (2) corporations in bankruptcy, (3) insurance companies, (4) foreign corporations, (5) corporations deriving 50% or more of their gross income from sources within possessions of the United

[50] This undistributed-profits tax was greatly modified by the Revenue Act of 1938, which provided for its expiration Dec. 31, 1939. It was not re-enacted by the Revenue Act of 1939. See below, Chaps. XIX and XX.

States, (6) corporations organized under the China Trade Act, and (7) joint stock land banks.

The rates of the penalty tax for improperly accumulating surplus were as follows: (1) in case of a corporation not subject to the surtax on undistributed profits, 25% of the amount of the retained net income not in excess of $100,000 plus 35% of the amount of the retained net income in excess of $100,000; (2) in case of a corporation subject to the surtax on undistributed profits, 15% of the amount of the retained net income not in excess of $100,000 plus 25% of the amount in excess of $100,000.

Because of the importance of dividend distribution in deciding the corporation surtax rates, several new sections were drafted to define "dividends." The general rule was laid down that a dividend paid by a corporation in stock or in rights to acquire stock was not to be treated as a dividend to the extent that it did not constitute income to the shareholder within the meaning of the Sixteenth Amendment to the Constitution. But whenever a corporation made a distribution payable in either stock or money, at the election of the shareholders, then the distribution was held to constitute a taxable dividend in the hands of all shareholders, regardless of the medium in which paid.

For failure to file a duplicate income tax return taxpayers were subject to an additional assessment of $5 in case of an individual and $10 in case of a partnership, fiduciary, or corporation. Returns were open to inspection by state tax officials for administration of state taxes.

Title IA — Additional Income Taxes. The tax rates on undistributed income of personal holding companies were reduced 12% in each bracket so that the minimum was 8% of the "undistributed adjusted net income" not in excess of $2000 and the maximum 48% of the amount in excess of $1,000,000.

Title II — Capital Stock and Excess-Profits Tax. The rate of the capital stock tax was reduced from $1.40 to $1 for each $1000 of value of capital stock. The rates of the excess-profits tax remained unchanged at 6% of the portion of net income in excess of 10% of the adjusted declared value of the capital stock and not in excess of 15% of the adjusted declared value, and 12% of the net income in excess of 15% of the adjusted declared value.

Title VIII — General Provisions. This title contained several definitions and the effective date of the Act, June 22, 1936. The provisions of Title I, however, were applicable to taxable years beginning after December 31, 1935.

CHAPTER XVIII

REVENUE ACT OF 1937 – PREVENTION OF TAX EVASION AND AVOIDANCE

ADMINISTRATION INTEREST IN TAX AVOIDANCE

In the President's budget message to Congress April 21, 1937, he stated that the deficit for the fiscal year would be greater than estimated in January, chiefly because the analysis of income tax returns received in March indicated that income tax collections would be $337,000,000 less than expected. He therefore urged Congress to be economical. No mention was made of the necessity of immediate tax revision, but it was announced that the Treasury was engaged in a study of the federal tax structure, directing particular attention to the closing of loopholes. Information upon which legislation could be based would be ready in November.

In the following two months, however, the President changed his plans and on June 1 sent a message to Congress urging immediate legislation to prevent evasion of the income tax laws. Most of the message consisted of a letter from Secretary Morgenthau, in which he enumerated eight devices for defeating the income tax, methods of moral fraud, and three "major instances" of inequalities in the law by which individuals and corporations were permitted "to avoid their equitable share of the tax burden." [1]

The Senate immediately passed a resolution to create a Joint Committee on Tax Evasion and Avoidance to consist of twelve members, six from the House Committee on Ways and Means and six from the Senate Committee on Finance. The House, however, did not look so favorably on the proposal and was very critical of parts of the Senate resolution. As soon as Chairman Doughton finished reading the resolution protests were voiced by several members. Chairman O'Connor (N. Y.) of the Rules Committee objected to two sections: (1) the provision that authorized officers or employees of the Treasury to conduct any part of the investigation and granted to them the right to subpœna witnesses, and (2) the section that gave the committee "the right to report." He characterized the first provision mentioned as "probably the greatest surrender and delegation of congressional power which has ever been suggested to the House of Representatives." The second section he disliked because of its

1 *Cong. Rec.* 81: 5124-25; 75th Congress, 1st Session, *Report of the Joint Committee on Tax Evasion and Avoidance.*

"gratuitous language." "They either should report or they should not report," he said.

Maverick (Dem., Tex.) protested at the request of Doughton for unanimous consent. He objected to rushing the measure through — to being a rubber stamp. "This is supposed to be a parliamentary body, not a door mat." [2] Therefore, the resolution was referred to the Rules Committee and not voted upon until the following Tuesday. In the meantime it was revised by two amendments. One placed upon the Joint Committee the responsibility for making public any information regarding the incomes of taxpayers under investigation. The second required the presence of at least two members of an investigating subcommittee to hold a public hearing. It was evident that only a few members, if any, had any enthusiasm for the proposal.[3]

Within a week the Committee opened public hearings, which were conducted at intervals throughout the summer. Secretary Morgenthau and Undersecretary Magill were the first witnesses. Their testimony was an elaboration of the main points set forth in the President's message of June 1. They called attention to the following three factors that encouraged tax avoidance: (1) the development of a group of clever attorneys and accountants who exercised every ingenuity in circumventing the law; (2) the fact that tax avoidance, as opposed to tax evasion, was considered by many a legitimate aim; and (3) the difficulty of distinguishing between tax avoidance "which is supposed to be proper and tax evasion which is supposed to be immoral."

The testimony of Undersecretary Magill was devoted to an explanation of seven types of schemes for tax avoidance, not all of which were commonly employed, to be sure, but each of which presented "a potential stumbling block in the administration of tax laws." These schemes were: (1) formation of foreign personal holding companies; (2) organization of foreign insurance companies with only nominal assets; (3) creation of domestic holding companies for creating surpluses and artificial deductions; (4) the incorporation of yachts and country estates; (5) the creation of multiple trusts for relatives and dependents; (6) the formation of husband-and-wife or father-and-children partnerships, and (7) the use of pension trusts.

The Committee listened to reports of how the Treasury ferretted out "dummy" insurance companies and saw pictures of empty shacks in the Bahamas that were the headquarters of various fictitious corporations. Questioning brought out the fact that these devices had been used by comparatively few individuals, that they were expen-

[2] *Cong. Rec.* 81: 5243-5244.

[3] *Cong. Rec.* 81: 5369-5370, 5442-5462; *Nation* 144: 667 (June 12, 1937).

sive, not new, and that they had been known to the Treasury for some time. Some of the members wondered why much more serious problems were not considered, for example, the problems connected with depletion and community property, or why the penalty sections of the income tax law had not been applied to those taxpayers who obviously intended to defraud. Before the hearings had ended the discussion became personal and political. Questions were asked about the Roosevelt family incomes. Mr. Robert Jackson, Assistant Attorney General, took the stand to defend the Bureau's unusual action in making a hypothetical ruling in regard to the tax exemption of Mrs. Roosevelt's earnings from radio broadcasts before she made her income tax return. Congressman Fish asked why the attacks had been concentrated on Republicans. He would have liked to know the names of some Democrats who were evading the income tax.

The hearings dragged on intermittently until August 10.[4] Unfriendly press reports indicated that the evidence presented made no such impression as that intended by the Treasury. Was this merely a face-saving device to distract attention from poor estimates, or from the Supreme Court issue ? Was it primarily a means of "smearing economic royalists" ? Columnists suggested that fraud cases should be handled by the Solicitor, that the tax rates were so high that evasion was encouraged, that personal holding companies were recognized as legal by the government, that the law was one-sided in taxing capital gains but not permitting the deduction of capital losses, and that there was double taxation in taxing corporation net income both in the hands of the corporation and again to the individual stockholders.[5]

THE BILL IN THE HOUSE

Early in August the Joint Committee on Tax Evasion made its report. This was the basis of the bill reported by the Committee on

[4] 75th Congress, 1st Session, *Hearings before the Joint Committee on Tax Evasion and Avoidance* 1937.

[5] New York *Times*, June 13, 20, 1937. The New York *Herald Tribune*, June 2, 1937, commented that the real blame for tax evasion lay with the Administration: first, for failing to make the law foolproof with respect to tax dodging; second, for not broadening the base of the income tax structure so as to include a larger share of the nation's income; third, for making estimates of receipts which were far too optimistic; and fourth, and most important, for failing to reduce government expenditures. Similar comments were made by *Business Week* (June 26, 1937), *Commercial and Financial Chronicle* (June 19, 1937), and such correspondents as Walter Lippmann and Westbrook Pegler. On June 7, Mr. J. P. Morgan declared that taxation was a legal question, pure and simple, and not a moral one. "Congress," he said, "should set about correcting the stupid mistakes in the income tax law which leave loopholes for the taxpayers instead of insulting them by seeking to make a moral issue of the onerous business of paying taxes." (New York *Times*, June 8, 1937.)

Ways and Means,[6] a measure largely drafted by the Treasury Department.[7] The bill was restricted to legislation for plugging the loopholes to which attention was called by the President, chiefly those connected with personal holding companies, both domestic and foreign, multiple trusts, artificial deductions for interest and business expense, and non-resident aliens. The House Committee made no recommendations on two subjects considered by the Joint Committee: (1) single premium life-insurance policies issued by fictitious foreign insurance companies, and (2) pension trusts, because it was thought that the existing law was adequate to reach cases of avoidance in the first case and because it was not evident that much revenue was lost in the latter.

The definition of a personal holding company was revised so that a corporation could not escape the special surtax merely by making a slight change in the character or source of its income. For example, under the 1936 law a corporation was taxable as a personal holding company for any year in which it derived 80% or more of its gross income from certain sources (mostly investments), and if at any time during the last half of the taxable year more than 50% of its stock was owned by not more than five individuals. Therefore a company could avoid the surtax by changing its investments so that only 79% of the income came from these specified sources. The Committee endeavored to prevent this by drafting stricter provisions as to changes in personal holding company income.

The definition of "personal holding company income" was amended to include, in addition to income from the sources specified in the 1936 law, income (1) from estates or trusts, (2) from personal service — to care for the "incorporated talent" loophole — and (3) from rents, unless they constituted 50% or more of the gross income of the corporation. The proposed draft also set forth new rules for determining ownership of stock.

The new definition of "undistributed adjusted net income" disallowed the deduction permitted under the 1936 Act for 20% of the excess of adjusted net income over the amount of dividends received from other personal holding companies. The subcommittee had also recommended that there be eliminated the deduction of amounts reserved for debt incurred before January 1, 1934, but the Committee on Ways and Means considered that such a rule would cause undue hardship.

[6] The membership of the Committee was the same as in the preceding session with the addition of A. Willis Robertson (Va.) and Otha D. Wearin (Ia.) by the Democrats, and appointment of Lloyd Thurston (Ia.) in place of Isaac Bacharach (N. J.) by the Republicans.

[7] 75th Congress, 1st Session, *House Report* 1546.

A new definition of "adjusted net income" was drafted so that personal holding companies could not deduct: (1) special taxes paid under the penalty provision for corporations improperly accumulating surplus, (2) unlimited contributions to charities, or (3) unlimited losses from sales or exchanges of capital assets. Allowable deductions for contributions were limited to an amount not over 15% of net income; losses from sale of capital assets, to the extent of $2000 plus gains from such sales. The rates of tax on income retained by such companies were increased to 65% on the amount of "undistributed adjusted income" not in excess of $2000 and 75% of the amount in excess of $2000. The Committee proposed that there be disallowed, as a deduction from gross income, the expense of operation and maintenance of property owned and operated by such personal holding companies to the extent that expenses exceeded rent or other compensation for the use of the property. To prevent deductions of fictitious losses from sales between members of a family, it was proposed that losses between a husband and his wife's corporation or vice versa should not be deductible.

No satisfactory method could be found to prevent the use of multiple trusts to accumulate income. The Committee proposed that the $1000 exemption granted under the previous law be disallowed unless the trust distributed all its income.[8]

The problem of foreign personal holding companies was also a poser. The new method of taxation proposed required American shareholders to report their distributive shares of a foreign personal holding company's net income whether distributed or not. Changes were also proposed in the sections relating to taxation of nonresident aliens so that the tax was 10% on income not in excess of $21,600 and at the regular surtax rates on income above that amount.

The purpose of the measure was described as follows by the Committee on Ways and Means:

> Your committee has pointed out that the major purpose of this bill is to close loopholes in the revenue laws of which numerous taxpayers have availed themselves, often by means of ingenious and complex devices, to escape the share of the burdens of taxation the Congress has intended that they should bear. The committee believes the proposed legislation is adequate for these purposes but also recognizes the difficulty of framing a tax law which is wholly proof against all the devices and schemes which legal ingenuity may evolve. Should time reveal that new stratagems are being devised to thwart the spirit and intent of the corrective legislation which the Congress may enact at this time, it is the purpose of your committee to frame such further legislation as may be necessary to checkmate them and, to whatever extent may be consistent with justice and sound policy, to recommend that the legislation be made retroactive. It believes

[8] In each prior income tax law trusts were granted the same exemption as single individuals.

that such measures of this kind as may be required to protect the integrity of the revenue laws are well within the scope of constitutional power and will be sustained by the courts.[9]

It is significant, however, that the measure omitted any reference to the following methods of tax avoidance: tax-exempt securities, undistributed profits, capital gains, single premium life insurance policies issued by fictitious companies, pension trusts, community property laws, percentage depletion, and multiple trusts to accumulate income.

The measure was reported out of Committee on August 13, and came up for debate on August 16. The chairman proposed a few verbal amendments which were agreed to with no discussion. Then the bill passed with no dissenting votes. Less than one column in the *Record* was used to cover the whole proceeding.

THE BILL IN THE SENATE

Two days later the bill was introduced into the Senate, with minor amendments,[10] by the Committee on Finance.[11] These were rushed through and, had it not been for Schwellenbach's objection, the measure would have been passed in fifteen minutes. Members were not familiar with the bill. Borah asked if there was anything in it relative to community property or depletion of mines. Chairman Harrison explained that the Committee had taken up only a limited number of subjects. Schwellenbach then said he would like to know the contents of the measure, at least; so it was agreed to postpone the vote until the following day. It then passed without a roll call. The only comment made was by Bridges (Rep., N. H.) who wanted to insert an amendment to authorize the Joint Committee on Internal Revenue Taxation to make a study of federal, state, and local tax systems "to discover their interrelationship and overlapping." Harrison explained that this was unnecessary because such an investigation was already in progress, so the amendment was withdrawn.[12]

The bill was signed by the President on August 26, 1937.

BRIEF SUMMARY OF THE LAW [13]

The Revenue Act of 1937 was written as an amendment to three titles of the Act of 1936, not as an independent Act.

[9] 75th Congress, 1st Session, *House Report* 1546, p. 32.

[10] The Senate Report merely embodied the House Report.

[11] The membership of the Committee was much the same as in 1936. The Democrats added Robert Bulkley (Ohio), Prentiss Brown (Mich.), and Clyde Herring (Ia.); the Republicans, Arthur Vandenberg (Mich.), John Townsend (Del.), and James Davis (Pa.). The following members in 1936 were no longer in the Senate: Gore (Okla.), Costigan (Colo.), Couzens (Mich.), and Keyes (N. H.).

[12] *Cong. Rec.* 81: 9042 (House debate); 9026-9029, 9031 (Senate debate).

[13] 50 *Statutes at Large* 813.

Title I — Personal Holding Companies. The tax rate on undistributed adjusted net income of such companies was increased from 8% to 65% on income not in excess of $2000, and from 48% to 75% on the remainder of the income. These changes made the highest rate the same as the maximum surtax rate on individuals.

The definition of a personal holding company was revised to remedy the defect of the 1936 law by which a corporation could escape the tax as a personal holding company by making a slight change in the character or source of its income, even though there was no change in stock ownership of the company.

The definition of personal holding company income was revised to include income from contracts for personal services (so as to care for the "incorporated talent" loophole) and rents which did not constitute 50% of gross income. To prevent a holding company from charging off expenses for maintenance of property, such as yachts, estates, etc., the definition of deductions was amended to exclude expense of operating and maintaining property to the extent that the expenses exceeded the rent.

Title II — Foreign Personal Holding Companies. This title presented a new method of taxing the undistributed income of such foreign corporations. It provided that such income should be included in the gross income of stockholders within the jurisdiction of the United States whether citizens, residents, corporations, or partnerships.

Title III — Disallowed Deductions. The sections defining losses from sales or exchanges of property were enlarged so as to disallow losses between: (1) members of a family; (2) an individual and a corporation, more than 50% of the stock of which was owned by the individual; (3) two corporations, more than 50% of the value of the outstanding stock of which was owned by the same individual; (4) a grantor and a fiduciary of any trust; (5) a fiduciary of a trust and fiduciary of another trust, if the same person was a grantor with respect to each trust; or (6) a fiduciary of a trust and any beneficiary of such trust.

Title IV — Trusts. This section amended the 1936 law so as to grant the $1000 exemption only if the trust did not require nor permit the accumulation of any portion of the income. Fiduciaries of such trusts were required to file returns no matter what the amount of the net income.

Title V — Nonresident Alien Individuals. The 1936 law imposed a flat tax of 10% on income from United States sources received by nonresident aliens. The 1937 law applied this rate only if the net income from such sources did not exceed $21,600 but, if it was greater, the regular and normal surtax rates were applied.

Title VI — Miscellaneous. This title dealt with amendments relating to exemption of personal holding companies from the surtax for improperly accumulating surpluses, and to the provisions for mutual investment companies.

The Act was applicable to taxable years beginning after December 31, 1936.

CHAPTER XIX

REVENUE ACT OF 1938 – REVISION OF THE TAX ON UNDISTRIBUTED PROFITS

THE SUBCOMMITTEE ON INTERNAL REVENUE TAXATION

The undistributed-profits tax first imposed in 1936 was responsible for only one of the many grudges held by "Business" against the New Deal. Charges of the disastrous economic effects of the tax were perhaps exaggerated, but they were persistent and could not be ignored. The House of Representatives heeded these complaints shortly before adjournment in August 1937 to the extent of authorizing the Committee on Ways and Means to make a study of needed revisions of the internal revenue laws. A subcommittee of eight members with Vinson as chairman was promptly appointed by Doughton, Chairman of the Committee on Ways and Means.

When the special session convened in the fall of 1937 rumors of tax legislation were current, but the subcommittee was not ready to report. In fact, it did not begin work until November, when it received basic material from the Treasury Department. About this time it became obvious to everyone that the slight decline in business first noticeable in August might presage a serious depression, euphemistically called a "recession" by the Administration when it eventually admitted a turn for the worse.

The subcommittee made sixty-three recommendations, over twenty of which concerned the corporation tax; seven, the tax on capital gains; thirty, other income tax and administrative changes; five, the estate and gift taxes; and four, the excise taxes.

The subcommittee proposed for smaller corporations, defined as those with net income of not more than $25,000, a tax equivalent to the graduated normal tax in the 1936 Act but with slightly increased rates; for corporations with net income over $25,000, a tax based on undistributed profits, as follows: from a tentative tax of 20% of adjusted net income, subtract (1) 16% of the "dividends received credit" and (2) 4% of the "dividends paid credit," but not over 4% of the adjusted net income. A special formula was devised for corporations with income slightly over $25,000.

It was estimated that the effective rates of the tax for larger corporations would be graduated from 16%, if all the "adjusted net" income was paid out in dividends, to 20% if no income was paid out in dividends.

In January the subcommittee report to the full Committee on Ways and Means [1] became the basis for public hearings. Influence, if not pressure, of the Administration and the Treasury was particularly obvious in the testimony of Undersecretary Magill, who appeared as official spokesman for the Secretary. He defended the action of the subcommittee in retaining the undistributed-profits tax despite tremendous propaganda to repeal it. One of his main arguments for retaining it was that if any taxes were repealed or modified so as to reduce the yield, it would be necessary to levy additional taxes to make up the loss. Such measures would impose new and unsettling obligations upon business. Furthermore the Undersecretary argued that there was no convincing evidence that the undistributed-profits tax or the tax on capital gains had been a major factor in the business recession.

Representatives of business firms, business associations, and the railroads appeared before the Committee to express their disapproval of the proposed corporation tax. Business was frankly disappointed that the undistributed-profits tax was kept even in a modified form. The chief objections were: (1) it was directly contrary to the principle of ability to pay; (2) it did not conform to any sound principle of taxation; (3) it was unfair and discriminating, "conferring advantages upon some and disadvantages upon others"; (4) it compelled unsound financing; (5) it aided monopoly; (6) it penalized initiative and enterprise; (7) it imposed on taxpayers conditions which they could not meet, and (8) it imposed penalties upon "a statutory, arbitrary, . . . concept of taxable net income whereas the only fund under State law which is available for the declaration of dividends is earnings and profits." [2]

Treadway expressed very briefly the objections of the minority members to the report, particularly to the statement of Mr. Magill that there was no convincing evidence that the operation of the undistributed-profits tax or of the tax on capital gains had been a major factor in the recent setback of business.[3] Majority members were also fully conscious of the possible connection between taxes and the "recession." The opening statement of the subcommittee report expressed the opinion that business would receive substantial stimulation by the enactment of the recommended changes; nevertheless, it was expected that government revenues from tax sources would not decline but would be stabilized.

[1] The members of the Committee were the same as in 1937, except that Samuel B. Hill (Dem., Wash.) had been appointed to the Board of Tax Appeals.

[2] 75th Congress, 3d Session, *Hearings before the Committee on Ways and Means . . . on Revenue Revision* 1938, pp. 504-505.

[3] 75th Congress, 3d Session, *Hearings*, p. 143.

The bill drafted by the majority members of the Committee on Ways and Means followed closely the recommendations of the subcommittee, but omitted some matters because they required more intensive study. The principle of the undistributed-profits tax was retained, but several important modifications were made in its application, as suggested by the subcommittee. In the first place, corporations with net incomes of $25,000 or less were exempt from this surtax and subject to a normal tax only, with rates graduated from 12½% to 16%. Secondly, corporations with net incomes of more than $25,000 were to be taxed at a flat rate of 20% but, in order to encourage the distribution of earnings, some credit was allowed for dividends paid out so that the tax might be reduced; but the maximum reduction was 4% of the net income. In case of a net loss, the corporation was permitted to carry the amount forward one year and treat it as a dividend in computing the 4% dividend credit.

The Committee proposed to add a new title, IB, which imposed an additional tax on corporations in which the stock was held by 10 or fewer individuals and which had a net income of $40,000 or over. Such corporations did not come within the class of personal holding companies as defined in Title IA of the existing law, yet it was thought that they were used by individuals to avoid the imposition of the surtax. This so-called "third basket" was therefore originated by Vinson in order to overcome the ineffectiveness of the penalty tax imposed on corporations used to accumulate earnings. The tax was 20% of the net income defined as "adjusted Title IB net income" which was net income, as defined by Title I, minus the undistributed-profits tax and also minus whichever of the following was the largest: (a) $60,000, or (b) 30% of the Title IB net income, or (c) amounts used or set aside to pay or retire indebtedness incurred prior to January 1, 1938.

Special treatment was proposed for the taxation of several groups of corporations including banks, life insurance companies, mutual investment companies, resident foreign corporations, and foreign personal holding companies, as in the existing law, but the rates were increased 1%, except that for foreign corporations they were reduced 2%.

Important changes were made in the treatment of individual capital gains and losses also, in order to meet the objections of taxpayers to the high rates and sharp annual reductions of percentages of gain taxable under the existing 1937 law.[4] One change that affected both corporations and individuals was a modification in the definition of capital assets so as to exclude property used in trade or business sub-

[4] See below, pp. 587, 588.

ject to depreciation allowances. Under this proposed change a taxpayer could include loss from sale or exchange of such property in the computation of net operating loss.

The following proposed changes were applicable to individuals only. For the purpose of separating speculative transactions from investment transactions, capital gains and losses were divided into two groups, "long-term capital gains and losses" from sale of assets held for more than a year, and "short-term capital gains and losses" from sale of assets held for not more than a year. It was proposed that short-term losses be offset against short-term gains only and not against ordinary income or against long-term gains. If the losses exceeded the gains, the excess could be carried forward one year and applied against the short-term capital gains of the next year. If the short-term gains exceeded the short-term losses, the excess was to be added to the ordinary income and taxed at the full normal and surtax rates.

It was proposed that long-term capital losses be offset against long-term capital gains; but, if the losses exceeded the gains, $2000 of the excess could be charged against ordinary income as under the 1937 law. Net long-term capital losses, reduced by $2000, could be carried forward for one year and applied to offset any long-term capital gains in such year.

New brackets were proposed for the percentages of taxable gains and losses. The taxable proportion of such gains began at 100% in case of assets held 13 months or less and was reduced by 2% for each month the asset was held until the rate became 76% of the gain or loss on assets held for more than 24 months but not more than 25 months. After the 76% bracket was reached, the rates were reduced 1% for each additional month until, in case of assets held over 5 years, the percentage became 40%. No further reduction was allowed.

The objectives of the new plan were summarized by the subcommittee as follows:

1. A smoother and more gradual step-down of the percentage of gain or loss to be taken into account for tax purposes, thus eliminating the inducement to concentration of transactions at certain intervals, with its accompanying accentuation of rises or declines in values.
2. Elimination, as to capital gains of individuals, of the highest surtax brackets provided for other income, thus accelerating liquidation of large blocks of overpriced securities and giving added mobility to the capital market, as well as encouraging investment of capital in new productive enterprises.
3. More liberal deductions of capital losses in the interest of greater equity and in order to minimize the tax risk of investment in new

enterprises (while at the same time preventing the loss of revenue which would result if such deductions were to be applied extensively to reduce taxable net income from sources other than capital gains).[5]

In order to simplify the estate tax law a single schedule of rates was proposed [6] and the credit for state death taxes made 16½%. To increase the yield the combined exemption for estate and gift tax purposes was reduced to $40,000. Under the 1937 and previous laws it was $40,000 for the estate tax and $40,000 for the gift tax, making a total of $80,000. The specific amount of annual exemption permitted for the gift tax was reduced from $5000 to $3000 for each gift.

The Committee proposed to eliminate most of the excise taxes. Many of them produced little revenue, some were difficult to administer, and some, which were imposed originally for regulatory purposes, no longer had any reason for being.[7]

The day before the report was made public Bernard M. Baruch, a prominent Democrat, testified before Senator Byrnes' Committee on Unemployment and Relief as to his belief in the unfortunate economic effects of the federal taxes on capital gains and on undistributed profits. He expressed his agreement with the purpose of the latter in preventing tax avoidance through unproductive accumulations of surplus, but thought evasion could be attacked without paralyzing the expansion of old business or the creation of new. He said:

The combined influence of high and unreasonable capital gains and unwise undistributed-profits taxes has almost stopped the development of new enterprises.[8]

THE BILL IN THE HOUSE OF REPRESENTATIVES

When Chairman Doughton presented the Committee draft of the bill to the House on March 3, 1938, he endeavored to explain the background of the measure, particularly to defend the somewhat anomalous decision to keep the undistributed-profits tax, while at the same time limiting its application to few corporations and reducing the rate to so insignificant a percentage. Doughton enumerated the principal complaints against the tax, chiefly that it dis-

[5] 75th Congress, 3d Session, *Hearings before the Committee on Ways and Means on Revenue Revision,* p. 41.

[6] The rates of the law then in force were based upon the Act of 1926 as amended in 1932 and 1935. The 1926 law permitted a credit of 80% of federal tax for death duties paid to states, but the succeeding laws made no such allowance with respect to the additions they imposed. The Treasury stated that the 16½ per-cent limit would allow the same benefit to states as under existing laws.

[7] 75th Congress, 3d Session, *House Report* 1860.

[8] 75th Congress, 3d Session, *Hearings Before the Senate Committee on Unemployment and Relief.*

couraged business, penalized corporations in debt, and was unfair to corporations with impaired capital which were restricted by state laws from declaring dividends. Most of these charges he dismissed as unproved. Some of them, however, he considered valid. Nevertheless the Committee thought it would be impractical to draft relief provisions without opening loopholes of a serious nature. Furthermore, no practical means had been devised to prevent accumulation of surplus and consequent evasion of surtax until the tax in question had been imposed. The solution therefore seemed to be to exempt small corporations from the tax and to impose a new special surtax on closely-held corporations that accumulated unreasonable surpluses.[9] He expected the bill to produce as much revenue as the existing law but to distribute the burden more equally so that business would be stimulated and encouraged. Vinson spoke over an hour, explaining the details of the proposed measure, but the small attendance of the House indicated little interest.[10]

Treadway and Reed led in presenting the minority objections to the bill. The latter facetiously commented on Vinson's adroitness, saying:

> I am sure that practically every person here is convinced not only that corporations and business men are not taxed but that the government is making them an annual contribution from these large appropriations.[11]

More effective opposition was launched by McCormack of the Committee on Ways and Means, a tall quick-tongued Irishman who criticized severely the so-called third basket, Section IB, the new tax on closely-held corporations.[12] Lamneck, also a Democrat, joined him in lining up votes against this provision,[13] on the grounds that the tax was unfair, that it was a penalty aimed at a few, and was proposed because of the ineffectiveness of Section 102. The Republicans were all too willing to aid in defeating this pet measure of the Administration.

Cooper, who aspired to Vinson's title of tax expert upon the latter's retirement at the end of the session to accept a federal judgeship, was the leading defender of the Committee plan.[14] This support was, however, insufficient. For three and a half hours the issue was debated. Majority leaders prevented the passage of several amendments that were introduced to strengthen Section 102 and thus remove the excuse for passing Title IB. They were, however, unable

[9] *Cong. Rec.* 83: 2761-2769.
[10] *Cong. Rec.* 83: 2777-2787.
[11] *Cong. Rec.* 83: 2787.
[12] *Cong. Rec.* 83: 2855-2860.
[13] New York *Times,* March 4, 1938.
[14] New York *Times,* March 8, 1938; *Tax Magazine,* June 1938 (Frontispiece).

to prevent the passage of McCormack's amendment to strike out Title IB.[15] This defeat was a blow to the Administration, but Doughton passed it off with the remark that he had no criticism to make of any individual member of the House and that the bill was a good one even without Title IB.[16]

Another amendment not sponsored by the Committee was that introduced by Fuller to require publicity of salaries of $75,000 or more. Doughton explained that the Committee had eliminated all such provisions in drafting the bill because the House had voted against a similar one in the previous session. Boileau (Dem., Wis.) urged the restoration of the existing provision, that is, publicity of salaries of $15,000 or over, but he was unsuccessful. Fuller's amendment was adopted after it had been amended, at Doughton's suggestion, to make the Treasury Department, not the Committee on Ways and Means, responsible for its publication.[17]

The elimination of Title IB and the consequent loss of expected revenue offered an excuse for the submission of numerous amendments proposing changes in excise taxes. Among them was an increased levy on distilled liquors. This passed easily. In order to prevent a flood of undigested and unwise measures,[18] Doughton closed the debate on the bill for that day. He told press representatives that it was his personal opinion that necessary additional revenue should be provided in a separate bill to be considered later because it was unwise and improper to draft such legislation before offering an opportunity to hear individuals or corporations who would be affected.[19] Such strategy was only partly successful. It could not defeat the amendment offered by Thompson for a tariff on imports of pork and pork products.[20]

Except for the deleting of the Administration-sponsored Title IB and the addition of a few comparatively unimportant amendments, the measure passed the House as introduced. The vote on the bill (March 11) was 293 yeas, 97 nays.[21]

15 The first vote on March 9 in Committee of the Whole was 180 yeas, 124 nays. The second in the House on March 11 was 234 yeas, 153 nays. (*Cong. Rec.* 83: 3136, 3265.)

16 New York *Times,* March 10, 1938.

17 *Cong. Rec.* 83: 3060.

18 Another reason for not wanting any new excise measures passed was that the revenue argument might be used to secure a reversal of the vote on eliminating Title IB.

19 New York *Times,* March 11, 1938.

20 *Cong. Rec.* 83: 3199.

21 *Cong. Rec.* 83: 3269.

THE BILL IN THE SENATE

The conservative Committee on Finance [22] under the leadership of Harrison quickly redrafted the House bill, chiefly to eliminate completely the undistributed-profits tax and to return to the flat tax on corporations.[23] The rate proposed by the Committee was 18%.

An important amendment was made in the method of computing gain and loss from the sale of capital assets. The Senate Committee discarded the House plan because it was "excessively" complicated and would obstruct the "free flow of capital into productive enterprises." The Committee therefore drastically changed the method of computing the tax on such investments and reduced the rates radically, not only as compared with the House bill but also as compared with the existing law. The method proposed was that used from 1924 to 1932, that is, the separation of capital gains of individuals from other income and the levy of a flat tax thereon. The proposed rate, however, was 15% as compared with 12½% in those years. The House definition of capital assets was retained. The Senate retained also the House limitation of deduction of losses from worthless securities, included as capital assets, when held by individuals, but it permitted corporations to deduct such losses in full on the supposition that they were incurred as a part of business expense. The House bill allowed corporations to revalue their stock for the purposes of the capital gains and excess-profits taxes in 1939 and every three years thereafter. The Senate proposed a revaluation in 1938 and every ten years thereafter.

The Finance Committee rejected the reductions made by the House in the exemption for the estate and gift taxes, and restored the existing exemptions of $40,000 each for the estate and gift taxes, and the $5000 annual exemption of gifts to each donee. The Com-

22 The members of the Senate Committee on Finance were:

Democrats	*Republicans*
Pat Harrison (Miss.), Ch.	Robert M. LaFollette, Jr. (Wis.)
William H. King (Utah)	Arthur Capper (Kan.)
Walter F. George (Ga.)	Arthur H. Vandenberg (Mich.)
David I. Walsh (Mass.)	John G. Townsend, Jr. (Del.)
Alben W. Barkley (Ky.)	James J. Davis (Pa.)
Tom Connally (Tex.)	
Josiah W. Bailey (N. Car.)	
Bennett Champ Clark (Mo.)	
Harry Flood Byrd (Va.)	
Augustine Lonergan (Conn.)	
Peter G. Gerry (R. I.)	
Joseph F. Guffey (Pa.)	
Robert J. Bulkley (Ohio)	
Prentiss M. Brown (Mich.)	
Clyde L. Herring (Ia.)	
Edwin C. Johnson (Colo.)	

23 75th Congress, 3d Session, *Senate Document* 177.

mittee proposed, however, that this specific annual amount of exclusion not be allowed for gifts in trust, a means of easy avoidance.

This Committee accepted most of the House draft of the section on excises, and even went farther in eliminating several taxes that the House had not disturbed. It deleted also the increased tax on distilled spirits and the tariff on pork, which had been added by the House.

An important revision made by the Committee was to strengthen the penalty Section 102, which was designed to prevent the accumulation of corporation earnings beyond the reasonable needs of business. It was to overcome the defects of this section that Vinson had drafted his "third basket" proposal, Title IB. According to Harrison, the Senate amendment was written "in as strong language as the experts could write and the committee could fashion." It stated that the fact that earnings or profits were permitted to accumulate beyond the reasonable needs of the business would be determinative of the purpose to avoid surtax upon shareholders unless the corporation by the clear preponderance of the evidence could prove the contrary. This shifted the burden of proof from the Treasury to the taxpayer.

The Senate accepted the draft of the Finance Committee with little debate. As the clerk speedily read the bill for amendments, the chairman punctuated his steady flow of words with the formula, "Without objection amendment agreed to," spoken as though it were one long word. At the end of 20 minutes Vice-President Garner turned the gavel over to Minton with the remark that they had already passed 224 pages of the measure.[24]

Harrison's explanation of the changes centered on the corporation tax and the capital gains sections. The undistributed-profits tax was a beautiful theory, he said, but it had proved harmful. An improvement had been made by the House, but the results were so complicated that hardly a lawyer in Washington could understand them. The Senate Committee bill attempted to simplify the law by levying a flat tax of 18% on corporate profits.

Majority leader Barkley, who had requested that the amendment deleting the undistributed-profits tax be passed over as the bill was read, defended the House provision and opposed the Senate Committee action because, in his estimation, the tax had not been tried out sufficiently.

In stronger terms La Follette also opposed the elimination of this surtax. Such action, he said, was a step backwards, a reversal of the principle of progressive taxation, which had been achieved only after long years of effort. He pointed out that the maximum surtax

24 New York *Times*, *Wall Street Journal*, April 8, 1938.

rate for individuals was 75%, hence if the corporation rate was made 18% as proposed there would certainly be every incentive to accumulate surpluses instead of to distribute earnings; accordingly, surtax avoidance would be more likely to occur than in previous years when corporation rates were lower. Furthermore, the proposed changes in the treatment of capital gains would accentuate the evil because they favored those with large incomes.[25] As usual, La Follette also wanted to increase the surtax rates and reduce the personal exemptions. His amendments for those purposes were rejected.[26]

Except for the majority and minority leaders, La Follette and one or two others, discussion of vital sections of the bill was almost nil. As in the House, those measures that were somewhat extraneous, but more easily understood, received much more attention.

Clark introduced an amendment to authorize the Treasury to conduct an investigation into "the desirability and practicability of the imposition of a tax on the use of labor saving and labor displacing machinery and to report to Congress at the beginning of the first session of the 66th Congress." This was passed.[27]

Vandenberg (Rep., Mich.) chided the majority for abandoning the tax on undistributed profits; nevertheless, he approved the move. He secured consent to print in the *Congressional Record* the conclusions of the recently published report by the Brookings Institution on the economic effects of this tax.[28]

At least two majority members seized the opportunity to criticize the tax policy of the government. Speaking of the limitations placed on corporations in determining valuations for the capital stock tax, Pittman (Nev.) remarked that it seemed to be the policy of the Treasury Department to get revenues no matter how it got them. Ashurst (Ariz.) went even farther, saying:

> The Treasury should not act as a spoilsman with a game bag engaged in an effort to see how much game he can get into the bag. . . We cannot continue to take a policeman's billet and pound the taxpayer on the head if we expect to achieve recovery.[29]

Several members — Hitchcock, Borah, and Clark — pressed for amendments to prevent the exemption of interest from government securities. Borah proposed to tax interest on obligations of the United States only if issued after the passage of the Revenue Act of 1938.[29] Clark wished to extend this policy to interest from bonds of states or any subdivision thereof.

[25] *Cong. Rec.* 83: 4929-4934, 5145-5148.
[26] *Cong. Rec.* 83: 5162, 5167.
[27] *Cong. Rec.* 83: 5175. This amendment was thrown out in conference.
[28] Kendrick, M. Slade, *The Undistributed Profits Tax.*
[29] *Cong. Rec.* 83: 4968.

Neither Harrison nor Barkley favored these amendments, doubtless because they opened the way to a long discussion of a controversial subject. Their main argument to the Senate was that the federal government would receive no fiscal advantage from such a policy because it would be necessary to raise the interest rate on securities issued thereafter. Lonergan (Conn.) stated that the Judiciary Committee was to meet the following Monday to consider a constitutional amendment dealing with tax-exempt securities, hence he also hoped that the Senate would take no action before then.[30] Ashurst saw no reason why the Senate action would interfere with the committee work. Borah's amendment was adopted,[31] but Clark's was rejected.

When the excise tax sections were under discussion, the debate became very lively and some interesting propositions were put forward, such as Pope's amendment for tariff equalization fees on manufactured cotton, synthetic fibers, wheat, rice, corn, etc. It was rejected. Lonergan proposed that in making inventories for certain industries taxpayers be allowed to make calculations of cost of raw material on the basis of "last in, first out," and received a favorable vote for his amendment.[32] Lodge (Rep., Mass.) offered an amendment to reduce the payroll tax for old-age insurance under the Social Security Act, but Harrison objected because such a change would reduce the reserve too drastically. Thirteen members voted for Lodge's proposal, sixty-one against.[33]

The bill passed the Senate on April 9 without a record vote and without an audible "nay." [34] It was estimated that it would produce $5,330,000,000, an amount $89,000,000 more than the House measure.

THE BILL IN CONFERENCE AND THE PRESIDENT'S ACTION

Because of the radical differences between the House and the Senate measures the Conferees had a difficult time. The House managers had the strategic advantage, because the undistributed-profits tax imposed by the previous law would remain on the statute

[30] *Cong. Rec.* 83: 5385.

[31] *Cong. Rec.* 75: 5181-5183. This was thrown out by the Conference Committee, but the issue was again brought up in 1939. Legislation was enacted to subject compensation of state officers and employees to the federal income tax, and to permit states to tax compensation of federal officers and employees. Legislation for taxation of securities was postponed. See below, Chap. XX.

[32] *Cong. Rec.* 83: 5042-5044. This method of taking inventories had been requested for several years by representatives of such industries as tanning and non-ferrous metal smelting and fabricating. The Treasury preferred to handle such matters by regulations instead of by law, but refused to grant the permission even by regulation.

[33] Such an amendment was adopted in 1939. See above, Chap. XVI.

[34] *Cong. Rec.* 83: 5183; New York *Times*, April 10, 1938.

books unless repealed. The Administration was throwing its support to the House measure and a two-thirds vote over a presidential veto would be difficult if not impossible to secure.

Senate conferees and leaders resented the pressure by the Administration, particularly when the President sent them a letter on April 13 requesting that the principle of the undistributed-profits tax be kept. Harrison issued a statement that the Senate would not yield in its determination to eliminate from the bill the particular sections to which business leaders objected.[35]

The Conferees worked for almost a month; often they were deadlocked. Their report was accepted by the Senate on May 9, and by the House on May 11.[36]

As is usually the case, the final draft was a compromise. The House managers won approval for their undistributed-profits tax but the Senate managers secured its limitation to the years 1938 and 1939. The second chief point of difference, treatment of capital gains and losses, was settled by the adoption of a method rather different from those of both House and Senate. It was rumored that Harrison swapped the undistributed-profits tax elimination for the capital gains tax plan. Senate managers secured the restoration of $40,000 exemption each for estate and gift taxes ($80,000 for both). Similarly, agreements were reached on other points of difference.

The President held the bill until May 27 before making known his decision. It was reported that even Congressional leaders were not informed as to what he would do. On that day at a small high school commencement at Arthursdale, W. Va., a resettlement project, he broadcast a speech in which he expressed his disapproval of many features of the bill. He objected particularly to the treatment of capital gains and the near elimination of the undistributed-profits tax. For these reasons, therefore, he could not sign the measure; nevertheless, he would not veto it because it contained certain improvements. This was the first time in his administration that he had taken this stand on any measure passed by Congress, and the first time since the adoption of the Sixteenth Amendment that any President had failed to sign a revenue bill.

In his speech the President gave examples to show that under the new law large and small taxpayers would be taxed at the same rate on profits from sales of capital assets. Chairman Harrison took exception to this statement in particular, as well as to the general implication that Congress was trying to ease taxes on the wealthy and

[35] New York *Times*, April 14, 1938.

[36] There was no roll call in the Senate. In the House the vote was 424 yeas, 89 nays. *Cong. Rec.* 83: 6441, 6699.

that the Senate was more responsible than the House for the bill. On May 28 he replied from the floor of the Senate, the first time in the history of the New Deal that a leading Democrat had taken the floor to dispute the accuracy of a specific statement of the President. Harrison showed how the President's example illustrating the tax on capital gains was only partly true, because he omitted to state that short-term capital gains were taxed as regular ordinary income at normal and surtax rates. Looking up to the reporters in the press gallery, he asked that the public hear the truth of the matter:

> Get that out to them. Tell the American people. Let the experts look into it.[37]

No one, however, could dispute the President's statement that there would be a new tax bill the next year. This was obvious from the fact that the corporation tax was limited in its application to the years 1938 and 1939. Unwelcome to many was the news that he would request a general tax revision to include the undistributed-profits tax and higher taxes on profits from capital gains. The prospect of another fight the next year over a tax bill dampened the hopes of many Congressmen that the measure would prove of value in stimulating business.[38]

SUMMARY OF THE IMPORTANT NEW PROVISIONS OF THE ACT [39]

The 1938 Revenue Act was a comprehensive law, not merely amendatory and superimposed upon prior statutes as was the 1937 Act. The new law contained seven titles: I — The Income Tax; IA — Personal Holding Companies; II — Estate and Gift Taxes; III — Capital Stock and Excess Profits Taxes; IV — Excise Taxes; V — Miscellaneous Provisions; VI — General Provisions. Following is a brief summary of the more important new features of each title.

Title I — Income Tax. The Act of 1938 introduced only one important change applicable to the income of individuals; namely, the computation of gain or loss from the sale of capital assets.[40] In order

[37] New York *Times*, May 29, 1938.

[38] *Wall Street Journal*, May 28, 1938. The Chamber of Commerce of the United States made the following comment on the bill: "Big and little business men together are clearly perturbed over trends in Washington. . . They are wondering if the practical and psychological benefits of the new law will not be lessened by official insistence on restoring the punitive higher rates of the discredited surplus tax and a steeply graduated capital gains tax in the next session of Congress." (Quoted in *Commercial and Financial Chronicle* 146: 3703, June 11, 1938.)

[39] 52 *Statutes at Large* 447.

[40] For a summary of the treatment of capital gains and losses since 1913 see below, Exhibit 7, Appendix.

to differentiate in the taxation of speculative and investment gains, an arbitrary period of ownership was taken as determinative. Profits from the sale of capital assets held for not more than 18 months, assumed to be speculative, were designated "short-term capital gains"; profits from sale of capital assets held for more than 18 months, assumed to be from investments, were designated "long-term capital gains."

Short-term capital gains were taxable in full at regular normal and surtax rates. Short-term capital losses were allowed only to the extent of short-term capital gains; but, if "short-term capital losses" exceeded "short-term capital gains" in any year, the resulting net loss might be carried forward for one year to the extent that it did not exceed the ordinary net income of the year in which such short-term net loss was sustained as an offset against short-term capital gains in such succeeding year. The following percentages of long-term capital gains and losses were recognized for tax purposes according to the length of time the asset had been held: 66⅔% if the asset had been held for more than 18 months but not more than 24 months; 50% if the asset had been held more than 24 months. Long-term capital losses were deductible from other income.

A new device was the alternative method for determining the tax in cases of long-term capital gains. If a taxpayer had realized a net long-term capital gain, the tax due was the lesser of that computed at regular normal and surtax rates and that derived by the following method: Compute a tentative tax on the net income exclusive of the net long-term gain; to this add 30% of the taxable long-term gain. It should be noticed that the 30% tax is not computed on the total amount of such gain, but on the fraction of the taxable gain, that is, on 66⅔% if the asset has been held over 18 months and not over two years, and on 50% if the asset had been held over two years. The tax, therefore, could not exceed 20% of the actual gain in the case of assets held 18 months to two years, and 15% in the case of assets held over two years.

There was also an alternative method for computing the tax in case of a net long-term capital loss. The tax due was the greater of that computed at regular normal and surtax rates and that computed as follows: Compute a partial tax on net income without regard to the capital loss; from this tentative tax deduct 30% of the taxable amount of the net long-term capital loss. As in the case of the tax on long-term gains mentioned above, this 30% was calculated on 66⅔% or 50% of the loss, depending on the length of time the asset had been held. The maximum deduction for such loss was therefore 20% or 15%.

The practical result of the change from the 1937 law was to increase the tax on gains from property held not more than 18 months but more than 12 months, but to reduce the tax on assets held longer than 18 months. The taxpayer whose income fell in the higher brackets received a greater advantage than the small taxpayer, particularly in the case of property held over two years. The law gave no inducement to a taxpayer to hold property more than two years.

This section contained also a new definition of "capital asset" so as to exclude property subject to depreciation allowances used in the taxpayer's trade or business. This was a relief provision, inasmuch as it allowed taxpayers to deduct the full loss from machinery or other equipment sold or abandoned.

Other sections, however, were more severe than in previous laws. Losses from worthless securities such as stocks, uncollectible bonds, notes, etc., issued by corporations, were restricted by the rules just given for calculation of capital gains and losses. That is, such securities were defined as capital assets, and therefore were subject to the limitations applicable to loss from sale of capital long-term or short-term assets. Previously such losses were deductible in full as bad debts from ordinary income.

New rules were established for partnerships. Every partnership must separate from other income gains or losses from sale of capital assets. The tax on capital gains was computed as though in the hands of an individual, on the basis of 100% of short-term gains and 66⅔% or 50% of long-term gains. Each member of the partnership must include with his individual income his distributive share of partnership ordinary net income and short-term capital gains or losses, and combine with his long-term capital gains his distributive share of partnership long-term gains or losses.

The most discussed and one of the most important changes made by the Act of 1938 related to the taxation of corporate net incomes. The new law retained the principle of the Administration-sponsored undistributed-profits tax, but with greatly reduced rates and only for the calendar years 1938 and 1939. Moreover, this surtax applied only to corporations with net incomes of over $25,000. The amount of tax varied according to the proportion and amount of earnings paid out in dividends, but the maximum rate was 2½%. In the previous law the maximum was 27%.

For corporations with net income over $25,000 the general rule was to compute a tax at 19% of the adjusted net income, that is, the net income minus interest from United States obligations. From this tax was deducted the sum of (1) 16½% of the credit for dividends received,[41] and (2) 2½% of the dividends paid credit [42] but not over 2½% of the adjusted net income.

An alternative method of computation was provided so that there would not be too sharp a tax differentiation between corporations with incomes of $25,000 and less, and those with incomes of slightly over $25,000. This very complicated "notch provision" affected only a few corporations. It is noted here, however, because it illustrates some of the characteristic complexities of the law.

This method for corporations with some income from interest on obligations of the United States (tax-exempt interest) provided for the division of the income into two portions, (1) the first $25,000 and (2) income over $25,000. A complicated rule was made for allocating certain dividends and interest. The tax was the sum of the following: (1) a tax on the $25,000 of the first division computed under the rule for corporations with income of not more than $25,000; (2) 12% of the dividends received, allocated by a specified rule to the second division; and (3) 32% of the remainder of the amount allocated to the second division, except certain interest. Corporations that came in this category were to pay the lesser of the tax computed according to this rule and that computed by the general rule described above.

The alternative method for corporations with income slightly over $25,000 but with no tax-exempt interest was simpler. The tax for such corporations was the lesser of that computed under the general rule and the following: $3525 plus 32% of the amount of net income in excess of $25,000.

For corporations with net income of $25,000 or less, that is, for those not subject to the undistributed-profits tax, the rates were graduated: 12½% on net income not in excess of $5000; 14% on net income over $5000 and not in excess of $20,000; 16% on the remainder.

Although the undistributed-profits tax was eliminated so far as most corporations were concerned, the law was not greatly simplified; in fact, the formulae for computing taxes in special cases were very complicated. For example, the "basic surtax credit," part of the "dividends paid credit," contained several factors, one of which was

41 "Dividends received" were defined as "85 per centum of the amount received as dividends from a domestic corporation which is subject to taxation under this title, but not in excess of 85 per cent of the adjusted net income."

42 The term "dividends paid credit" was defined as the sum of (1) the basic surtax credit (dividends paid during the year reduced by the amount of interest from United States obligations); (2) "the dividend carry over" (as defined at length in another section); (3) the amount by which a deficit in the earnings at the close of the preceding taxable year exceeded the amount of the credit for net losses as defined in the Act, and (4) amounts reserved to pay indebtedness.

the "consent dividends credit." This credit was based on signed consents that the shareholders would include in their taxable income as dividends the amounts specified. Such consents were to be filed with the Commissioner.

For certain classes of corporations, special methods of taxation were imposed; for example, the incomes of banks, insurance companies, corporations organized under the China Trade Act, and some others were taxed at 16½% regardless of the amount of income; incomes of resident foreign corporations were taxed at 19%. These rates were higher than in the previous law, except for the last group, resident foreign corporations, for which the rate was lower.

Every trust with net income of $100 or more for the taxable year was required to file a return. The Act of 1937 had eliminated any exemption for trusts that permitted the accumulation of income. The Act of 1938 allowed an exemption of $100 regardless of the type of trust.

Contributions made by corporations were restricted to those paid within the taxable year. Contributions made by individuals were restricted to those paid to domestic institutions, a requirement made in the 1936 law for corporations.

The section imposing a surtax on corporations improperly accumulating surplus was revised so as to place on the taxpayer the burden of proving that the surplus was not accumulated to prevent the imposing of surtax on individual shareholders.

Certain taxpayers, namely producers and processors of such nonferrous metals as copper and brass, and tanners, were permitted to inventory in the order of acquisition of raw materials.

Title IA — The Surtax on Personal Holding Companies. The rates remained as in the previous law at 65% and 75%, but the method for computing undistributed net income was changed so that such companies could distribute additional dividends after the close of the taxable year and thus escape at least part of the heavy taxes on undistributed net income. Some relief provisions were granted; for example, certain personal finance companies were exempted from the imposition of the tax. The law did not allow personal holding companies that owned or operated property to deduct depreciation and expense charges which exceeded the amount of rent unless the Commissioner could be satisfied that the property was held as a business operated for profit, or that there was reasonable expectation that it could be operated at a profit.

Title II — Estate and Gift Taxes. The previous law was not changed, except that the annual individual gift-tax exemption for donor was reduced from $5000 to $4000 for each gift, and gifts in trust were granted no exemption. A total exemption of $80,000 for estate and gift taxes was allowed as before, that is, $40,000 for each tax.

Title III – Capital Stock and Excess-Profits Taxes. This title also received only slight amendment. A corporation was permitted to make a new declaration of the value of its capital stock in 1938 and every third year thereafter. Corporations coming out of bankruptcy were permitted to make their declarations irrespective of the three-year period. The capital stock tax rate remained at $1 for each $1000 of the fair value. The excess-profits tax rates were kept at 6% of the portion of net income in excess of 10% and not in excess of 15% of the adjusted declared value of the stock and 12% of the portion of net income in excess of 15% of such value.

Title IV – Excise Taxes. Many excise taxes were repealed, for example, those on chewing gum, furs, toilet soaps, mouth washes, phonograph records, sporting goods, and cosmetics; but the tax on colored wooden matches was retained. The tax on theater tickets was made 10% of the actual price paid, instead of the face value or box office price. The tax on market transactions in commodities for future delivery was eliminated after June 30, 1938. The tax on distilled spirits was increased from $2 to $2.25 a gallon.

Titles V and VI – Miscellaneous and General Provisions. These titles dealt with technical matters mostly relating to administration and the effective dates of the Act. One important new provision was that permitting closing agreements between the taxpayer and the Commissioner as to the basis for computing gain or loss in future transactions. Corporations subject to Title I were required to report to the Secretary of the Treasury all officers and employees to whom they paid $75,000 or more for personal services. In the 1936 Act the corresponding minimum amount was $15,000. The law became effective at midnight May 27, 1938, but the provisions of Title I applied to taxable years beginning after December 31, 1937.

CHAPTER XX

CODIFICATION, PUBLIC SALARY TAX, AND REVENUE ACTS OF 1939

IMPORTANT CHANGES IN POLICY AND PRACTICE

The tax legislation passed by Congress in 1939 covered a wide range of subjects, and was significant in that it involved several fundamental changes of policy and, also, because most of it was passed primarily to improve the fundamental structure of the tax laws and to remove tax irritants and inequities rather than to raise additional revenue. In addition to the amendments of the Social Security Act to reduce payroll taxes and extend the benefits of old-age insurance, discussed elsewhere,[1] three important measures were enacted. The adoption of the Internal Revenue Code, consisting of a codification of the internal revenue laws, was intended to remove inconsistencies therein and to simplify reference thereto. The Public Salary Tax Act of 1939 was passed for the purpose of abolishing federal tax immunity of state government officers and employees and removing obstacles to state taxation of compensation of federal officers and employees. The Revenue Act of 1939 was enacted to extend certain excises about to expire and to revise the corporation normal income tax in view of the early expiration of the bitterly opposed undistributed-profits tax.[2] Fundamental changes in the administration of the law by decentralizing the Income Tax Unit are explained in Chapter XXIII below.

THE INTERNAL REVENUE CODE

Simplification of the income tax law was one of the aims of those who established the Joint Committee on Internal Revenue Taxation in 1926, but this purpose was found almost impossible of achievement because of the nature of the income tax. In 1928 the Joint Committee took an important step in this direction by rearranging the form of the income tax law, as explained in Chapter XI above, and commenced work on the removal of inconsistencies in the laws and simplification of reference from one law to another. With aid from the legal department of the Treasury and the Department of Justice, this codification of internal revenue laws was completed in 1939 and submitted to Congress.

[1] See above, Chap. XVI.

[2] Three other measures were under consideration by subcommittees: (1) a bill for "incentive taxation," to encourage business, (2) a stringent law to prevent profiteering in time of war, and (3) tax exemption of government securities.

Chairman Doughton presented the measure to the House on January 23, with the full approval of the Committee on Ways and Means.[3] Some apprehension was expressed by certain Republican Congressmen that taxpayers and laymen would find it more difficult to use the Code than to refer to past legislation. Doughton explained that without the Code it was necessary to go through thirty-five volumes of statutes to find all the references to existing internal revenue laws. Furthermore, the law was not always easy to understand, because inconsistencies had crept in during the course of years. The experts who drafted the Code had weeded out such matter but in other respects had not changed the law.

The House passed the bill on January 25, with a vote of 355 to 16. The Senate passed it on February 2, without a roll call, and the President signed it on February 10. (53 *Statutes at Large,* Part I.)

Public Salary Tax Act

Reference was made in the preceding chapter to the President's request for legislation to prevent further tax immunity of income from government salaries. His main purposes were: (1) abolition of the federal and state tax immunity of state and federal officers and employees;[4] (2) discontinuance of the narrowing of the tax bases as the federal and state governments broaden their activities and employ larger personnels; and (3) the securing of somewhat more revenue. In January 1939 the President sent another message to Congress calling attention to the importance of removing tax exemption, and especially to the need for immediate legislation occasioned by the recent decision of the Supreme Court that employees

[3] The members of the Committee on Ways and Means were:

Democrats	*Republicans*
Robert L. Doughton (N. C.), Ch.	Allen T. Treadway (Mass.)
Thomas H. Cullen (N. Y.)	Frank Crowther (N. Y.)
Christopher D. Sullivan (N. Y.)	Harold Knutson (Minn.)
John W. McCormack (Mass.)	Daniel A. Reed (N. Y.)
Jere Cooper (Tenn.)	Roy O. Woodruff (Mich.)
John W. Boehne, Jr. (Ind.)	Thomas A. Jenkins (Ohio)
Wesley E. Disney (Okla.)	Donald H. McLean (N. J.)
Frank H. Buck (Cal.)	B. W. Gearhart (Cal.)
Richard M. Duncan (Mo.)	Frank Carolson (Kan.)
John D. Dingell (Mich.)	Benjamin Jarrett (Pa.)
A. Willis Robertson (Va.)	
Paul H. Maloney (La.)	
Patrick J. Boland (Pa.)	
Milton H. West (Tex.)	
Raymond S. McKeough (Ill.)	

[4] Contrary to the belief of many, government employees have not heretofore been exempt from all income taxes. The federal government has taxed federal officers and employees but not state officers and employees engaged in performing essential governmental functions; the states having income taxes have taxed state officers and employees but not federal officers and employees.

of the Port of New York Authority were liable for the federal income tax.[5] Unless Congress took action before March 15, the Bureau of Internal Revenue would be forced to collect back taxes for at least three years from employees of many state agencies.[6]

The Committee on Ways and Means conducted hearings in January, at which time a representative of the Department of Justice encouraged the members to proceed in the enactment of a measure to impose the federal income tax on state officers and employees in order to lay the mooted question of constitutionality squarely before the Court.[7] Such procedure would secure results much more quickly than a constitutional amendment if the measure were upheld by the Court.

In the Senate a subcommittee, which had been authorized in the preceding session, studied the matter for some months.[8] This subcommittee also conducted hearings and received many briefs and memoranda on the subject. Because of the probability of state antagonism, as well as because of constitutional difficulties, it was agreed to confine legislation at that time to taxation of salaries of government officers and employees and to defer action relative to tax immunity of government securities.

The bill, known as the Public Salary Tax Act, provided for the taxation of salaries of judges of the United States who took office on or before June 6, 1932, permitted federal taxation of salaries of state officers and employees, and made it possible for the states to tax federal officers and employees. It was not expected that the measure would bring in much revenue, probably about $16,000,000 to the federal government. Estimates of additional revenue for the states had not been made at the time of enactment of the law because of the wide diversity of state income tax laws ; but it was thought that fed-

[5] *Helvering* v. *Gerhardt,* 304 U. S. 405 (1938).

[6] The legal limitation to the period for collecting taxes under the 1935 Act expired March 15, 1939. According to the Chief Counsel of the Bureau of Internal Revenue: "The Commissioner of Internal Revenue, it seems to me, would be derelict in his duty if he permitted several million dollars of taxes to slip out of his hands, with nothing before him, and no mandate from Congress authorizing him to do it. As a matter of fact, he could be impeached." 76th Congress, 1st Session, *Hearings before the Committee on Ways and Means on Tax-Exempt Salaries,* Jan. 26, 1939, p. 74.

[7] 76th Congress, 1st Session, *Hearings before the Committee on Ways and Means on Tax-Exempt Salaries,* pp. 49-57. The measure was then being drafted by the Treasury Department (*Hearings,* p. 70).

[8] This subcommittee consisted of three members of the Committee on Finance (Senators Byrd, Townsend, and Brown) and three members of the Committee on Judiciary (Senators Logan, Austin, and Miller). Hearings were conducted by this subcommittee January 18, February 7-16. The Senate Committee on Finance also conducted hearings on proposed amendments to increase the tax on certain imported vegetable and fish oils.

The members of the Senate Committee on Finance were the same in 1939 as in 1938, except that Radcliffe (Md.) was added to the Committee by the Democrats, while Lonergan (Conn.) and Bulkley (Ohio) were no longer members ; Lodge (Mass.) was added by the Republicans.

eral employees would pay more state income taxes than state employees would pay to the federal government, inasmuch as federal salaries were higher than those paid by the states, and state exemptions were generally lower, although there were fewer in the federal service and state income tax rates did not run so high as federal income tax rates.[9] Undersecretary of the Treasury Hanes, in his testimony before the Committee on Ways and Means, laid great stress on the unfairness of allowing certain classes of citizens to escape their tax responsibilities because they were government employees. With the great extension of the use of the income tax by states (34 in 1939) the problem was of increasing importance.

This measure was passed by the House on February 9, and by the Senate on April 4; in neither house were there important amendments or objections. Its passage marked an important development not only in the income tax law but in breaking down supposedly time-honored barriers between the states and the national government. Inasmuch as this subject has been one of much controversy almost ever since the adoption of the Constitution, a brief summary will be given of the important judicial and legislative developments that have led to the new point of view exemplified in the Public Salary Tax Act.

INCOME FROM GOVERNMENT SOURCES EXEMPT FROM THE FEDERAL INCOME TAX

Prior to this Act of 1939 the federal income tax was not imposed on salaries of state officials and employees engaged in performing essential governmental functions,[10] on salaries of federal judges taking office on or before June 6, 1932, or on interest from certain securities, namely: (1) obligations of a state, territory, or any political subdivision thereof, or the District of Columbia, (2) obligations of certain corporations organized under act of Congress to the extent provided in the authorizing act, and (3) some obligations of the United States and of its possessions.

Interest on all federal obligations is exempt from both individual and corporation normal income tax. In addition, interest from obligations issued prior to September 1, 1917 is also exempt from the federal surtax. Interest on obligations issued after September 1, 1917

[9] In 1937 there were approximately 1,200,000 federal officers and employees receiving $1,900,000,000 in annual compensation and 2,600,000 state and local officers and employees receiving annual compensation of $3,600,000,000 according to Undersecretary Hanes. (76th Congress, 1st Session, *Hearings before the Committee on Ways and Means on Tax-Exempt Salaries*, p. 5.) Of course, non-governmental income of government officers and employees has had no special immunity. For federal and state tax rates and personal exemptions see Chapter XXII and Appendix, Exhibits 14-17, below.

[10] See below, pp. 460, note 12, and 467, notes 33-36.

is exempt to the extent provided by the terms of the authorizing acts. For example, interest on Treasury certificates of indebtedness is entirely exempt from federal income taxes but interest on Treasury bonds is exempt from the surtax only on an aggregate of not over $5000 principal amount of such obligations held by a taxpayer.

Interest on obligations of corporations organized under acts of Congress is exempt only to the extent provided by the terms of the acts that authorized their issue. The first of such obligations to be exempt from federal taxation were those of the Federal Farm Loan Banks. Under the Act of 1916 not only the federal land banks but also federal intermediate credit banks and national farm-loan associations, including the capital and reserve and the income derived therefrom, were exempt from all taxation except death taxes and state taxes on real estate. Also under that Act first mortgages executed to federal land banks, federal intermediate credit banks, or to joint stock land banks and farm loan bonds and debentures issued by intermediate credit banks with the income therefrom were exempt.[11]

The revenue acts are not specific as to the taxation of dividends from Federal Reserve Banks but the Federal Reserve Act provides that the Federal Reserve Banks, including the capital stock and surplus and income therefrom, shall be exempt from taxation, except taxes on real estate. Dividends received from stock of Federal Reserve Banks are also exempt from the income tax, but dividends paid by member banks are treated like dividends of ordinary corporations.

Interest on postal savings accounts is exempt from the income tax. Bonds issued by the Federal Deposit Insurance Corporation are exempt from all taxation except estate or inheritance taxes of the United States or any local taxing authority.

Issues exempt from the federal normal income tax but not from the surtax are: (1) Federal Farm Mortgage Corporation Bonds; (2) Home Owners Loan Corporation Bonds; (3) Reconstruction Finance Corporation (2 per-cent notes series H, 1½ per-cent notes series K, ⅞ per-cent notes series N); and (4) Federal Housing Administration bonds.

Interest on mortgages insured by the FHA and debentures issued by the FHA in exchange for existing mortgages on property are not exempt from federal income taxation, except that debentures issued after the amendments of the National Housing Act of 1938, in exchange for property covered by mortgages issued after the date of the amendment, are exempt from the normal income tax.

Salaries of state officials and employees engaged in essential govern-

[11] Accordingly, income derived from dividends on stock of federal land banks, federal intermediate credit banks, and national farm loan associations and from interest on promissory notes secured by such first mortgages or from such farm loan bonds or debentures was not subject to income tax.

TABLE 17

TAX-EXEMPT SECURITIES

ESTIMATED AMOUNT OF SECURITIES OUTSTANDING, INTEREST ON WHICH IS WHOLLY OR PARTIALLY EXEMPT FROM THE FEDERAL INCOME TAX, JUNE 30, 1938 [a]

(In millions of dollars)

	Total	*Wholly exempt* [b]	*Partially exempt* [c]
A. U. S. Government, Federal agencies and instrumentalities:			
1. Interest-bearing securities outstanding:			
(*a*) U. S. Government	$36,579	$13,492	$23,087 [d]
(*b*) Federal agencies and instrumentalities [e]	7,989	2,151	5,838
Total	44,568	15,643	28,925
2. Interest-bearing securities held by:			
(*a*) U. S. Government, Federal trust funds and agencies	6,465	3,621	2,844
(*b*) Federal Reserve banks	2,564	1,820	744
(*c*) State and local sinking funds	59	......	59
(*d*) State and local trust and investment funds	210	......	210
Total	9,298	5,441	3,857
3. Net outstanding interest-bearing securities	35,270	10,202	25,068
B. State and local governments:			
1. Interest-bearing securities outstanding	19,170	19,170	......
2. Interest-bearing securities held by:			
(*a*) U. S. Government, Federal trust funds and agencies	538	538	......
(*b*) State and local sinking funds	1,501	1,501	......
(*c*) State and local trust and investment funds	2,393	2,393	......
Total	4,432	4,432	......
3. Net outstanding interest-bearing securities	14,738	14,738	......
C. Territories and insular possessions:			
1. Interest-bearing securities outstanding	146	146	......
2. Interest-bearing securities held by:			
(*a*) Territorial and insular sinking funds	23	23	......
3. Net outstanding interest-bearing securities	123	123	......
D. Recapitulation:			
1. Interest-bearing securities outstanding	63,884	34,959	28,925
2. Interest-bearing securities held by:			
(*a*) U. S. Government, Federal trust funds and agencies	7,003	4,159	2,844
(*b*) Federal Reserve banks	2,564	1,820	744
(*c*) State and local sinking funds	1,560	1,501	59
(*d*) State and local trust and investment funds	2,603	2,393	210
(*e*) Territorial and insular sinking funds	23	23	......
Total	13,753	9,896	3,857
3. Net outstanding interest-bearing securities	50,131	25,063	25,068

[a] *Report of the Secretary of the Treasury* 1938, p. 543; and 76th Congress, 1st Session, *Hearings before the Committee on Ways and Means on Tax-Exempt Securities* 1939, pp. 21-24.

[b] Exempt from normal income tax and surtax.

[c] Exempt from normal income tax.

[d] Includes United States savings bonds and Treasury bonds, but interest derived from the first $5000 of principal amount of these securities owned by any single holder is exempt from both the normal tax and surtax.

[e] These issues were as follows:

(In millions)	*Total*	*Wholly Exempt*	*Partially Exempt*
Federal Farm Loan System	$3561	$2151	$1410
Federal Home Loan System	3029	.....	3029
Reconstruction Finance Corporation	1163	.....	1163
Commodity Credit Corporation	206	.....	206
Federal National Mortgage Association	30	.....	30
Total	$7989	$2151	$5838

mental functions were exempt from the federal income tax, not because of specific provisions in the law,[12] but because of the Supreme Court interpretations of the Constitution. It had been generally held for many years that the federal government might not tax the agencies or instrumentalities of the states, and conversely that the states might not tax the agencies and instrumentalities of the federal government.

Because it has been considered unconstitutional to tax them, the obligations of states and their political subdivisions have been exempted from the income tax by specific provisions in the federal income tax laws.

TAXATION OF THE COMPENSATION OF THE PRESIDENT AND FEDERAL JUDGES

Compensation of the President of the United States and of the federal judges is now taxable because of specific legislation. Whereas the Revenue Act of 1932, by an indirect circumventing clause, provided in effect for the taxation of salaries of federal judges and presidents taking office after June 6, 1932, the Public Salary Tax Act of 1939 provided directly and specifically for the taxation of the salaries of federal judges who took office on or before that date. Congress proceeded on the assumption that the Court would reverse its former decision in the case of *Evans* v. *Gore* (253 U. S. 245, 1920).

The Civil War income tax laws did not exempt the compensation of the President and of the federal judges, therefore the Justices of the Supreme Court sent a communication to the Secretary of the Treasury in which they stated that in their opinion their salaries were not legally subject to the tax. In reply the Attorney General issued an opinion that the income tax could not be imposed on judges who were in office at the time of the enactment of the income tax law.[13] This opinion was based on the theory that the tax was a reduction of income, and hence was contrary to the following section of the Constitution :

> Art. III, Sec. 1 . . . The judges . . . shall . . . receive for their services, a compensation, which shall not be diminished during their continuance in office.

[12] The Acts of 1913, 1916, and 1917 specifically exempted the salaries of officers and employees of a state and of any political subdivision thereof. The Regulations applicable to years 1934-1939 read : "Compensation received for services rendered to a state is to be included in gross income unless the person receives such compensation from the State as an officer or employee thereof and such compensation is immune from taxation under the Constitution of the United States."

[13] 13 Op. Attorney General 162 (1869).

A similar section applied to the compensation of the President:

> Art II, Sec. 1. The President shall . . . receive for his services, a compensation, which shall neither be increased nor diminished during the period for which he shall have been elected.

Doubtless because of the opinions of the Court and the Attorney General the income tax laws of 1913, 1916, and 1917 specifically exempted the compensation of the federal judges then in office and of the President during the term of office for which he was elected. The Treasury issued a ruling in 1914 that the salaries of judges appointed after October 3, 1913 and judges who had been retired were subject to the income tax.[14] In the War Revenue Act of 1918 Congress specifically taxed the compensation of the President and of the federal judges in order that the legality of the section might be tested, inasmuch as it did not seem equitable that these officers be exempt.[15] The Revenue Acts of 1921, 1924, and 1926 also specifically taxed the compensation of the President and the federal judges. In 1920 the Supreme Court heard a case brought by a federal judge appointed in 1899 for a refund of income tax paid under the Act of 1918 on the grounds that the effect of the act was to diminish his salary and that this was repugnant to the third article of the Constitution.[16] The Court agreed with this reasoning. Thereupon the Treasury issued a ruling that salaries were taxable in the cases of presidents elected, and of judges taking office, after the enactment of the law of 1918.[17]

In 1925 the Supreme Court ruled that the compensation of a judge appointed after the enactment of the Revenue Act of 1918 was not subject to the income tax on the ground that Congress had "no power to tax a judge of a court of the United States on account of the salary prescribed for him by law." [18]

When the Senate drafted its amendments to the House Revenue bill in 1928 it omitted any reference to federal judges because of these decisions, but inserted a section to tax the compensation of the President taking office after the enactment of the law. This was rejected by the Conference Committee because the House managers

[14] See above, p. 97.

[15] See above, Chap. VII.

[16] *Evans* v. *Gore*, 253 U. S. 245.

[17] The Regulations applicable to the 1921 Act read as follows:

"The salaries of Federal officers and employees are subject to tax, except that, in view of the provisions of the Constitution of the United States as construed by the Supreme Court, the salaries of the President of the United States and Federal judges are not subject to a new tax or an increased tax if elected or appointed to office prior to the passage of the taxing statute. The Revenue Act of 1921, however, imposes no new or increased tax upon such salaries; hence the salaries of all Federal judges appointed since February 24, 1919, are subject to the tax imposed by the Revenue Act of 1921."

[18] *Miles* v. *Graham*, 268 U. S. 501.

insisted that "in so far as this compensation can be taxed under the Constitution it is covered in the general definition of income."

The Revenue Acts of 1932 and succeeding years have contained the following clause :

> In the case of President of the United States and judges of courts of the United States taking office after June 6, 1932, the compensation received as such shall be included in gross income; and all Acts fixing the compensation of such Presidents and judges are hereby amended accordingly.

In May 1939 the United States Supreme Court upheld the validity of this section [19] in a decision that "removed another landmark," according to Justice Frankfurter. It rejected the traditional view that a tax on salary, even if general and non-discriminatory, acted as a reduction of compensation within the meaning of the Constitution.

THE THEORY OF FEDERALISM AND THE SCOPE OF TAX IMMUNITY

The doctrine of immunity from state taxation of the agencies and instrumentalities of the federal government and immunity from federal taxation of state agencies and instrumentalities rests upon the theory of division of powers between the state and national governments, and the independence of each sovereign government of this dual system within its sphere.

The scope of the doctrine of inter-governmental tax immunity has been discussed at great length,[20] but can be sketched only briefly here. Historically the limitations of the taxing power may be traced to the federal structure of the government, to the doctrine of states rights, and the delegated powers of the national government. They are among the implied, not expressed, limitations of the Constitution.

One of the earliest and most far-reaching decisions of Chief Justice Marshall delineated the boundary of state and federal rights and laid down the doctrine that the power to tax involves the power to de-

[19] *O'Malley* v. *Woodrough,* 59 S. Ct. 838 (1939).

[20] Legislators, historians, and lawyers have contributed an enormous amount of literature on the subject. Bibliographies have been issued by the Library of Congress. In 1924 the Senate Committee on Finance published a study made by the Federal Trade Commission in which is a limited list of pertinent articles and law opinions. (68th Congress, 1st Session, *Sen. Doc.* 148.) In 1938 the Department of Justice published a report with an appendix of 6 volumes entitled *Taxation of Government Bondholders and Employees* (The White Book). The point of view of the states, opposing taxation of governmental securities, was presented by Lutz, H. L., *The Fiscal and Economic Aspects of the Taxation of Public Securities* (The Yellow Book) reprinted in 76th Congress, 1st Session, *Hearings before the Special* (Senate) *Committee on Taxation of Governmental Securities,* . . . Jan. 18, Feb. 7-16, 1939.

For a concise summary of the issues see Seligman, E. R. A., *The Income Tax,* Chap. VI.

stroy. In this case, *McCulloch* v. *Maryland*,[21] the Court held that a State of Maryland stamp tax on notes issued by a branch of the Bank of the United States was invalid. Marshall stated that if the states taxed one instrument employed by the government in the execution of its powers, they could tax any and every other instrument, for example, the mails, the mint, patent rights, papers of the custom house, in fact "all the means employed by the government to an excess which would defeat all the ends of government." Therefore, careful consideration of this subject by the Court resulted in the conviction that:

> . . . the States have no power, by taxation or otherwise, to retard, impede, burden, or in any manner control, the operations of the Constitutional laws enacted by Congress to carry into execution the powers vested in the general government.

The converse, that the federal government could not tax an agent or instrumentality of a state, was decided somewhat later in the case of the *Collector* v. *Day*. In this case the Court said:

> It is admitted there is no express provision in the Constitution that prohibits the general government from taxing the means and instrumentalities of a State, nor is there any prohibiting the State from taxing the means and instrumentalities of the government. In both cases exemption rests upon necessary implication and is upheld by the great law of self preservation, as any Government whose means employed in conducting its operations, if subject to the control of another and distinct Government, can exist only at the mercy of that Government.[22]

Pollock v. *Farmers' Loan and Trust Co.*, the famous income tax case of 1895, which has been discussed in some detail in Chapter I above, involved, among other things, the question of the power of Congress to tax income from municipal bonds in the hands of an individual taxpayer. With respect to this matter the Court said:

> The Constitution contemplates the independent exercise by the Nation and the State, severally, of their constitutional powers.
>
> As the States cannot tax the powers, the operations, or the property of

[21] 4 Wheat. 316 (1819).

Much has been made of Marshall's statement that "the power to tax involves the power to destroy." It should also be noted that he made the following comments in the same case:

"It is admitted, that the power of taxing the people and their property, is essential to the very existence of government, and may be legitimately exercised on the objects to which it is applicable, to the utmost extent to which the government may choose to carry it. The only security against the abuse of this power is found in the structure of the government itself."

In this connection should be noted also the following excerpt from the decision of Justice Peckham in *Nicol* v. *Ames* (173 U. S. 509, 1899).

"The power to tax is the one great power upon which the whole national fabric is based. It is as necessary to the existence and prosperity of a nation as is the air he breathes to the natural man. It is not only the power to destroy, but it is also the power to keep alive!"

[22] 11 Wall. 113 (1870).

the United States nor the means which they employ to carry their powers into execution, so it has been held that the United States have no power under the Constitution to tax either the instrumentalities or the property of a State. . .[23]

After this decision the question was in abeyance until the resolution for the Sixteenth Amendment was before the states for ratification.

PREVIOUS INTERPRETATIONS OF CONSTITUTIONAL LIMITATIONS QUESTIONED

The Sixteenth Amendment reads :

The Congress shall have power to lay and collect taxes on incomes, from whatever source derived, without apportionment among the several States, and without regard to any census or enumeration.

At the time of the passage of the joint resolution there was no discussion in the Senate or in the House on the exemption or taxation of income from government sources. In the following year Governor Hughes of New York requested the state Assembly not to ratify the amendment because it gave the federal government power to tax instrumentalities of a state. Senator Root [24] replied for the Administration. He denied that the amendment gave the federal government any extension of power ; it merely removed the necessity for apportionment of the tax among the states according to population.

On the floor of the Senate in January 1910 Brown (Rep., Neb.), who had introduced the resolution for the amendment in the preceding session, and Borah, a member of the Judiciary Committee, also replied to the governor. They objected to his interpretation on the grounds that the amendment did not deal with power but "with the manner of exercising that power which is already complete."

Nelson (Rep., Minn.), who urged the insertion in the amendment of the words "from whatever source derived," made no comment on Borah's interpretation. In fact, he apparently made no mention of the fact that he wrote that phrase until some ten years later.[25]

No interest was shown in a resolution introduced by Borah in 1910 to have the Judiciary Committee report to the Senate its interpretation of the question of whether or not the amendment au-

[23] 157 U. S. 429 ; 158 U. S. 601.

[24] In a brief for the contention that the federal government has the power to tax income from state sources without a constitutional amendment, the Department of Justice made the point (1939) that Root was a new Senator and that he was not on the Judiciary Committee. The fact is, however, that Root was probably more conversant than any other member of the Senate with the entire controversy, inasmuch as he was the President's confidante and had taken a very significant part in this legislation. See above Chap. II, text and footnotes 103, 135, 156, 157, 171-178.

[25] Hubbard, Harry, "From Whatever Source Derived," *Am. Law Journal* VI (b) : 220-227 (Sept. 1920).

thorized Congress to tax the income of state and municipal bonds and the salaries of state officers.[26]

In June 1910 Borah published an article explaining that the income tax amendment added nothing to the power of Congress, that "the sole purpose and only effect" was to relieve Congress from the necessity of apportionment. He said that the taxation of state bonds and other securities would be no different with the amendment from what it would be without it. The power of Congress to tax was full and complete, but it must be construed in the light of the Constitution as a whole. The "scope, purpose and design" of this instrument was "to create two separate, and within their granted and reserved powers, independent sovereignties." The rule by which state bonds and state instrumentalities have been exempted from taxation for a hundred years was "untouched and unchanged" by this amendment. The Senator explained that the words "from whatever source derived" added nothing to the amendment, and in his opinion it probably would have been better not to have used them.[27]

Some years later (1920) the majority opinion in a decision of the Supreme Court, in commenting on the theory of Governor Hughes, contained this sentence:

> his message promptly brought forth from statesmen who participated in preparing the amendment such convincing expositions of its purpose . . . that the apprehension was effectively dispelled and ratification followed.[28]

When the first case under the Sixteenth Amendment arose, the Supreme Court, upholding the constitutionality of the income tax sections of the Tariff Act of 1913 (*Union Pacific R. R.* v. *Brushaber*), took occasion to comment on the meaning of the amendment as follows:

> It is clear on the face of this text that it does not purport to confer power to levy income taxes in a generic sense . . . but . . . to relieve all income taxes when imposed from apportionment, from a consideration of the source whence the income was derived. . .
>
> The purpose was not to change the existing interpretation except to the extent necessary to accomplish the result intended. . .[29]

In another case, decided about the same time, the Chief Justice made a similar comment:

> . . . the 16th Amendment conferred no new power of taxation but simply prohibited the previous complete and plenary power of income taxation possessed by Congress from the beginning from being taken out

[26] See above Chap. II.

[27] Borah, William E., "The Income Tax Amendment," *No. Am. Review* 191: 755-764 (June 1910).

[28] *Evans* v. *Gore*, 253 U. S. 245.

[29] 240 U. S. 1 (1916).

of the category of indirect taxation to which it inherently belonged and being placed in the category of direct taxation, subject to apportionment. . . Hark, of course, in saying this we are not here considering a tax not within the provisions of the 16th Amendment, that is . . . one entirely beyond the scope of the taxing power of Congress. . .[30]

That Congress in 1913 thought the Sixteenth Amendment granted no further powers to Congress is indicated by a speech of Cordell Hull, who was in the House in 1909 when the joint resolution was passed. He drafted a section for the income tax law that specifically exempted salaries of state and local officers and interest from state and local bonds. In explaining this section to the House, the author said :

The Supreme Court has often held that under our form of government the States have no power to tax the instrumentalities of the federal government and conversely that the federal government has no power under the Constitution to tax the instrumentalities of the States ; not desiring to raise any constitutional question, or to arouse the antagonism of any of the States this provision was inserted.[31]

Thereupon a Representative from the South (Bartlett, Ga.) commented that at the time of the ratification of the amendment there was some opposition to it because it did not contain a specific statement that state and municipal bonds were exempt ; but that friends of the amendment assured the voters that "except in great stress, except in time of war, Congress would never think it wise to tax the bonds of the states or subdivisions thereof."

In the case of *Evans* v. *Gore* the Court followed its interpretations made in the previous decisions just cited and held that the Sixteenth Amendment merely removed the necessity for the apportionment of income taxes among the states according to population and did not grant additional power to Congress. Justices Holmes and Brandeis dissented from this conclusion.

As pointed out by Mr. Wenchel, Chief Counsel for the Bureau of Internal Revenue :

Tax immunity became too all-inclusive as a result of the earlier decisions and the court soon became conscious of the fact that the doctrine of implied immunities had swelled itself to such proportions that the taxing powers of both the State and the Nation were in danger of becoming impotent.[32]

It became increasingly clear that this doctrine created an unjust distribution of the tax burden. Furthermore, the levying of certain taxes by one governmental jurisdiction could not be considered such

[30] *Stanton* v. *Baltic Mining Co.*, 240 U. S. 103 (1916).
[31] *Cong. Rec.* 50: 508.
[32] 76th Congress, 1st Session, *Hearings before the Special* (Senate) *Committee on Taxation of Governmental Securities and Salaries* 1939, p. 77.

a burden as to threaten to destroy the other's sovereignty, even though it added to the costs of services.

Therefore, in the course of the years the Court has steadily given greater emphasis to the need for an interpretation of the doctrine of inter-governmental immunity that would protect the taxing power of both the nation and the states.[33] By regulation the Treasury Department has defined those services that are essential to the exercise of governmental functions. In 1938 the Supreme Court rendered two important decisions that further emphasized the changing doctrine of the immunity of state instrumentalities, and declared valid the imposition of the federal income tax on employees of the Port of New York Authority [34] and the federal excise tax on admissions to state university football games.[35] In 1939 the Court almost completely broke with the traditional view in declaring that a state could tax the compensation of an officer of an agency of the federal government so long as the tax did not discriminate against such an officer because of the source of such compensation.[36]

ARGUMENTS FOR AND AGAINST TERMINATION OF TAX EXEMPTION

Most of the discussion of tax exemption has centered on exemption of interest from government securities, rather than on exemption of government salaries, partly because of the greater fiscal importance of the former, and partly for other reasons. The arguments for and against termination of these exemptions will be only briefly outlined here.

It is held that by reason of the issuance of such securities the federal government has suffered a serious fiscal loss ; and worse, the basic justification of the federal income tax, taxation according to ability to pay, has been circumvented by providing a means of escape for incomes in the higher surtax brackets. From the point of view of national economy it is argued that capital is diverted from investment in private business and therefore potential new enterprises are not started. Furthermore, by withdrawing money from private enterprise the interest rate for all non-government enterprises has been raised, and therefore the cost of living has been increased. From the standpoint of society, it is argued that such tax exemption creates

[33] In 1905 the Supreme Court distinguished between the governmental activities of a state and those that were of a private or business nature. (*So. Car.* v. *U. S.*, 199 U. S. 437). In more recent years state employees engaged in the sale of liquor were subject to the Federal income tax (*Ohio* v. *Helvering*, 292 U. S. 360, 1934) ; so also were employees of public utilities owned and operated by a state (*Helvering* v. *Powers*, 293 U. S. 214, 1934) and contractors supplying services or materials to a state (*Metcalf & Eddy* v. *Mitchell*, 269 U. S. 514, 1926).

[34] *Helvering* v. *Gerhardt*, 304 U. S. 405.

[35] *Allen, Collector* v. *University of Georgia*, 304 U. S. 439.

[36] *Graves* v. *N. Y. ex. rel. O'Keefe*, 59 Sup. Ct. 595.

social unrest because a subsidy is granted to certain privileged individuals. It has also been argued that such tax exemption encourages extravagance of states and municipalities because it enables these jurisdictions to borrow funds at subnormal rates of interest.

Estimates of the amount of loss of governmental revenue from exemption of government bond interest depend, of course, on the amount of the issues of such bonds, on the ownership, and on the rates of interest that the government would have had to pay if the bonds had not been tax-exempt.[37]

Treasury experts estimated in 1923 that the government lost $120,000,000 a year. Mr. Ogden Mills estimated that the government lost $242,000,000 a year on the assumptions: (1) that there were outstanding eleven billion dollars of wholly tax-exempt securities, twenty billion dollars partially exempt; (2) that 37% were held by corporations, 23% by people who pay no income tax, and the balance by those whose average income tax rate was 35%.[38]

Professor Seligman gave an estimate of loss of $300,000,000 to the Senate Finance Committee at the time of the hearings on the tax-exemption question in 1922. He based his figure on the assumption that 75% of the outstanding tax-exempt securities were held by individuals and that the average rate of income tax was between 40% and 50%.[39] The 1922 estimate of loss by the Federal Trade Commission was $100,000,000.[40] Undersecretary Hanes testified in 1939 that the federal government lost between $179,000,000 and $337,000,000 annually.[41] Recent estimates of the amount of such bonds outstanding are shown in Table 17 and estimates of federal tax gains from removel of exemptions are shown in Table 18.

On the other hand, some students of the problem have pointed out that there is little conclusive evidence that the federal government has lost much, if anything, through tax exemption of government securities. They hold that the federal government probably has saved in interest as much as it has lost in taxes. The state governments have saved as much interest or more than they have lost in revenue, according to a study made some years ago by Dr. C. O. Hardy. In 1939

[37] The arguments against tax-exempt securities are briefly summarized in 67th Congress, 2d Session, *House Report* 969 and fully considered in Hardy, C. O., *Tax-Exempt Securities and the Surtax.* See also the testimony of Mr. James W. Morris, Assistant Attorney General, and Professor H. L. Lutz in 76th Congress, 1st Session, *Hearings before the Special* (Senate) *Committee on Taxation of Government Securities and Salaries* 1939.

[38] *Proceedings* National Tax Association 1923, p. 335.

[39] 67th Congress, 3d Session, *Hearings before the Committee on Ways and Means on Tax-Exempt Securities* 1922.

[40] The Commission secured data on the ownership of tax-exempt securities by sending out questionnaires to corporations. 68th Congress, 1st Session, *Senate Document* 148.

[41] 76th Congress, 1st Session, *Hearings before the Special* (Senate) *Committee on Taxation of Governmental Securities* 1939, p. 10.

TABLE 18

ESTIMATED ANNUAL ADDITIONAL INCOME TAX
RESULTING FROM THE REMOVAL OF TAX-EXEMPTION [a]

(by type of taxpayer and type of security held)

(million dollars)

	Present holders of obligations of State and local governments, territories and possessions	*Present holders of obligations of the U. S. Government and Federal agencies*	*Total*
Minimum estimates			
Individuals	92	39	131
Corporations	15	33	48
Total, individuals and corporations	107	72	179
Maximum estimates			
Individuals	184	84	268
Corporations	14	55	69
Total, individuals and corporations	198	139	337

[a] 76th Congress, 1st Session, *Hearings before the Committee on Ways and Means on Tax-Exempt Securities*, p. 39.

Undersecretary Hanes estimated much lower savings, $19,000,000 to $50,000,000 for the federal government, and $40,000,000 to $105,000,000 for state and local governments.[42]

The most important reason that tax exemption of securities has continued is the practical one that the states want it, and the federal government has also wanted to borrow as cheaply as it could. They fear that if their securities were taxed their credit would be impaired. Even if they were not seriously hindered in securing funds, interest costs would be increased at the very time they have most difficulty in securing adequate tax revenue. Garner pointed out the real obstruction when he, as a member of the House in 1922, asked McFadden, then appearing before the Committee on Ways and Means to

[42] Using 1937 data, Professor Lutz estimated the net loss of the states at $96,000,000 (loss of $113,000,000 less gain of $17,000,000), the net gain of the federal government, $90,000,000 (gain of $120,000,000 less loss of $30,000,000), if tax exemption were abolished. Undersecretary Magill placed the latter figure at $40,000,000. Mr. Roy Blough of the Treasury criticized Professor Lutz's estimates. 76th Congress, 1st Session, *Hearings before the* [Senate] *Committee on Taxation of Government Securities and Salaries* 1939, p. 188.

urge a constitutional amendment, just how long it would take the several states to ratify an amendment to tax their own securities.

EXECUTIVE AND CONGRESSIONAL INTEREST IN PREVENTING TAX AVOIDANCE

As long as the income tax rates were low, and while the federal government was interested in disposing of large amounts of bonds at the beginning of the World War, there was little inclination to raise the issue of tax-free income from bonds. When, however, income tax rates, especially the war surtax rates, were raised to unprecedented heights, non-taxable income became a matter of importance. Some taxpayers received more benefit from the exemption than others. In other words, from the standpoint of the taxpayer, the possession of tax-exempt securities was a legal means of tax avoidance. From the standpoint of the federal government, such avoidance meant a loss of revenue when the costs of borrowing had to be met.

Several secretaries of the Treasury gave the subject some passing reference, but Secretary Mellon made it an issue. He considered it a "grave economic evil," and during his entire term of office agitated for restriction of further issues of tax-exempt securities. To this end he wrote articles – even a book – sent appeals to important committees in Congress, and saw to it that the President mentioned the subject in his speeches. He coupled his plea for elimination of tax exemption with that for reduction of the surtax on the ground that such high rates drive taxpayers to seek means of escape. He succeeded in getting reductions of the surtax rates, but no effective legislation on tax-exempt securities. Many resolutions for constitutional amendments were introduced, but little interest was shown.

With the advent of the New Deal, and the imposition of higher surtax rates, interest was again revived in preventing tax avoidance, including that which was made possible by investing in government securities. President Roosevelt, however, was hampered during the first five years of his administration by a conservative Supreme Court, and apparently he considered it futile to urge legislation contrary to the traditional intergovernmental-immunity doctrine. He also knew that a constitutional amendment would be a slow if not an impossible achievement.

An opportune time for some legislation, at least, on tax-exempt salaries, was offered after the decision of the Court in the case of the Port of New York Authority, cited above. In January 1939 the President sent a special message to Congress at a time when a special Senate Committee on Tax Exemption was conducting hearings. He asked for immediate legislation (1) to subject to federal and state taxes private income from all future government salaries and from all government securities issued thereafter, and (2) to prevent retroactive taxation of salaries of employees of the Port of New York Authority. As already mentioned, the result was the passage of the Public Salary Tax Act of 1939.

SUMMARY OF THE ACT [43]

The Public Salary Tax Act is in the form of an amendment to the Internal Revenue Code and contains two titles : Title I amends the definition of gross income (1) to include compensation of personal services of officers and employees of a state or political subdivision thereof received after December 31, 1938 ; (2) to repeal the exemption of compensation of teachers in Alaska and Hawaii ; (3) to include compensation of judges of courts of the United States who took office before June 6, 1932. The fourth section of the title permits non-discriminatory state taxation of compensation of federal employees and officers received after December 31, 1938.

Title II specifies that income tax upon compensation of state officers or employees cannot be collected under certain circumstances for any taxable year beginning prior to January 1, 1939, and provides for refunds in certain cases, within the applicable period of limitation, of any such tax paid for prior years. It forbids state taxation of compensation of federal officers and employees received prior to January 1, 1939.

The Act was approved April 12, 1939.

THE REVENUE ACT OF 1939 — END OF THE UNDISTRIBUTED-PROFITS TAX

Persistent objections to the undistributed-profits tax continued even after the passage of the Revenue Act of 1938 reduced the rate to 2½% and restricted its application to corporations with net income of more than $25,000. The agitation against this levy was doubtless strengthened by business conditions which failed to show much improvement prior to the end of the fiscal year 1939. Part of the continuing recession was probably the result of the uncertainties in international affairs, but much of it was due to fear of New Deal measures. Even the "business appeasement" talks given by Secretary Morgenthau, Secretary of Commerce Hopkins, and Undersecretary Hanes failed to relieve the "jitteriness" of business convinced that a permanent change of policy could not be inaugurated under the Administration in power.

[43] 53 *Statutes at Large* 574.

The President, in fact, was very insistent that the undistributed-profits tax be continued. It will be recalled that he refused to sign the Revenue Act of 1938 largely because Congress had retained only a remnant of this tax. Throughout the spring of 1939 he defended the basic theory of the tax and challenged Congress to find a substitute that would encourage distribution of dividends equally well.

Meanwhile a subcommittee of Congress was working on a comprehensive program in harmony with Undersecretary Hanes' plan to "make it clear that it is the intention of the Government to establish a tax system which preserves and increases the incentives that are essential to the perpetuation of a system of free enterprise in a nation of free men." [44] The President hoped to sidetrack this plan by pushing through Congress a concurrent resolution to continue existing taxes. Chairman Harrison, however, was opposed to this maneuver.

For some months this deadlock continued. The President finally agreed not to insist on retaining the undistributed-profits tax, if Congress would strengthen the penalty sections for undue accumulation of corporate surpluses, and if it would not reduce the revenue below that to be obtained from existing laws. Inasmuch as Congress was thereby restricted from removing any important taxes or reducing important tax rates, plans were abandoned for a comprehensive revision of the tax structure at that session.[45]

Fair taxation in harmony with economic recovery was the underlying theme of the speech of the Secretary of the Treasury before the Committee on Ways and Means late in May 1939. Although the immediate need was for legislation to continue taxes scheduled to

[44] Hanes' recommendations were set forth by himself and by Secretary Morgenthau as follows: (1) formation of a joint committee on fiscal policy, to consider the over-all prospects of the expenditure and revenue programs; (2) creation of a small temporary national commission to report, as soon as feasible, on the subject of overlapping Federal, State, and local taxes; (3) the renewal of the present excise taxes; (4) stopping the issuance of tax-exempt securities by Federal, State, and local governments; (5) revision of the social security taxes; (6) removal from the tax laws of any manifest inequities or other defects; (7) consideration of certain features of the tax structure which have been characterized as "deterrents" to business expansion and investment, such as (*a*) the absence of provision in our income tax laws for carry-over of net business losses to be deducted from business profits in future years, and (*b*) the surtax rates in the higher brackets; (8) reexamination of another group of features in our tax system that have been described as "tax irritants," such as (*a*) the undistributed-profits tax, and (*b*) the capital stock and excess profits tax; and (9) revision of the laws to eliminate inequities such as the limitation on the deduction of corporation capital losses. (76th Congress, 1st Session, *Hearings before the Committee on Ways and Means on Revenue Revision* 1939, p. 250.) After the Revenue Act of 1939 was passed the Chairman of the Committee on Ways and Means appointed a subcommittee under the chairmanship of Cooper to study (1) removal of business deterrents from the tax law, and (2) revision of surtax brackets to lessen the punitive effects of high rates. The work already started on the taxation of government securities was continued.

[45] New York *Times*, March 23, May 14, 15, 26, 1939. Congress did not amend the penalty sections, hence the Treasury drafted more stringent regulations. They are described by Godfrey Nelson, New York *Times*, Aug. 27, 1939.

expire in 1939 (excise taxes, June 30; undistributed corporation profits taxes, December 31) the Secretary emphasized the broad aspects of a fiscal policy to insure the successful operation of a democratic form of government. To this end he advocated a fiscal program with the following four objectives:

> (1) Promotion of free enterprise and private investment, (2) attainment of full business recovery, (3) maintenance of our public finances in a sound and unassailable position, and (4) a just distribution of tax burdens and a more equitable distribution of national income.

The Secretary recognized that a comprehensive revision of the tax structure was not feasible at that time; nevertheless, he admonished the Committee to give serious attention to removing from the tax laws "any manifest inequities or other defects," particularly the features of the tax system that (1) hindered business expansion and investment, (2) were irritating, and (3) were inequitable. In the first category the Secretary referred to the absence of provision in the income tax laws for carrying over net business losses as deductions in succeeding years, and to the inequity of permitting tax exempt securities to "nullify our progressive surtax rates." In the second group, "tax irritants," the Secretary included the taxes on undistributed profits, capital stock, and excess profits. The undistributed-profits tax he characterized as a "psychological irritant, largely because of the widespread and emotional criticism which has been directed against it." As an example of inequitable provisions, the Secretary cited the limitation restricting deductions of corporate capital losses to $2000 in excess of capital gains. In concluding his testimony the Secretary repeated "with deep conviction" a sentence from his statement of November 1937:

> The basic need is to foster the full application of the driving force of private capital. We want to see capital go into the productive channels of private industry. We want to see private business expand.

Questions from Committee members failed to secure from the Secretary an estimate of the corporation tax rate that would be needed to make up the $17,500,000, estimated as the yield of the 2½ per-cent undistributed-profits tax for the fiscal year 1939, and the $17,600,000 from the capital stock and excess-profits taxes if these levies were repealed, as the Secretary "timidly" suggested.[46] Republican members, especially Jenkins and Treadway, were less timid in chiding their opponents for coming around at last to see the mistake of the tax on undistributed earnings. The Secretary and Democratic members took this banter in good spirits, so the first

[46] Everyone present was aware of the President's long insistence on retention of the undistributed-profits tax.

session ended in general good will and agreement as to the nature of the bill that should be reported. The remaining days of the hearings were occupied with testimony from business men, most of whom urged the abolition of the undistributed-profits tax.

READY ACCEPTANCE OF THE BILL BY THE COMMITTEE AND THE HOUSE

All ten Republican Committee members signed the report of the Committee on Ways and Means, although they expressed regret over the following three features: (1) continuance of the nuisance taxes and the three-cent postage rate, (2) delay of repeal of the undistributed-profits tax from January 1, 1939 to January 1, 1940, and (3) non-allowance of loss-carryover provision applicable to 1939 income.

The Committee report was very short and devoted chiefly to the discontinuance of the small segment of the undistributed-profits tax on corporations with income in excess of $25,000, and the substitution of a flat-rate 18 per-cent net income tax for the 1938 graduated normal rates applicable to such corporations. Other income tax rates of the Act of 1938 were left unchanged. More liberal allowance was made for corporation losses from sale of capital assets. Several technical improvements were made to remedy the confusion caused by recent court decisions.[47] The excess-profits and capital-stock taxes were not repealed.

After a four-hour debate and rejection of the few amendments offered, the bill passed the House on June 19, with only one dissenting vote, that of Tinkham (Rep., Mass.).

SUMMARY OF HOUSE MEASURE

The House measure extended the excise taxes but dealt mostly with corporation tax changes occasioned by the early expiration of the undistributed-profits tax; it scarcely touched individual income taxes. The principal changes it made in the existing law may be outlined briefly.

1. For taxable years beginning after December 31, 1939, taxpayers were permitted to carry over their net operating business losses for two years.

2. Corporations were given the right to increase their capital-stock tax valuations for the fiscal years 1939 and 1940 but not to decrease them.

3. The undistributed-profits tax was allowed to expire December 31, 1939. A tax of 18% of net income was imposed on corporations with incomes above $25,000. No change was made in the tax im-

[47] 76th Congress, 1st Session, *House Report* 855.

posed by existing law on other domestic corporations, nor in that on foreign corporations not engaged in trade or business within the United States.

4. A "notch" provision was designed to prevent unduly heavy levies on corporations with income slightly in excess of $25,000.

5. Banks, insurance companies, China Trade Act corporations, and corporations in the possessions of the United States were taxed at the same rates as other corporations.

6. Foreign corporations engaged in a trade or business within the United States and mutual investment companies were taxed at 18%, regardless of the amount of their income.

7. Corporations in bankruptcy or receivership and joint-stock land banks were treated like other corporations. The special treatment in the 1938 law necessitated by the undistributed-profits tax was abandoned.

8. The $2000 limitation to capital losses of corporations was repealed except for domestic and foreign personal holding companies.

9. At the request of the American Railroad Association and the American Bar Association, a provision was enacted to allow a corporation in an unsound financial condition to redeem its bonds at less than face value for the next three years, without recognition of gain.

10. At the suggestion of the American Bar Association provision was made for a corporation to assume the debts of another corporation in the process of reorganization without tax liability. This provision was made to clarify the law in view of the Supreme Court decision in *U. S.* v. *Hendler* (303 U. S. 564, 1938) which established a rule contrary to that which had been followed generally by the Treasury.

11. A provision was enacted to validate a Treasury regulation for establishing a basis for computing gain or loss from sale of stock received as a dividend. Because of confusion resulting from divergence of Treasury rulings and decisions of the Supreme Court, a taxpayer might have had to pay a very high tax because he was deprived of any cost basis (*Helvering* v. *Gowran,* 302 U. S. 238, 1937), or he might have paid a very low tax if he had been allowed an excessively high basis. The Treasury ruled that, where a stock dividend was declared, the basis for determining gain or loss in case of sale was to be determined by allocating between the old stock and the new stock the adjusted basis of the old stock, under regulations of the Commissioner.

12. The excise taxes scheduled to expire in June and July 1939 were extended for two years.

THE BILL QUICKLY PASSED IN THE SENATE

A filibuster by currency expansionists who were trying to get a higher price for silver delayed Senate consideration of the tax bill until a truce was arranged.[48] The tax measure as introduced was very little different from that passed by the House.

La Follette surprised Administration forces by getting acceptance of his amendment to increase individual surtaxes on incomes between $6000 and $100,000 but, on a recapitulation of votes, Tydings shifted from "yea" to "nay," so a tie resulted and his amendment failed.

Daneher (Rep., Conn.) secured support for an amendment to penalize the commercial use of income tax lists and Walsh offered a successful amendment to extend to Guam and Samoa the same internal revenue laws relating to exemption of goods shipped from the United States as applied to Puerto Rico.

The measure was passed without a roll call and without a dissenting vote. It was sent to the House for quick approval of the few Senate changes, and was signed by the President on June 29. Revenue yield was estimated at $1,644,300,000,[49] about $5,000,000 less than expected from the House bill or from the existing law.

SUMMARY OF THE REVENUE ACT OF 1939 [50]

This Act consists of four titles amending the Internal Revenue Code: Title I – Excise Taxes and Postal Rates; Title II – Income Tax Amendments; Title III – Capital Stock and Excess Profits Taxes; Title IV – Miscellaneous Amendments.

Title I – Excise Taxes and Postal Rates. Existing excise taxes and postal rates were continued to 1941.

Title II – Income Tax Amendments. This title dealt chiefly with the corporation sections of the income tax law. For corporations with net income of more than $25,000 there was imposed the lesser of the following taxes:

(1) 18% of net income; or

(2) a tax of $3525 plus 32% of the amount of the normal tax net income in excess of $25,000.

[48] In order to improve relations with the Treasury, according to current gossip. (New York *Times*, June 23, 1939.)

[49] *Cong. Rec.* 84: 7463-7503 (House debate); 7685-7708 (Senate debate).

[50] 53 *Statutes at Large* 862.

For corporations with net income of not more than $25,000 the tax was left as in the existing law, that is, as follows:

(1) upon net income not in excess of $5000, 12½%;
(2) $625 on net income of $5000 and on net income in excess of $5000 and not in excess of $20,000, 14%;
(3) $2725 on net income of $20,000, and 16% upon net income in excess of $20,000.

Long-term capital losses of corporations could be deducted from any income, but short-term capital losses were allowable only to the extent of short-term capital gains. An additional allowance was granted by permitting corporations to carry over net short-term capital losses to the succeeding taxable year.

Individuals and corporations were permitted to carry over net operating losses for two years, beginning in 1940. A new provision was enacted to tax individual compensation received for personal services covering a five-year period, so that after December 31, 1938 the tax would not be greater "than the aggregate of the taxes attributable to such compensation had it been received in equal portions in each of the years included in such period."

Title III – Capital Stock and Excess Profits Taxes. This title made no changes in the rates of either of these taxes, but merely provided for new declarations of capital stock value, 1939 and 1940, under certain specified conditions.

Title IV – Miscellaneous Amendments. One important change of this title was to clarify the provisions in regard to freeing purchasers of securities from federal liens on securities when they were purchased in good faith and without knowledge of the existence of the lien.

It was made unlawful to sell any information derived from income tax returns.

The Act went into effect when signed, June 29, 1939. The income tax sections were applicable to taxable years beginning after December 31, 1939.

CHAPTER XXI

EVOLUTION OF THE DEFINITION OF TAXABLE INCOME

SPECIAL CONSIDERATION OF CERTAIN SUBJECTS

Each of the important federal income tax laws enacted since the Civil War has been discussed in the preceding chapters; that is, the various laws have been discussed chronologically, and the various issues taken up at each revision have been discussed in their relation to each other as well as in their relation to various political and economic pressures of the times. If space permitted, it would be desirable also to treat each of the most important issues topically; that is, to devote a long chapter or even a volume to rates and exemptions, another to capital gains and losses, another to depreciation, obsolescence, and depletion, another to corporate reorganizations, and so on. Though it is not possible to give such a complete cross section or double treatment in the present volume, it does seem desirable to have a brief topical discussion of the development of: (1) the definition of taxable income, (2) rates and exemptions, and (3) the administration of the law. This will serve to summarize and unify to some extent a few points and issues already touched upon from time to time in different chapters and, besides, it will offer the opportunity to mention some additional related and significant considerations that will aid in understanding the evolution of the income tax.

In discussing various phases of the development of the federal income tax in the preceding chapters only fragmentary references have been made to the concept of income or to the evolution of the definition of taxable income. Our first federal income tax was provided for in a single short paragraph of the general revenue Act of 1861; the income tax Act of 1938 covered 152 pages, and the Commissioner's regulations for its administration ran to 741 pages.[1] The framers of our first income tax law, aside from making a few general statements and implications, refrained from defining the tax base; in the Act of 1938 Congress approached the other extreme — statutory income was proliferated into more than a dozen varieties, each defined in highly technical phraseology.

It is not possible nor even desirable to discuss exhaustively in this volume all of the details of the evolution in definition since 1861;

[1] The latest revenue act at this writing, that of 1939, was drafted as an amendment to the Internal Revenue Code and affected only a few sections of the law.

in fact, all that seems feasible here is a brief sketch of some of the outstanding developments, particularly of those developments which relate to some of the more difficult or controversial problems that have arisen since the adoption of the Sixteenth Amendment, though with some references to a few of the Civil War precedents. Perhaps a few samples of the technical provisions should be included so that the lay reader may get some idea of the character of the present law but, in order to keep within limitations of space, the treatment here must be illustrative and suggestive rather than detailed and comprehensive. Many other treatises are available for practitioners wishing to examine the law in all of its details. It seems desirable in this study to help the less specialized reader find the main currents of the stream.

SOME CONCEPTS OF ECONOMISTS

The following discussion relating to the development of the income tax law and its administration will be somewhat clearer if the reader keeps in mind not only the problems and ideas of the lawmakers and administrators but also certain basic doctrines and definitions of economists.[2] It is impossible to state briefly and at the same time adequately the economists' concepts and definitions, but the characteristic ideas of some of their representative schools of thought may be indicated.[3]

What may be called the traditional school, the one largely influenced by English ideas and practices, stresses recurrence and more or less regularity of income flow. This school would not normally include in taxable income occasional gains or receipts such as gifts, inheritances, profits from sale of one's residence or capital gains,

[2] "There are, therefore, reasons why the legal theory of income for income tax purposes cannot be expected to conform exactly to any of the various theories advanced by economists, but the character of the problem makes it desirable to take these latter at least as points of departure in developing the former. However much the economists' views may lack that definiteness that is essential to exact classification of situations into those that do, and that do not, involve income, they do represent the views of those best qualified to deal with such questions. Resort to the economists' theories in evaluating the legal theory is, therefore, legitimate, particularly in so far as the courts have supported their theory by economic analysis." (Rottschaefer, Henry, "Concept of Income in Federal Taxation," *Minnesota Law Review* 13: 638, June 1929.)

[3] Inasmuch as taxable income is defined by law, this discussion does not relate primarily to developments of economic concepts. See Hewett, William W., *The Definition of Income,* and Wueller, Paul H., "Concepts of Taxable Income," *Pol. Sci. Quart.* 53: 83, 557 (March, Dec. 1938) for much more adequate treatment from the standpoint of economists; Magill, *Taxable Income* and Rottschaefer, "Concept of Income in Federal Taxation," *Minnesota Law Review* 13:637 (June 1929), for summary analyses of the legal concept. See also Chapter XXIV, below, and *American Economic Review,* 28: Sup. 102 (March 1928).

Those who want fuller discussions can, of course, go to the official sources which run to many volumes. See bibliography in Appendix below. Important handbooks are Montgomery, Robert H., *Federal Tax Handbook* (for each Revenue Act) and Paul, Randolph E., and Mertens, Jacob, *Law of Federal Income Taxation* (1935, with Supplement 1938) 6 vol.

except those made by a regular dealer whose gains normally recur. One of the representative exponents of this theory is Professor Plehn of the University of California.[4]

Professor Haig of Columbia University may be taken as a representative of a quite different and more modern point of view. Haig's definition is: "Income is the money value of the net accretion to economic power between two points of time." He would include all realizable net economic gains, recurring and non-recurring, whether "realized" or not. Realizable capital appreciations and other gains, gifts, inheritances, windfalls, etc., would be included from the viewpoint of his economic theory, though Haig would probably grant that, under some conditions, economic considerations might well give way to legal "realization" requirements for the sake of administrative advantage.[5]

Professor Irving Fisher of Yale University may be taken as a representative of the "psychic income" school. For him, income is a flow of psychic satisfactions, rather than money or goods. Inasmuch as the measurement of psychic satisfactions presents insuperable administrative difficulties, Fisher suggests, as a practicable substitute, the taxing of consumption expenditures. He would exclude from income all receipts which are invested or saved during the taxable year. If, however, savings are consumed in a later year they are considered income of that year.[6]

None of these schools of economic thought has been followed closely or consistently either by American lawmakers or by American courts, but all of them have influenced the legal — the authoritative — definition of taxable income. Their ideas may be taken, therefore, as points of departure for the ensuing discussion of the development in connection with our federal tax.

Most of the issues which have been chosen to illustrate the evolution of the definition of taxable income in the following pages can be divided into a few groups. Perhaps they can be indicated by the following questions and examples, though the problems cut across or

[4] Plehn, Carl, "The Concept of Income, Recurrent Consumable Receipts," *American Economic Review* XIV: 1 (March 1924).

Professor E. R. A. Seligman of Columbia University, who has written much on income taxation and who has had a large influence on income tax legislation in the United States, has been much influenced by British theory and practice.

[5] Haig, Robert M., ed., *The Federal Income Tax* (Columbia University Lectures, 1921). G. von Schanz presented a similar theory in "Der Einkommensbegriff und die Einkommensteuergesetze," *Finanz Archiv* 1896, p. 1; cited in Wueller, Paul H., "Concepts of Taxable Income," *Political Science Quarterly,* 53: 83, 557 (March, Dec. 1938.)

[6] Fisher, Irving, *The Nature of Capital and Income* (1906); *Income Concept in the Light of Experience* (1928); "Income in Theory and Income Taxation in Practice," *Econometrica* V: 1. (Jan. 1937).

merge into each other so that there is no such definite demarcation between them as some may infer.

TYPICAL QUESTIONS AND PROBLEMS

1. Does taxable income mean gross receipts, gross income, net income, or something else?

2. Does taxable income mean receipt of gain in the form of money (cash), or money equivalent (income in kind—goods and services), or "real income" (gain in purchasing power), or "psychic income" in the sense of satisfaction from utilization of goods and services, or something else?

3. In order to qualify as income, must receipts be recurrent, or are occasional, irregular, or non-business receipts income? Consider, for example, windfalls, gifts, inheritances, lottery winnings, profits from sale of residence once in a lifetime, etc. Are corresponding outgoes negative income and properly deductible?

4. When, where, and by whom is income "realized" (or legally recognized) and therefore taxable? For example, is the amount of one's income to be determined by cash or by accrual accounting? When, if ever, are appreciations in the value of land, plant, or other capital properly taxable? Annually as they accrue, all in the year of sale, or when and how? Do exchanges and reorganizations, as well as sales, result in "realization" of income? What effects have the creation, operation, and reorganization of legal entities such as corporations and trusts on the "realization" of income?

5. Who defines income or determines taxable income? What are the respective roles of the legislative, executive, and judicial branches of the government? Do economists, accountants, business men, or laymen generally have any voice in the matter, or is everything decided by the lawmakers and the courts? [7]

GROSS INCOME, NET INCOME, OR SOMETHING ELSE?

Does taxable income mean gross receipts, gross income, net income, clear income, or something else?

The taxing power of Congress, though limited by the Constitution, has always been held broad enough to permit the levying of an income tax. The restriction emphasized, if not imposed, by the Pollock Case [8] related to the manner in which Congress exercised this power. The Court held that the tax on income from land and from certain other sources was a direct tax and therefore was invalid be-

[7] Logically this question may not belong with the others but it is relevant in any case.
[8] 157 U. S. 429; 158 U. S. 601. See above, Chap. II.

cause not apportioned among the states according to their respective populations as required by the Constitution. This restriction relative to apportionment of income taxation was removed by the Sixteenth Amendment, but it was not thus specifically removed from any other kind of taxation that the Court might hold to be direct; for example, a direct tax on capital would be subject to apportionment if capital is not income. Hence the importance of determining whether or not any tax base in controversy is income.

In the Civil War era, Congress levied gross receipts taxes as well as various other kinds of excises and fees on corporations; on individuals it imposed an income tax which was apparently intended to be on a net basis, though the statutes were not very specific. For the fiscal emergency created by the Spanish American War, Congress imposed an excise tax on the gross receipts of sugar refiners. The Supreme Court held this valid.[9] The corporation excise Act of 1909 provided for "net income" as a measure of that excise and net income has been the base for corporations as well as individuals under all federal income tax laws passed since the adoption of the Sixteenth Amendment.

Despite the statutory provision of "net income" in the Act of 1909, the Court did not permit the deduction of mine depletion in *Stratton's Independence* v. *Howbert*[10] which came under that Act. The Court said:

> It was reasonable that Congress should fix upon gross income, without distinction as to source, as a convenient and sufficiently accurate index of the importance of the business transacted. And from this point of view, it makes little difference that the income may arise from a business that theoretically or practically involves a wasting of capital.

Similar decisions under statutes passed after the adoption of the Sixteenth Amendment left considerable doubt as to the meaning of "income" as used in that amendment. For example, did it mean gross income as well as net income? Could Congress tax gross receipts as income if it so desired? This latter question as to the power of Congress has never been decided definitely and clearly, perhaps chiefly because the statutes under the Sixteenth Amendment say what shall be excluded and what may be deducted from gross income to arrive at the net which Congress wants to tax, but the income tax laws do not attempt to define or tax gross receipts. That is, most of the cases involving a definition of income require an interpretation of the intent of Congress rather than of its power under the Constitution.

[9] *Spreckels* v. *McLain*, 192 U. S. 397 (1904). An indirect tax is required to be uniform throughout the United States but is not required to be apportioned among the states according to population.

[10] 231 U. S. 399 (1913).

Eisner v. *Macomber* [11] was an exception; in that case it was held that Congress had attempted to exceed its powers by levying this tax on stock dividends, by taxing as income what was not income in fact. The assertion in that decision that income is *gain* would appear to rule out both gross receipts and gross income, but possibly this interpretation in this and various other decisions was of the statutory intent rather than of the constitutional authority. It appears more probable, however, that the Court intended to define a "constitutional concept" and that it phrased its definition with reference to the facts of the case before it without envisaging other situations.

In *Doyle* v. *Mitchell Bros. Co.,*[12] a case under the 1909 excise Act decided a few years after *Stratton's Independence* v. *Howbert,* the Court rendered the first of a series of decisions interpreting the intent of Congress as to gross receipts, gross income, and net income. It rejected the contention of the Solicitor General that "gross income" was equivalent to "gross receipts" and said that the intent of the law was not to tax the entire proceeds from the conversion of capital assets.

There was a distinction between capital and income "either as a subject of taxation or as a measure of the tax." The Court held:

> In order to determine whether there has been gain or loss, and the amount of the gain, if any, we must withdraw from the gross proceeds an amount sufficient to restore the capital value that existed at the commencement of the period under consideration.[13]

With a few exceptions, some of which will be mentioned below, the general trend of decisions has been to permit Congress to tax what gross income it sees fit to tax, particularly in view of the fact that in practice it attempts to tax little if anything more than certain parts of net income (as it defines net), which is only a fraction of the total gross income which it might tax, so far as constitutional limitations are concerned.

In 1920 the Court held invalid the section of the 1918 Act that specifically included in gross income the compensation of the President of the United States and also that of federal judges. This section was held to violate the provisions of Article 3 of the Constitution which stated that salaries of these officials should not be reduced during the terms of office for which they had been elected or appointed.[14]

11 252 U. S. 189 (1920).

12 247 U. S. 179 (1918).

13 *Doyle* v. *Mitchell Bros. Co.*, 247 U. S. 179 (1918).

14 *Evans* v. *Gore,* 253 U. S. 245. This case involved the tax on salary of a judge appointed in 1899. In 1925 the Court ruled that the tax could not be imposed on the salary of a judge taking office after the enactment of the 1918 law. (*Miles* v. *Graham,* 268 U. S. 501.) In 1939 the Court rejected the reasoning that payment of the income tax involved a reduction of compensation within the meaning of the Constitution (*O'Malley* v. *Woodrough,* 59 S. Ct. 838, May 22, 1939.)

This judicial restriction was circumvented by the following clause which was incorporated in the 1932 and succeeding revenue acts.

> In the case of Presidents of the United States and judges of courts of the United States taking office after June 6, 1932, the compensation received as such shall be included in gross income; and all Acts fixing the compensation of such Presidents and judges are hereby amended accordingly.

Another important type of gross income excluded from taxable income for implied constitutional reasons has been the income from bonds of states and their subdivisions. In view of the Court's decisions relative to one government's interference with another government's functions, Congress has specified that such income is not taxable.[15] For the same reason the Treasury Regulations have exempted from the tax salaries of officials and employees of states and their subdivisions. But in 1938 and 1939 the Court made several important decisions that opened the way for reciprocal federal and state taxation of government officers and employees.[16] In 1939, therefore, Congress imposed the income tax on compensation of state officers and employees received after December 31, 1938, and permitted non-discriminatory state taxation of federal officers and employees.[17]

Thus the Court has indicated some of the boundaries of Congressional power to tax gross income. It has not, however, attempted to delimit the deductions from gross income to arrive at a taxable net basis. Such deductions have been held to be within the sphere of Congressional action, the Constitution does not require Congress to grant them. In fact, it has been held that so far as the Constitution is concerned the income tax could be levied on gross income. In a 1934 opinion the Supreme Court said:

> Unquestionably Congress has power to condition, limit, or deny deductions from gross income in order to arrive at the net that it chooses to tax.[18]

15 Until 1938 the Court followed the course of reasoning laid down in *McCulloch* v. *Maryland*, 4 Wheat. 316 (1819); *Collector* v. *Day*, 11 *Wall.* 113 (1870). The historical argument and the recent objections to it are summarized in U. S. Dept. of Justice, *Taxation of Government Bondholders and Employees*, 1938.

16 *Helvering* v. *Gerhardt*, 304 U. S. 405 (1938); *Allen, Collector* v. *University of Georgia*, 304 U. S. 439 (1938); *Graves et al* v. *N. Y. ex rel O'Keefe*, 59 S. Ct. 595 (1939); *O'Malley* v. *Woodrough*, 59 S. Ct. 838 (1939).

17 See above, Chap. XX.

18 *Helvering* v. *Independent Life Ins. Co.*, 292 U. S. 371 (1934). See also *Burnet* v. *Thompson Oil and Gas Co.*, 283 U. S. 301 (1931); *Doyle* v. *Mitchell Bros. Co.*, 247 U. S. 179 (1918); *Stanton* v. *Baltic Mining Co.*, 240 U. S. 103 (1916); *Stratton's Independence* v. *Howbert*, 231 U. S. 399 (1913).

In 1929 Professor Henry Rottschaefer thought that no one could determine definitely from the apparently conflicting decisions under what conditions the Court would decide that income might be gross and under what conditions it must be net income, in order to be taxable without apportionment, especially in view of the emphasis on "gain" in

In general, the deductions allowed under the laws have been business or professional, but not personal expenses. A few exceptions have been made, for example, the following personal expenses may be deducted: taxes on the taxpayer's home; contributions to organizations for philanthropic, educational, or religious purposes; and interest paid out, regardless of the reason for the debt incurred, except for purchase of tax-exempt securities.

Since the depression of the 1930's, with the consequent decline in income tax yield accompanied by increased needs for government revenue, there has been a tightening of the laws and regulations, especially a closer scrutiny of depreciation and depletion. The English income tax law does not permit deductions for depreciation of buildings but does allow expenditures for repairs when made.[19] All of the United States laws since 1913 have provided for deductions of estimated depreciation of tangible property and of such intangibles as copyrights, patents, and contracts when the life of the asset is limited as to time. These deductions are the largest permitted by the law on a basis of estimate and are contrary to the general principle that loss, like gain, must be "realized" by sale, exchange, or some other definite transaction.[20] The Treasury and the Joint Committee on Internal Revenue Taxation have frequently been concerned over the enormity of these deductions and in 1934 Congress proposed rather drastic legislative reductions. The Treasury, however, preferred to handle the matter by administrative regulations.[21]

To summarize: Congress is not required to tax all of the income which it may tax; it has chosen to tax net income as it defines net income. After saying certain things shall be excluded from gross income, the law says that net income is gross income less certain specified deductions. Thus we have a very technical legal definition that does not correspond exactly with the definitions of accountants, economists, or anybody else. It is supposed to approximate what is generally understood as net income but, because of personal exemptions granted, the income that is actually taxed is a rough approximation of what some economists designate "clear income," that is, net

---

Eisner v. *Macomber* (252 U. S. 189, 1920) and *Goodrich* v. *Edwards* (255 U. S. 527, 1921). "The Concept of Income in Federal Taxation" (*Minnesota Law Review*, 13: 642, June 1929.)

[19] Konstam, E. M., *The Law of Income Tax*, p. 157.

[20] For the last six years for which data are available depreciation deductions taken by all corporations were as follows: 1930, $3,986,000,000; 1931, $4,003,000,000; 1932, $3,693,000,000; 1933, $3,496,000,000; 1934, $3,362,000,000; 1935, $3,352,000,000. The "compiled net profit or loss" of these corporations for the same years were: 1930, +$4,649,000,000; 1931, —$777,000,000; 1932, —$3,829,000,000; 1933, —$930,000,000; 1934, +$2,970,000,000; 1935, +$5,423,000,000.

The average annual "compiled net income" for these years was $1,084,500,000, after deducting average annual depreciation of $3,648,000,000. (U. S. Treasury *Statistics of Income* 1935, pp. 11, 24, 40.)

[21] See above, Chap. XIV.

income in excess of a minimum of subsistence or a minimum of efficiency.[22]

MONEY INCOME, REAL INCOME, OR PSYCHIC INCOME?

Controversies have arisen as to whether taxable income should be confined to income received in the form of money or whether it should include income in kind, usances, and other valuable considerations. A somewhat similar controversy is involved in the suggestion that money income should be converted into "real income," and certain economists go so far as to advocate the use of "psychic income" as the proper tax base.

The framers and administrators of modern income tax laws have almost always thought of the tax base as money income or its equivalent, that is, cognizance has been taken of income in kind and of "real income" at times, though, in practice, many exceptions have been made for administrative and other reasons. For example, allowance has not been made for increase or decrease in real income caused by fluctuations in the purchasing power of United States money. The failure to do this causes much injustice, and would cause much more if we should have serious inflation or deflation, but general application would lead to endless administrative difficulties, many of them very serious. The taxation of "psychic income" has appealed to certain theorists only and even they would modify their definition radically to meet administrative difficulties.[23]

In fact, most legislators and administrators think it unwise to tax even all usances and incomes in kind. The rental value of a home occupied by the taxpayer was specifically excluded from gross income in several of the Civil War Acts and, by administrative ruling, it has not been considered taxable income under later laws.[24] Simi-

[22] Magill's conclusion on this aspect of taxable income is as follows: The several lines of cases discussed above do not outline very definitely the boundaries of the term "income," with reference to the necessity for deductions, largely because Congress has, in general, allowed those deductions which business practice dictates, and thus the question has not been put to the test. Notwithstanding the *Pollock* case, it is likely that the Court today would accept the view that an income tax is an excise tax. Such a tax can constitutionally be measured by gross income. The Court, apparently following this analysis, has repeatedly stated, and in some cases it has held, that deductions are wholly within the power of Congress to grant, condition, or deny; and a number of instances where gross income has been taxed can be cited. Hence, "income," as used in the amendment, has in effect been given at times the meaning of "gross income." Nevertheless, the general emphasis the Court has placed upon the necessity for a gain or profit, coupled with such decisions as *Doyle* v. *Mitchell Bros. Co.*, indicates that it would be unwise to assume that "income" in the amendment means gross receipts. With the possible exception of the mining depletion cases, which seem to stand upon a peculiar footing of their own, some provision for the recoupment of the cost of goods sold, or of the investment, must be made. (Magill, *Taxable Income*, p. 329. Quoted by express permission of The Ronald Press).

[23] What they advocate as practical is the taxation of expenditures for things consumed within the taxable year. But see footnote 29, below.

[24] In 1911 the Wisconsin state income tax law included such income.

larly, neither cash value of farm produce consumed by the farmer's family, nor estimated value of service of a housewife or member of the family (agricultural or other) has been included in gross income.

The laws have, however, always recognized some income received in forms other than money. For example, the 1938 and other laws use the phrase "in whatever form paid"; thus farm rent received from a tenant whether paid in cash or in crops, and the value of corporation stock, meals, living quarters, or other perquisites with which services are paid for are considered taxable income. Certain exceptions are made to this rule, however. The value of quarters for officers and enlisted personnel of the Army, Navy, Coast Guard and Geodetic Survey, and Public Health Service are excluded from gross income. In one case the Court of Claims held that such rental value should not be included in gross income because living quarters were furnished for the convenience of the employer. This rule of convenience has been adopted by the Bureau of Internal Revenue.[25] When property is exchanged for other property, the rule adopted by the Treasury is that the fair market value of the thing taken in payment is the basis for computing the amount to be included in taxable income. The difficulties encountered in administering and interpreting "fair market value" are illustrated in the complexities of the reorganization and exchange provisions discussed elsewhere in this chapter.[26]

In general the statutes and regulations have provided that taxpayers must report income "constructively received" as well as that actually received. For example, interest received is income when due and payable, even though the coupons are not actually cashed until the next fiscal year; dividends from corporation stock are income when unqualifiedly made subject to demand of the shareholder, even though the dividend check may be cashed in a later year; [27] interest on savings bank deposits is income when credited, even though not drawn by the depositor until later.

On the other hand, not all monetary receipts are considered taxable income. Examples are gifts, bequests, and alimony. If, however, gifts are really payments for services rendered, they are taxable. In the case of an alleged gift by a corporation it is generally held that there is a heavy burden of proof on both the donor and the donee, on the theory that the directors would not give away the corporation's money. Commissions, fees, and tips received are taxable also.

[25] *Jones* v. *U. S.*, 60 Ct. Cl. 522 (1925). The 1938 regulations state: "If living quarters such as camps are furnished to employees for the convenience of the employer, the ratable value need not be added to the cash compensation of the employees. . ."

[26] See below, pp. 492-495.

[27] If a dividend check is received too late to cash within the year declared, it may be counted as income of the next year, if taxpayer reports on a cash basis. See Regulations 101 (1938), Art. 42—3.

The Supreme Court sustained the statutory requirement that income from an irrevocable trust used to pay insurance premiums on the life of the grantor for the benefit of relatives, employees, and others after his death was taxable income of the grantor.[28] According to Magill, it was "Justice Cardozo's basic conception that Congress may tax as income a benefit to the taxpayer essentially similar to the economist's flow of satisfactions. . . Hence we come to the core of the decision – that the 'economic realities of enjoyment or fruition' may validly be treated by Congress as the equivalent of ownership of the income." [29] This, perhaps, is as near an approach to validation of the psychic income concept as we shall find in practical application. It is also an illustration of the force of economic realities in shaping the evolving definition of income.

RECURRENCE AND REGULARITY OF INCOME

It has been a common view that, to be included in income, receipts should be of the type that recur more or less regularly, that most occasional and casual receipts should not normally be used for current consumptive expenditures but should be saved and added to capital, particularly if such receipts or gains are inherited or arise from the "realization" of capital assets.

The first three Civil War income tax laws (Acts of 1861, 1862, 1864) provided for the taxation of "annual" income. Even these laws as administered, however, provided for the taxation of certain irregular income and capital gains. The Act of 1894 added another category of income, money and personal property acquired by inheritance or gift. The Act of 1909 specified that the tax was measured by "the entire net income . . . received . . . from all sources."

Since the adoption of the Sixteenth Amendment, the income tax laws have assumed an annual accounting but, with a few exceptions, casual as well as regular gains have been considered income. Most gifts and inheritances have been excluded, presumably because they have been considered transfers of capital rather than income and probably partly because inheritances, and recently certain gifts, have been subject to special taxes.[30] Nevertheless, the law is not entirely consistent on this point. In certain cases, gifts in the form of income from a trust may or may not be taxable; [31] a government bonus to a

28 *Burnet* v. *Wells*, 289 U. S. 670 (1933).
29 Magill, *Taxable Income*, p. 240.
30 But see Magill, *Taxable Income*, p. 390.
31 The subject of trusts is a complicated one. The general underlying principle is that income is taxable to the beneficiary if the income is distributed to him but to the grantor if he remains in control of the income or if the income is used for his benefit or satisfaction. It is sometimes taxed to the trustee.

railroad company in Cuba for construction was not considered a gift or taxable income but a capital contribution to promote public interest; [32] contributions by a chamber of commerce in the form of land, buildings, etc., to corporations for encouragement of new industries are not considered income.

From the viewpoint of some economists there is a difference between income derived from capital and profit derived from the sale of capital. From the viewpoint of the taxpayer, it is questionable justice to tax in a single year appreciation in value of capital or earnings accumulated over a period of years. In drafting revenue measures, however, Congress has been guided by the thought that such receipts represent taxpaying ability, even though they may be difficult to allocate to years of accrual as equity might require; [33] moreover, much revenue might be lost if they were disregarded. Therefore, the laws have been administered on the theory that capital gains are taxable income for the year of "realization," even though the statutes made no specific reference to such income until 1921.

The courts have generally upheld this interpretation of the law and, since the adoption of the Sixteenth Amendment, there has been no insistence on regularity or recurrence of income, although a Civil War case [34] and one in 1915 [35] indicated a trend towards the British point of view, namely, that income is recurrent and that capital gain is merely an increase in capital and not subject to tax as income. These cases have not been followed, however, as precedents for recent decisions.

The question of including as income of the year sold the gain from an isolated investment in stock bought in 1902 and sold in 1911 came up under the corporation excise Act of 1909.[36] The Circuit Court of Appeals, relying on *Gray* v. *Darlington,* held the profit not taxable, but it was overruled by the Supreme Court which held that the measure of this tax, "income *received during* such year . . . looks to the time of realization rather than to the period of accrue-

[32] *Edwards* v. *Cuba RR. Co.,* 268 U. S. 628 (1925). For comments on the fallacious reasoning and inconsistencies in this and other decisions see Rottschaefer, Henry, "Concept of Income in Federal Taxation," *Minnesota Law Review,* 13: 637-674, especially p. 668 (June 1929).

[33] The Revenue Act of 1939 amended the Internal Revenue Code by adding Section 107, which provides that the tax on income received in one year in payment for personal services covering a period of five years or more shall not be greater than if spread over the years earned.

[34] In *Gray* v. *Darlington* (15 Wall. 63) the Court upheld the contention of a taxpayer that his capital gains from the exchange and sale of United States securities held several years were not taxable to him in the year of sale, under the 1867 Act. The 1867 Act did provide, however, for the taxation of gains from the sale of real estate held two years.

[35] In *Lynch* v. *Turrish* (247 U. S. 221) the Court held that ". . . advance in value is not income at all, but merely increase of capital and not subject to a tax as income."

[36] *Hays* v. *Gauley Mountain Coal Company,* 247 U. S. 189 (1918). See also *U. S.* v. *Cleveland, Cincinnati, Chicago, St. Louis Railway Company,* 247 U. S. 195 (1918).

ment, except as the taking effect of the act on a specified date (January 1, 1909), excludes income that accrued before that date." [37]

In the case of *Eisner* v. *Macomber* the Supreme Court developed and summarized its definition of income as follows:

The fundamental relation of "capital" to "income" has been much discussed by economists, the former being likened to the tree or the land, the latter to the fruit or the crop; the former depicted as a reservoir supplied from springs, the latter as the outlet stream, to be measured by its flow during a period of time. For the present purpose we require only a clear definition of the term "income," as used in common speech. . .

After examining dictionaries in common use we find little to add to the succinct definition adopted in two cases arising under the Corporation Act of 1909. . . "Income may be defined as the gain derived from capital, from labor, or from both combined," provided it be understood to include profit gained through a sale or conversion of capital assets. . .[38]

The validity of taxing casual gains was questioned in the case of *Merchants' Loan and Trust* v. *Smietanka.* In answer to the contention that the word "income" in the Acts under the Sixteenth Amendment referred not to gain realized by a single isolated sale of property, but only to profits derived from buying and selling as a business, the Court said:

no such distinction was recognized in the Civil War Income Tax Act of 1867 or in the Act of 1894 . . . that it was not recognized in determining income under the Excise Tax Act of 1909, as the cases cited . . . show; that it is not to be found, in terms, in any of the income tax provisions of the Internal Revenue Acts of 1913, 1916, 1917, or 1919; that the definition of the word "income" as used in the Sixteenth Amendment, which has been developed by this Court, does not recognize any such distinction; that in departmental practice, for now seven years, such a rule has not been applied; and there is no essential difference in the nature of the transaction or in the relation of the profit to the capital involved, whether the sales or conversion be a single, isolated transaction, or one of many.[39]

Probably the most frequent cases of isolated transactions have been those involving sales of capital assets. English law, as is well known, has followed a policy of disregarding generally both gain and loss from sale of capital assets except in the case of those who make a business of buying and selling investments. The income tax laws of the United States have pursued a very different policy.

Each income tax law from the time of the Civil War to the present has contained some provision for the taxation of gains from sale of capital assets, although that term was not used in the statutes before 1921. From 1913 to 1916 gains realized by individuals from the sale

[37] See Magill, *Taxable Income,* pp. 92, 93.
[38] 252 U. S. 189 (1920).
[39] 255 U. S. 520 (1921).

of capital assets were taxable as ordinary income, that is, at the regular normal and surtax rates. No mention was made of losses except those incurred in trade; hence capital losses were not deductible. In 1916 the law was relaxed somewhat to allow deduction of such losses, but it restricted those of individuals to the amount of the capital gains. This was the rule in 1917 also. With respect to corporations the law remained unchanged from 1913 to 1931, all gains were taxable and all losses were deductible. In the Act of 1918 capital gains of individuals were taxable in full, and capital losses were deductible in full against income of any kind.

In drafting the Revenue Act of 1921 Congress was impressed not only by the complaints of taxpayers that the war taxes were too high and that they retarded normal business transactions,[40] but also by the argument of the Treasury that the government was not getting so large a yield of revenue as it would if rates were lower. The Administration adopted the policy of tax reduction after the World War and Congress changed radically the method of computing the tax on capital gains of individuals. For the first time the income tax law contained specific provisions for the taxation of gains from the sale of capital assets. If an individual so chose, gain from the sale of capital assets, defined as assets held more than two years, could be segregated from ordinary income and taxed at the special rate of 12½%, under certain conditions. This method, with some additional restrictions relative to the deduction of losses, was continued until 1934. At that time Congress adopted a schedule of percentages of gain to be included which decreased as the length of time the asset was held increased. A variation of this method was adopted in 1938.[41]

Difficulties in finding a satisfactory method of treating capital gains and losses are accentuated, on the one hand, by the Treasury fear of tax avoidance and smaller revenues and, on the other hand, by taxpayers' protests that business transactions are hampered.

REALIZATION OF GAIN OR LOSS

Is gain, including appreciation in capital assets, income as it accrues or only when it is "realized" by sale, exchange, or other definite transaction? The answer to this question often determines whether a gain is taxable in one year or another, in one tax jurisdiction or another, and/or to one person or another.

The Court has held that "realization" is an essential attribute of taxable income. This idea was developed at some length in the

40 67th Congress, 1st Session, *House Report* 350, *Senate Report* 275.

41 See above, Chaps. VIII, XIV, and XVIII and, below, Exhibit 7, Appendix.

decision of the case of *Eisner* v. *Macomber* in which it was stated that the stock dividend represented no segregation of profits:

> Here we have the essential matter: *Not* a gain *accruing* to capital; not a *growth* or *increment* of value *in* the investment; but a gain, a profit, something of exchangeable value, *proceeding from* the property, *severed* from the capital, however invested or employed. . .[42]

Three years previously the Court decided two cases in which dividends declared by subsidiary corporations and transferred to holding companies were held not to be income for income tax purposes.[43] In the first, Justice Pitney, delivering the opinion of the Court, stated:

> We base our conclusion in the present case upon the view that it was the purpose and intent of Congress, while taxing "the entire net income arising or accruing from all sources" during each year commencing with the 1st day of March, 1913, to refrain from taxing that which in mere form only, bore the appearance of income accruing after date, while in truth and substance it accrued before. . .[43]

Nevertheless, in succeeding cases involving corporate distributions the Court emphasized the form of the transaction. For instance, in *Hornby* v. *Lynch* a corporation dividend paid in 1914 was held taxable income of an individual shareholder, even though much of the corporation income had been earned prior to March 1, 1913. Part of the opinion read:

> Just as we deem the legislative intent manifest to tax the stockholder with respect to such accumulations only if and when, and to the extent that, his interest in them comes to fruition as income, that is, in dividends declared, so we can perceive no constitutional obstacle that stands in the way of carrying out this intent when dividends are declared out of a preexisting surplus.[44]

This same reasoning was followed in *Peabody* v. *Eisner*.[45] A few years later in the reorganization cases the emphasis was put on form rather than substance in determining tax liability.[46]

In determining the amount of gain or loss, an important consideration is the basis of computation. The Supreme Court decided in *Lynch* v. *Turrish*[47] that the cost of the property was the basis for determining such gain if the property was acquired after March 1,

42 252 U. S. 189 (1920).

43 *Southern Pacific Co.* v. *Lowe*, 247 U. S. at 338 (1918); *Gulf Oil Co.* v. *Llewellyn*, 248 U. S. 71 (1918).

44 247 U. S. 345 (1918).

45 247 U. S. 347 (1918).

46 See below, p. 495.

47 247 U. S. 221 (1918). This was a logical deduction from the previous decisions in such cases as *Hays* v. *Gauley Mountain Coal Company* (247 U. S. 189) and *U. S.* v. *Cleveland, Cincinnati, Chicago and St. Louis Railway Co.* 247 U. S. 195 (1918).

1913 but, if acquired before that date, the basis should be the value on March 1, 1913. This was the date on which the income tax law went into effect. This general rule was adopted in each revenue Act, with certain exceptions.

Congress and the courts, as well as the Treasury, have recognized the difficulty and the importance of defining "gain" and "loss" and of determining when income is "realized." In the course of years the definitions of gain and loss have been more closely drawn so that, instead of cost, the basis is that provided in the statute. The 1924 Act formally approved the Treasury practice of providing an "adjusted" basis for computing gain or loss by allowing the item of "cost" to be increased by the amount of items properly chargeable to capital account and decreased by depreciation and similar deductions previously allowed with respect to the property. This rule has been reenacted in all succeeding laws as the basic principle, but it has been amplified and refined. There are now eighteen specific exceptions to this rule, applicable chiefly to transactions in connection with property acquired by gift, bequest, "wash" sales, corporate liquidations, and reorganizations.

RECOGNITION OF GAIN OR LOSS IN EXCHANGE OF PROPERTY

For income tax purposes a "sale" of property is a transaction in which property is exchanged for money; an "exchange" is a transaction in which property is exchanged for other property. The general rule is that the transaction in both cases is completed, and the gains and losses must be accounted for, as of the time the transfer of property occurs.

In the case of a sale of property the taxable gain or loss is computed on an "adjusted gain or loss basis," defined by law as just explained. In the case of an exchange the amount of taxable gain is not so easily determined. It may not be possible to place a value on the property received in the transaction. It is obvious too that not all transactions result in taxable gain.

Prior to the Act of 1918 the income tax laws did not deal specifically with taxability of gain or allowance of loss from the exchange of property. The Acts of 1913, 1916, and 1917 provided that gross income included "gains, profits, and income derived from . . . sales, or dealings in property . . ." It became clear, however, that this provision was too broad because it failed to take into account transactions such as trades or exchanges in which a taxpayer may have realized a gain but no cash profit. In drafting the Act of 1918 the Senate Finance Committee inserted a provision to establish a rule in cases of exchanges of property and "to negative the assertion of tax in the case of certain purely paper transactions."[48] As enacted this section of the law read:

When property is exchanged for other property the property received in exchange shall for the purpose of determining gain or loss be treated as the equivalent of cash to the amount of its fair market value if any.[49]

The regulations issued by the Commissioner for the administration of the law stated that gain or loss was realized when property was converted into cash or into property that (a) was essentially different from that disposed of and (b) had a market value.

The statutory provision was unsatisfactory because it was productive of litigation and seriously interfered with postwar business readjustments. The Secretary of the Treasury pointed out that the law failed to take account of all transactions in which it was difficult to determine the gain or loss in absence of an actual sale and urged that exchanges under the following conditions be added to those already exempted: (1) when market value of property received could not be satisfactorily determined; (2) when property was exchanged for all or substantially all of the stock of a corporation; (3) when property was exchanged between affiliated corporations, and (4) when a corporation, partnership, or person received stock in connection with a reorganization.[50]

Therefore in drafting the 1921 Act the exchange provision was completely rewritten to incorporate some of these suggestions. It provided that exchanges of property would not be taxable unless the property received in exchange had a readily realizable market value, with certain exceptions.[51]

The Treasury soon discovered, however, that taxpayers were taking undue advantage of one clause of this section, the provision that property held for investment could be exchanged for other prop-

[48] 65th Congress, 3d Session, *Senate Report* 617.

[49] The Supreme Court has defined the term "fair market value" to mean "the price at which a seller willing, but not compelled to sell, and a buyer willing, but not compelled to buy, both having reasonable knowledge of all the material circumstances, will trade." Montgomery, *Federal Income Tax Handbook* 1938-1939, p. 60. Some of the pertinent cases are *Burnet* v. *Logan,* 283 U. S. 404; *Helvering* v. *Tex-Penn Oil Co.,* 300 U. S. 48; *Heiner* v. *Crosby,* 224 Fed. (2d) 191 and *Helvering* v. *Walbridge,* 70 F (2) 683, cert. den. 293 U. S. 594.

[50] 67th Congress, 1st Session, *House Report* 350.

[51] Four cases were enumerated in which gain from the transaction was not taxable even though the property received had a readily realizable market value:

(1) When property held for investment, or for productive use in trade or business (not including stock-in-trade or other property held primarily for sale), was exchanged for property of a like kind or use;

(2) When a taxpayer received securities as the result of a corporation reorganization;

(3) When property was exchanged in connection with a transfer of property to a corporation, if the transferor was in control of the corporation immediately after the transfer;

(4) When there was a compulsory conversion of property into other property similar to the property so converted.

erty of like kind without the realization of taxable income. Brokers advertised that they would exchange securities for their customers in such a way as to avoid tax. The Secretary therefore requested Congress to limit tax-free exchanges to those in which securities were received or exchanged in connection with reorganizations, consolidations, or mergers of corporations.[52] This revision was made in 1923. Other amendments were made in 1924, notably the change of the phrase "readily realizable market value" to "fair market value."

Similar difficulties were encountered in drafting legislation to cover exchanges of property occasioned by corporate reorganizations, mergers, or consolidations. The income tax laws prior to 1918 contained no special provisions with respect to such transactions and the courts ruled in several important cases that taxable income resulted when the exchange of securities took place.

Presumably the Court wanted some definite act by which to determine time of realization, partly as an administrative device. When corporate mergers and consolidations became frequent, much business was carried on without the normal realizations that take place when transactions are made "at arm's length"; that is, when the number of objective valuations become relatively small, the usual realization requirements lose much of their alleged validity and administrative justification.

Congress saw, however, that the requirements respecting realization made taxpayers liable for substantial income taxes as a result of paper transactions which had little economic significance in producing income. Therefore the income tax laws were amended to make it clear that income was "realized" only after a sale or some other definite transaction. The result of this specific legislation, however, was a very technical and complicated section, so involved, in fact, that the Treasury requested a complete change in procedure — a simple legislative statement with ample administrative power. This Congress was unwilling to grant. When, however, revenue became more important because of the economic depression of the 1930's, Congress became conscious of the possibilities of tax avoidance permitted by these sections and drafted some restrictions.[53]

The complexities cited above in connection with "realization" of income are, of course, multiplied by the creation of such artificial entities as trusts and corporations. Either very detailed law or much administrative discretion is needed to determine just when, where, and how much income is taxable to such entities, their creators,

[52] *Report of the Secretary of the Treasury* 1922, p. 15. Also published in 67th Congress, 4th Session, *House Report* 1432.

[53] The reorganization provisions are explained at greater length in Magill, *Taxable Income,* pp. 52-58 ; Miller, Hendricks and Everett, *Reorganizations and Other Exchanges in Federal Income Taxation.*

managers, controllers, beneficiaries, and other individuals and corporations connected with them.

Thus we see that the definition of taxable income has evolved from the very simple to the very complex. The actual administration and adjudication of a general income tax in a complex industrial society reveals the naïveté of the pioneer advocates, legislators, and courts and makes it clear that no one can give a brief, accurate, legal definition that will not require discriminating interpretations at hundreds of difficult points.

A SUMMARY OF THE LEGAL DEFINITION

After essaying the task and coming to a somewhat similar conclusion, Professor Magill, who has made a notable study of the legal definition of taxable income, summarizes his findings as follows:

> The taxable income of an individual consists of (1) his total gross receipts during the period (other than gifts, bequests, and devises), after subtracting its cost from the proceeds of any sale or other disposition of stock-in-trade or any investment, plus (2) any increase in his economic worth resulting from the discharge of his obligations.
>
> 1. Income so determined is considered to belong to the person who earned it, or who owned or controlled the investment which produced it.
>
> 2. The gross receipts of an individual include: (1) any item of money; and (2) any interests in property, having a money value, and differing in kind or in extent from those previously held by the recipient, which he has actually received, which he may obtain upon demand, or which have accrued during the period according to a recognized method of accounting employed in keeping his books.
>
> 3. Obligations for this purpose include not only one's debts, but recognized obligations to support and maintain one's family.[54]

WHO DETERMINES TAXABLE INCOME?

One who has followed the discussion above may ask, In the last analysis, who or what really determines what income shall be taxed, the Treasury, the Congress, the Courts, the economic verities, or somebody or something else?

Under the United States form of government the Supreme Court is supposed to be the final authority in interpreting what the Constitution permits Congress to tax. As mentioned earlier, in the cases that arose under the Act of 1909 and the income tax laws enacted after the ratification of the Sixteenth Amendment, the Court ruled that Congress could tax gross income, but its position with

[54] Magill, *Taxable Income*, pp. 398-399. Quoted by express permission of the author and the publisher, The Ronald Press.

reference to gross receipts is not wholly clear.[55] The Court has not, however, required Congress to tax all income that it might tax but has permitted it to authorize such deductions as it has chosen to grant.[56]

Another important step in the Court's definition of income was the establishment of the requirement of "realization." The necessity for "separation" of income from capital, or "realization," was emphasized in *Eisner* v. *Macomber*,[57] but the full significance of this requirement was not brought out until decisions were rendered in cases relating to trust distributions, corporate reorganizations, and other involved transactions.[58] The importance of Court interpretations of "realization" and insistence on the form of a transaction have just been cited in connection with the reorganizations of corporations and exchanges of property.

But the income tax decisions exhibit numerous inconsistencies and departures from precedents despite Court emphasis on "stare decisis." One interesting illustration of a complete change of view is found in recent cases [59] referred to above relative to reciprocal state and federal exemption of salaries of government employees. These decisions overturn more than a century of precedents dating from Chief Justice Marshall's famous decision in *McCulloch* v. *Maryland* (1819). *Pollock* v. *Farmers Loan and Trust Co.*[60] invalidated the income tax of 1894, although the Court had upheld the Civil War tax.[61] In *Collector* v. *Hubbard* [62] the Court upheld the section of the law that taxed as individual income profits of corporations even though they were not distributed. Later cases, particularly *Eisner* v. *Macomber*,[63] established the opposite rule that income must be "separated" from capital, it must be "realized" by the stockholder before it can be considered taxable income. Since this decision the Court has modified its interpretation of "realization." Some of the factors stressed as essential in *Eisner* v. *Macomber* have not been required in all subsequent cases. For example, the separation of assets analogous to the

[55] See discussion in text and footnote 18 above.
[56] 292 U. S. 371 (1924).
[57] 252 U. S. 189.
[58] See above, pp. 492-495.
[59] *Helvering* v. *Gerhardt*, 304 U. S. 405 ; *Allen, Collector* v. *University of Georgia*, 304 U. S. 439 ; *Graves* v. *N. Y. ex rel O'Keefe*, 59 Sup. Ct. 595 and *O'Malley* v. *Woodrough*, 59 Sup. Ct. 838.

The propriety of treating these "inter-governmental immunity" cases as income tax decisions may be questioned by some on the ground that they involve changes in theory as to the scope of immunity, not in theory of what constitutes income. Practically, however, they do define, delimit, determine what is, and what is not, taxable income under federal law and, probably, to a large extent, under state laws of the future.

[60] 157 U. S. 429, 158 U. S. 601 (1895).
[61] *Pacific Insurance Co.* v. *Soule* (7 Wall. 433) and *Springer* v. *U. S.* (102 U. S. 586).
[62] 12 Wall. 1 (1870).
[63] 252 U. S. 189 (1920).

separation of the fruit from the tree was not held necessary in some of the reorganization decisions.

The number of judges dissenting from various decisions exhibits the division of opinion found in the Court itself. In fact, few of the important tax decisions have been unanimous. Apparently some of the justices have felt that the taxpayers are frequently not given due consideration. On the other hand, others apparently have been inclined to think that Congress should be given more freedom of action, also that the states should be less hampered by federal restrictions. In recent years the Court has apparently been influenced also by the revenue needs of the government and by the necessity of preventing tax avoidance.[64] Some of the differences of opinion among members of the Court are due, of course, to personal bias, psychological traits, social attitudes, economic and other interests.

In fact, the Court has frequently if not always been influenced by other considerations than those of strictly legal character. The administrative problems have been recognized from the time of the earliest decisions. The economic verities were recognized in the distinctions made between gross receipts and gross income, in the distinctions made between capital and income, and also in other instances involving economic issues, despite the remark of Justice Clarke:

> In determining the definition of the word "income" – this Court has consistently refused to enter into the refinements of definition of lexicographers and economists.[65]

Because, presumably, the opinions of the Supreme Court represent the final interpretations they have been cited most frequently in this study. It should not be overlooked, however, that there are many other courts of law making tax decisions. These also have their influence on the developing definition of taxable income.[66]

Although the courts have indicated the meaning of taxable income, Congress has not always been willing to accept judicial interpretations as final. The decision in the Pollock case led to a constitutional amendment.[67] The Court prohibition of the taxation of com-

64 The needs of the government have affected many decisions other than those in tax cases. A good example is the decision in the Gold Clause Case, *U. S.* v. *Banker's Trust Co.*, 294 U. S. 240 (1935).

65 *Merchants' Loan and Trust Co.* v. *Smietanka*, 255 U. S. 509 (1921).

66 The Board of Tax Appeals, the Court of Claims, and Federal District Courts hear tax cases. Their decisions are often at such variance that the Treasury as well as taxpayers take suits lost in one court to others in the hope of winning decisions.

67 As mentioned in earlier chapters herein, the Pollock case decisions did not deal primarily with the definition of income in a generic sense but rather with the validity of the method of taxing income under the 1894 law. Practically, however, the Court did define "taxable income," or that the income in question was not "taxable income" under the existing law. This was a 5 to 4 decision, and was practically repudiated by dicta in later decisions. A 5 to 4 decision for the 1894 law, such as probably would

pensation of the President and federal judges was circumvented in part by legislation. On the other hand, in some cases Congress has been unwilling to tax court-defined income when that meant accepting form for substance. Efforts of Congress to prevent taxation of paper profits in connection with corporate reorganizations have been mentioned. Thus we see, on the one hand, that the Court may invalidate acts of Congress and, on the other hand, that Congress may circumvent decisions of the Court.

But the passing of a law or the rendering of a court decision is not the end of the definition of income nor the determination of just what income is taxed or will be taxed in actual practice. As mentioned elsewhere, Congress has left much of the determination of taxable income to the administrators of the law. Moreover, the Treasury has taken an important part in directing legislation because of its responsibility for the administration of the law and also because of its interest in the yield. The Treasury, and often the President, have been further interested in shaping the revenue laws because of their importance in carrying out semi-fiscal and other economic and social policies of the Administration in power.

For example, Secretary Mellon was interested in relieving business of unnecessary tax burdens; President Roosevelt asked for tax legislation to bring about more equitable distribution of the nation's wealth.

Of course there have been great contrasts in the attitudes of the presidents toward tax problems. Woodrow Wilson was very much interested in the drafting of the first income tax law under the Sixteenth Amendment, but in later years he was too engrossed in the war to give revenue matters much personal attention. Neither Harding nor Coolidge knew much of tax problems, hence left them to a very aggressive Secretary of the Treasury. At the other extreme is President Roosevelt, who has sponsored several important tax proposals and programs, some of them considered very radical and unwelcome to "business."

Neither the President nor the Secretary of the Treasury can give to tax problems the day-to-day study they demand. Therefore, the Treasury has sought special technical advice on tax matters and in recent years has developed a large research staff. As tax measures have increased in complexity, the Treasury has taken an active and aggressive part in drafting legislation. In 1926 Congress decided,

---

have been rendered by the Court as constituted most years since 1900, would have brought within the ring of "taxable income" the income ruled outside of this ring in 1895. That is, in either case, the Court would define "taxable income" if "define" is used in a broad sense. (See Chapters I, II, III, and XX, above, including the pertinent cases cited therein, particularly the decisions of the Court on the constitutionality of the early laws enacted under the Sixteenth Amendment.)

however, to have its own tax research organization. Since then it has depended to a great extent on technical help from the staff of the Joint Committee on Internal Revenue Taxation.

Administration of the law is the responsibility of the Commissioner of Internal Revenue who is in the Treasury Department, although the Commissioner and other important members of the Treasury do not always agree.[68] The War Revenue Acts have been cited as granting unusual power to the Commissioner to define taxable net income but he has always had authority to interpret the law. For instance, in 1911 the Commissioner ruled that depletion allowance was deductible under the Act of 1909 although the law did not so provide. This is only one example; the Regulations and Rulings of the Commissioner fill volumes.[69]

Of course, the Commissioner personally makes few rulings. Most of his powers are delegated to the Chief Counsel and others of the staff. The auditors and other employees make countless decisions as to the meaning of the law.[70] Their powers will doubtless be extended under the recent plan for the decentralization of the work of the Income Tax Unit.

The taxpayer also influences the definition of taxable income. Before each revenue act is drafted, an opportunity is usually offered to the public to attend hearings conducted by the House Committee on Ways and Means and the Senate Committee on Finance, and to criticize or comment on needed amendments to former laws or proposed drafts of new ones. For example, changes made by the Senate Committee in the 1936 Act were largely the result of evidence presented at the public hearings. Even greater influence is exerted, however, by the taxpayer in accepting or protesting rulings of the Commissioner, in taking cases to the Board of Tax Appeals and to the Courts, and in making his wants known to his representatives in Congress.

In this connection mention should be made also of the part played by lawyers and accountants.[71] In 1937 the Secretary of the Treas-

68 The Commissioner is appointed by the President.

69 The rulings of the Treasury are issued weekly in the *Internal Revenue Bulletin*, and semi-annually in the *Internal Revenue Cumulative Bulletin*.

70 In the fiscal year 1938 the legal division of the Treasury handled 5689 income, estate and gift tax appeals involving $134,519,452; prepared for review 363 cases involving overassessments, prepared data for the Department of Justice in prosecution or defense of 3948 tax cases, prepared more than 2449 regulations, Treasury decisions, and rulings, and reviewed more than 1900 cases involving offers in compromise. (*Report of the Secretary of the Treasury* 1938, pp. 182-183).

71 An interesting attempt of accountants to change the wording of the law was made in 1909. At that time the excise tax bill provided for taxing income actually received and expenses actually paid, and made no provision for accrual accounting. Although the accountants protested that this was an unworkable basis, their protests were not heeded. The difficulties they cited had to be taken care of later by the Regulations. See Chap. II above.

ury and the President of the United States were particularly disturbed by the cleverness of lawyers who specialized in finding methods of tax avoidance. Congress has been cognizant of this difficulty and has tried to plug loopholes as fast as they are discovered and disclosed by ingenious taxpayers and their advisors. The administrative angle is discussed elsewhere in this study, particularly in Chapter XXIII.[72]

Who then, shall we conclude, determines what income shall be taxed? Is it true, as commonly thought, that Congress defines income in the first place but that ultimate decisions are made by the Supreme Court? So far as general formal definitions are concerned, this common opinion may be substantially correct. As the authors interpret developments, however, the definitions as actually applied are a composite in which the legislature, the executive, and the judiciary have participated. Indirect influence has been exerted by economists, lawyers, accountants, and others. Administrators have most to do with the law and with the taxpayers and, on the whole, the executive branch of the government is perhaps in the most strategic position to determine what income is actually taxed and also to influence the trend of the future definition of taxable income. Fundamentally, however, the definition of taxable income is determined by biological, economic, and other natural forces which affect society; that is, it is determined by the public, by pressure groups, by public opinion commonly expressed through political channels. Mr. Dooley once remarked that even the Supreme Court follows the elections.

In other words, the meaning of income is not static.[73] It is always evolving as a result of the dynamic forces operating in society. This truth was well stated by Justice Holmes:

> But it is not necessarily true that income means the same thing in the Constitution and the Act. A word is not a crystal, transparent and unchanged, it is the skin of a living thought and may vary greatly in color and content according to the circumstances and the time in which it is used.[74]

[72] We are thinking of the definition and determination of income here in rather broad terms and attributing to the executive not only the activities and interpretations outlined above but also the actual application of the law by administrators. As one example consider the substitution of Treasury administration of depreciation allowances for proposed legislation in 1934.

[73] For some additional consideration see the note appended to this chapter and the Conclusion, Chap. XXIV below.

One reader of this chapter, whose opinion the authors value highly, questions their interpretation of this extract from Justice Holmes' opinion. Nevertheless, regardless of what Justice Holmes meant, the authors believe that the quotation as they interpret it is a very effective statement of a very important truth that many do not appreciate.

[74] *Towne* v. *Eisner*, 245 U. S. 418 (1918).

RECAPITULATION

The Civil War laws imposing income taxes on individuals [75] gave every evidence of hurried drafting. They were naïve, general authorizations; indeed, the first Act (1861) was so indefinite that it is impossible to tell from its phraseology whether a gross or net income tax was intended. The Secretary of the Treasury hesitated to enforce it, so Congress enacted a new law before the first was put into effect.[76] Fragmentary reports of congressional debates and references to British practice in 1861 indicate it was intended that net income should be the tax base, but suggestions that the word "net" be inserted in the bill were countered by the objection that if this were done too many deductions might be taken.[77] The Act of 1862 was not much more definite, though it provided for the annual taxation of "annual gains, profits, or income." The Commissioner of Internal Revenue, who was given much freedom of interpretation, administered the tax as one on net income, or an approximation to net income as now understood. All succeeding laws (Acts of 1864, 1865, 1866, 1867, 1870) were drafted more carefully and provided more specifically for deductions. The 1864 law used the term "net profits." Nevertheless, these laws were somewhat vague and much discretion was left to the Commissioner of Internal Revenue.

The last Civil War Act expired January 1, 1872. The next income tax Act, that of 1894, was almost a copy of that of 1867, except that it applied a general income tax to corporations as well as to individuals, taxed inheritances of personal property as income, increased the individual exemption to $4000, and made some minor changes.[78]

Technically the Act of 1909 was not an income tax but an excise. It takes on significance in this connection because the measure of the tax was "net income" and the definition of income established by the Court under this Act was later carried over as the definition of income applicable to laws enacted under the Sixteenth Amendment.[79]

In drafting the 1913 Act, the first of the present series of income tax laws, there were many matters which Congress overlooked, or about which it was uncertain, and which were, therefore, left vague in the statute. For example, it did not make clear what distinction, if any, was to be made between capital gains and current income,

75 Corporations were subject to gross receipts taxes, license fees, etc.

76 *Report of the Secretary of the Treasury* 1861, p. 13.

77 *Congressional Globe*, 37th Congress, 1st Session, p. 315.

78 See above, Chap. I.

79 The thirty-sixth and thirty-seventh states ratified the amendment Feb. 3, 1913. The Secretary of State certified the adoption of the amendment Feb. 25, 1913. 37 *Statutes at Large* 1785. See above, Chap. II.

though the chief authors of the bill pointed out specifically that the intention was to tax income, not capital. The drafters were cautious in order to avoid phraseology or definite commitments that would raise constitutional objections, administrative difficulties, and popular disapproval that would endanger the income tax before it was given a fair trial. For these reasons Hull was inclined to follow Civil War statutes, already partially adjudicated, and British law and practice which had been tested for many years, though the bill as phrased by Hull and his colleagues in the House was amended considerably in the Senate.

This law of 1913 specified that, subject to certain exemptions and deductions, net income included gains, profits, and income derived from salaries, wages, or compensation for personal services, or from professions, vocations, trade, sales, etc. Much the same phraseology was followed in 1916, but an important question was raised by an addition which specifically included corporation stock dividends in taxable income. This was declared unconstitutional in 1920,[80] hence such dividends were specifically excluded in the 1921 and later Acts.[81]

In 1918 and succeeding Acts net income was defined as gross income minus certain deductions. "Gross income," in turn, was defined as "gross profits and income . . . from any source whatever." Specific classes of income were enumerated at some length and certain items were excluded. Examples of the latter were gifts, proceeds of insurance policies, interest on state obligations, compensation of military and naval forces, income derived from publicly-owned utilities and essential government functions.

Since 1918 the laws have followed the same general practice of specifying net income in terms of gross income minus certain allowable deductions. In the 1934 Act, however, a new method was introduced, that of employing specialized technical definitions of income. This law imposed a special tax on personal holding companies in order to prevent the evasion of surtax on individual income by incorporation. This tax was levied on "the undistributed adjusted net income" of such corporations. "Adjusted net income" was defined as

> the net income computed without the allowance of the dividend deduction, otherwise allowable, but minus the sum of (A) Federal income taxes . . . , (B) Contributions or gifts . . . , (C) Losses from sale of capital assets . . .

80 *Eisner* v. *Macomber,* 252 U. S. 189.

81 Inasmuch as the Court has narrowed its interpretation of taxable corporate distributions, as explained above, the 1936 and subsequent Acts restated the rule as to stock dividends so as to tax whatever dividends could be reached constitutionally.

In other words, while continuing the same basic method of defining income in general, Congress, with the assistance of the Treasury and others, has been developing numerous specialized definitions for special purposes and situations.

When the 1936 Act revised the method of taxing corporations in order to force distribution of earnings, the use of technical definitions initiated in 1934 for certain corporations was carried further. The law defined four different kinds of corporation income: (1) "normal tax net income," (2) "adjusted net income," (3) "undistributed adjusted net income," and (4) "retained net income." In 1938 this scheme of technical definitions was applied to the section defining individual income also. This Act of 1938 defined fifteen kinds of income: (1) "surtax net income" [Sec. 12]; (2) "adjusted net income" [Sec. 13a]; (3) "special class net income" [Sec. 14(a)]; (4) "Section 102 net income" [Sec. 102(d)(1)]; (5) "undistributed Section 102 net income" [Sec. 102(d)(2)]; (6) "foreign personal holding company income" [Sec. 332]; (7) "undistributed Supplement P net income" [Sec. 335]; (8) "Supplement P net income" [Sec. 336]; (9) "personal holding company income" [Sec. 401]; (10) "Title IA net income" [Sec. 402]; and (11) "undistributed Title IA net income" [Sec. 405]. In addition to this list were the general definitions of gross and net income of individuals and special definitions of gross and net income of insurance companies. The House bill had one more variety, "Title IB net income."

Thus the definition of income has been expanded in length and complexity from 1861 to 1938. So technical has it become that only experts can interpret it. No longer could a Supreme Court justice comment on the simplicity of the law and the nature of taxable income as did Justice McKenna in 1918:

> And this in resolution of a statute which concerns the activities of men, and intended, it might be supposed, to be without perplexities and readily solvable by the off-hand conceptions of those to whom it was addressed.[82]

Some considerations of economic and social forces, rather than those primarily of a legal nature, will be discussed briefly in the concluding chapter.

Note

Inasmuch as the definition of taxable income is a legal rather than an economic definition, the discussion above has paid primary attention to the development of the legal definition. A thoroughgoing discussion of the economic concepts of income, also of the nature and functions of income and capital, and of the economic effects of various tax provisions and measures would be very desirable, in fact, necessary to a full under-

[82] *Lynch* v. *Turrish*, 247 U. S. 221 (1918).

standing of the many points raised in the preceding pages. Without such an understanding one cannot appreciate the harm that is done by faulty legislation, poor administration, and unenlightened court decisions.

Limitations of space, however, have confined this study mostly to an exposition of what has taken place and have permitted little more than suggestions concerning effects of the character just mentioned. The present authors are of the opinion that sketchy inadequate discussions of such recondite and controversial matters are not very helpful, that in many cases adequate data to substantiate general conclusions are not yet available, and that in most important cases special studies and monographs are called for. As a matter of fact, numerous monographs and articles on economic definitions and economic effects have long been available, others are being turned out in unprecedented volume, and in time we shall probably have the bases for more comprehensive and convincing conclusions, at least, more convincing to the disinterested and open-minded. Despite the previous remarks, a few footnote comments on definition may be permissible.

In our opinion the definitions of income, capital, etc., depend primarily upon the purposes of the definers. A suitable definition of capital for consideration of interest-rent-wage controversies may not be suitable for tax purposes. An appropriate definition of income for tax purposes may not be the best for certain credit and trust purposes; or one that is reasonably satisfactory for tax purposes in a primitive self-sufficient agricultural society may be far from adequate for a modern industrial-financial society.

The differences in the definitions of income by economists and lawyers arise largely from their different points of view and purposes. Their ideas are related, but they emphasize different things, or different aspects of the same problems. Economists focus their attention on the principles that govern the maximization of income, wealth, human satisfactions; hence, for example, the emphasis of Fisher and others upon satisfactions, "psychic income." Economists naturally favor taxes and fiscal systems that further the ends they deem desirable.

Lawyers, on the other hand, particularly lawmakers, judges, and administrators, are concerned with making and executing the rules of the game of life in society. But if these rules are to serve their purposes, they must be sufficiently definite, understandable, and acceptable for practical administration. Economists or others may say that men should share the paying of taxes according to their respective abilities, or according to benefits received, but legislators, courts and administrators have to be more definite; they must make and administer the rules (laws) which determine just how many dollars John Smith, Chris Jensen, and others must pay in taxes, and just how many dollars or days in prison they must pay in penalties if they do not pay their specified taxes within the specified time. This indicates why courts want "realization" or some other definite act or event as a basis or point of time for making a decision or taking stock.

But when a rule is set up for one purpose it is often used or misused for some other purpose, also. If we consider all the facts, all the different points of view, all interests, biases, etc.; if we consider the social survival value as well as the special interests in reducing taxes and in maintaining capital (or the government's and other beneficiaries' interests in increasing taxes), it is not very difficult to find plausible explanations of many seeming inconsistencies. "Realization" may be justifiable in many cases for administrative purposes; it may be used or misused in other cases to put off or avoid taxes. The valuation of capital assets is often very difficult and hence impractical, particularly if it means increased taxes: for example, when it involves the inclusion of estimated appreciation in taxable income; but, however inconsistent, it is not held administratively impossible for the purpose of ascertaining estimated depreciation which means lower taxes. The accountant often includes inventory at cost or market, whichever is lower, an illogical practice but possibly a desirable offset to usual over-optimism.

Thus we see that lurking behind the definition of income, the graduation of rates, the special treatment of this or that class of individuals or corporations, are the purposes of those determining or trying to determine policy. Taxable income is what it is defined to be by law, and law is what it is by virtue of all the influences and forces which operate upon it. Economic income is something else, something different though closely related, perhaps less definite, and differing in the minds of different economists.

The present authors think of a person's income as his receipts of economic value (goods and services) within a period of time; net income, as his economic gains within the income period; capital, as his stock of wealth at a point of time. The same things or values might be one's income of 1939 and also one's capital at 12:00 P. M., December 31, 1939. We think of both income and capital in terms of *value* more commonly than in terms of *things* (*res*) and consider increases and decreases in values more significant for tax purposes than increases or decreases in physical quantities of things. We think the "psychic income" concept very useful for certain purposes but not usually the most desirable and practical for tax purposes. We like Haig's "net accretion" definition for tax purposes, insofar as it is administratively feasible, that is, as we understand and interpret it, though it is somewhat ahead of the times and is ambiguous with respect to the exact meaning of "net accretion." Moreover, we believe that it is desirable and possible to make taxable income approach much more closely than at present to Haig's definition and thus reduce manipulation, evasion, avoidance, and also injustice. For example, some of the present "realization" requirements smack too much of form rather than substance; some present capital-loss provisions are indefensible;[83] some usances such as rental values of owner-occupied residences might be included in taxable income; and numerous inconsistencies might be eliminated. We are not discussing here rates and provisions for regulatory purposes, some of which we would change.

Much could be said about simplification of the income tax if there were space, though we have discussed that elsewhere.[84] We cannot wholly agree with, though we think we can understand, Dr. O. C. Stine of the Bureau of Agricultural Economics and others who have urged the adoption of one definition of income, and the use of no other, so that Congress, the press, and others would understand the data of research organizations and use them accurately and intelligently instead of in the

[83] The Revenue Act of 1939 made a partial return to more equitable law after this was written.

[84] See p. 479, note 3, above, and p. 562, note 2, below.

customary misleading ways. We agree with Stine that everything feasible should be done to promote understanding and prevent misuse, and we think that economists, at least, might take the definition of income most commonly referred to (if they can agree on it) and never give out data on other kinds of income without using proper qualifying designations.

But if it had not already been obvious, it is certainly clear from the discussions in this study, particularly from those in this chapter and in Chapter XXIV below, that there are numerous varieties and shades of income, much as there are different varieties and shades of color. No all-inclusive definition can be very helpful in a difficult situation, except as a starting point. Perhaps the only all-inclusive definition of income is that income is what comes in, but this definition would satisfy few without interpretation and qualification, and the more it is interpreted and qualified the greater is the number of the kinds and amounts of income that are excluded by the refined definition of the class or variety selected.

The study of income for various purposes has received an unprecedented impetus in recent years. The restricted concepts and discussions are no longer adequate for present purposes and are becoming less adequate every year. This is particularly evident in the investigations of national, state, and local income (social income) and in the allied studies of consumption, capital formation, national wealth, and social progress. For purposes of scientific discussion and analysis we should not confine our attention to the one income of most common usage (if there is such) but rather we should recognize the different varieties appropriate for different purposes.

It would facilitate the discussions and analyses if different varieties of income were divided systematically into classes and subclasses and designated by some systematic terminology. For example, gross receipts might be designated "income 1"; gross income, as "income 2"; net income, as "income 3"; clear income as "income 4"; and so on. There are many subclasses, for example, many kinds of net income, depending upon just what deductions are made from gross income to arrive at net income. These subclasses might be designated, according to the different deductions authorized, as "income 3.1," "income 3.2," "income 3.3," . . . "income 3.n." Similarly the exclusions from gross receipts to arrive at gross income are not always the same, so different varieties of gross income might be designated "income 2.1," "income 2.2," . . . "income 2.n."

The system of designation could be amplified to provide for differentiations of all kinds; for example, it could take account of money income, income in kind, usances, psychic income, etc. The foregoing suggestions are merely illustrative; we leave to others for the time being, at least, the development of the best classification and the most appropriate system of designations. If it were decided that net income of the variety designated above as "income 3.3," or "Income A4.671," is the variety which is most generally understood when the term *income* is used, perhaps because it is the kind of income that most people report for tax purposes, it could be agreed upon as *the* income for general public usage. Research organizations could give out data on such income without any qualifying term. But specialists would still want to discuss other varieties and they would have need for an accurate differentiating terminology. Sometimes they might even want to expose to public view, with proper qualifying terms, some varieties of income other than *the* income most commonly considered. If Congress still wanted to tax as many varieties of income as it did when it passed the Act of 1938 these varieties could be referred to by the proper differentiating designations. But the naïve idea that there is just one correct definition of income for all times, places, and purposes belongs to the same age and place as the idea that there is only one rheumatism or one variety of the "common cold." In the good old days one remedy, also, might have been sufficient, bleeding or a drink of whiskey, but this generation is more discriminating and wants more variety.

(Logically, parts of Chapter XXIV should precede this note, but to make this a part of that chapter would interrupt a sequence developed there.)

CHAPTER XXII

RATES AND EXEMPTIONS

A brief consideration of the changes in rates [1] and exemptions will make it easier to understand the problems encountered in the definition of taxable income and the administration of the federal tax upon it. If the rate or rates of such a tax are very low it makes comparatively little difference whether the definition of income is very accurate or not. For example, if the rate is one-tenth of 1% an individual having a taxable net income of $10,000 will be liable to a tax of $10. If the definition or administration of the tax should be so faulty as to include $1000 that should not be included, the taxpayer and the government would be affected to an extent of $1 only, not enough to make much ado about. But if the rate is 25%, or 50%, or 79%, it is quite a different matter. It is obvious that when rates are advanced to high percentages protests, litigation, delinquency, tax strikes, avoidance, evasion, tax law complexity, and serious problems of administration increase rapidly.

INCOME TAX RATES UNDER EARLY LAWS

The Civil War income taxes were adopted during an emergency, when national affairs were in much confusion and when maximum revenues were an urgent need. The first law, that of 1861, provided for a tax of 3% on annual income in excess of $800 in cases of individuals residing in the United States, except that the rate for both residents and nonresidents was 1½% on interest received from United States securities, and a tax of 5% was levied on incomes of citizens residing abroad. The only deduction specified was for national, state, and local taxes on property from which the income was derived. Doubtless the lower rate upon interest from United States securities was to facilitate borrowing, the main source of Civil War funds.

Before it was put into effect the 1861 income tax law was superseded by the 1862 law. The rates of the 1862 law were 3% on individual income in excess of $600 and not in excess of $10,000, and 5% on income over $10,000. Salaries of government officials were taxed at 3% on income over $600, collected at the source, and certain corporations (railroads, banks, trust companies, insurance companies)

[1] U. S. Treasury, *Sources and Rates of Federal Taxation*, corrected to Jan. 1, 1939. See also Hendricks, H. G., "Federal Income Tax Rates 1913-1932," *Bulletin* National Tax Association, Dec. 1932 ; Jan., Feb., March 1933 ; Wells, David A., "The Communism of a Discriminating Income Tax," *North American Review* 130: 236 (March 1880).

TABLE 19

RATES AND BRACKETS — FEDERAL INDIVIDUAL INCOME TAX
1861–1870, 1894

Act of	*Exemption* [b]	*Rate %*	*Brackets of "Taxable Net Income"*
1861 [a]	$800	3[c]	$600–10,000
1862	600	3	600–10,000
		5	10,000–
1864 [a]	600	5	600–5,000
		$7\frac{1}{2}$	5,000–10,000
		10	10,000–
1864 [d] (additional)	600	5	600–
1865	600	5	600–5,000
		10	5,000–
1867	1000	5	1,000–
1870	2000	$2\frac{1}{2}$	2,000–
1894	4000	2	4,000–

[a] Superseded by succeeding laws before they went into effect.
[b] These laws did not discriminate between single and married persons as have the Acts since 1913.
[c] There was a special tax of 1½% on interest from government bonds. The rate for non-residents was 5%.
[d] A special additional war tax.

were required to withhold and pay to the government a tax of 3% on interest and dividends which they paid. Income from government bonds was taxed at 1½%. Citizens living abroad were taxed at 5% on income over $600.

In 1864 the rates were increased to 5% on income in excess of $600 and not over $5000; 7½% on the excess over $5000 and not over $10,000; and 10% on the excess over $10,000. Government salaries were taxable at 5%, and so were dividends and interest. No distinction was made between citizens living in the United States and abroad, and the lower rate for the interest from government bonds was eliminated. Late in October 1864 a special additional income tax of 5% was levied on all income over $600 received in 1863. Before the first 1864 law was put into effect it was amended in 1865, so that the rates became 5% on income over $600 and not over $5000, and 10% on income over $5000.

In 1867, inasmuch as the war was over, the rates were reduced to 5% on all income over $1000. In 1870 the rate was further reduced to 2½% on all income over $2000 for the years 1870 and 1871. Because of confusion in the laws in regard to the withholding of the tax on dividends, interest, and salaries, the 5 per-cent rate was imposed on such income until August 1, 1870, no tax was imposed from August 1 to December 31, 1870, and the new 2½ per-cent rate applied only for the calendar year 1871.

The Civil War net income tax was applicable to individuals only. Corporations were subject to various license fees and gross receipts taxes. For example, the 1864 law imposed gross receipt taxes of 2½% on steamboat and canal companies, 3% on toll roads, ferries and bridges; but it was provided that the tax could be added to the fare charged passengers and users. The rate for express companies was 3%, insurance companies 1½%, telegraph companies 5%, lotteries 5%, and advertisements 3%.

The Act of 1894 imposed a tax of 2% on the net income of individuals in excess of $4000 and on corporations doing business for profit in the United States. The Act of 1909 imposed on corporations engaged in business an excise tax of 1% measured by net income in excess of $5000.

INDIVIDUAL INCOME TAX RATES SINCE ADOPTION OF SIXTEENTH AMENDMENT

One of the first things Congress had to decide about rates in the first law enacted after the adoption of the Income Tax Amendment (1913) was whether or not to graduate them. Our legislators were greatly influenced by the experience of the British; the latter had struggled long over the issue of "graduation." From the adoption of Peel's income tax in 1842 until the approval of the super-tax in Lloyd George's historic budget of 1909 (adopted in 1910) the British rates had been flat or ungraduated, though in 1907 "differentiation" – a reduction of 25% in rate, in this case – had been provided for "earned" income not in excess of £2000.[2] But until 1910 the rate on other income was the same regardless of amount, except that there was some indirect graduation, through exemptions and abatements. After thirty years of experience with graduation, it is difficult for this generation to appreciate the strength of the earlier opposition to it.

But even after many were convinced of the equity of progressive rates, adoption of them was delayed in England for administrative reasons. The British attributed much of their unusual success with administration of the income tax to the collection-at-the-source method. The payer of wages, rent, interest, or other income sub-

[2] "Differentiation" is variation in rate according to *source* or *kind* of income; for example, the low rate of 1½% on interest from federal securities in the 1861 law is an example of differentiation. "Graduation" refers to variation in the rate according to *amount* of income. The present income taxes of most American states are "graduated" but not differentiated, though Massachusetts' income tax is characterized by differentiation—different rates of tax on income from different sources—rather than by graduation, rates varying according to *amount* of income.

TABLE 20

NORMAL RATES AND EXEMPTIONS — INDIVIDUAL INCOME TAX — UNDER THE ACTS OF 1913 TO 1939

Act of	*Exemption*			*Rate %*	*Bracket*
	Single person	*Married couple*	*Dependent*		
1913	$3000	$4000	none	1	[a]
1916	3000	4000	none	2	[a]
1917	1000	2000	$200	2 4	First $2000 $2000–
1918 (for 1918)	1000	2000	200	6 12	First $4000 $4000–
(for 1919 and 1920)	1000	2000	200	4 8	First $4000 $4000–
1921 (for 1921, '22, '23)	1000	2500 [b]	400	4 8	First $4000 $4000–
1924	1000	2500	400	2 4 6	First $4000 Second $4000 $8000–
1926 (for 1925, '26, '27)	1500	3500	400	1½ 3 5	First $4000 Second $4000 $8000–
1928 (for 1928, '30, '31)	1500	3500	400	1½ 3 5	First $4000 Second $4000 $8000–
(for 1929)	1500	3500	400	½ 2 4	First $4000 Second $4000 $8000–
1932	2500	1000	400	4 8	First $4000 $4000–
1934	2500	1000	400	4	[a]
1936	2500	1000	400	4	[a]
1938 [c]	2500	1000	400	4	[a]

[a] Only one normal rate under these Acts, hence no brackets for different rates.
[b] For incomes of $5000 and over, the exemption was $2000.
[c] These rates and exemptions were not changed by the Revenue Act of 1939.

CHART 6

INDIVIDUAL INCOME TAX RATES *
For Selected Years
Combined Normal and Surtax Rates

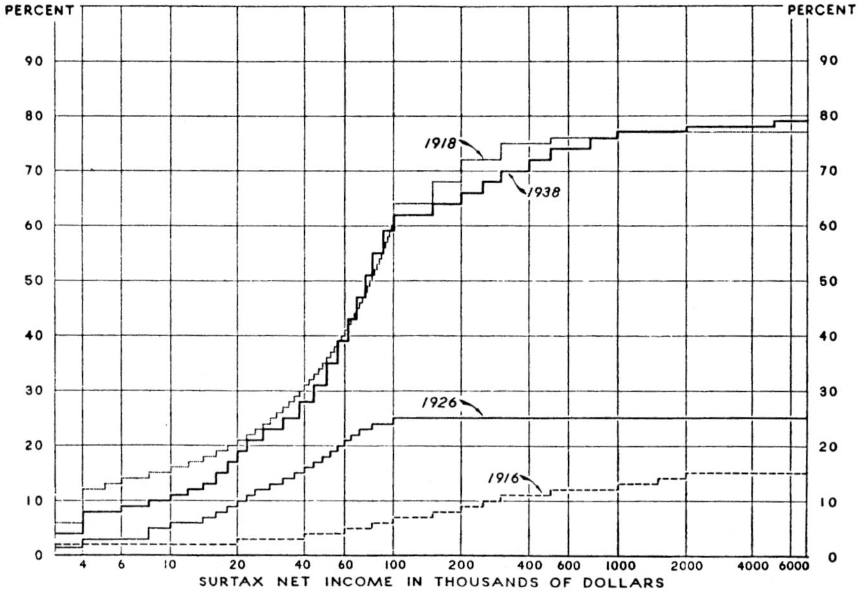

* 76th Congress, 1st Session, *Hearings before the Committee on Ways and Means on Tax-Exempt Securities*, 1939, p. 10.

tracted the income tax, forwarded it to the government, and paid the remainder to the one whom he owed. Thus the actual payer in such cases had no special inducement to evade the tax, because it was not at his expense. Under this system it was not necessary for any "source" of income to know what other income a certain taxpayer had, nor was it necessary for the taxpayer to make a summation of all his income and report to the government just how much his income was. Thus the taxpayer largely avoided having officials prying into his private affairs,[3] and the government minimized evasion of the tax. But this system of collection was dependent upon a flat or ungraduated rate; if rates were graduated, the "source" would not know what rate or rates to deduct unless he knew just how much income the taxpayer had from all sources. When the supertax on

[3] The greatest difficulties of administration in England were in connection with the independent shopkeepers, professional men, and others not receiving their incomes through "sources" which could be checked by tax officials. These independents had to make their own returns, but they were much fewer in England where rented real estate and investments in stocks and bonds were much more common than in the United States before the World War.

TABLE 21

INDIVIDUAL SURTAX RATES 1913–1939 [a]

Net income [b]		*Revenue Act*									
		1913		1916		1917		1918		1921	
Exceeding	*Not Exceeding*	*On incomes for Mar.* 1, 1913, *to Dec.* 31, 1915, *inclusive*		*On incomes for* 1916		*On incomes for* 1917		*On incomes for* 1918, 1919, 1920 *an act of* 1921, *on incomes for* 1921		*On incomes for* 1922, 1923 [c]	
Thousands of dollars	*Thousands of dollars*	*Rate (per cent)*	*Total surtax*	*Rate (per cent)*	*Total surtax*	*Rate (per cent)*	*Total surtax*	*Rate (per cent)*	*Total surtax*	*Rate (per cent)*	*Total surtax*
4	5	....	....	....	....	....	....	....	....	....	....
5	6	....	....	....	....	1	$10	1	$10	....	....
6	7.5	....	....	....	....	1	25	2	40	1	$15
7.5	8	....	....	....	....	2	35	2	50	1	20
8	10	....	....	....	....	2	75	3	110	1	40
10	12	....	....	....	....	3	135	4	190	2	80
12	12.5	....	....	....	....	3	150	5	215	3	95
12.5	13	....	....	....	....	4	170	5	240	3	110
13	14	....	....	....	....	4	210	5	290	3	140
14	15	....	....	....	....	4	250	6	350	4	180
15	16	....	....	....	....	5	300	6	410	4	220
16	18	....	....	....	....	5	400	7	550	5	320
18	20	....	....	....	....	5	500	8	710	6	440
20	22	1	$20	1	$20	8	660	9	890	8	600
22	24	1	40	1	40	8	820	10	1,090	9	780
24	26	1	60	1	60	8	980	11	1,310	10	980
26	28	1	80	1	80	8	1,140	12	1,550	11	1,200
28	30	1	100	1	100	8	1,300	13	1,810	12	1,440
30	32	1	120	1	120	8	1,460	14	2,090	13	1,700
32	34	1	140	1	140	8	1,620	15	2,390	15	2,000
34	36	1	160	1	160	8	1,780	16	2,710	15	2,300
36	38	1	180	1	180	8	1,940	17	3,050	16	2,620
38	40	1	200	1	200	8	2,100	18	3,410	17	2,960
40	42	1	220	2	240	12	2,340	19	3,790	18	3,320
42	44	1	240	2	280	12	2,580	20	4,190	19	3,700
44	46	1	260	2	320	12	2,820	21	4,610	20	4,100
46	48	1	280	2	360	12	3,060	22	5,050	21	4,520
48	50	1	300	2	400	12	3,300	23	5,510	22	4,960
50	52	2	340	2	440	12	3,540	24	5,990	23	5,420
52	54	2	380	2	480	12	3,780	25	6,490	24	5,900
54	56	2	420	2	520	12	4,020	26	7,010	25	6,400
56	58	2	460	2	560	12	4,260	27	7,550	26	6,920
58	60	2	500	2	600	12	4,500	28	8,110	27	7,460
60	62	2	540	3	660	17	4,840	29	8,690	28	8,020
62	64	2	580	3	720	17	5,180	30	9,290	29	8,600
64	66	2	620	3	780	17	5,520	31	9,910	30	9,200
66	68	2	660	3	840	17	5,860	32	10,550	31	9,820
68	70	2	700	3	900	17	6,200	33	11,210	32	10,460
70	72	2	740	3	960	17	6,540	34	11,890	33	11,120
72	74	2	780	3	1,020	17	6,880	35	12,590	34	11,800
74	75	2	800	3	1,050	17	7,050	36	12,950	35	12,150
75	76	3	830	3	1,080	17	7,220	36	13,310	35	12,500
76	78	3	890	3	1,140	17	7,560	37	14,050	36	13,220
78	80	3	950	3	1,200	17	7,900	38	14,810	37	13,960
80	82	3	1,010	4	1,280	22	8,340	39	15,590	38	14,720
82	84	3	1,070	4	1,360	22	8,780	40	16,390	39	15,500
84	86	3	1,130	4	1,440	22	9,220	41	17,210	40	16,300
86	88	3	1,190	4	1,520	22	9,660	42	18,050	41	17,120
88	90	3	1,250	4	1,600	22	10,100	43	18,910	42	17,960
90	92	3	1,310	4	1,680	22	10,540	44	19,790	43	18,820
92	94	3	1,370	4	1,760	22	10,980	45	20,690	44	19,700
94	96	3	1,430	4	1,840	22	11,420	46	21,610	45	20,600
96	98	3	1,490	4	1,920	22	11,860	47	22,550	46	21,520
98	100	3	1,550	4	2,000	22	12,300	48	23,510	47	22,460
100	150	4	3,550	5	4,500	27	25,800	52	49,510	48	46,460
150	200	4	5,550	6	7,500	31	41,300	56	77,510	49	70,960
200	250	4	7,550	7	11,000	37	59,800	60	107,510	50	95,960
250	300	5	10,050	8	15,000	42	80,800	60	137,510	50	120,960
300	400	5	15,050	9	24,000	46	126,800	63	200,510	50	170,960
400	500	5	20,050	9	33,000	46	172,800	63	263,510	50	220,960
500	750	6	35,050	10	58,000	50	297,800	64	423,510	50	345,960
750	1000	6	50,050	10	83,000	55	435,300	64	583,510	50	470,960
1000	1500	6	80,050	11	138,000	61	740,300	65	908,510	50	720,960
1500	2000	6	110,050	12	198,000	62	1,050,300	65	1,233,510	50	970,960
2000	5000	6	290,050	13	588,000	63	2,940,300	65	3,183,510	50	2,470,960
5000	....	6	....	13	....	63	....	65	....	50	....

a United States Treasury, *Sources and Rates of Federal Taxation*, corrected to Jan. 1, 1939, pp. 34, 35.

b In arriving at the net income subject to surtax for 1934 and subsequent years, the sum of the persona exemption and credit for dependents is allowed as a credit; prior to 1934 no such credit was allowed.

c Tax for 1923 reduced 25% by credit or refund under sec. 1200 (a), Revenue Act of 1924.

TABLE 21 (*Continued*)

INDIVIDUAL SURTAX RATES, 1913–1939 [a]

Net income		*Revenue Act*									
		1924		1926		1932		1934		1935, 1936, 1937, 1938	
Exceeding	*Not exceeding*	*On incomes for 1924*		*On incomes for 1925, 1926, 1927, and act of 1928 on incomes for 1928, 1929, 1930, and 1931*		*On incomes for 1932, 1933*		*On incomes for 1934, 1935*		*On incomes for 1936, 1937, 1938, 1939*	
Thousands of dollars	*Thousands of dollars*	*Rate (per-cent)*	*Total surtax*	*Rate (per-cent)*	*Total surtax*	*Rate (per-cent)*	*Total surtax*	*Rate (per-cent)*	*Total surtax*	*Rate (per-cent)*	*Total surtax*
4	5	....	....	....	....	....	....	4	$40	4	$40
5	6	....	....	....	....	....	....	4	80	4	80
6	7.5	....	....	....	....	1	$15	5	155	5	155
7.5	8	....	....	....	....	1	20	5	180	5	180
8	10	....	....	....	....	1	40	6	300	6	300
10	12	1	$20	1	$20	2	80	7	440	7	440
12	12.5	1	25	1	25	3	95	8	480	8	480
12.5	13	1	30	1	30	3	110	8	520	8	520
13	14	1	40	1	40	3	140	8	600	8	600
14	15	2	60	2	60	4	180	9	690	9	690
15	16	2	80	2	80	4	220	9	780	9	780
16	18	3	140	3	140	5	320	11	1,000	11	1,000
18	20	4	220	4	220	6	440	13	1,260	13	1,260
20	22	5	320	5	320	8	600	15	1,560	15	1,560
22	24	6	440	6	440	9	780	17	1,900	17	1,900
24	26	7	580	7	580	10	980	17	2,240	17	2,240
26	28	8	740	7	720	11	1,200	19	2,620	19	2,620
28	30	9	920	8	880	12	1,440	19	3,000	19	3,000
30	32	10	1,120	8	1,040	13	1,700	19	3,380	19	3,380
32	34	10	1,320	9	1,220	15	2,000	21	3,800	21	3,800
34	36	11	1,540	9	1,400	15	2,300	21	4,220	21	4,220
36	38	12	1,780	10	1,600	16	2,620	21	4,640	21	4,640
38	40	13	2,040	10	1,800	17	2,960	24	5,120	24	5,120
40	42	13	2,300	11	2,020	18	3,320	24	5,600	24	5,600
42	44	14	2,580	11	2,240	19	3,700	24	6,080	24	6,080
44	46	15	2,880	12	2,480	20	4,100	27	6,620	27	6,620
46	48	16	3,200	12	2,720	21	4,520	27	7,160	27	7,160
48	50	17	3,540	13	2,980	22	4,960	27	7,700	27	7,700
50	52	18	3,900	13	3,240	23	5,420	30	8,300	31	8,320
52	54	19	4,280	14	3,520	24	5,900	30	8,900	31	8,940
54	56	19	4,660	14	3,800	25	6,400	30	9,500	31	9,560
56	58	20	5,060	15	4,100	26	6,920	33	10,160	35	10,260
58	60	21	5,480	15	4,400	27	7,460	33	10,820	35	10,960
60	62	21	5,900	16	4,720	28	8,020	33	11,480	35	11,660
62	64	22	6,340	16	5,040	29	8,600	36	12,200	39	12,440
64	66	23	6,800	17	5,380	30	9,200	36	12,920	39	13,220
66	68	24	7,280	17	5,720	31	9,820	36	13,640	39	14,000
68	70	25	7,780	17	6,060	32	10,460	39	14,420	43	14,860
70	72	26	8,300	18	6,420	33	11,120	39	15,200	43	15,720
72	74	26	8,820	18	6,780	34	11,800	39	15,980	43	16,580
74	75	27	9,090	18	6,960	35	12,150	42	16,400	47	17,050
75	76	27	9,360	18	7,140	35	12,500	42	16,820	47	17,520
76	78	28	9,920	18	7,500	36	13,220	42	17,660	47	18,460
78	80	28	10,480	18	7,860	37	13,960	42	18,500	47	19,400
80	82	29	11,060	19	8,240	38	14,720	45	19,400	51	20,420
82	84	30	11,660	19	8,620	39	15,500	45	20,300	51	21,440
84	86	31	12,280	19	9,000	40	16,300	45	21,200	51	22,460
86	88	31	12,900	19	9,380	41	17,120	45	22,100	51	23,480
88	90	32	13,540	19	9,760	42	17,960	45	23,000	51	24,500
90	92	33	14,200	19	10,140	43	18,820	50	24,000	55	25,600
92	94	34	14,880	19	10,520	44	19,700	50	25,000	55	26,700
94	96	35	15,580	19	10,900	45	20,600	50	26,000	55	27,800
96	98	36	16,300	19	11,280	46	21,520	50	27,000	55	28,900
98	100	36	17,020	19	11,660	47	22,460	50	28,000	55	30,000
100	150	37	35,520	20	21,660	48	46,460	52	54,000	58	59,000
150	200	37	54,020	20	31,660	49	70,960	53	80,500	60	89,000
200	250	38	73,020	20	41,660	50	95,960	54	107,500	62	120,000
250	300	38	92,020	20	51,660	50	120,960	54	134,500	64	152,000
300	400	39	131,020	20	71,660	51	171,960	55	189,500	66	218,000
400	500	39	170,020	20	91,660	52	223,960	56	245,500	68	286,000
500	750	40	270,020	20	141,660	53	356,460	57	388,000	70	461,000
750	1000	40	370,020	20	191,660	54	491,460	58	533,000	72	641,000
1000	1500	40	570,020	20	291,660	55	766,460	59	828,000	73	1,006,000
1500	2000	40	770,020	20	391,660	55	1,041,460	59	1,123,000	73	1,371,000
2000	5000	40	1,970,020	20	991,660	55	2,691,460	59	2,893,000	74	3,591,000
5000	....	40	....	20	....	55	....	59	....	75	....

CHART 7

NET INCOME, TAX, AVERAGE RATE, AND MAXIMUM BRACKET RATE OF TAX *

For Taxable Individual Income Tax Returns

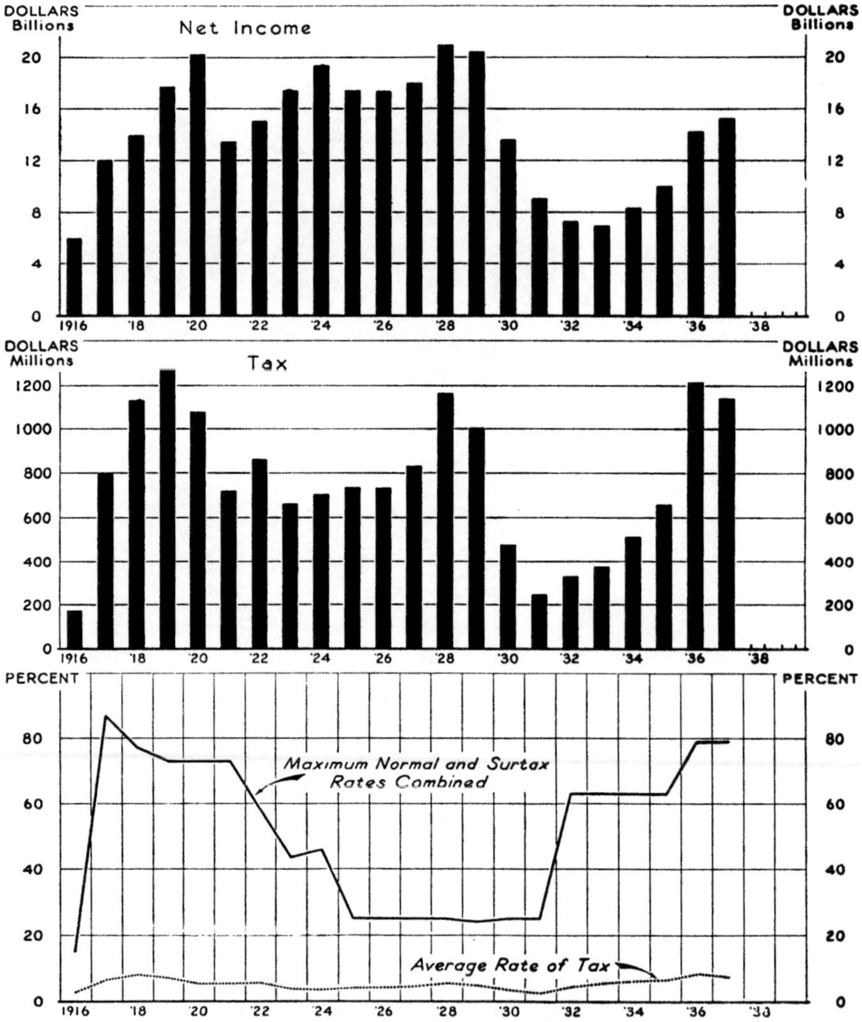

* 76th Congress, 1st Session, *Hearings before the Committee on Ways and Means on Tax-Exempt Securities,* 1939, p. 13.

Table 22

Great Britain

Individual Income Surtax, 1938–1939 [a]

Amount of surtax net income (thousands of dollars)	*Rate %*	*Total surtax cumulative*
Under 10	....	....
10– 12	5.75	$115.00
12– 12.5	5.75	143.75
12.5– 14	7.1875	251.56
14– 15	7.1875	323.44
15– 16	11.5	438.44
16– 18	11.5	668.44
18– 20	11.5	898.44
20– 22	17.25	1,243.44
22– 25	17.25	1,760.94
25– 26	20.125	1,962.19
26– 30	20.125	2,767.19
30– 32	23	3,227.19
32– 38	23	4,607.19
38– 40	23	5,067.19
40– 44	30	6,267.19
44– 50	30	8,067.19
50– 56	33	10,047.19
56– 62	33	12,027.19
62– 68	33	14,007.19
68– 74	33	15,987.19
74– 75	33	16,317.19
75– 80	36	18,117.19
80– 90	36	21,717.19
90– 100	36	25,317.19
100– 150	39	44,817.19
150– 200	42	65,817.19
200– 250	42	86,817.19
250– 300	45	109,317.19
300– 400	45	154,317.19
400– 500	45	199,317.19
500– 750	45	311,817.19
750–1000	45	424,317.19
1000–over	45	

[a] 76th Congress, 1st Session, *Hearings before the Committee on Ways and Means on Tax-Exempt Securities* 1939, p. 60. Compiled from Budget Proposals in Parliamentary Debates, vol. 346, No. 88, April 25, 1939.

The normal tax is 8⅓% on net income of $675 (£135) or less, and 27½% on income in excess of that amount. The surtax is applicable to total income before personal exemption and credits for dependents and "earned income" credit. See Table 25, notes.

Pound converted at $5.

TABLE 23

MAXIMUM SURTAX RATES IN GREAT BRITAIN [a]
1909–1938

Year	*Maximum top bracket surtax net income*	*Maximum rate %*
1909–10 to 1913–14	$15,000	2.50
1914–15	40,000	8.89
1915–16 to 1917–18	50,000	17.50
1918–19, 1919–20	50,000	22.50
1920–21 to 1924–25	150,000	30.00
1925–26 to 1928–29	150,000	30.00
1929–30	250,000	37.50
1930–31 to 1937–38	250,000	41.25
1938–39	250,000	45.00

[a] 76th Congress, 1st Session, *Hearings before the Committee on Ways and Means on Tax-Exempt Securities* 1939, p. 61. See Table 25, notes.
Pound converted at $5.

income in excess of £5000 was added in 1910, the old ungraduated tax with its collection-at-the-source was retained and is still referred to as the income tax; the supertax is thought of as a separate tax and is referred to as such. An Englishman referring to the income tax would not generally expect his auditor or reader to think the supertax was included in his reference as would an American. Collection-at-the-source does not, and could not very well, apply to the supertax, but inasmuch as the larger incomes are relatively few, and because their receivers are relatively "easy marks" and also because British tax officials are expert at their business, the supertax is administered efficiently and collection-at-the-source can still be retained for the income tax, that is, for the one we would call the "normal" tax.

When our first law under the Sixteenth Amendment was under consideration, Congressman Cordell Hull and other proponents of the tax were strongly impressed with the desirability of employing collection-at-the-source. Most of them favored progressive rates also, though some of them did not favor graduation at first because they thought it expedient to simplify administration as much as possible, especially when introducing such an important new tax into a nation of such large numbers scattered over such an extensive territory.

All of them had long witnessed the poor administration of local personal property taxes and some of them knew of the farcical administration of colonial and state income taxes.

They compromised their various proposals by adopting a low "normal" tax with a flat rate (1%) and made provision for as much collection-at-the-source as they thought expedient; but they adopted also an "additional" graduated tax (now called "surtax") which should apply to large incomes, those in excess of $20,000 in the first law. The normal rate on individuals was raised to 2% in 1916 and to 4% in 1917. The three laws of 1913, 1916, and 1917 were the only ones to have a single normal rate until 1934. In 1918 the normal rates were 6% on the first $4000 of taxable income and 12% on the remainder for 1918, and 4% and 8%, respectively, for 1919 and 1920. The 1921 law re-enacted these lower rates. From 1924 to 1931 there were three "normal" rates. For 1924 they were 2% and 4% on the first and second $4000's of taxable income, and 6% on the remainder. In 1925, 1926, and 1927 these rates were reduced to 1½, 3, and 5%, respectively. The lowest normal rate (½%) was in 1929. The other two rates for that year were 2% and 4%. This reduction was made at the request of Secretary Mellon because of the financial crash and also because of the large surplus of government receipts over current expenses. The 1928 rates were again effective in 1930 and 1931. In 1932 two normal rates of 4% and 8% were imposed. Since 1934 there has been one normal rate of 4%. (See Table 20.)

Early administration was simplified, though at some sacrifice of equity and revenue, by granting the large personal exemption of $3000 to an unmarried individual and $1000 more ($4000) to a man and wife regardless of the number of dependents. It is obvious that such large exemptions removed all but a small percentage of the population from income tax liability, and focused the labors of the limited and inexperienced administrative staff where they counted most, that is, upon the smaller number with larger incomes, who were generally easy to discover, who had the best accounting records, and who would provide the most revenue for the government. The introduction of statutory complexities in order to make the tax more equitable could be left till later when administrative experience had been developed and revenue needs had become greater. Unfortunately the unexpected war brought almost overwhelming demands before adequate staff and experience had been developed.

Collection-at-the-source and the crediting of the corporate tax against the individual normal tax, as explained below, were the main reasons for having both a "normal" tax and also a "surtax." Collection-at-the-source was never so important here as in England. With

CHART 8

UNITED STATES AND BRITISH INCOME TAX LIABILITY
MARRIED PERSON, NO DEPENDENTS, 1938

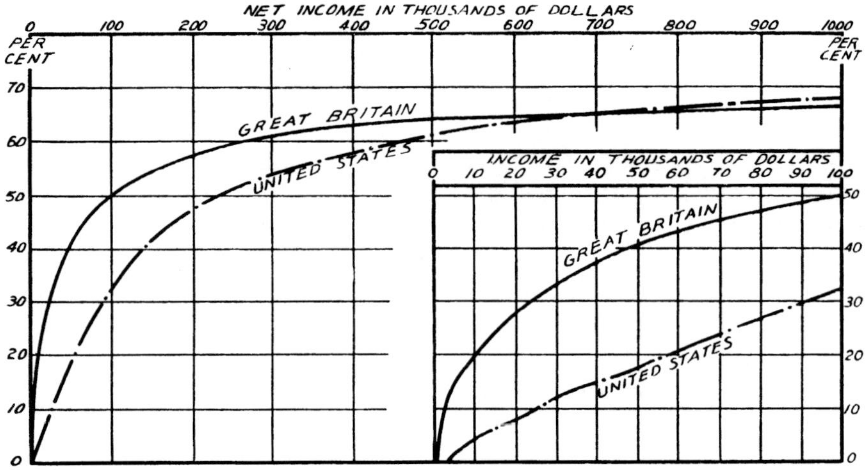

Based on Table 24.

the substitution of "information-at-the-source" in 1916,[4] with the continuation of disparities between the corporation and individual normal taxes since the war, and particularly with the abolition of credit for corporation dividends against the individual normal tax since 1935, there seems to be little or no excuse for retaining a double system of rates and distinguishing between a normal tax and a surtax on individuals. Few of the 34 American states having income taxes have such a combination and most of these result in patchwork rather than in systematic schedules of rates (See Appendix, Exhibits 16 and 17).

From the Tables 20 and 21 herein it will be seen that the rates of both normal tax and surtax were increased, and personal exemptions were decreased as more revenue was needed for the war. These trends were naturally reversed following the war, though neither rates nor exemptions were ever restored to their original positions. With the depression of the 1930's and greater need for relief and other funds, both normal and surtax rates again tended upward, though personal exemptions have remained almost stationary for several years. (For state data see Exhibits 14-17, Appendix, below.)

[4] Collection-at-the-source is still retained in the administration of taxes on some incomes going to non-residents.

TABLE 24

COMPARISON OF THE AMOUNT OF INCOME TAX LIABILITY OF A MARRIED PERSON WITH NO DEPENDENTS UNDER THE UNITED STATES REVENUE ACT OF 1938 AND UNDER THE BRITISH FINANCE ACT OF 1938, FOR SELECTED AMOUNTS OF NET INCOME.

Net income before exemptions	*Amount of Tax* [a]			
	United States		*Great Britain* [b]	
		%		%
$1,000	....	....	....	....
1,500	....	....	$25.00	1.67
2,000	....	....	63.13	3.16
2,500	....	....	173.13	6.93
3,000	$5	.17	283.13	9.44
3,500	26	.74	393.13	11.23
4,000	44	1.10	503.13	12.57
4,500	62	1.38	613.13	13.62
5,000	80	1.60	723.13	14.46
6,000	116	1.93	943.13	15.71
7,000	172	2.45	1,163.13	16.61
8,000	248	3.10	1,410.63	17.63
9,000	329	3.65	1,685.63	18.72
10,000	415	4.15	1,960.63	19.60
12,000	602	5.01	2,620.63	21.83
14,000	809	5.77	3,301.25	23.58
16,000	1,044	6.52	4,030.00	25.18
18,000	1,299	7.21	4,800.00	26.66
20,000	1,589	7.94	5,570.00	27.85
25,000	2,489	9.95	7,770.00	31.08
30,000	3,569	11.89	10,107.50	33.69
40,000	5,979	14.94	15,057.50	37.64
50,000	8,869	17.73	20,557.50	41.11
60,000	12,329	20.54	26,332.50	43.88
70,000	16,449	23.49	32,107.50	45.86
80,000	21,269	26.58	38,020.00	47.52
100,000	32,469	32.46	50,120.00	50.12
200,000	95,344	47.67	114,745.00	57.37
500,000	304,144	60.82	319,620.00	63.92
1,000,000	679,044	67.90	663,370.00	66.33

[a] Maximum earned income allowed. Basis of computations: for U. S. earned income credit 10% (maximum credit $1400), personal exemption, $2500; for Great Britain earned income credit 20% (maximum credit $1500), personal exemption, $900. It should be noted that British taxable income differs from U. S. taxable income. The British exclude certain items that we include; and they differ from the U. S. in the deductions they allow. The British surtax rates are applicable to total income before personal exemption and credits for dependents and "earned income" credit, whereas the U. S. surtax rates apply after deduction of personal exemption and credits for dependents, but before "earned income" credit. See Table 25, notes.

[b] Pound converted at $5. Chart 8 presents the data above in graphic form.

TABLE 25

UNITED STATES AND GREAT BRITAIN

Top bracket normal tax and surtax rate combined and effective rate of tax for a married man with two dependents (1938–1939)[a]

Selected net income[b]	*Top bracket normal tax and surtax rate combined, %*		*Effective rate of tax, % (normal and surtax)*	
	United States	*Great Britain*[c]	*United States*	*Great Britain*
$5,000	4	27.5	1.0	11.2
10,000	9	27.5	3.4	18.0
20,000	15	39.0	7.3	27.2
30,000	23	47.625	11.3	33.5
40,000	25	50.5	14.4	37.8
50,000	31	57.5	17.2	41.7
100,000	59	63.5	32.0	51.9
200,000	64	69.5	47.4	59.9
300,000	68	72.5	53.9	63.6
400,000	70	72.5	57.9	65.8
500,000	72	72.5	60.7	67.2
750,000	74	72.5	65.1	68.9
1,000,000	76	72.5	67.8	69.8
5,000,000	78	72.5	75.8	72.0
Over 5,000,000	79	72.5		

[a] 76th Congress, 1st Session, *Hearings before the Committee on Ways and Means on Tax-Exempt Securities.* June 28, 1939, pp. 59, 61.

[b] Net income before personal exemption and credits for dependents and earned income credit. Maximum earned income assumed.

[c] Surtax as proposed for 1938-1939 from Budget Proposals in *Parliamentary Debates, Volume* 346, *No.* 88, *April* 25, 1939. The British surtax rates are applicable to total income before personal exemption and credits for dependents and "earned income" credit, whereas the United States surtax rates apply after deduction of personal exemption and credits for dependents, but before "earned income" credit. The normal tax is 8⅓% on net income of £135 ($675) or less and 27½% on income in excess of that amount. Pound converted at $5.

War was declared by Great Britain against Germany Sept. 3, 1939. In October Parliament reduced the income tax exemptions, increased the (normal) income tax rate to 35% immediately and to 37½% effective April 1, 1940. It also added two brackets to the surtax, making the maximum slightly under 50%. (New York *Times,* Sept. 28, 1939.)

For income tax rates of various foreign countries see *Tax Systems of the World,* 7th and later editions.

CORPORATION RATES AND EXEMPTIONS

The law of 1913 provided for a one per-cent tax on the income of corporations, replacing the 1909 excise tax of the same rate on corporations doing business, but the $5000 exemption enjoyed under this excise tax was not included in the 1913 law. Corporation dividends paid to a holding company were not again subject to tax when received by the latter, and dividends paid to individuals, already having been subjected to the corporation income tax, were not again liable to the one per-cent "normal" tax applicable to individuals, but were included in individual income for surtax purposes on the theory that a levy corresponding to the surtax had not been paid on this income before distribution by the corporation. For several years, whenever the rate of normal tax on individual income was revised the rate on corporations was changed correspondingly, so that the tax credit for dividends in the hands of individuals continued to correspond with the tax previously paid by the corporation.

War needs and excessive profits made by some corporations soon led to special additional taxes, first to taxes on munitions manufacturers, and later to war-profits and excess-profits taxes on corporations generally and, in the 1917 law, on partnerships and individuals. The graduation and the heights to which these special taxes and the surtaxes on individuals were carried and the trends following the war and since are shown in the Tables herein and have been mentioned in earlier chapters. Attention may be called here, however, to the fact that after the war the corporation income tax was always higher than the normal tax on individual income, although until 1935 the law permitted the exclusion of corporate dividends from individual income subject to normal tax, but not from income subject to the surtax.

It will be noted that during all of the period from 1913 to 1938, except for a short time when the rates of the war-excess-profits tax reached a maximum of 80%, the surtaxes on the upper brackets of individual income have been higher, usually much higher, than the combined federal taxes on corporate income. It has been pointed out elsewhere [5] how these great differences in individual and corporate rates have stimulated the formation of family and other corporations, and also how they have encouraged wealthy directors of corporations to retain corporate earnings in the corporation rather than distribute them and thus subject them to higher individual surtaxes. On the other hand, many partnerships (none of which is subject to the federal income tax *per se*) and individual entrepreneurs having small or moderate incomes have been favored as com-

[5] See above, Chap. XVII (1936 Act).

TABLE 26

CORPORATION TAXES UNDER THE ACTS OF 1909 TO 1939, INCLUSIVE [a]

Act	*Income Tax*		*Excess Profits Tax*		*Capital Stock Tax*	
	Rate (Per Cent)	*Exemption*	*Rate Per Cent*	*Income Taxable*	*Rate per $1000*	*Exemption*
1909	1	$5000				
1913	1	none				
1916	2	none	12½	munition manufacturers,	$.50	$99,000
1917	6	none	20–60	net income above exemption of $3000 plus percentage of invested capital [b]	.50	99,000
1918	12 (1918) 10 (1919, '20)	2000 2000	30–80 20–40	net income above exemption of $3000 plus percentage of invested capital [c]	1.00	5,000
1921	10 (1921) 12½ (1922)	2000	....	....	1.00	5,000
1924	12½	2000	....	....	1.00	5,000
1926	13 (1925) 13½ (1926, '27)	2000	....	....	1.00 (1925) repealed (1926)	5,000
1928	12 (1928, '30, '31) 11 (1929)	3000				
1932	13¾	none				
NIRA (1933)	13¾	none	5	net income in excess of 12½ per cent of adjusted declared value of capital stock	1.00	none
1934	13¾	none	5	same as above	1.00	none
1935	12½–15	none	6 12	net income in excess of 10 per cent but not in excess of 15 per cent of adjusted declared value of capital stock net income in excess of 15 per cent of adjusted declared value of capital stock	1.40	none
1936 1937	(*a*) Normal tax, 8–15 (*b*) Undistributed-profits, 7–27 (*c*) Special corporations Banks, insurance companies, non-resident foreign corporations, 15 Resident foreign corporations, 22	none	6 12	same as 1935 Act ..	1.00	none

[a] Compiled from official sources. See also Exhibit 8, Appendix.

[b] $3000 plus an amount equal to the same percentage of invested capital for the taxable year as the average annual prewar income was of prewar invested capital (not less than 7% nor more than 9%); or, if corporation was not in existence during at least 1 whole year of the prewar period, 8% of invested capital for taxable year; or, if during prewar period, corporation had either no net income or a very small net income or, if invested capital cannot be determined, same per cent as that of representative corporations.

[c] $3000 plus either an amount equal to the average prewar net income plus or minus 10% of the increase or decrease of invested capital for the taxable year as compared with average pre-war invested capital, or 10% of the invested capital for the taxable year, whichever is greater.

[d] This was the undistributed-profits tax. A special "notch" provision was drafted to care for cases in which the net income was only slightly over $25,000.

TABLE 26 (*Continued*)

CORPORATION TAXES UNDER THE ACTS OF 1909 TO 1939, INCLUSIVE [a]
(*Continued*)

Act	*Income Tax*		*Excess Profits Tax*		*Capital Stock Tax*	
	Rate (Per Cent)	*Exemption*	*Rate Per Cent*	*Income Taxable*	*Rate per $1000*	*Exemption*
1938	General					
	(*a*) Net income over $25,000: 19 less 16½ per cent of dividend received and 2½ per cent of dividend paid [d]	none	6 12	same as 1935 Act	$1.00	none
	(*b*) Net income $25,000 or less, 12½–16	none				
	Special corporations					
	Banks, insurance and mutual investment companies, 16½					
	Resident foreign corporations, 19					
	Non-resident foreign corporations, 15					
1939	General					
	(*a*) Net income over $25,000, 18	none	6	same as 1935 Act	1.00	none
	(*b*) Net income not over $25,000, 12½–16		12			
	Special corporations					
	Mutual investment, foreign corporations, 18					
	Banks, insurance, China Trade Act companies—same as for general corporations					
	Resident foreign corporations, 18					

[a] Compiled from official sources. See also Exhibit 8, Appendix.

pared with corporations ever since the repeal of the excess-profits tax in 1921, because corporate income tax rates have exceeded normal rates plus lowest surtax rates on individual incomes.

For a good many years the orthodox view has been that graduation of taxes on individuals is justified as a means of adjusting tax burden somewhat according to ability to pay, but that graduation of taxes on corporate income is not justifiable because the stockholders are the ultimate bearers of such taxes and the several stockholders of a corporation usually have such different abilities that a rate or set of rates that would accord with the abilities of some stockholders would not accord with the abilities of others.

Until relatively recently most income taxes on corporations have not been graduated. The Wisconsin income tax adopted in 1911 was an exception, and a few other states have adopted graduated corporation income taxes in recent years. It is true that the war-profits and excess-profits taxes of 1917-1921 were graduated, but they were emergency measures and were soon repealed as undesirable if not obnoxious in ordinary times. The corporate excise tax of 1909 and the regular or normal federal taxes on corporate incomes from 1913 to 1935 were not graduated. But the 1935 law introduced one innovation in the form of mild graduation of this tax, that is from 12½% to 15%,[6] and it also graduated the relatively light excess-profits tax that had been re-introduced as a flat tax by the National Industrial Recovery Act in 1933. The 1935 law provided also an extensive graduation of the penalty tax rates on undistributed income of personal holding companies. Some preceding penalty taxes had had two rates, but no such schedule of graduated rates as the 1935 law.

The 1935 law introduced also the innovation of taxing 10% of the dividends received by a corporation from another corporation; the 1936 law increased this percentage to 15%, thus discouraging the formation or continuation of holding companies. This was in line with the recommendations of President Roosevelt, though it did not go so far as he suggested. All of the above-mentioned graduations of federal taxes on corporate income have been continued to date, with some slight changes in rates; and, moreover, the 1936 Act introduced an additional extensively graduated tax on undistributed corporate income. The latter tax was continued in principle but was much reduced and modified by the 1938 Act; rates were lowered and exemptions increased, not to mention other important changes. To say that the corporate income tax was revolutionized by the Roosevelt administration is a very conservative statement. The revolution in range and height of rates has not been greater than that in the underlying philosophy, though there were many who were not convinced of the equity or wisdom of the changes. In fact, active opposition to the undistributed-profits tax was so effective that Congress permitted the much-berated levy to expire December 31, 1939, according to the terms of the Act of 1938.[7]

Table 26 shows the exemptions that have been granted to corporations to ease the burdens of those having small incomes. Such exemptions are practically equivalent to a certain graduation of rates; they aid the great majority of corporations, the small ones. Corporations having large incomes form a small minority of the total number, though their output, profits, and income tax payments are relatively significant.

[6] Graduation of corporation rates was advocated by Garner for many years and, in 1928, was adopted by the House. See above, Chap. XI, p. 285.

[7] See above, Chapters XIX and XX.

CHAPTER XXIII

ADMINISTRATION [1]

THE CIVIL WAR ACTS

The office of Commissioner of Internal Revenue was established in 1862 to administer the income tax, the excise taxes on commodities, and taxes on corporation gross receipts. The states and territories were divided into collection districts,[2] in the chief city of which an office was established. A collector and an assessor were appointed for each district, and these officers were authorized to select such deputies and assistants as they needed. At first collectors were paid on a commission basis, that is, 4% of the first $100,000 collected and 2% on additional amounts, but the maximum was set at $10,000.

[1] The chief sources for this chapter are the *Reports* of the Commissioner of Internal Revenue, unpublished data in the Bureau, other materials referred to herein, personal experience as auditor in the Bureau and interviews with staff members and others. The authors are particularly indebted to Mr. W. T. Sherwood, Assistant Deputy Commissioner.

[2] The 1862 law restricted the maximum number of districts to the number of representatives in Congress. In 1939 there were 65 collection districts in the United States. The difficulties of collecting revenue in the southern states in 1864 are exemplified in the following letter:

Memphis, Tenn., 1-20-64

Com'r. of Taxes for Tenn. to Lewis, Commissioner.

Sir. Your favour on the subject of a personal bond has been duly considered. My home is 300 miles from this place. I tryed to go to it a few days since, in order to enable myself to properly respond, and it only led to the realization of the fact, that my family had just been *robed* and damaged to the amount (as a military court has said) of $10,000 — and the family driven within the federal lines for protection and subsistance. The robery was perpetrated at midnight, whilst my wife was compelled to stand on the pazza barefoot in her night cloathes, beging the rebles not to burn the house over her head, which they declared was their intention.

There are no clerks — no Judges — no justices of the peace or other officers in authority, whereby a bond could be authenticated. I dare not go beyond the federal lines to find a friend or anyone with whom I might have business. I had to obtain a military escort for 40 miles before I could reach my family, whom I found destitute of every article of cloathing, taken by the rebles extending to the under cloathing of my wife and daughter. (You cannot as is ever the case around this city) go five miles beyond our picket lines without a reasonable prospect of being robed of the cloathes on your back, if you escape with your life (if a union man). it may be difficult for you, that you are safe at your homes, to appreciate our situations and the State of things as they exist here, but so are the facts.

I have given the Hon. Secretary the best security in the country. I could offer no better, but if the public service is likely to suffer thereby, I will give up my office willingly. It is simply an impossibility to do otherwise just now the office has no facenations for me, its true it gives me a support, since the rebles have destroyed for me, or deprived me of the use of three saw and grist mills, my former source of income, but I have the consolation to know that God has tempered the wind to the shorn lamb.

Respectfully

John B. Rodger
Com'r.

(U. S. Treasury, Secretary's File, Series AB, 9: 13, 14.)

Assessors were paid $3 a day for making arrangements and giving instructions to assistant assessors ; $5 a day for hearing appeals, revising valuations, and making out lists. In 1863 the President was authorized to appoint Revenue Agents to aid the enforcement of the law.

In order to ferret out tax evaders informers were allowed a share of fines or penalties imposed for violation of the internal revenue laws. This offered so much temptation to employees of the Bureau, and to some outside the government service, that it led to a notorious system of "racketeering."

Taxpayers complained of the prying, inquisitorial methods of the employees of the Bureau, but the same problems evidently faced those who enforced the law in Civil War days as now. Writing of these difficulties in 1894, David A. Wells, who made a special study of the administration of the law, 1866-1869, wrote:

> American ingenuity was never more strikingly illustrated — not even by the exhibits of the Patent office — than it was at that time in devising and successfully carrying out methods for evading the taxes on incomes and distilled spirits.[3]

Although the income tax was discontinued in 1871, the excises on liquor and tobacco were retained, hence the activities of the Bureau were limited to the enforcement of these taxes. The expansion of the office is shown in Exhibit 6, Appendix.

PRE-WORLD-WAR INCOME TAX ADMINISTRATION

In 1909 the staff in Washington, including clerical and technical employees, numbered less than 300. In the field were 65 collectors in charge of districts, about 1150 deputy collectors, and 40 revenue agents. The total budget was less than $5,000,000.[4]

The passage of the Corporation Excise Act necessitated not only additional staff but the development of a new technique. The dominant character of the work became accounting rather than policing. Corporation income tax returns had to be audited in Washington and, to verify them, corporation books of record had to be examined in the field. Some effort was made to check tax liability by securing lists of corporations from state officials. Certain cities were selected as fields for special examination in 1911, 1912, and 1913. Even with this intensive work, the number of corporation filings in 1913 was only slightly over 300,000, of which only 61,116 showed taxable net income. The yield of the corporation excise tax

[3] Wells, David A., "An Income Tax: Is it desirable?" *Forum* 17: 8 (March 1894).

[4] The Compensation of the Commissioner was then $6000 ; it was increased to $10,000 by the Revenue Act of 1918. For salaries of other officers of the Bureau see *Official Register of the United States* (annual).

and the number of returns filed is shown above in Chapter II, Table 5.

The first income tax act under the Sixteenth Amendment (1913) necessitated an extension of staff and an enlargement of quarters, but not a fundamental change in procedure. A new office, that of third deputy commissioner, was established with the title "Income Tax Deputy Commissioner." Under his direction the new Income Tax Unit was organized. Two divisions were formed: the personal income tax division and the corporation tax division. Tax returns from corporations were handled much as before.

All income tax returns were forwarded by the collectors of the several districts to Washington where they were examined for mathematical errors. Little else in the way of a careful audit was possible, since many of the clerks were not selected because of their especial accounting or legal proficiency. Fortunately the 1913 Act was comparatively simple in its terminology and the rates were not high enough to create serious temptation to evasion. The only sections that caused administrative difficulty were those in regard to the withholding of the tax at the source. They necessitated a great deal of referring from one return to another in the Bureau. Taxpayers were often confused about this matter in filling out their returns and hence made many errors.

Continuing the procedure that had been started under the Corporation Excise Tax Act, revenue agents made field audits of certain returns and submitted their reports to the Bureau. They had no authority, however, to make any tax adjustments and, in fact, they were not under the direction of the Income Tax Unit until 1920. This staff of field men was deficient not only as to numbers but also as to training. The Commissioner of Internal Revenue reported in 1915 that a preliminary audit in Washington indicated that 5% of the returns of individuals and 15% of the returns of corporations were in need of further investigation but that even those few were greatly in excess of the number that could be cared for by the field force; in fact, it would require three-and-a-half years to complete the work that would be submitted to them in the following year. The small number of filings, 375,515 individual returns in 1915, indicated that many were not complying with the law, partly of course because of ignorance.

The Revenue Act of 1916 introduced two new principles: (1) a tax on a special industry, munition manufacturers, and (2) allowance for special amortization of plant and machinery for making war equipment. Because of the complexity of the tax on munition makers, the Income Tax Unit did not attempt to audit returns of such companies until an examination had been made of the taxpayers' books. A special corps of revenue agents was organized for this work. The second problem, that of obsolescence, was to plague the Bureau for many years.

WAR EXPANSION

The war income taxes were levied to secure a vast amount of revenue for the prosecution of the War and to get it as quickly as possible. The Revenue Act of 1916 yielded approximately $410,000,000; that of 1917, $3,694,000,000. Of this latter amount two-thirds was from the income and excess-profits taxes, the remainder from additional levies on excises already in force and from numerous new taxes on documents, admissions, club dues, and certain commodities. The Bureau of Internal Revenue was responsible for the administration of all these taxes.

The new income tax law was especially involved because of the increased rates, lowered exemptions, and new bases for computing income. The excess-profits tax, applicable to income of both individuals and corporations from invested capital, was particularly difficult to interpret and administer. It involved the determination of capital values, including the interpretation of the meaning of invested capital, depreciation of property, and similar complicated and somewhat vague concepts.[5] It was exceedingly difficult, not only for the Bureau to interpret the law, but also to draft regulations that could be readily understood by taxpayers many of whom had not been subject to the law before. Even in the issuance of the forms and blanks the Bureau ran into snags. Because of the war disruption of the transportation system, paper supplies were low. When finally the thirty-one different kinds of returns required by the Act were printed, distribution proved to be a serious problem. Because of innumerable delays the filing date was postponed a month.

The Income Tax Unit, small and poorly organized, was not prepared for the tremendous flood of returns that poured in during 1918; in fact, the returns for 1916 had not yet been audited. In his report for 1917 the Secretary of the Treasury commented that, because of so much delay, in numerous cases inquiry for additional information brought the reply that the taxpayer had been "long since deceased!"

[5] Speaking before the Academy of Political Science (New York) George O. May, who had been in England studying the income tax, said that the blame for administrative difficulties in the United States should be placed on Congress. He cited the work of the Interstate Commerce Commission in valuing railroads; the Internal Revenue Bureau had a much more difficult task with less money and "without any general recognition of the enormous task they were trying to perform." (*Proceedings* of the Academy of Political Science, 11: 146, April 1921.)

CHART 9

INCOME TAX DIVISION, 1917

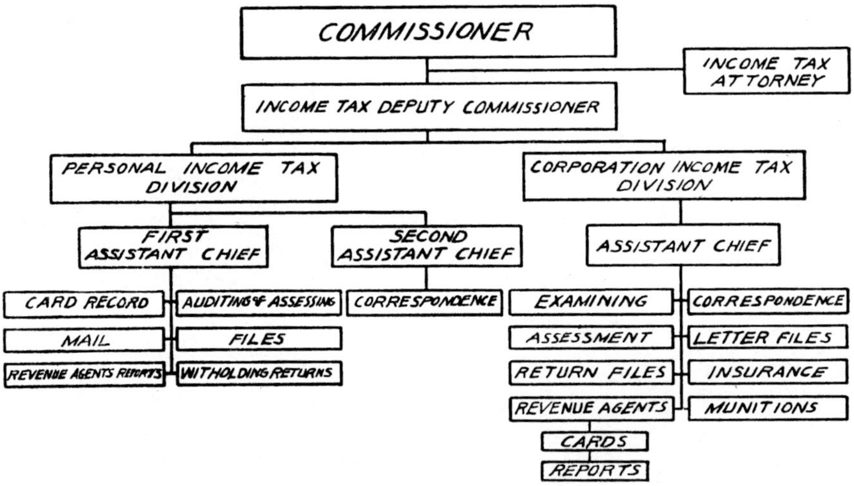

The number of returns filed in 1918 was five times that of 1917, but the work was multiplied by ten. The first question confronting administrators, that of space in which to handle the unit, was answered in a most unsatisfactory way by moving from the main Treasury building to the old Convention Hall at 5th and K streets, N.W., the ground floor of which was occupied by a public meat and vegetable market. The space was probably as ample as could be secured in crowded wartime Washington, but the building was inconveniently located, dirty, and odorous. It was a vast open auditorium, noisy, poorly adapted to the work that had to be done, besides being a fire hazard. In such a place the fundamental physical problem of merely caring for the returns seemed insoluble. They had to be protected, and at the same time be available for ready reference.

Much more perplexing was the question of personnel. During the year 1918 the staff of the Income Tax Unit was increased from 380 to 1200, and in the first six months of 1919, to 2692 – much too rapid a growth for proper assimilation. Due to competition from other war work and the drafting of men into the army, it was not possible to secure an adequate number of employees with proper legal and accounting experience. Every effort was made to train employees in courses given after work hours and eventually by establishing a special day course.

TABLE 27

NUMBER OF TAXABLE INDIVIDUAL INCOME TAX RETURNS
1916–1937 [a]
(By net income classes in thousands of dollars)

Year	*Net income classes*						
	Under 100	100–200	200–500	500–1000	1000 *and over*	*Total* 100 *and over*	*Total*
1916	348,702	4,184	1867	376	206	6,633	355,335
1917	1,584,854	4,604	1604	315	141	6,664	1,591,518
1918	3,388,364	3,224	1030	178	67	4,499	3,392,863
1919	4,225,655	4,075	1197	189	65	5,526	4,231,181
1920	5,514,661	2,781	712	123	33	3,649	5,518,310
1921	3,587,633	1,817	451	63	21	2,352	3,589,985
1922	3,677,218	2,934	869	161	67	4,031	3,681,249
1923	4,265,939	3,089	878	141	74	4,182	4,270,121
1924	4,483,983	4,149	1249	242	75	5,715	4,489,698
1925	2,491,606	6,517	2357	479	207	9,560	2,501,166
1926	2,461,408	6,569	2314	468	231	9,582	2,470,990
1927	2,429,819	7,383	2892	557	290	11,122	2,440,941
1928	2,507,086	10,099	4384	983	511	15,977	2,523,063
1929	2,443,233	9,205	4122	976	513	14,816	2,458,049
1930	2,031,443	4,281	1453	318	150	6,202	2,037,645
1931	1,522,362	2,250	708	149	77	3,184	1,525,546
1932	1,934,259	1,351	379	86	20	1,836	1,936,095
1933	1,745,689	1,490	430	81	50	2,051	1,747,740
1934	1,794,013	1,346	442	86	33	1,907	1,795,920
1935	2,108,243	1,918	579	109	41	2,647	2,110,890
1936	2,856,389	3,515	965	178	61	4,719	2,861,108
1937	3,367,293	3,046	893	162	49	4,150	3,371,433

[a] 76th Congress, 1st Session, *Hearings before the Committee on Ways and Means on Tax-Exempt Securities* 1939, p. 62. See Table 28, note b.

THE ADMINISTRATIVE CRISIS

Although the Reports of the Commissioner for these years warily admitted some "congestion" they did not state the full truth. In August 1918, however, Commissioner Roper testified before the Committee on Ways and Means that four million returns for 1916 and 1917 were still unaudited.[6] Congress increased the appropriation for the Bureau from $12,000,000 in 1918 to $20,000,000 in 1919, but even with these additional funds and the tremendous increase in personnel mentioned above no perceptible progress was made in catching up with the work. In fact, the Revenue Act of 1918 in-

[6] 65th Congress, 2d Session, *Hearings before the Committee on Ways and Means on the Proposed Revenue Act of 1918.*

TABLE 28

NET INCOME FOR TAXABLE INDIVIDUAL INCOME TAX RETURNS
1916–1937 [a]
(Net income classes and money figures in thousands of dollars)

Year	*Net income* [b] *classes*						
	Under 100	100–200	200–500	500–1000	1000 *and over*	*Total* 100 *and over*	*Total*
1916	$4,181,045	$580,905	$554,247	$256,771	$464,264	$1,856,187	$6,037,233
1917	8,986,471	624,474	460,575	214,631	306,836	1,606,516	10,592,987
1918	12,902,537	432,850	300,827	119,076	137,487	990,240	13,892,776
1919	16,522,067	546,209	342,403	128,290	152,650	1,169,552	17,691,620
1920	19,501,955	366,478	203,486	79,964	77,078	727,006	20,228,960
1921	12,946,681	240,957	129,855	42,780	49,411	463,003	13,409,685
1922	14,127,919	385,320	250,291	106,243	141,287	883,140	15,011,058
1923	16,563,878	406,036	254,307	94,320	152,072	906,736	17,470,613
1924	18,170,275	544,478	349,534	149,910	154,174	1,198,105	19,368,381
1925	15,111,401	855,708	676,735	319,582	416,543	2,268,575	17,379,975
1926	15,000,035	876,867	674,705	315,004	494,034	2,360,610	17,360,645
1927	15,213,998	985,755	843,535	372,514	593,410	2,795,222	18,009,220
1928	16,546,370	1,358,089	1,285,567	666,855	1,105,025	4,415,545	20,961,915
1929	16,087,185	1,240,755	1,220,245	665,502	1,207,862	4,334,373	20,421,558
1930	12,062,326	547,187	406,292	202,841	353,130	1,509,442	13,571,767
1931	8,414,806	248,427	171,965	81,793	142,793	644,978	9,059,785
1932	7,148,956	77,300	49,593	18,396	21,032	166,329	7,315,284
1933	6,642,454	126,150	81,458	46,316	69,089	323,013	6,965,468
1934	7,923,783	180,087	122,450	59,464	57,775	419,776	8,343,558
1935	9,462,467	256,433	167,765	73,811	73,630	517,639	10,034,106
1936	13,244,719	467,356	276,375	122,762	107,641	974,134	14,218,854
1937	14,401,882	404,779	257,686	114,399	85,416	862,280	15,264,162

[a] 76th Congress, 1st Session, *Hearings before the Committee on Ways and Means on Tax-Exempt Securities* 1939, p. 63.

[b] Gross income less deductions as specified in the revenue act effective for each income year, and including, for the years 1922 through 1933, the capital net gains and net losses subject to the flat 12½ per-cent rate. The various credits against net income allowed during the period have not been deducted.

creased administrative difficulties by requiring not only valuations of invested capital, depletion, obsolescence, but also estimates of amortization of war equipment and other computations that could not be made by ordinary mathematical rules. The Bureau reached an impasse.

T. S. Adams, then an advisor in the Treasury, commented on the situation in the spring of 1921 in these words:

No federal administration, in my opinion, is capable during the next five or six years of carrying with even moderate success two such burdens as the income tax and the excess profits tax. . . As a matter of fact, it seems to be beyond doubt that the administration of these two taxes is in danger of collapse. . .

Why not improve the administration? The reply is that it will take years to improve it. The intricacy of the excess profits tax is such that it is hardly an exaggeration to say that it takes more time to teach an accountant to master its mysteries than the average accountant can be retained in the service after he has attained such mastery.[7]

A basic reason for the crisis was the complicated nature of the law, as stated above, particularly the relief and regulatory provisions for determining the excess-profits tax. They permitted a special determination of the tax due by the Commissioner when it was impossible to compute the amount of deduction based on invested capital, either because the invested capital was difficult to determine or because there was no other comparable corporation. This determination was time-consuming and usually unsatisfactory, opening the door to endless litigation.[8] It is significant that at this time (1939)

7 Adams, T. S., "The Excess Profits Tax," *Quarterly Journal of Economics*, 35: 372-73 (May 1921).

8 The following case record may give a clearer idea of the course of procedure and reasons for delay.

The "A" Lumber Company

Chronological history of 1917 return in connection with the audit:

May 1, 1918. The 1917 return of the above-mentioned case was filed.

Dec. 18, 1919. Taxpayer requested 60-day extension of time for filing general forest-industries questionnaire.

Dec. 30, 1919. Extension for 30 days granted.

Aug. 14, 1920. General forest-industries questionnaire mailed; received August 17, 1920.

Sept. 4, 1920. Further information requested.

Oct. 28, 1920. Conference.

Dec. 1, 1920. Information requested from M Co.

Feb. 23, 1921. Conference.

(March to August. Correspondence.)

Feb. 13 and 14, 1922. Conference. Additional information requested.

Mar. 8, 1922. Taxpayer requested extension of time for filing information called for in conference of February 14, 1922.

Mar. 13, 1922. Time extended until March 31.

Mar. 27, 1922. Reply to request for information in conference of February 14, 1922. A revenue agent's report dated September 30, 1922, covering the years 1917 and 1918 was forwarded during this time.

Nov. 11, 1922. Taxpayer advised that value of March 1, 1913, was then under advisement.

Nov. 23, 1922. Taxpayer requested that no values be set until receipt of further information, which it will furnish by December 1, 1922.

Nov. 23, 1922. Final extension of filing information granted until December 1, 1922.

(January, April, 1923. Two conferences.)

Nov. 30, 1923. Original valuation report on 1917 and 1918.

Dec. 8, 1923. Case returned to Section G. (Handled returns involving natural resources) . . .

Mar. 11, 1924. An A-2 letter covering the years 1917 and 1918 based on the R. A. R. dated September 30, 1922, was mailed to the taxpayer. Brief No. 3 was submitted protesting audit and valuation adjustments.

May 9 and 10, 1924. Conference was held. At this conference the taxpayer requested that time be granted in which to furnish additional data and a further hearing given.

May 21, 1924. Additional information requested. Reply June 10.

July 16, 1924. Conference as per request. [*Continued at bottom of next page.*]

the Bureau is still working on cases from 1917 and 1918. Table 29 shows the number of returns for each tax year that remained unaudited in succeeding years.

Even in the sections of the Bureau where the work was not so complicated seemingly inextricable confusion prevailed. The audit and claims sections of the Income Tax Unit settled claims made by taxpayers for abatement of income tax assessed and refund of income tax paid. These sections handled the general run of the returns; difficult ones were sent to special technical sections. Decision of taxpayers' cases was reached only after much delay, partly because of necessary correspondence with the taxpayer and partly because of many reviews by supervisors in the income tax unit. Some of this verification was necessary because of the incompetence of auditors, but some was due to unwillingness of the chiefs of the sections to place responsibility on their subordinates. The system in the Bureau became annoyingly trivial and sometimes seemed futile to the auditors.[9]

Even when a claim was settled, it was not a closed transaction. Frequently the government reopened the case because of change in Bureau rulings, a new Treasury decision, or a verdict by a court of law. The taxpayer too had the privilege of reopening without any formality. Hence the continued influx of returns to be audited and of claims to be adjusted and readjusted nearly wrecked the Bureau. The number of cases reopened is shown in Table 30.

In order to relieve the congestion in Washington, it was arranged in 1919 to audit in the local offices returns showing net income of $5000 or less. It was decided to classify returns audited in Washington according to importance and to audit first those involving the

---

Oct. 8, 1924. In accordance with taxpayer's request and T. D. 3616, the file containing the years 1917 and 1918 was transmitted to the review division of the solicitor's office. In this office numerous conferences were granted the taxpayer in accordance with his requests, some lasting several days. Additional data were furnished by the taxpayer.

Nov. 11, 1924. Additional information requested. Reply November 13.

Aug. 2, 1926. The case was returned to section G.

Sept. —, 1926. The taxpayer requested that, if the values contended for were not allowed by the review division, the case be sent to special assessment section. Case prepared and forwarded to special assessment section.

Oct. 7, 1926. On learning the case was in special assessment section, the taxpayer wrote to this office requesting the case be withdrawn from special assessment. Immediately after receipt of this letter the taxpayer in an oral hearing requested that the mailing of the NP-2 letter be held up in order that he could submit information in connection with installment sales. This request was granted.

Dec. 17, 1926. NP-2 letter mailed.

Apr. 1, 1927. At request of general counsel conference set for April 11, 1927.

Apr. 7, 1927. At request of taxpayer conference postponed to May 23, 1927.

May —, 1927. Appeal to the United States Board of Tax Appeals filed.

(Joint Committee on Internal Revenue Taxation, *Report* 1927, III: 144.)

[9] As an example, a letter to a taxpayer notifying him of the settlement of a claim was held many weeks on desks of various "chiefs" and finally returned to the auditor to revise because the word "therefore" in the last line was incorrectly placed.

TABLE 29

NUMBER OF RETURNS UNAUDITED IN THE INCOME TAX UNIT JUNE 30, 1923 TO JUNE 30, 1939 BY TAX YEARS [a]

Years	On Hand June 30, 1923	On Hand June 30, 1924	On Hand June 30, 1925	On Hand June 30, 1926	On Hand June 30, 1927	On Hand June 30, 1928	On Hand June 30, 1929	On Hand June 30, 1930	On Hand June 30, 1931	On Hand June 30, 1932	On Hand June 30, 1933	On Hand June 30, 1934	On Hand June 30, 1935	On Hand June 30, 1936	On Hand June 30, 1937	On Hand June 30, 1938
1917	28,916	8,773	3,417	1,372	622	294	185	147	142	150	293	116	167	80	102	112
1918	84,323	19,364	6,002	1,877	861	389	232	222	180	207	248	85	119	69	70	71
1919	103,198	61,327	12,155	2,628	1,184	493	299	270	174	251	267	118	125	84	79	90
1920	458,205	166,484	90,746	7,121	2,081	637	400	367	298	275	240	116	163	115	107	85
1921	1,190,902	353,781	171,221	8,192	2,020	668	409	305	249	261	239	96	146	105	114	89
1922	1,167,000	719,702	380,045	141,084	5,136	1,109	575	466	276	307	245	148	209	130	118	90
1923	....	1,100,624	372,200	154,329	35,316	2,531	1,111	754	423	373	315	157	232	149	138	111
1924	....	....	975,298	170,786	107,607	15,662	5,019	1,828	735	517	536	212	281	157	162	123
1925	....	....	....	255,351	289,275	38,067	7,305	2,556	1,001	677	1,028	277	352	204	212	154
1926	....	....	....	....	30,433	120,248	17,104	5,814	1,630	1,101	1,265	388	435	226	276	204
1927	....	....	....	....	....	148,088	122,286	18,529	5,061	3,713	2,939	634	507	336	337	253
1928	....	....	....	....	....	....	115,522	166,800	10,172	4,380	2,632	1,033	823	517	439	317
1929	....	....	....	....	....	....	......	23,835	237,868	10,496	5,236	3,246	2,214	1,162	803	616
1930	....	....	....	....	....	....	......	......	106,491	209,921	9,929	4,298	2,993	1,539	1,012	790
1931	....	....	....	....	....	....	......	......	......	22,142	208,111	9,522	4,562	2,096	1,243	877
1932	....	....	....	....	....	....	......	......	......	83	92,211	297,803	13,643	4,229	2,100	1,285
1933	....	....	....	....	....	....	......	......	......	......	......	45,421	339,235	14,996	4,912	2,559
1934	....	....	....	....	....	....	......	......	......	......	......	......	36,188	123,752	25,318	10,841
1935	....	....	....	....	....	....	......	......	......	......	......	......	......	200,151	144,459	28,508
1936	....	....	....	....	....	....	......	......	......	......	......	......	......	......	354,629	236,513
1937	....	....	....	....	....	....	......	......	......	......	......	......	......	......	......	308,884
1938	....	....	....	....	....	....	......	......	......	......	......	......	......	......	......	186
Total	3,032,544	2,430,055	2,011,084	742,740	474,535	328,186	270,447	221,893	364,700	254,854	325,734	363,670	402,394	350,097	536,630	592,758

[a] Numbers of such returns on hand June 30, 1939 were:

1920 and earlier	99	1924	43	1929	220	1934	3,450
1921	30	1925	72	1930	315	1935	10,086
1922	34	1926	80	1931	422	1936	42,112
1923	36	1927	103	1932	520	1937	98,775
		1928	112	1933	1114	1938	281,366
							438,989

TABLE 30

REOPENING OF CASES [a]

Fiscal year ended June 30	On hand beginning fiscal year	Number reopened	Number closed	Number on hand, end of fiscal year
		1917 RETURNS		
1922	....	....	....	123,308
1923	123,308	9,209	92,872	39,645
1924	39,645	27,350	56,768	10,227
1925	10,227	11,481	18,291	3,417
1926	3,417	7,594	9,639	1,372
1927	1,372	2,366	3,116	622
		58,000	180,686	
		1918 RETURNS		
1922	....	....	....	114,956
1923	114,956	53,585	71,675	96,866
1924	96,866	17,771	75,845	38,792
1925	38,792	3,055	35,845	6,002
1926	6,002	9,870	13,995	1,877
1927	1,877	5,398	6,414	861
		89,679	203,774	
		1919 RETURNS		
1922	....	....	....	354,947
1923	354,947	59,999	234,818	180,128
1924	180,128	76,090	151,441	104,777
1925	104,777	31,020	123,642	12,155
1926	12,155	20,980	30,507	2,628
1927	2,628	7,976	9,420	1,184
		196,065	549,828	
		1920 RETURNS		
1922	....	....	....	1,045,674
1923	1,045,674	95,516	682,985	458,205
1924	458,205	281,716	520,099	219,822
1925	219,822	28,953	158,029	90,746
1926	90,746	79,297	162,922	7,121
1927	7,121	16,932	21,922	2,081
		502,414	1,548,088	
		1921 RETURNS		
1923	....	....	....	1,190,902
1924	1,190,902	10,093	837,121	363,874
1925	363,874	53,374	245,027	171,221
1926	171,221	178,088	341,117	8,192
1927	8,192	22,818	28,990	2,020
		263,373	1,452,255	
Grand Total..................		1,109,531	3,934,631	6,768

[a] *Report of Joint Committee on Internal Revenue Taxation,* 1927, III: 33-34.

most money and usually those involving also the most difficult questions of law. It was hoped that this would result in a body of valuable precedents for the decision of other cases but it resulted chiefly in much delay. Most of the returns had to be sent to the field for complete verification from the taxpayers' records, not only for the tax year in question, but also for the prewar years 1911 to 1913, if invested capital, depreciation, or depletion of property was involved. This took a vast amount of time, years in some instances; hence, when it seemed obvious from a preliminary audit that there was a tax deficiency, additional tax was assessed before the field report was completed because of the statute of limitations. This procedure added to the administrative muddle.

ADMINISTRATIVE IMPROVEMENTS

With hopes of restoring order a further increase was made in the number of employees in the Bureau and the routine in the Bureau was revised in 1920. During that year almost two thousand additional auditors were employed. The personnel problem was, however, not much simpler after the War than before. As in previous years, it was almost impossible to secure a staff adequately trained at the low salaries offered. It was even more difficult to keep employees after they had had valuable training and experience in the Bureau. Complexities of the law caused such difficulties for taxpayers that the demand for tax lawyers and accountants exceeded the supply. Salaries paid by business firms were so attractive that the government could not compete with them. The Bureau became known as an excellent training school for highly skilled tax experts. Furthermore, some Bureau employees lacking ethical standards left the Bureau with knowledge of profitable cases which they offered to handle for the taxpayer for a percentage of the tax refund secured. It was found necessary to rule that no one who left the Bureau to become a tax advisor would be re-instated.

On October 1, 1919 there were 2779 in the Income Tax Unit in Washington. Before June 30, 1920, 944 had left the service. The Bureau employed 2482 during the period. In the following fiscal year 1479 left the Bureau. The staff that year numbered 4317 in June 1920 and 5376 in June 1921. The next year 1087 left the service. The total number of appointments and separations in the field service as well as in Washington from October 1, 1919 to June 30, 1927 is shown in Table 31. The total number of employees in the Bureau of Internal Revenue and in the Income Tax Unit 1909-1938 is shown in Table 32.

Table 31

Appointments and Separations, Income Tax Unit 1919–1927 [a]

Period	Number at beginning of period			Separations during period			Additions during period			Number at end of period		
Washington												
Fiscal year ending June 30	Technical	Clerical	Total	Technical	Clerical	Total	Technical	Clerical	Total	Technical	Clerical	Total
1920	1532	1247	2779	451	493	944	1002	1480	2482	2083	2234	4317
1921	2083	2234	4317	517	962	1479	973	1565	2538	2539	2837	5376
1922	2539	2837	5376	448	639	1087	441	709	1150	2532	2907	5439
1923	2532	2907	5439	377	594	971	471	453	924	2626	2766	5392
1924	2626	2766	5392	500	542	1042	95	229	324	2221	2453	4674
1925	2221	2453	4674	312	737	1049	133	500	633	2042	2216	4258
1926	2042	2216	4258	577	543	1120	24	202	226	1489	1875	3364
1927	1489	1875	3364	297	587	884	6	135	141	1198	1423	2621
Total	......	......	......	3479	5097	8576	3145	5273	8418			
Field												
1921	1720	241	1961	......	......	......	......	......	......	2100	341	2441
1922	2100	341	2441	331	124	455	718	210	938	2487	427	2914
1923	2487	427	2814	327	206	533	427	272	699	2589	493	3080
1924	2587	493	3080	406	179	585	64	165	229	2245	479	2724
1925	2245	479	2724	140	76	216	205	118	323	2310	521	2831
1926	2310	521	2831	310	94	404	442	184	626	2442	611	3053
1927	2442	611	3053	185	84	269	514	197	711	2771	724	3495
Total, Washington and Field												
1921	3803	2475	6278	......	......	......	......	......	......	4369	3178	7817
1922	4639	3178	7817	779	763	1542	1159	919	2078	5019	3334	8353
1923	5019	3334	8353	763	800	1504	898	725	1623	5213	3259	8472
1924	5213	3259	8472	906	721	1627	159	394	553	4466	2932	7398
1925	4466	2932	7398	452	813	1265	338	618	956	4352	2737	7089
1926	4352	2737	7089	887	637	1524	466	386	852	3931	2486	6417
1927	3931	2486	6417	482	671	1153	520	332	852	3969	2147	6116
Total	......	......	......	5178	5860	11,083	5515	6419	11,934			

[a] *Report of the Joint Committee on Internal Revenue Taxation,* 1927, III: 155. The data for the fiscal years ending June 30, 1920 and 1921 are incomplete. They include data for the Washington staff only from October 1, 1919 and do not include figures showing separations and additions in the field from September 30, 1920 to June 30, 1921.

The cost to the Bureau of this constant shift of personnel cannot be measured accurately. In 1927 it was estimated to have been over $13,000,000 for the period since 1919, and this was "insignificant in comparison with the actual cost resulting from loss of ability, experience, and judgment." [10] Taxpayers also found it expensive because of the constant changes of rules and regulations that accompanied changes in the personnel that drafted them. In 1921 T. S.

[10] *Report of the Joint Committee on Internal Revenue Taxation,* 1927, III: 35.

TABLE 32

PERSONNEL IN THE OFFICE OF THE COMMISSIONER OF INTERNAL REVENUE AND THE INCOME TAX UNIT 1909–1939

Fiscal Year Ending June 30	*Office of the Commissioner*			*Income Tax Unit*		
	Washington	*Field*	*Total*	*Washington*	*Field*	*Total*
1909	285	3,536	3,821			
1910	281	3,576	3,857			
1913	277	3,729	4,006			
1914	277	3,695	3,972			
1915	530	4,200	4,730			
1916	560	4,158	4,718			
1917	585	4,529	5,114			
1918	2245	7,257	9,502			
1919	4088	9,967	14,055	2672		
1920	5912	12,528	18,440	4317		
1921	6996	13,145	20,141	5376	2413	7789
1922	7275	14,113	21,388	5439	2914	8353
1923	7239	13,756	20,995	5392	3080	8472
1924	6447	12,756	19,203	4674	2731	7405
1925	6176	13,157	19,333	4258	2831	7089
1926	4843	13,060	17,903	3364	3071	6435
1927	3798	9,474	13,272	2630	3447	6077
1928	3671	9,310	12,981	2280	3640	5920
1929	3584	8,689	12,273	2214	3379	5593
1930	3448	8,531	11,979	2110	3334	5444
1931	3461	8,372	11,833	2105	3313	5418
1932	3405	8,371	11,776	2046	3275	5321
1933	3378	8,282	11,660	1965	3229	5194
1934	3798	12,720	16,518	1985	3202	5187
1935	4300	14,732	19,032	2043	3567	5610
1936	4294	14,180	18,474	2043	4175	6218
1937	4935	18,666	23,601	2270	4113	6383
1938	5189	19,226	24,415	2179	4406	6585
1939	4669	19,377	24,046	2116	4499	6615

The personnel of the Income Tax Unit is included in the personnel of the Office of the Commissioner. There are slight discrepancies between Tables 31 and 32, though both are from official sources; possibly the periods covered are slightly different.

Adams commented on this fundamental weakness of American government, that is, the failure to make public positions attractive to men of ability by offering adequate salaries, security, and prestige.[11]

The change of routine within the Bureau involved both a shift in

[11] Adams, T. S., "The Excess Profits Tax," *Quarterly Journal of Economics*, 35 : 372 (May 1921).

work from one division to another and an increase in the number of divisions. Some of these changes were temporary or not of a nature to be of interest to the general reader; one important development was the creation of a Field Audit Division to direct the work of the revenue agents who were used by the Income Tax Unit, the first important move in the direction of decentralization.

Another development was the result of congressional agitation over the situation in the Bureau. The Board of Tax Simplification was created in 1921 to hear taxpayers' complaints, study the procedures of the Income Tax Unit and make recommendations for its improvement. Six men were selected, three by the President to represent the public and three by the Secretary of the Treasury to represent the Bureau of Internal Revenue. The latter were employees of the Bureau. Their report, published in December 1923, was in three parts: (1) Recommendations to the Bureau, (2) Discussion of the condition of work, and (3) Recommendations as to legislation.[12] In the first, the Board recommended several important changes in procedure to eliminate duplication of work and reopening of claims. It urged that the work of the claims and audit division be decentralized so that some of the work could be done in the local offices, thus aiding the taxpayer and preventing the congestion in Washington.

The Commissioner adopted some of the suggestions. He gave orders that "cases once closed should not be reopened except in case of fraud or gross error." Legislation to this effect was incorporated in the Revenue Act of 1921. Changes to eliminate duplication of work and evasion of responsibility were made in the procedure of the Bureau. The Commissioner was not convinced, however, that decentralization would be of any value, hence this recommendation was not carried out.

There were three recommendations for legislation. One for the establishment of an independent quasi-judicial body to hear tax cases was the official origin of the Board of Tax Appeals created three years later.[13] The second recommendation, one of the most important, was for a new building;[14] the third was the elimination of profits and losses from sale of capital assets in the computation of net income. The new building was constructed in the course of time, but Congress was never favorable to the third proposal.

[12] 68th Congress, 1st Session, *House Document* 103. Various parts of the Report were issued during the previous two years in mimeographs.

[13] See below, p. 544.

[14] After moving from Convention Hall the Unit was scattered to six different places, some divisions to the New Treasury Annex, some to the Interior Building, and some to temporary buildings. The new Internal Revenue Building on Constitution Avenue was occupied in 1932.

THE COUZENS REPORT

In 1924 Congress again took official notice of the state of affairs in the Bureau and appointed a Select Committee on Investigation of the Bureau of Internal Revenue.[15] The undercurrent of hostility between the Treasury and Congress which existed during most of the decade from 1920 to 1930 came to the surface occasionally. A few Senators, especially Couzens (Rep., Mich.) and McKellar (Dem., Tenn.) bitterly criticized the Bureau of Internal Revenue. Couzens and Secretary Mellon were engaged in a series of petty but bitter personal tilts. The Senate was in a muckraking mood in 1924, hence it was hardly to be expected that the Bureau would escape.[16]

The resolution for a special committee to investigate the Bureau was passed after the Finance Committee had refused to undertake the task and after the original preamble had been toned down.[17] The members of the committee were Couzens (Rep., Mich.), Watson (Rep., Ind.), Jones (Dem., N. M.), King (Dem., Utah), and later, Ernst (Rep., Ky.). Watson and Couzens were the only active members at the start, and even Watson soon became so irritated because Couzens employed an attorney to assume charge of the investigation that he introduced a resolution to discharge the committee. The whole idea was political, he claimed, to belittle Mellon and through Mellon to besmirch President Coolidge. The debate was bitter, but the conclusion was to let the investigation continue. A staff of workers was organized under the direction of Couzens and fifteen months later the report was made.

Three lines of investigation were pursued by the Committee: (1) the administration of the prohibition laws, (2) the extent to which income was escaping taxes, and (3) the administration of income and estate taxes, particularly with respect to deductions for depletion and amortization of war facilities.

The Report severely criticized the "practically unlimited discretionary power vested in the Commissioner," the failure of the Commissioner to publish many of the rulings, and the granting to the taxpayer of "innumerable extensions of time for furnishing information required to determine the validity of deductions." In other

15 *Cong. Rec.* 65: 4013-4023.

16 At least 50 Senators were working on 16 special committees looking into the affairs of the Veterans Bureau, oil leases of the Navy, the Interior Department, and the Department of Justice—investigating chiefly the scandals of the Harding régime.

17 This stated that the government lost millions of dollars because of the improper organization or gross inefficiency of the Bureau of Internal Revenue, that taxpayers were oppressed, that corruption or the opportunity for corruption existed, and that numerous tax-attorneys, agents, and tax advisors in the employ of taxpayers claimed to have special influence with officers of the Bureau and were carrying on negotiations with them.

words, the Bureau was taken to task for abuse of the very administrative flexibility it was criticized for not using in the earlier days.

The most serious charges were those of laxity in interpreting the sections of the law allowing deductions for depletion and amortization. According to the cases studied and reported, those deriving the greatest benefit from the deduction of discovery depletion were not newly formed "wildcat" oil companies for whose benefit the law was passed, but old, well-established corporations. The criticism was made also that, in the adjudication of cases involving obsolescence, there were no rulings nor instructions for the guidance of either the engineers of the Income Tax Unit or taxpayers until after the expiration of the time fixed by law for determination of claims. As a result there had been "the grossest kind of discrimination among taxpayers." [18]

A short reply to these charges was made by the minority members of the Committee, introduced into the Senate by Ernst. He stated that many of the cases had been explained by the Bureau and that the Committee did not accept the invitation of the Bureau to see the entire procedure at first hand. The report was discounted, also, because much of the information was secured from disgruntled, discharged employees and because of the Mellon-Couzens "feud."

Although little official attention seemed to be paid to the investigation, the press played it up and it had its influence in Congress. In drafting the 1926 Revenue Act members of the Committee on Ways and Means consulted Couzens and accepted his suggestions to the extent of establishing a permanent committee to study internal revenue taxes, although it was not set up exactly as he desired. This was known as the Joint Committee on Internal Revenue Taxation and its establishment may be looked upon as the official reply of Congress to Couzens.

SPECIAL BOARDS AND COMMITTEES

This permanent Joint Committee was only one of a number of special boards and committees selected during the course of the years to aid the Bureau, but it was unique in that it was made up of members of Congress. The first of these special committees was appointed in 1918. It was a group of economists and business men under the direction of T. S. Adams, and was called the Excess-Profits Tax Advisors. They endeavored to interpret the law for the Treasury and at the same time to secure the good will of taxpayers. Adams remained as official and unofficial advisor to the Treasury for a number of years.

[18] 69th Congress, 1st Session, *Senate Report* 27.

In 1919 a similar body, known as the Tax Advisory Board, was established. The five members of this group assisted in interpreting the sections of the law applicable to such difficult problems as reorganization, net losses, and amortization inventory losses. When this body disbanded in seven months because several of the members were obliged to return to their own businesses, the work was carried on by a special group of lawyers and accountants, ostensibly outside the Income Tax Unit but in the Bureau. This was called the Committee on Appeals and Review. The chief purpose of this committee was to hear taxpayers' complaints and cases in which refunds were claimed or additional assessments were protested. This committee continued until 1924, though with various changes in personnel.

Appeal to the Commissioner, represented by the Committee on Appeals and Review, was unsatisfactory for several reasons: (1) the committee was in the Bureau and hence was not an impartial body; (2) the person who decided the appeal acted as both advocate and judge, since he had to protect the interests of the government and decide the questions involved; (3) if the decision was in favor of the government, the taxpayer could test the decision in the courts; but, if it was not in favor of the taxpayer, the action of the Bureau was final; therefore on doubtful points the decision was likely to be in favor of the government; and (4) the taxpayer was forced to go to Washington for a hearing.

THE BOARD OF TAX APPEALS

The next step, therefore, was the creation in 1924 of a body independent of the Bureau and the Treasury to hear taxpayers and review their cases before deficiency assessments were paid. This was the Board of Tax Appeals.

When the Treasury draft of the section proposing such an organization was first written, the Board of Tax Appeals was defined as an administrative body, with members appointed by the Treasury for life terms. During the public hearings preceding the drafting of the bill by the Committee on Ways and Means, objections were made to several of these provisions. The fact that the Board was to be in the Treasury indicated that it would not be the unprejudiced body that was needed. The provision that members were to be appointed by the Treasury added to this fear. It was argued, too, that if the body were not judicial the Board would not be any improvement over the Committee on Appeals and Review.[19]

[19] 68th Congress, 1st Session, *Hearings before the Committee on Ways and Means on H. R.* 6715.

These considerations received much attention in the House of Representatives. Before the bill came up for debate the Democrats, especially Garner and Blanton, and some of the Progressives objected to having the Secretary of the Treasury appoint the members and they objected also to the amount of salary, $10,000 each. In the committee meetings and on the floor of the House much stress was placed on the necessity of keeping the Bureau independent, free of bias toward or against either the taxpayer or the government.[20]

The House amended the bill so as to provide for the appointment of members by the President, with the advice and consent of the Senate, with salaries at $7500.[21] These changes were accepted by the Senate and written into the bill. The Senate further amended the measure by making the Board a quasi-judicial instead of an administrative body. When the constitutionality of this section of the law was reviewed, the Supreme Court held that the Board was not a court but an executive or administrative body.[22]

From the outset the Board was handicapped by several restrictions. The low-salary scale for members and also for assisting attorneys made it difficult for the Board to secure competent men outside of the Treasury. Another restriction was that members of the Board were forbidden to practice before the Board for a period of two years after leaving office. The object was to prevent the turnover in personnel experienced by the Income Tax Unit which had spent much of its energies training attorneys for more lucrative practice outside.

The jurisdiction of the Board was limited to claims for abatement of taxes; it had no authority over claims for refund.[23] Within 60 days of receipt of notice of additional assessment the taxpayer could file an appeal with the Board. A copy of the taxpayer's petition was sent to the Commissioner, who had 20 days in which to make his reply. In order to relieve taxpayers of the necessity of coming to Washington, arrangements were made to send divisions of the Board to cities in various parts of the country for short periods of time.

Before the Board had completed its first year of work it became clear that the number of cases it could handle was only a small per-

[20] *Cong. Rec.* 65: 3281-3287.

[21] In 1926 the salaries were increased to $10,000. It was probably not accidental that this increase was voted after 1925 when salaries of Congressmen were raised from $7500 to $10,000.

[22] *Old Colony Trust Co.* v. *The Commissioner,* 279 U. S. 716 (1929). Ogden Mills, who was looked upon as Mellon's spokesman in the House, told his colleagues that in changing the nature of the Board Congress had wrecked the administrative machinery. An informal group, he said, could reach decisions much more quickly than a formal judicial one. (*Cong. Rec.* 65: 9540.)

[23] When this was discussed in the Senate, McKellar proposed that the Board adjudicate claims for refund as well as abatement when the amount involved exceeded $10,000. Smoot replied that if such an amendment were adopted the Board would need 300 judges. (*Cong. Rec.* 65: 7696.)

TABLE 33

NUMBER OF PETITIONS FILED WITH THE BOARD OF TAX APPEALS DURING THE FISCAL YEARS 1928 TO 1939, BY TAX YEARS [a]

Tax Year	1928	1929	1930	1931	1932	1933	1934	1935	1936	1937	1938
1917	174	62	16	30	18	10	24	8	8	13	20
1918	339	89	47	38	28	35	21	11	7	7	22
1919	476	118	67	50	28	32	18	12	7	9	36
1920	966	198	99	127	86	65	37	15	13	10	28
1921	823	166	67	86	29	37	58	20	16	10	28
1922	1,844	265	79	105	82	35	33	39	33	20	32
1923	4,638	579	159	174	66	37	60	52	37	29	37
1924	3,274	1845	679	452	108	52	76	47	55	37	41
1925	3,000	2514	1094	617	161	65	95	92	56	40	46
1926	825	1947	2054	1,288	246	113	128	98	69	45	46
1927	17	348	1233	3,164	849	175	172	143	95	59	51
1928		13	211	5,643	1493	297	223	169	180	97	64
1929			5	378	5107	1827	589	282	209	155	129
1930				5	269	3574	1632	442	272	170	124
1931				1	4	236	2023	1002	530	269	156
1932					1	6	156	2001	1369	584	238
1933						1	2	104	2213	1315	682
1934								3	126	1465	2165
1935									2	228	1571
1936										5	360
1937											5
Total	16,376	8144	5810	12,158	8575	6597	5347	4540	5297	4567	5881

[a] The corresponding numbers of petitions filed in 1939 for the years indicated were:

1917	17	1922	32	1927	80	1932	149	1937	413
1918	7	1923	44	1928	80	1933	273	1938	10
1919	13	1924	42	1929	93	1934	837		——
1920	28	1925	47	1930	80	1935	2044	*Total*	6197
1921	15	1926	57	1931	102	1936	1734		

centage of those appealed to it; for example, in the first ten months it decided about 1000 of the 4000 cases submitted. The number of appeals filed is shown in Table 33.

THE JOINT COMMITTEE ON INTERNAL REVENUE TAXATION

In accordance with the provisions of the Revenue Act of 1926, ten members of Congress were selected to form the Joint Committee on Internal Revenue Taxation. The law stated that five members were to be appointed from the House Committee on Ways and Means and five from the Senate Committee on Finance, of whom three from each House were to be from the majority party and two from the minority party. The members organized in the summer of 1926 with Chairman Green (Iowa) of the Committee on Ways and Means as Chairman of the Joint Committee also. They provided for a technical staff and directed that the work be along two lines, simplification of the law, and improvement of administration. In

August, L. H. Parker, an engineer, was made Chief of the Division of Investigation.[24] Other members of the technical staff were selected; at first, three auditors and an assistant. In the following spring C. D. Hamel was made Chief of the Division of Simplification. A voluntary advisory committee was chosen to assist both divisions temporarily.[25] Later this division of work was changed and the staff enlarged. The function of the Committee has been that of studying ways and means of improving the tax laws, advising Congress and its tax committees, acting as a liaison between the Treasury and Congress on tax matters and in drafting revenue legislation.

In the fall of 1927 the Joint Committee submitted to Congress a report dealing with: (1) certain difficult phases of the law, such as earned income, capital gains and losses, surtax evasion, and consolidated returns; (2) proposed rearrangement of the text of the law for clarification and simplification, and (3) administration of the law. The report was invaluable to Congress and to the Bureau. This was followed by other studies and by an important codification of the Internal Revenue Laws (1939), but in recent years the greatest service of the Committee's staff has been in advice and aid to Congress by more direct and less formal methods than through printed reports.

THE LEGAL STAFF — THE OFFICE OF CHIEF COUNSEL

No account of the administration of the income tax would be complete without some mention of the work of the legal staff. At the time of the establishment of the Income Tax Unit an attorney designated Solicitor was appointed to the legal staff of the Bureau to care for the income tax work. With the expansion of work the Solicitor's office became more and more involved in income tax cases. By the Revenue Act of 1926 the title of Solicitor was changed to General Counsel, the staff was enlarged, and salaries were increased. In 1934 the organization was slightly changed by establishing the office of General Counsel for the Treasury and that of Assistant General Counsel for the Bureau of Internal Revenue.

The duties of the Assistant General Counsel embrace the preparation and presentation of the government's case in all appeals before the Board of Tax Appeals; the review of refunds, credits, and abatements in excess of $20,000; decision and advice on tax questions submitted by the Secretary, Undersecretary, or Assistant Secretary of the Treasury, the General Counsel of the Treasury, the Commis-

[24] Mr. Parker remained in office until 1937, with the title Chief of Staff. He was succeeded by Mr. Colin F. Stam, an attorney who had been on the staff for a number of years.

[25] The members were T. S. Adams, A. A. Ballantine, George E. Holmes, George O. May, and Thomas W. Page.

sioner or heads of administrative units of the Bureau, Collectors of Internal Revenue, and other branches of the government.

The activities of the office are allocated to six divisions: Appeals, Civil, Interpretative, Penal, Review, and Legislation and Regulations. The Appeals Division has charge of cases filed with the Board of Tax Appeals and those appealed from the Board to Appellate Courts. The Civil Division prepares statements of facts for the Department of Justice, obtains witnesses and assists at trials when requested by the Department of Justice. The Interpretative Division considers for administrative purposes the various statutes relating to the internal revenue and passes upon questions of law arising under them. The Penal Division prepares opinions construing criminal statutes and deals with tax cases involving criminal liability. The Review division reviews overassessments and proposed refunds in excess of $20,000. It prepares reports to the Joint Committee on Internal Revenue Taxation when the overpayment exceeds $75,000. The Legislation and Regulations Division prepares regulations issued under the internal revenue laws and makes reports on suggested changes in the internal revenue laws and regulations.[26]

The handicaps under which the legal staff competes with taxpayers were thus cited by Secretary Morgenthau in his testimony before the Joint Committee on Tax Evasion in 1937:

> We have now a bar of registered attorneys and tax accountants numbering approximately 45,000. Against them are pitted some 2,800 field agents actively engaged in tax investigations for the Government. The contest is, of course, unequal. The fees of the tax lawyer exceed by thousands of percent the pay of his opponent employed by the Government. In this manner the most resourceful brains of the legal world are engaged actively in trying to avoid taxes for their clients. Among these are men who received their early training from the Government, and who use the skill they acquired in that service against the younger men who take their places. The Government then becomes a training school for many of its opponents.[27]

ADMINISTRATION BECOMES A LEGAL BATTLEGROUND

The brief chronicle of the developments in the Bureau in the first part of this chapter was interrupted by the accounts of the various legal and review bodies. It has been shown that the great mass of returns filed under the war revenue acts raised audit problems and legal problems that were almost insuperable. By 1923 the Bureau had worked out a semblance of order.[28] The great war rush was

[26] *Report of the Secretary of the Treasury* 1937, pp. 161-168.

[27] 75th Congress, 1st Session, *Hearings on Tax Evasion and Avoidance* (1937) Part 1, p. 10.

[28] The staff was gradually reduced from a maximum of 8472 in 1923 to 6077 in 1927 and to 5187 in 1934. Since then it has been increased. See Table 32.

over; the law of 1921 was much simpler than that of 1918. Gradually the audit sections cleared out the old returns. Unfortunately, however, this did not mean a final settlement of cases. In too many instances it meant their transfer to litigation, particularly to the Board of Tax Appeals. The Joint Committee on Internal Revenue Taxation, in its study of the situation in 1927, analyzed the problem and made many recommendations based upon the following "truisms":

> (1) At root the major problem is one of personnel.
> (2) All tax cases cannot be closed upon a basis of absolute accuracy. To attempt to do so is to sacrifice accomplishment to unattainable ideal. Prompt and final settlement is often more important than meticulous accuracy.
> (3) The collection of revenues is primarily an administrative and not a judicial problem. As far as the Federal income tax is concerned, a field of administration has been turned into a legal battle field.[29]

The fact that the Board of Tax Appeals was unable to keep up with the cases filed was some evidence that the Bureau was not doing its job.[30] This was further indicated by the fact that the Board sustained the Bureau in only 40% of the amount of tax claimed by the government in cases heard between July 1, 1927 and June 30, 1928.[31]

Several suggestions were made for the improvement of routine in the Bureau and for the employment of several high-salaried technical advisors. A Special Advisory Committee was established in the Bureau in 1927 "to afford the public a more direct and expeditious procedure for the settlement of its tax disputes." The aim of the Bureau became settlement of tax cases even at the sacrifice of some revenue. Before June 30, 1931 the Advisory Committee had secured settlement without trial in 12,696 cases which represented 19.8% of the cases docketed with the Board of Tax Appeals.

The success of this procedure led to an important step in the decentralization of the work of the Bureau, the training of revenue agents in key positions to represent the Advisory Committee in the field. The Field Procedure Division was created in the Income Tax Unit to form a contact between Washington and the field. Field divisions included representatives of the Special Advisory Committee (succeeded by the Technical Staff in 1933) and the office of the General Counsel. Every effort was made to reach the taxpayer by personal contact. This decentralization policy has been continued and expanded.

This policy of aggressive settlement of tax cases became a target

29 *Report of the Joint Committee on Internal Revenue Taxation*, 1927, III: 2.

30 On June 30, 1927 there were pending more than 18,000 cases involving more than $550,000,000 in taxes.

31 *Report of the Secretary of the Treasury* 1928, p. 174.

for Congressional charges that the Treasury was showing favoritism to certain large taxpayers. Publication of the news that the United States Steel Company had been granted a refund of $53,000,000 in 1928 was used as a case in point.[32] At that time (prior to 1934) it was necessary to pass special appropriation measures for tax refunds. In the early 1920's these special bills contained a proviso that the Treasury report all refunds to Congress. The Revenue Act of 1926 also required that such refunds be reported. Some of the senators, particularly those hostile to the Bureau, thought this was inadequate as a check on possible abuse. The requests of large sums ($43,000,000 in December 1927; $103,000,000 in January 1928; $75,000,000 in 1929) stirred Heflin, McKellar, and others to introduce amendments for drastic changes in procedure. In 1928 McKellar proposed that refunds in excess of $50,000 be approved by the Comptroller General. This was a direct affront to the Bureau of Internal Revenue and contrary to the wishes of Congress, as expressed in prior legislation forbidding a review of claims by administrative or accounting officers outside the Bureau.

When this proposal was rejected after a tremendous controversy between the House and the Senate,[33] McKellar introduced others, such as requiring all refunds over $10,000 to be certified to the Board of Tax Appeals, and requiring an open hearing before an officer or committee of the Treasury department. These also were rejected. The provision of the 1928 Revenue Act that grew out of this controversy required the Commissioner to report to the Joint Committee on Internal Revenue Taxation all refunds or credits of income, estate, or gift tax in excess of $75,000 at least thirty days before paying them, and required the Joint Committee to report annually to Congress the names of all persons and corporations to whom such payments were made.

EMPHASIS ON REVENUE RATHER THAN SETTLEMENT

With the decrease in tax revenue because of the depression and with the initiation of the New Deal efforts to prevent tax avoidance, the Bureau of Internal Revenue changed its policy in 1933. A drive

32 This enormous case covered the years 1918, 1919, and 1920. The Treasury had worked on it for a decade. Some of the study on invested capital covered sixty years of the company's history. There were 195 companies involved. The records took all the shelf space in two rooms. There were thirty volumes on amortization alone. The final letter of the Bureau covered 2400 pages. (*Cong. Rec.* 70: 1195-1234, 1315-1321, 2064; 72: 5747-5766.)

33 When this amendment was introduced the members of the Committee on Ways and Means summoned representatives of the Treasury Department to a hearing. 69th Congress, 2d Session, *Hearings . . . on Amendments to H. Res.* 16462. The Senate was very insistent that the measure be passed but the House voted down the proposition seven times. (*Cong. Rec.* 68: 2294, 3642, 4420, 4664.)

TABLE 34

COLLECTION OF BACK TAXES, 1934–1939 [a]

	1934	1935	1936	1937	1938
1. Assessments based on agreements secured by field agents	$18,897,448	$23,797,542	$45,224,651	$57,279,977	$53,877,036
2. Assessments based on agreements executed prior to mailing of 60 or 90 day letter	41,742,943	66,846,866	85,454,752	117,705,315	95,809,170
3. Agreements subsequent to mailing 60 or 90 day letter	38,503,163	4,312,969	5,411,975	4,508,826	4,982,029
4. Assessments listed in cases where taxpayers neither executed agreements nor filed appeals	23,420,736	13,786,480	21,763,393	16,059,924	14,495,181
5. Assessments listed in appealed cases, after decision by Board of Tax Appeals	69,330,359	69,408,401	57,546,236	43,186,950	34,994,503
6. Abatement and credit claims rejected	2,136,097	887,310	2,743,431	4,020,879	1,254,323
Total	$194,030,746	$179,039,568	$222,099,314	$242,761,874	$205,862,242

[a] From *Reports of the Commissioner of Internal Revenue.* Jeopardy assessments are excluded.

The corresponding collections in 1939 were: item 2, $144,506,648; item 3, $4,249,916; item 4, $13,517,938; item 5, $35,381,557; items 1 and 6, distributed among other items; total, $197,656,059.

was inaugurated to check loss of revenue by closing loopholes in the law. For example, deductions for loss from sales between members of the same family were no longer allowed, and an order was issued that certain agreements on final settlement of tax must be approved by the Secretary or Undersecretary of the Treasury. Brokers' records were checked. Collectors, revenue agents, and other field officials were called to Washington for a special meeting, at which time a "quota" was set for $200,000,000 in back tax collections for the calendar year 1934.

In June 1933 the House of Representatives authorized a study of the methods of tax evasion. Many of the recommendations of this subcommittee's report have been mentioned in connection with the

CHART 10. INCOME TAX UNIT, 1939

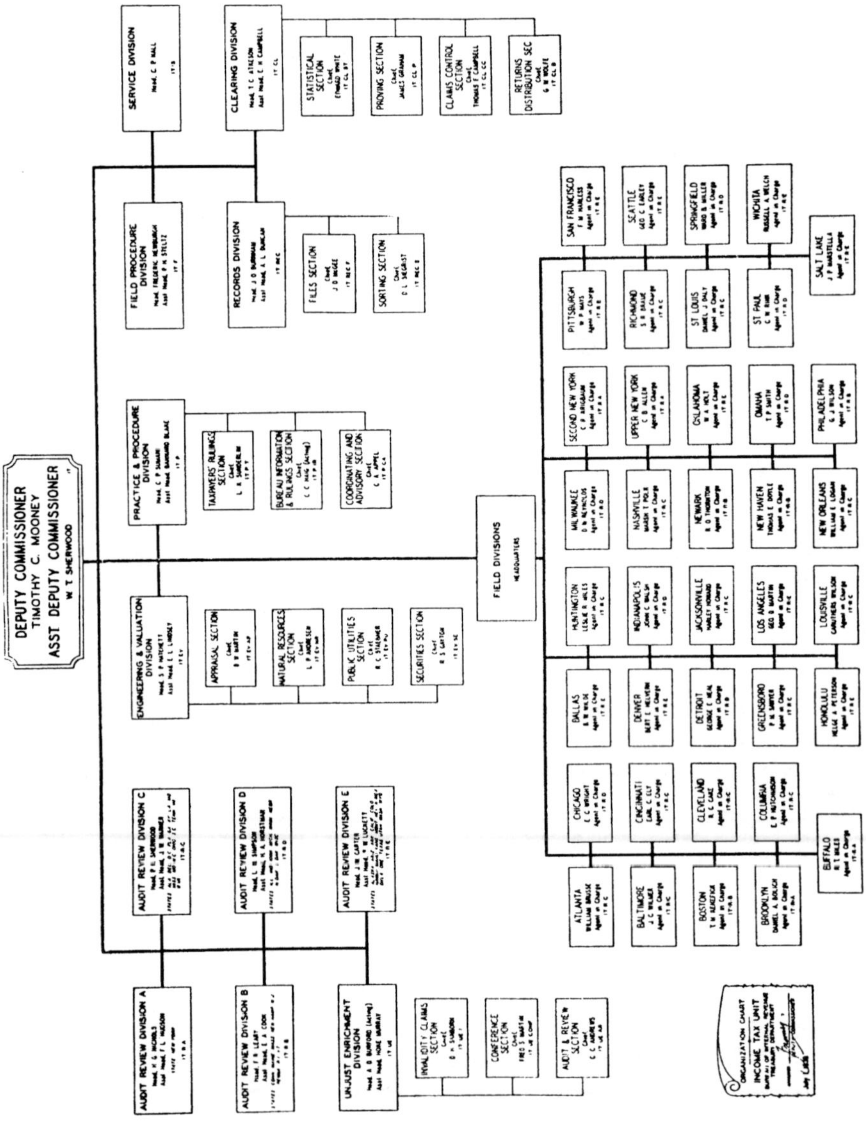

drafting of the Revenue Act of 1934.[34] Several recommendations were made in regard to routine in the Bureau. The result was a stricter interpretation of the regulations with respect to depreciation and depletion. In the first six months of 1934 the Bureau disallowed depreciation deductions of over $248,000,000 which resulted in increased taxable income of over $242,000,000 and deficiency assessments of over $29,000,000. This policy of stricter enforcement has been followed since 1933. The consequent additional taxes collected are shown in Table 34.[35]

DECENTRALIZATION OF THE INCOME TAX UNIT

From the point of view of administrative procedure, the most important recent development is the decentralization of the Bureau. In 1936 an experiment was started at Cleveland. There a division was organized in which the agent in charge was delegated to represent the Commissioner and to assume the usual duties in negotiations for settlement. To this office were assigned a staff of engineers and attorneys from the office of the General Counsel. Arrangements were made with the traveling units of the Board of Tax Appeals for speedy trials when negotiations with the taxpayers were unsuccessful.

In 1938 a policy was inaugurated of establishing field divisions of the Technical Staff.[36] The first was set up on the Pacific Coast, with jurisdiction over cases originating in the states of Washington, Oregon, California, Idaho, Montana, Nevada, Utah, and Arizona and the territories of Alaska and Hawaii, with offices at Los Angeles, San Francisco, Seattle, Salt Lake City, and Honolulu. The second was established in New York City to handle cases originating in the state of New York; a third in Chicago with jurisdiction over cases in Illinois, Indiana, Wisconsin, Minnesota, and North and South Dakota. The fourth central division covers Michigan, Ohio, and Kentucky, with local offices at Detroit, Cleveland, Cincinnati, and Louisville. The fifth, the New England division, maintains offices at Boston and New Haven. These divisions now cover the entire country (See Chart 10).

[34] See above, Chap. XIV.

[35] The amounts of additional tax for the five preceding years were: 1929, $260,227,744; 1930, $172,304,837; 1931, $242,893,238; 1932, $218,521,219; 1933, $169,629,610. It must be noted that these collections were from the much larger amounts of income received by taxpayers in the pre-depression era.

[36] As stated above, this organization succeeded the Special Advisory Committee in 1933, with enlarged staff and increased duties. It considers settlement without further litigation of income, estate and gift taxes, questions involving determination of Bureau policy, specific cases and other matters assigned or submitted to it by the Commissioner of Internal Revenue, certain classes of compromise of income tax cases and applications for extension of time. (*Report of the Secretary of the Treasury* 1935, p. 115.)

Under this decentralization plan, cases in which the taxpayer disagrees with the findings of the internal revenue agent are referred to the local office of the Technical Staff. Here the taxpayer is given a hearing and his tax liability finally determined. Appeal can be made only to the Board of Tax Appeals and the courts — not to the Bureau or the Treasury Department at Washington.

The Bureau has issued the following statement of the advantages of the arrangement:

> It will eliminate the repetitious steps and protracted delays which it seems impossible to avoid under the old plan of centralizing the settlement of tax disputes in the Bureau of Internal Revenue at Washington. It will permit prompt action on all contested cases at a point near to the taxpayer and to the sources of evidence regarding his transactions. It will provide an able and impartial administrative body to which the taxpayer can have recourse in his own community should he wish to contest the findings of the agency which examined his tax return in the first instance. The plan is expected to result not only in greater convenience to taxpayers but also in quicker administrative decisions and in fewer appeals from the Bureau of Internal Revenue to the Board of Tax Appeals and the Courts. It will be of special benefit to taxpayers who are financially unable to employ counsel.[37]

It has been suggested that it would have been better if the decentralization had been carried out more gradually because there were insufficient adequately trained and experienced experts in the Bureau to fill properly all the technical staff positions in all of the field divisions and also to leave an adequate staff in Washington. Some fear has been expressed, also, that administration of the tax will be less uniform throughout the United States, taxpayers in different sections are more likely to be treated differently. There were, however, disadvantages of slow, gradual, reorganization.

CONCLUSIONS

Consideration of the subjects discussed in this chapter leads to the question: How competent is the administration of the income tax? There are a few criteria by which the efficiency of the Bureau may be measured; for example: Is the auditing of returns fairly up to date? Does the taxpayer get an even chance to have his side of a case presented? Is the Bureau used for political purposes? Is the personnel chosen on a merit basis?

Great improvement has been made in recent years in keeping the auditing of returns current. By June 30, 1937 the returns for 1934 and 1935 had been completely audited, and practically two thirds of the returns for 1936 had been examined and closed. At that time

[37] Treasury Department, *Press Release* Nov. 7, 1938.

TABLE 35

COST OF ADMINISTRATION AND COLLECTIONS OF THE OFFICE OF INTERNAL REVENUE [a]

Fiscal Year	*Total Cost*	*Collections*	*Cost per $100*
1909	$4,975,238	$246,212,719	$2.02
1910	5,044,520	289,957,220	1.74
1911	5,411,658	322,526,299	1.68
1912	5,509,984	321,615,895	1.71
1913	5,584,654	344,424,453	1.59
1914	5,779,329	380,008,894	1.52
1915	6,804,688	415,681,023	1.63
1916	7,199,163	512,723,287	1.40
1917	7,699,031	809,393,640	.95
1918	12,003,214	3,698,955,820	.32
1919	20,573,771	3,850,150,078	.53
1920	29,647,439	5,407,580,251	.55
1921	40,203,716	4,595,357,061	.87
1922	41,577,374	3,197,451,083	1.30
1923	45,316,312	2,621,745,227	1.39
1924	42,895,625	2,796,179,257	1.24
1925	47,631,893	2,584,140,268	1.44
1926	39,948,483	2,835,999,892	1.23
1927	32,967,764	2,865,683,129	1.15
1928	32,599,845	2,790,535,537	1.17
1929	34,377,082	2,939,054,375	1.17
1930	34,352,063	3,040,145,733	1.13
1931	33,997,785	2,428,228,754	1.40
1932	33,870,903	1,557,729,042	2.17
1933	30,031,722	1,619,839,224	1.85
1934	28,826,225	2,672,239,194	1.25
1935	42,719,338[b]	2,773,213,213	1.44
1936	51,783,386	3,520,208,381	1.47
1937	51,797,735	4,653,195,315	1.12
1938	58,204,050	5,658,765,314	1.03
1939	58,662,969	5,181,573,953	1.13

[a] From *Reports of the Commissioner of Internal Revenue.* From the data available it is not possible to separate costs of collecting the income tax from costs of collecting other internal revenue taxes.

[b] Includes approximately $10,700,000 for administrative expenses of the Alcohol Tax Unit and $4,000,000 for administering revenue provisions of the AAA.

(June 30, 1937) there remained in the Bureau to be closed 536,630 cases some of which dated back to 1917, but over 350,000 were for 1936. On June 30, 1938 there were 590,000 cases on hand of which 540,000 were for 1936 and 1937. It is the policy of the Bureau to audit the returns within fifteen months following the filing date. Another forward step in administration during the past few years has been the effort to obtain more prompt payment of back taxes. As a means to this end, the Bureau has endeavored to come to an agreement with the taxpayer without recourse to litigation.

This leads to the second query: Does the taxpayer have an even chance? The available evidence on this point indicates that for the most part the Bureau employees aim to be fair in so far as the law permits. It has been pointed out in other sections of this study that the law itself gives certain advantages to the government. Until the 1938 law this was true in the taxation of gains and non-deductibility of losses. The contest throughout has been between the shrewd taxpayer or tax evader, on the one hand, and the legislator and administrator, on the other hand. In fact, it is almost a game of hide and seek in which clever lawyers find loopholes more quickly than Congress can stop them. This is one reason why the law cannot be simplified.

In recent years the Administration has gone somewhat farther in castigating taxpayers who have obeyed the letter of the law but have taken advantage of the loopholes. This was particularly evident in the President's message to Congress in 1937 and the Congressional hearings held preparatory to amending the law. The courts, on the other hand, have consistently recognized distinctions between evasion and avoidance.[38] They have not viewed cases from the "moral" point of view which the President emphasized. Perhaps the Administration, too, has recently decided to be less antagonistic to the taxpayer, if one may judge by the utterances of Assistant Secretary Hanes.[39]

The possibilities and temptations of using the weapons of the Bureau for political purposes must be obvious to anyone.[40] The evidence as to the extent of this abuse is not easily available. It is impossible to sift the exact truth from rumors and political talk. A few well-known cases were generally thought to have been tinged

[38] For example " . . . the courts have held that a purpose to minimize or avoid taxation is not unlawful if permissable under a strict construction of a taxable statute." [*Helvering* v. *Bowen* C C A (4th)]; "A taxpayer may resort to any legal method available to him to diminish the amount of his tax liability." [*Commissioner* v. *Eldridge*, 79 F (2d) 629, 631]. See also *Bullen* v. *Wisconsin*, 240 U. S. 625; *Jones* v. *Helvering*, 71 F (2d) 214; *Sautell* v. *Commissioner*, 82 F (2d) 221; *General Utilities and Operating Co.* v. *Helvering*, 296 U. S. 200.

[39] Speech in Minneapolis, Oct. 14, 1938, at the School of Business Administration of the University of Minnesota. See also the "business appeasement" speeches of Secretary Morgenthau.

[40] In 1929 Couzens said on the floor of the Senate:

"I have repeatedly said that if I were Commissioner of Internal Revenue . . . I could perpetuate any political party in power. . . It is entirely possible, and I believe to an extent practiced, that every contribution to a political party may be secured out of the Treasury of the United States through a refund or an abatement or a credit to those corporations or individuals who want to contribute to campaign expenses." (*Cong. Rec.* 70: 2109.) (As has been mentioned, Couzens was a bitter critic of the Treasury, and, particularly, of Secretary Mellon.)

with political and personal bias if not venom ; for example, in the so-called Couzens-Mellon feud (1925-1926) and the New Deal action against Senator Huey Long which was dropped shortly after his death. Cases that did not appear quite so obvious but which aroused suspicion, nevertheless, were those of the New Deal Administration against Mellon, du Pont, and Raskob. Congressman Fish openly accused the Democrats of ferreting out rich Republican campaign contributors and foes of the Administration in the publicity on tax evasion in 1937.[41]

Such political abuse of the Bureau, at least, in the opinion of some, has usually been instigated and fostered by those high in political authority, generally by those entirely outside of the Bureau, rather than by those directly in charge of tax administration. In this connection it might be mentioned that since 1909 the Commissioner has been appointed by the President instead of by the Secretary of the Treasury. The Assistant to the Commissioner and the Special Deputy Commissioner are likewise political appointees. The Secretary and the Commissioner do not always agree on policies. For example, it was rather obvious that the Bureau had little enthusiasm for the tax avoidance propaganda and the publicity methods used by the Administration in 1937.

All employees of the Bureau in Washington from the Assistant Deputy Commissioner down to the clerks and messengers are under Civil Service. They appear to be conscientious, well-trained, and, for the most part, experienced. In recent years there has been little difficulty in keeping good men. Most of the confusion brought in by the war work was cleared out by 1927. The economic depression ended most of the competition from outside employers and, during the course of the years, more experienced accountants have become available for public service. The Bureau has improved its training of employees in the service. The salary scale, too, has been made attractive. But Collectors in the district offices, their staffs, the internal revenue agents in the field, the General Counsel and his staff in Washington are not on Civil Service. One of the few examples of interference with employees, according to the press, was the requested resignation of the Chief Counsel and his assistant in September 1937 because of their refusal to present names of tax avoiders during the Congressional hearings.[42] It is, of course, impossible for anyone outside the Bureau to know what pressure is put on employees or how much political activity exists.

When the Board of Tax Appeals was first established the members

[41] Press comments are numerous. Minneapolis *Tribune*, Oct. 27, 1938 ; Westbrook Pegler in a syndicated column, Minneapolis *Journal*, Feb. 5, 1938, entitled "Power to Ruin Lurks in Abuse of Income Tax."

[42] New York *Times*, Sept. 17, 1937.

were selected primarily on the basis of training and ability. Most of the members appointed during the last two administrations, however, appear to have been selected primarily for political reasons. This has meant that in trying cases and rendering decisions they have had to rely mostly on their trained staff of assistants.

The comments above indicate where some improvements could be made. A few additional suggestions might be in order. The merit system might be extended to collectors, field agents, and the Board of Tax Appeals. Constant attention should be given to improving the qualifications of the Bureau staff.

At the present time, the Income Tax Unit does not attempt a careful audit of all returns. About one third of the corporation returns are sent to the field. The experience of the Wisconsin Tax Commission indicates that a more nearly complete audit of all returns would be fruitful. Consideration might be given also to the desirability of special federal courts of tax appeals in which the judges were especially trained in tax law and not required to divert their talents and energies to hear all other sorts of cases.

The problem of simplifying the law seems insoluble, but none the less desirable. In any case, extreme complexity should be avoided, even at the sacrifice of some revenue. Whatever else may be said of discontinuing the undistributed-profits tax, it was at least a step in the direction of simplicity. The very height of the tax rates makes the law difficult to administer. The elimination of tax-exempt securities and the consequent modification of tax schedules might help a good deal.

Much of the complexity of the law has resulted from the attempt to check evasion and avoidance, and much has resulted from the attempt to achieve more equity between taxpayers. But some changes that would increase equity would also make for simplicity. Every effort should be made to gain the confidence of the taxpayer and secure his co-operation rather than his resentment. This can be accomplished by removing the glaring inequities — consider the existing one-sided gains and loss provisions — and by administering the law competently and with courtesy.[43]

The income tax is basically as fair a tax as has been devised. Its future success depends upon keeping it equitable and maintaining its administration upon the highest plane possible.

43 In 1939 Secretary Morgenthau listed a number of "tax irritants" and inequities to be corrected. Some improvement in that direction was made by the Revenue Act of 1939; for example, the carry-over of net operating losses to a succeeding year was allowed and the amount of deductible corporate loss from sales of capital assets was increased.

CHAPTER XXIV

CONCLUSION

Now that we have traced the evolution of the federal income tax, how shall we evaluate it? What judgment shall we place upon it? Is it the most efficient and effective measure that we could adopt for raising necessary revenue? Or, is it just another tax, another device, to squeeze funds from the people, a cunning method of extracting revenue? Or, does our adoption and development of the income tax have some deeper significance, some fundamental relation to basic economic and political issues in the United States?

We have seen how the first federal income taxes, those of the Civil War period, were emergency measures which were allowed to lapse soon after the emergency had passed. The next income tax, that of 1894, was the result of a great equalitarian movement which grew out of the economic stresses and the rising industrialism that followed the Civil War. The submission of the Sixteenth Constitutional Amendment and the adoption of the corporation excise tax in 1909 were results of the momentum of the same equalitarian and industrial movements. These two steps toward income taxation were accepted by astute opponents, not as a first choice, but in an attempt to outmaneuver and head off the sponsors of a general and comprehensive income tax.[1] The long series of statutes enacted under the authority of the Sixteenth Amendment following its adoption in 1913 have been the natural fruit of the continuing economic revolution in the United States, that is, natural to such a revolution developing in the atmosphere and environment of this hemisphere.

Indeed, the adoption and evolution of our income tax have brought about a revolution in national taxation. For the 72 years of our national existence prior to the Civil War, customs duties were almost the only important source of federal funds. (See Tables 1 and 2, Chapter I.) From the Civil War until the World War such duties still played the main role and excises from liquor and tobacco were the only other important national taxes. The yields of the 1909 corporation excise were small, and even those of the 1913 income tax were only a fraction of total federal receipts. (See Table 5, Chapter II, above, and Table 39, Appendix, below.)

But the necessities of the World War, particularly after we entered it in 1917, led to the development of the income tax, with its variations — war-profits, and excess-profits taxes — into a veritable engine

[1] See Chap. II, above.

of taxation. These new measures were the mainstay of war finance. With them the United States raised eight to ten times as much tax revenue as had ever been raised before and, moreover, laid the basis for far the largest flotation of loans that this or any nation ever issued in so short a time. It was indeed fortunate for our national finances that the income tax law had been passed and that at least a small staff had gained some little administrative experience before we entered the war.

But if the war demonstrated the great values of income taxation, the postwar depression revealed its weaknesses. Large declines in business and business profits, accompanied by similar declines in individual incomes, were sufficient to account for reductions in collections; but the peculiar structure of our income tax magnified the decline so that United States yields shrank far more than those of the British and others, even after making allowance for the greater severity of the depression in the United States. But despite the weaknesses of the income tax, there is now no thought of abandoning it; at least, no serious thought of such action by responsible persons. In fact, the evolution of the attitude toward the income tax is an interesting development in the evolution of the tax itself. Whereas its introduction was attacked 45 and 30 years ago as an entering wedge of communism, socialism, and all ugly *isms*, the tax is now accepted by practically all; it has become indispensable. In other words, the

CHART 12

RECEIPTS OF THE FEDERAL GOVERNMENT, 1928-1939

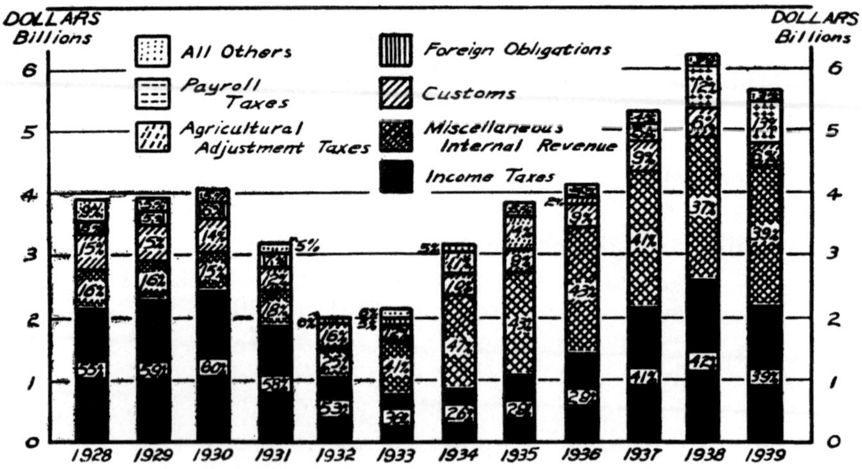

Based on *Reports of the Secretary of the Treasury.*

question today is not, "Shall we adopt an income tax or shall we continue it ?" but rather, "How may we improve it, how make it still more serviceable ?"

EVALUATION OF THE TAX

Whether a tax is good or poor depends upon how it meets needs. This monograph is devoted primarily to one special tax; it cannot discuss all taxes, much less the whole field of public finance. It should not be forgotten, however, that the unusual seriousness of tax problems today is largely the result of war and depression, of vastly increased public expenditures, recurring deficits and mounting public debts. (See accompanying Tables 36, 37 and 38, and Tables 39 and 40 in the Appendix; also, Charts 12 and 13.) Obviously, the amount of taxes required is a function of public expenditures and the amount of taxes that can be paid is a function of available income. Taxes cannot be greatly reduced if expenditures are not reduced (unless deficits are to increase), though they can be rendered less burdensome if properly arranged, just as the load on one's back may be

CHART 13

EXPENDITURES OF THE FEDERAL GOVERNMENT, 1928-1939

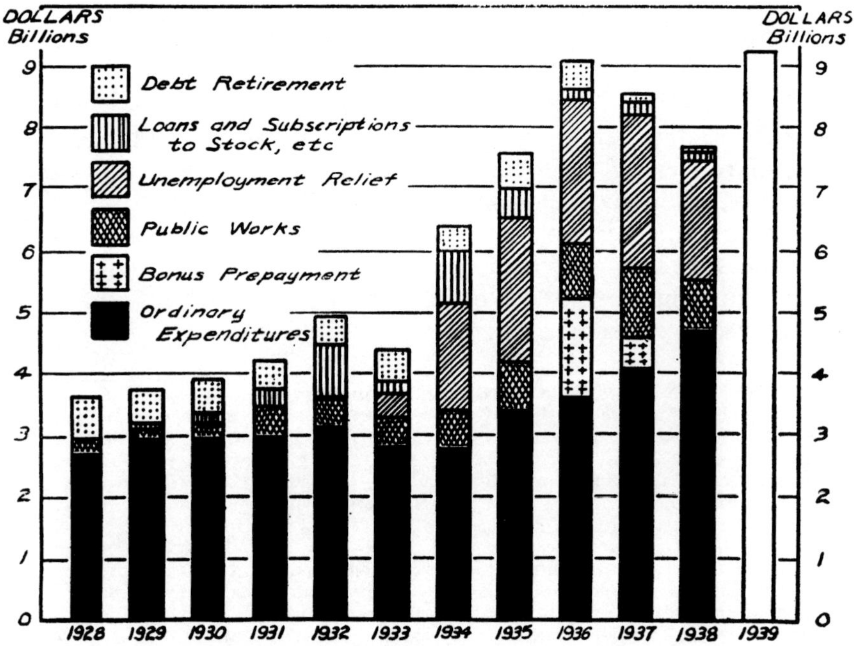

Based on *Reports of the Secretary of the Treasury*. For 1939 see Table 38, note a.

TABLE 36

FEDERAL AND ESTIMATED STATE AND LOCAL TAX REVENUES
FISCAL YEAR ENDING IN 1938

(In millions of dollars)

Source	*Federal*	*State*	*Local*	*Total*	
				Amount	*Per cent*
Customs	359	.....	.....	359	2.4
Property	.....	214	4531	4,745	32.0
Individual income	1313	249	.....	1,562	10.6
Estate, inheritance and gift	417	145	.....	562	3.8
Corporate income and privilege	1449	313	.....	1,762	12.0
Pay rolls	743	707	.....	1,450	9.8
Motor fuel and vehicle	293	1163	25	1,481	10.0
Liquor and tobacco	1136	298	32	1,466	9.9
Sales and other excises	287	717	302	1,306	8.8
Other tax revenue	37	51	30	118	0.7
Total	6034	3857	4920	14,811	100.0
Per capita tax revenues [a]	$46.48	$29.71	$37.90	$114.09	
Tax revenues as per cent of national income [b]	8.9%	5.7%	7.2%	21.8%	

[a] On the basis of the estimated population (129,818,000) as of January 1, 1938.
[b] On the basis of the average ($67,923,000,000) of the estimated national income for calendar years 1937 and 1938.
Bulletin of the Treasury Department, August 1939, p. 4.

less burdensome if the knapsack is properly adjusted. The principal hope of rendering taxes less burdensome, however, is through the increasing of the national income.[2]

The central question of public expenditure is, To whom and in what measure shall government (Society Organized) distribute benefits? The central question of taxation is, From whom and in what measure shall government require contributions to pay for the bene-

[2] We cannot go into all the niceties and refinements of definition and theory here but, in general, income consists of what comes in, what is received, which on the whole is much the same as what is produced, though we are not discussing here whether or not each individual receives exactly what he produces. National income or social income is the sum of all individual incomes, plus group or other incomes not attributed to individuals, if any. Taxation according to ability to pay usually has reference to individual or personal ability. Transfer of income or capital from one person to others may not affect the total of social or national income though usually it does affect the total of each of the several persons concerned and it also affects their respective abilities to pay taxes. Except in the cases of transfers, most increases of individual income increase the social income also and most things which destroy or reduce individual income lessen social income. Much confusion relative to capital gains and losses and relative to the definition of income results from the confusion over social *versus* individual income, and over social *versus* individual ability and welfare. Commonly, increases of all run in the same direction, but not always.

TABLE 37

FEDERAL AND ESTIMATED STATE AND LOCAL GENERAL GOVERNMENT EXPENDITURES FISCAL YEAR ENDING IN 1938

(In millions of dollars)

Function	Expenditures from own sources[a]				Intergovernmental grants[b]				Expenditures for own functions[c]			
	Federal	State	Local	Total	Federal to State	Federal to Local	State to Local	Local to State	Federal	State	Local	Total
1. Education	177	818	1418	2,413	58	102	628	..	17	248	2148	2,413
2. Highways and streets	260	900	510	1,670	219	24	300	23	17	842	811	1,670
3. Agriculture and natural resources[d]	1000	73	3	1,076	27	..	2	..	973	98	5	1,076
4. National defense	1610	12	...	1,622	2	..	..	..	1608	14	...	1,622
5. Police and other protection	44	138	566	748	...	..	...	..	44	138	566	748
6. Relief, welfare, and social security	2182	637	266	3,085	260	..	315	9	1922	591	572	3,085
7. Net additions to social security reserves[e]	489	516	...	1,005	41	..	...	..	448	557	...	1,005
Social security reserves	(574)	(707)	...	(1,281)	(41)	..	..	..	(533)	(748)	..	(1,281)
Withdrawals included in (6) above	(85)	(191)	...	(276)	..	..	...	..	(85)	(191)	...	(276)
8. Health and hospitals	36	270	265	571	16	..	7	..	20	279	272	571
9. Interest	926	121	592	1,639	..	..	...	..	926	121	592	1,639
10. All other	902	738	2001	3,641	10	46	136	..	846	612	2183	3,641
11. Total expenditure	7626	4223	5621	17,470	633	172	1388	32	6821	3500	7149	17,470
12. Debt retirement	65	135	529	729	...	...	12	..	65	123	541	729
13. Total disbursement, including debt retirement	7691	4358	6150	18,199	633	172	1400	32	6886	3623	7690	18,199

Note: The classification of expenditures here used varies from and is not as detailed as classifications employed in the reports of the Bureau of the Census and elsewhere. The differences are necessitated by the inadequacy of the data available for estimating purposes. The class "all other" comprises the aggregate of all the unclassified expenditures. *Bulletin* of the Treasury Department, August 1939, p. 4.

[a] Excludes expenditures from grants received from another jurisdiction.

[b] Includes shared taxes and comprises part of "Expenditures from own sources."

[c] Includes expenditures from own sources and from "Intergovernmental Grants" received, but excludes grants paid other jurisdictions.

[d] Includes such items as flood control, reclamation, river and harbor improvement and Panama Canal expenditures.

[e] Interest on invested social security reserves is included in item (9)

TABLE 38

EXPENDITURES, DEFICITS, AND DEBTS OF THE FEDERAL GOVERNMENT [a]

(In millions)

Fiscal Year	*Expenditures*	*Surplus (+) or Deficit (−)*	*Principal of the Public Debt (Total Gross)*
1900	$621.39	+ $63.07	$1,263.42
1905	719.63	+ 24.78	1,132.36
1910	915.13	− 18.11	1,146.94
1915	1052.53	− 62.68	1,191.26
1920	6900.69	+ 212.48	24,297.92
1925	4145.76	+ 250.51	20,516.27
1930	4706.14	+ 183.79	16,185.31
1931	4748.48	− 901.96	16,801.49
1932	5538.62	−2942.05	19,487.01
1933	4907.78	−2245.45	22,538.67
1934	6949.71	−3255.39	27,053.09
1935	8216.07	−3782.97	28,701.17
1936	9736.51	−4952.93	33,545.38
1937	9277.29	−3252.54	36,427.09
1938	8319.47	−1449.63	37,167.49
1939	9268.34	−3600.51	40,439.53

[a] *Report of the Secretary of the Treasury* 1938, pp. 413, 416, 490. Daily Statement of the Treasury, June 30, 1939. Because of change in method of reporting, the items of expenditures for 1938 and 1939 are not exactly comparable.

fits? The federal income tax and the system [3] of which it forms a part should be judged upon the basis of whether or not they tap individual and national income in the most effective and socially desirable ways; that is, whether they distribute the burdens and other effects of tax contributions in such ways as to do the least harm and the most good to the members of society, to the national economy and, finally, to society as a whole.

How well, it may be asked, does the federal income tax meet the requisites of a good tax? How satisfactorily does it meet the tests of fiscal adequacy, elasticity, and stability of yield, or the administrative tests of practicability, simplicity, economy, convenience of payment, minimization of evasion and avoidance? Moreover, is it really equitable and does it promote or retard general economic and social progress? Obviously, these questions, which must be considered in any adequate evaluation of the federal income tax, cannot be discussed very fully here; about all that is feasible in this chapter is to

[3] If such an unsystematic combination of taxes can be called a "system."

mention certain facts and considerations rather briefly, perhaps apparently more dogmatically than is intended, and leave the reader to make decisions after he has had adequate time to pursue and ponder the issues. In any case, many of these matters involve imponderables and personal opinions about which there are bound to be disagreements, regardless of how exhaustive or how profound the discussion might be.

Fiscal adequacy is, of course, a relative matter ; no tax ever brought in over a long period all that was needed or wanted, but, judged by usual standards, the federal income tax has been a good producer of revenue. The war yields have been mentioned already, also the smaller but still large postwar yields. Only property [4] and excise tax yields rival those of the income tax.[5] (See Table 36.)

The income tax compares favorably also with other important taxes in the matter of elasticity or adjustability. Normally, yields can be increased or decreased according to needs by means of practicable rate and other adjustments. Because this tax is usually on surpluses rather than on margins, changes in its rates usually affect business and prices to consumers less than do changes in rates of gross earnings, excise, customs, and some other taxes. But no tax has much elasticity upward after it has already been extended to the limit of what is practicable; in other words, income, property, and some excise taxes have been pushed so near the limit in many cases in recent years that much of their former elasticity has been exhausted. Obviously, elasticity may be restored by increasing national income or by reducing government expenditures. In periods of rapid and extensive changes in the value of money (inflation or deflation), however, sales taxes or excises have certain great advantages of adjustability over usual income and property taxes which involve long lapses of time between dates of receipt or assessment and dates of tax payment.[6]

Instability of revenue, particularly the failure to furnish adequate revenue in time of depression, is commonly considered the most serious weakness of the income tax. This is a shortcoming of practically all taxes, though some exhibit it in much higher degree than others. For example, yields of United States cigarette taxes held up remarkably well during the depression of the 1930's. On a tax base for which the demand is inelastic, almost any sale or similar tax

[4] Used mostly for local rather than for national purposes.

[5] The Social Security payroll taxes may be considered income taxes, though often differentiated from ordinary income taxes originated under earlier laws.

[6] Obviously, advantages to government and taxpayer might run in different directions under inflation and also under deflation ; moreover, questions of equity and social welfare, as well as government revenue and individual advantage, would be involved. See Viner, Jacob, "Taxation and Changes in Price Levels." *Journal of Political Economy* XXXI : 494-520 (Aug. 1923).

will produce a stable yield, whether the thing taxed is a prime necessity, a luxury, or a vice.[7]

Mention has already been made of the great decline in income tax revenues during the postwar depression. Although instability is inherent in the income tax, the extent of the weakness in the case of the federal tax was increased by several provisions peculiar to our tax law, some of which have since been modified somewhat. One was the treatment of capital gains and losses which are disregarded in the British system except for those engaged in the trade or business of buying and selling investments. Another was concerned with "realization" requirements and options which encourage manipulation in order to reduce tax liability. Other reasons for the greater fluctuation in yields of our tax as compared with the British are our much greater dependence upon high surtaxes, lesser reliance upon "normal" tax rates, our relatively high scale of personal exemptions, our capital gains and loss provisions, and restrictions on carrying over other losses.[8] These features not only tend to reduce yields, especially during depressions, but they also lessen the pressure of "tax-conscious" brakes on expenditures because such a large proportion of the population is wholly exempted and another important segment is not subject to the rates of the higher brackets. To change our system very substantially in the direction of the British income tax might lessen equity to a certain extent, that is, might conflict with the idea of ability to pay, which was largely responsible for our adoption of this tax; nevertheless, certain modifications might result in much more stable revenues with little sacrifice of equity and might also simplify administration.[9]

It should be remembered, also, that alternatives to the income tax are also more or less unstable. Property, excise and other taxes that are usually considered more stable, and therefore better in some respects, are not fundamentally so much superior as they may appear to be. In the last analysis, practically all taxes have to be paid out of current or past income, whatever the measure of the tax. If rates, exemptions, and other features were properly adjusted, it might be more equitable and more feasible to raise five billion dollars on the basis of income even in time of depression than to raise the same amount on the basis of property or consumption. One of the best

7 Napoleon is reputed to have advised his finance minister, "Tax the vices, they have the broadest shoulders." It is usually considered that luxuries have elastic demands but that necessities have inelastic demands. Definitions of necessities vary, however; sometimes conventional ideas and harmful tastes and desires may affect demand as much as do physical necessities.

8 These provisions vary in different laws; some of them were modified by the Revenue Act of 1939. See Chap. XXII above for comparisons of United States and British tax rates.

9 Some argue for some instability to force borrowing in depression.

ways to meet the difficulties caused by fluctuations in income tax revenues is by proper budget and debt policies,[10] although certain abuses already indicated might be eliminated and bring additional improvement.

DIFFICULTIES OF ADMINISTRATION

The income tax has often been rated higher than the property tax on the ground that it minimizes the making of capital valuations. This merit has been exaggerated by those who fail to recognize that American income tax administration requires the valuation of the bases upon which estimates of depreciation, depletion, and obsolescence are calculated. On the other hand, the income tax has been criticized frequently because of the difficulties of administration. There is no doubt that proper administration is rather complex and difficult, but whether the income tax should be condemned on this ground or not depends upon the balance of advantages and disadvantages in comparison with those of alternative taxes.

It has long been assumed that the income tax was simple enough to be self-assessed. Nevertheless, the law has become so complex that a taxpayer with income of much size, especially if it is derived from various sources, is almost compelled to secure expert help in making out his return. From the point of view of the administrator the method of self-assessment offers difficulties because of opportunities for evasion. Much investigation is necessary and some decisions seem rather arbitrary. Fair administration of the law is important not only in attaining good will of the taxpayer but in establishing the fundamental equity of the law. Decentralization of the Income Tax Unit now under way should make possible closer co-operation between taxpayers and collectors.

Doubtless much of the complaint of taxpayers of the unfairness of the Bureau of Internal Revenue is due to the inconsistencies and some real inequities in the law. The realization and exchange provisions are artificial in some respects; losses cannot be carried forward except under certain conditions and in specified limited amounts; capital gains must be counted as taxable income, but not all capital losses can be deducted; certain income, such as interest on government bonds, is exempt; certain industries seem to have been favored, for example, the oil and mining industries have been granted special depletion deductions.

The creation and maintenance of legal entities such as corporations and trusts maximize the difficulties of administration. The "realization" provisions decrease some difficulties but add to others.

[10] Such policies are, however, fraught with serious difficulties.

They were drafted to prevent the taxation of paper profits as well as to prevent tax avoidance. The Treasury has occasionally suggested that extremely difficult matters be provided for in general terms in the statute and that details be left to administrative discretion, but such a plan has rarely been acceptable to Congress. In any case, no simple general income tax can be equitable, and no equitable income tax can be simple. The federal income tax is far from simple, and its proper administration is a very large, complex, technical undertaking.[11]

Considering all of the complexities and difficulties, the administration of the federal income tax appears reasonably efficient and economical. The average costs of administration reported by the Bureau of Internal Revenue do not seem excessive when compared with the receipts or when compared with the costs of administering other taxes. (See Table 35, Chapter XXIII.)

On the basis of equity the great majority of the public probably rank the income tax far above all other taxes which approximate it in fiscal adequacy and other essential qualities. Its correspondence with the equalitarian idea of ability to pay is considered by many to be its *raison d'être*. Its relation to American ideals of democracy is sensed by all, but relatively few have grasped the full significance of such a tax with its strong and universal appeal to the spirit of fair play. This significance is fully recognized only by those who appreciate the transcendent importance of social vision and genuine social co-operation on a vast scale in a rising industrialism characterized by mass production for large markets, which modern economies and standards of living require, especially if civilization is to go forward.

But whether or not income is really a good criterion of ability to pay depends upon how income is defined; and, besides, there are tests of taxpaying ability other than income. Moreover, ability to pay is itself very difficult to determine, and it is also only one of several criteria of a good tax, and not always the best one,[12] despite the fact that it has become almost a fetish. A further important fact is that an income tax is susceptible of great abuse. By legal definition and interpretation it is possible to load the law with inequities and handicaps to progress; in fact, if great care is not taken, pressure groups are likely to pervert it to their special interests, so that instead of furthering the spirit of fair play, it may arouse class feeling,

[11] For more extended discussions of this topic see Blakey, Roy G., "Simplification of the Income Tax," *American Economic Review*, 18: Supplement 102 (March 1928), and "Revenue Act of 1938," *American Economic Review*, 28: 447 (Sept. 1938).

[12] This is too large a subject to discuss in detail here. Most authors of texts and many others discuss it; the present writers have discussed it in various places, particularly in *Taxation in Minnesota*, Chap. 2.

increase social friction, and destroy rather than promote industrial harmony, social co-operation, and the general welfare.[13]

Another matter which it is not feasible to discuss at length here but which should be considered in any evaluation, or in any program for improving the federal income tax, is its place in the federal tax "system" and, also, its place in a co-ordinated system of federal, state, and local finance. No tax should be judged singly, by itself, but rather after consideration of how harmoniously and effectively it can be combined with others. American customs duties, so long the mainstay of our federal finances, have been regressive levies on consumption, though they probably hastened American industrialization despite their encouragement of more or less inefficiency, monopoly, and political corruption. The federal excises also have been regressive. Since its adoption the federal income tax has offset the regressivity of the other federal taxes; in fact, with its large personal exemptions and high surtax rates, many think that it has more than offset them, that it has become a dangerous class tax voted by the great majority of nonpayers upon a relatively small fraction of the few thriftiest, ablest, and most enterprising. In any case, it seems clear that the proper sort of income tax is valuable in correcting the regressivity and other faults of our old mainstays. It may be true, as some claim, that excises and tariffs are administratively superior to income taxes for reaching those with small incomes who should make some contribution to government support. There is, however, no very definite accepted line of division where yield, administrative, and other advantages and disadvantages of one tax just balance those of an alternative tax.

A most pressing problem, already alluded to, is the co-ordination of federal, state, and local taxes though it would take us too far afield to do more than mention this problem here. A few, though not many, assert that the states have a prior right to the use of the income tax because they had employed such taxation long before it was adopted by the federal government. They cite also the rejuvenation and modernization of state income taxation by Wisconsin before the adoption of the Sixteenth Amendment. Most tax students, however, do not take this priority claim very seriously, but they do recognize the important problems raised and magnified by the developments of the last thirty or forty years. Whereas, before 1900 (and even prior to 1913) practically all government expenditures and taxes were very light compared with what they are now and, whereas, the federal government relied mainly on two taxes — customs

[13] It has been suggested that a democracy that votes a very heavy tax upon a small minority from which it exempts the great majority is marching down the road to free "bread and circuses."

duties and excises — and states and local units had only one main source — the property tax, mostly on real estate — now expenditures and taxes have become multiplied several fold and both federal and state governments, as well as local subdivisions, are searching for every conceivable practicable source of revenue. They are invading each other's fields and seriously hampering each other's operations, despite (or partly because of) the substantial offsetting grants by larger jurisdictions to smaller ones. It is obvious that if all taxes are derived ultimately from income, huge federal drafts on the national (social) income lessen the ability of states to raise what they need by means of income taxes, and even by means of any other kinds of taxes. So far no one has been able to propose a practicable comprehensive plan of co-ordination, or even a generally satisfactory plan for allocation of collections. Not only do the interests of the federal government diverge from those of the states; the interests of the several states are also far from harmonious in various respects.

In judging taxes and tax systems one should look even beyond national and local fiscal systems and so-called fiscal results. It is important that the tax system and every important tax which enters into it should be considered in relation to the national economic and social *milieu.* Even when taxes are designed for maximum revenue they have incidental repercussions that are frequently very significant. When more and more taxes, particularly the most important varieties, are used purposely and often primarily for economic and social regulation, the significance of these broader effects may become serious. Most fiscal authorities agree that it is sometimes proper to use a tax for non-fiscal purposes if the direct and indirect advantages of such use more than counterbalance the disadvantages. But there is much disagreement as to where the balance is struck, and some believe there are altogether too many reformers and would-be reformers who are willing to use any tax if it will serve to further their hobbies or issues, regardless of almost all other considerations. The danger is that such abuse may spoil good taxes for better purposes.[14]

As suggested above, balancing of advantages and disadvantages is always in order, but it takes a sane, far-sighted, judicially-minded individual to read the scales aright. Who can and will read the scales to suit most of us in deciding to what extent the federal income tax shall be used to control the business cycle; to regulate the policies of corporations, including those relating to the distribution of earn-

[14] Under conceivable circumstances even a well-balanced person might be justified in using a pocket knife for a screw-driver, or in burning the furniture to avoid freezing, but such employment would not usually improve such articles for their normal uses.

ings; to encourage or discourage certain forms of business organization, for example, partnerships *versus* corporations, holding companies *versus* mergers, small businesses *versus* big businesses? In short, to what extent shall this or other taxes be used to redistribute wealth; or to promote *laissez-faire,* private enterprise, democracy, communism, socialism, fascism, or whatever else some individual, interest, group, or party favors? There is little doubt, however, that the income tax can be used to further or check progress toward most of the suggested ends.[15]

Regardless of one's opinion of the use of taxes for non-fiscal purposes, it is quite important sometimes to raise revenue, even very substantial revenue, if government is to carry on both the traditional functions and also the many new ones. It is, therefore, important for those who plan taxes to be something more than tax specialists with such narrow focuses that they can see nothing but the tax system. Unfortunately some tax men, including some writers and some planners, seem to lose sight of the rest of the world. Of course, no one can be a specialist in every field of economics and politics, but it does not take such a specialist to see that, however meritorious the federal income tax may be, or however much it may be improved, it is not a panacea; moreover, it can be nullified largely or completely by an unsound program in almost any other important field of national policy. How much would the best possible income tax avail in the face of grossly unsound expenditure and debt policies, or banking and monetary policies, or agricultural policies, or wage and labor policies, or even international policies? No tax nor tax system can long be adequate or satisfactory if national income is low and declining; on the other hand, a prosperous nation with generally sound economic policies — one with a large and expanding income — can secure adequate revenues through various combinations of taxes, though some combinations are undoubtedly much superior to others. A good income tax should be an important part of any system for Americans of this generation.

[15] The authors have some opinions on these matters but further discussion of them is reserved for the future. Among the many existing discussions, attention may be called to a few. See 75th Congress, 3d Session, *Hearings before the Committee on Ways and Means on Revenue Revision* and *Hearings before the Senate Committee on Finance* 1938; Kendrick, M. Slade, *The Undistributed Profits Tax,* Brookings Institution; Lutz, Harley L., "The Principle of the Undistributed Profits Tax," *Bulletin of the National Tax Association,* 23: 200 (April 1938); Magee, James D., *Investment of Capital,* Brookings Institution; Simons, H. C., *Personal Income Taxation,* and *A Positive Program for Laissez-Faire: Some Proposals for a Liberal Economic Policy;* Twentieth Century Fund, *Facing the Tax Problem*; Smith, J. G., "The Undistributed Profits Tax," *American Economic Review,* 28: 305 (June 1938); Round Table, *Fortune* XIX: 67 (May 1939); Colm, Gerhard, and Lehman, Fritz, "Economic Consequences of Recent American Tax Policy," *Social Research,* Supplement I (1938). See also Chaps. XVII and XIX above.

SOCIAL SIGNIFICANCE

In the preceding pages we have been appraising the federal income tax on the basis of long-tested and generally accepted standards. In the next few pages we wish to consider further, though briefly, its fundamental social significance. This consideration will give further support to the conclusion of the preceding section.

Those who have studied modern economic evolution and who have also traced the development of income taxation are struck with the interrelations between these two developments. In fact, the evolution of income taxation, particularly, the evolution of the definition of income, reflects most faithfully and interestingly the development of modern industrialism. This parallel will become clearer to the layman if he will consider a few basic facts and principles. The first is that, from one point of view, income is the most important thing in the world to every individual in it. Everybody devotes all of his efforts and thoughts to one thing, namely, to satisfying his needs or wants. Almost the only thing with which he can satisfy them is income, using the term in a broad sense. In other words, it may be said that practically all human thoughts and efforts are devoted to securing and utilizing income.

Moreover, income is scarce in comparison with what is wanted and probably always will be. Therefore, it is important to use available income economically and to increase the amount produced in order to satisfy needs more adequately. Economists naturally focus their attention upon principles and methods of economical use and maximum production of income; they consider how the satisfaction of human needs may be maximized.[16] The Industrial Revolution, which has not yet begun to be appreciated by most people, impressed upon economists the great role of capital in increasing income.[17] In the course of time practically all responsible leaders have come to sense something of the importance of increasing and conserving capital if the consumption and wastage of natural resources is to be offset and the standard of living advanced at anything like the rate of the last century.

The increasing development of capital has emphasized also the great importance of proper organization of the human as well as of the material factors of production. But real appreciation of the great

[16] Economists are sometimes said to be materialists; they are not necessarily materialists exclusively but realize that a certain amount of food, clothing, and shelter are necessary prerequisites if man is to get satisfaction from the so-called higher things of life as well as from the so-called material things.

[17] World income has probably been increased more in the last two centuries than in the twenty preceding centuries.

significance of specialization, capitalistic mass production, free exchange of products, proper money and credit systems, and real general social co-operation has percolated slowly among the peoples of all countries. Indeed, modern technical progress has outdistanced progress in social organization and control. The great desideratum today is effective social co-operation, effective organization of "The Great Society." This is especially obvious and urgent in industrial and international relations.[18] Standards of living throughout the world, and even in the most fortunate nations of the world are far below what they might be if men generally had solved the problems of social organization.[19]

In tracing the manner in which the definition and the taxation of income have reflected the course of economic evolution, we must not forget the importance of capital, or the consequent importance of uninterrupted production, the further consequent importance of uninterrupted exchange, and the consequent necessity of industrial and international co-operation as opposed to industrial and international friction and warfare. These necessities of exchange suggest, moreover, the importance of money, and the valuation of everything in terms of money, when production is primarily for the market rather than for home consumption. That is, the modern concept of capital evolves from the primitive concept of capital as a *thing* (*res,* for example, a tool) with which to increase production to a concept of capital as a *value* embodied in, or represented by, the capital good. In a money economy where exchanges are frequent, this value is readily transmutable into an equivalent value embodied in any other exchangeable thing. The concept of income also is now generally in terms of *value* rather than *things* (*res*) and, with modern exchange facilities, the unit of exchange (dollar, franc, pound) is a common denominator of both capital and income, regardless of the form in which either may be embodied for the moment.

Moreover, capitalistic production is indirect or roundabout; it involves calculations of probable yields a long time in advance, and it also involves frequent *estimates* of current depreciation and obsolescence in order to estimate current income. These estimates bring in the problems of accrual *versus* cash accounting, the problems of "realization" and the associated administrative problems connected with frequent appraisals of fixed and other capital assets. The future

18 More or less lack of social cooperation is evident in almost all groups and organizations. For example, what we call "politics," corruption, and graft in government and what we call "soldiering," or "railroading" on the job, in the army, and in the large private railroad or other corporations is a failure or breakdown of effective group or social co-operation. Indeed, every anti-social act or failure to act, whether of high or low degree, evidences lack of social co-operation.

19 Of course, such problems can never be solved finally in an evolving society, but they can be solved progressively, step by step, if the race is equal to the challenge.

values which the producer of (and investor in) long-life fixed capital[20] must estimate suggest the role of law, precedents, and courts. Dependable rules of the game and some continuity of policy upon which entrepreneurs can rely are indispensable in order to bring the necessarily great risks within the realm of practical action. In other words, a definite, dependable decision as to "realization," even though it lags behind economic evolution and is contrary to the economic realities, may have some merit not only for purposes of tax administration but also for other practical reasons; a larger measure of certainty may sometimes justify the sacrifice of a little equity.

With these points in mind we are better prepared to understand why controversies have arisen relative to taxing income *versus* capital, gross income *versus* net income, money income *versus* real income or *versus* income in kind, recurrent and regular receipts *versus* casual gains, accrued values *versus* "realized" gains. We are also better prepared to understand why the questions raised have been answered as they have been, why the definition of income and the taxation of income have evolved as they have.

Our earliest ancestors probably had a gross-receipts concept of income — if they had concepts — any and every valuable thing that came in might be used for immediate consumption; little thought was taken of the morrow. It was not until later that primitive man appreciated the value of implements and tools (capital), and perhaps still later before he realized that some of his gross receipts (income to him) should be applied to the maintenance of his capital if his long-time income was not to diminish, at least, if it was to increase.

Moreover, his wants were recurrent. He desired to eat several times a day, perhaps as often as he could. Because of the need of something to meet these recurring wants, it is obvious that it has been natural for recurrence and regularity to be thought of as two of the primary, if not two of the indispensable, characteristics of income.

But it took a long time for primitive man, and even for some moderns, to take much cognizance of depreciation until actual repairs had to be made. It has taken even longer for many to recognize depletion and obsolescence. Some of these phenomena were not generally recognized when the British income tax was established — in fact, have not been fully legally recognized in the administration of their income tax as yet — and some have been only tardily recognized by laymen and even by the American courts.

20 For example, consider the chances of error in calculating the advisability of constructing a railroad, a public utility plant, or any other large plant that is presumed to involve incomes 30, 50, or 100 years hence. One can never know exactly what the real net income is or will be until the whole has been worn out or liquidated.

The growing recognition of the importance of maintaining capital is seen in the evolving distinction between gross receipts and gross income. A further step in the same direction occurs when some of the less obvious forms of capital wastage or consumption, such as depreciation, depletion, and obsolescence, are recognized.[21] When this recognition becomes general, we arrive at a concept of net income.

But even the concept of net income — that which is left after business expenses or cost of production is deducted from gross income — is still vague rather than clear — except when some statute or ruling arbitrarily makes it clearer than the economic facts justify. For example, there is no clear line of demarcation between personal expenditures and business expenditures, between the cost of clothing, food, and shelter that is for personal use and that which is necessary to maximize production. Hence some economists have gone further than net income to the concept of "clear income," which involves the deduction of at least a minimum of subsistence or a minimum for efficiency from what is generally designated "net income." "Clear income" has not yet been adopted in such terms in our tax laws, but it is there in fact. We allow flat personal exemptions and in effect tax an approximation of "clear income" rather than net income. This flat exemption has great administrative advantages. For example, it does not necessitate the determination of just what is a minimum of subsistence or a minimum of efficiency for every individual; it disregards peculiarities of individual needs and variations in costs of living in different parts of the United States. Most of what has just been said holds in the cases of numerous exemptions that are graduated rather than flat.

There are many other modifications of the definition of taxable income for the sake of administrative feasibility. For example, most of the laws, rules, and technicalities about "realization," "separation," etc., are to be justified primarily, if at all, on that ground.

Haig's definition of income, the net accretion definition,[22] which largely disregards recurrence and the arbitrary application of the Supreme Court's ideas of "realization" and "separation," is a natural product of the later developments of capitalistic organization and finance. The situation today is in great contrast with a Robinson Crusoe or even a pioneer, self-sufficient economic regime typical of much of America until half a century ago. Now any realizable value may become capital (production goods) through exchange, or it may be translated into income (consumable goods) by any person, if not

[21] Note the lags and inconsistencies of statutes and court decisions, a few of which are mentioned in Chap. XXI above.

[22] See above, Chap. XXI.

by society as a whole. The appreciation in the value of a farm or a lot can be transmuted into consumable food, clothes, or automobiles, and its consumption may be distributed over as many days or weeks or years as the one who controls it chooses. That is, Haig's definition of income fits into the modern industrial and financial world. Any net accretion of realizable value that comes in between two points of time is income for that period; by virtue of modern exchange facilities the modern man may consume it almost immediately or use it for further production, just as he chooses. The old ideas about recurrence, casual and capital gains, as they relate to income taxation, have, therefore, lost much of their former justification.[23]

Thus, we see that the growing recognition of the importance of capital to the individual, to the business man, and to others, as well as to social organizations, led to the modification of the concept of income from gross receipts to gross income, then to net income, and now to "clear income," almost. We see also that developments of the capitalistic system nullified much of the distinction formerly made between capital and income without necessarily weakening the reasons for maintaining and increasing capital; in fact, while increasing the ability of individuals and society to increase capital and hence the ability to meet human needs.[24] We have seen also that capitalistic production requires close co-ordination, not only of vast amounts of capital but also of great numbers of workers, of producers and consumers. All parts of the process must articulate, must operate almost continuously, without serious interruption, much as all parts of a modern harvester combine must articulate and function continuously or the potentially efficient machine becomes less effective than an old-fashioned sickle.

A good income tax, considered as most in accord with ability to pay by most people, promotes the distribution that maximizes social good will, which is a *sine qua non* of the operation of a highly complex industrialism; thus, at the same time that it tends to maximize the utility of the goods and services distributed, it also tends to maximize the quantity of income produced and hence increases want satisfaction in a twofold manner.

But to the extent that the income tax or any other tax is abused, or perverted, for example, to the extent that it encourages the masses of the voters to mulct the minority, to the extent that it discourages the feeling of individual responsibility to the group — the sense

[23] See note at end of Chap. XXI.

[24] Today the actuary can easily furnish a few simple tables showing how anyone can transmute any present casual or recurring sum or sums into equivalent future recurring installments or lump sums, as desired — and almost vice versa. He cannot, however, supply will power and business ability to all.

of solidarity — to that extent it fails to maximize quantity and utilization of income and becomes anti-social.

At one stage in our social evolution the building up of capital was vital. Perhaps we are not yet so far past this stage as some think, but at the present time our greatest difficulties are those of articulating and organizing the various members and groups of society so that we can make the best use of our resources, material and human. Because of its appeal to the sense of justice, if properly planned and administered, no important tax is better qualified than the income tax to minimize social friction and promote social co-operation. That is, no other important tax is more in harmony with the ideals of democracy. It fits into our national *milieu* because it has grown up in it and with it. Its evolution has paralleled our general economic evolution, partly as effect but partly as cause; in other words, it is of the warp and woof of modern industrial civilization, particularly of the variety that has developed upon American soil and in American atmosphere.

APPENDIX

EXHIBIT 1

PROVISIONS OF THE CONSTITUTION RELATING TO TAXATION [1]

Art. 1, sec. 2, cl. 3: "Representatives and direct taxes shall be apportioned among the several States which may be included within this Union, according to their respective numbers, which shall be determined by adding to the whole number of free persons, including those bound to service for a term of years, and excluding Indians not taxed, three-fifths of all other persons." [2]

Art. 1, sec. 8, cl. 1: "The Congress shall have power to lay and collect taxes, duties, imposts, and excises, to pay the debts and provide for the common defense and general welfare of the United States, but all duties, imposts, and excises shall be uniform throughout the United States."

Art. 1, sec. 9, cl. 4: "No capitation or other direct tax shall be laid, unless in proportion to the census or enumeration hereinbefore directed to be taken."

Art. 1, sec. 9, cl. 5: "No tax or duty shall be laid on articles exported from any State."

Art. 1, sec. 10, cl. 2: "No State shall, without the consent of the Congress, lay any imposts or duties on imports or exports, except what may be absolutely necessary for executing its inspection laws; and the net produce of all duties and imposts, laid by any State on imports or exports, shall be for the use of the Treasury of the United States; and all such laws shall be subject to the revision and control of the Congress."

Amendment XVI: "The Congress shall have power to lay and collect taxes on incomes, from whatever source derived, without apportionment among the several States, and without regard to any census or enumeration."

[1] 53 *Statutes at Large* LXXXI, *Internal Revenue Code* (1939).

[2] The part of this clause relating to the mode of apportionment of Representatives among the several States was amended by the Fourteenth Amendment, section 2, and as to taxes on incomes, by the Sixteenth Amendment, which is quoted above.

Exhibit 2

Secretaries of the Treasury
1861–1939

Term of Service	Secretaries of Treasury	Presidents
Mar. 7, 1861 – June 30, 1864	Salmon P. Chase, Ohio	Lincoln
July 5, 1864 – Mar. 3, 1865	Wm. P. Fessenden, Maine	Lincoln
Mar. 9, 1865 – Mar. 3, 1869	Hugh McCulloch, Indiana	Lincoln, Johnson
Mar. 12, 1869 – Mar. 16, 1873	Geo. S. Boutwell, Massachusetts	Grant
Mar. 17, 1873 – June 3, 1874	Wm. A. Richardson, Massachusetts	Grant
June 4, 1874 – June 20, 1876	Benj. H. Bristow, Kentucky	Grant
July 7, 1876 – Mar. 9, 1877	Lot M. Morrill, Maine	Grant, Hayes
Mar. 10, 1877 – Mar. 3, 1881	John Sherman, Ohio	Hayes
Mar. 8, 1881 – Nov. 13, 1881	Wm. Windom, Minnesota	Garfield, Arthur
Nov. 14, 1881 – Sept. 4, 1884	Chas. J. Folger, New York	Arthur
Sept. 25, 1884 – Oct. 30, 1884	Walter Q. Gresham, Indiana	Arthur
Oct. 31, 1884 – Mar. 7, 1885	Hugh McCulloch, Indiana	Arthur, Cleveland
Mar. 8, 1885 – Mar. 31, 1887	Daniel Manning, New York	Cleveland
Apr. 1, 1887 – Mar. 6, 1889	Chas. S. Fairchild, New York	Cleveland, Harrison
Mar. 7, 1889 – Jan. 29, 1891	Wm. Windom, Minnesota	Harrison
Feb. 25, 1891 – Mar. 6, 1893	Chas. Foster, Ohio	Harrison, Cleveland
Mar. 7, 1893 – Mar. 5, 1897	John G. Carlisle, Kentucky	Cleveland, McKinley
Mar. 6, 1897 – Jan. 31, 1902	Lyman J. Gage, Illinois	McKinley, Roosevelt
Feb. 1, 1902 – Mar. 3, 1907	L. M. Shaw, Iowa	Roosevelt
Mar. 4, 1907 – Mar. 7, 1909	George B. Cortelyou, New York	Roosevelt
Mar. 8, 1909 – Mar. 5, 1913	Franklin MacVeagh, Illinois	Taft
Mar. 6, 1913 – Dec. 15, 1918	W. G. McAdoo, New York	Wilson
Dec. 16, 1918 – Feb. 1, 1920	Carter Glass, Virginia	Wilson
Feb. 2, 1920 – Mar. 3, 1921	David F. Houston, Missouri	Wilson
Mar. 4, 1921 – Feb. 12, 1932	Andrew W. Mellon, Pennsylvania	Harding, Coolidge, Hoover
Feb. 13, 1932 – Mar. 3, 1933	Ogden L. Mills, New York	Hoover
Mar. 4, 1933 – Dec. 31, 1933	William H. Woodin, New York	Roosevelt
Jan. 1, 1934 –	Henry Morgenthau, New York	Roosevelt

Exhibit 3

Commissioners of Internal Revenue
1862–1939

Term of Service	*Commissioners*	*Presidents*
July 17, 1862 – Mar. 4, 1863	George S. Boutwell, Massachusetts	Lincoln
Mar. 18, 1863 – June 30, 1865	Joseph J. Lewis, Pennsylvania	Lincoln, Johnson
July 1, 1865 – Oct. 31, 1865	William Orton, New York	Johnson
Nov. 1, 1865 – Mar. 10, 1869	Edward A. Rollins, New Hampshire	Johnson
Mar. 11, 1869 – Jan. 2, 1871	Columbus Delano, Ohio	Grant
Jan. 3, 1871 – Aug. 8, 1871	Alfred Pleasonton, Missouri	Grant
Aug. 9, 1871 – May 14, 1875	John W. Douglass, Pennsylvania	Grant
May 15, 1875 – July 31, 1876	Daniel D. Pratt, Indiana	Grant
Aug. 2, 1876 – April 30, 1883	Green B. Raum, Illinois	Grant, Hayes, Garfield, Arthur
May 21, 1883 – Mar. 19, 1885	Walter Evans, Kentucky	Arthur, Cleveland
Mar. 20, 1885 – Mar. 20, 1889	Joseph S. Miller, West Virginia	Cleveland, Harrison
Mar. 21, 1889 – April 18, 1893	John W. Mason, West Virginia	Harrison, Cleveland
Apr. 19, 1893 – Nov. 26, 1896	Joseph S. Miller, West Virginia	Cleveland
Nov. 27, 1896 – Dec. 31, 1897	W. St. John Forman, Illinois	Cleveland, McKinley
Jan. 1, 1898 – Feb. 28, 1899	Nathan B. Scott, West Virginia	McKinley
Mar. 1, 1899 – Nov. 27, 1900	George W. Wilson, Florida	McKinley
Dec. 20, 1900 – April 30, 1907	John W. Yerkes, Kentucky	McKinley, T. Roosevelt
June 5, 1907 – Aug. 31, 1909	John G. Capers, South Carolina	T. Roosevelt, Taft
Sept. 1, 1909 – April 27, 1913	Royal E. Cabell, Virginia	Taft, Wilson
Apr. 28, 1913 – Sept. 25, 1917	William H. Osborn, North Carolina	Wilson
Sept. 26, 1917 – Mar. 31, 1920	Daniel C. Roper, South Carolina	Wilson
Apr. 1, 1920 – April 11, 1921	William M. Williams, Georgia	Wilson, Harding
May 27, 1921 – May 31, 1929	David H. Blair, North Carolina	Harding, Coolidge
June 1, 1929 – Aug. 15, 1930	Robert H. Lucas, Kentucky	Hoover
Aug. 20, 1930 – May 15, 1933	David Burnet, Ohio	Hoover
June 6, 1933 –	Guy T. Helvering, Kansas	F. D. Roosevelt

In addition, the following were Acting Commissioners for the time specified: John W. Douglass, from November 1, 1870 to January 2, 1871; Henry C. Rogers, from May 1 to 10, 1883; John J. Knox, from May 11 to 20, 1883; Robert Williams, Jr., from November 28 to December 19, 1900; Millard F. West, from April 12 to May 26, 1921; H. F. Mives, from August 16 to August 19, 1930; and Pressly L. Baldridge, from May 16 to June 5, 1933.

Exhibit 4

Chairmen of the House Committee on Ways and Means 1861–1939

Name	*Term of Service*	*President*
Thaddeus Stevens (Pa.)	July 8, 1861 – Mar. 3, 1865	Lincoln
Justin S. Morrill (Vt.)	Dec. 11, 1865 – Mar. 4, 1867	Johnson
Robert C. Schenck (Ohio)	Nov. 25, 1867 – Jan. 5, 1871 (date of resignation)	Johnson – Grant
Godlove S. Orth (Ind.)	Jan. 5, 1871 – Mar. 4, 1871	Grant
Henry L. Dawes (Mass.)	Dec. 4, 1871 – Mar. 4, 1875	Grant
William R. Morrison (Ill.)	Dec. 20, 1875 – Mar. 3, 1877	Grant
Fernando Wood (N. Y.)	Oct. 29, 1877 – Mar. 4, 1881	Hayes
William D. Kelley (Pa.)	Dec. 21, 1881 – Mar. 3, 1883	Arthur
William R. Morrison (Ill.)	Dec. 24, 1883 – Mar. 3, 1887	Arthur – Cleveland
Roger Q. Mills (Tex.)	Jan. 5, 1888 – Mar. 2, 1889	Cleveland
William McKinley, Jr. (Ohio)	Dec. 9, 1889 – Mar. 3, 1891	Harrison
William M. Springer (Ill.)	Dec. 19, 1891 – Mar. 3, 1893	Harrison
William L. Wilson (W. Va.)	Aug. 21, 1893 – Mar. 2, 1895	Cleveland
Nelson Dingley, Jr. (Me.)	Dec. 21, 1895 – Mar. 3, 1899	Cleveland – McKinley
Sereno E. Payne (N. Y.)	Dec. 18, 1899 – Mar. 4, 1911	McKinley – Roosevelt – Taft
Oscar W. Underwood (Ala.)	Apr. 11, 1911 – Mar. 4, 1915	Taft – Wilson
Claude Kitchin (N. C.)	Dec. 14, 1915 – Mar. 4, 1919	Wilson
Joseph W. Fordney (Mich.)	May 19, 1919 – Mar. 4, 1923	Wilson – Harding
William R. Green (Iowa)	Dec. 17, 1923 – Mar. 4, 1929	Coolidge
Willis C. Hawley (Oregon)	Apr. 16, 1929 – Mar. 4, 1931	Hoover
James W. Collier (Miss.)	Dec. 7, 1931 – Mar. 4, 1933	Hoover
Robert L. Doughton (N. C.)	Mar. 9, 1933 –	Roosevelt

Exhibit 5

Chairmen of the Senate Finance Committee 1861–1939

Name	*Term of Service*	*President*
William Pitt Fessenden (Me.)	July 6, 1861 – July 4, 1864	Lincoln
John Sherman (Ohio)	Dec. 7, 1864 – Mar. 3, 1865	Lincoln
William Pitt Fessenden (Me.)	Dec. 6, 1865 – Mar. 4, 1867	Johnson
John Sherman (Ohio)	Mar. 7, 1867 – Mar. 3, 1877	Johnson – Grant
Justin S. Morrill (Vt.)	Mar. 9, 1877 – Mar. 4, 1879	Hayes
Thomas F. Bayard (Dela.)	Mar. 19, 1879 – Mar. 4, 1881	Hayes
Justin S. Morrill (Vt.)	Oct. 13, 1881 – Mar. 3, 1893	Arthur – Cleveland – Harrison
Daniel W. Voorhees (Ind.)	Mar. 15, 1893 – Mar. 2, 1895	Cleveland
Justin S. Morrill (Vt.)	Dec. 30, 1895 – Mar. 3, 1899 (continued through Dec. 15, 1900)	Cleveland – McKinley
Nelson W. Aldrich (R. I.)	Dec. 15, 1900 – Mar. 4, 1911	McKinley – Roosevelt – Taft
Boies Penrose (Pa.)	Apr. 27, 1911 – Mar. 4, 1913	Taft
Furnifold McL. Simmons (N. C.)	Mar. 15, 1913 – May 28, 1919	Wilson
Boies Penrose (Pa.)	May 28, 1919 – Dec. 31, 1921 (date of death)	Wilson – Harding
Porter J. McCumber (N. C.)	Jan. 19, 1922 – Mar. 4, 1923	Harding
Reed Smoot (Utah)	Dec. 10, 1923 – Mar. 4, 1933	Coolidge – Hoover
Pat Harrison (Miss.)	Mar. 9, 1933 –	Roosevelt

EXHIBIT 6

DEVELOPMENT OF THE STAFF OF OFFICE OF THE COMMISSIONER OF INTERNAL REVENUE 1862–1894 [a]

1862	*A Commissioner of Internal Revenue* authorized, to superintend the collection of internal duties, stamp duties, licenses, or taxes imposed by law, and of assessing the same, at an annual salary of	$4000	1862 July 1
1866	The salary increased to	$6000	1866 July 13 1875 Mar. 3
	Deputy Commissioners:		
1863	A Deputy Commissioner authorized, at an annual salary of	$2500	1863 Mar. 3
1866	The salary increased to	$3500	1866 July 13 1875 Mar. 3
1876	The salary appropriated for, fiscal years 1877 to 1894, inclusive, at the annual rate of	$3200	1876 Aug. 15
1866	Two additional Deputy Commissioners authorized, at annual salaries each of	$3000	1866 July 13
1874	One Deputy Commissioner abolished		1874 Jan. 29
	The remaining Deputy Commissioner, at $3000, not appropriated for after fiscal year 1876		
	Solicitor of Internal Revenue:		
1866	A Solicitor of Internal Revenue authorized, in the office of the Commissioner of Internal Revenue, at an annual salary of	$4000	1866 July 13
1870	The office transferred to the Department of Justice and the salary increased to	$5000	1870 June 22
1876	The salary appropriated for, fiscal years 1877 to 1894, inclusive, at the annual rate of	$4500	1876 Aug. 15
1886	*A Chemist* authorized, at an annual salary of	$2500	1886 Aug. 2
	A Microscopist authorized, at an annual salary of	$2500	
	Heads of Division:		
1866	Seven heads of division authorized, at annual salaries each of	$2500	1866 July 13 1875 Mar. 3
1876	Two heads of division appropriated for, fiscal years 1877 to 1894, inclusive, at annual salaries each of	$2500	1876 Aug. 15
1876	Five heads of division appropriated for, fiscal years 1877 to 1891, inclusive, at annual salaries each of	$2250	1876 Aug. 15
1891	Six heads of division appropriated for, fiscal years 1892 to 1894, inclusive, at annual salaries each of	$2250	1891 Mar. 3
1875	*A Stenographer* authorized, at an annual salary of	$2000	1875 Mar. 3
1876	The salary appropriated for, fiscal years 1877 to 1894, inclusive, at the annual rate of	$1800	1876 Aug. 15
1882	*A Superintendent of Stamp Vault* appropriated for, fiscal years 1883 to 1894, inclusive, at an annual salary of	$2000	1882 Aug. 5

[a] 53d Congress, 1st Session, *Senate Report* 41 (1893).

1893 *The appropriations* for salaries in the office of the Commissioner of Internal Revenue for the fiscal year 1894 are as follows: 1893 Mar. 3

Salaries, Office of Commissioner of Internal Revenue:

1	Commissioner of Internal Revenue	$ 6,000
1	Deputy Commissioner	3,200
1	chemist	2,500
1	microscopist	2,500
2	heads of division, at $2500 each	5,000
6	heads of division, at $2250 each	13,500
1	superintendent of stamp vault	2,000
25	clerks of class four	45,000
25	clerks of class three	40,000
35	clerks of class two	49,000
25	clerks of class one	30,000
14	clerks at $1000 each	14,000
41	clerks at $900 each	36,900
3	messengers at $840 each	2,520
14	assistant messengers at $720 each	10,080
13	laborers, at $660 each	8,580
209	*Total*	$272,580

Salaries, Office of Commissioner of Internal Revenue (reimbursable):

1	stamp agent	$1600
1	counter	900
	The same to be reimbursed by the stamp manufacturers.	
2	*Total*	$2500

Exhibit 7

Historical Summary of Tax Treatment of Capital Gains and Losses, 1913–39, Inclusive[a]

PART I. INDIVIDUALS

Revenue Act	Income year	Treatment of: Gains from sale or exchange of assets	Treatment of: Losses from sale or exchange of assets
1913	Mar. 1, 1913, to Dec. 31, 1915.	Included with other income subject to full normal and surtax rates.	Not allowed.
1916	1916	do.	Allowed only to the extent of the gains from such sales.
1917	1917	do.	do.
1918	1918–21	do.	Allowed in full against income of any kind.
1921	1922, 1923	*Assets held 2 years or less*	
		Included with other income subject to full normal and surtax rates.	Allowed in full against other income, but not against capital net gains.
		Assets held over 2 years	
		At the election of the taxpayer, capital net gains were taxable at 12½% in lieu of the normal and surtax rates; but if such election were made, the total tax, including the tax on capital net gains, could in no case be less than 12½% of the total net income.	Allowed in full against income of any kind.
1924	1924	*Assets held 2 years or less*	
		Same as 1921 act	Allowed in full against income of any kind.
		Assets held over 2 years	
		At the election of the taxpayer, capital net gains were taxable at 12½% in lieu of the normal and surtax rates.	Could be segregated from ordinary net income, and a tax credit of 12½% of the capital net loss taken, but in no case could the tax be less than the tax (computed at normal and surtax rates) would be if the capital net loss were deducted from ordinary net income.
1926	1926–27	Same as 1924 act	Same as 1924 act.
1928	1928–31	do.	do.

[a] Treasury Department, *Sources and Rates of Federal Taxation,* Jan. 1, 1939.

EXHIBIT 7 (*Continued*)

HISTORICAL SUMMARY OF TAX TREATMENT OF CAPITAL GAINS AND LOSSES, 1913–39, INCLUSIVE [a]

PART I. INDIVIDUALS (*Continued*)

Revenue Act	Income year	Treatment of: Gains from sale or exchange of assets	Treatment of: Losses from sale or exchange of assets
1932	1932	*Assets held 2 years or less*	
		Same as 1924 act.	Losses from sales or exchanges of stocks, and bonds were limited to the gains from such sales. It was provided, however, that such losses disallowed in 1 year (to an amount not in excess of the net income) could be carried over and applied against gains from such transactions in the succeeding taxable year.[b] Other losses were allowed in full against income of any kind.
		Assets held over 2 years	
		Same as 1924 act.	Same as 1924 act.
N. I. R. A.	1933	*Assets held 2 years or less*	
		Same as 1924 act.	Losses from sales or exchanges of stocks and bonds were limited to the gains from such sales. Other losses were allowed in full against income of any kind.
		Assets held over 2 years	
		Same as 1924 act.	Same as 1924 act.
1934–36	1934	*Percentages of gains or losses recognized*	
		Period assets are held	Percentages
		1 year or less	100
		Over 1 year but not over 2 years	80
		Over 2 years but not over 5 years	60
		Over 5 years but not over 10 years	40
		Over 10 years	30
		Capital gains so computed are included in net income subject to full normal and surtax rates.	Capital losses so computed are recognized in determining net income to the amount of the recognized capital gains plus $2000.

[b] The provision relating to the carry-forward of disallowed losses from sales or exchanges of stocks and bonds held 2 years or less was repealed by the National Industrial Recovery Act before it became effective.

EXHIBIT 7 (*Continued*)

HISTORICAL SUMMARY OF TAX TREATMENT OF CAPITAL GAINS AND LOSSES, 1913–39, INCLUSIVE [a]

PART I. INDIVIDUALS (*Continued*)

<table>
<tr><th rowspan="2">Revenue Act</th><th rowspan="2">Income year</th><th colspan="2">Treatment of</th></tr>
<tr><th>Gains from sale or exchange of assets</th><th>Losses from sale or exchange of assets</th></tr>
<tr><td rowspan="5">1938</td><td rowspan="5">1938, 1939</td><td colspan="2">Percentages of gains or losses recognized
Period assets are held — Percentages
18 months or less — 100
Over 18 months but not over 24 months — $66\frac{2}{3}$
Over 24 months — 50</td></tr>
<tr><td colspan="2">Assets held 18 months or less (short-term)</td></tr>
<tr><td>Capital gains not offset by allowed losses included with other income subject to full normal tax and surtax rates.</td><td>Capital losses allowed only to the extent of gains of such transactions but losses disallowed in 1 year (to an amount not exceeding net income) may be carried forward and applied against gains from such transactions in the succeeding taxable year.</td></tr>
<tr><td colspan="2">Assets held more than 18 months (long-term)</td></tr>
<tr><td>Net capital gains computed on basis of foregoing percentages are included with other income and subject to normal tax and surtax rates or segregated and taxed at 30%, whichever method results in lesser total tax.</td><td>Net capital losses computed on basis of foregoing percentages are deducted from other income or 30% of such losses is credited against the tax, computed on net income before deducting the net loss, whichever method gives the greater tax.</td></tr>
<tr><td colspan="4">PART II. CORPORATIONS</td></tr>
<tr><td>1913–28</td><td>1913–31</td><td>Included with other income subject to full rate.</td><td>Allowed in full against income of any kind.</td></tr>
<tr><td>1932</td><td>1932</td><td>do.</td><td>Losses from sales or exchanges of stocks and bonds held 2 years or less were limited to the gains from such sales. It was provided, however, that such losses disallowed in 1 year (to an amount not in excess of the net income) could be carried over and applied against gains from such transactions in the succeeding taxable year.[b]
Other losses were allowed in full against income of any kind.</td></tr>
<tr><td>N. I. R. A.</td><td>1933</td><td>do.</td><td>Losses from sales or exchanges of stocks and bonds held 2 years or less were limited to the gains from such sales.
Other losses were allowed in full against income of any kind.</td></tr>
<tr><td>1934–38</td><td>1934–39</td><td>do.</td><td>Allowed only to extent of $2000 plus capital gains.</td></tr>
<tr><td>1939</td><td>1940–</td><td>do.</td><td>Same as individuals.</td></tr>
</table>

Exhibit 8

Summary of Statutory Provisions to Prevent Use of Corporations for Surtax Evasion

Act of 1913 (section II (A) (2)

"For the purpose of this additional tax [the surtax] the taxable income of any individual shall embrace the share to which he would be entitled of the gains and profits of all corporations, joint stock companies, or associations . . . formed or fraudulently availed of for the purpose of preventing the imposition of such tax through the medium of permitting such gains and profits to accumulate instead of being divided or distributed. . ."

Act of 1916 (section 3)

"For the surtax the taxable income of an individual shall include his share of all profits (whether distributed or not) of corporations formed or availed of to prevent the imposition of the surtax, but the fact that gains and profits are permitted to accumulate shall not be construed as evidence of purpose to escape the tax unless the Secretary of the Treasury shall certify that in his opinion such accumulation is unreasonable for the purposes of the business."

Act of 1917 (section 1206)

Additional tax of 10% on amount undistributed six months after end of each calendar or fiscal year — "but not upon portion of undistributed net income actually invested in business or retained for employment in reasonable requirements of the business" — Provided, if Secretary of Treasury finds any amount so retained is not so employed or is not reasonably required in the business, tax of 15% shall be levied.

Act of 1918 (section 220)

If a corporation was formed or availed of for the purpose of preventing the imposition of the surtax by permitting its gains and profits to accumulate, the corporation was not subject to the ordinary income tax, but individual stockholders were subject to tax upon their proportionate share of the net income under the individual income tax.

Act of 1921 (section 220)

Penalty additional tax of 25% of net income if corporation was formed or used to enable stockholders to evade surtax. If stockholders agreed, tax could be imposed on their distributive share of the net income as in the case of partnerships.

Act of 1924 (section 220)

Penalty additional tax of 50% of net income. "Net income" defined to include corporation dividends and interest on government securities.

Acts of 1926 (section 220), 1928 (section 104), and 1932 (section 104)

Penalty additional tax of 50% of net income if corporation was formed or used to enable stockholders to evade surtax. But the tax was not to be imposed if stockholders included in their gross income at the time of filing their returns their proportionate share of the corporate net income, whether distributed or not.

Act of 1934

Tax on "undistributed, adjusted net income" of personal holding companies (section 351):

30% of amount not in excess of $100,000

40% of amount over $100,000

Penalty surtax on improperly accumulated surpluses (section 102):

25% on "retained net income" not over $100,000

35% on amounts over $100,000

The tax was not to be imposed if (1) all the shareholders (at the time of filing their returns) included in gross income their entire *pro rata* shares, whether distributed or not, of the retained net income, and (2) 90% or more of such retained net income is so included in the gross income of shareholders other than corporations.

Act of 1935

Penalty surtax on improperly accumulated surplus (section 102) same as 1934. Surtax on undistributed adjusted net income, personal holding companies (section 351):

20%, first $2000

30%, over $2000 but not over $100,000

40%, over $100,000 but not over $500,000

50%, over $500,000 but not over $1,000,000

60%, over $1,000,000

Act of 1936

Surtax on retained net income (section 102):

(1) Corporations not subject to undistributed-profits tax

25%, retained net income not over $100,000

35%, retained net income over $100,000

(2) Corporations subject to undistributed-profits tax

15%, retained net income not over $100,000

25%, retained net income over $100,000

Surtax on undistributed adjusted net income personal holding companies (section 351):

8%, first $2000

18%, over $2000 but not over $100,000

28%, over $100,000 but not over $500,000

38%, over $500,000 but not over $1,000,000

48%, over $1,000,000

Acts of 1937, 1938, 1939

Surtax on retained net income

(1) Corporations not subject to undistributed-profits tax

25% if retained net income not over $100,000

35% if retained net income over $100,000

(2) Corporations subject to undistributed-profits tax

15% if retained net income not over $100,000

25% if retained net income over $100,000

Surtax on undistributed adjusted net income, personal holding companies:

65%, first $2000

75%, over $2000

EXHIBIT 9

TABLE 39

RECEIPTS OF THE FEDERAL GOVERNMENT FISCAL YEARS 1908–1939 [a]

Year	Ordinary receipts							Postal revenues, exclusive of surplus postal receipts covered into the Treasury	Total ordinary receipts and postal revenues	Surplus (+) or deficit (−) of ordinary receipts covered into the Treasury compared with expenditures chargeable against ordinary receipts
	Customs (including tonnage tax)	Internal revenue		Sales of public lands	Surplus postal receipts covered into the Treasury	Miscellaneous	Total ordinary receipts			
		Income and profits taxes	Miscellaneous							
1908	$286,113,130	....	$251,711,127	$9,731,560	....	$54,306,090	$601,861,907	$191,478,663	$793,340,570	−$57,334,413
1909	300,711,934	....	246,212,644	7,700,568	....	49,695,352	604,320,498	203,562,383	807,882,881	−89,423,387
1910	333,683,445	$20,951,781	268,981,738	6,355,797	....	45,538,954	675,511,715	224,128,658	899,640,373	−18,105,350
1911	314,497,071	33,516,977	289,012,224	5,731,637	....	59,075,002	701,832,911	237,879,824	939,712,735	+10,631,399
1912	311,321,672	28,583,304	293,028,896	5,392,797	....	54,282,535	692,609,204	246,744,016	939,353,220	+2,727,870
1913	318,891,396	35,006,300	309,410,666	2,910,205	....	57,892,663	724,111,230	266,619,526	990,730,756	−400,733
1914	292,320,014	71,381,275	308,659,733	2,571,775	$3,800,000	55,940,370	734,673,167	284,134,566	1,018,807,733	−408,264
1915	209,786,672	80,201,759	335,467,887	2,167,136	3,500,000	66,787,373	697,910,827	283,748,165	981,658,992	−62,675,975
1916	213,185,846	124,937,253	387,764,776	1,887,662	....	54,759,011	782,534,548	312,057,689	1,094,592,237	+48,478,346
1917	225,962,393	359,681,228	449,684,980	1,892,893	5,200,000	81,903,301	1,124,324,795	324,526,116	1,448,850,911	−853,356,956
1918	179,998,385	2,314,006,292	872,028,020	1,969,455	48,630,701	247,950,012	3,664,582,865	295,845,261	3,960,428,126	−9,033,253,840
1919	184,457,867	3,018,783,687	1,296,501,292	1,404,705	89,906,000	561,203,585	5,152,257,136	274,941,126	5,427,198,262	−13,370,637,569
1920	322,902,650	3,944,949,288	1,460,082,287	1,910,140	5,213,000	959,508,024	6,694,565,389	431,937,212	7,126,502,601	+212,475,198
1921	308,564,391	3,206,046,158	1,390,379,823	1,530,439	....	718,412,150	5,624,932,961	463,491,275	6,088,424,236	+86,723,772
1922	356,443,387	2,068,128,193	1,145,125,064	895,391	81,494	538,430,622	4,109,104,151	484,772,047	4,593,876,198	+313,801,651
1923	561,928,867	1,678,607,428	945,865,333	656,508	....	820,077,345	4,007,135,481	532,827,925	4,539,963,406	+309,657,461
1924	545,637,504	1,842,144,418	953,012,618	522,223	....	670,727,939	4,012,044,702	572,948,778	4,584,993,480	+505,366,987
1925	547,561,226	1,760,537,824	828,638,068	623,534	....	642,788,033	3,780,148,685	599,591,477	4,379,740,162	+250,505,239
1926	579,430,093	1,982,040,088	855,599,289	754,253	....	544,931,967	3,962,755,690	659,819,801	4,622,575,491	+377,767,816
1927	605,499,983	2,224,992,800	644,421,542	621,187	....	653,858,929	4,129,394,441	683,121,989	4,812,516,430	+635,809,921
1928	568,986,188	2,173,952,557	621,018,666	384,651	....	678,006,094	4,042,348,156	693,633,921	4,735,982,077	+398,828,281
1929	602,262,786	2,330,711,823	607,307,549	314,568	....	492,653,499	4,033,250,225	696,947,578	4,730,197,803	+184,787,035
1930	587,000,903	2,410,986,978	628,308,036	395,744	....	551,250,041	4,177,941,702	705,484,098	4,883,425,800	+183,789,210
1931	378,354,005	1,860,394,295	569,386,721	230,302	....	381,273,309	3,189,638,632	656,463,383	3,846,102,015	−901,959,088
1932	327,754,969	1,057,335,853	503,670,481	170,339	....	116,793,795	2,005,725,437	588,171,923	2,593,897,360	−2,942,051,451
1933	250,750,251	746,206,445	858,217,512	102,561	....	224,419,973	2,079,696,742	587,631,364	2,667,328,106	−2,245,452,981
1934	313,434,302	817,961,481	1,822,642,347	99,336	....	161,416,584	3,115,554,050	586,733,166	3,702,287,216	−3,255,393,297
1935	343,353,054	1,099,118,638	2,178,571,390	86,757	....	179,337,363	3,800,467,202	630,795,302	4,431,262,504	−3,782,966,360
1936	386,811,594	1,426,575,434	2,086,276,174	74,355	....	216,219,058	4,115,956,615	665,343,356	4,781,299,971	−4,952,928,957
1937	486,356,599	2,157,526,981	2,439,613,122	71,218	....	210,272,317	5,293,840,237	726,201,110	6,020,041,347	−3,252,539,719
1938	359,187,249	2,634,618,139	3,039,700,298	95,649	....	208,059,892	6,241,661,227	728,634,051	6,970,295,278	−1,449,625,881
1939	318,837,311	2,192,300,487	2,978,919,660	b	....	187,765,468	5,667,823,626	b	b	−3,600,514,405

[a] *Report of the Secretary of the Treasury* 1938, p. 413; Daily Statement of the Secretary of the Treasury, June 30, 1939. Footnotes of original table are omitted.

[b] Not reported in Daily Statement of the Treasury, June 30, 1939.

Exhibit 10

Table 40 — Expenditures of the Federal Government, 1908–1939 [a]

Year	Expenditures chargeable against ordinary receipts										Postal expenditures exclusive of postal deficiencies	Total ordinary and postal expenditures
	Ordinary								Public debt retirements chargeable against ordinary receipts	Total expenditures chargeable against ordinary receipts		
	Civil and miscellaneous	War Department (including rivers and harbors and Panama Canal)	Navy Department	Indians	Pensions	Postal deficiencies	Interest on the public debt	Total ordinary expenditures				
1908	$162,532,368	$175,840,453	$118,037,097	$14,579,756	$153,892,467	$12,888,041	$21,426,138	$659,196,320	....	$659,196,320	$195,500,901	$854,697,221
1909	167,001,087	192,486,904	115,546,011	15,694,618	161,710,367	19,501,062	21,803,836	693,743,885	....	693,743,885	201,541,092	895,284,977
1910	171,580,830	189,823,379	123,173,717	18,504,132	160,696,416	8,495,612	21,342,979	693,617,065	....	693,617,065	221,514,528	915,131,593
1911	173,838,599	197,199,491	119,937,644	20,933,869	157,980,575	....	21,311,334	691,201,512	....	691,201,512	237,660,705	928,862,217
1912	172,256,794	184,122,793	135,591,956	20,134,840	153,590,456	1,568,195	22,616,300	689,881,334	....	689,881,334	246,961,344	936,842,678
1913	169,802,304	202,128,711	133,262,862	20,306,159	175,085,450	1,027,369	22,899,108	724,511,963	....	724,511,963	261,081,506	985,593,469
1914	170,530,235	208,349,746	139,682,186	20,215,076	173,440,231	....	22,863,957	735,081,431	....	735,081,431	283,558,103	1,018,639,534
1915	200,533,231	202,160,134	141,835,654	22,130,351	164,387,942	6,636,593	22,902,897	760,586,802	....	760,586,802	291,944,881	1,052,531,683
1916	191,752,692	183,176,439	153,853,567	17,570,284	159,302,351	5,500,000	22,900,869	734,056,202	....	734,056,202	300,728,453	1,034,784,655
1917	1,144,448,923	377,940,870	239,632,757	30,598,093	160,318,406	....	24,742,702	1,977,681,751	....	1,977,681,751	319,889,904	2,297,571,655
1918	6,143,916,172	4,869,955,286	1,278,840,487	30,888,400	181,137,754	2,221,095	189,743,277	12,696,702,471	$1,134,234	12,697,836,705	322,628,094	13,020,464,799
1919	6,627,726,263	9,009,075,789	2,002,310,785	34,593,257	221,614,781	343,511	619,215,569	18,514,879,955	8,014,750	18,522,894,705	362,160,763	18,885,055,468
1920	2,771,141,778	1,621,953,095	736,021,456	40,516,832	213,344,204	114,854	1,020,251,622	6,403,343,841	78,746,350	6,482,090,191	418,607,441	6,900,697,632
1921	1,916,122,018	1,118,076,423	650,373,836	41,470,808	260,611,416	130,128,458	999,144,731	5,115,927,690	422,281,500	5,538,209,190	489,506,490	6,027,715,680
1922	1,091,652,312	457,756,139	476,775,194	38,500,413	252,576,848	64,346,235	991,000,759	3,372,607,900	422,694,600	3,795,302,500	481,316,006	4,276,618,506
1923	1,166,634,334	397,050,596	333,201,362	45,142,763	264,147,869	32,526,915	1,055,923,690	3,294,627,529	402,850,491	3,697,478,020	524,366,214	4,221,844,234
1924	1,131,154,606	357,016,878	332,249,137	46,754,026	228,261,555	12,638,850	940,602,913	3,048,677,965	457,999,750	3,506,677,715	574,773,905	4,081,451,620
1925	1,183,882,296	370,980,708	346,142,001	38,755,457	218,321,424	23,216,784	881,806,662	3,063,105,332	466,538,114	3,529,643,446	616,119,721	4,145,763,167
1926	1,293,702,536	364,089,945	312,743,410	48,442,120	207,189,622	39,506,490	831,937,700	3,097,611,823	487,376,051	3,584,987,874	640,235,690	4,225,273,564
1927	1,204,375,974	369,114,122	318,909,096	36,791,649	230,556,065	27,263,191	787,019,578	2,974,029,675	519,554,845	3,493,584,519	687,364,998	4,180,949,518
1928	1,340,702,732	400,989,683	331,335,492	36,990,808	229,401,462	32,080,202	731,764,476	3,103,264,855	540,255,020	3,643,519,875	693,674,815	4,337,194,690
1929	1,471,452,939	425,947,194	364,561,544	34,086,586	229,781,079	94,699,744	678,330,400	3,298,859,486	549,603,704	3,848,463,190	687,709,010	4,536,172,200
1930	1,597,512,107	464,853,515	374,165,639	32,066,628	220,608,931	91,714,451	659,347,613	3,440,268,884	553,883,603	3,994,152,487	711,985,635	4,706,138,122
1931	1,800,641,110	478,418,974	354,071,004	26,778,585	234,402,722	145,643,613	611,559,704	3,651,515,712	440,082,000	4,091,597,712	656,885,960	4,748,483,672
1932	2,639,280,130	477,449,816	357,617,834	26,125,092	232,521,292	202,876,341	599,276,631	4,535,147,138	412,629,750	4,947,776,888	590,846,193	5,538,623,081
1933	2,000,129,912	449,395,013	349,561,925	22,722,347	234,990,427	117,380,192	689,365,106	3,863,544,922	461,604,800	4,325,149,722	582,626,064	4,907,775,786
1934	4,153,843,625	408,894,976	297,029,291	23,372,905	319,322,034	52,003,296	756,617,127	6,011,083,254	359,864,093	6,370,947,347	578,763,705	6,949,711,052
1935	4,797,651,840	489,155,454	436,447,860	27,918,899	373,804,501	63,970,405	820,926,353	7,009,875,312	573,558,250	7,583,433,562	632,632,848	8,216,066,410
1936	6,254,317,517	618,919,108	529,031,666	28,875,773	399,065,694	86,038,862	749,396,802	8,665,645,421	403,240,150	9,068,885,572	667,620,819	9,736,506,391
1937	5,715,914,252	628,348,231	556,884,449	36,933,148	396,047,400	41,896,945	866,384,331	8,442,408,756	103,971,200	8,546,379,956	730,918,898	9,277,298,854
1938	4,978,321,400	644,525,410	596,278,301	33,378,389	402,779,083	44,258,861	926,280,714	7,625,822,158	65,464,950	7,691,287,108	628,186,746	8,319,473,854

[a] Report of the Secretary of the Treasury, 1938, pp. 416–417. Footnotes of the original table are omitted.
For the fiscal year 1939 expenditures were reported on a different basis, namely: I. General, $5,327,746,418; II. Recovery and relief, $3,104,687,554; III. Revolving funds, (net), $92,453,595; IV. Transfers to trust accounts, $685,204,013; V. Debt retirements, $58,246,450; Total, $9,268,338,031. (U. S. Treasury, Daily Statement, June 30, 1939.)

Exhibit 11

Table 41

Individual Income Tax Returns, 1937 [a]

(Including returns filed for estates and trusts for prior years)

(Net income classes and money figures in thousands of dollars)

Net income classes	Number of returns	Net income	Tax	Average rate of tax
Under 5 (est.) [b]	2,977,959	5,970,414	......	.....
Under 5 (est.)	2,667,156	6,452,099	72,254	1.12
5– 10 [b]	746	3,998	......	.....
5– 10	470,425	3,166,572	83,529	2.64
10– 11	31,316	328,136	14,933	4.55
11– 12	25,034	287,417	14,312	4.98
12– 13	20,496	255,899	13,843	5.41
13– 14	16,909	227,961	13,207	5.79
14– 15	14,551	210,821	12,992	6.16
15– 20	45,967	791,103	57,637	7.29
20– 25	24,173	538,181	48,785	9.06
25– 30	14,505	396,275	43,967	11.10
30– 40	16,140	554,352	74,968	13.52
40– 50	8,303	368,804	60,460	16.39
50– 60	4,877	266,408	51,224	19.23
60– 70	3,090	200,165	44,320	22.14
70– 80	2,026	151,288	37,990	25.11
80– 90	1,363	115,370	32,618	28.27
90– 100	962	91,029	28,355	31.15
100– 150	2,269	272,264	102,062	37.49
150– 200	777	132,516	59,587	44.97
200– 250	375	83,769	41,631	49.70
250– 300	206	56,440	29,842	52.87
300– 400	207	71,168	39,988	56.19
400– 500	105	46,309	27,501	59.39
500– 750	106	64,942	41,095	63.28
750–1000	56	49,457	33,061	66.85
1000–1500	29	35,309	24,555	69.54
1500–2000	5	8,505	6,096	71.67
2000–3000	12	27,008	19,737	73.08
3000–4000	1	3,162	2,355	74.46
4000–5000	1	4,446	3,357	75.50
5000 and over	1	6,985	5,358	76.71
Total........	6,350,148	21,238,574	1,141,619	5.38
Nontaxable returns	2,978,705	5,974,412	....	.....
Taxable returns...	3,371,443	15,264,162	1,141,619	7.48

[a] 76th Congress, 1st Session, *Hearings before the Committee on Tax-Exempt Securities*, 1939, p. 64.
[b] Nontaxable returns.

EXHIBIT 12

TABLE 42

CONSOLIDATED RETURNS FOR 1930 SHOWING ESTIMATED INCREASE IN THE AMOUNT OF TAX LIABILITY HAD MEMBER CORPORATIONS BEEN TAXED SEPARATELY AT 13¾% COMPARED WITH THE TAX LIABILITY ON THE CONSOLIDATED RETURNS TAXED AT 14½%.

	Number	Consolidated Returns		Member Corporations Separately		Increase in Tax Had Member Corporations Been Taxed Separately
		Net Income	Tax Liability at 14½%	Net Income	Tax Liability at 13¾%	
Consolidated returns showing net income with member corporations showing net income or deficit.....	511	$447,100,000	$64,829,500	$526,100,000	$72,338,750	$7,509,250
Consolidated returns showing net income with member corporations showing net income only.........	97	115,400,000	16,733,000	115,400,000	15,867,500	865,500 (dec.)
Consolidated returns showing deficit with member corporations showing net income or deficit........	488	317,150,000 (def.)	None	95,200,000	13,090,000	13,090,000
Consolidated returns showing deficit and with no deficit or no separate data for member corporations.	554	None	None	None	None	None
Totals..................................	1650	....	$81,562,500	$736,700,000	$101,296,250	$19,733,750
Estimated total increase in the tax liability for 1930, based on this tabulation, representing 16⅔% of the total increase in the amount of the tax liability that would have resulted had the member corporations of consolidated returns been taxed separately.....						$118,402,500

See above, Chapter XIV, pp. 352, 353, 360-363.

EXHIBIT 13

TABLE 43

CONSOLIDATED RETURNS FOR 1933 SHOWING ESTIMATED INCREASE IN THE AMOUNT OF TAX LIABILITY HAD MEMBER CORPORATIONS BEEN TAXED SEPARATELY AT 13¾% COMPARED WITH THE TAX LIABILITY ON THE CONSOLIDATED RETURNS TAXED AT 14½%

	Number	Consolidated Returns		Member Corporations Separately		Increase in Tax Had Member Corporations Been Taxed Separately
		Net Income	Tax Liability at 14½%	Net Income	Tax Liability at 13¾%	
Consolidated returns showing net income with member corporations showing net income or deficit.....	557	$269,650,000	$39,099,250	$381,000,000	$52,387,500	$13,288,250
Consolidated returns showing net income with member corporations showing net income only.........	166	21,905,000	3,176,225	21,905,000	3,011,938	164,287 (dec.)
Consolidated returns showing deficit with member corporations showing net income or deficit........	965	450,000,000 (def.)	None	101,750,000	13,990,625	13,990,625
Consolidated returns showing deficit and with either deficit or no separate data for member corporations.	2452	None	None	None	None	None
Total....................................	4140	....	$42,275,475	....	$69,390,063	$27,114,588
Estimated total increase in the tax liability for 1933 for all consolidated returns had the member corporations been taxed separately and based on the net income of the returns tabulated for this study representing 46⅔% of the total net income for all consolidated returns for 1933, is..................						$58,525,000

See above, Chapter XIV, pp. 352, 353, 360-363.

EXHIBIT 14

TABLE 44

FEDERAL AND STATE INCOME TAXES ON THE TOP $100 FOR SELECTED AMOUNTS OF SURTAX NET INCOME AND FOR SELECTED STATES [a]

State	$100,000			$1,000,000		
	Federal tax	State tax	Combined Federal and state taxes	Federal tax	State tax	Combined Federal and state taxes
*Arizona[b]......	$57.88	$1.90	$59.78	$75.15	$1.12	$76.27
California[b]....	51.92	12.00	63.92	64.60	15.00	79.60
*Georgia.......	57.24	2.99	60.23	74.65	1.77	76.42
*Idaho[b]........	56.97	3.44	60.41	74.45	2.04	76.49
*Iowa.........	57.76	2.11	59.87	75.05	1.25	76.30
*Louisiana[b] ...	57.50	2.55	60.05	74.85	1.51	76.36
*Minnesota....	56.43	4.36	60.79	74.02	2.60	76.62
Mississippi....	55.17	6.50	61.67	71.06	6.50	77.56
*Montana.....	58.01	1.68	59.69	75.25	.99	76.24
New York[c]...	54.28	8.00	62.28	69.92	8.00	77.92
North Carolina	54.87	7.00	61.87	70.68	7.00	77.68
*Oklahoma....	56.70	3.90	60.60	74.24	2.32	76.56
Virginia......	57.23	3.00	60.23	73.72	3.00	76.72

* States marked with asterisk allow Federal income tax as a deduction; other States do not. It should be noted that in the States allowing the Federal income tax as a deduction for the State income tax, the State tax on the top $100 of $100,000 income is greater than the State tax on the top $100 of $1,000,000 income. This results from the fact that State income tax rates, unlike the Federal rates, are not progressive at the high levels of income and that the deduction of Federal tax for State income tax purposes is greater for the top $100 of $1,000,000 income than for the top $100 of $100,000 income.

[a] 76th Congress, 1st Session, *Hearings before the Committee on Ways and Means on Tax-Exempt Securities* 1939, p. 11.

[b] Tax on stated amount considered as one share of community property.

[c] Includes 1 per-cent emergency tax.

Exhibit 15

Table 45

Extent of State Taxation of Net Income [a]

January 1, 1939

Alabama	Louisiana	Ohio [d]
Arizona	Maryland	Oklahoma
Arkansas	Massachusetts	Oregon
California	Minnesota	Pennsylvania [b]
Colorado	Mississippi	South Carolina
Connecticut [b]	Missouri	South Dakota
Delaware [c]	Montana	Tennessee [e]
Georgia	New Hampshire [d]	Utah
Idaho	New Mexico	Vermont
Iowa	New York	Virginia
Kansas	North Carolina	West Virginia
Kentucky	North Dakota	Wisconsin

[a] Statement of the Undersecretary of the Treasury before the Committee on Ways and Means, June 28, 1939 (mimeographed).

Of the 32 States which tax all corporate net income, all apply flat rates except Arizona, Idaho, Mississippi, North Dakota, South Dakota, and Wisconsin. Ohio imposes a flat rate on intangibles. Of the 31 States that levy taxes on individuals, all but three (Maryland, Massachusetts, and Vermont) levy progressive rates.

On Jan. 1, 1939, there were 34 states having more or less general income taxes, besides Ohio and New Hampshire which had taxes on income from intangibles, only. In 1939 an income tax on individuals and corporations was adopted for the District of Columbia. See Exhibits 16 and 17, including notes.

[b] Applicable to corporations only.

[c] Applicable to individuals only.

[d] Applicable only to income from intangibles.

[e] Applicable to all corporate net income, but only to intangibles of individuals.

EXHIBIT 16—TABLE 46

RATES OF STATE INDIVIDUAL INCOME TAXES, JANUARY 1, 1939 [a]

State	Applicable to—	Percentage rates	Applicable to—	Percentage rates	Special rates or features
Alabama	First $1000	1.5	$3001–$5000	4.5	
	$1001–$3000	3	Over $5000	5	
Arizona	First $2000	1	$6001–$7000	3	
	$2001–$3000	1.25	$7001–$8000	3.5	
	$3001–$4000	1.5	$8001–$9000	4	
	$4001–$5000	2	Over $9000	4.5	
	$5001–$6000	2.5	....	....	
Arkansas	First $3000	1	$11,001–$25,000	4	
	$3001–$6000	2	Over $25,000	5	
	$6001–$11,000	3	....	....	
California	First $5000	1	$50,001–$60,000	9	
	$5001–$10,000	2	$60,001–$70,000	10	
	$10,001–$15,000	3	$70,001–$80,000	11	
	$15,001–$20,000	4	$80,001–$100,000	12	
	$20,001–$25,000	5	$100,001–$150,000	13	
	$25,001–$30,000	6	$150,001–$250,000	14	
	$30,001–$40,000	7	Over $250,000	15	
	$40,001–$50,000	8	....	....	
Colorado	First $2000	1	$6001–$8000	4	Surtax on dividends, royalties, interest —2%.
	$2001–$4000	2	$8001–$10,000	5	
	$4001–$6000	3	Over $10,000	6	
Delaware	First $3000	1	Over $10,000	3	
	$3001–$10,000	2	....	....	
Georgia	First $1000	1	$7001–$10,000	5	Minimum $2.
	$1001–$3000	2	$10,001–$20,000	6	
	$3001–$5000	3	Over $20,000	7	
	$5001–$7000	4	....	....	
Idaho	First $1000	1.5	$3001–$4000	5	
	$1001–$2000	3	$4001–$5000	6	
	$2001–$3000	4	Over $5000	8	
Iowa	First $1000	1	$3001–$4000	4	
	$1001–$2000	2	Over $4000	5	
	$2001–$3000	3	....	....	
Kansas	First $2000	1	$5001–$7000	3	
	$2001–$3000	2	Over $7000	4	
	$3001–$5000	2.5	....	....	
Kentucky	First $3000	2	$4001–$5000	4	
	$3001–$4000	3	Over $5000	5	
Louisiana	First $10,000	2	Over $50,000	6	
	$10,001–$50,000	4	....	....	
Maryland [b]	All net income	0.5	Imposed as a temporary tax on 1936 and 1937 incomes.		
Massachusetts	Earned income and annuities.	1.5	Interest and dividends.	6	Plus surtax of 10% computed on tax amount.
	Capital gains	3	....	....	
Minnesota	First $1000	1	$5001–$7000	6	
	$1001–$2000	2	$7001–$9000	7	
	$2001–$3000	3	$9001–$12,500	8	
	$3001–$4000	4	$12,501–$20,000	9	
	$4001–$5000	5	Over $20,000	10	
Mississippi	First $2000	3	$5001–$15,000	5.5	
	$2001–$5000	4	Over $15,000	6.5	
Missouri	First $1000	1	....	....	
	$1001–$2000	1.5, less $5	....	....	
	$2001–$3000	2, less $15	....	....	
	$3001–$5000	2.5, less $30	....	....	
	$5001–$7000	3, less $55	....	....	
	$7001–$9000	3.5, less $90	....	....	
	Over $9000	4, less $135	....	....	
Montana	First $2000	1	$4001–$6000	3	
	$2001–$4000	2	Over $6000	4	

[a] 76th Congress, 1st Session, *Hearings* before the Committee on Ways and Means on Tax-Exempt Securities 1939, pp. 30–31. (See note b at bottom of this table on next page.)

Exhibit 16—(*Continued*)

Rates of State Individual Income Taxes, January 1, 1939 (*Continued*)

State	Applicable to—	Percentage rates	Applicable to—	Per-centage rates	Special rates or features
New Hampshire	Average property tax rate on intangibles.	....	....	....	1938 rate: 3.48.
New Mexico...	First $10,000	1	$20,001–$100,000	3	
	$10,001–$20,000	2	Over $100,000	4	
New York.....	First $1000	2	$5001–$7000	5	Emergency tax, 1%. Capital gains taxed at one-half the rates. On unincorporated business, 4%.
	$1001–$3000	3	$7001–$9000	6	
	$3001–$5000	4	Over $9000	7	
North Carolina	First $2000	3	$6001–$10,000	6	
	$2001–$4000	4	Over $10,000	7	
	$4001–$6000	5	....	....	
North Dakota .	First $2000	1	$6001–$8000	7.5	
	$2001–$4000	2	$8001–$10,000	10	
	$4001–$5000	3	$10,001–$15,000	12.5	
	$5001–$6000	5	Over $15,000	15	
Ohio..........	Income from intangibles.	5	....	....	
Oklahoma.....	First $1000	1	$5001–$6000	6	
	$1001–$2000	2	$6001–$7000	7	
	$2001–$3000	3	$7001–$8000	8	
	$3001–$4000	4	Over $8000	9	
	$4001–$5000	5	....	....	
Oregon [b]	First $1000	2	$3001–$4000	5	Income from intangibles, 8%.
	$1001–$2000	3	$4001–$5000	6	
	$2001–$3000	4	Over $5000	7	
South Carolina.	First $2000	2	....	....	Surtax on: Interest and dividends: $500–$800, 3%; $801–$1200, 4%; over $1200, 5%.
	$2001–$4000	3	....	....	
	$4001–$6000	4	....	....	
	Over $6000	5	....	4	
South Dakota..	First $1000	1	$18,001–$68,000	5	
	$1001–$3000	2	$68,001–$318,000	6	
	$3001–$8000	3	Over $318,000	8	
	$8001–$18,000	....	....	....	
Tennessee......	Interest and dividends.	6	Dividends from corporations if at least 75% of their property is assessable for property tax, 4%.		
Utah..........	First $1000	1	$3001–$4000	4	
	$1001–$2000	2	Over $4000	5	
	$2001–$3000	3	....	....	
Vermont.......	Interest and dividends.	4	....	....	
	All other income	2	....	....	
Virginia.......	First $3000	1.5	Over $5000	3	
	$3001–$5000	2.5	....	....	
West Virginia..	First $1000	1	$2001–$3000	3	
	$1001–$2000	2	Over $3000	4	
Wisconsin......	First $1000	1	$7001–$8000	4	Surtax: Normal tax less $37.50 divided by 6. Temporary surtax equal to 60% of normal tax rates.
	$1001–$2000	1.25	$8001–$9000	4.5	
	$2001–$3000	1.5	$9001–$10,000	5	
	$3001–$4000	2	$10,001–$11,000	5.5	
	$4001–$5000	2.5	$11,001–$12,000	6	
	$5001–$6000	3	Over $12,000	7	
	$6001–$7000	3.5	....	....	

[b] The rates of the new (1939) District of Columbia tax begin at 1% on income in excess of $5000 and reach a maximum of 3% on the excess over $20,000. In 1939 the Oregon rates were raised. They are graduated from 2% on the first $500 to 7% on the excess over $4000. An additional tax of 2% is imposed on "surtax net income." The Maryland rates also were raised in 1939.

EXHIBIT 17

TABLE 47

PERSONAL EXEMPTIONS UNDER STATE INDIVIDUAL INCOME TAXES

JANUARY 1, 1939[a]

State	Single	Married couple or head of family	Dependent	State	Single	Married couple or head of family	Dependent
1. Where exemptions are deducted from the otherwise taxable base							
Alabama	$1500	$3000	$300	New Hampshire	$200	$200	None
Arkansas	1500	2500	400	New Mexico	1500	2500	$200
California	1000	2500	400	New York	1000	2500	400
Colorado	1000	2500	400	North Carolina	1000	2000[c]	200
Delaware	1000	2000	200	North Dakota	500	1500	200
Georgia	1000	2500	400	Ohio	None	None	None
Idaho	700	1500	200	Oklahoma	850	1700	300
Kansas	750	1500	200	Oregon	800	1500	300
Kentucky	1000	2500	400	South Carolina	1000	1800	200
Louisiana	1000	2500	400	Tennessee	None	None	None
Maryland	1000	2500	400	Utah	600	1200	300
Massachusetts	2000[b]	2500[b]	250	Vermont	1000[d]	2000[d]	250
Mississippi	1000	2500	400	Virginia	1000	2000	200
Missouri	1000	2000	200	West Virginia	1000	2000	300
Montana	1000	2000	300				
2. Where exemptions take the form of tax credits							
Arizona	$10	$20	$4	Wisconsin			
Iowa	10	20	5	(a) Normal income tax	$8	$17.50	$4
Minnesota	10	30	5	(b) Regular surtax, normal tax exemptions, plus	..	37.50	..
South Dakota	6	12	2	(c) Temporary surtax	10	25.00	2

a 76th Congress, 1st Session, *Hearings before the Committee on Ways and Means on Tax-Exempt Securities* 1939, p. 32.

b For income from intangibles the exemption is $1000 if total income does not exceed $1000 or if total income of husband and wife does not exceed $1500.

c An additional exemption of $1000 is provided for a married woman with separate income.

d For incomes from intangibles, the exemption is $400 and $800 for a single or a married individual respectively, with provision that this exemption applies only if the total income does not exceed $1000 in case of a single man and $2000 in case of a married person.

BIBLIOGRAPHY

Bibliographies

Osaka University of Commerce, Institute for economic research, Bibliography of economic science. Tokyo, Maruzen Co., Ltd., 1934-35. 2 vol.

U. S. Library of Congress. Division of Bibliography. Select list of works relating to taxation of inheritances and of incomes. Washington, Govt. Printing Office 1907.

——— Additional references relating to taxation of incomes. Washington, D. C. 1911.

——— List of references on excess profits taxation. Washington, D. C. 1917.

——— War taxation of incomes, excess profits, and luxuries in certain foreign countries. Washington, D. C. 1918.

——— List of recent references on the income tax. Washington, D. C. 1921.

——— List of references on tax exemption of securities (mimeographed). Washington, D. C. 1922.

——— List of references on income tax evasion (typewritten). Washington, D. C. 1924.

——— List of references on the Mellon plan of tax reduction (typewritten). Washington, D. C. 1924.

——— Federal income tax in the United States (mimeographed.) Washington, D. C. 1931.

——— List of references on tax exemption of securities (mimeographed). Washington, D. C. 1931.

——— Federal income tax in the United States (mimeographed.) Washington, D. C. 1934.

——— Selected list of recent references on inheritance taxation in the United States and foreign countries (mimeographed). Washington, D. C. 1935.

——— Rates of income and inheritance taxes : United States, Great Britain, and France (typewritten). Washington, D. C. 1935.

——— Federal income tax in the United States (mimeographed). Washington, D. C. 1937.

——— List of references on tax exemption of securities (mimeographed). Washington, D. C. 1938.

Congressional Documents

U. S. Congress

Congressional Globe (1789-March 3, 1873)

Congressional Record (March 4, 1873-)

—— Committee Reports

36th Congress, 2d Session (1861)

Letter of the Secretary of the Treasury to the Chairman of the Committee on Ways and Means on the condition of the Treasury. *House Misc. Doc.* 20.

39th Congress, 1st Session (1866)

Report of the U. S. Revenue Commission. *House Exec. Doc.* 34.

39th Congress, 2d Session (1867)

Report of the Special Commissioner of the Revenue. *Sen. Exec. Doc.* 2.

40th Congress, 2d Session (1867)

Report of the Special Commissioner of the Revenue. *House Exec. Doc.* 81.

40th Congress, 3d Session (1868)

Report of the Special Commissioner of the Revenue. *House Exec. Doc.* 16.

41st Congress, 2d Session (1869)

Report of the Special Commissioner of the Revenue. *House Exec. Doc.* 27.

53d Congress, 1st Session (1893)

Report of the Joint Committee on laws organizing the executive departments. *House Report* 49; *Senate Report* 41.

Senate

Committee on Finance. The tariff and administrative customs acts of 1890 and the bill H. R. 4864 as reported to the Senate from the Finance Committee, March 20, 1894. (Pages 279-290 contain comparison of the income tax laws of 1864 and 1867 with the provisions of House bill 4864 as amended by subcommittee of Senate Finance Committee.)

61st Congress, 2d Session (1910)

Senate

Proposed income-tax amendment. Letter from Hon. Elihu Root to Hon. Frederick M. Davenport on the subject of the scope and effect of the proposed income-tax amendment. *Sen. Doc.* 398.

62d Congress, 2d Session (1912)

House of Representatives

Committee on Ways and Means. The excise tax bill. Report to accompany H. R. 21214. *House Report* 416.

Decisions of the U. S. Supreme Court in corporation tax cases and income tax cases. *House Doc.* 601.

63d Congress, 1st Session (1913)

House of Representatives

Report (of the Committee on Ways and Means) to accompany H. R. 3321. . . *House Report* 5.

Report of the Conference Committee to accompany H. R. 3321. *House Report* 86.

Senate

Finance Committee. Tariff schedules, briefs, and statements filed with Committee on Finance on H. R. 3321. (Hearings)

—— To reduce tariff duties and to provide revenue for government. . . *Sen. Rep.* 80.

—— Opinions of Shields, Hull, Gordon on the proposed income-tax provision of the (1913) . . . tariff bill. *Sen. Doc.* 171.

63d Congress, 2d Session (1914)

House of Representatives

To increase internal revenue, report to accompany H. R. 18891. *House Report* 1163.

Senate

War revenue bill. Comparison of additional revenues derived in 1900 with additional revenues to be derived for a year under H. R. 18891 . . . as reported to the Senate. *Sen. Doc.* 596.

63d Congress, 3d Session (1915)

House of Representatives

Refund of certain penalties collected under the Act of October 3, 1913. *House Report* 1456.

64th Congress, 1st Session (1916)

House of Representatives

Hearings before the Committee on Expenditures in the Treasury Department on H. Res. 221, directing the Secretary of the Treasury to submit certain information pertaining to the collecting of the income tax. June 1, 2, and 17, 1916.

To increase revenue, and for other purposes. Report (of the Committee on Ways and Means) to accompany H. R. 16763. *House Report* 922.

Revenue bill. Conference report to accompany H. R. 16763. *House Report* 1200.

Senate

Hearings before the subcommittee of the Committee on Finance on H. R. 16763, an act to increase the revenue. . . (July 17-August 1, 1916).

To increase revenue, Report of Senate Committee on Finance to accompany H. R. 16763. *Sen. Rep.* 793.

64th Congress, 2d Session (1917)

Senate

Hearings before the Committee on Finance on H. R. 20573.

65th Congress, 1st Session (1917)

House of Representatives

Report of the Committee on Ways and Means, to accompany H. R. 4280. *House Report* 45.

Report of the Conference Committee on H. R. 4280. *House Rep.* 172.

Senate

Hearings and briefs before the Senate Committee on Finance on H. R. 4280. (May 11, 14, 15, 1917)

Report of the Senate Committee on Finance on H. R. 4280. *Sen. Report* 103.

65th Congress, 2d Session (1918)
House of Representatives
Hearings before the Committee on Ways and Means on the Proposed Revenue Act of 1918. June 7, July 17, August 5, 14, 15, 1918.
Report of the Committee on Ways and Means on the revenue bill of 1918. *House Report* 767.
Senate
Hearings before the Committee on Finance on H. R. 12863 to provide revenue for war purposes. September 1918.

65th Congress, 3d Session (1919)
Senate
Report of the Senate Finance Committee on H. R. 12863. *Sen. Rep.* 617.
Report of the Conference Committee on H. R. 12863. *Sen. Rep.* 1037.

66th Congress, 2d Session (1920)
House of Representatives
Simplification of the Revenue Act of 1918. *House Report* 1035. May 22, 1920.
Hearings before the Committee on Ways and Means on stock dividends. March 18, 19, 1920.

67th Congress, 1st Session (1921)
House of Representatives
Revenue bill of 1921. *House Report* 350.
Report of the Conference Committee on the revenue bill of 1921. *House Report* 486.
Report of the Committee on Ways and Means on tax-exempt securities. *House Report* 969.
Hearings on Internal Revenue revision, 1921.
Hearings before the Committee on Ways and Means on tax-exempt securities, January 16-March 7, 1922.
Senate
Report of the Senate Finance Committee on Revenue bill of 1921. *Sen. Rep.* 275.

67th Congress, 4th Session (1923)
House of Representatives
Capital losses, hearings on H. R. 13413 to amend revenue act of 1921 in respect to capital gains and losses. January 8, 1923.
Capital losses, report to accompany H. R. 13770, January 12, 1923. *House Report* 1388.
Exchange of property, report to accompany H. R. 13774. January 19, 1923. *House Report* 8157.
Senate
Refunds of taxes, to accompany H. R. 13775. *Sen. Rep.* 1137.

68th Congress, 1st Session (1924)
House of Representatives
Hearings before the Committee on Ways and Means on internal revenue revision. January 14-19, 1924.
Report of the Committee on Ways and Means on the revenue bill of 1924. *House Report* 179.
Senate
Taxation and tax-exempt income. Letter from the chairman of the Federal Trade Commission transmitting a report on taxation and tax-exempt income in partial response to Sen. Res. 451, 67th Congress, 4th Session. *Sen. Doc.* 148.
Hearings before the Select Committee on Investigation of the Bureau of Internal Revenue.
Comparison of the Mellon, Garner, and Longworth tax plans. *Sen. Doc.* 62.
Hearings before the Senate Committee on Finance on revenue revision.
Statement of changes made in the Revenue Act of 1921 by H. R. 6715 and the reasons thereof [Gregg Report].
Report of the Senate Finance Committee on the revenue bill of 1924. *Sen. Rep.* 398.

69th Congress, 1st Session (1926)
House of Representatives
Internal revenue bill of 1926. *House Report* 1.
Senate
Report of the select committee on investigation of the Bureau of Internal Revenue [Couzens Report]. *Sen. Rep.* 27.
Report of the Senate Finance Committee on the internal revenue bill of 1926. *Sen. Rep.* 52.

69th Congress, 2d Session (1927)
House of Representatives
Hearings before the Committee on Ways and Means on amendments proposed to H. R. 16462 (*re* approving of income tax refunds by Comptroller).

Interim, 69th-70th Congress
House of Representatives
Hearings before the Committee on Ways and Means on revenue revision. October 31-November 10, 1927.
Hearings on amendments proposed to H. R. 16462 (tax refunds) January 28, 1927.

70th Congress, 1st Session (1928)
House of Representatives
Internal revenue bill of 1928, *House Report* 2.
Report of the Joint Committee on internal revenue taxation (1927). *House Doc.* 139.
Senate
Report to accompany H. R. 1. *Sen. Rep.* 960.

71st Congress, 2d Session (1929)
House of Representatives
Hearings before the Committee on Ways and Means on H. J. Res. 133 reducing rates of income tax for . . . 1929. December 4, 1929.
Senate
Tax relief for 1929. Report to accompany H. J. Res. 133. *Sen. Rep.* 48.

71st Congress, 3d Session (1931)
Senate
Data on ratification of the Constitution and amendments by the states. *Sen. Doc.* 240.

72d Congress, 1st Session (1932)
House of Representatives
Hearings before Committee on Ways and Means on revenue revision, 1932. January 13-27, February 2-4, 1932.
Report to accompany H. R. 10236. The revenue bill of 1932. *House Report* 708.
Senate
Hearings before Senate Finance Committee on H. R. 10236, revenue act of 1932. April 6-21, 1932.
Report to accompany H. R. 10236, revenue act of 1932. *Sen. Rep.* 665.

73d Congress, 1st Session (1933)
Senate
Report to accompany H. R. 5755 (N I R A). *Sen. Rep.* 114.
Hearings before the Committee on banking and currency and stock exchange practices 1933.

73d Congress, 2d Session (1934)
House of Representatives
Prevention of tax avoidance. Preliminary report of a sub-committee . . . relative to . . . preventing the avoidance and evasion of the internal revenue laws 1933.
Hearings before the Committee on Ways and Means on revenue revision 1934. December 15-21, 1933; January 9-11, 1934.
Report to accompany H. R. 7835, revenue bill 1934. *House Report* 704.
Hearings on H. R. 8396 (community property), May 1-5, 7, 9, 21, June 12 and 13, 1934.
Senate
Hearings before the Senate Finance Committee on H. R. 7835 (revenue bill 1934). March 12-15, 1934.
Report to accompany H. R. 7835. *Sen. Rep.* 558.
Hearings before the Committee on the Judiciary proposing an amendment to the Constitution of the United States relative to taxes on certain incomes. *Sen. Rep.* 738.
National income in the United States 1929-1932. *Sen. Doc.* 124.

74th Congress, 1st Session (1935)
House of Representatives
Hearings before the Committee on Ways and Means. Proposed taxation of individual and corporate incomes, inheritances, and gifts. July 8-13, 1935.
Report of the Committee on Ways and Means on the revenue bill of 1935. *House Report* 1681.
Repeal certain provisions relating to publicity of certain statements of income. Report to accompany H. R. 6359. *House Report* 313.
Hearings before the Committee on Ways and Means on H. R. 4120 (social security).
Report of the Committee on Ways and Means on H. R. 4120. *House Report* 615.
Hearings before the Committee on Ways and Means on taxation of interstate carriers and employees. August 15-20, 1935.
Excise tax upon carriers and income tax upon their employees. *House Report* 1882.
To exempt from taxation official compensation of certain foreign representatives and to provide for deductibility from income of certain dividends on preferred stocks owned by the U. S. *House Report* 1759.
Senate
Report on H. R. 4120 (social security). *Sen. Rep.* 668.
Hearings on H. R. 8974, an act to provide revenue, equalize taxation, and for other purposes. July 30, 31, August 1, 2, 6, 7, 8, 1935.
Revenue bill of 1935. Report to accompany H. R. 8974. *Sen. Rep.* 1240.
Taxation of interstate carriers and employees. Hearings on S. 3150. August 22, 23, 1935.
74th Congress, 2d Session (1936)
House of Representatives
Hearings before the Committee on Ways and Means on the revenue act of 1936. March 30, 31, April 1-7, 1936.
The revenue bill of 1936. Report to accompany H. R. 12395. *House Report* 2475.
The revenue bill of 1936. Report of the subcommittee of the Committee on Ways and Means relative to proposed tax revision.
Report to the Committee on Finance to accompany H. R. 5529, War Revenue Act.
Senate
The revenue act of 1936, hearings on H. R. 12395. . . April 30-May 12, 1936.
The revenue bill of 1936. *Sen. Rep.* 2156.
75th Congress, 1st Session (1937)
House of Representatives
Extension of excise tax upon carriers and income tax upon their employees. *House Report* 219.
Hearings before the Joint Committee on Tax Evasion and Avoidance.

June 17, 18, 22-24, 29, 30; July 1, 2, 9, 13, 28; August 5, 9, and 10, 1937.

Report of the Committee on Ways and Means on H. R. 8234, revenue bill of 1937. *House Report* 1546.

Senate

Report of the Senate Finance Committee on revenue bill of 1937. *Sen. Rep.* 1242.

75th Congress, 3d Session (1938)

House of Representatives

Hearings before the Committee on Ways and Means on revenue revision 1938. January 14-25, 1938.

Report of the Committee on Ways and Means on the revenue bill of 1938. *House Report* 1860.

Senate

Hearings before the Senate Finance Committee on H. R. 9682, revenue act 1938. March 17-22, 1938.

Report of the Senate Finance Committee on revenue bill 1938. *Sen. Rep.* 1567.

76th Congress, 1st Session (1939)

House of Representatives

Hearings before the Committee on Ways and Means on revenue revision 1939. May 27, 29, June 2, 3, 5, 1939.

Report of the Committee on Ways and Means on publicity of compensation of corporate officers. *House Report* 27.

Hearings before the Committee on Ways and Means on tax-exempt salaries. January 26, 1939.

Hearings before the Committee on Ways and Means on Social Security. 3 vol. 1939.

Hearings before the Committee on Ways and Means on tax-exempt securities, June 28-July 11, 1939.

Report on the revenue bill of 1939. *House Report* 855.

Report of the Committee on Ways and Means on the public salary tax act 1939. *House Report* 26.

Report of the Committee on Ways and Means on the codification of the internal revenue laws. *House Report* 6.

Report of the Committee on Ways and Means on amendments to the Social Security Act. *House Report* 728.

Senate

Hearings before the special Committee on taxation of governmental securities and salaries. January 18, February 7-16, 1939.

Hearings before the Committee on Finance on taxes on fats and oils. March 6-9, 1939.

Hearings before the Committee on Finance on H. R. 3790 (Public Salary Tax Act 1939).

Report of the Committee on Finance on H. R. 3790. *Sen. Rep.* 112.

Hearings on the consolidation and codification of the internal revenue laws. January 30, 1939.

Report of the Committee on Finance on codification of the internal revenue laws. *Sen. Rep.* 20.
Report of the Committee on Finance on the amendments to the Social Security Act. *Sen. Rep.* 734.

Joint Committee on Internal Revenue Taxation
Federal and state death taxes 1933
Internal revenue collections from specified sources 1918-1938
Million dollar incomes 1938
Preliminary report on depletion 1929
Report on internal revenue taxation 1927
Supplemental report on capital gains and losses 1929

Official Departmental and Court Reports

U. S. Board of Tax Appeals
Reports (38 vol., 1926 to 1938)
U. S. Department of Commerce
Company law and business taxes in Great Britain, by Walter Jaeger. Trade promotion series, No. 147. Washington, D. C., Govt. printing office 1933.
Comparative law series (monthly) Division of commercial law.
Digest of state laws relating to net income taxes 1938. Washington, D. C., Govt. printing office 1938. Supplement 1939.
National income in the United States 1929-1932. Washington, D. C., Govt. printing office 1933. (Also, 73d Congress, 2d Session, Senate Doc. 124.)
National income in the United States 1929-1935. Washington, D. C., Govt. printing office 1936.
State tax collections, 1939
Preliminary report, state and local government, Special study No. 7. Washington, D. C., Oct. 31, 1939.
Taxation of business in Great Britain, by M. B. Carroll. Trade promotion series, No. 60. Washington, D. C., Govt. printing office 1928.
U. S. Department of Justice
Taxation of government bondholders and employees 1938
U. S. Department of State
Statutes at Large
U. S. Supreme Court Reports
U. S. Treasury Department
Annual reports of the Secretary of the Treasury
Annual reports of the Commissioner of Internal revenue
German income tax laws 1938
History of the internal revenue service 1930
Income tax laws of France 1938
Inheritance and gift tax laws of Sweden 1938
Internal revenue bulletin (weekly summary of Treasury decisions, court decisions, opinions of the Chief Counsel, etc.)

Internal revenue cumulative bulletin (semi-annual compilation of decisions and rulings)
Regulations (for administration of each income tax law)
Sources and rates of federal taxation (corrected to January 1, 1939)
Statistics of income, annual, 1916-1937
Statement of the Acting Secretary of the Treasury on the report of the sub-committee of the Committee on Ways and Means on tax avoidance 1933

Books

Acheson, Sam Hanna, Joe Bailey, the Last Democrat. N. Y., Macmillan 1936.
Adarkar, B. H., Principles and Problems of Federal Finance. London, King 1933.
Allix, E., Traité élèmentaire de science des finances et de legislation financiere française. 6th ed. Paris, Rousseau 1931.
American Academy of Political and Social Science (Philadelphia) Readjustments in Taxation, Annals, vol. 58, 1915. Financing the War, Annals, vol. 75, 1918. Government Finance in the Modern Economy, vol. 183, 1936.
American Federal Tax Reports. N. Y., Prentice-Hall (annual) 20 vol. to 1939.
Annual Encyclopedia.
Black, Henry Campbell, Treatise on the Law of Income Taxation. 2d ed. Kansas City, Mo., Vernon Law Book Co. 1916.
Blakey, Roy G., The State Income Tax. Minneapolis, U. of Minn. Press 1932.
Blakey, Roy G., and Associates, Taxation in Minnesota. Minneapolis, U. of Minn. Press 1932.
Blakey, Roy G. and Gladys C., Digest and Index of the Proceedings of the National Tax Association 1907-1925. N. Y. The National Tax Association 1927.
Bogart, Ernest L., Direct and Indirect Costs of the Great World War. N. Y., Oxford 1919.
Boutwell, George S., Manual of the Direct and Excise Tax System of the United States. Boston, Little, Brown 1863.
—— Reminiscences of 60 years in Public Affairs. N. Y., McClure Phillips 1902. 2 vol.
Bowers, Claude G., Beveridge and the Progressive Era. Boston, Houghton Mifflin 1932.
—— The Tragic Era, Cambridge, Mass., Houghton Mifflin 1929.
Brown, H. G., Economics of Taxation. Columbia, Mo., Lucas 1938.
Buehler, Alfred G., Public Finance. N. Y. and London, McGraw-Hill 1936.
—— The Undistributed Profits Tax. N. Y. and London, McGraw-Hill 1937.
Bump, Orlando F., Internal Revenue Statutes Now in Force. N. Y., Baker Voorhis 1870.

Butt, Archibald W., Taft and Roosevelt: Letters to His Sister Clara. Garden City, N. Y., Doubleday 1930. 2 vol.

Clark, Champ, My Quarter Century of American Politics. N. Y., Harper 1920. 2 vol.

Commerce Clearing House, Standard Federal Tax Service. Chicago (current loose-leaf reporting service).

Dewey, Davis R., Financial History of the United States. N. Y., Longmans 1936.

Douglas, Paul, Social Security in the United States. N. Y., McGraw-Hill 1936.

Einaudi, L., Corso di scienza della finanza. Torino, La Riforma Sociale 1926.

Emerson, Charles H., The Internal Revenue Guide. Springfield, Mass., Samuel Bowles 1866.

Estee, Charles F., The Excise Law. N. Y., Fitch, Estee 1863.

Fisher, Irving, Nature of Capital and Income. N. Y., Macmillan 1906.

Friday, David, Profits, Wages, and Prices. N. Y., Harcourt Brace 1920.

Frost, Thomas Gold, Treatise on Federal Income Tax Law of 1913. Albany, N. Y., Bender 1913.

Gerloff, W. and Meisel, F., Handbuch der Finanzwissenschaft. Tubingen, Moll 1926-29. 3 vol.

Grady, Henry, British War Finance 1914-19. New York, Columbia U. Press 1930.

Great Britain, Report of Committee on National Debt and Taxation (Colwyn Committee), Cmd. 2800. London, H. M. S. Off. 1927.

——— Report of the Royal Commission on the Income Tax, Cmd. 615. London, H. M. S. Off. 1920.

Green, William R., The Theory and Practice of Modern Taxation. 2d ed. N. Y. and Chicago, Commerce Clearing House 1938.

Groves, H. M., Financing Government. N. Y., Holt 1939.

Haig, Robert Murray, Seligman, E. R. A., Adams, T. S., and others, The Federal Income Tax. (Columbia University Lectures 1920.) N. Y., Columbia University Press 1921.

Hart, Albert Gailord, Debts and Recovery. N. Y., The Twentieth Century Fund 1938.

Haynes, Fred E., Third Party Movements. Iowa City State Historical Society 1916.

Hewett, William Wallace, The Definition of Income. Philadelphia, U. of Pa. 1925.

Hicks, John D., The Populist Revolt. Minneapolis, U. of Minn. Press 1931.

Holmes, George E., Federal Income Tax. 6th ed. Indianapolis, Bobbs Merrill 1925.

Hunter, M. H., Outlines of Public Finance. Rev. ed. N. Y. and London, Harper 1926.

Interstate Commission on Conflicting Taxation, Conflicting Taxation, 1935 progress report. By the Research Staff of the Commission, James W. Martin, Research Director. Chicago, Ill., Published jointly by The American Legislator's Association and The Council of State Governments 1935.

Jensen, Jens P., Problems of Public Finance. N. Y., Crowell 1924.

——— Government Finance. N. Y., Crowell 1937.

Jèze, G., Cours de finances publiques 1923-33. Paris, Giard 1933.

Kendrick, M. Slade, The Undistributed Profits Tax. Washington D. C., The Brookings Institution 1937.

Ketcham, Earle H., The Sixteenth Amendment. Urbana, Ill., U. of Ill. 1926.

King, W. I., The National Income and Its Purchasing Power. N. Y., National Bureau of Economic Research 1930.

Konstam, E. M., K. C. The Law of Income Tax. 7th ed. London, Stevens 1936.

Kuznets, S. S., National Income and Capital Formation. N. Y., National Bureau of Economic Research 1937.

La Follette, Robert Marion, Autobiography: A Personal Narrative of Political Experiences. Madison, Wis., The Robert M. La Follette Co. 1913.

Leven, Maurice, The Income Structure of the United States. Washington, D. C., The Brookings Institution 1938.

——— Your Income and Mine. N. Y., Public Affairs Committee, Inc. 1938.

Lotz, W., Finanzwissenschaft. 2 umgearb. Aufl. Tubingen, Mohr 1931.

Lutz, H. L., Public Finance. 3d ed. N. Y., Appleton-Century 1936.

Magill, Roswell, ed., Columbia University lectures on taxation: T. S. Adams, A. A. Ballantine, M. B. Carroll, Ed. H. Green, R. M. Haig, W. E. Hope, R. H. Montgomery. N. Y., Commerce Clearing House 1932.

——— Taxable Income. N. Y., Ronald 1936.

——— and others, Summary of the British Tax System. U. S. Govt. printing office 1935.

McAdoo, William G., Crowded Years. Boston, N. Y., Houghton Mifflin 1931.

McCall, Samuel W., Thaddeus Stevens (American Statesmen Series). Boston, N. Y., Houghton Mifflin 1899.

McElroy, R. M., Grover Cleveland, the Man and the Statesman. N. Y., Harper 1923. 2 vol.

Mellon, Andrew, Taxation: The People's Business. N. Y., Macmillan 1924.

Miller, Robert N., Hendricks, Homer, and Everett, Ewing, Reorganizations and Other Exchanges in Federal Income Taxation. N. Y., Ronald 1934.

Montgomery, Robert H., Excess Profits Tax Procedure. N. Y., Ronald 1921.

——— Federal Tax Handbook : Revenue Act of 1932. N. Y., Ronald 1932.

——— Income Tax Procedure. N. Y., Ronald 1917-1922. 6 vol.

——— Federal Income Tax Handbook 1935-1936. N. Y., Ronald 1935.

——— Federal Income Tax Handbook 1936-1937. N. Y., Ronald 1936.

——— Federal Income Tax Handbook 1938-1939. N. Y., Ronald 1938.

Moulton, Harold G., Income and Economic Progress. Washington, D. C., The Brookings Institution 1935.

——— and Pasvolsky, Leo, War Debts and World Prosperity. N. Y., Century for the Brookings Institution 1933.

National Bureau of Economic Research, Income in the United States, Its Amount and Distribution 1909-1919. N. Y., Harcourt Brace 1921. 2 vol.

National Industrial Conference Board

Federal Finances, 1923-32. N. Y. 1933.

Federal Fiscal Emergency. N. Y. 1932.

Income in Agriculture 1929-1935. N. Y. 1936.

Income Received in the Various States 1929-1935. N. Y. 1937.

National Income and Its Elements. N. Y. 1936.

Proceedings, National Industrial Tax Conference. N. Y. 1920.

Proposals for Changes in Federal Income Tax Administration. N. Y. 1924.

Proposals for Changes in the Federal Internal Revenue System. N. Y. 1927.

Proposals for Changes in the Federal Revenue Act of 1924. N. Y. 1925.

The Shifting and Effects of the Federal Corporation Income Tax. N. Y. 1928-30. 2 vol.

Nevins, Allan, Grover Cleveland: A Study in Courage. N. Y., Dodd, Mead 1933.

——— Letters of Cleveland. Boston, N. Y., Houghton Mifflin 1933.

New York Tax Commission, Allocation of Corporate Income for the Purpose of State Taxation. Special report No. 6. Albany, N. Y. 1933.

Paul, Randolph E., and Mertens, Jacob, The Law of Federal Income Taxation. Chicago, Callaghan 1934-1938. 6 vol.

Pigou, A. C., A Study in Public Finance. London, Macmillan 1928.

Prentice-Hall, Federal Tax Service. N. Y., Prentice-Hall (looseleaf, current service.)

Pringle, Henry F., The Life and Times of William Howard Taft. N. Y., Farrar & Rinehart 1939. 2 vol.

Schmeckebier, Laurence F., and Eble, Francis A., The Bureau of Internal Revenue, Its History, Activities, and Organization. Institute for Government Research Service Monographs of the U. S. Government, No. 25. Johns Hopkins University Press 1923.

Seidman, J. S., Legislative History of Federal Income Tax Laws 1938-1861. N. Y., Prentice-Hall 1938.

Seitz, Don C., Joseph Pulitzer. N. Y., Simon and Schuster 1924.

Seligman, E. R. A., Double Taxation and International Fiscal Co-operation. N. Y., Macmillan 1928.

—— The Income Tax. 2d ed. N. Y., Macmillan 1914.

—— Essays in Taxation, 10th ed. N. Y., Macmillan 1925.

—— Progressive Taxation in Theory and Practice. 2d ed. Princeton, American Economic Review 1908.

—— Shifting and Incidence of Taxation. 5th ed. N. Y., Columbia University Press 1927.

—— Studies in Public Finance. N. Y., Macmillan 1925.

Sherman, John, Recollections of 40 Years in the House, Senate, Cabinet. Chicago, Werner 1895. 2 vol.

Shirras, G. Findlay, The Science of Public Finance. 3d ed. London, Macmillan 1936.

Shoup, Carl, Blough, Roy, Newcomer, Mabel, and others, Studies in Current Tax Problems. N. Y., The Twentieth Century Fund 1937.

—— Facing the Tax Problem. N. Y., The Twentieth Century Fund 1937.

Shultz, William J., American Public Finance. 2d ed. N. Y., Prentice-Hall 1938.

Simons, Henry C., Personal Income Taxation. Chicago, University of Chicago Press, 1938.

Smith, Harry Edwin, The United States Federal Internal Tax History from 1861 to 1871. Boston, N. Y., Houghton Mifflin 1914.

Spaulding, H. B., The Income Tax in Great Britain and the United States. London, King 1927.

Stamp, Sir Josiah, The Fundamental Principles of Taxation in the Light of Modern Developments. London, Macmillan 1936.

—— British Income and Property. London, P. S. King and Sons 1916.

—— Taxation During the War. London, Oxford U. Press 1932.

Stephenson, Nathaniel W., Nelson W. Aldrich, a Leader in American Politics. N. Y., Scribner 1930.

Stewart, Paul W. and Tucker, Rufus S., The National Debt and Government Credit. N. Y., Twentieth Century Fund 1937.

Studenski, Paul, ed., Taxation and Public Policy: A Discussion of the Current Problems of American and European Public Finance. Contributors: F. L. Bird, A. E. Buck, Gerhard Colm and others. N. Y., R. R. Smith 1936.

Tax Policy League, How Shall Business Be Taxed? Symposium (E. C. Alvord, A. G. Buehler, Roy Blough, and others). N. Y., Tax Policy League 1936.

—— Tax Relations among Governmental Units. Symposium (Roy Blough, Philip Cornick, L. Ecker-R and others). N. Y., Tax Policy League 1938.

Tax Research Foundation, Tax Systems of the World. 7th ed. Chicago, Commerce Clearing House 1938. (Annual.) Also, Supplement 1939.

Underwood, Oscar W., Drifting Sands of Party Politics. N. Y., Century 1928.
United States Tax Cases, 1913- . Chicago, Commerce Clearing House. (1913-1934, 4 v.; annual since 1935.)
Villard, Oswald Garrison, Fighting Years. N. Y., Harcourt Brace 1939.
Warren, George F. and Pearson, Frank, Prices. N. Y., Wiley 1933.
Wells, David A., The Theory and Practice of Taxation. N. Y., Appleton 1900.
Woodley, Thomas F., Thaddeus Stevens. Harrisburg, Pa., The Telegraph Press 1934.
World Peace Foundation, Subject Index to the Economic and Financial Documents of the League of Nations 1927-1930. Boston, World Peace Foundation 1932.

Periodicals and Pamphlets

Adams, T. S., Economic and social basis of tax reduction, Proceedings Academy of political science, xi: 30 (May 1924).
—— Immediate future of the excess profits tax, American economic review, X: Sup. 15 (March 1920).
—— Should the excess profits tax be repealed? Quarterly journal of economics, 35: 364 (May 1921).
—— Sources of federal revenue readjustment and federal tax, Proceedings, National tax association 1919, p. 300.
American bar association, Report of the committee on the income tax law. 39: 533 (October 1914).
Anderson, Benjamin M., Jr., Eating the seed corn: the proposed penalty tax on corporate savings, Chase economic bulletin, vol. 16, May 1936.
Blakey, Roy G., Effects of bonds and taxes on war finance, South Atlantic quarterly, xvi: 236 (July 1917).
—— Amending the federal income tax, Annals of the American academy of political and social science, 58: 32-43 (1915).
—— State income taxation (pamphlet). Minneapolis, League of Minnesota municipalities 1930.
—— The income tax exemption, Outlook, 106: 256 (January 31, 1914).
—— The revenue act of 1913, American economic review iv: 25 (March 1914). Succeeding Acts are discussed in later issues of the American Economic Review, as follows: 1916 Act, vi: 837-50; 1917 Act, vii: 791-815; 1918 Act, ix: 213-43; 1921 Act, xii: 75-108; 1924 Act, xiv: 475-504; 1926 Act, xvi: 401-25; 1928 Act, xviii: 428-48; 1932 Act, xxii: 620-40; 1934 Act, xxiv: 450-61; 1935 Act, xxv: 673-90; 1936 Act, xxvi: 466-82; 1937 Act, xxvii: 698-704; 1938 Act, xxviii: 447-58; 1939 Acts, xxix: 695-707. (Gladys C. Blakey is co-author of most of these articles.)
—— Shifting the war burden upon the future, Annals of the American academy of political and social science, 75: 90 (January 1918).
—— Simplification of the income tax, American economic review, xviii: Sup. 102. (March 1928.)

Blakey, Roy G. and Gladys C., Founders and builders of the income tax, Tax magazine 18: — (March, April 1940).

Borah, William E., The income-tax amendment, North American review, 191: 760 (June 1910).

Breadner, R. W., Canadian business profits and war tax acts, Bulletin National tax association 4: 93-97, 116-119 (January, February 1919).

Bullock, Charles J., Conscription of wealth, North American review, 205: 895 (June 1917).

——— War finance, Proceedings of the National tax association, 1917, p. 146.

Chamber of Commerce of the U. S. A. (pamphlets)

Comparison of the tax program of the national chamber with the provisions of the Revenue Act of 1926 as passed by the House of Representatives.

Federal taxation: Technical and administrative features with special bearing on pending revenue bill (1928).

Federal taxation: Suggestions of the President's tax message; statements of members before the House Ways and Means Committee (1935).

Miscellaneous bulletin, revenue bill 1939.

Proposed revenue legislation, January 1934.

Referendum No. 34, Federal taxation (1920).

Referendum No. 67 on report of special committees on federal expenditures, October, December 1934.

Report to the board of directors . . . by the . . . committee on taxation, November 1925.

Choate, Joseph H., William Guthrie, Victor Morawitz, Austen G. Fox, John G. Milburn. The proposed 16th article of amendment to the Constitution of the United States. Memorandum submitted to the Legislature of the State of New York in opposition to the amendment (pamphlet) April 11, 1910.

Colm, Gerhard, and Lehman, Fritz, Economic consequences of recent American tax policy (pamphlet). Social research Sup. I 1938.

Cummins, Albert B., The reason for the income tax, Independent 67: 178 (July 1909).

Disney, Wesley, The depletion allowance, Tax magazine 16: 262 (May 1938).

Dun's Review, Business enterprise as tax collector and taxpayer, July 1939.

——— Taxes paid by business, April 1939.

——— Taxes paid by business compared with value of service rendered, August 1939.

——— Undistributed profits tax (September 1937, May, July 1939).

Edmunds, George F., The salutary results of the income tax decision, Forum 19: 513 (July 1895).

Fetter, Frank A., Reformulation of the concepts of capital and income in economics and accounting, Accounting review XII: 3-12 (March 1937).

Fisher, Irving, Income in theory and income taxation in practice, Econometrica 5: 1 (January 1937).

——— Income concept in the light of experience (pamphlet). New Haven, Conn., The author 1928.

——— A practical schedule for an income tax, Tax magazine 15: 379 (July 1937).

Fortune survey: Taxpayer's money's worth, Fortune 19: 88 (February 1939).

Gibson, Lloyd C., The Bureau's new depreciation policy, Tax magazine 12: 279 (June 1934).

Groves, H. M., A tax policy for the United States, New republic 77: 297, 327, 357 ; 78: 78 (January 24, February 14, 1934).

Haensel, Paul, Public Finance of the Union of Soviet Socialist Republics, Tax magazine 16: 517, 591, 659, 724 (September, October, November, December 1938).

Haig, Robert M., British war excess profits tax, American economic review, 10 : Sup., 108 (December 1920).

Hall, U. S., The income tax : reasons in its favor, Forum 17: 14 (March 1894).

Hendricks, H. G., Federal income tax rates, 1913-1922, Bulletin National tax association 18: 74, 104, 137, 166 (December 1932 ; January, February, March 1933).

Holcomb, A. E., Pending federal war revenue taxes, Bulletin National tax association 2: 245 (June 1917).

Holmes, George E., Excess profits tax, American economic review 10: Sup., 22 (March 1920).

Houston, David F., What you need to know about federal taxation, World's work 42: 586 (October 1921).

——— Where our taxes go and why, World's work 42: 480 (September 1921).

——— Taxes, which and why, World's work 43: 103 (November 1921).

Hubbard, Harry, From whatever source derived, American law journal vi (b): 202 (September 1920).

Hull, Cordell, Proceedings of the New York state bar association (January 1914).

Income tax legislation, Independent 74: 384 (February 13, 1913).

Journal of Accountancy, The Morgan investigation, 56: 1 (July 1933).

Kendrick, M. S., Ability-to-pay theory of taxation, American economic review 29: 92 (March 1939).

La Follette's Magazine, especially editorials 1909, 1913, 1917.

Leupp, F. E., President Taft's own view, Outlook 99: 816 (December 2, 1911).

Littleton, A. C., Concepts of income underlying accounting, Accounting review XII: 13-22 (March 1937).

Lutz, H. L., The privilege of personal income taxation, Bulletin National tax association, 23: 14 (October 1937).

—— The principle of the undistributed profits tax, Bulletin National tax association 23: 200 (April 1938).

Machen, Arthur W., The strange case of *Florida* v. *Mellon*, Cornell law quarterly (April 1928).

Magee, James D., Taxation and capital investment, Washington, D. C. The Brookings Institution 1939 (pamphlet).

Magill, Roswell, The too well remembered man, Fortune 11: 100 (April 1935).

May, George O., Administration of the British income tax law, Proceedings of the academy of political science 11: 146 (April 1921).

Miller, A. C., National finance and the income tax, Journal of political economy 3: 255-288 (June 1895).

National Industrial Conference Board, Experience under the undistributed profits tax, Bul. 11: 11 (October 13, 1937).

—— Proceedings of the national industrial tax conference, Chicago, April 16, 1920, Special report 9 (May 1920).

National Tax Association, Proceedings of the first national conference on inheritance and estate taxation, Washington, D. C., February 1925.

—— Proceedings of the second national conference on inheritance and estate taxation, New Orleans, November 1925.

—— Report of the committee on federal taxation, Proceedings 1919, p. 317.

—— Report of the committee on simplification of the income tax, Proceedings 1927, p. 110. Also published as a pamphlet.

—— Final report of committee on federal taxation of corporations (R. M. Haig, Chair.), Proceedings 1939. Reprint, 131 pp.

Nelson, G. N., Taxation of corporate surplus, Tax magazine 15: 15 (January 1937).

Parker, L. H., Capital gains and losses, Tax magazine 14: 609 (October 1936).

Paton, William A., Proprietors' salaries, Journal political economy 28: 240 (March 1920).

Peffer, William A., The farmers' defensive movement, Forum 8: 464 (December 1889).

Plehn, Carl C., War profits and excess profits taxes, American economic review 10: 283 (June 1920).

Ratchford, B. W., Fisher's concept of taxable income, Tax magazine 15: 646 (November 1937).

Roper, Daniel C., Administrative problems in United States internal revenue taxation, South Atlantic quarterly 21: 97 (April 1922).

—— Basis for reform of federal taxation, Annals of the American Academy of political and social science 95: 164 (May 1921).

—— Taxation problems, North American review 222: 12 (September, October, November 1925).

—— The war revenue act of 1917, Annals of the American Academy of political and social science 75: 159 (1918).

Rothschild, M. D., The gross sales or turnover tax, Proceedings of the National tax association 1920, p. 180.

Rottschaefer, Henry, Concept of income in federal taxation, Minnesota law review 13: 637 (June 1929).

Satterlee, Hugh, The income tax definition of reorganization, Tax magazine 12: 639 (December 1934).

—— Some suggestions for simplification of federal taxation, Proceedings of the National tax association 1920, p. 117.

Schanz, G. v., Der Einkommensbegriff und die Einkommensteuergesetze, Finanz archiv 1896: 1.

Schiff, Mortimer L., Some aspects of the income tax, Annals of the American academy 58: 24 (March 1915).

Seligman, E. R. A., The federal income tax. Political science quarterly 29: 1 (March 1914).

—— Taxes versus bonds, New York times (April 15, 1917).

—— Tax reduction and tax exemption, North American review 219: 433-48 (April 1924).

—— Income tax, Encyclopiedia of the social sciences VIII: 626-639.

Seligman, E. R. A., Durand, E. D., Moulton, H. G., Bogart, E. L. and others, Financial mobilization for war. Chicago, University of Chicago press 1917. (pamphlet)

Shoup, Carl, Taxing for social security, Annals of the American academy 202: 165 (March 1939).

—— The corporation tax and the normal tax, Bulletin of the National tax association 19: 106 (January 1934).

Simons, H. C., A positive program for laissez faire : some proposals for a liberal economic policy, Public policy pamphlets No. 5, University of Chicago press 1934.

Smith, J. G., Economic significance of the undistributed profits tax, American economic review 28: 305 (June 1938).

Smith, Gerald L. K., Or superman? New republic 82: 15 (February 13, 1935).

Sprague, O. M. W., Conscription of wealth once more, New republic 11: 300 (July 14, 1917).

—— Loans and taxes in war finance, American economic review 7: Sup. 199 (March 1917).

Taussig, F. W., The financial situation, Annals of the American academy of political and social science 75: 9 (January 1918).

—— The war tax act of 1917, Quarterly journal of economics 32: 25 (November 1917).

Tunnell, George B., Legislative history of the second income tax law, Journal of political economy 3: 311 (June 1895).

Viner, Jacob, Taxation and changes in price levels, Journal of political economy 31: 494 (August 1923).

——— Who paid for the war? Journal of political economy 28: 46 (January 1920).

Walker, John E., Simplification of the federal income tax, Proceedings of the National tax association 1920, p. 209.

Washington notes, Journal of political economy 32: 91 (January 1914).

Wells, David A., An income tax: is it desirable? Forum 17: 1 (March 1894).

——— The Communism of a discriminating income-tax, North American review, 130: 236 (March 1880).

Williamson, K. M., The literature on the sales tax, Quarterly journal of economics 35: 618 (August 1921).

Winston, Garrard B., Changes made by the revenue act of 1924, Proceedings of the National tax association 1924, p. 267.

Wueller, Paul H., Concepts of taxable income, Political science quarterly 53: 83, 557; 54: 555 (March, December 1938; December 1939).

Newspapers

Annalist
Baltimore Sun
Commercial and Financial Chronicle
Minneapolis Tribune
Newark Evening News
New York Evening Post
New York Herald
New York Sun
New York Times
New York Tribune
New York World
Richmond (Virginia) *Times Dispatch*
St. Paul Representative
Syracuse (New York) *News*
Wall Street Journal
Washington Daily News
Washington Post
Washington Star

Unpublished Material

Bryan Papers, Library of Congress
Chase Papers, Library of Congress
Cleveland Papers, Library of Congress
Nightingale, Edmund A., Taxation in Great Britain. M. A. Thesis. Minneapolis, U. of Minn. 1936.
United States Bureau of Internal Revenue Files
United States Treasury Department, Secretary's Files

INDEX

Printed in the USA/Agawam, MA
November 30, 2010
555354.003